Syria & Lebanon

Terry Carter, Lara Dunston
Amelia Thomas

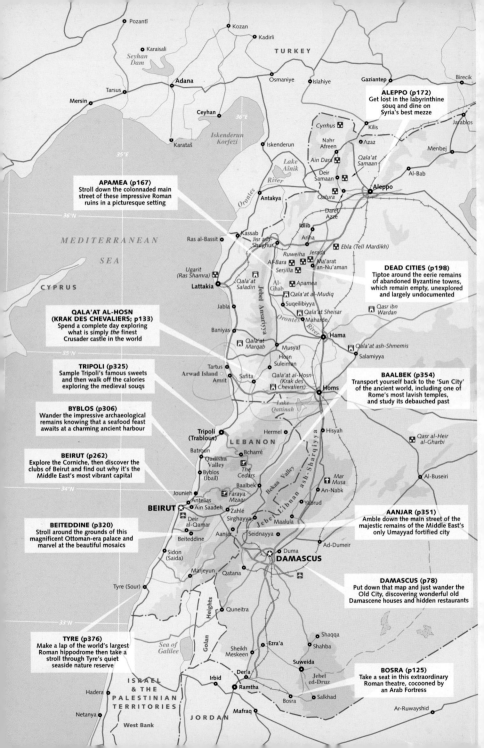

ALEPPO (p172)
Get lost in the labyrinthine souq and dine on Syria's best mezze

APAMEA (p167)
Stroll down the colonnaded main street of these impressive Roman ruins in a picturesque setting

DEAD CITIES (p198)
Tiptoe around the eerie remains of abandoned Byzantine towns, which remain empty, unexplored and largely undocumented

QALA'AT AL-HOSN (KRAK DES CHEVALIERS; p133)
Spend a complete day exploring what is simply *the* finest Crusader castle in the world

TRIPOLI (p325)
Sample Tripoli's famous sweets and then walk off the calories exploring the medieval souqs

BAALBEK (p354)
Transport yourself back to the 'Sun City' of the ancient world, including one of Rome's most lavish temples, and study its debauched past

BYBLOS (p306)
Wander the impressive archaeological remains knowing that a seafood feast awaits at a charming ancient harbour

BEIRUT (p262)
Explore the Corniche, then discover the clubs of Beirut and find out why it's the Middle East's most vibrant capital

AANJAR (p351)
Amble down the main street of the majestic remains of the Middle East's only Umayyad fortified city

BEITEDDINE (p320)
Stroll around the grounds of this magnificent Ottoman-era palace and marvel at the beautiful mosaics

DAMASCUS (p78)
Put down that map and just wander the Old City, discovering wonderful old Damascene houses and hidden restaurants

TYRE (p376)
Make a lap of the world's largest Roman hippodrome then take a stroll through Tyre's quiet seaside nature reserve

BOSRA (p125)
Take a seat in this extraordinary Roman theatre, cocooned by an Arab Fortress

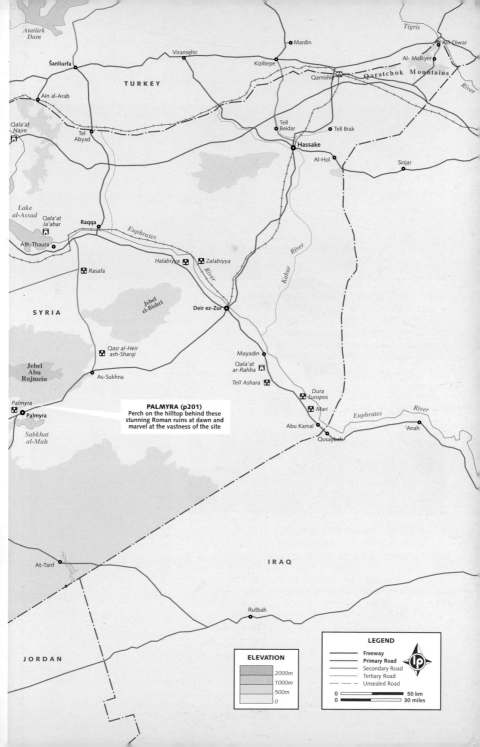

PALMYRA (p201)
Perch on the hilltop behind these stunning Roman ruins at dawn and marvel at the vastness of the site

LEGEND

	Freeway
	Primary Road
	Secondary Road
	Tertiary Road
— — —	Unsealed Road

ELEVATION

2000m
1000m
500m
0

0   50 km
0   30 miles

On the Road

TERRY CARTER Coordinating Author

It had been one of those days as a traveller where things just didn't go to plan. We had been driving for hours in the desert looking for a little-visited set of ruins. Our driver, having managed to get off course by a couple of hundred kilometres, declared he was too tired to drive. After I steered us to Palmyra we dumped our bags and headed straight to the ruins. The touts had thankfully retired for the day and we had Palmyra all to ourselves. The light was Palmyra perfect.

LARA DUNSTON Coordinating Author

The Euphrates is one of *the* great Middle East rivers, like the Tigres and the Nile. For me, it's one of those must-sees. I love the way it gives life to the desert, blanketing its otherwise arid banks in green. And there's nothing like viewing the Euphrates from atop the massive walls of a magnificent Arab castle, such as this one at Qala'at Najm, built by Nureddin in the 12th century. It had been a long hot drive to get here and when we clambered to the top and took in that view, it was all worth it.

AMELIA THOMAS
At Baalbek's creaky old Palmrya Hotel – one of the world's greatest old-timer hotels – I met charming tour guide Charbel Saliba who, with a grin, insisted on taking me up to the town's old Roman quarry to see the world's largest cut stone. It was only on getting there that he confided its local name, Hajar al-Hubla (Stone of the Pregnant Woman). 'Go on', he giggled, 'Stand on top!' Obligingly, I clambered its age-worn slope, carved with ancient graffiti, to the Lebanese flag at the pinnacle – no easy feat when, as I was then, you're six months pregnant.

See full author bios on p422

Highlights

There is no single essence to distil from these most ancient of lands. Thousands of years of tired travellers, obstinate invaders and optimistic settlers have left a patchwork kilim of history in the region's chaotic cities, isolated hilltops, verdant countryside and bare deserts. Through this, both countries have accumulated the physical evidence of civilisations and their cultures, some long buried or reduced to rubble, others discarded, some still cherished. The joy of the journey through Syria and Lebanon is detecting the influences and connecting the dots, through the customs and cuisine, the myths and monuments and, above all, the nature of the people, accustomed to greeting visitors – whatever their intention – for thousands of years.

MARK DAFFEY

1 DAMASCUS' OLD CITY

The lanes of the Old City (p85) can hold your interest for hours, making you wonder what lies behind the doors of the old Damascene houses. With many structures dating back to medieval times, and houses with overhanging features dating from the Ottoman era, a walk here is akin to a stroll in a living museum.

MARK DAFFEY

DAMASCUS' SOUQ

Every day at this busy souq (p115) the customary haggling for goods is played out time and time again, as it has been for hundreds of years. Everybody knows the game – whether it's negotiating over the price of a piece of brocade, a gold chain, or a bag of spices – and everyone participates.

3

ANDREW BURKE

2

INTERIOR COURTYARD, UMAYYAD MOSQUE

This mosque (p88) is one of the most important structures in Islam. After spending time admiring the mesmerising gold mosaics, you begin to notice the many nationalities of Muslims who come on pilgrimage to this site, which has been attracting worshippers for over 3000 years.

JANE SWEENEY

4

RUINS AT PALMYRA

Syria's greatest set of ruins (p202) is both monolithic and majestic. At the magic hour before sunset, you can savour the silence and sublime golden light as it falls on the massive colonnades that remain of this once vastly important city.

OLD QUARTER & NORIAS OF HAMA

You'll probably first hear the *norias* (water wheels; p162) before you see them – their excruciating wail reverberates around the Old Quarter's cobblestone streets. While most of the Old Town was destroyed in 1982, the turning *norias* signify how life goes on. Modern methods of irrigation may have passed the *norias* by, yet they still serve as symbols of the town's resilience.

5

MARK DAFFEY

BOSRA'S THEATRE

Everyone who visits Bosra's perfectly preserved Roman theatre (p126), dating back to the 2nd century AD, can't help but picture themselves as one of 15,000 theatregoers that this once white-marble structure held. During a performance, the entire area was covered in white fabric and the scent of perfumed water wafted over the crowd.

6

JANE SWEENEY

MICHAEL NICHOLSON/CORBIS

Aleppan cuisine (p190) is rich and complex, with Turkish, Jewish and Armenian influences that make it unique in the Middle East.

8

BON APPETIT/ALAMY

7

APAMEA'S MAIN STREET

As you pass the massive colonnades on your way down Apamea's cardo maximus (p168), it's easy to lose count of how many there are. Here, on one of the longest main streets of the ancient world, you can see grooves in the stones where horse-drawn carriages made their way down the road at the time of Christ, when the city boasted some half-a-million inhabitants.

KEVIN LANG/ALAMY

9

DEAD CITIES

The crumbling ruins of the abandoned stone buildings at Syria's eerie Dead Cities (p198) are even more enigmatic when you consider that historians don't exactly know why these complex cities were deserted.

LAKE AL-ASSAD

One of Hafez al-Assad's pet projects had the unexpected side effect of producing a wonderful lake (p214), with gorgeous azure waters more akin to the Mediterranean Sea. The presence of Qala'at Ja'abar – a castle highlighted by its island setting – makes this a sight that's worth the considerable effort it takes to get there.

PATRICK HORTON

QALA'AT SAMAAN

It's ironic that one man's quest to be left alone resulted in what is one of Syria's most important tourist attractions. The ruins of the tower that St Simeon once sat atop to evade pilgrims are little more than rubble today. However, the ruins of the church (p195) that celebrated his devotion are well preserved and in a peaceful setting – despite the pilgrims who still flock here to pay respects.

12

JOHN ELK III

JOHN ELK III

ALEPPO'S SOUQ

It's easy to step back in time in Aleppo's medieval souq (p191), where commerce continues just as it has for hundreds of years and the donkey is still the preferred means of transporting goods and customers. Bedouins doing their monthly shopping, North Africans trading and locals just here to pick up household items – all keep the souq alive.

BYBLOS HARBOUR

The days of the first jet-setters throttling back their speedboats as they enter the tiny harbour (p306) might today appear as ancient as the nearby ruins, but it doesn't require a vivid imagination to picture celebrities gorging on seafood and downing champagne as they sit in a waterfront restaurant at this petite and pretty harbour.

14

JEAN-BERNARD CARILLET

13
BEITEDDINE'S MOSAICS

BETHUNE CARMICHAEL

Beiteddine Palace (p320) might be a fascinating mix of Druze hermitage, Ottoman-sponsored architecture, Italian architects and Syrian workmanship, but the Byzantine mosaics displayed are the most extraordinary part of this palace puzzle.

15
BEIRUT'S BARS & CLUBS

AMELIA THOMAS

Visit any of Beirut's clubs (p289) before 11pm and you'll wonder what the fuss is about. Visit around midnight and you'll find groups of clubbers settled in for supper accompanied by copious wines or abundant bottles of premium spirits. Once the plates are cleared and spirits are raised, tables become dance floors, dancing becomes mandatory and dawn comes quickly.

SKIING AT FARAYA MZAAR

Come late December, the ski hounds of Lebanon take bets on when the ski lifts of the Faraya Mzaar resort (p299) will start their motors running. When they do, so do the engines of Beirut's entire skiing population, with sets of skis and skintight snow suits hastily tossed in the back of a sports car or a fashionable 4WD. On the slopes, the race continues, but with copious breaks for coffee, people watching, reapplication of make-up, and taking mobile phone calls where you pretend you're at the office.

16

CHRISTIAN ASLUND

TRIPOLI'S SOUQS

Tripoli's medieval souqs (p336) transcend time. Forget the guide-book and spend a few hours here getting lost, as hammams, khans, madrassas and mosques vie for your attention, along with the souqs' stallholders. Some of the wares displayed might have changed, but there are still plenty of those famous soaps and the souqs remain as vibrant as ever.

17

BETHUNE CARMICHAEL

18

AMELIA THOMAS

PALMYRA HOTEL, BAALBEK

The monumental ruins of Baalbek might loom large, but the historic Palmyra Hotel (p360) has just as many stories to tell. While this colonial-era relic was host to the German army in WWI and the British army in WWII, it's more fun to imagine characters such as Jean Cocteau and General de Gaulle enjoying a sundowner overlooking the ruins. *Santé!*

BAKLAVA & OTHER PASTRIES

Tasting Tripoli's sweet treats for the first time is a revelation. Syrup and honey stick desperately to the fingers, while the pastry and pistachios crunch in your mouth. You can find them elsewhere, but there is a good reason why Lebanese expats all over the world keep Tripoli's pastry shops busy with fax orders – they're the best.

20

BETHUNE CARMICHAEL

JANE SWEENEY

19 **RUINS AT AANJAR**

Wandering Aanjar's Ummayad ruins (p351) can be a somewhat spooky affair, despite the very picturesque location. The mix of influences in the remains of the buildings and the fact that it was a one-era city lend it an air of mystery.

JEAN-BERNARD CARILLET

21 **HIKING IN THE QADISHA VALLEY**

Far from the madness of Beirut, the serene Qadisha Valley (p337) provides an antidote to the fast-living and fog of fumes that inhabit the capital. Just as many religious minorities escaped persecution by fleeing to the valley, for hikers the valley is a form of paradise – with religious monasteries, hermitages and churches from which to offer praise for the respite.

Swiss

Bouij Al-Ghazal
Ave. Fouad
Chehab
Achrafie

961-1324129

Contents

Regional Map Contents

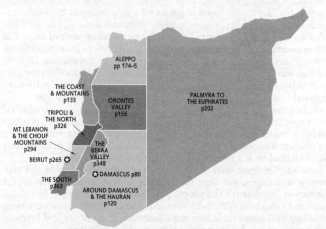

ALEPPO pp 174–5

THE COAST & MOUNTAINS p133

TRIPOLI & THE NORTH p326

MT LEBANON & THE CHOUF MOUNTAINS p294

BEIRUT p265

THE SOUTH p363

ORONTES VALLEY p155

THE BEKAA VALLEY p348

AROUND DAMASCUS & THE HAURAN p120

DAMASCUS p80

PALMYRA TO THE EUPHRATES p202

Destination Syria & Lebanon

The rise and fall of myriad civilisations in Syria and Lebanon and, indeed, in the whole of the Levant (also encompassing Jordan, Israel and the Palestinian Territories), has contributed to creating a region as diverse as it is venerable, and as vulnerable as it is invincible.

With the world's most precious of ancient ruins, medieval souqs that hum incessantly with the banter of hagglers, cities that pulsate with life day and night, and Islamic mosques and Byzantine churches so sublime and sacred that worshippers of all religious persuasions make pilgrimages to them – not to mention mountain forests thick with cedar, pine and eucalypt, sparkling Mediterranean bays, blazing desert moonscapes, and luxuriant river plains – Syria and Lebanon are tailor-made to be tourism magnets.

And in the past, they were. The 'road to Damascus' (the conversion of St Paul to Christianity) attracted Westerners as early as the 1800s to discover Syria's mysterious charms, while in the 1960s there was no more swinging place than Beirut, known then as the 'Paris of the Middle East'.

Today, unfortunately, the vilification of Syria in the West, Israel's 2006 bombardment of Lebanon, and a series of assassinations and explosions in Lebanon in 2007, have had government travel advisories periodically listing the countries as no-go areas. It's perhaps ironic then that these are two of the friendliest countries on the planet. Both are the embodiment of the hospitality and generosity for which the Middle East is renowned.

Despite the warmth of the Syrian people and a back door that's always been ajar to pilgrims, traders, archaeologists and travellers, Syria was pretty much closed to 'the West' under the late President Hafez al-Assad. While there were hopes the country would open up more under the leadership of his son Bashar al-Assad, it's really only the economy that has seen significant liberal reforms and talk of political reform has remained just that.

The generosity of spirit of the Lebanese is just as striking. This is a country where doors are flung open, where people love to socialise. But unfortunately Lebanon has had its fair share of guests who've overstayed their welcome (Syrians) and gatecrashers who were never welcome (Israelis). The 2006 war added another brutal chapter to Lebanon's never-ending story of woes. The 2005 assassination of Prime Minister Rafiq Hariri, who was responsible for Lebanon's reconstruction and revitalisation after the devastating 1975–90 civil war, was one of an ongoing series of assassinations. Since then, the government has been in a state of flux, with the presidency and the parliament paralysed in a standoff that could degenerate into another civil war.

While travelling amid this political conflict and turmoil it's paradoxical that you will never feel safer or more at home. Don't be surprised if you're handed a bag of pistachio nuts as they're being passed around a bus, if you're invited to share a pot of tea at a ruins ticket office, or if a family you've chatted to at a restaurant offers to pay for your meal.

Syria and Lebanon offer an abundance of compelling sights and captivating landscapes, yet here the journey is just as important as the destination, because it's the people you'll meet in the streets, bus stops, souqs and cafés who will make your experience all the more enriching, rewarding and memorable. See these fascinating countries and befriend their people now – before politics takes another ugly turn.

FAST FACTS

Population:
Syria 20,000,000;
Lebanon 4,100,000

GDP per capita:
Syria US$5350;
Lebanon US$6100;
USA US$43,444

Inflation:
Syria 10%; Lebanon 4%

Unemployment:
Syria 20%; Lebanon 20%

Life expectancy:
Syria 70; Lebanon 73

Iraqi refugees in Syria:
1,500,000

Palestinian refugees in Lebanon: 395,000

Literacy rates:
Syria, male 86%,
female 74%;
Lebanon, male 91%,
female 82%

Itineraries

CLASSIC ROUTES

SYRIAN SOJOURN
Two Weeks / Syria

Spend three days in **Damascus** (p78), exploring its atmospheric **Old City** (p85), Umayyad Mosque, souqs and historic houses. Visit the **National Museum** (p95) in preparation for Syria's archaeological sites. Do day trips to **Maalula** (p121), the convent at **Seidnayya** (p121), the monastery at **Mar Musa** (p123) and visit **Bosra** (p125) for its Roman theatre.

From Damascus, travel to **Aleppo** (p172), allowing two days to explore its citadel, souqs and Al-Jdeida quarter. From Aleppo, take day trips to the basilica ruins of **Qala'at Samaan** (p195) and the **Dead Cities** (p198) of Jerada, Ruweiha, Serjilla and Al-Bara, and the Roman ruins of **Apamea** (p167), before taking the train to the lively seaside city of **Lattakia** (p144). Stop by **Tartus** (p137) on the way to **Hama** (p160) and stay for a couple of days to see its *norias* (wooden waterwheels) and visit **Qasr ibn Wardan** (p169) and the **beehive villages** (p171). Head to **Homs** (p155) and **Qala'at al-Hosn (Krak des Chevaliers**; p133) for the night, then allow a day or two in **Palmyra** (p202) to see the spectacular ruins, before returning to Damascus.

Your Syrian Sojourn is a busy but satisfying two-week trip that covers the best Syria has to offer. Starting off at Damascus the trip takes in the country's most captivating sights, ending with two of the best, Qala'at al-Hosn (Krak des Chevaliers) and Palmyra.

LEVANTINE ADVENTURE
Four Weeks / Syria & Lebanon

Begin in Beirut so you only enter Syria once, avoiding a multiple entry visa. Spend two days in **Beirut** (p262), travelling north to **Byblos** (p306) for a night, then **Tripoli** (p326) for another, before heading to the **Qadisha Valley** (p337), **Bcharré** (p339) and **the Cedars** (p342) for a day, then across the mountains (impossible during winter) to **Baalbek** (p354) for a night. Go south to **Aanjar** (p351), the Chouf Mountains and **Beiteddine Palace** (p320); stay overnight in **Deir al-Qamar** (p317). Heading south, spend a night each in **Sidon** (p363) and **Tyre** (p372), bussing back to Beirut and across to Damascus. Dawdle for five days in **Damascus** (p78), doing day trips to **Maalula** (p121), **Mar Musa** (p123) and **Bosra** (p125). Head to **Homs** (p155) and **Qala'at al-Hosn** (**Krak des Chevaliers**; p133) overnight, then to **Hama** (p160) to spend a couple of days doing day trips to **Qasr ibn Wardan** (p169), **beehive villages** (p171), **Apamea** (p167) and the **Dead Cities** (p198). From Hama, cruise across to **Qala'at Marqab** (p143) and **Lattakia** (p144) to catch your breath before taking the train to **Aleppo** (p172) for a few days. Do a day trip to **Ain Dara** (p196) and **Qala'at Samaan** (p195) before setting out to the Euphrates, best-explored using your own wheels and sharing the cost of a hire car or driver. Cruise up to **Qala'at Najm** (p216), then via Raqqa to **Qala'at Ja'abar** (p214) on **Lake al-Assad** (p214) and camp overnight. Leave early to allow detours to **Rasafa** (p217) and **Halabiyya** (p218) on the way to **Deir ez-Zur** (p219). Stay two nights, visit **Dura Europos** (p222) and **Mari** (p223), then hightail it via **Qasr al-Heir al-Sharqi** (p213) to **Palmyra** (p202) and back via Damascus to Beirut. Phew!

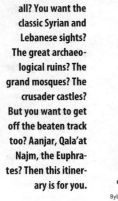

You want to see it all? You want the classic Syrian and Lebanese sights? The great archaeological ruins? The grand mosques? The crusader castles? But you want to get off the beaten track too? Aanjar, Qala'at Najm, the Euphrates? Then this itinerary is for you.

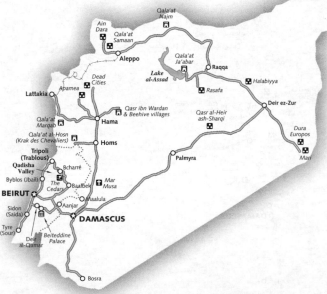

ROADS LESS TRAVELLED

COMPLETELY LEBANON   Two Weeks / Lebanon

What was once a classic route has become a bit of an off-the-beaten-track trip for some travellers, unnerved by the political tensions in Lebanon. The country is still as captivating as ever and its great sights haven't gone anywhere so get out there and see the best it offers in one complete journey.

Begin by spending a few days in beguiling **Beirut** (p262) before cruising up the coast to **Byblos** (p306) for its picturesque old port, timing your explorations so that you are strolling around the ruins at sunset – a sublime experience. Next, head to **Tripoli** (p326), taking a few days to explore its ancient khans, mosques, hammams, souqs and the crusader castle in nearby Enfe.

Enjoy the dramatic vistas and charming villages of the **Qadisha Valley** (p337) on your way to **Bcharré** (p339) and **the Cedars** (p342). Outside of winter, take the mountain road to the Bekaa Valley and **Baalbek** (p354) to enjoy the best-preserved Roman temples in the world. Drop in to Zahlé for lunch and to one of the **Bekaa Valley's vineyards** (p352) for some wine-tasting.

Next, visit the exquisite Umayyad ruins of **Aanjar** (p351) before heading to the Chouf Mountains and the charming village of **Deir al-Qamar** (p317). Nearby is the lavish **Beiteddine Palace** (p320) and its delightful gardens with Byzantine mosaics. Make your way to **Sidon** (p363) to see its stylish **Museé Du Savon** (p367), **labyrinthine souq** (p367) and **Sea Castle** (p366).

Head south to **Tyre** (p372) for its pretty bay and ruins, which include the world's largest **Roman hippodrome** (p376). Head back along the coast to Beirut for one last taste of the city's vibrant nightlife.

Unfortunately fewer travellers are doing this former classic route trip these days due to political tensions in the country. Completely Lebanon takes you to the country's most captivating sights, starting and finishing in the capital. Note, during winter you usually can't cross from Bcharré to Baalbek.

THE EUPHRATES & THE EMPTINESS   Five Days / The Euphrates River

Alongside the Nile and Tigris, the Euphrates is one of the great rivers of the Middle East. Flowing through the northeastern region of Syria, bordering Turkey and Iraq, this area is known as the Jezira, or 'island'. As the Euphrates cuts through the dry rocky desert, nourishing the landscape, it blankets its banks and surrounding flood plains in green, its fertile soil yielding wheat, cotton, sunflowers and oil. To explore this region, from **Aleppo** (p172), head northeast to **Qala'at Najm** (p216) for your first spectacular view of the river, before veering southeast via **Raqqa** (p216), a dusty little town, to the dramatic **Qala'at Ja'abar** (p214), a Mesopotamian citadel overlooking **Lake al-Assad** (p214), where you can swim, eat freshly caught fish and camp for the night.

Leave early to allow detours to **Rasafa** (p217), an immense walled city with basilica ruins that rises dramatically out of the empty desert, and **Halabiyya** (p218), a unique fortification that sprawls down a hill, on the way to **Deir ez-Zur** (p219).

Base yourself here for a couple of days, so you can visit the archaeological sites along the Euphrates River towards the Iraqi border. **Dura Europos** (p222), an extensive Hellenistic/Roman fortress city, offers breathtaking views of the Euphrates and desert, while the mud-brick ruins of **Mari** (p223) might not offer beautiful vistas, but are one of the most important ancient Mesopotamian sites. Take time in Deir ez-Zur to enjoy the riverside setting and bustling little souq, before heading via the remote and dramatic desert palace of **Qasr al-Heir al-Sharqi** (p213) to the spectacular Roman ruins of **Palmyra** (p202), before travelling southwest to vibrant Damascus.

This trip is best made with your own transport, by driving yourself or hiring a car and driver. Some have even done this journey by bicycle. You can still follow this route using public transport, but you should allow an extra couple of days.

TAILORED TRIPS

ARCHAEOLOGICAL ADVENTURE

If you're interested in archaeology, then Syria and Lebanon have some of the world's most important sights, including a long list of ruins easily as impressive as Pompeii or Persepolis.

From **Damascus** (p78) you can travel north to visit **Apamea** (p167) with its 2km-long colonnades, and the eerie Byzantine **Dead Cities** (p198). **Qala'at al-Hosn** (**Krak des Chevaliers**; p133) and **Qala'at Marqab** (p143) are musts for fans of Crusader castles, while the city of **Palmyra** (p202) is one of the world's greatest sites. **Bosra** (p125), in the south, was once the capital of the Roman province of Arabia.

In Lebanon, the city of **Tyre** (p372) boasts Roman and Byzantine ruins and the world's largest **Roman hippodrome** (p376). At **Sidon** (p363), the **Sea Castle** (p366) dates back to Phoenician times, although the present structure was built by the Crusaders. The **Temple of Echmoun** (p370) is the best preserved of the Phoenician ruins.

In **Beirut's Downtown** (p274) you'll find excavations from the Bronze Age and Roman remains. In the north, **Byblos** (p306) has 7000 years of history to explore in its Phoenician, Greek, Roman and Crusader ruins. Although **Tripoli** (p326) was settled around 1400 BC, its Crusader castle and medieval structures are mostly intact. **Baalbek** (p354), with its monumental temples, is the most impressive ancient site in Lebanon, followed by the Umayyad ruins of **Aanjar** (p351).

THE GOOD LIFE

Good food, good wines, good hotels. After checking in to Beirut's **Hotel Albergo** (p283), make a booking to dine on superb Italian at chic little **Olio** (p283). Stop at Jounieh's legendary **Chez Sami** (p305) for succulent seafood before an overnight stay (in a room with sea views) at **Byblos Sur Mer** (p311) in Byblos. Reserve a table for dinner at **Bab El Mina** (p311). Over lunch at Pepe's **Byblos Fishing Club** (p312), pay homage to the '60s jet set whose pics adorn the walls. If you like winters in the Alps, you'll love the lodge style of **L'Auberge des Cèdres** (p343) at the Cedars. Outside winter, take the mountain road to the Bekaa Valley and the **Ksara Winery** (p351), picking up some wines before heading to Damascus.

In Damascus, a room in elegant Old City boutique **Hotel Talisman** (p105) is a must, as is dinner at the city's finest restaurants **Al-Hallabi** (p107) and **Aldar Restaurant** (p107). Fly to Aleppo for an Oriental palace experience and stay at **Beit Salahieh** (p187) in the Governor's Suite. Lunch at **Cordoba** (p189) for tasty Armenian food, and for dinner feast on delicious cherry kebabs at **Beit Wakil** (p189) and **Beit Sissi** (p189). True foodies should line up with the locals in the early morning for hot steaming bowls of Syria's best **foul** (fava bean soup; p189).

History

EARLY EMPIRES

The area of modern-day Syria and Lebanon lays claim to having one of the oldest civilisations in the world. The shores of Lebanon were settled from around 10,000 BC. Archaeological finds at Ugarit (c 6600 BC), on the Mediterranean coast, and at Mari (c 4500 BC), on the Euphrates River, bear evidence of advanced settlements that would later become sophisticated city-states, in evidence at Byblos (p307).

By around 2500 BC the coast was colonised into city-states by a Semitic group who came to be known as the Phoenicians. For over 1500 years they would watch the ebb and flow of great civilisations before the tide ebbed for them, too.

The emerging city-states were very much independent entities. They were first brought together under the rule of the Akkadians, who marched out of Mesopotamia (modern-day Iraq) in search of conquest and natural resources. Under the rule of Sargon of Akkad (r 2334–2279 BC) the eastern Mediterranean area flourished, particularly ports such as Byblos, which grew wealthy on trade with the Egyptians, who needed plentiful supplies of timber (from Mt Lebanon), a resource lacking in their own country.

By about 1550 BC Egypt had removed itself from under the occupation of Asiatic Hyksos invaders, who had fought to control the country for over a century. To completely banish the threat, the pharaohs pursued their former tormentors north, leading to a period of expansion of the Egyptian empire.

In 1480 BC, a revolt organised by more than 300 local rulers was easily crushed as Egypt was firmly established in what is now Palestine and southern Syria. In the north, however, the various principalities coalesced to form the Mitanni empire. They held off all Egyptian attempts at control, helped in part by their invention of the horse-drawn chariot.

The Mitanni empire was subsumed by the encroachments of the Hittites (1365 BC) from a region corresponding with today's central Turkey. By 1330 BC all of Syria was firmly under Hittite control. The region became a battleground for the Egyptian and Hittite superpowers. They clashed at the bloody Battle of Kadesh on the Nahr al-Aasi (Orontes River) in Syria around 1300 BC, the battle seeing the Egyptians retreat south. Finally, the two opposing forces signed a treaty of friendship in 1284 BC. It left the Egyptians with the south and the Hittites with what corresponds to modern-day Syria and Lebanon.

Still living in tandem with the Egyptians and Hittites were the Phoenicians, who occupied several towns along the Mediterranean coast and

Some Lebanese today refer to themselves as 'Phoenician', and reject that notion that they are 'Arab', a subject that can start a fascinating debate.

The word Palestine is derived from the word 'Philistine', the name of the enigmatic 'Sea Peoples', who were most probably from Crete.

TIMELINE

6600 BC
First evidence of advanced human settlement at Ugarit; fortifications found there indicate that it was already an important settlement at this time.

2500 BC
The Lebanese coast is colonised by a people who came to be known as the Phoenicians, settling in coastal towns that are modern-day Tyre, Sidon and Byblos.

2340 BC
The region flourishes under the rule of Sargon of Akkad, an imperial power whose empire covered all of southern Mesopotamia (modern-day Iraq), as well as most of Syria and western Iran.

successfully traded with Egypt to the south, Mesopotamia to the east and Anatolia to the north. Having no military ambitions, they were not seen as a threat to the great powers of the region. Despite their innovations and skills as artisans and traders, the Phoenicians never became unified politically, and instead remained independent city-states along the Lebanese coast. Gebal (Byblos, later Jbail) and Tyre (also known as Sour) were the most important of these cities, followed by Sidon (Saida) and Berytus (Beirut).

A SPOIL OF WAR

By the 13th century BC the Egyptian empire was in decline and was under threat on several fronts. In the eastern Mediterranean this threat came from the 'Sea Peoples', of whom little is known, except that one group was the Philistines, who settled on the coastal plain in an area that came to be known as the Plain of Philistia. These sea peoples – possibly from the Aegean or Crete – overthrew the Hittites, destroying Ugarit in the process.

Adding to the melange was a further influx of new people, the Aramaeans, a semi-nomadic race from the deserts to the south. The Aramaeans settled mainly in the north including Halab (Aleppo) and Hamath (Hama). Although the Aramaeans stood their ground against the expansionist ambitions of the kingdoms of Judea and Israel to the south, they were unable to repel the attentions of the powerful Assyrian empire (1000–612 BC) to the east and by 732 BC all of Syria was under the command of Sargon II.

For the next 400 years Syria was little more than a spoil of war, being ceded to the Babylonians after their king Nebuchadnezzar defeated the Assyrians, then to the Achaemenid Persians who captured Babylon in 539 BC.

THE GREEKS & ROMANS

Alexander the Great defeated the forces of King Darius III at Issus (333 BC) in what is now southeast Turkey, opening the way for his armies to storm through Syria and Palestine on his way to Egypt. On his death,

Alexander the Great died at the tender age of 33 in Babylon, taking ill after a feast of epic proportions and dying several days later.

> **FOLLOWING THE SCRIPT**
>
> One of the most important contributions to world history during the Late Bronze period was the development of written scripts. The ancient sites of Ugarit in Syria and Byblos in Lebanon have yielded the oldest alphabets yet known. Until then only Egyptian hieroglyphics and Mesopotamian cuneiform existed and both required hundreds of symbols that were far too difficult for anyone but scribes to use. By 1000 BC, scripts that were linear, rather than pictorial, were in general use. It is from these alphabets that today's scripts are derived.

1550 BC	1365 BC	1000 BC
Egyptians control much of Lebanon and southern Syria. In the north, the Mitanni empire blends with the Hurrians and fight for regional dominance against the Egyptians and the Hittites.	The Hittites spread their rule to include modern-day Syria and Lebanon, making pacts with both the Egyptians and the Mitanni; the Phoenician golden age begins.	Writing in linear script, superior to Egyptian hieroglyphics and Mesopotamian cuneiforms, emerges at Ugarit in Syria and Byblos in Lebanon. Tablets at Ugarit bear texts in Ugaritic, Sumerian, Hurrian and Akkadian.

his nascent empire was divided among his bickering generals. Ptolemy I gained Egypt and southern Syria, while Seleucus I Nicator established a kingdom in Babylonia that spread to include the north Syrian centres of Antioch, Apamea, Lattakia and Cyrrhus.

Queen Zenobia was led into Rome in chains, but clearly charmed everyone and was set free. She married a Roman senator and lived out her days in Tibur (now Tivoli), close to Rome.

The Seleucids disputed the Ptolemaic dynasty's claim to Palestine and finally succeeding in ousting them in 198 BC, under the leadership of Antiochus III. A further aggressive campaign of expansion by the Seleucids brought them up against the new power of Rome. In the resulting clash, the Seleucids were defeated and in 188 BC Antiochus was forced to cede all his territories in Asia Minor. However, it wasn't until 64 BC that the Roman legate Pompey finally abolished the Seleucid kingdom, making it a province of Rome with its capital at Antioch.

Antioch became the third-most important imperial city after Rome and Alexandria, and Syria grew rich on trade and agriculture. New trade routes were developed and towns such as Palmyra, Apamea, Bosra, Damascus and Lattakia were replanned and expanded.

In the 3rd century AD the Sassanian Persians (Sassanids) invaded northern Syria, but were repelled by the Syrian prince Odainat of Palmyra. He was granted the title *dux orientalis* (commander of the east) by his Roman overlords for his efforts, but died shortly afterwards. Suspected of complicity in his death, his widow, the beautiful and ambitious Zenobia, assumed the title Augusta and, with her sights set on Rome, invaded western Syria, Palestine and Egypt. In 272, the Roman emperor Aurelian destroyed Palmyra and carted Zenobia off to Rome as a prisoner (for more details, see p203).

After emperor Constantine converted to Christianity in 313, the new religion, now legitimised, soon dominated the empire. This rosy state of affairs was abruptly shattered in the 7th century when the Persians once again descended from the north, taking Damascus and Jerusalem in 614 and eventually Egypt in 616, although Byzantine fortunes were revived when the emperor Heraclius invaded Persia and forced the Persians into a peace agreement. In the south, however, the borders of the empire were being attacked by Arab raiders. This was no new thing, but these Arabs were different. They were ambitious followers of the teachings of a prophet named Mohammed and they called themselves Muslims.

Muslim pilgrimages to Mecca began in 632 AD, but pilgrimages to the ancient city began as early as 2000 BC.

THE ADVENT OF ISLAM

With the Byzantine empire severely weakened by the Persian invasion, the Muslims met with little resistance and in some cases were even welcomed.

In 636 the Muslim armies led by Khaled ibn al-Walid (see p157) won a famous victory at Yarmouk, near the modern border between Jordan and Syria. The Byzantine forces could do little but fall back towards Anatolia. Jerusalem fell in 638 and soon all of Syria was in Muslim hands.

856 BC	539 BC	333 BC
The powerful Assyrian empire takes over parts of northern Syria and Phoenician city-states, later pushing into Damascus and ending independent rule there in 732.	The Achaemenid Persians take over much of Syria after defeating the Babylonians and Syria is made a province. The only real evidence of their reign remains at Amrit.	Alexander the Great defeats the forces of Darius III and storms Syria. Darius III, who fled and left his family to be captured, twice offers Alexander incentives to stop his march into Mesopotamia. Alexander declines.

Because of its position on the pilgrims' route to Mecca, Syria became the hub of the new Muslim empire that, by the early 8th century, stretched from Spain across northern Africa and the Middle East to Persia (modern Iran) and India. Mu'awiyah, the governor of Damascus, had himself declared the fifth caliph (successor to Mohammed) in 658 and then went on to found a dynasty, the Umayyads, which would last for nearly 100 years.

Umayyad rule was overthrown in 750, when the Abbasids seized power. This new and solemn religious dynasty moved the capital of the Arab world to Baghdad, relegating Syria to backwater status. By 980, all of Palestine and part of Syria, including Damascus, had fallen under the rule of the Fatimid dynasty, whose capital was Cairo.

Emperor Constantine (sometimes known as Constantine the Great) attributed his success to his belief in a Christian God and became the first Roman emperor to profess his beliefs.

THE CRUSADES

A plea from Pope Urban II in November 1095 for the recapture of the Church of the Holy Sepulchre in Jerusalem resulted in a Crusade of hundreds of thousands of people on the road to the Holy Land. All along their route, cities such as Antioch, Aleppo, Apamea, Damascus, Tripoli, Beirut and Jerusalem, weakened by their own rivalries and divisions, were exposed to the invaders' untempered violence.

The atrocities inflicted on the population of Ma'arat an-Nu'aman (see p198) in December 1098 were perhaps the nadir of Crusading behaviour, but the same excesses of savagery also marked the taking of Jerusalem on 15 July 1099, when only a handful of Jewish and Muslim inhabitants escaped alive.

SALADIN (1138–93)

Salah ad-Din Yusuf ibn Ayyub is the first and most salient historical Arab hero. He was born in Tikrit (in modern Iraq, the same birthplace as Saddam Hussein) to Kurdish parents, and the family moved to Aleppo after Saladin was born. At the age of 14 he joined other members of his family in the service of Nureddin of the ruling Zangid dynasty. Saladin rose to the rank of general and had already taken de facto control of Egypt by the time Nureddin died in 1174. Saladin quickly took control of Syria and in the next 10 years extended his control into parts of Mesopotamia, being careful not to infringe too closely on the territory of the by-then largely powerless Abbasid caliphate in Baghdad.

In 1187 Saladin crushed the Crusaders in the Battle of Hittin and stormed Jerusalem. By the end of 1189, he had swept the Franks out of Lattakia and Jabla to the north and from castles such as Kerak and Shobak (both in Jordan) inland. This provoked Western Europe into action, precipitating the Third Crusade and matching Saladin against Richard I 'the Lionheart' of England. After countless clashes and sieges, the two rival warriors signed a peace treaty in November 1192, giving the Crusaders the coast and the Muslims the interior. Saladin died three months later in Damascus.

---

64 BC	AD 272	313
Pompey the Great abolishes the Seleucid Kingdom and annexes Syria. The region becomes a principal province of the Roman Empire with its main city at Antioch (now Antakya in Turkey).	After trying to take Egypt and Antioch, Zenobia of Palmyra flees Antioch, is defeated by the Roman Emperor Aurelian, is captured while fleeing again and sent to Rome as a prisoner.	Tolerance of Christianity is declared by Roman emperor Constantine I (Constantine the Great) and Emperor Licinius. The Edict of Milan seeks to end persecution for Christians and Constantine encourages it as the state religion in Syria.

Following the capture of the Holy City, the Crusaders built or took over a string of castles, including the well-preserved Qala'at al-Hosn (Krak des Chevaliers; p133). Nureddin (Nur ad-Din), the son of a Turkish tribal ruler, was able to unite all of Syria not held by the Franks and defeat the Crusaders in Egypt. His campaign was continued by Saladin (Salah ad-Din; see p25), who recaptured Palestine and most of the inland Crusader strongholds. Saladin's compromise with the Assassins (see p170) led to the Crusaders remaining on the coast.

The Crusades through Arab Eyes (1984), by Amin Maalouf, offers an antidote to the 'traditional' Western histories of the Crusades. Essential reading for students of Middle Eastern history.

Prosperity returned to Syria with the rule of Saladin's dynasty, known as the Ayyubids, who parcelled up the empire on his death. They were succeeded by the Mamluks, the freed slave class of Turkish origin that had taken power in Cairo in 1250, just in time to repel the onslaught from the invading Mongol tribes from Central Asia in 1260. Led by the fourth of their sultans, Beybars – a great warrior hero of Islam – the Mamluks finally managed to rid the Levant of the Crusaders by capturing their last strongholds, taking Acre in 1291 and the fortified island of Ruad (Arwad; see p139) in 1302. Not quite as chivalrous as Saladin, Beybars torched Antioch, a devastation from which the city never recovered. Beybars also separated the Crusaders from their castles and put them to flight.

However, more death and destruction was not far off and in 1401 the Mongol invader Tamerlane sacked Aleppo and Damascus, killing thousands and carting off many artisans to Central Asia. His new empire lasted for only a few years but the rout sent Mamluk Syria into decline for a century.

THE OTTOMAN TURKS

By 1516 the Ottoman Turks occupied Palestine and Syria and would remain there for the next four centuries. Most of the desert areas of modern Syria, however, remained the preserve of Bedouin tribes.

The Young Turks were a group of reformers who ruled the Ottoman Empire from 1913 to 1918. Both the Armenian and Assyrian 'genocides' occurred during their rule – the use of the term genocide is still debated within Turkey and globally.

Up until the early 19th century, Syria prospered under Turkish rule. Damascus and Aleppo were important market towns for the surrounding desert as well as being stages on the desert trade routes and stops on the pilgrimage route to Mecca. Aleppo was also an important trading centre with Europe.

By the 19th century, though, groups of Arab intellectuals in Syria and Palestine, many influenced by years of study in Europe, had set an Arab reawakening in train. The harsh policies of the Young Turk movement of 1908 further encouraged both opposition to Turkish rule and growth of Arab nationalism.

WWI & THE FRENCH MANDATE

During WWI, the region was the scene of fierce fighting between the Turks, who had German backing, and the British based in Suez. The enigmatic British colonel TE Lawrence, better known as Lawrence of

The Byzantine era, three centuries of rule from Constantinople (today's Istanbul), begins in Syria, with strong prosperity and cultural activity only limited by Persian aggression.

After the Prophet Mohammed's death, the Caliphate, Abu Bakr takes the expansion of the Muslim faith to the next level and Arab conquest begins. Syria is claimed in 636 after the decisive battle at Yarmouk.

The dawn of the Umayyad Caliphate ushers in a period of great invention starting with the Sufyanid reign (661–84), where Damascus was the centre of the action, followed by the Marwanid reign (684–750).

Arabia (see p188), and other British officers involved with the Arab Revolt encouraged Arab forces to take control of Damascus, and Emir Faisal, the leader of the revolt, to set up a government in 1918.

When Arab nationalists proclaimed Faisal king of Greater Syria (an area that included Palestine and Lebanon) and his Hashemite brother, Abdullah, king of Iraq in March 1920, the French moved swiftly to force Faisal into exile. Later the French were formally awarded the mandate over Syria and Lebanon by the League of Nations.

Under pressure from the Lebanese Christian Maronites, the French employed what amounted to a divide-and-rule policy. They split their mandate into Lebanon (including Tyre, Beirut and Tripoli); a Syrian Republic, whose Muslim majority resented their presence; and the two districts, Lattakia and Jebel Druze.

The French attempt to create a Lebanese nation fell foul of growing Arab nationalist sentiment, which held that Arabs should live in a greater Arab homeland, rather than arbitrarily drawn nation states. For the Maronites, who looked towards Europe, Arab nationalism was a threat. Hostility to the French led to uprisings in 1925 and 1926 and France twice bombarded Damascus.

Scant attention was paid to the opposition and in 1926 the French and their Maronite allies drew up and passed a new constitution for Lebanon, sowing the seeds of the country's troubled future. The document formalised a largely symbolic power-sharing formula, but Maronites still managed to secure a virtual monopoly on positions of power. Sunni Muslims boycotted the constitution, which was suspended in 1932. In 1936, the Franco-Lebanese treaty was signed, promising eventual independence for Lebanon; the following year a new constitution was drawn up but not ratified by the French.

In Syria, a Constituent Assembly set up in 1928 to hammer out a constitution for partial independence was dissolved because it proposed a single state, including Lebanon, as the successor to the Ottoman province. This was unacceptable to the French.

In 1932 the first parliamentary elections took place in Syria. Although the majority of moderates elected had been hand-picked by Paris, they rejected all French terms for a constitution.

Finally, in 1936, a treaty was signed but never ratified; under the deal, a state of Syria would control Lattakia and Jebel Druze as well as the sanjak (subprovince) of Alexandretta, the present-day Turkish province of Hatay. After riots by Turks protesting against becoming part of Syria, the French encouraged Turkey to send in troops to help supervise elections.

The outcome favoured the Turks and the sanjak became part of Turkey in 1939. Syria has never recognised the outcome, and at the time it further sharpened feeling against France.

Many Maronites left the Middle East in the 1800s and there are large Maronite communities in Europe and in North and South America.

A Peace to End All Peace: The Fall of the Ottoman Empire and the Creation of the Modern Middle East (2001), by David Fromkin, chronicles Middle East meddling by Europe during WWI and the mess that ensued.

750 **1097** **1260**

Incompetent rule by the Umayyads sees the Abbasids assume power. A more Eastern-leaning, sombre and devout Persian rule, they transfer the Caliphate to what is modern-day Iraq.

The Crusaders come to Syria and find the resistance lacking in cohesion and strength overall. However, Antioch only falls after a protracted struggle and Tripoli's resistance finally crumbles in 1109.

The Mamluks rule the region and usher in a renewed vigour in the fight against the Crusaders, taking back Antioch in 1268, Qala'at al-Hosn (Krak des Chevaliers) in 1271 and later Latakia (1287) and Tripoli (1289).

WWII & INDEPENDENCE

When France fell to the Germans in 1940, Syria and Lebanon came under the control of the puppet Vichy government until July 1941, when British and Free French forces took over. The Free French promised independence – and delivered another five years later – but only after violent clashes (and French bombing) in Syria in 1945 had compelled Britain to intervene. Syria took control of its own affairs when the last of the British troops pulled out in April 1946.

For more on the religious makeup of Lebanon, see the Religion chapter (p42).

In Lebanon, the various religious and political factions came together in 1943 to draw up the Lebanese National Covenant, an unwritten agreement dividing power along sectarian lines on the basis of the 1932 census. The president was to be Maronite, the prime minister a Sunni, and the speaker of the house a Shiite. Parliamentary seats were divvied-up between Christians and Muslims in the ratio of six to five. The Maronites were also given control of the army, with a Druze chief of staff.

In November 1943, the fledgling Lebanese government of President Bishara al-Khouri went a step further and passed legislation removing all references to French Authority in the constitution. The French retaliated by arresting the president and members of his cabinet, and suspending the constitution. Britain, the US and the Arab states supported the Lebanese cause for independence, and in 1944 the French began the transfer of all public services to Lebanese control, followed by the withdrawal of French troops. Independence was declared in 1946.

POST-INDEPENDENCE SYRIA
A Land of Confusion

Civilian rule in Syria was short-lived, and was terminated in 1949 by a series of military coups that brought to power officers with nationalist and socialist leanings. By 1954, the Ba'athists in the army, who had won support among the Alawite and Druze minorities (see p44), had no real rival.

The ruling al-Assad family are Alawites – an offshoot of Shiite Islam that only makes up 11% of Syria's population.

Founded in 1940 by a Christian teacher, Michel Aflaq, the Arab Ba'ath Socialist Party was committed to the creation of a greater Arab state. In a merger with Egypt under President Nasser in 1958, Syria became the Northern Province of the United Arab Republic. Although this was at first a popular move with many Syrians, the Egyptians treated them as subordinates, and after yet another military coup in September 1961, Damascus resumed full sovereignty. Although outwardly civilian, the new regime was under military control and it made few concessions to Ba'ath and pro-Nasser pan-Arabists, resulting in yet another change of government in March 1963.

A month before the Ba'ath takeover in 1963, which first propelled an air force lieutenant-general, Hafez al-Assad, into a government headed by General Amin al-Hafez, the Iraqi branch of the party seized power

1401	1516	1918
The Mamluks, weakened by civil war, succumb to the Mongol invader Tamerlane. Also know as Timur, he is from modern-day Uzbekistan and a student of the strategies of Genghis Khan. Tamerlane sacks Aleppo and Damascus, killing thousands.	The Ottoman Turks occupy the Syrian region, with Süleiman the Magnificent taking charge in 1520; he systematically gets taxes and administration in order and makes Aleppo, Damascus and Raqqa provinces.	The Allies and Arab Nationalists enter Damascus on 1 October after the Turkish flee the day before. Emir Faisal is declared king, but the French mandate sees the French rule by force. Faisal departs in 1920.

in Baghdad. Attempts were made to unite Iraq, Egypt and Syria, but the parties failed to agree on the tripartite federation. The Ba'ath Party in Iraq was overthrown in November 1963.

Syria now stood alone. The Ba'ath Party's economic policy of nationalisation was meeting with much dissatisfaction, expressed in a disastrous and bloodily repressed revolt in the city of Hama in 1964. Worse, the Ba'athists' pan-Arabism implicitly gave non-Syrians a significant say in Syrian affairs, an issue that led to a party split. In February 1966, the ninth coup saw Amin al-Hafez ousted and the self-proclaimed socialist radical wing of the party took control of the government. Hafez al-Assad, the rising strongman, was instrumental in bringing about the fall of the party old guard.

The war between Israel and Syria and Egypt in 1973 is often called the 'Yom Kippur War' as the Syrians and Egyptians attacked on the holiest day of the Jewish calendar.

War But No Peace
The socialist government was severely weakened by defeat in two conflicts. The first disaster came at the hands of the Israelis in the June 1967 war. Later known as the Six Day War, it was launched by Israel partly in

THE SECOND SON
It was never meant to happen. Bashar al-Assad, born on 11 September, 1965, was the second son of Hafez al-Assad, president of Syria since seizing power in November 1970. But Bashar's elder brother, Basil, was always groomed for the throne. While Basil was outgoing, Bashar was introspective; while Basil was driving fast cars, Bashar was studying to become a doctor. That all changed in 1994, when Basil was killed in a car accident. 'Doctor Bashar', who was in London studying ophthalmology, came home. With his soft-spoken nature and bookish appearance, the doctor was looking forward to running his own ophthalmologists' surgery, but instead he entered the military academy at Homs and rose to the rank of colonel in the elite Presidential Guard.

Upon his father's death in 2000, Bashar assumed power. Expectations were unreasonably high, both from Syrian intellectuals hungry for change and from Western interests keen to see moves towards Western-style democracy. While Bashar made cautious progress, political freedoms were not forthcoming and early signs of media freedom were soon curtailed – perhaps he was his father's son after all.

However, this lack of progress remains at odds with his personal profile. He likes to drive his own car (safely), eat at restaurants sans cronies and attend arts events with his British-born wife, Asma. A Syrian Sunni from West London, she was known as Emma and worked as a financial analyst before marrying Bashar. Both are apparently charming, grounded and well rounded. They married in a low-key civil ceremony in Damascus on New Year's Day 2001 and only alerted the press the next day.

The most common question asked of this enigma is, 'is he really in control?' Bashar's always accused of being either a dictator or a puppet. He has heard the criticism many times and once stated that the questioners should choose, because he certainly cannot be both at once. The question remains though, could he be one thing while pretending to be the other?

1922   **1940**   **1946**

The French Mandate for Syria and Lebanon is ratified by the League of Nations. Lebanon's separate status is confirmed; Syria, with its predominately Muslim population, proves harder to manage.

Syria and Lebanon come under control of the puppet Vichy government. In June 1941 British and other Allied forces, along with the Free French forces, invade Syria. Independence is near for both states.

Complete Lebanese independence is finally declared. In Syria, the French Mandate that had ended in 1945 and saw Syria join the UN finally sees the French forces leave Damascus – after a farewell bombing.

retaliation for raids by Syrian guerrillas on Israeli settlements and also because the Egyptians were massing troops near the Israeli border. The result was a severe political and psychological reversal for the Arab states and saw vast areas of land fall into Israeli hands. Syria lost the Golan Heights and Damascus itself was threatened.

Next came the Black September hostilities in Jordan in 1970. In this clash, the Jordanian army smashed Syrian-supported Palestinian guerrilla groups who were vying for power in Jordan. At this point Hafez al-Assad, who had opposed backing the Palestinians against the Jordanian army, seized power in November 1970. He was sworn in as Syria's president in 1971.

On 6 October 1973, Syria, in a surprise offensive coordinated with Egypt, sent 850 tanks across the 1967 cease-fire line to regain the lost Golan Heights. It was also an attempt to regain *karama* (dignity) after previous ignominious defeats. Three days after hostilities started, Israeli planes bombed Damascus. The Arab offensive failed; an Israeli counter-attack was halted only 35km from Damascus. Although Assad grudgingly accepted a UN cease-fire on 22 October (as Egypt had done), his troops kept up low-level harrying actions in the Golan area. Egypt signed an armistice in January 1974 but it was not until the end of May that Syria did the same.

Syria Today

After 30 years of iron-fisted and often bloody presidential rule, Hafez al-Assad died on 10 June 2000, aged 69. His replacement was his son, 34-year-old Bashar al-Assad (see The Second Son, p29), for whom the constitution had to be amended to allow the swearing in of a president younger than 40.

The unopposed election of Bashar al-Assad gave Syria's budding reform movement hope, but they were to be sorely disappointed with the new leader, who clearly was either unable or unwilling to affect change as quickly as expected. Assad, however, did implement a mandatory retirement age of 60 for the military (thereby retiring some of his father's cronies) and tackled corruption in the public service. Elections in March 2003 saw 178 mostly fresh new faces elected to the 250-member People's Assembly. Relations with the US reached an all-time low with the invasion of Iraq, as did relations with Israel, with border skirmishes and bombings.

In 2004, growing dissent by intellectuals about human rights sparked Assad to discuss reforms to the Ba'ath Party, but any activities that were deemed against the regime were quickly put down. Relations with Israel remained tense and relations with the US reached a new nadir, with the US applying sanctions to Syria in May. The US saw Syria as supporting Hezbollah and other groups that they deemed terrorist organisations and

After the death of Hafez al-Assad in 2000, passionate political and social debates raged across Syria. The short-lived period of openness was dubbed the 'Damascus Spring'.

In late 2007, Syrian authorities blocked Facebook, the popular social networking website, over fears that Israelis had 'infiltrated' groups there. Web-savvy Syrians believe that it is actually because of the government's fear of political dissent.

1948	1957	1958
The State of Israel is declared; Lebanese troops join a pan-Arab army to invade Israel. Thousands of Palestinian refugees flood into Lebanon and are housed in temporary refugee camps. Later, many camps will become permanent.	Lebanon's Maronite President Camille Chamoun signs the Eisenhower Doctrine, which offers US aid to Middle Eastern countries to oppose 'communist' threats. He then supports Western troops against Egypt's President Nasser. Both acts anger Arab leaders.	Lebanon's first civil crisis erupts, with Muslim supporters of pan-Arabism facing pro-Western Maronites. US troops land in Beirut to intervene at President Chamoun's behest and succeed in crushing disturbances.

began focussing on Lebanon, asking Syria to remove its military and intelligence presence from the beleaguered country. While Syria continued to accept refugees from Iraq, the US was more concerned with just who was crossing the border: the situation on the border remained tense.

Things did not improve in 2005. On February 14, former Lebanese prime minister and outspoken heavyweight Rafiq Hariri was assassinated in Beirut. Given that Syria stood to gain from this, agents working for the government of Syria were immediately suspected, despite the Syrian president's condemnation of the act. The response in Lebanon brought down the pro-Syrian government: by April 26 the last Syrian soldiers had left Lebanese soil. This, in turn, left a power vacuum in Lebanon that the Iranian-backed Hezbollah was more than ready to exploit. With Damascus under pressure to hand over Iraqi Ba'athist's who had fled Iraq, as well as to reduce the flow of weapons and fighters crossing the border, Assad was placed in a no-win situation on several fronts.

During 2006, Assad strengthened ties with Iran and Russia and managed to stay out of the war between Israel and Hezbollah forces in Lebanon, warning Israel that and move towards the border would result in conflict. After a tense summer in 2007, relations with Israel worsened on September 6, when Israeli aircraft bombed a site in the north of Syria. Syria's hushed response and rumours that a shipment from North Korea – possibly containing nuclear material – was the target of the top-secret operation make this an intriguing chapter in Syria–Israel relations.

In 2007 a presidential election saw Bashar al-Assad returned to power with an overwhelming vote of 97.62%, predictable considering there was no other candidate. While Assad has weathered a crisis (or three) over

---

BORDER CROSSING CRISIS

As the fallout of the invasion of Iraq drags on, Arab hospitality has been sorely tested by the exodus of Iraqi refugees. It's estimated that 2 million people have fled Iraq, with 1.5 million going to Syria and at least 500,000 going to Jordan – on top of over 2 million internally displaced Iraqi citizens. The refugees in Syria were granted three-month visas renewable within Syria, but as of 2007 the rules changed: every three months refugees now have to cross to the border and get stamped to return for up to three months, after which they must repeat the process. The experiences are diverse; wealthy Iraqi's have been buying apartments and houses, prompting a serious rise in rents. Poorer refugees have scrambled to make a living, working as cheap labour, while some young women are being forced to join the sex trade and there are concerns about child prostitution and trafficking. Towards the end of 2007, some Iraqis began to move back and while many attributed this 'success' to the improved security situation, the UN High Commission for Refugees stated that 46% of returning refugees could no longer afford to stay in Syria, 25% could not obtain new visas and only 14% said that it was because of the improved security situation.

1963	1967	1967
After numerous coups, Ba'athists seize power in Syria, a month after the Ba'athists have come to power in Iraq. A union between the two countries is only thwarted after talks in Cairo do not bear fruit.	The aggressive foreign policies of the Ba'athist regime see Syria lose the Golan Heights in the Six Day War with Israel. For Syria, it is only the first of several military humiliations to come.	The Six Day War brings a new influx of Palestinians into Lebanon. Some are members of the Palestinian Liberation Organisation (PLO), which formed in 1964.

GOVERNMENT & ECONOMY SNAPSHOTS

Syria

Syria is a presidential republic, and its 1973 constitution declares that its legislative powers lie with the people and that freedom of expression and equality before the law is guaranteed, as is universal suffrage, although it is only the last of these that's evident. Syria has 14 governorates, divided into districts and subdistricts, and while these are elected, the real power lies with the president. All political parties are huddled under the one umbrella, the National Progressive Front, a coalition of parties dominated by the Ba'ath Party. The president is nominally elected (and must be a Muslim) and appoints a cabinet that exercises legislative and executive powers.

The country functions essentially as a socialist state, the government operating the oil refineries, electricity production and mass manufacturing plants. Taxes are mainly indirect. Associations of workers look after workers rights and some social service aspects of employment. The economy is at a crossroads, having relied too long on now-dwindling oil reserves to prop up the lack of investment money coming into the country. Reforms, such as private banking and a toe in the water towards free trade, were stymied by war and the US government sanctions, both of which slowed tourism and investment. With over 20% unemployment and heavy debt, Syria's key issues are now regional stability and a willingness to open the country to investment.

Lebanon

Lebanon is a republic with a unique parliamentary system that was devised during the French mandate in 1926, with a few alterations since to reflect the religious make-up of the country. Parliamentary seats are split evenly between Christian and Muslim sects. The president, who always is a Maronite Christian, is the head of state and is elected by a two-thirds majority of the National Assembly for a single term of six years. The president may stand again after another six years have elapsed. The Prime Minister must be a Sunni Muslim and the speaker of parliament a Shiite Muslim. The cabinet also reflects the sectarian mix. The country is divided into governorates, which in turn are divided into districts and smaller municipalities, all of which have elected officials.

Former Prime Minister Rafiq Hariri went a long way to putting the economy back on track after the civil war, but the spate of assassinations, war and political unrest since then make Lebanon an unlikely target for the foreign investment needed to get the country back on its economic feet. The lack of political consensus to privatise government-owned businesses has further hampered an economic upswing, as has rampant government corruption and massive budget deficits. Until there is political stability both within the country and with its neighbours, the negative outlook is not set to change. However, given the opportunity, Lebanon has a knack of bouncing back, both in investment and tourism.

the preceding seven years, the posters and paintings of his father, Hafez, still hang proudly across the country. Until he can make a clean break with the past and put more of his own stamp on the country through economic, diplomatic, political and media reforms, the shadow cast by his father will not fade.

1969	1970	1970
On 3 February Yasser Arafat is appointed PLO chairman. In November, the Cairo Agreement is signed, guaranteeing Palestinian militants greater autonomy over Palestinian refugee camps in Lebanon.	The Alawite leadership of both the Ba'athist Party and Syria continues; Hafez al-Assad is promoted to the leadership role and sworn in as Syria's president on 14 March 1971.	Black Sunday sees PLO militants driven out of Jordan, along with a third wave of Palestinian civilian refugees, and the PLO subsequently establishes headquarters in Beirut. Palestinian guerrilla raids into northern Israel from southern Lebanon increase.

POST-INDEPENDENCE LEBANON
The Covenant's First Years
The early years of the National Assembly were not easy for a system that would soon prove a political pressure cooker. Beset by economic problems, the first major political crisis for the government came on 14 May 1948 with the declaration of Israeli independence in former Palestine.

Immediately, a delegation of Lebanese soldiers joined forces with pan-Arab armies and Palestinian fighters. Israel, however, proved unconquerable. Lebanon accepted an armistice on 23 March 1949. By July, a final agreement had been signed with Syria, and Israel's new borders were secured.

During 1948 and 1949, while war raged, Palestinian refugees flooded into Lebanon. Amnesty International puts Lebanon's 1949 refugee population at around 100,000, indicating that it absorbed more Palestinian refugees than any other country. Though the 1948 UN Resolution 194 stated that refugees who wished to return home in peace should be allowed to do so, this was largely not to be. Initially welcomed into Lebanon, the Maronite majority soon became uneasy about the refugees, mostly Sunni Muslims, who threatened to tilt the balance of power established by the 1932 census.

The Turbulent '50s
By the 1950s, the National Assembly was struggling against economic crisis and growing support for pan-Arabism. In 1951, Prime Minister Riad al-Solh was assassinated and in 1952, amid heated public protests, the government resigned, with pro-Western president Camille Chamoun stepping in. Staunchly disregarding the position of non-Christian Lebanese, Chamoun garnered substantial opposition from Muslim sectors and in 1956 became the only Arab leader to support the Western invasion of Egypt following the Suez Canal crisis. In 1957, he signed the Eisenhower Doctrine, allowing the USA to 'use armed forces to assist any nation…in the Middle East requesting assistance against armed aggressors from any country controlled by international communism', and topped it off by refusing to unite with Syria and Egypt as part of their newly formed United Arab Republic, or with Jordan and Iraq as part of their Arab Federation.

In 1958, with Chamoun's unpopular presidency due to run out, he nevertheless managed to win the elections, provoking allegations of fraud. His attempt to extend his presidency to a second consecutive term was widely considered unconstitutional, and Lebanon's first civil crisis soon erupted, with pro-Western Maronites pitted against largely Muslim, pro-Arab opponents. Chamoun, panicking, asked US president Eisenhower to intervene. On 15 July 1958, Operation Blue Bat saw 15,000 US troops land in Beirut.

The presence of US troops quelled the opposition, though the government was severely weakened and Chamoun was persuaded to resign by a US envoy. Chief of Staff Fouad Chehab, his replacement as president, was popular with Christians and Muslims and more even-handed in leadership.

Riad al-Solh was the first of three Lebanese prime ministers, two presidents and 10 politicians to be assassinated – before, during, or following their term of office – between 1951 and 2007.

Chamoun was the first of several presidents to extend their terms of duty. Recent president Émile Lahoud extended his term in 2004; pro-democracy campaigners argue this is illegal and unconstitutional.

1973
Egypt and Syria launch a surprise attack on Israel on their Yom Kippur holiday; after early gains Syria ends up with another humiliating defeat.

1975
Full-scale civil war breaks out in Lebanon, with tit-for-tat killings between Phalangist and Muslim militias. Beirut is divided along the front-line Green Line and will remain that way for 15 years.

1976
At the request of Lebanon's president Suleiman Franjieh, thousands of Syrian troops intervene on the Maronites' behalf in the fighting in Lebanon, angering the Arab world. Syria will switch allegiance frequently during the conflict.

THE DISPLACED & THE DISPOSSESSED

Though some middle-class Palestinian refugees found it possible to integrate into mainstream Lebanese society, tens of thousands of others were relegated to refugee camps administered by the UN Relief and Works Agency (UNRWA). Today, 12 of the original 16 camps still house most of Lebanon's Palestinian population. According to UNRWA, there are now about 410,000 registered Palestinian refugees in Lebanon, while Amnesty International estimates that there are another 3000 to 5000 second-generation unregistered refugees living illegally and without rights.

Palestinian refugees in Lebanon still suffer from a lack of opportunities. They are prohibited from entering professions governed by a professional syndicate, such as engineering and medicine, are largely barred from owning property and have only limited access to public health care, education and welfare programmes. Most are still provided for by UNRWA, which runs the camps' schools, hospitals, women's centres and vocational training.

They are not, however, Lebanon's only disadvantaged group. The Geneva-based Internal Displacement Monitoring Centre (IDMC) estimates there are between 216,000 and 800,000 Internally Displaced Persons in Lebanon, defined as individuals forced out of their homes due to war, persecution or natural disaster. It states 200,000 people are displaced as a result of the 2006 war between Hezbollah and Israel, which saw the destruction of infrastructure, livelihoods and hundreds of homes. The remainder, says the IDMC, are still displaced following Lebanon's civil war and Israeli invasions and occupation of southern Lebanon.

For more information, visit the IDMC website www.internal-displacement.org, or the UNRWA website www.un.org/unrwa.

He presided over the withdrawal of American forces, and appointed Rashid Karami, leader of the Muslim insurrection in the north, prime minister. Karami formed a National Reconciliation government, order was temporarily restored, and Beirut developed as the banking capital of the Arab world.

Paradise Lost & the Six Day War

In 1964, Charles Hélou became President Chehab's successor and pressed on with reforms in the newly crowned 'Paris of the East'. Beirut blossomed, attracting a hard-partying international jet set, but most of the prosperity remained concentrated in the city and its environs, while the southern Shiites and Palestinian refugees remained in poverty. While Beirut basked in newfound riches, the less fortunate grew bitter and restless.

Stability was not to last. In 1966 the country's largest bank collapsed, then in 1967 the Six Day War brought a fresh influx of Palestinian refugees into Lebanon, and refugee camps soon became centres of guerrilla resistance. The government, too weak to suppress guerrilla operations, watched impotently as Palestinian attacks on Israel rapidly increased from Lebanese soil.

In May 1968 Israeli forces retaliated across the border, frequently targeting Lebanese villages which, against their will, often sheltered guerrillas. In December, a plane of the Israeli carrier El Al was machine-gunned by

Chamoun, undaunted after his resignation, formed the National Liberation Party and was re-elected president in 1960, 1968 and 1972. He later became Deputy Prime Minister from 1984 until his death in 1987.

1978

Israel launches Operation Litani and occupies southern Lebanon. The UN creates an Interim Force in Lebanon (Unifil) to ensure peace and oversee Israel's withdrawal, while Israel forms the proxy South Lebanon Army (SLA) to protect its interests in the 'buffer zone.'

1982

In Lebanon, Syrian forces get pushed back by Israeli forces. Back in Syria, the massacre of thousands of supporters of the Muslim Brotherhood at Hama sees Assad globally castigated and losing popularity at home.

1982

In June Israel invades Lebanon; Israeli troops attack Syrian soldiers in the Bekaa Valley and surround Beirut. In September, Lebanon's president Bashir Gemayel is assassinated; reprisals include massacres at Sabra and Shatila camps. International peacekeepers arrive in Lebanon.

Palestinian militants at Athens airport; Israel responded by destroying 13 Lebanese passenger aircraft in Beirut. With sectarian tensions growing, polarising the Lebanese population, the army clashed violently with Palestinian guerrillas. The guerrillas proved too strong, and in November 1969 army leader General Emile Bustani cemented the Egyptian-brokered Cairo Agreement with the Palestinian Liberation Organisation (PLO). Bustani agreed to most of their terms, including large-scale autonomy of the camps and the freedom 'to participate in the Palestinian revolution'.

Maronite opposition to the agreement was immediate: as the country's demographic balance steadily tipped towards a Muslim majority – due to a higher Muslim birth rate and large numbers of Christians relocating overseas – they complained that parts of Lebanon had become a Palestinian 'state within a state'. Many Muslims, however, felt an innate sympathy to their fellow Palestinian Sunnis. In response, Christian Phalangists began to arm and train young men around the Qadisha Valley; by March 1970, fighting between Phalangists and Palestinians had erupted on Beirut's streets.

In the Black September hostilities of the same year, the Jordanian army drove Palestinians out of Jordan, prompting a third influx of refugees into Lebanon, many of them members of the PLO. Meanwhile, southern Lebanon suffered under Israeli reprisals against relentless guerilla attacks. Rapidly, the country factionalised and took up arms, with newly elected, fiercely militant Maronite president Suleiman Franjieh doing little to soothe tensions.

Meanwhile, the newly formed National Movement, led by Kamal Jumblatt, called for a new census and a subsequent alteration of governmental structure. The National Movement allied itself to the Palestinians against the Maronites, while Phalangists, armed by Israel, joined the Lebanese army in opposing them. It wouldn't be long until the country erupted in flames.

Civil War Begins

Though a long time coming, it's widely agreed that civil war began on 13 April 1975, when Phalangist gunmen attacked a Beirut bus, killing 27 Palestinian passengers. Soon, it was outright chaos. In December, four Christians were found shot dead in a car, and in response Phalangists stopped Beirut traffic and killed Muslim travellers. Muslims did the same, prompting 'Black Saturday' during which around 300 people died.

The slaughter rapidly reached horrific proportions. In January 1976, Phalangists led a massacre of some 1000 Palestinians in Karantina, a Beirut slum. Two days later, Palestinians attacked the coastal town of Damour, killing over 500 Christians. In August, Phalangists set their sights on the Tel al-Zaatar refugee camp, killing between 2000 and 3000 Palestinian civilians.

Soon Beirut was divided along the infamous Green Line, with Christian enclaves to the east and Muslims to the west. Though allegiances and alliances along its border would shift many times in the coming strife, the Green Line would remain in place for another 15 years.

The officially secular Phalange army was established in 1936 by Pierre Gemayel as a youth movement, inspired by his observations on Nazi party organisation at the 1936 Berlin Olympic Games.

Suleiman Franjieh is widely considered one of Lebanon's most ruthless presidents, responsible for numerous murders that began with the massacre of 22 Christians of a rival clan inside a church.

1983	1985	1988
On 23 October, 56 French paratroopers and 241 US marines are killed in suicide bombings in Beirut, after US warships shell Muslim areas in support of President Amin Gemayel. Militant Shiite groups take responsibility.	Israeli troops withdraw south from Sidon and Tyre, leaving some support forces in the South Lebanon 'security zone', and impose a fierce policy of military repression. Shiite Amal forces attack Palestinian camps in Beirut.	Holding little power, the Lebanese government splinters in two; the Christians are led by Chief of Staff General Michel Aoun in East Beirut, and Muslims by former deputy Prime Minister Selim al-Hos in the West.

Syria & Israel Intervene

The late 1960s saw Syrian displeasure building towards its neighbour, as Lebanon's army attempted to prevent Palestinian guerrilla attacks. Though Syria didn't want Palestinian aggression on its own soil, it objected to Lebanon's official retaliation and in 1973 closed its Lebanese borders in protest. The outbreak of civil war soon gave Syria the opportunity to intervene more actively in Lebanon and in 1976 it sent in troops, initially sympathetic to Jumblatt's National Movement and the Palestinians. It wasn't long, though, before Syria switched allegiance to the Maronite cause, sending in tens of thousands of troops countrywide, occupying all but the far south, and angering other Arab countries. Syrian aid also helped Phalangists finally break the Tel al-Zaatar siege, resulting in the August 1976 massacre.

In October 1976 the Arab League brokered a deal with Syria, allowing it to keep 40,000 troops in Lebanon as part of a peacekeeping Arab Deterrent Force. Syria was left in primary control of Lebanon, and the first of the civil war's 150 cease-fires was declared. Despite Syria's policing, Palestinian attacks on Israel continued, causing Israel to launch Operation Litani in 1978, swiftly occupying most of southern Lebanon and causing the evacuation of around 100,000 civilians. Immediately, the UN demanded Israel's withdrawal and formed the UN Interim Force in Lebanon (Unifil) to 'restore international peace'. Though Israel withdrew to a 20km-wide 'Security Zone', it also installed the South Lebanon Army (SLA), led by pro-Israeli Christian Major Saad Haddad, and proclaimed a region comprising 1800 sq km south of the Litani River as 'Free Lebanon'. Soon, the area was knee-deep in war.

Regardless of attempts at an American-brokered cease-fire in 1981, Israel appeared keen to eradicate the PLO and, with tensions between Syria and the Phalangists mounting, moved closer towards its Lebanese Christian allies. Thus, on 6 June 1982, when Israeli troops involved in Operation Peace for Galilee marched into Lebanon, pushing Syrian forces from the Bekaa Valley and heading north to Beirut, they were supported tacitly by Maronite and Phalangist leaders. By 15 June, Israeli forces had surrounded and besieged West Beirut, bombarding 16,000 PLO fighters entrenched there.

By the end of the summer, the city was in ruins and 20,000 people, from both sides of the Green Line, were dead. On 21 August, the PLO left Beirut, guaranteed safe passage by multinational forces. Phalange leader Bashir Gemayel was elected president on 23 August, though most Muslims boycotted the voting session. Less than a month later, he was assassinated.

A Decade from Peace

News of the Sabra and Shatila massacres (see p37) shocked the world; multinational forces soon returned to attempt, unsuccessfully, to keep the peace. Amin Gemayel, brother of murdered Bashir, took the presidency and on 17 May 1983 an agreement was finalised with Israel whereby Israeli troops would withdraw once Syria did the same. Syria, unsurprisingly, refused.

Kamal Jumblatt, from a powerful Druze Chouf Mountains clan, was the principal leader of anti-government forces in the civil war until his assassination, allegedly by Syrian nationalists, in 1977.

Unifil was established by the UN in 1978 as a temporary peacekeeping force. Around 10,000 Unifil troops and personnel remain in Lebanon today.

1989	1990	1992
In Lebanon, the Taif Accord is endorsed by the National Assembly on 22 October and ratified on 5 November. It transfers executive power to the cabinet to reduce the power of the president and equalises the parliamentary Muslim-to-Christian ratio.	On 13 October the civil war in Lebanon ends after a Syrian air force attack on the Lebanese presidential palace and the exile of General Aoun. The subsequent reconstruction of Beirut is supervised by a millionaire entrepreneur, Rafiq Hariri.	The first elections since 1972 are held in Lebanon. In October Rafiq Hariri becomes prime minister and Nabih Berri, secretary general of Shiite Amal, becomes the National Assembly speaker.

SABRA, SHATILA & SINCE

The day after Gemayel's assassination in September 1982, Israeli forces moved into West Beirut in violation of the US-brokered agreement. The next day, Phalangists entered Beirut's Sabra and Shatila refugee camps, ostensibly looking for 'terrorists', killing in the process between 1000 and 3000 Palestinians, mostly women and children. Though the Sabra and Shatila massacres were no bigger than that of Tel al-Zaatar six years before, they are better remembered internationally today. This is probably due to the suspect part Israel played in the incident; an Israeli report, known as the Kahan Report, later found Israeli troops were aware that a massacre was in progress and even offered logistical help, lending bulldozers to dig mass graves and dropping flares at night to illuminate the camp. The then defence minister Ariel Sharon denied all knowledge of the massacres while they were taking place. Further conflict later hit both troubled camps, with two more massacres claiming hundreds of lives.

Today the 1-sq-km Shatila camp houses over 12,000 people in poor conditions with unreliable drinking water. Life for survivors and their descendents remains bleak, with little prospect of jobs and slim chances of returning to what they still proudly refer to as their 'homeland'.

Nevertheless, Israeli troops began to retreat southward, while 40,000 Syrian soldiers continued to occupy the north. Yasser Arafat and PLO fighters returned briefly to Lebanese soil to wage war in Tripoli, before being evacuated – again under multinational protection – in December 1983.

Battle also raged in the central Chouf Mountains, the historic preserve of Druze and Christians, until now free from the ravages of war. The area was occupied by Israel, with Phalangist support, and the harassment of Druze citizens led to wide sectarian violence. The Lebanese army joined the Phalangists against the Druze, who themselves were aided by the Shiite militia Amal, until the US intervened and another cease-fire was called.

The US, however, was becoming increasingly entrenched in the war, appearing to favour Israel and Gemayel's beleaguered government. In 1983 came the reprisals. In April an Islamic Jihad suicide attack on the US embassy in Beirut left 63 dead. In October suicide bombers hit the US and French military headquarters in Beirut, killing over 300. In 1984, abductions of foreigners began. The following year, international forces left Lebanon.

Battle of the Camps

In early 1985 the last Israeli troops finally withdrew to their 'security zone', leaving their interests in the hands of the SLA and Christian militias, who immediately clashed with Druze and Shiite opponents around Sidon. In West Beirut, fighting continued between Shiite, Sunni and Druze militias.

In the midst of the chaos, PLO forces began to return to Lebanon. Concerned, however, that this would lead to a renewed Israeli invasion of the south, the Shiite Amal fought to remove them. Heavy fighting battered the Palestinian refugee camps during 1986, causing many more thousands of casualties. Though Syrian forces returned to West Beirut in

1993

Israel launches Operation Accountability on southern Lebanon in an effort to end the threat from Hezbollah and Palestinian militias, while Lebanon struggles to rebuild and recover from the civil war.

1996

On 11 April Israel launches Operation Grapes of Wrath, again bombing southern Lebanon, southern Beirut and the Beqaa Valley and targeting Hezbollah bases. One hundred and six civilians die in a UN compound at Qana.

2000

Syrian president Hafez al-Assad passes away unexpectedly and is replaced by his son Bashir. Grand expectations of a more liberal governing style are mostly dashed within 12 months.

increasing numbers and were able to stem the worst of the fighting, the camps would remain under Amal control until early 1988.

To add to the confusion, in 1987 the National Assembly government finally fell apart. Prime Minister Rashid Karami was assassinated on 1 June; by September, President Gemayel's term was almost up, but MPs couldn't reach parliament to vote for a replacement. With just hours to go before his term expired, Gemayel chose Chief of Staff General Michel Aoun to head an interim military government. Muslims opposed the decision and the government divided, with a Muslim government formed under former deputy prime minister Selim al-Hoss to the west and a Christian administration under Aoun to the east. Al-Hoss found support in the ranks of the Syrian army and Muslim militias, while Aoun enjoyed strong Christian backing.

Fighting along the Green Line continued as Aoun, staunchly anti-Syrian, attempted to drive Syrian forces from Lebanon, angering Syria still more by accepting arms from Iraq, Syria's gravest enemy. It wasn't until 1989 that a road to peace seemed a viable option, with the drafting of the Taif Accord.

The Road to Peace
The Taif Accord was the product of a committee consisting of the Saudi and Moroccan kings, along with President Chadli of Algeria, who proposed a comprehensive cease-fire and a meeting of Lebanon's fractured parliament to discuss a Charter of National Reconciliation. Under their plan the confessionalist system would remain, but the balance of power would be redressed. On 23 September a cease-fire was implemented and Lebanon's government met in Taif, Saudi Arabia. Despite Aoun's opposition, the accord was formally ratified on 5 November 1989. René Mouawad was elected president, but was assassinated just 17 days later by Taif Accord opponents and Elias Hwari took his place. Constitutional amendments included the expansion of the National Assembly from 99 to 128 seats, equally divided between Christians and Muslims. Many analysts also assert that the Accord formalised Syria's control over Lebanon, in return for promising internal stability.

Aoun continued to oppose the agreement and fighting broke out between his supporters and those of rival Christian militias. Infighting also began between Hezbollah and Amal militias, backed by Iran and Syria respectively, first in Beirut and then the south.

In August 1990 the National Assembly voted to accept the terms of the Taif Accord. After Syria supported the US-led military campaign in the Gulf War, the US allowed Syrian aircraft to bomb Lebanon's presidential palace and Syrian and SLA troops succeeded in deposing Aoun. With the exception of the still occupied south, Aoun's departure saw peace in Lebanon for the first time in 15 years. The civil war officially ended on 13 October 1990.

Syria's continued presence in Lebanon beyond the civil war was justified with reference to Lebanon's weak national army and the government's inability when acting alone to carry out Taif Accord reforms,

After leaving Lebanon, the PLO set up its base in Tunis with the blessing of President Habib Bourguiba, who, despite initial misgivings, waved the first influx in at the harbour.

The Lebanese governmental system of power-sharing along religious lines is known formally as 'confessionalism'; Lebanon is currently the only country in the world to make this its policy.

2000	2002	2002
On 24 May Israel, under Prime Minister Ehud Barak, pulls all troops out of southern Lebanon due to ongoing Hezbollah attacks on Israeli army bases. Hezbollah deems it a victory.	Syria is declared a 'rogue state' by the US administration. Relations with both the US and Israel deteriorate in the lead up to the invasion of Iraq.	Elie Hobeika, a key figure in the 1982 Sabra and Shatila massacres in Lebanon, is killed in a bomb blast shortly after disclosing that he possesses documents and videotapes challenging Israel's account of the massacres.

including dismantling militias. Some criticised Syria's continued interference in Lebanese military and intelligence matters; others felt that Syria's presence would prevent a renewed Israeli invasion or civil war. Syria later maintained that it would have withdrawn troops had the Lebanese government officially requested it do so. Lebanon, it said, never did.

In 1990, Syria formalised its dominance over Lebanon with the Treaty of Brotherhood, Cooperation and Coordination, followed in 1992 by a defence pact. In May 1991, most militias – except Hezbollah, whose existence was justified by continuing Israeli occupation – were dissolved, and all but the SLA-controlled south brought back under central control. In line with Taif Accord conditions, Syria began its military pull-out in March 1992, taking another 13 years to complete the job. The last Westerners kidnapped by Hezbollah were released in 1992.

Beirut's international airport has been damaged or destroyed three times by Israel, in 1968, 1982 and again in 2006.

Post-war Reconstruction

From 1993 onwards the Lebanese army slowly rebuilt. Rafiq Hariri, a Lebanese-born multimillionaire and entrepreneur, became prime minister in October 1992. Immediately he set about ambitious rebuilding plans; Solidere, the company established to rebuild Beirut's historic centre, quickly became a symbol of hope and rebirth for the whole country.

Meanwhile, however, the south remained impoverished and the ground for Israeli and Hezbollah offensives. In 1993 Israel launched Operation Accountability and in 1996 Operation Grapes of Wrath, the latter a land-sea-air offensive that devastated newly rebuilt structures, destroyed Beirut's power station and killed around 106 civilians in the beleaguered southern village of Qana. The offensive ended 16 days later, with a 'Ceasefire Understanding' brokered by American diplomats.

Although both sides initially respected the agreement, it wasn't long until fighting broke out once more. In 1999 Israel launched attacks targeting Beirut's power stations, while Hezbollah continued offensives against Israel and the SLA. Sustained losses led to calls within Israel for military withdrawal, and its army withdrew from southern Lebanon on 24 May 2000. Hezbollah stated that Israel would remain its target until Israeli troops were withdrawn from Shebaa Farms, a 31-sq-km area southeast of Lebanon captured by Israel in the 1967 Six Day War. In the years since the civil war, this bone of contention has frequently led to Hezbollah violence and Israeli retaliation.

In 1990 Aoun went into exile in France, and continued to fight Syrian influence in Lebanon. He returned to Lebanon in May 2005, 11 days after the final withdrawal of the Syrian army.

Despite countrywide celebration at Israel's pull-out, internal difficulties rumbled on. Maronite groups opposed Syria's refusal to leave, while Shiites and Hezbollah continued to support its presence. Pressure, moreover, was growing from overseas, with the USA urging Syria to leave Lebanon, a stance echoed by the UK, Germany and France after Syria allegedly supported pro-Syrian Emile Lahoud's bid for a third term in presidential office. In the wake of Lahoud's re-election, Rafiq Hariri resigned and was replaced as prime minister by pro-Syrian Omar Karami. On 2 September 2004, the

2003	2004	2005
War in Iraq begins and Syria is accused of aiding foreign fighters. Despite its handing over of intelligence and suspected terrorists, the US castigates Syria, even as Syria absorbs the thousands of refugees fleeing Iraq's chaos.	Lebanon's parliament votes 96 to 29 to amend the constitution to extend President Lahoud's term for another three years. In the aftermath, three cabinet ministers resign, along with Prime Minister Rafiq Hariri.	On 14 February former Lebanese president Rafiq Hariri is killed in a powerful car bombing in Beirut, prompting renewed calls for Syria to immediately withdraw its army from Lebanon and the creation of the Cedar Revolution movement.

THE RISE OF HEZBOLLAH

The 1983 suicide attacks heralded the first public appearance of Islamic Jihad, the armed wing of the radical, Iran-backed Shiite Hezbollah. Though relatively new, the group would soon prove a key figure in the civil war. Historically, the Shiites had always been Lebanon's poor, being concentrated in the south and having borne the brunt of Israeli retaliation against Palestinian guerrillas. As a minority group, they had little say in the country's government and had been displaced in vast numbers without adequate Lebanese governmental aid.

With Syrian approval, Iranian revolutionary guards began to preach to the disaffected, who proved fertile ground for its message of overthrowing Western imperialism and the anti-Muslim Phalange. Alongside suicide bombings, its ruthless armed wing also resorted to hostage-taking. CIA bureau chief William Buckley was tortured and killed, while Associated Press bureau chief Terry Anderson and UK envoy Terry Waite were held for almost seven and five years respectively.

Today, while Hezbollah's armed tactics revolve around rocket attacks on Israel and kidnap missions against its soldiers, it also concentrates on welfare projects in the still-stricken south, and holds 14 seats in the Lebanese parliament. For more on the party's social policies, see The Party of God (p356).

UN issued Security Council Resolution 1559, which called 'upon all remaining foreign forces to withdraw from Lebanon'. Syria did not comply.

The Killing of Rafiq Hariri

On 14 February 2005 a massive car bomb near Beirut's St George Yacht Club killed its target, former prime minister Rafiq Hariri. The event triggered a series of demonstrations, particularly in Beirut, with protestors placing blame firmly on Syria. Tens of thousands of protestors called for Syrian withdrawal from Lebanon, an independent commission to investigate the murder, the return of exiled Aoun and the organisation of free parliamentary elections. Together, these events became known as the Cedar Revolution. Prime Minister Karami and his government resigned on 28 February and demonstrators rejoiced. On 14 March, Lebanon's largest ever public demonstration was held in Place des Martyrs, with between 800,000 and one million attendees spanning sectarian divisions. The result was the March 14 Alliance, an anti-Syrian governmental alliance led by Samir Geagea, Walid Jumblatt and Saad Hariri, the son of the murdered ex-prime minister.

With the UN, USA, Russia and Germany backing Lebanese calls for withdrawal, Syria finally bowed to pressure, withdrawing its 14,000 remaining troops from Lebanon on 27 April 2005 after almost 30 years of occupation. Lebanon was completely free from military forces other than its own. This, however, was destined not to last.

The 2006 Conflict & Beyond

The months after Syria's withdrawal were characterised by a spate of car bombs and targeted assassinations of anti-Syrian politicians and

The 33-Day War: Israel's War on Hezbollah in Lebanon and its Consequences, by Gilbert Achcar and Michel Warschawski, makes an interesting read on the 2006 Israeli offensive in Lebanon.

2005	**2006**	**2006**
Bowing to Lebanese pressure, Syrian troops completely withdraw from Lebanon. The anti-Syrian March 14 alliance led by Saad Hariri wins control of the Lebanese parliament following the elections and Fouad Siniora is chosen as Lebanon's prime minister.	In July Israel's Operation Summer Rain falls on Lebanon after Israeli soldiers are killed and abducted by Hezbollah. Southern Lebanon, south Beirut, the Bekaa Valley and major infrastructures are severely damaged; over 1000 civilians are killed.	In November Hezbollah and Amal ministers resign from the Lebanese government just before the cabinet approves UN plans for a tribunal to try Hariri murder suspects. Prominent Lebanese Christian politician and government minister Pierre Gemayel is shot dead.

journalists, with growing calls for the expedition of a UN probe into Hariri's murder.

The 2005 parliamentary elections, the first after Syria's withdrawal, saw a majority win for the March 14 Alliance led by Saad Hariri, with Fouad Siniora elected Lebanon's new prime minister. The elections also saw Hezbollah become a legitimate governmental force, winning 14 seats in parliament, while in the south its fighters continued to launch attacks on Israeli troops and towns. Though Siniora publicly denounced the attacks, it seemed that once again Lebanese authorities were powerless to stop them.

In October 2005 the UN published an official report into Hariri's death, but the investigation remained ongoing. The UN Security Council, along with the Lebanese cabinet, approved a special tribunal to prosecute those responsible for the crime. Despite Syrian and Hezbollah protests, this is scheduled for some time in 2008 in The Hague. It's estimated to cost US$120 million and take around three years. Like many things in Lebanon, however, no-one knows for certain exactly when, how or if at all it will happen.

On 12 July 2006, days after a Hezbollah incursion resulted in the deaths and kidnappings of several Israeli soldiers, Israel once again invaded Lebanon with the aim, this time, of destroying Hezbollah. For the following 33 days, Israeli warplanes pounded the country, resulting in the deaths of over 1000 Lebanese civilians. On 14 August fighting finally came to an end, though Israel maintained an air and sea blockade until 8 September.

Following the war Lebanon has once again struggled to its feet. Its tourist industry has been hard hit, and homes and infrastructure countrywide damaged or destroyed. Major contributors towards Lebanese reconstruction include Saudi Arabia, the European Union and a number of Gulf countries.

Lebanon's problems, however, are far from over. In December 2006 Hezbollah, Amal and various smaller opposition parties overran Beirut's centre in an attempt to bring down Siniora's government. Summer 2007 saw fierce fighting near Tripoli, with the Lebanese army battling Palestinian militants, while car bombs during the early part of the year killed two anti-Syrian MPs. In November 2007, President Emile Lahoud stepped down, and presidential elections, postponed and repostponed more than a dozen times, are now expected some time in 2008, leaving Lebanon, in the interim, without an elected president. In February 2008, one of Hezbollah's high-level and most wanted leaders, Imad Mughniyeh, was assassinated in Damascus, leading Hezbollah to declare 'open war' with Israel and accuse the Lebanese establishment of complicity. At the end of February, Hezbollah was further dismayed when the US sent a warship to patrol off Lebanon's coastline, in a show of support for 'regional stability'. With the upcoming prospect of the controversial Hariri tribunal, and Syria and Iran once again becoming slowly embroiled in Lebanese affairs, only the most optimistic of Lebanese are able to believe that such 'regional stability', or an end to Lebanon's long, dark days, could be in the making any time soon.

Two excellent accounts of Lebanon's post-independence history are *A History of Modern Lebanon* by Fawwaz Trablousi and Robert Fisk's classic *Pity the Nation: Lebanon at War*.

Lebanon's last census was held in 1932, when Christians made up the population's majority at 55%. The CIA World Factbook estimates that Muslims now comprise Lebanon's religious majority at 59.7%

2007

In Syria, elections result in a predictably overwhelming victory for Bashar al-Assad. A mysterious Israeli attack on Syrian soil in September raises questions about the transfer of nuclear material through Syria from North Korea.

2007

In Lebanon, fighting breaks out in a refugee camp near Tripoli; a militant group linked to Al-Qaeda takes responsibility. Two anti-Syrian MPs are assassinated in car bomb attacks. President Lahoud steps down in November, with no successor.

2008

In February Hezbollah's second-in-command, Imad Mughniyeh, is assassinated in Damascus. Hezbollah, Syria and Iran variously blame Israel and Lebanon; the US sends a warship to patrol off Lebanon's coast. Lebanese presidential elections and the Hariri tribunal remain forthcoming.

Religion

While many people incorrectly assume that both Lebanon and (especially) Syria are Islamic states, both are nominally republics. In Lebanon, Muslims make up around 59% of the population, and Christians 40%, with 1% being of other religions. In Syria, Muslims make up around 90% of the population and Christians around 10%. What makes the religious make-up of both countries interesting is the role of the minorities. The president of Syria, for instance, is an Alawite, an offshoot of Shiite Islam that only makes up 11% of Syria's population. In Lebanon, the intriguing Druze (another offshoot of Shiite Islam) have an influential and outspoken leader, Walid Jumblatt, despite only being 7% of the population. In these two countries, where faith plays such an important role in the everyday lives of most inhabitants, understanding the complexities of the religious puzzle leads to a greater understanding of the politics and lives of the people you'll meet.

Muslims are prohibited from eating or drinking anything that contains pork or alcohol. Nor are they allowed to consume the flesh or blood of any animal that has died by natural causes. Meat must be halal (permitted), meaning slaughtered in a prescribed manner.

ISLAM

Islam was founded in the early 7th century AD by the Prophet Mohammed (570–632), born in Mecca. The basis of Islam is a series of divine revelations in which the voice of the archangel Gabriel revealed the word of God to Mohammed. These revelations started when he was 40 and continued throughout the rest of his life. The transcribed versions of these revelations form the Quran, literally meaning 'recitation', and great care is taken not to change a single letter of the holy Quran.

Mohammed started preaching in 613, three years after the first revelation, but only attracted a few dozen followers. Having attacked the ways of Meccan life – especially the worship of idols – he also made many enemies. In 622 he and his followers retreated to Medina, an oasis town some 360km from Mecca. It is this Hejira, or migration, which marks the beginning of the Muslim calendar.

In Medina, Mohammed quickly became a successful religious, political and military leader. After several short clashes with the Meccans, he finally gathered 10,000 troops and conquered his home town, demolished

---

THE FIVE PILLARS OF ISLAM

Shahada (The Profession of Faith) 'There is no God but Allah and Mohammed is his prophet.' *'La il-laha illa Allah Mohammed rasul Allah.'* The fundamental tenet of Islam, this is often quoted at events such as births and deaths.

Salat (The Call to Prayer) This is the obligation to pray in the direction of Mecca five times a day, when the muezzins call the faithful to prayer from the minarets (see opposite). Prayers can be performed anywhere if a mosque is not available and Muslims often travel with a prayer mat and pray wherever they can. The midday prayers on Friday are the most important of the week and this is when the weekly sermon is given.

Zakat (The Giving of Alms to the Poor) A fundamental part of the social teaching of Islam, it has become formalised in some states into a tax, which is used to help the poor. In other countries it is a personal obligation to give and is a spiritual duty rather than the Christian idea of charity.

Sawm (Fasting) Ramadan, the ninth month of the Islamic calendar, commemorates the month when the Quran was revealed to Mohammed. In a demonstration of Muslims' renewal of faith, they are asked to abstain from sex and from letting *anything* pass their lips from dawn to dusk for an entire month.

Hajj (Pilgrimage) The pilgrimage to Mecca is the ultimate profession of faith for the devout Muslim. Ideally, the pilgrim should go to Mecca during the last month of the year, Zuul-Hijja, to join with Muslims from all over the world in the pilgrimage and subsequent feast. See also The Hajj (p44) for more details.

THE CALL TO PRAYER

One of the most delightful aspects of travelling through the Middle East is the engaging sound of the muezzins' call to prayer (adhan). In some cities and towns, as one muezzin (the man whose voice leads the call) starts, others in the area follow and as the mesmerising note-bending calls intertwine and reverberate through the streets, they create a unique soundscape. This is not to say that it's always pleasant, if you've been woken at 4am by a not particularly gifted muezzin whose speaker is right outside your window, you might not find it as entrancing!

You'll hear the call to prayer five times a day:

Fajr Between dawn and sunrise
Zuhr Just after the height of the midday sun
Asr In the afternoon
Maghrib Just after sunset
Isha During the evening

---

the idols worshipped by the population and established the worship of the one God.

After his death the new religion continued its rapid spread, through the remarkable wave of conquests achieved by Mohammed's successors, the four caliphs (or Companions of Mohammed). By the end of the 7th century Islam had reached across North Africa to the Atlantic and, having consolidated its power, invaded Spain in 710.

The Faith

Conversion to Islam is simply achieved by a profession of faith (the shahada) in front of two witnesses. This is the first of the five pillars of Islam, the five tenets that guide Muslims in their daily life – see The Five Pillars of Islam (opposite) for more details.

To Muslims, Allah is the same God that Christians and Jews worship. Adam, Abraham, Noah, Moses and Jesus are all recognised as prophets, although Jesus is not recognised as the Son of God. According to Islam, all these prophets partly received the word of God, but only Mohammed received the complete (and final) revelations.

Sunnis & Shiites

Not long after the death of Mohammed, Islam suffered a major schism that divided the faith into two main sects: the Sunnis and the Shiites. The split arose over disputes about who should succeed Mohammed, who died without an heir.

The main contenders were Abu Bakr, who was the father of Mohammed's second wife Ayesha and the Prophet's closest companion, and Ali, who was Mohammed's cousin and husband to his daughter Fatima. They both had their supporters, but Abu Bakr was declared the first caliph, an Arab word meaning 'successor'.

Ali finally became the fourth caliph following the murder of Mohammed's third successor, Uthman. He in turn was assassinated in 661 after failing to bend to the military governor of Syria, Mu'awiyah. A relative of Uthman, Mu'awiyah had revolted against Ali over the latter's alleged involvement in Uthman's killing and set himself up as caliph.

Ali's supporters continued to hold fast to their belief in the legitimacy of his line and became known as the Shiites (Partisans of Ali). They believe in 12 imams (spiritual leaders), the last of whom will one day appear to create an empire of the true faith.

The Sunnis are followers of the succession of the caliphs.

The New Encyclopaedia of Islam: A Revised Edition of the Concise Encyclopaedia of Islam is the newly revised edition of this highly regarded study of the Islamic religion by Cyril Glasse. Authoritative and eminently readable.

Muezzins used to climb the minaret to perform the call, but these days, technology sees the muezzin using a microphone, with speakers mounted on the minaret and a touch of reverb for more atmosphere.

THE HAJJ

The hajj, or pilgrimage to Mecca, is the fifth pillar of Islam (see The Five Pillars of Islam, p42) and it is the duty of all Muslims to perform at least one hajj in their lifetime. The traditional time for the hajj is during the month of Zuul-Hijja, the 12th month of the Muslim year.

The high point of the pilgrimage is the visit to the Kaaba, the construction housing the stone of Ibrahim in the centre of the haram, the sacred area into which non-Muslims are forbidden to enter. The pilgrims, dressed in a plain white robe, circle the Kaaba seven times and kiss the black stone.

After several more acts of devotion, the hajj culminates in the ritual slaughter of a lamb (in commemoration of Ibrahim's sacrifice) at Mina. This marks the end of the pilgrimage and the beginning of Eid al-Adha, or the Feast of Sacrifice. This act of sacrifice is repeated throughout the Islamic world and part of the sheep is always given to the poor. The holiday runs from 10 to 13 Zuul-Hijja. The returned pilgrim can be addressed as *hajji* (if male) or *hajjia* (if female). In Syria you may see murals of Mecca painted on the exterior walls of houses – this indicates that the people who live there have performed the hajj.

Islamic Minorities

ALAWITES

The Alawites are an offshoot of the Shiite branch of Islam. It is believed the sect was founded on the Arabian Peninsula in the 9th century by a preacher named Mohammed ibn Nusayr. Their basic belief is that there is one God with a hierarchy of divine beings, the highest of whom is Ali (see Sunnis & Shiites, p43), hence the name Alawites, or 'followers of Ali'.

Like the Ismailis (see The Assassins, p170), the mountain-dwelling Alawites have always suffered persecution at the hands of ruling Sunni dynasties. Saladin (Salah ad-Din) and his Ayyubid dynasty, the Mamluks and the Ottoman Turks massacred Alawite communities, forced them to convert or imposed crippling taxes. Alawites traditionally worked the poorest lands or held down the least skilled jobs. That situation radically changed early in the 20th century when the French courted the Alawites as allies and granted them a self-ruled enclave in the mountains around Lattakia. From there the Alawites entrenched themselves in Syrian national politics – with Hafez al-Assad, an Alawite, taking power in 1970.

The Druze believe that God is too sacred to be called by name, is amorphous (or fluid) and will reappear in other incarnations.

DRUZE

The Druze religion is another offshoot of Shiite Islam and was spread in the 11th century by Hamzah ibn Ali and other missionaries from Egypt who followed the Fatimid caliph Al-Hakim. The group's name is derived from one of Hamzah's subordinates, Mohammed Darazi. Darazi had declared Al-Hakim to be the last imam and God in one. When Al-Hakim mysteriously died, Darazi and his companions fled to Egypt.

The hajj in Mecca is the world's largest annual gathering and over four million *hajjis* and *hajjias* travelled to Mecca in 2007.

Most Druze live in the Lebanese mountains, although there are some small Druze towns in the Hauran, around the Syria–Jordan border. Their faith has survived mainly because of the secrecy that surrounds it. Not only is conversion to or from the faith prohibited, but only an elite, the *'uqqal* (knowers), have full access to the religious doctrine, the *hikmeh*. The *hikmeh* is contained in seven holy books that exist only in handwritten copies.

CHRISTIANITY

There are many different churches and rites representing the three main branches of Christianity – Eastern Orthodox, Catholic and Protestant – but the main Christian sect in Lebanon is Maronite, a Roman Catholic church of Eastern origin.

Maronite Church

The Maronite church traces its origins back to the 4th century AD and to the monk, St Maro (also called St Maron), who chose a monastic life on the banks of Nahr al-Aasi (Orontes River) in Syria. It is said that 800 monks joined his community and began to preach the gospel in the surrounding countryside. After his death, his followers built a church over his tomb, which became an important sanctuary. Later, a monastery grew around the church and from here early missionaries set out to convert the people.

The Byzantine emperor Heraclius visited the monastery in 628 to discuss his ideas for mending the rifts in Christianity. His new doctrine was that of monothelitism, according to which the will of Jesus Christ, both divine and human, was defined as one and indivisible. The Western orthodoxy later condemned this idea as heretical. But the Syrians of Lebanon remained attached to monothelitism, which grew to be identified with their national and religious aspirations. This led to their isolation from both the Orthodox and Jacobite (Syrian Orthodox) sections of the Lebanese community.

Two major events charted the course of the Maronites. Firstly, the Arab conquest put an end to Christian persecutions of heretical groups. Secondly, serious differences led to the expulsion of the Patriarch of Antioch, and at the end of the 8th century, the Maronites elected their own national patriarch, who took the title Patriarch of Antioch and the East – a title still held today.

During the Crusades, the Maronites were brought back into contact with the Christian world and the Church of Rome. A gradual process of Romanisation took place, but the church still worshipped in Syriac (a dialect of Aramaic spoken in Syria) and maintained its own identity. Today the Maronite sect is considered a branch of Roman Catholicism.

Eastern Orthodox Church

This branch of Christianity is well represented in Lebanon. There are many Greek and Armenian Orthodox Churches, as well as a small Jacobite (Syrian Orthodox) community.

Greek Orthodox has its liturgy in Arabic and is the mother church of the Jacobites (Syrian Orthodox), who broke away in the 6th century. Jacobites use only Syriac, which is closely related to Aramaic, and was the language of Christ. Armenian Orthodox (also known as the Armenian Apostolic Church) has its liturgy in classical Armenian and is seen by many to be the guardian of the national Armenian identity.

Catholic Churches

The largest Catholic group in Lebanon is the Maronites, but other Catholic rites represented include Greek Catholics (also know as Melchites), who come under the patriarch of Damascus; Syrian Catholics, who still worship in Syriac; and Armenian Catholics, whose patriarch lives in Beirut. There is also a small community of Catholics who worship in either the Chaldean rite or the Latin rite. The Middle East–based patriarchs are often responsible for the worldwide members of their churches.

With estimates ranging from one to two billion faithful, Islam is the second-largest religion, behind Christianity. For around 50 countries Islam is the majority religion, but it is not a Middle Eastern country that has the most Muslims – it's Indonesia.

The museum of the Armenian Catholicosate of Cilicia, in Antelias, Beirut, documents the ejection of the Armenians by the Turks in 1915. The religious (Armenian Orthodox) and cultural treasures of the museum are breathtaking; see p278.

Food & Drink Greg Malouf & Geoff Malouf

There is no better way to gain an understanding of the Syrian and Lebanese psyches than by observing the role that food, and in particular entertaining, plays in everyday life. It would be an understatement to say that for the people of the Levant, life revolves around food. From the cradle to the grave, a dish or a feast marks every milestone in life. If you're travelling with children, they will fall in love with this gregarious, family-oriented culture, and they'll always be welcome in restaurants.

Lebanese food has often been described as the 'pearl of the Arab kitchen'. The country is the gateway to the Mediterranean, linking the cultures of East and West, and it has stylised its cuisine to appeal to Western palates. Lebanon inherited the art of trading and the ability to please from the Phoenicians, and from the Arabs, the art of hospitality.

A host's generosity is measured by the amount of food on the table, and it's often the subject of gossip. An old rule of entertaining advises people to serve up twice the amount of food that they expect their guests to eat. A word of advice, then, to a guest in the home of a Syrian or Lebanese – take everything offered, because to decline will greatly offend your host.

While Syrians and Lebanese generally love their meat, if you're vegetarian you can still eat very well in the region (much mezze is vegetarian), and you won't have to survive solely on felafels. The abundance of fresh local produce means that there's almost always a meat-free option.

> Greg Malouf is one of Australia's most admired chefs and food writers. Born into a Lebanese-Australian family, he is an acknowledged champion of modern Middle Eastern cuisine. He is the co-author of *Arabesque, Moorish, Saha* and *Turquoise,* and his restaurant ventures have included Mo Mo (Melbourne, Australia) and Malouf's Arabesque Cuisine (Hong Kong). Geoff Malouf, Greg's brother, is also an accomplished restaurateur, running Arabesque (Melbourne) and Mama Ganoush (Melbourne).

STAPLES & SPECIALITIES
Mezze

The core of Syrian and Lebanese hospitality is typified by mezze. This huge array of small starters precedes the main course. Dishes range from pickled vegetables to offal and savoury pastries *(samboosik)*. In a normal *azeemieh* (invitation) or *hafli* (party), the preferred way of entertaining is a banquet.

The dips – hummus (chickpea and tahini) and *baba ghanoug* (smoky eggplant) – are served on long oval platters and garnished with chopped parsley, paprika and olive oil. In Damascus, *baba ghanoug* (which means 'father's favourite') takes the form of an eggplant salad with diced tomato, onion, parsley, garlic and lemon.

The ever-popular *tabbouleh* (a salad of bulgur wheat, parsley and tomato, with a sprinkling of sesame seeds, lemon and garlic) is accompanied with bowls made of lettuce cups, enabling diners to dispense with cutlery and scoop up the tangy olive oil and lemon. Vine leaves are also popular – they're rolled with spiced lamb and rice and served with platters of fresh greens.

For the daring, there's finely chopped, fresh lamb's fry served raw with a piece of fat *(liyye)* found only in the tail of a regional breed of sheep. Or try chicken livers and frogs legs sautéed in lemon, garlic and coriander.

Bastoorma, an Arabic pastrami coated with fenugreek, garlic and chilli, is made by Turkish and Armenian butchers. It's a breakfast favourite, usually fried in paper-thin slices with eggs. At breakfast you may also find *labneh,* a thick and creamy yogurt cheese, sprinkled with fruity olive oil.

Traditionally all meals are eaten with *khoobz Arabi,* the ancient flat bread of the Arabic world, often used as a scoop.

These are just some of the many mezze dishes. The best advice for the *ajnabi* (foreigner) is to not go in hard at this stage of the meal – the best is yet to come!

Mains

Just when you are rising to wish your host warm thanks and goodnight, the main course arrives on the table. In a private home this might be a whole oven-roasted lamb, stuffed with spiced mince, rice, almonds and pine nuts. This is served on the birth of a male in the family, or on the arrival of an honoured guest.

In a restaurant the mains usually consist of a variety of skewered meats. Chicken and lamb kebabs, barbecued on charcoal, arrive on the table covered with *khoobz Arabi*. Another main course dish, *kafta*, is made of minced lamb, onion and spices, topped with a tossed salad of parsley, onions, olive oil and sumac (a tangy, lemony spice). The celebrated chicken and rice dish, *roz a djaj*, always completes the banquet. Rice is cooked in chicken stock with aromatic spices such as cinnamon and allspice, and roasted chicken pieces are placed on top with toasted almonds and pine nuts.

In Damascus, don't miss *makhlooba* (literally 'upside-down') rice. It's cooked in stock and spices with chickpeas, onions and off-the-bone lamb shanks, then pressed in a deep bowl and turned upside down to reveal a delicious work of art. The vegetarian version incorporates eggplants with almonds and pine nuts.

Moolookhiye is a triumph of textures and flavours, combining fragrant rice with chicken, lamb and slimy but sexy spinach-like leaves called mallow. Don't let the slime fool you, this is comfort food at its Bedouin best, and an aphrodisiac to boot! Generally, *moolookhiye* is garnished with toasted *khoobz Arabi*, cumin and onions soused in vinegar. It can be hard to find in restaurants, but sometimes appears as a lunch special on Sunday. The dish originated in Egypt, and was adapted in Syria and Lebanon to suit local tastes. Another dish starting with the letter M is *moghrabiye* (which means 'Moroccan'). It's made of steamed, spiced semolina pellets, like a giant couscous, and is served with chicken, lamb shanks and little pickled onions. It's a popular dish, especially in Lebanon's Tripoli and Syria's Damascus.

In Syria, *labneh* is spread on thick *khoobz Arabi* and rolled up – it's then called *arus* (the bride).

Kibbeh

A cook's skills are judged by their success in preparing Lebanon's national dish, *kibbeh*. These croquettes of ground lamb, cracked wheat, onion and spices are served in many regional variations. In Damascus they're shaped into mini footballs and stuffed with spiced lamb, pine nuts and walnuts, then shallow-fried until golden brown. In Beirut they're served raw like a steak tartare, accompanied with fresh mint leaves, olive oil and spring onions.

Raw *kibbeh* (*kibbeh nayye*) has many variations. In northern Lebanon you often find mint and fresh chillies mixed through the meat. In Aleppo, a chilli paste is layered on top of the *kibbeh* with walnuts and onions.

Kibbeh saniye is *kibbeh* flattened out on a tray with a layer of spiced lamb and pine nuts in between. This is served with natural yogurt on the side.

Before the arrival of food processors, the matron of the household or village pulverised lamb for the *kibbeh* in a mortar and pestle. To produce an even texture requires great skill and strength in the arms. Driving through the mountains of Lebanon on a Sunday morning you can hear the chimes of these stone 'food processors' like church bells calling the faithful to eat.

Fish

The warmer waters of the Mediterranean Sea are home to an abundance of fish species. Most popular are the red mullet *(Sultan Ibrahim)*, sea bass *(lookoz)* and sole *(samak moossa)*. Although very simple to prepare, whole fish dishes are probably the most loved. There are two standout favourites. *Samak sa'ayadiye* is a seafood paella made of rice cooked in fish stock, brown onions and spices. Onions are caramelised and scattered on top of the rice with toasted pine nuts. *Sammki harra* is usually a whole fish (sea bass), oven-baked with a mixture of coriander, fresh chillies, walnuts and onions stuffed inside. When it's almost cooked, tahini sauce is poured on top and it's returned briefly to the oven. This is a firm favourite along Lebanon's coast, especially in Tripoli where the dish originated.

Samak bi loz is a dish that reflects the influence of French cuisine. It's a whole trout baked with almonds and it's served in restaurants near trout farms, such as in Aanjar and at Nahr al-Aasi in the Bekaa Valley.

> British soldiers in the Middle East during WWII used to call *kibbeh* 'Syrian torpedoes', which describes their shape rather well.

Desserts

Diners in Syria and Lebanon usually opt for fresh fruit after a meal. When in season, fruit is in plentiful supply. Lebanon's good soil and abundant snowfalls guarantee a flavoursome crop season after season.

Regional fruits to look out for include: oranges and tangerines from Lebanon's southern coastal strip; apples and pears from the elevated hinterland of northern Lebanon and the banks of Syria's Nahr al-Aasi; grapes and melons from the Bekaa Valley; and sweet cherries and figs of different varieties from Mt Lebanon. In Syria, don't miss the white mulberry as well as the conventional purple variety *(toot shami)*. The fruit of the prickly pear is always plentiful in the hot, dry conditions.

If dessert is offered it will be *mahalabiye,* which is a milk custard similar to blancmange, laced with orange blossom essence, almonds and pistachios. *Halawat bi djeben* is a stringy, sweet cheese with dollops of *ashta* (clotted cream skimmed from the top of boiling milk) and sugar syrup. *Asmaleyye* (literally 'gold sovereign') is a sandwich of *kataifi* pastry filled with *ashta* and sprinkled with pistachios.

The traditional baklava usually makes an appearance. These sweet filo pastry morsels of crushed pistachios, almonds, cashews or peanuts come in all shapes – try lady fingers *(asabeeh),* the nest of the nightingale *(aash el-bulbul)* or eat and give thanks *(kol wa shkor)*. Syria is renowned for *barazi,* a large biscuit of sesame seeds and pistachios. Also popular in Syria is *bor'ma,* a mosaic of pistachios wrapped in angel hair noodles and sliced into discs.

PRESERVING THE HARVEST

Due to the rugged terrain in the Levant, especially in Lebanon, communities often thrived in isolation for centuries, giving rise to wonderful regional cuisines. The climate and availability of produce also influenced the menu. High altitudes and snowed-out winters led to the development of ingenious food preservation methods that could take a family through the harsh winter months.

All this changed with the arrival of refrigeration and modern food-storage technologies. Nevertheless, traditional food preservation techniques are kept alive in rural areas and are relished by urban dwellers who look suspiciously on food they know is not in season.

When something is in season, Syrians and Lebanese always take full advantage of the situation. Fruits and vegetables from the summer harvest are blanched and pickled to be stored in the *moonay* (food cellar or pantry).

Bayt injen makdoos are baby eggplants blanched, then split open and stuffed with garlic, chilli and walnuts. They're put into jars of olive oil and pickled for a month. No table is complete without olives, which are pickled in brine. Long thin cucumbers and beetroot-coloured turnips are also pickled.

Huge pots of cubed and fried lamb with onions and spices are kept in rendered fat to be brought out and cooked with eggs in winter, or added to a stew of winter vegetables, pulses and rice.

Labneh (a type of yogurt cheese) is rolled into individual balls and stored in jars filled with olive oil. In summer cracked wheat mixed with yogurt is laid out to dry and then stored for the winter. It makes a hearty bowl of *kishik,* which is served like porridge in the mornings.

DRINKS
Spirits & Beer
Arak (lion's milk) is always drunk with mezze, a process that usually takes a couple of hours. This aniseed-based cousin to ouzo is the preferred drink of the region. It's combined with water and ice into a potent mixture served in small glasses. See Arak (p350) for more information.

Next on the list of favourites, especially in Beirut, is scotch – always an upmarket brand served straight with ice. There are breweries producing beer for the locals in both countries. The favourite is Almaza, a light brew made under licence from the popular Dutch brewer Amstel. In Syria the next most popular labels are Barada in Damascus and Al Chark in Aleppo.

Wine
Recently wine has become an acceptable part of a meal in the region. Lebanon has produced some excellent wines, based on the 'old-world' style, which have gained some popularity among connoisseurs.

Winemaker Gaston Hochar took over an 18th-century castle, Château Musar (p352), in Ghazir, 24km north of Beirut, in 1930. Together with his sons, Hochar created a wine that, despite the civil war, was able to win important awards in France, including the prestigious Winemaker's Award for Excellence. Ninety percent of their produce is exported. The main wine-growing areas are Kefraya and Ksara in the Bekaa Valley. The success of these wines can be attributed to the climate and soil composition of the region. In 1857 Jesuit fathers introduced quality viticulture at the Ksara Winery (p351), using European growing techniques. A natural wine cellar that was discovered and used by the Romans was enlarged, creating a series of tunnels with the ideal temperature for storing wine.

See Lebanese Vineyards (p352) for more information on Lebanon's thriving wine industry.

Nonalcoholic Drinks
As in many societies, coffee *(ahwa)* is an important social lubricant. The black, syrupy Arabic coffee is served in small Chinese teacups. It's usually laced with cardamom and sweetened according to taste: *moorra* (no sugar), *wasat* (a little sugar) or *helwi* (sweet). See also Coffee, Coffee Everywhere, p287. In Syria, unlike Lebanon, tea is popular. A distinct Arabic blend is served sweet and black in small glasses. At night *zhurat* (chamomile tea with dried wild flowers and rosehip) is prepared. In Beirut one might ask for *ahwa bayda* (a few drops of rose-water added to boiling water).

There are many street stalls in both Syria and Lebanon selling freshly squeezed juice, just the thing in summer. As Lebanon is an important citrus-growing area, orange juice is very popular. *Limonada* is a simple drink of lemon juice and sugar, which sounds basic enough until the orange blossom essence is added. This gives the drink a refreshing, perfumed quality. In Syria, lemon and mint is the most popular combination. For a revitalising, delicately flavoured drink, try *jallab* (a date drink with floating pine nuts and pistachios), or *ma'wared* (distilled rose petals served with ice).

CELEBRATIONS
Holy Days
Food plays an important part in the religious calendar of the region. Holy days usually involve hours of preparation in the kitchen.

The Muslim fasting period of Ramadan offers a good insight into the diversity of festive food. Once the sun sets, a feast is spread on the table with an emphasis on sweet energy foods, to get the believers through the next day

Sole is known as *samak moossa*, or Moses fish. Because of its thinness, it is said to have been cut in half when Moses divided the Red Sea.

Traditionally, yogurt is not put on the same table as fish – an old wives' tale claims eating the two together will poison the diner.

There is only one correct way to pour a glass of arak: first pour about two fingers of arak, then add the water and finish off with one ice cube. Any other order will provoke frowns from onlookers.

of fasting. At this time of year the pastry shops of Tripoli and Damascus are full of special Ramadan sweets. The traditional colour for Ramadan food is white, and desserts are filled with *ashta*. Beverages like *kharroob* (carob) and *tamar hindi* (a tamarind drink) accompany great feasts of grilled lamb and chicken with almond rice. Platters of dates on the table remind diners of the Prophet Mohammed's only source of food while fasting in the desert.

Easter is the most important time in the calendar for eastern Christians. Good Friday's abstinence from meat brings out dishes such as *m'jaddara*, a dish of spiced lentils and rice. Another Easter dish is *shoraba zingool* (sour soup with small balls of cracked wheat, flour and split peas). The sourness reminds Christians of the vinegar on the sponge offered by the Roman centurion to Christ on the cross. *Selak,* rolls of silver beet (Swiss chard) stuffed with rice, tomato, chickpeas and spices, are also served. The fast is broken on Easter Sunday with round semolina cakes called *maamoul,* stuffed with either walnuts or dates.

The Armenian Christmas, the Epiphany (6 January), has the women busy making *owamaut* (small, deep-fried honey balls). On Eid el-Barbara, a Christian feast day similar to the American Halloween, a bowl of boiled barley, pomegranate seeds and sugar is offered to masquerading children.

Arabesque: Modern Middle Eastern Food by Greg and Lucy Malouf lists the 42 most essential ingredients from the region and offers insights into how they can be used to create authentic dishes.

Special Occasions

Food in the region is associated with different milestones in an individual's life. When a baby is born a pudding of rice flour and cinnamon called *mighlay* is served to family and friends. Sugar-coated almonds and chickpeas are the celebratory treats when the baby's first tooth pushes through.

At death a loved one is remembered with a banquet. This takes place after the burial in Christian communities, and one week later in Muslim communities. The only beverage offered is water and unsweetened *ahwa*.

It is believed that the spirit of the departed stays among the living for 40 days before it travels on to the afterlife. At this point the family offers another banquet to relatives and friends.

WHERE TO EAT & DRINK

Syria and Lebanon offer a unique eating experience. Restaurants in both countries serve the traditional mezze-and-main-course banquet, and a variety of other cuisines are available in Lebanon. The mezze component is much the same wherever you eat, however some restaurants specialise in particular main courses, for example grilled meats or seafood.

Claudia Roden's *The New Book of Middle Eastern Cooking* is filled with mouth-watering recipes from across the Middle East.

At *kebabji ahwa* (restaurants that specialise in kebabs), you will find long metal troughs, the width of a skewer, filled with lighted charcoal. Skewers of lamb, chicken and beef *kafta* are evenly cooked to customers' tastes (Arabs like their meat well done). In Beirut the restaurant scene is all about keeping up appearances – wearing the right clothes and being seen in the right establishment. Prices reflect these upmarket tastes.

In Syria you can get the same meal you would get in Lebanon for a quarter of the price. Its presentation might lack finesse, but the quality will be just as good and in some cases, even better. In Damascus you can say to the waiter *'ah zowaak'* (I'll leave it up to you) and still pay only a moderate amount, no matter how many dishes are placed on the table. In Lebanon this isn't the case and you need to be specific when ordering.

Quick Eats

You don't need to blow your budget eating out in expensive restaurants with the vast array of takeaway food on offer. For breakfast nothing beats a big, hot bowl of fava beans drizzled with olive oil, lemon and cumin, especially on a cold Damascus morning. This is the traditional *foul m'damas* served throughout the Middle East, but it takes on a distinctly Syrian flavour with the addition of chickpeas and tomatoes. In Beirut, breakfast is *k'nefi bi djeben* (sweet cheese and semolina in a doughy sesame roll with a sugar syrup and orange blossom).

In the mountains of Lebanon, a porridge-like dish called *kishik* is served with fried lamb pieces and onions. It's designed to warm you from the inside during the snowed-out winters. Shwarma is strips of lamb or chicken sliced from a vertical turning spit and served with tahini and greens in *khoobz Arabi*. To enhance the flavour and moistness of the meat, fat from the sheep's tail is skewered to the top of the pyramid and dribbles down slowly and evenly while the spit is turning.

Felafel balls are one of the world's most widely recognised snack foods. These golden spheres of ground chickpeas, coriander, onions, garlic and heaps of cumin are usually stuffed in a sandwich of *khoobz Arabi* with tahini, lettuce, pickled turnip and tomato. Fabulous *farooj mishwee* is hard to beat. A whole chicken is split, placed in a wire rack, barbecued on charcoal and served with copious amounts of garlic that has been whipped to a mayonnaise consistency. Down it with Almaza beer, *khoobz Arabi* and a few greens while watching the sun set over the Mediterranean Sea.

Other delicious fast-food options are savoury pastries eaten straight out of the oven. *Manaeesh* is the name given to the variety of pizza-like snacks eaten for breakfast or at any other time of the day. The most popular *manaeesh* is *manaeesh bi-zaatar*, a mixture of dried wild thyme and sesame seeds mixed with olive oil, which is spread on dough and baked. *Fatayer bi jibne* is like a pasty stuffed with *haloumi* cheese. The speciality from the town of Baalbek is lamb *sfeeha* (spiced lamb with onion, tomato and chilli baked on a thin pastry crust and side-served with yogurt).

Food from Biblical Lands by Helen Corey is an easy-to-use guide to Syrian and Lebanese cooking. A video is also available.

Sonia Uvezian's *Recipes and Remembrances from an Eastern Mediterranean Kitchen* includes anecdotes, proverbs and recipes from Syria, Lebanon and Jordan.

HABITS & CUSTOMS

The age-old Arabic custom of respect and hospitality to guests puts certain obligations on both host and guest. A lot of these obligations are really just good manners; however, there are certain subtle patterns of behaviour that you should follow if you are invited to eat in a private home.

In most homes, whether Christian or Muslim, the men usually gather separately from the women. This is not a strict religious or social requirement (though this may not be the case in rural Muslim areas), just a social practice that has evolved over time. Men and women come together at the table where the host will welcome you with a toast. You should follow this with a reciprocal toast, wishing the host and the family good health. If appropriate, you could also congratulate the family on a birth, or offer commiserations on the sudden death of a loved one. When the meal begins, it is important to accept as much food as possible when it is offered to you. If you say 'no thanks' continually, it can offend the host.

A Taste of Syria by Virginia Jerro Gerbino and Philip Kayal consists of recipes from Aleppo, as handed down by the authors' grandparents.

EAT YOUR WORDS
Useful Phrases

Bring a variety of dishes for the mezze please.	jeebelna tishkeeli mezza a'amil ma'aroof
Bottoms up!	kassak!
After you.	tfaddal (m) tfaddali (f).
The bill, please.	al hessab, a'amil ma'aroof.
Open/Closed.	maftooh/m'sakar.
Is that dish very spicy?	hal akle-harra?
I don't eat meat.	anna ma baqel laham.

What's the special of the day?   shoo al sah'an al yomi?
Do you have a table?   undak tawle?

Menu Decoder

Note that because of the imprecise nature of transliterating Arabic into English, spellings on menus vary. For example, what we give as *kibbeh* may appear variously as 'kibba', 'kibbe', 'kibby' or even 'gibeh'.

attoosh al-batinjan – Damascus version of fattoosh using fried eggplant tossed with pomegranate

bamiye – okra stewed with tomatoes, onions and spices served with fragrant rice

fattoosh – a Lebanese bread salad with purslane, tomatoes, cucumbers and sumac dressing

harak isbao – a Damascus favourite of green with tamarind and pomegranates

kibbeh – minced lamb, bulgur wheat and pine nuts shaped into a patty and deep fried

kibbeh nayye – ground lamb and cracked wheat served raw like steak tartare

labneh – thick yogurt cheese with olive oil

loobiye bi zhet – green beans cooked in garlic, onions and crushed tomatoes

mahashi – stuffed vine leaves, eggplant or silver beet rolls

mashawi – grilled meats on charcoal

m'jaddarah – lentil and rice with caramelised onions, served with cabbage salad

moosa'a' – eggplant, chickpea and onion with crushed tomatoes

selek – silverbeet stuffed with chickpeas and rice

The Lebanese Kitchen by Abla Ahmed is a cornucopia of centuries-old Lebanese recipes for modern chefs.

FOOD GLOSSARY

Basics
foorn – bakery
helwanji – pastry shop
ma'alaka – spoon
mataam – restaurant
showki – fork
sikeen – knife

Cooking Terms
halal – Islamic meat; meaning that the animal has been slaughtered using the halal method
labaniyye – cooked in yogurt
maa le – salty
mi'klay – fried
mishwee al-faham – charcoal grilled
mooghli – boiled
muhammar – roasted
nayye – raw
sayniye – baked
yabis – dried (herbs)

Dishes & Ingredients
adas – lentils
ashta – clotted cream

baharat – spices
ejja – omelette
filfil – pepper
jibna – cheese
khoobz – bread
khoobz Arabi – Arabic flatbread
lahame – meat
ma'al-ward – rose-water
mele – sal
naana – mint
roz – rice
samak – fish
shoraba – soup
tahini – sesame paste
toom – garlic
za'atar – spice mix
zaytoon – olives, olive oil

Drinks
ahwa – Arabic coffee
arak – aniseed-based spirit, similar to ouzo
chai – tea

The Word on the Street

Shoe repairer, Damascus
CLINT LUCAS

Bridging Cultures

NAME	Banoura Awad
OCCUPATION	Marketing manager
RESIDENCE	Damascus, Syria

'We have a great Old City that's in good shape, but we also have modern Damascus that's open, liberal and relaxed.'

My dad's Palestinian and mum's German. I grew up in the Palestinian refugee camp in Damascus. I went to school here but went to university in Germany. It was difficult at first, but I got used to it; now I find it easy to move between cultures and countries. I returned to Syria to work with my family. I handle marketing for Anat. It's a nonprofit organisation mum created to provide a bridge between the traditional Palestinian embroidery the women were creating in the camp and the international market. We have a workshop in the camp and a shop in the Old City. I work with my mother to reinterpret the designs and make them more contemporary. I love Damascus – it's more open now, more liberal, more relaxed. We have pubs where you can dance, drink and have fun, and Syrians are so friendly, it's easy to start conversations.

Start your night at the pub and music venue Marmar (p111)
LYNSEY ADDARIO/CORBIS

Stop for sheesha in a
Damascene café (p109)
LYNSEY ADDARIO/CORBIS

Catch up with
contemporary art at
Atassi Gallery (p97)
LYNSEY ADDARIO/CORBIS

DAMASCUS MUST-DOS

Two essential Damascus
experiences are visiting
a traditional hammam
for the full scrub and
steam (p100), and
having nargileh at
Al-Nawfara coffeehouse
(p110) – both are very
relaxing after a tiring
day in the Old City.

Eating in the Old City
is a must. Al-Khawali
(p106) is in a typical old
Damascene house, the
food is excellent, and
it's mostly locals there.
Aldar Restaurant (p107)
is a mix of old and
new, in a modernised
Arabian house.

Drinking coffee is
important. My favourite
café is Art Café Ninar
(p108). There's art on
the walls, changing
exhibitions, and lots of
Syrian artists and
intellectuals go there.

Escape to the peaceful Bekaa Valley (p347)

BETHUNE CARMICHAEL

DARE TO EXPLORE

The best time to visit the Bekaa Valley and Baalbek is in spring, between April and May, when it's warm but there's no rain. If you want to take pictures of the ruins, get there early, as they look most spectacular around sunrise.

The afternoons are good for exploring the ancient sites, as any tourists on day trips will have got back on their buses and left by then.

There are lots of things to discover outside Baalbek, too: you'll find the Hermel Pyramid, the Nahr al-Aasi (Orontes River), ancient rock-cut monasteries (all p361) and such friendly local people, if you just dare to explore a little.

Contemplate the mysteries of the Hermel Pyramid (p361)

DE AGOSTINI PICTURE LIBRARY/GETTY IMAGES

A Guide's Life

AGE	Charbel Salibad
OCCUPATION	Official Baalbek tour guide and night manager of the Palmyra Hotel
RESIDENCE	Baalbek, Lebanon

I'm a third-generation Baalbek guide. My grandfather was born in the USA and came to Lebanon when he was seven; by the 1930s, he had become the first English-speaking guide in the town. My father was his eldest son, so he studied the same profession and became a guide in the 'golden years' of the '60s, guiding tourists in four different languages. My elder brother didn't want to continue in the profession, so I took over and studied history at university to do it. The 1990s were good years, but times have been harder recently since tourists have been quite scared to come here. But visitors shouldn't be afraid: this town isn't the frightening terrorist-filled place they imagine. And even through the difficult times, I love my job: for me, walking among these ancient monuments is like a drug. Once it's in your blood, it's impossible to get it out.

'Visitors shouldn't be afraid: this town isn't the frightening terrorist-filled place they imagine.'

Take in the temple ruins at Baalbek (p354)

JOHN ELK III

The Best of Both Worlds

NAME	Zena Boufakhreddine
OCCUPATION	Kitsch boutique and tearoom manager, Beirut
RESIDENCE	A tiny village in the Metn mountains, Lebanon

'Beneath all the political problems we all get on very well. I wish the whole world could be like our little Lebanon in that respect.'

I love my work here at Kitsch, which – and I'm not biased – is definitely the funkiest boutique in Beirut. We have the best clothes, the cutest cupcakes and eggs Florentine like you've never tasted. I live up in the mountains, and it takes me half an hour to get to work every day. This balance is the great thing about Lebanon being so small: I can work in this 24/7 city, which is so crazy and alive, then go home to my little village in the countryside with its beautiful views and calm, nature-loving people. What I like most about Beirut is that there are so many kinds of people here, from so many different religious and cultural backgrounds. Beneath all the political problems we all get on very well. I wish the whole world could be like our little Lebanon in that respect: that would be just great.

Shop beyond the souqs at Beirut's ABC Mall (p290)

VIEW PICTURES LTD/ALAMY

Cruise subterranean caverns at Jeita Grotto (p303)

HOLGER LEUE

Dine out in Downtown at Place d'Étoile (p274)

MARK DAFFEY

THE RIGHT BALANCE

Explore Lebanon's little villages as well as the big cities, and combine city shopping and nightlife with a few days in the countryside.

Go to Baalbek (p354) for history; head to Jeita Grotto to see how amazing nature can be.

In Beirut, you should definitely explore Gemmayzeh (p278) and Hamra (p271), and do some shopping at the ABC Mall.

Consider visiting at Christmas. It's the best time in the whole year, with all the Christmas lights and excitement in the air, and you can even go skiing, too. That's when you see people at their happiest, and their best.

A Beautiful Mix

AGE	Naim Turki
OCCUPATION	Entrepreneur
RESIDENCE	Palmyra, Syria

'Sunrise is best for a Palmyra visit: the light is perfect for pictures, it's not hot, nobody's around; just walk around, you'll feel so relaxed.'

I grew up in Palmyra but studied business in London. I returned home to manage the family business and help develop tourism. Palmyra is amazing. Just walking around, you see a complete ancient city – the theatre, souq, parliament – it's amazing. I love Damascus also. I split my time between the two, between city and country. When I'm in Damascus I go to the cafés in old houses; they have lots of atmosphere. I go to Marmar pub; it attracts a mix of locals and foreigners. That's the thing I love most about my country. Syrians are friendly, we're open to foreigners, we're tolerant. When you drive through the Syrian countryside you notice the beautiful mix of religions: one village is Christian, one Alawite, another Druze, then Sunni. What we believe is: 'God is for you, but the country is for everyone'. Syria shows how people can live together peacefully.

Step into an ancient city at Palmyra (p202)

CHRISTOPHER WOOD

Syria

Getting Started in Syria

With ancient ruins from many great civilisations, medieval souqs, fascinating cities and beautiful mountains and valleys all located in a reasonably compact area, you can cover a lot of territory in a small amount of time in Syria. If you're time is limited, however, we can't emphasise enough how important logistics are. Trying to cover *every* Roman ruin in a week will see you, well, ruined. Make sure to leave yourself enough time in your itinerary to wander the souqs of Aleppo and Damascus. For advice, see our suggested itineraries (p17).

In general terms, Syria is suited to all budgets, but there are cities and towns that some travellers prefer to visit on a day trip, as there's no suitable accommodation within their price range.

For online currency conversions, go to www.xe.com.

WHEN TO GO

The best time of year to visit Syria is spring (March to May) when the weather is mild and wildflowers are in bloom. During May the weather can be warm enough for swimming and the mountains are carpeted with colour. In Damascus, the winter rains clear the haze that obscures the city for some of the year. The rain swells the rivers, so the wooden *norias* (waterwheels) in Hama are turning and fresh, clean water flows through Damascus. If you can't make the spring, aim for autumn (September to November), between the intense heat of summer and the cloud of winter.

Temperatures soar from June to the middle of September, and summers can be uncomfortably hot. On the coast at Lattakia, it can be extremely humid, while the interiors will be very hot and dry. This may be fine if you want to lie on a Mediterranean beach, but it is not ideal

See Climate (p229) for more information.

TRAVELLING SUSTAINABLY IN SYRIA

Sustainable travel is about minimising your impact and maximising your connection with the people and the environment. It's about making a positive contribution and having the most rewarding and inspiring travel experiences of your life. Travelling by the sustainable travel ethos is one of the most direct and personal ways you can make a difference to two of the biggest issues affecting our world, especially the Middle East: poverty and peace.

- Do ask before taking close-up photographs of people – use sign language if you have to.
- Learn the traditional Arabic greeting, *salaam alaykum*. It really makes a difference – the fact that it means 'peace be upon you' makes it all the more compelling.
- Do have respect for local etiquette. Men should shake hands when formally meeting other men, but not women unless the woman extends her hand first. If you are a woman and uncomfortable with men extending their hand to you (they don't do this with local women), just put your hand over your heart and say hello.
- Learn at least a little about Islam (such as remembering the Five Pillars of Islam, p42).
- Don't wear revealing clothing – what's fine at a club in Beirut is not OK in the souqs of Aleppo. Syrians and Lebanese take pride in their appearance; it's good manners to do so as well.
- Don't display overt affection in public.
- When haggling in the souqs, always do it in a good-humoured manner (see The Art of Bargaining, p235).
- Buying locally made crafts and curios means your money goes directly to the community.

DON'T LEAVE HOME WITHOUT...

- Checking the latest travel advisory warnings.
- Checking the status of border crossings in the region.
- Getting a new passport if your current one contains an Israeli stamp.
- Ensuring you have proof of the relevant vaccinations (see p405) for the region.
- Applying for a Syrian visa (see p237).
- Making copies of important documents – main passport pages, travel insurance details and original receipt for travellers cheques.
- Carrying an Arabic phrasebook – an *'al salaam 'alaykum'* (peace be upon you) works wonders in turning suspicion to a smile.

---

for exploring the large exposed ruins at Palmyra, Apamea or Bosra. Travel in the northeast of the region and through the desert can become a real endurance test. Heading out early and returning to the hotel for an afternoon siesta is necessary to avoid heat stroke and exhaustion (for more advice, see p409). The winter rains can make sightseeing difficult, but if you're lucky enough a blanket of snow may cover Damascus and the mountains.

If you are heading to Syria during school holidays, you should book accommodation well in advance. Religious and state holidays shouldn't seriously disrupt any travel plans. Some services may be cut back, but transport, hotels, restaurants and many businesses function as normal – well, as normal as they do in this lackadaisical country.

The Muslim fasting month of Ramadan may require a bit more planning: make sure you eat breakfast at your hotel, as some cafés and restaurants close during the day, and some offices operate reduced and erratic hours. Despite the inconveniences, it is a fascinating time of year to visit and Ramadan nights, particularly during the final three days of Eid al-Fitr, can be particularly lively. You may wish to schedule your trip around annual festivals, such as those in Damascus, Palmyra and Bosra. For details on these and other special events, see p231; for more information on holidays, see p231.

COSTS & MONEY

Once you're on the ground, Syria is a great-value destination. If you're visiting on a 'time-poor, cash-rich' vacation, you can live it up at elegant restaurants and top-end hotels in Syria for far less than you could in Europe. At the finest Damascene restaurants, a feast with wine for two will cost around US$40, while a romantic room in a boutique hotel can be had for US$120. At the other extreme, a delicious shwarma and fresh fruit juice can be had for US$4 for two. You can spend as little as US$5 to US$10 at a decent sit-down restaurant.

Staying in dorms in hostels and living on shwarma, you could scrape by on an average of US$25 per day – making Syria a popular destination to learn Arabic (see Dialling In Your Dialect In Damascus, p102). A more comfortable budget – staying in hotels as opposed to pensions or hostels and eating in restaurants as opposed to street food – would be US$70 to US$80 (per person, travelling as a couple).

You can live very well indeed for US$100 a day. Travel is also inexpensive, with a bus ride from Aleppo to Damascus costing S£150 – and it's been that price for years.

HOW MUCH?

Postcard S£40

Newspaper S£10

Fresh fruit-juice cocktail S£75

Bottle of Lebanese wine S£600

Short taxi ride S£40

LONELY PLANET INDEX

Litre of petrol S£6.85

Litre of bottled water S£30

Bottle of Barada/Almaza beer S£75

Souvenir T-shirt S£200

Shwarma S£75

TOP PICKS

SYRIA

MUST-SEE MOVIES

Pre-departure dreaming can be done from the comfort of your sofa, preferably with some mezze. If you can't find the following movies in your local video store, art-house cinema or on the foreign movie channel, you can probably find them at www.arabfilm.com. See p70 for more details on Syrian film.

- *Under the Sky of Damascus* (1931)
  Director: Ismail Anzur
- *Dreams of the City* (1984)
  Director: Mohamed Malas
- *The Extras* (1993) Director: Nabil Maleh

- *Listener's Choice* (2002)
  Director: Abdullatif Abdulhamid
- *Sacrifices* (2002)
  Director: Oussama Mohammad

TOP READS

Perusing these titles is a short-cut to understanding the hopes, dreams and observations of life and love in Syria. For more details on literature in Syria, see p69.

- *On Entering the Sea: The Erotic and Other Poetry* (1996) Nizar Qabbani
- *Damascus Nights* (1997) Rafik Schami
- *Sabriya: Damascus Bitter Sweet* (1997) Ulfat Idilbi

- *Menstruation* (2001)
  Ammar Abdulhamid
- *Just Like a River: from Syria* (2003)
  Muhammed Kamil Al-Khatib

LISTENING TO THE LEVANT

Music plays an important role in Syrian culture and was the birthplace of one of the true legends of Middle Eastern music, Farid al-Atrache (see p72). Here's some old and new *oud* (lute) music, some contemporary Syrian pop and Aleppan sung poetry to get you in the mood. All are available on iTunes.

- *Aghany Film El Hob El Kebeer/El Khorog men El Gana* (1964) Farid al-Atrache
- *Eastern Strings: The Art Of Arabian Oud Solos* (2002) Amer Ammouri
- *The Very Best of George Wassouf* (2003) George Wassouf

- *Syrie Wasla d'Alep Syria Wasla d'Aleppo* (2005) Sabri Moudallal et Son Ensemble
- *Hayati* (2006) Asalah

TRAVEL LITERATURE

As there are very few travelogues focused solely on Syria, you may find yourself selectively reading chapters from foreigner's accounts of travels through the Middle East.

Paul Theroux cleverly writes about his travels to Aleppo, Tartus, Lattakia, Qala'at al Hosn (Krak des Chevaliers), Damascus and Maalula in *The Pillars of Hercules* (1996).

While it's only one chapter, Theroux's serendipitous style of travelling is inspiring. *The Street Philosopher and the Holy Fool: A Syrian Journey*

(2006), by Marius Kociejowski, is a humorous and insightful tale of five trips to the Levant.

Robert D Kaplan eruditely writes about his journeys in Syria and Lebanon in *Eastward to Tartary* (2001), cleverly weaving together historical and contemporary characters and stories as he did in *Balkan Ghosts* (1993).

A bittersweet, evocative and quirky account of a gay man's travel in Syria can be found in Robert Tewdwr Moss' *Cleopatra's Wedding Present* (2003). Heartbreakingly, Moss was murdered the day after he finished the manuscript.

Janet Wallach's *Desert Queen* (2001) is a decent account of the often sensuous adventures of feisty Victorian traveller (and friend to TE Lawrence), Gertrude Bell. Bell gives her own gossipy account of carousing with Bedouin tribesmen in *The Desert and the Sown*, first published in 1907.

In *Travels with a Tangerine* (2001), Tim Mackintosh Smith engagingly documents his travels to Damascus, the Crusader and Assassin castles, Hama and Aleppo, as he retraces the journeys of the famous 14th-century Arab traveller, Ibn Battuta. William Dalrymple follows in the footsteps of another earlier traveller – a 6th-century monk – in *From the Holy Mountain* (1998). Dalrymple's visits to Aleppo, Damascus, Beirut and Bcharré offer some keen observations.

For vivid local perspectives on the Syrian capital, read Siham Tergeman's *Daughter of Damascus* (1994), a personal account of growing up in the atmospheric Souq Saroujah in the first half of the 20th century.

There are some wonderful cookbooks on Syria. *Aromas of Aleppo: The Legendary Cuisine of Syrian Jews* (2007) by Poopa Dweck, Michael J Cohen and Quentin Bacon is simply beautiful, and *Saha: A Chef's Journey Through Lebanon and Syria* (2007) by Greg and Lucy Malouf has splendid photography.

INTERNET RESOURCES

Lonely Planet (www.lonelyplanet.com) Succinct summaries on travelling to Syria and Lebanon and, of course, the Thorn Tree bulletin board, where you can ask about the latest border openings and closings.

Syria Planet (www.syplanet.com) The best place to go to find Syrian bloggers writing on Syria.

Syria's Ministry of Tourism (www.syriatourism.org) Quite good official travel site.

The Syria News Wire (http://saroujah.blogspot.com) A good source of what's happening in Syria, with excellent links to other sites of interest.

Emusic (www.emusic .com) has an excellent selection of Middle East Mp3s.

Syria's Culture

THE NATIONAL PSYCHE

The first thing you'll notice in Syria is the hospitality. Those travelling from Western countries with preconceived ideas about the country being a 'rogue state' or part of an 'axis of terror and hate' will find little to support these notions on the streets of Syria. While Syrians might intensely dislike some Western governments' actions, they make a distinction between the government and the people. The friendliness and offers of tea and a chat are constant and only occasionally linked to the sale of a carpet! However, underneath this hospitality, the Syrians can be a little reserved on some topics, such as their own government's actions. This is tied to the fact that most people still believe someone's always listening, and during Hafez al-Assad's reign they were probably right. Until you really get to know a local well, discussing *their* politics is generally off the table.

Don't be surprised, however, at how many questions *you* are asked – about your family, where you live, your life and how much you earn. While many visitors consider the constant questions about family as being too personal, remember that family is of paramount importance throughout the Middle East. Having a large, healthy family is seen as a gift from God and in traditional Arab greetings it's the first thing you ask about after saying hello.

LIFESTYLE

Family is the core unit of Syrian life, regardless of religious sect or ethnic background. Several generations of the one family will often live together. The elderly are greatly respected and are not placed in nursing homes, as there are usually enough family members willing to take care of them. When a person dies there are three days of mourning when friends and relatives pay their respects. Family and individual pride is very strong and this is one reason that, despite being a relatively poor country, you'll rarely see begging on the streets.

Marriage is a major social event in Syria. There is pressure on women to marry young, and more than a little advice on prospective marriage partners is forthcoming from the family – especially from the older women. These days young people have a greater say in whom they marry; however, many living in rural areas still have partners chosen for them. Young couples who are engaged usually meet under supervision, generally a male member of the girl's family, and in the Muslim population they never live together before marriage. It's common for a couple to save money to buy their own place and they'll often delay marriage until they are financially stable; others will marry and stay at home for a few years until they are able to have a place on their own.

The conduct of young women is constantly scrutinised and they are expected to uphold the standing of their family. Bringing shame on the family can occur through something as simple as being alone with a man not from her immediate family – when girls marry they are expected to be virgins.

For most of the desert-dwelling Bedouin of Syria, the seminomadic life has been replaced by a more settled life in a town or city. There are still a few who keep to the old lifestyle – albeit often with a 4WD parked next to their goat-hair tent. Many work a 'normal' job, but get out to the desert as often as possible to enjoy its peace and solitude. For more on the fascinating Bedouin, see p212.

'Having a large, healthy family is seen as a gift from God'

POPULATION

Nearly two-thirds of Syria's total population of around 18.5 million live in a city, concentrated in Damascus (1.6 million in the city itself), Aleppo (2 million) and between Lattakia and Tartus on the coast. Syria's Muslims make up around 90% of the population and this statistic includes the Ismailis, Alawites and Druze, as well as the Sunnis and Shiites. The Alawites have traditionally occupied the mountainous ranges along the coast, which to this day are known as the Jebel Ansariyya, or Jebel an-Nusariyya, after the founder of the Alawite sect, Ibn Nusayr. The other 10% of the population mainly consists of Armenian and Greek Orthodox Christians. For more on religion, see p42.

Syria has a Palestinian population of around 300,000. The invasion of Iraq also saw an incredible influx of Iraqi refugees, who numbered more than 1.5 million before Iraqis began timorously tricking back to their devastated country (see Border Crossing Crisis, p31).

Syria has a youthful population, with over 36% under 15 years of age. Population growth is around 2.5%, down from previous decades but still one of the region's highest. Life expectancy is 69 years of age for men and 71 for women and has been steadily increasing over the last few years.

'Syria has a youthful population, with over 36% under 15 years of age'

SPORT

By far the most popular sport in Syria is football (soccer) and it still remains a male-dominated pastime for participants and armchair fans alike. While results on the international stage have been less than stellar (they've never made it past the qualifying stage of the World Cup, for instance), they do reasonably well in regional tournaments such as the West Asian Football Federation Championships. The national competition, the Syrian League, has existed since 1966 and popular teams to look out for are Al-Jaish (Damascus), Al-Karamah (Homs) and Al-Ittihad (Aleppo). The Syrian Cup, a knockout tournament, is exciting to watch. The only other sport that's overtly popular on the national stage is basketball – but it runs a poor second to football.

MULTICULTURALISM

To the casual observer, Syria appears to be a homogeneous, Arab-Muslim country. However, around 10% of the population is Christian, and a proportion of the Muslim community is Alawite or Druze. In terms of ethnic background the largest minority group in Syria is the Kurds, who make up around 7% of the population and remain a people without a homeland, with the rest of the Kurdish population based in Turkey, Iraq and Iran.

The Armenian community, mainly based in Aleppo, maintain their traditions and culture. The Armenian language is widely spoken and mass is celebrated in the classical Armenian dialect. Much of Syria's large Palestinian population lives on the outskirts of Damascus. While Syria's Arab hospitality has been sorely tested by the influx of Iraqi refugees and the lack of support provided for these refugees by the governments that invaded Iraq, the country has coped reasonably well. All across Syria you'll hear people say that they don't care about ethnicity or religion, nor enquire about it when meeting people, but generally they'll know – either by the dress, accent or name of the person.

WOMEN IN SYRIA

The place of women in Syria today defies traditional classification, although these women must tackle many of the same problems facing women globally. Key issues of concern to women include, but are not

---

THE THOUSAND & ONE NIGHTS

Long before the novel, a deeply rooted tradition of Arabic literature existed in the form of oral storytelling. Before print, professional storytellers circulated tales, epics, fables and histories. A standard entertainment was to entrance audiences with tales attributed to Sheherezade from *The Thousand and One Nights*, or *Arabian Nights*, a mixed bag of colourful and fantastic tales that were periodically committed to manuscript from the 12th century onwards. Collectively they comprise thousands of stories, sharing a core of 271 common tales that employ the same framing device. A Persian king, Shahriyar, discovers his new wife was unfaithful, executes her and marries a succession of virgins only to dispatch them the next morning. Sheherezade, the daughter of the vizier who is helping locate virgins, offers herself as a bride. To save herself, every night she tells fascinating stories to the king, but withholds the ending, thus giving herself another day to live. In the earliest written versions available, the adventures, enchantments and goings-on take place in the semi-fabled Baghdad of Haroun ar-Rashid (r 786–809), and in the Damascus and Cairo of the Mamluks (1250–1517). The *Nights* provides a wealth of rich period detail, from shopping lists and slave prices, through to vivid descriptions of the practices of assorted conjurers, harlots, thieves and mystics. The best-known stories from the book are *Aladdin*, and *Ali Baba and the Forty Thieves*. The best translations are the Penguin Classics version, translated by NJ Dawood and the colourful version by Sir Richard Francis Burton – see Richard Burton, Renaissance Man (p100).

---

limited to, human rights, access to education, gender discrimination, equal opportunity, fairer laws relating to household expenses, violence against women, annulment, divorce, alimony, and custody laws.

Perhaps due to their socialist leanings and connections to the former Soviet Union, women in Syria have long had equitable employment opportunities, have excelled in fields such as education and health and have attained good positions in the legal and political fields. Thirty of the 250 members of parliament are women, and there is a female vice-president – something that never would have happened under Bashar Al-Assad's father's regime. The General Union of Syrian Women, established in 1967, has branches across the country, and has worked hard to encourage women to take a more active social and political role in society. Overall though, there is a strong expectation that women will conform to 'traditional' roles.

MEDIA

Liberalisation of the media appeared likely when Bashar al-Assad came to power, but regional tensions and government interference have seen plans fall far short of expectations. The introduction of the internet opened the floodgates for educated Syrians looking to broaden their knowledge, but a concerted campaign against outspoken bloggers, opinion forums, independent news outlets and even Facebook doesn't bode well.

For most Syrians, news still comes via traditional means. The dailies – three in Arabic and one in English – are mouthpieces for the government and its Ba'ath Party. It's possible for private citizens to start a newspaper, but it's easy for the government to shut it down via 2001's press laws. See p226 for general information on newspapers and magazines available.

Television is state-run, and the only time you'll find anything approaching a critique of life under the Al-Assad regime is during Ramadan programming. Comedies and soap operas attempt to cast a critical eye over life in Syria, but are edited before screening.

Radio doesn't fare much better. While there are no privately owned Syrian radio stations, private Lebanese companies can broadcast in Syria.

ARTS

Syria has a vibrant arts scene, both traditional and contemporary, with Syrian artists and cultural practitioners producing provocative works. Contemporary Middle Eastern culture has been the flavour of the month for a while in Europe, which has meant you were more likely to stumble across an interesting Middle Eastern exhibit or film in Paris or London than you were in Damascus or Beirut. That's starting to change, with the revitalisation of the Damascus International Film Festival, the flourishing of the contemporary arts scene and the growth of the music industry.

Literature

The first great literature in Arabic came from the Arabian Peninsula. The Holy Quran is considered to be the finest example of classical Arabic writing.

Al-Mu'allaqaat, a collection of the earliest Arabic poetry, predated the Quran, and was a celebrated text. Al-Mu'allaqaat means 'the suspended', and refers to the tradition of hanging poems for public view. That explains those pages you see decoratively hanging across the street during *eid* (Islamic feasts; see p231).

Syria didn't become the focal point of classical Arabic poetry until the 10th century. However, as the Arab world came to be dominated by the Ottoman Turks, its literature faded and continued to stagnate until the 19th century. The most popular recent poet was a Damascene, Nizar Qabbani (1923–98), who transformed formal Arabic poetry with the use of everyday language, and was adored in the 1950s for his love poems and, later, for his expressions of the Arabs' collective feelings of humiliation and outrage after the wars with Israel.

The novel as an art form emerged with the awakening of Arab national consciousness after WWII. Since then, Egyptians (including Nobel Prize winner Naguib Mahfouz), Lebanese, Palestinians and Syrians have dominated the Middle Eastern literary scene, although in Syria repression has kept most writing banal or forced authors into exile. Zakariya

---

THE GREATEST ARAB POETS

Abu Nuwas (756–815) Considered *the* greatest of all Arab poets, he was companion to 8th-century Baghdad Abbasid caliph Haroun ar-Rashid. Abu Nuwas spent his summers at Raqqa on the Euphrates River, where he wrote humorous accounts of court life and countless odes to the wonders of wine – his 'research' landed him in jail more than once. His reputation earned him a few mentions in *The Thousand & One Nights* (see opposite).

Al-Mutanabbi (915–65) The Syrian 'Shakespeare of the Arabs' was born in Al-Kufah, in modern-day Iraq. Having spent his youth bragging to local Bedouin that he was a prophet (hence the nickname al-Mutanabbi, which means one who wants to become a prophet), a stint in prison was where he found his voice as a poet. The prince of northern Syria, Sayf al-Dawlah, became his patron and many of his best works were written while he was part of his court at Aleppo. Not without ego, al-Mutanabbi's lyrical style would fit right in with the hip-hop crowd today, boasting that his poetry was so powerful blind men could read it.

Abu Firas al-Hamdan (932–68) An Aleppan who wrote most of his poetry while a prisoner in Byzantium, his notable works were part of the genre called *habsiyah* (prison poem), where the lament of the author's personal life was the overarching theme of the work.

Abu Ala al-Ma'ari (973–1057) Born in Ma'arat an-Nu'aman, the near-blind 'philosopher of poets and poet of philosophers' was a recluse, having refused to ever sell his work. His writings are marked by a heavy scepticism about the decadent, fragmented society surrounding him, and in one poem he suggests that people not reproduce to save the children the pain of existence.

Tamir (b 1931), Syria's master of the children's story, deals with everyday city life marked by frustration and despair born of social oppression, which may explain why he ended up in London. Initially his work was realist in manner, but increasingly he turned to fantasy and surrealism. Having been virtually forced to leave Syria in 1980, he was awarded the Syrian Order of Merit in 2002. Of the noted writers who remained in Syria, the most celebrated and outspoken was Ulfat Idilbi (1912–2007), who wrote about the late Ottoman Empire and French Mandate and the drive for liberation and independence. *Sabriya: Damascus Bitter Sweet* is critical of the mistreatment of women by their families. Much of its anger stemmed from Idilbi's own experience of being married off at 16 to a man twice her age.

In 2007 the release of *A Story Called Syria*, a collection of pieces by 40 writers, was celebrated, and was quickly followed by calls from Syria's writers and intellectuals to reinvigorate the literature scene.

'Syrian and Lebanese filmmakers have created films of great beauty that speak to their countries, peoples and region.'

Cinema & Television

Middle Eastern movies have often been treated as products of a single, unified 'Arab world', yet the unifying factors – Pan-Arab identity, Arab nationalism and Islam – also represent the range of identities characteristic of the region. The most successful industries are those in Egypt, Iran and Turkey; however, countries less developed in terms of film production, such as Syria and Lebanon, have produced carefully crafted movies that reflect upon issues specific to their cultures and countries. Despite Hollywood's dominance of their cinema screens, Syrian and Lebanese filmmakers have created films of great beauty that speak to their countries, peoples and region.

Syria was one of the first Arab countries to develop a cinema industry, yet its production has always been intermittent, with only a handful of films made each year. It got off to a dazzling start in 1928 with Ismail Anzur's stunning silent film, *Under the Sky of Damascus*. However, after a flurry of filmmaking activity following independence in the 1940s, nothing much was made until the 1960s, when a state organisation was created to promote film production and distribution.

Ever since, the government has supported screen education, sending many of its filmmakers to Moscow's excellent cinema academies for training, and financing first feature films. Successful filmmakers include Omar Amiralay, an active director, curator and critic, who made a groundbreaking documentary, *Daily Life in a Syrian Village* (1974) and Mohamed Malas, who directed *Dreams of the City* (1984), an evocative fictional study of Damascus. Abdulatif Abdulhamid, whose brilliant first feature was *The Nights of the Jackal* (1989), has garnered critical praise in recent years for *Two Moons and an Olive Tree* (2001) and *Listeners Choice* (2003), both of which screened at the November 2007 Damascus International Film Festival. The festival screened eight new Syrian feature films under the banner 'New Syrian Cinema', a programme that was the talk of the festival, sparking excited whispers about the rebirth of local film production.

While the handful of movies Syria produces have earned the tiny film industry critical acclaim, it hasn't been able to compete with the production levels of television drama, which has delivered a constant output of quality programming since the 1980s when the government allowed independent companies to produce television content. Since then, Syrian television has boomed, developing a reputation as the indisputable leader of soap opera and series production in the Arab world. Many Syrian

SYRIAN SOAP OPERAS

Soap operas have always been popular in the Arab world and Syria has a reputation for produc-ing the best of them. The peak period for soap watching around the region is Ramadan, when families spend quality time together around the TV set in the evenings. Whereas historical epics once dominated the small screen, a recent trend is for directors to tackle subjects such as Islamic militancy, terrorism, the Arab–Israeli conflicts and the US occupation of Iraq. Two of the most recently popular soap operas were *Al-Hur Al-Ayn* (The Beautiful Maidens) and *Al Tareeq Al-Waer* (The Rugged Path), which dealt with Islamic extremism. Made by Syria's most revered television director Najdat Anzour, the critically acclaimed *Al-Hur Al-Ayn* (the title of which refers to the beautiful virgins that martyrs will be rewarded with in Paradise) had Arab families across the region glued to their screens during Ramadan in 2007. Based on the Al Qaeda bombing of a Saudi Arabian compound that killed mostly Arabs, Anzour's aim was to show the brutal results of extremism and, in doing so, diminish support for calls for jihad among an audience who might ordinarily be sympathetic. The series received critical acclaim and was one of the most watched around the region.

series have sold successfully abroad, not only in other Middle Eastern countries, but – somewhat unexpectedly – in Latin American countries, where there is a great fondness for the melodrama and epic drama in which Syria specialises.

Most of the talent graduating from the National High Institute for Drama head straight for lucrative television work rather than into film as they do in most countries. One of the most successful Syrian television dramas was *The Silk Market,* by Nihad Sirees, an Aleppan novelist and screenwriter, which presented the city of Aleppo, its culture and dialect, on television for the first time. During Ramadan 2007, Bassam Al-Malla's *The Neighbourhood Gate,* a nostalgic portrayal of Damascus during the wars, captivated audiences across the Arab world. More recently, how-ever, Syrian productions have dealt with Islamic militancy, terrorism, and conflict in the region. See Syrian Soap Operas (above).

Music

From the sounds of contemporary Arab pop to the myriad tunes of the adored Farid al-Atrache, music is everywhere in Syria. Contemporary Arab music today reflects a successful synthesis of indigenous harmony, taste and instruments, combined with some Western instruments and influences. In the Syrian desert the Bedouin have long had simple, but mesmerising, musical traditions. However, the music you hear on the Arab street has little to do with timeless desert traditions. Its roots are in Egypt which, for much of the past hundred years, has been the un-disputed musical capital of the Arab world. If the artists weren't always Egyptian-born, they were Egyptian-bred, groomed and broadcast. Syria's most famous performer, Farid al-Atrache, spent most of his career in Cairo. See Farid al-Atrache, (p72).

The most popular style of music focuses on a star performer backed by anything from a small quartet to a full-blown orchestra. The all-time great remains Umm Kolthum, an Egyptian diva renowned in the Arab world as the Kawkab ash-Sharq (Nightingale of the East), who died in 1975. The only singer who has come close to supplanting her in the affections of the Arabs is Fairouz, a Lebanese torch singer who has enjoyed star status since first recording in Damascus in the 1950s. Although the kind of orchestra that backs such a singer is a curious cross-fertilisation of East and West – instruments such as violins, piano,

FARID AL-ATRACHE

This legend of 20th-century Arabic music was born in Suweida in the Hauran region of Syria, in 1915. A Druze, his prominent family were fighting the French at the time of his youth and his mother took the young Farid and brother and sister to Egypt, where they were granted permission to stay, with his mother earning money as a singer and *oud* player. Music ran in the family and Farid and his sister, Amal (later Asmahan) were soon playing to rapt audiences themselves and starred in their first feature film together, *Intisar al-Chabab* in 1941. Farid's sister tragically died during filming of their second movie together, but Farid went on to appear in more than 30 films during the '40s and '50s, several with his girlfriend and belly dancer, the seductive, always smiling, Samia Gamal. Far more than just an 'Arab Sinatra', he was a highly accomplished *oud* player and composer, who succeeded in updating Arabic music by blending it with Western scales and rhythms and the orchestration of the tango and waltz. His melodic improvisations on the *oud* (he is still known as 'King of the Oud') and his *mawal* (a vocal improvisation) were the highlights of his live performances and recordings of these are treasured. Suffering ill health in later life, he still performed until his death in 1974 in Beirut and was buried in his adopted home of Egypt. Of all the male performers of Arabic music in the last century, Farid is the best-known and most respected. His music still reverberates through the streets of the Middle East and especially his birthplace, Syria.

wind and percussion instruments predominate, next to such local species as the *oud* (lute) – the sounds that emanate from them are anything but Western. There is the seduction of the East in the backing melodies and the melancholic, languid tones you'd expect from a sun-drenched and heat-exhausted region.

Held in such esteem as they still are, singers like Farid al-Atrache, Umm Kolthum and Fairouz have little appeal to younger generations of Syrians who have grown up on a sugary diet of Arabic pop. Characterised by a clattering, hand-clapping rhythm overlaid with synthesised twirlings and a catchy repetitive vocal, the first Arab pop stars came out of Cairo. While the Arab world's biggest selling song ever, Amr Diab's 'Nour al-Ain' (1998), was an Egyptian product, these days the Egyptians are being beaten at their own game by Syrian and Lebanese artists.

There were a number of signs in 2007 that the emerging Syrian music industry could be about to experience a boom with the local success of albums by Kulna Sawa (All Together), Lena Chamamian, Itar Shameh, Anas and Friends, Gene, and InsaniT, and a sell-out Woodstock-type concert that toured the country featuring many of these bands.

Hailed as Syria's new diva, charismatic Lena Chamamian released her second CD, *Shamat*, one of 2007's most successful. Its heartfelt folk songs focused on social issues of concern to Syria's youth, such as Syrians having to leave their country to fulfil their dreams, and lovers weary of their families' interference in their romance.

To catch live music performances, check out the *What's On Syria* magazine listings (see p84).

Architecture

The earliest architectural efforts undertaken by Muslims were mosques, which inherited much from Christian and Graeco-Roman models. The Umayyad Mosque (p88) in Damascus was built on the site of a Christian basilica, which itself had been the successor of a Roman temple, and is one of the earliest and grandest of Islam's places of worship.

With the spread of Islam, various styles soon developed and the vocabulary of Islamic architecture quickly became very sophisticated and expressive, reaching its apotheosis under the Mamluks (1250–1517). The Mamluks extended the types of buildings to include the madrassa (theological school), *khanqah* (Sufi monastery) and mausoleum complex. These were typically characterised by the banding of different coloured stone (a technique known as *ablaq*) and by the *muqarnas*, the elaborate stalactite carvings and patterning around windows and in recessed portals. The Mamluks were also responsible for the transformation of the minaret from the Umayyad Mosque's square tower into a slender cylindrical shape. The Ottoman Turks defeated the Mamluks, and during the Ottoman era Damascus and Aleppo flourished, growing rich on trade monopolies. Much of the architecture from this time reflects that wealth. The most prevalent Ottoman building type is the khan, or travellers' inn.

The most notable development in architecture in Aleppo and Damascus is the restoration of Ottoman-era houses and their conversion into restaurants and hotels.

Painting, Visual Arts & Photography

If you think of painting in the Western sense, you may think there is little artistic tradition in the Arab world. Islam's taboo on the depiction of living beings (which clearly doesn't extend to political figures) means that the Arabs have traditionally limited their artistic endeavours to calligraphy and patterning, hence the term 'arabesque'. In the late 19th century a smattering of educated Levantines travelled abroad and returned to form schools of fine art, although their styles were all imported.

In Syria, many of its best artists and photographers have studied, and continue to study, at the Department of Fine Arts at the University of Damascus. One of Syria's most successful artists, Homs-born Abdulla Murad (b 1944) was initially inspired by the European modern masters such as Kandinsky and Miro. Others went overseas to study, such as the prize-winning sculptor Abdel Rahman Mouakket (b 1946), who studied at the Fine Arts Academy of Rome. Murad gradually developed his own style, combining abstract forms with arabesque. A distinctive style and identity began to emerge in the region in the latter half of the 20th century and in recent years a vibrant contemporary art scene has developed in Damascus.

Damascus has half a dozen dynamic and influential independent art galleries, and a handful of others that show local art. Two galleries that have been most supportive of Syria's artistic talent are Atassi and Ayyam galleries (p97), which regularly show the work of renowned Syrian masters such as Mahmoud Hamad, Louay Kayyali, Naseer Chaura, Safwan Dahoul, Fateh Moudarres, Yousef Abdelke, Mouneer Al-Sharaani, Fadi Yazigi, Mouonzer Kamnakache and Abdulla Murad, and acclaimed sculptors such as Mustapha Ali and Abdel Rahman. Art House (p97) recently joined them with its regular exhibitions of work and open-door policy to artists – artists can even go and work there. These are the best galleries to visit to experience quality Syrian art.

Theatre & Dance

With a limited number of theatre venues and little funding in Syria, young dramatists and performers find it difficult to get a start in theatre yet Syria does have a lively Arab theatre scene. Unlike practitioners in the West, Syrian actors, writers and directors are fairly fluid and tend to move easily between working in theatre, television and film. If you can understand Arabic, you can see local theatre at Dar Al Assad for

'in recent years a vibrant contemporary art scene has developed in Damascus'

Arts and Culture (p112). Performances are often filmed and broadcast on television.

Syria's elite love nothing more than to catch a performance by the Russian Ballet, a French contemporary dance group or even Cirque de Soleil at Dar Al Assad, but seeing contemporary Syrian dance is virtually impossible. Travellers have a greater chance of seeing the traditional Levantine dance, the *dabke*. This energetic folk dance is performed at weddings and celebrations throughout the region. People join hands and are led by a 'master' dancer. The dance can also be seen in tourist-oriented restaurants where dancers wear the traditional costume of the mountains and portray aspects of village life. Far more fun is when a spontaneous *dabke* erupts at a wedding or social occasion, and people form circles and start to move. You may also catch a glimpse of some raqs sharki (belly dancing) at a wedding or a 'women only' social occasion. Belly dancers, with their gyrating hips and spangled bikinis, are one of the Middle East's most famous sights, and belly dancing is still very popular in the region, although these days many dancers are not even Arab.

'far more fun is when a spontaneous *dabke* erupts at a wedding or social occasion'

Syria's Environment

From its urban soup of smog, traffic and dusty, littered streets, to the arid deserts, Syria's environment is in a brittle state. Much of Syria's scant vegetation has been depleted by tree felling, farming and grazing, and water bottles, plastic bags and empty shell casings from hunters litter the landscape in some of the more remote areas. While Syria set up the Arab world's first environment ministry in 1991, it's clear that priorities do not lie with 'keep clean campaigns', understandable when you have a faltering economy, war at your doorstep and well over a million neighbours who have moved in to escape it.

One of the key issues for Syria is water conservation. Syria is located in a very arid area of the Middle East. Water scarcity is compounded by the demands of a rapidly growing population, development and by pollution of natural water supplies. A huge proportion of Syria's water is used for agriculture; however, the amount of money that Syria earns from agriculture is small. Water pollution is a problem throughout the country, but the greatest risk is industrial and household waste polluting water intended for agricultural use.

Syria's land types: arid lands 20%; pastures 45%; fertile lands 32%; forests 3%

In the larger urban areas of Syria almost 30% of housing is illegally built or occupied, mainly due to people migrating from rural areas to look for work. These dwellings often lack basic amenities (running water and waste disposal) leading to waterborne diseases such as cholera, typhoid and diarrhoea. Occupation of and damage to historic buildings is also a concern in both Aleppo and Damascus.

Air quality is a problem in urban areas, where air pollution, often visible as smog, exceeds Syrian allowable limits most of the time. Rapid industrialisation on the outskirts of the cities, high-density living, and aged transport vehicles belching smoke are the main contributors, with carbon monoxide levels sometimes double the maximum allowable. In the Old City of Damascus, health problems such as pulmonary diseases have been attributed to this. In addition, vegetation (what little there is) and fragile historic buildings are affected.

Syria has borders with Turkey to the north, Iraq to the east and southeast, Jordan to the south, and Lebanon and Israel and the Palestinian Territories to the southwest.

Arable land issues are also pertinent in Syria, where only around one-third of the total land is suitable for growing crops. Poor use of land and unsustainable development are causing widespread soil degradation, while wind and water erosion are causing further losses of fertile land. Many residential and commercial developments (both legal and illegal) are located near land used for agriculture: it doesn't take a biologist to work out that building houses without sufficient plumbing or cement plants adjacent to fruit farms is not a great idea.

Solid and hazardous wastes are a major concern. While domestic waste is collected at a high rate within the cities, in rural areas the figures are only a little better than half. Open burning and uncontrolled landfill is as unsightly as it is harmful and often domestic waste is mixed with medical waste.

Visit www.ecotourism syria.com, an ecotourism company that has some good information on wildlife- and bird-watching areas in Syria.

Population growth, developments and expansion of agricultural activities have had an adverse effect on Syria's biodiversity. Forests are shrinking, desert ecosystems are under pressure, and hunting and destruction of habitat are threatening bird and mammal species. Aquatic fauna is under threat from over-fishing and the use of illegal fishing methods.

The Syrian National Environmental Action Plan (NEAP), completed in 2003, clearly recognised the significant challenges of protecting Syria's environment – however, funding the recommendations is an ongoing issue.

THE LAND

There are four broad geographical regions of Syria: a coastal strip, backed by mountains, which then flatten out into cultivated plains, quickly giving way to desert.

The coastline is not particularly extensive, stretching for just 180km between Turkey and Lebanon. In the north, the coast is almost fronted by the Jebel Ansariyya.

This range of peaks, with an average height of 1000m, forms a formidable and impenetrable north–south barrier and dominates the whole coast. In the south, the mountains angle inland somewhat to give space to the Sahl Akkar (Akkar Plain). Deep ravines mark the western side of the range, while to the east the mountains fall almost sheer into Al-Ghab, a fertile valley through which the Nahr al-Aasi (Orontes River) flows on its way north into Turkey.

The Jebel Libnan ash-Sharqiyya (Anti-Lebanon Range) marks the border between Syria and Lebanon and averages 2000m in height. Syria's highest mountain, Jebel ash-Sheikh (the Bible's Mt Hermon), rises to 2814m. The main river flowing from this range is the Barada, which has enabled Damascus to survive in an otherwise arid region for over 2000 years.

Other smaller ranges include the Jebel Druze, which rises in the south near the Jordanian border, and the Jebel Abu Rujmayn in the centre of the country, north of Palmyra.

The Fertile Crescent is, as the name suggests, Syria's main agricultural region and forms an arc in which are cradled the major centres of Damascus, Homs, Hama, Aleppo and Qamishle.

The Euphrates and Nahr al-Aasi provide water for intensive farming, while away from the water sources, dry-land wheat and cereal crops are grown.

The Syrian desert, a land of endless, largely stony plains, occupies the whole southeast of the country. The oasis of Palmyra is on the northern edge of this arid zone. As with other oases, it used to be an important centre for the trade caravans plying the routes between the Mediterranean and Mesopotamia.

WILDLIFE

ANIMALS

Officially, wolves, hyenas, badgers, wild boar, jackals, deer, bears and even polecats still roam some corners of Syria, but don't expect to see these on your travels.

The number of bird species found in Syria and their population densities are both low. While Syria has only a small number of major wetlands, they are significant for globally threatened species of birds.

Syria's big claim to faunal fame is as the original home of the golden hamster (see below).

A global alliance of conservation organisations with a fantastic database of birds is www.birdlife.net

Threatened bird species in Syria are the Houbara bustard, Griffon vulture, black frankolin/partridge and the Syrian woodpecker.

Threatened mammals in Syria are the striped hyena, fallow deer and the roe deer.

CAN YOUR HAMSTER SPEAK ARABIC?

It's hard to believe, but nearly every cute little *Mesocricetus auratus* (golden or Syrian hamster) you'll see in the window of a pet shop is a descendent of a pregnant female trapped near Aleppo in 1930. The pups were bred in a laboratory and then released into the British pet market in the 1940s. Breeding as they do (a female can produce a litter of up to 20 pups), they're now tugging at kids' heartstrings all over the world. The irony is that the hamster is almost extinct in the wild in Syria.

PLANTS

Heavy clearing has all but destroyed the once plentiful forests of the mountain belt along the coast of Syria, although some small areas are still protected. Yew, lime and fir trees predominate in areas where vegetation has not been reduced to scrub. Elsewhere, agriculture dominates, and there's little or no plant life in the unforgiving stretches of the Syrian desert.

NATIONAL PARKS & RESERVES

Syria has one of the lowest ratios of protected areas to total land area of any country in the Mediterranean region. However, Syria has a significant protected wetland, the Sabkhat al-Jabbul Nature Reserve. This large, permanent saline lake is located in Halap province, 30km east-southeast of Aleppo. The area is important for a large number of water birds, including the greater flamingo.

A new reserve near Palmyra, Al-Talila, is being developed to protect the region's biodiversity.

Three of a small group of the critically endangered northern bald ibises have been tagged in Syria. Satellites so far have tracked Sultan, Salam and Zenobia on a 3100km journey to Ethiopia.

Damascus   دمشق

Legend has it that on a journey from Mecca, the Prophet Mohammed cast his gaze from the mountainside onto Damascus but refused to enter the city because he wanted to enter paradise only once – when he died. In a place that vies for the title of the world's oldest continually inhabited city, this is but one of thousands of stories.

With its position as the first stop for travellers from the east, and with the Barada River flowing down freely from the mountains where the Prophet stood, Damascus has always been a coveted capital. The machinations of those wishing to claim the city as their own is as fascinating as the wealth of architecture and culture they left behind, with Damascus collecting the calling cards of myriad civilisations. There is hardly a city in the world that has packed so much history into such a small space as the Old City. Thankfully, the Old City is still the Damascus that sustains the romantic notion of the Orient, filled with bazaars and blind alleys, minarets, mosques and fountain courtyards, street-cart vendors and coffeehouses.

While the Barada may not flow as it once did, today Damascus is finding a new spring of life. Boutique hotels now flourish in delightful old Damascene addresses, restaurants refine what is one of the world's most complex cuisines, and art galleries are riding an incoming tide of creativity. There is a new modern sophistication in the city, but for those looking for the Damascus of countless stories, it's still right where it's always been.

HIGHLIGHTS

- Lose yourself in the labyrinthine lanes of Damascus' **Old City** (p85), where thousands of years of history confront you around every corner
- Marvel at the architectural magnificence of **Umayyad Mosque** (p88), one of Islam's most notable buildings
- Haggle for Oriental handicrafts on **Straight St** (p112) or in the hustle and bustle of **Souq al-Hamidiyya** (p115)
- Admire the decorative interiors of the **old Damascene houses** (p92)
- Dine on the Middle East's tastiest cuisine at an atmospheric **Old City restaurant** (p106)
- Be amazed by the traditional storyteller's ability to engage his audience at the coffeehouse **Al-Nawfara** (p109

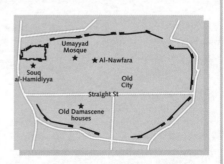

| ■ AREA CODE: 011 | ■ POPULATION: 4.5 MILLION |

HISTORY

'...no recorded event has occurred in the world but Damascus was in existence to receive news of it. Go back as far as you will into the vague past, there was always a Damascus... She has looked upon the dry bones of a thousand empires and will see the tombs of a thousand more before she dies.'

> Mark Twain,
> The Innocents Abroad, *1869*

Damascus lays a strong claim to being the oldest continuously inhabited city in the world. Hieroglyphic tablets found in Egypt make reference to 'Dimashqa' as one of the cities conquered by the Egyptians in the 15th century BC, but excavations from the courtyard of the Umayyad Mosque have yielded finds dating back to the 3rd millennium BC. The name Dimashqa appears in the Ebla archives and also on tablets found at Mari (2500 BC).

In the earliest times it was a prize city, constantly fought over. Early conquerors include the fabled King David of Israel, the Assyrians in 732 BC, Nebuchadnezzar around 600 BC and the Persians in 530 BC. In 333 BC it fell to Alexander the Great. Greek influence declined when the Nabataeans occupied Damascus in 85 BC. Just 21 years later, Rome's legions sent the Nabataeans packing and Syria became a Roman province.

Under the Romans Damascus became a military base for the armies of legionnaires fighting the Persians. Hadrian declared the city a metropolis in the 2nd century AD and during the reign of Alexander Severus it became a Roman colony.

With the coming of Islam, Damascus became an important centre as the seat of the Umayyad caliphate from 661 to 750. When the Abbasids took over and moved the caliphate to Baghdad, Damascus was plundered once again.

After the occupation of Damascus by the Seljuk Turks in 1076, the Crusaders tried unsuccessfully to take the city. They made a second attempt in 1154; this time a general of Kurdish origin, Nureddin (Nur ad-Din), came to the rescue, occupying Damascus himself and ushering in a brief golden era.

During his time business prospered, triggering a corresponding building boom. Notable monuments from the era include the Maristan Nureddin, Madrassa an-Nuri and the Hammam Nureddin, one of the oldest public baths in Syria.

A brief occupation by the Mongols separates the successors of Nureddin as rulers from the Mamluks of Egypt, who rose to power in 1260. During the Mamluk period, Damascene goods became famous worldwide and attracted merchants from Europe. This led to the second Mongol invasion under Tamerlane, when the city was flattened and the artisans and scholars were deported to the Mongol capital of Samarkand. The Mamluks returned soon afterwards and proceeded to rebuild the city.

From the time of the Ottoman Turk occupation in 1516, the fortunes of Damascus started to decline and it was reduced to the status of a small provincial capital in a large empire.

The Turkish and German forces used Damascus as their base during WWI. When they were defeated by the Arab Legion and the Allies, a first, short-lived Syrian government was set up in 1918.

The French, having received a mandate from the League of Nations, occupied the city from 1920 to 1945. They met with massive resistance and at one stage in 1925 bombarded the city to suppress rioting. French shells again rained on the city in the unrest of 1945, which led to full independence a year later when French and British forces were pulled out and Damascus became the capital of an independent Syria.

ORIENTATION

There are two distinct parts to Damascus: the Old City and everything else. The Old City lies largely within its imposing walls, but also extends southwest of the walls, past Cemetery Bab al-Saghir and Bab Mousala (Saahat Yarmouk or Al Yarmouk Sq) to Sharia al-Midan. Modern Damascus sprawls around the Old City, stretching in all directions, climbing the slopes of Jebel Qassioun (Mt Qassioun) to the north and petering out towards the plains to the south. All the parts likely to be of most interest to visitors are contained in roughly 4 sq km and are accessible on foot. The official street signs do not always

DAMASCUS

GREATER DAMASCUS

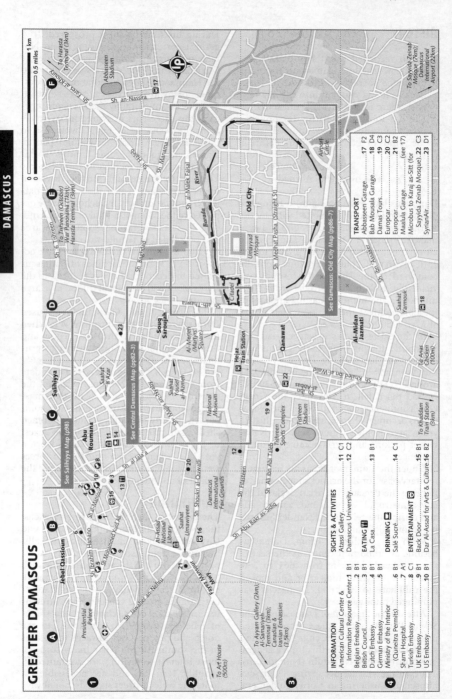

correlate with the commonly known names of various streets and squares – we give both where appropriate.

The Old City lies on the lowest ground around the banks of the Barada River. It's still partially walled and oval in form. The main access from the new city is via the covered Souq al-Hamidiyya, which leads directly to the centrepiece, Umayyad Mosque. South of the mosque is Sharia Medhat Pasha, the ancient Straight St, which bisects the Old City on an east–west axis.

The heart of the modern city is Al-Merjeh, also known as Saahat Shohada (Martyrs' Sq), a landscaped traffic island about 500m west of the Old City walls. Many cheap hotels and restaurants are around here.

The rest of 'downtown' Damascus lies north and west of Al-Merjeh. You'll find the closest thing Damascus has to a 'main street' two blocks west of here, beginning at the old Hejaz train station as Sharia Said al-Jabri (the main post office is here), and continuing for a couple of kilometres via Saahat Yousef al-Azmeh (Yousef al-Azmeh Sq), near the main tourist office. You'll find many airline offices and banks on this street, which changes its name twice en route, becoming Sharia Bur Said after Saahat Ash-Sham until Saahat Yousef al-Azmeh, and Sharia 29 Mai (29 May St) between there and Saahat Al Tajrideh Al Maghribiyeh (also known as Saahat as-Sabe Bahrat or 17 April Sq).

Saahat Yousef al-Azmeh is a focal point for the modern city centre, into which all roads run. The road running to the west, Sharia Maysaloun, has more airline offices and the swish Cham Palace, and off Maysaloun runs Sharia al-Hamra, Damascus' main shopping street. This area is known commonly as Salihiyya.

At its extreme western end, Maysaloun intersects with Sharia al-Jala'a, which is the main thoroughfare through the wealthy diplomatic district known as Abu Roumana. Here you are already on the lower slopes of Jebel Qassioun; there's plenty of greenery and the air seems distinctly fresher and more breathable than it is down below.

Maps

For information regarding maps of Damascus and Syria, see p232.

INFORMATION
Bookshops

Librairie Avicenne (Map pp82–3; ☎ 221 2911; 4 Sharia Attuhami; ☑ 9am-8.30pm Sat-Thu) One block south of Cham Palace, Damascus' best bookshop stocks foreign-language publications including a decent range of Syria guidebooks, coffee-table books on the Middle East, phrase books, and novels in English and French.

Librairie Universelle (Map pp82–3; ☎ 230 0744; ☑ 9am-8pm Sat-Thu) Just west of Sharia Yousef al-Azmeh, it has a smattering of novels plus Middle East gift books.

The Cham Palace (p105) also has a small but good bookshop, with a selection of guidebooks and gift books related to Syria and the Islamic world.

Time, Newsweek, the *International Herald Tribune* plus a limited selection of international publications are available at Librairie Avicenne, the Cham Palace bookshop, and a couple of newsstands, including one near the end of Sharia Majlis an-Nyaby, close to the intersection with Sharia al-Jala'a, and another (the best) one block north of the main tourist office.

Cultural Centres

The city's cultural centres offer language courses, libraries, resource centres, and vibrant programmes of performance, music and film.

In some cases only citizens of those countries can access facilities; call ahead and take your passport.

American Cultural Center & Information Resource Centre (Map p80; ☎ 3391 4444; http://damascus .usembassy.gov/cultural_programs.html; 87 Sharia Ata al-Ayyoubi; ☑ 1-5pm Sun-Thu) The Cultural Center hosts lectures, events, exhibitions and courses, while the Information Resource Center has a library where US citizens can read American press, among other things.

British Council (Map p80; ☎ 333 0631; fax 332 1467; www.britishcouncil.org/syria; Sharia Maysaloun; ☑ 8.30am-8.30pm Sat-Thu) Primarily a teaching and resource centre, the Council occasionally hosts cultural events. Visit the website for details.

Centre Culturel Français de Damas (Map pp82–3; ☎ 231 6192; fax 231 6194; www.ccf-damas.org; off Sharia Yousef al-Azmeh; ☑ 8.30am-9pm Mon-Sat) French speakers should check out the Centre's comprehensive programme of films and lectures. It also offers a stimulating programme of theatre and music performances, many of which are free.

CENTRAL DAMASCUS

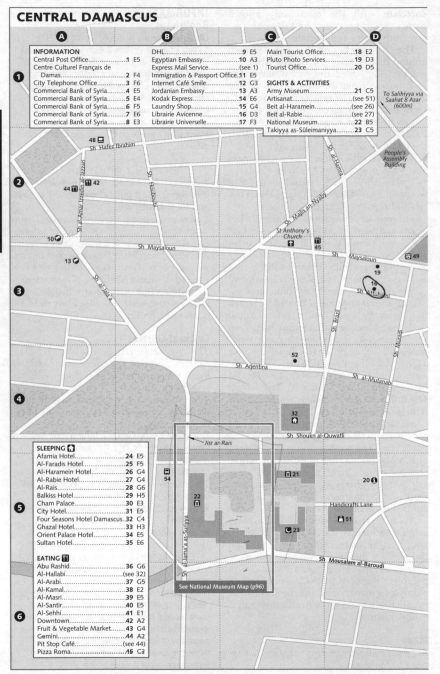

INFORMATION
Central Post Office...................**1** E5
Centre Culturel Français de
   Damas...............................**2** F4
City Telephone Office...............**3** F6
Commercial Bank of Syria.......**4** E5
Commercial Bank of Syria.......**5** E4
Commercial Bank of Syria.......**6** F5
Commercial Bank of Syria.......**7** E6
Commerical Bank of Syria........**8** E3
DHL......................................**9** E5
Egyptian Embassy..................**10** A3
Express Mail Service...........(see **1**)
Immigration & Passport Office.**11** E5
Internet Café Smile................**12** G3
Jordanian Embassy................**13** A3
Kodak Express......................**14** E6
Laundry Shop........................**15** G4
Librairie Avicenne..................**16** D3
Librairie Universelle................**17** F3

Main Tourist Office...............**18** E2
Pluto Photo Services.............**19** D3
Tourist Office........................**20** D5

SIGHTS & ACTIVITIES
Army Museum......................**21** C5
Artisanat...........................(see **51**)
Beit al-Haramein...............(see **26**)
Beit al-Rabie.....................(see **27**)
National Museum.................**22** B5
Takiyya as-Süleimaniyya.......**23** C5

SLEEPING 🏠
Afamia Hotel........................**24** E5
Al-Faradis Hotel....................**25** F5
Al-Haramein Hotel................**26** G4
Al-Rabie Hotel......................**27** G4
Al-Rais................................**28** G6
Balkiss Hotel.........................**29** H5
Cham Palace........................**30** E3
City Hotel............................**31** E5
Four Seasons Hotel Damascus.**32** C4
Ghazal Hotel........................**33** H3
Orient Palace Hotel..............**34** E5
Sultan Hotel.........................**35** E6

EATING 🍴
Abu Rashid..........................**36** G6
Al-Hallabi.........................(see **32**)
Al-Arabi..............................**37** G5
Al-Kamal.............................**38** E2
Al-Masri..............................**39** E5
Al-Santir.............................**40** E5
Al-Sehhi..............................**41** E1
Downtown...........................**42** A2
Fruit & Vegetable Market......**43** G4
Gemini................................**44** A2
Pit Stop Café.....................(see **44**)
Pizza Roma..........................**45** C3

To Salihiyya via
Saahat 8 Azar
(600m)

People's
Assembly
Building

Sh Hafez Ibrahim

Sh al-Amar Izzedin al-Hazzari

Sh al-Hamra

Sh Holboubi

Sh Majlis an-Nyaby

St Anthony's
Church

Sh Maysaloun

Maysaloun

Sh al-Jala'a

Sh al-Jala'a

Sh al-Ittuhami

Sh Bazal

Sh Murad

Sh Argentina

Sh al-Mutanabi

Sh Shoukri al-Quwatli

Jisr ar-Rais

Handicrafts Lane

Sh al-Jama'a as-Suriyya

Sh Mousalam al-Baroudi

See National Museum Map (p96)

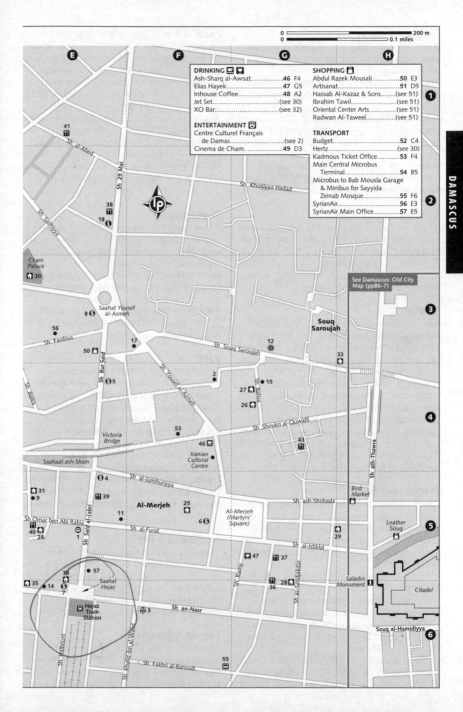

0 ━━━━━ 200 m
0 ━━━━━ 0.1 miles

DRINKING 🍷 🍸
Ash-Sharq al-Awsat...............**46** F4
Elias Hayek.......................**47** G5
Inhouse Coffee..................**48** A2
Jet Set..........................(see 30)
XO Bar..........................(see 32)

ENTERTAINMENT 🎭
Centre Culturel Français
de Damas.......................(see 2)
Cinema de Cham...............**49** D3

SHOPPING 🛍
Abdul Razek Mousali............**50** E3
Artisanat........................**51** D5
Hassab Al-Kazaz & Sons........(see 51)
Ibrahim Tawil...................(see 51)
Oriental Center Arts............(see 51)
Radwan Al-Taweel..............(see 51)

TRANSPORT
Budget..........................**52** C4
Hertz...........................(see 30)
Kadmous Ticket Office...........**53** F4
Main Central Microbus
Terminal.......................**54** B5
Microbus to Bab Mousla Garage
& Minibus for Sayyida
Zeinab Mosque.................**55** F6
SyrianAir........................**56** E3
SyrianAir Main Office...........**57** E5

See Damascus: Old City
Map (pp86–7)

Cham
Palace

Souq
Saroujah

Saahat Yousef
al-Azmeh

Sh. Fardous

Sh. 29 Mai

Sh. al-Abed

Sh. Saliniyya

Sh. Baltis

Sh. Bur Said

Sh. Khorjiyya Hadad

Sh. Souq Saroujah

Sh. Yousef al-Azmeh

Sh. Babel

Sh. Shoukri al-Quwatli

Sh. ath-Thawra

Victoria
Bridge

Saahaat ash-Sham

Iranian
Cultural
Centre

Sh. al-Jumhuriyya

Al-Merjeh

Al-Merjeh
(Martyrs'
Square)

Sh. ash-Shohada

Bird
Market

Sh. Omar ben Abi Rabia

Sh. Said al-Jabri

Sh. al-Furat

Sh. al-Istiklal

Leather
Souq

Saahat
Hejaz

Sh. Ramy

Sh. as-Saodiatkar

Saladin
Monument

Citadel

Hejaz
Train
Station

Sh. an-Nasr

Sh. Talibouni

Sh. Khalid Ibn al-Walid

Sh. Fakhri al-Baroudi

Souq al-Hamidiyya

Internet Access

There are internet cafés all over Damascus, and most charge the same rates, roughly S£50 to S£60 per hour.

Amigo Net (Map pp86-7; ☎ 542 1694; Sharia al-Kassaa; ☷ 10am-midnight) Just north of Bab Touma and the Old City.

Internet Café Smile (Map pp82-3; ☎ 232 6239; Sharia Souq Saroujah; ☷ 11am-midnight Sat-Thu, 2pm-midnight Fri) Convenient for Souq Saroujah's budget hotels; also organises parcel shipping.

Spotnet Café (Map pp86-7; ☎ 543 3374; www.spot netcafe.com; opposite Elissar, Bab Touma; ☷ 10am-2am) Friendly staff and reasonably fast access for the Old City.

Laundry

There are laundries all over Damascus, but long-term travellers like the **laundry shop** (Map pp82-3; Sharia Bahsa; per item S£25-35) in Souq Saroujah. Staff take about 24 hours to turn around your washing. Most hotels can arrange to have laundry done.

Media

The national, government-owned, English-language daily newspaper, the *Syria Times* (www.syriatimes.tishreen.info), provides an intriguing insight into Syrian politics, society and everyday life. More helpful to travellers is the glossy *What's On Syria* magazine (www.whatsonsyria.com), with features on everything from Syria's video-game culture to the popularity of ballroom dancing in Damascus, along with reviews of cultural performances, art exhibitions and films, as well as entertainment listings. It's available at hotels, cafés and bars.

Medical Services

There are numerous pharmacies dotted around Saahat Yousef al-Azmeh.

Shami Hospital (Map p80; ☎ 373 5090-94; Sharia Jawaher an-Nehru) This private hospital has an excellent reputation among expats, with many doctors speaking English.

Money

Very few banks will change travellers cheques so it's best to leave them at home and bring US dollars instead, withdraw cash using your ATM card or get cash advances on your credit card.

There are dozens of branches of the Commercial Bank of Syria (CBS) all over Damascus, with the main branches at **Saahat**

Yousef al-Azmeh (Map pp82-3; ☷ 8.30am-8pm Sat-Thu, to 2pm Fri), opposite the Hejaz train station (Map pp82-3), on Sharia Bur Said (Map pp82-3), at the corner of Sharia Said al-Jabri and Sharia Jumhuriyya (Map pp82-3), on the west side of Al-Merjeh (Map pp82-3) and at Bab ash-Sharqi (Map pp86-7). Branches keep the same opening hours. Most have ATMs, as do the many new private banks that have opened in recent years, including Bank Audi, Byblos Bank and the Real Estate Bank of Syria. There is also an ATM at the airport, although it often runs out of money.

Photography

Along Sharia al-Jumhuriyya are a few camera stores selling memory cards, mini-tripods and other accessories; they also do camera repairs if you're desperate.

Kodak Express (Map pp82-3; Sharia Mousalam al-Baroudi; ☷ 9am-7pm Sat-Thu) About 100m west of Hejaz train station. Stocks memory cards and film.

Pluto Photo Services (Map pp82-3; Sharia Maysaloun; ☷ 9am-8pm Sat-Thu) Just west of Cham Palace; good for emergency camera repairs or spares.

Post

Central post office (Map pp82-3; Sharia Said al-Jabri; ☷ 8am-7pm Sat-Thu, 9am-noon Fri & national holidays) Just down from Hejaz train station, there is a poste restante office inside (passport required; S£10 charge per letter) and a parcel post office outside and around the corner.

DHL (Map pp82-3; ☎ 096-345 345; Sharia Omar ben Abi Rabia; ☷ 8am-8pm Sat-Thu, 9am-2pm Fri) Not far from the post office, and west towards Sharia Shoukri al-Quwatli; a better option if sending carpets or valuables home.

Express Mail Service (EMS; Map pp82-3; ☷ 8am-5pm Sat-Thu) A faster and more secure mail service than the regular post; located in the parking lot behind the central post office.

Telephone & Fax

There are card phones scattered around Damascus, but you're better off buying a SIM card for your own mobile. For more details on card phones and phonecards, see p236.

City telephone office (Map pp82-3; Sharia an-Nasr; ☷ 24hr) A block east of the Hejaz train station.

Tourist Information

The staff at the tourist offices are friendly and speak some English. However, beyond free maps and a monthly brochure of cultural events they have little to offer and are poorly informed on the sorts of things that most visitors might want to know.

Main tourist office (Map pp82-3; ☎ 232 3953, 221 0122; www.syriatourism.org, damascus@syriatourism .org; Sharia 29 Mai; ☼ 9.30am-7pm Sat-Thu) Just north of Saahat Yousef al-Azmeh.

Tourist office (Map pp82-3; Ministry of Tourism Bldg, Sharia Shoukri al-Quwatli; ☼ 9am-2pm Sat-Thu) Despite being in the Ministry of Tourism building, this office is often closed. It's near the National Museum and Takiyya as-Süleimaniyya.

Visa Extensions

Immigration & Passport Office (Map pp82-3; ☎ 221 9400; Al-Merjeh; ☼ 8am-2pm Sat-Thu) Take your passport and several photocopies of your main passport pages, and pay S£25 for the forms and process. Fill out the forms on the spot, then return to collect your passport the next day. There are dozens of shops doing passport photos and photocopies in the surrounding streets.

SIGHTS
Old City المدينة القديمة

Although settlement of the Old City dates back to as early as the 15th century BC, and there's strong evidence of both Hellenic and Roman city styles, the Old City's character is essentially medieval Islamic. It remains unchanged from that time to an astonishing degree.

The Old City can be confusing for the first-time visitor but it's a magical, meandering place to explore. If possible, allow a couple of hours each for the sights listed here.

CITY WALLS & CITADEL

First erected by the Romans, the **Old City walls** (Map pp86-7) have been flattened and rebuilt several times over the 2000 or so years since. What stands today dates largely from the 13th century. They are pierced by a number of gates (the Arabic for gate is *bab,* plural *abwab*), only one of which dates from Roman times, the restored **Bab ash-Sharqi** (East Gate). Until the 20th century there were 13 gates in the city walls, all closed at sunset, and there were inner gates dividing the Christian, Jewish and Islamic quarters. These inner gates are now gone, as are several of the main city gates. Most impressive of those remaining are the northern **Bab al-Farag** (Gate of Joy); **Bab al-Faradis** (Gate of Paradise), with a short stretch of market enclosed within its vaulting; **Bab as-Salaama** (Gate of Peace), the best-preserved of the

gates and a beautiful example of Ayyubid military architecture; and, in the south, **Bab as-Saghir** (Little Gate).

For most of their length, the walls are obscured by later constructions. It's not possible to do a circuit of the walls, nor get up on the ramparts. However, there is a fine short walk between Bab as-Salaama and **Bab Touma** (Thomas' Gate) along the outside of the walls by a channel of the Barada River.

The **citadel** (Map p114; ☼ 9am-3pm Sun-Thu, open later for concerts) anchors the northwest corner of the Old City, its imposing stone walls confronting the six lanes of traffic on Sharia ath-Thawra. Built by the Seljuks between 1076 and 1193, the citadel was further fortified by the Zangid ruler Sultan Nur al-Din and by the Ayyubid Sultan Saladin in the 12th century to resist Crusader attacks. Modifications were added by the Mamluks and Ottomans, and during the French mandate it became a prison, which it remained until 1985. The citadel has been recently restored, and it's possible to wander the grounds (allow two hours) for free, although some time in 2008 ticket offices will be installed and a visitors centre will open, featuring a bookshop, interactive kiosks and a mosaic exhibition. Guided tours will be conducted. Concerts are held frequently in the citadel grounds, especially during summer evenings, when you might see anything from a symphony orchestra to jazz bands. The Jazz Festival is held here in July.

SOUQ AL-HAMIDIYYA سوق الحميدية

Just to the south of the citadel, **Souq al-Hamidi-yya** (Map p114) is the long, covered market that leads into the heart of the Old City. A cross between a Parisian passage, a department store and a Middle Eastern bazaar, its main thoroughfare is lined with clothes emporiums and handicrafts shops (see Shopping the Damascus Souq, p115), while its narrow side streets are crowded with stalls selling everything from cheap shoes to kids' toys. A vault of corrugated-iron roofing blocks all but a few torch-beam-like shafts of sunlight, admitted through bullet holes punctured by the machine-gun fire of French planes during the nationalist rebellion of 1925.

Although the street dates back to Roman times, its present form is a product of the late 19th century: the two-storey shops, the roof and the generously wide street

DAMASCUS: OLD CITY

DAMASCUS

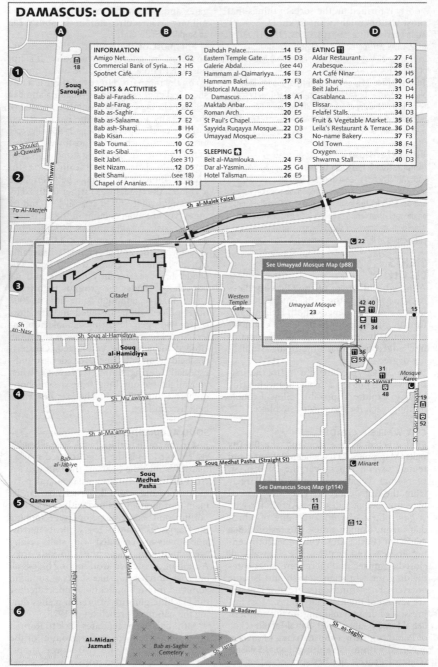

INFORMATION
Amigo Net.............................1 G2
Commercial Bank of Syria......2 H5
Spotnet Café..........................3 F3

SIGHTS & ACTIVITIES
Bab al-Faradis.......................4 D2
Bab al-Farag..........................5 B2
Bab as-Saghir........................6 C6
Bab as-Salaama......................7 E2
Bab ash-Sharqi......................8 H4
Bab Kisan.............................9 G6
Bab Touma...........................10 G2
Beit as-Sibai.........................11 C5
Beit Jabri........................(see 31)
Beit Nizam..........................12 D5
Beit Shami......................(see 18)
Chapel of Ananias.............13 H3

Dahdah Palace.....................14 E5
Eastern Temple Gate...........15 D3
Galerie Abdal...................(see 44)
Hammam al-Qaimariyya.....16 E3
Hammam Bakri....................17 F3
Historical Museum of
  Damascus.........................18 A1
Maktab Anbar.....................19 D4
Roman Arch........................20 E5
St Paul's Chapel..................21 G6
Sayyida Ruqayya Mosque....22 D3
Umayyad Mosque...............23 C3

SLEEPING
Beit al-Mamlouka...............24 F3
Dar al-Yasmin....................25 G4
Hotel Talisman...................26 E5

EATING
Aldar Restaurant.................27 F4
Arabesque..........................28 E4
Art Café Ninar....................29 H5
Bab Sharqi..........................30 G4
Beit Jabri...........................31 D4
Casablanca.........................32 H4
Elissar...............................33 F3
Felafel Stalls.......................34 D3
Fruit & Vegetable Market.....35 E6
Leila's Restaurant & Terrace..36 D4
No-name Bakery..................37 F3
Old Town............................38 F3
Oxygen..............................39 F4
Shwarma Stall....................40 D3

DAMASCUS

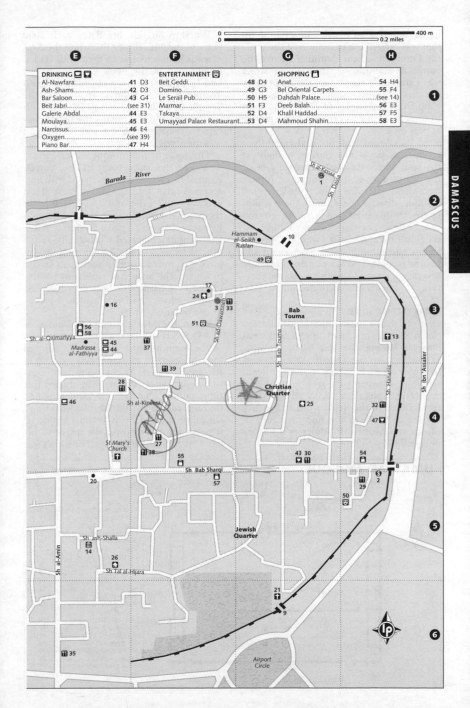

0   400 m
0   0.2 miles

DRINKING 🍺🍷
Al-Nawfara........................41 D3
Ash-Shams.......................42 D3
Bar Saloon.......................43 G4
Beit Jabri.....................(see 31)
Galerie Abdal...................44 E3
Moulaya..........................45 E3
Narcissus........................46 E4
Oxygen.......................(see 39)
Piano Bar........................47 H4

ENTERTAINMENT 🎭
Beit Geddi........................48 D4
Domino............................49 G3
Le Serail Pub....................50 H5
Marmar............................51 F3
Takaya.............................52 D4
Umayyad Palace Restaurant...53 D4

SHOPPING 🛍
Anat.................................54 H4
Bel Oriental Carpets............55 F4
Dahdah Palace................(see 14)
Deeb Balah......................56 E3
Khalil Haddad....................57 F5
Mahmoud Shahin..............58 E3

are all due to a bit of civic smartening up that was carried out in honour of the visiting Ottoman sultan, Hamid II (hence the name, Al-Hamidiyya). In 2002 the street was extensively renovated, stripping away decades of messy signage and random shop-front accretions, to restore the souq to something like its original 19th-century appearance.

At its eastern end, Souq al-Hamidiyya re-emerges back into glaring sunlight at the spot where the **western temple gate** of the 3rd-century Roman Temple of Jupiter once stood. The outer walls of the Umayyad Mosque, directly ahead, mark the position of the temple itself, but here, on ground now occupied by stalls selling Qurans and religious paraphernalia, was the propylaeum (the monumental gateway to the temple complex). What remains today are several enormous Corinthian columns carrying fragments of a decorated lintel.

UMAYYAD MOSQUE   الجامع الاموي

One of Islam's most important buildings (its first great mosque), the magnificent **Umayyad Mosque** (Map pp86-7; admission S£50; ☪ dawn until after sundown prayers, closed 12.30-2pm Fri for noon prayers) is Syria's most significant religious structure. Its architectural and decorative splendour ranks with Jerusalem's Dome of the Rock, while in sanctity it's second only to the holy mosques of Mecca and Medina. It possesses a history unequalled by all three.

Worship on this site dates back 3000 years to the 9th century BC, when the Aramaeans built a temple to their god, Hadad (mentioned in the Book of Kings in the Old Testament). It was a cousin to the great Temple of Bel at Palmyra (p207) and the Temple of Jupiter at Baalbek (p358). With the coming of the Romans the temple became associated with the god Jupiter and was massively expanded.

The walls of the mosque as seen today were just the inner court of the temple. Around this was a large courtyard with four access points – traces of two of these grand gateways still exist and are described in the Souq al-Hamidiyya (p85) and Sayyida Ruqayya Mosque (p90) sections. After Constantine embraced Christianity as the official religion of the Roman Empire, Jupiter was ousted from his temple in favour of Christ. The former pagan shrine was replaced by a basilica dedicated to John the Baptist, whose head was said to be contained in a casket here.

When the Muslims entered Damascus in AD 636 they converted the eastern part of the basilica into a mosque but allowed the Christians to continue their worship in the western part. This arrangement continued for about 70 years. But, during this time, under Umayyad rule Damascus had become capital of the Islamic world and the caliph, Khaled ibn al-Walid, considered it necessary to empower the image of his city with 'a mosque the equal of which was

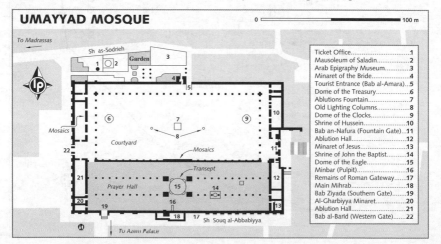

UMAYYAD MOSQUE

0 ————————————————— 100 m

To Madrassas

Sh as-Sodrieh

Garden

To Azem Palace

Sh Souq al-Abbabiyya

Mosaics

Courtyard

Mosaics

Transept

Prayer Hall

Minbar (Pulpit)

Ticket Office	1
Mausoleum of Saladin	2
Arab Epigraphy Museum	3
Minaret of the Bride	4
Tourist Entrance (Bab al-Amara)	5
Dome of the Treasury	6
Ablutions Fountain	7
Old Lighting Columns	8
Dome of the Clocks	9
Shrine of Hussein	10
Bab an-Nafura (Fountain Gate)	11
Ablution Hall	12
Minaret of Jesus	13
Shrine of John the Baptist	14
Dome of the Eagle	15
Minbar (Pulpit)	16
Remains of Roman Gateway	17
Main Mihrab	18
Bab Ziyada (Southern Gate)	19
Al-Gharbiyya Minaret	20
Ablution Hall	21
Bab al-Barid (Western Gate)	22

never designed by anyone before me or anyone after me'.

Consequently, the Christians were elbowed out of the basilica while the Roman and Byzantine constructions were flattened. For the next 10 years more than 1000 stonemasons and artisans were employed in building a grand new mosque. According to historical accounts, practically every wall was covered with rich mosaics, precious stones were set into the prayer niches, and the wooden ceiling was inlaid with gold and hung with 600 gold lamps. It cost seven years of taxes from the whole of Syria to build. While the mosque has been ravaged by invading Mongols, rocked by earthquakes and gutted by fire, what remains is impressive.

Visiting the Mosque
The tourist entrance is through the northern Bab al-Amara, and the ticket office is on the left; look for the amusing sign that says 'Putting on Special Clothes Room'. Here, women are provided with a hooded cloak that must be worn in the mosque, while men in shorts or sleeveless shirts will also be asked to don one. As in all mosques, shoes must be removed at the threshold. Photography is permitted.

Mausoleum of Saladin (Salah ad-Din)
قبر صلاح الدين
In the small archaeological garden that lies along the north wall of the Umayyad Mosque are a few columns dating back to the original Roman Temple of Jupiter, and a small white building topped by a rust-red dome, which is the **Mausoleum of Saladin** (🕑 10am-5pm). The famed, chivalrous adversary of the Western Crusaders died in Damascus in 1193, and the original mausoleum was erected on this site that same year. It was restored with funds made available by Kaiser Wilhelm II of Germany during his visit to Damascus in 1898.

For a man who was famed for his austerity, the mausoleum is a fittingly modest affair. Inside are two cenotaphs. The walnut-wood one on the right, richly decorated with motifs of the Ayyubid period, contains Saladin's body, while the modern tomb in marble on the left was donated by Kaiser Wilhelm.

Admission is included in the ticket for Umayyad Mosque.

Arab Epigraphy Museum
For most visitors this will be a case of a building being more engaging than its contents. The **Arab Epigraphy Museum** (adult/student S£75/10; 🕑 9am-2pm Wed, Thu & Sat-Mon, 9-11.30am Fri) has a small but fascinating calligraphic exhibit of illuminated manuscripts, while the 15th-century Madrassa al-Jaqmaqiyya in which the collection is exhibited is a fine example of Mamluk-era architecture.

Courtyard
The northern part of the mosque is an expansive, open courtyard with a white limestone floor, flanked on three sides by a two-storey arched arcade. The fourth side is the façade of the prayer hall, dominated by a central section covered with enchanting, shimmering, golden **mosaics**.

A larger expanse of mosaic also remains on the western arcade wall. Stretching some 37m in length, and executed in shades of green and lime on a background of gold, the mosaic depicts fairytale-like towers, domes and forests. Damascenes believe it's the Barada Valley and the paradise Mohammed saw in Damascus.

In the centre of the courtyard is an odd square-shaped **ablutions fountain** topped by a wooden-canopied pulpit, while flanking it are two old **columns** that used to hold lamps. The small octagonal structure on the western side, decorated with intricate 14th-century mosaics and standing on eight recycled Roman columns, is the **Dome of the Treasury**, once used to keep public funds safe from thieves. It's counterbalanced by a domed structure on the eastern side, built in the 18th century and known as the **Dome of the Clocks** because it's where the mosque's clocks used to be kept.

Minarets
There are three minarets dating from the original construction, each of which was renovated and restored by the Ayyubids, Mamluks and Ottomans. The one on the northern side, the **Minaret of the Bride**, is the oldest; the one in the southwestern corner, the Mamluk-styled **Al-Gharbiyya minaret**, is the most beautiful; while the one on the southeastern corner, the **Minaret of Jesus**, is the tallest, and so named because local tradition has it that this is where Christ will appear on earth on Judgment Day.

Prayer Halls
On the southern side of the courtyard is the rectangular prayer hall, its three aisles divided by a transept. The hall as seen today is the Ottoman reconstruction that took place after the devastating fire of 1893. At the centre of the hall, resting on four great pillars above the transept, is the **Dome of the Eagle**, so called because it represents the eagle's head, while the transept represents the body and the aisles are the wings.

Looking somewhat out of place in the sanctuary is the green-domed, marble-clad **shrine of John the Baptist** (Prophet Yehia to Muslims). The story goes that during the building of the mosque, back in the early 8th century, a casket was discovered buried under the old basilica floor. It contained the biblical character's head, still with skin and hair intact, and that's what's in the shrine. However, this is one of several claimed final resting places for the relic, and unless the saint was endowed with multiple heads, the authenticity of claims has to be seriously doubted.

To the eastern side of the courtyard, but a part of the mosque building itself, is the **shrine of Hussein**, son of Ali and grandson of the Prophet. He was killed by the Umayyads at Kerbala in Iraq. The shrine attracts large numbers of Shiite Muslims (Ali is regarded as the founder of Shiism), and black-clad Iranians are a common sight, making straight across the courtyard for this part of the mosque.

NORTH OF THE MOSQUE
Two fine old madrassas (schools where Islamic law is taught) face each other across a narrow alley less than 100m northwest of the Umayyad Mosque. Both of these schools were erected in the 13th century during the ascendancy of the Ayyubids. On the left (west), **Madrassa al-Adeliyya** (Map p114) was begun under Nureddin and continued under a brother of Saladin, Al-Adel Seif ad-Din, whose grave it contains. Its façade is considered a classic example of Ayyubid architecture.

Madrassa az-Zahariyya (Map p114), on the eastern side of the alley, was originally a private house belonging to the father of Saladin. Following the death in 1277 of the great Mamluk sultan and nemesis of the Crusaders, Beybars, the building was converted into his **mausoleum** (قبر بيبرس; ⏲ 9am-5pm, closed Fri). Someone will usually be around to let you in for a look. Note the band of splendid mosaic decoration in a style similar to that in the Umayyad Mosque.

From the madrassas, head north, past the doorway of Hammam az-Zahariyya, and then bear right; following this narrow alley leads you to a small square at the main entrance to Sayyida Ruqayya Mosque.

Sayyida Ruqayya Mosque
جامع السيدة الرُقية
For centuries the mausoleum of Ruqayya bint al-Hussein ash-Shaheed bi-Kerbala (Ruqayya, the Daughter of the Martyr

---

DIY DAMASCUS

It's time to put away the guidebook and get lost in some of the city's fascinating neighbourhoods – try these for starters:

■ Christian Quarter, Old City (Map pp86–7) – the streets parallel to Sharia Bab Touma are where the sights and shops are; instead, cruise the cross-streets and little cul-de-sacs to see how the locals live.

■ Jewish Quarter, Old City (Map pp86–7) – avoid Straight St and stroll the labyrinthine backstreets around Bab Sharqi, through the Jewish Quarter's dusty, dilapidated lanes by Dahdah Palace to Beit Nizam.

■ Salihiyya's old quarter (Map p98) – after exploring Sharia Madares Assad al-Din, meander the ramshackle streets north of here before exploring the streets south; Sharia al-Nawa'eer is charming, with a few Ottoman-era buildings.

■ Salihiyya's new city and Abu Roumana (Map p80) – from Salihiyya's old quarter, stroll downhill via posh Abu Roumana's elegant apartments and embassies to new Salihiyya and Sharia Maysaloun; on the backstreets you'll enjoy all kinds of architectural styles, from grand Art Deco to pretty wrought iron from the French mandate period.

Hussein of Kerbala) was hidden among the clutter of tumbledown Damascene housing just to the north of Umayyad Mosque. In 1985 the Iranians (Ruqayya being a Shiite saint) began construction of a **mosque** (Map pp86–7) around the mausoleum, designed very much in the modern Persian style. While the portico, courtyard and main 'onion' dome are relatively restrained and quite beautiful, the interior is a riot of mirror mosaics. Except during Friday prayers, non-Muslim visitors are welcome (modest dress is required and women must cover their heads).

From the mosque, follow the lane that runs due east, and turn right (south) at the T-junction leading to a crossroad marked by the half-buried remains of the **eastern temple gate** (Map pp86–7). The gate served as the eastern entrance to the compound of the Roman Temple of Jupiter, the site now occupied by Umayyad Mosque.

Sharia al-Qaimariyya

Running from the Umayyad Mosque all the way to Hammam Bakri near Bab Touma, Sharia al-Qaimariyya is a bustling artery that's worth wandering, and its loveliest stretch is between the eastern temple gate and the mosque. Shaded with vines and its walls hung with vividly coloured carpets, the lane winds slightly to accommodate a burbling fountain and Al-Nawfara and Ash-Shams, two atmospheric **coffeehouses** (p110). The former has been around for more than 200 years.

Beside the coffeehouses, a broad flight of stairs carries the alley up to the eastern wall of Umayyad Mosque, shaped by elements of what was originally part of the main Roman-era monumental entrance to the inner courts of the temple – now the mosque's **Bab al-Nafura** (Fountain Gate). The street loops around the southern wall of the mosque and reconnects with Souq al-Hamidiyya.

SOUTH OF THE MOSQUE

South of Umayyad Mosque is the heart of the **Damascus souq** (Map p114), with stretches of stalls devoted to spices, gold, sweets, perfume and fabrics. If you can drag yourself away from the colourful and fragrant displays, there are also wonderful examples of architecture, including numerous khans, or travellers' inns, and a beautiful palace complex.

One of the liveliest thoroughfares, with its glittering gold and silver sellers, is **Souq as-Silah**, running due south from Bab Ziyada (set into the southern wall of Umayyad Mosque), out of which crowds of people continually emerge. After 100m, turn right (west) to Azem Ecole, Madrassa an-Nuri and Maristan Nureddin, or left to the splendid Azem Palace. Continue due south and you're in **Souq al-Bzouriyya** (literally the Seed Bazaar, but in reality the Spice Souq), heavily scented with cumin, coffee and perfumes. Halfway along, on the left, is Hammam Nureddin (p100), the most elegant of Damascus' old bathhouses. Just beyond the hammam is the grand entrance to **Khan As'ad Pasha** (Map p114; ☻ 8am-2pm Sat-Thu), arguably the finest and most ambitious piece of architecture in the Old City – a cathedral among khans. Built in 1752 under the patronage of As'ad Pasha al-Azem, it encompasses a vast space achieved through a beautiful arrangement of eight small domes around a larger circular aperture, allowing light to stream in above a circular pool. The domes are supported on four colossal grey-and-white piers that splay into elegant arches. Beyond the khan, the souq intersects with Straight St.

Azem Ecole   مدرسة العظم

Built in 1770 by a member of the Azem family (successive generations of whom governed Damascus from 1725 to 1809), **Azem Ecole** (Map p114) is a former madrassa and a gem of urban Ottoman architecture. It has a beautiful little courtyard, hemmed in by a delicate three-storey gallery, the upper floor of which is wood. Currently it houses a souvenir store (see p113).

Madrassa an-Nuri   المدرسة النورية

Just 50m beyond Azem Ecole, **Madrassa an-Nuri** (Map p114) is easy to pick out because of its crimson domes. The structure is fairly modern and not particularly noteworthy but inside is a surviving part of a madrassa dating from 1172, which houses the mausoleum of Nureddin, the uncle of Saladin, who united Syria and paved the way for his nephew's successes against the Crusaders. It's not necessary to enter the building to see the tomb chamber. Instead, walk down the narrow market alley beside the madrassa and peer in through a big iron-grille opening in the wall.

Azem Palace   قصر العظم

If you are only going to visit one building
in Damascus, in addition to the Umayyad
Mosque, then it should be this, a stunning
tour de force of all that's wonderful about
Damascene architecture.

Azem Palace (Map p114; adult/student S£150/15;
9am-5.30pm Wed-Mon Apr-Sep, 9am-3.30pm Wed-
Mon Oct-Mar, closed 12.30-2.30pm Fri) comprises a
complex of splendid buildings, courtyards
and gardens that were built between 1749
and 1752 as a private residence for the governor of Damascus, As'ad Pasha al-Azem.
It remained the Azem residence until the
beginning of the 20th century, when the
family moved outside the Old City and the
house was sold to the French to become an
Institute of Archaeology and Islamic Art.
Badly damaged by fire during uprisings
against the French in 1925, it has since been
beautifully restored.

After buying your tickets turn left, then
right, into a small leafy courtyard, before
entering the main courtyard, which has
a serene central pool and fountain. The
courtyard is fringed by low-rise buildings,
all boasting the beautiful black basalt, limestone and sandstone banding technique
known as *ablaq*, a characteristic of Mamluk
architecture typically found throughout the
Levant and Egypt, and later adopted by Ottoman masons.

Off the courtyard are a number of sump-
tuously decorated rooms with wooden panelling, lustrous blue tiling, painted ceilings
and coloured paste work – a technique in
which a pattern is incised into stone and
then filled in with pastes made from different coloured stones to give the effect of an
immensely complicated stone inlay. This
area served as the *haramlik* (family or wom-
en's quarters).

Also known as the Museum of the Arts
& Popular Traditions of Syria, the rooms
contain rather kitsch mannequin displays,
each with a different theme (the wedding,
pilgrimage etc), and displays of exquisite
ceramics, costumes, textiles and musical
instruments.

STRAIGHT STREET (WESTERN END)
Known also as Souq Medhat Pasha (the covered western part) and Sharia Bab Sharqi
(the eastern part), the main east–west street
that bisects the Old City has historically

been known as **Straight St** (Map pp86–7),
from the Latin, Via Recta.

While it's not exactly straight these days,
this street was the main thoroughfare of
Damascus during Greek and Roman times,
when it would have appeared something
like the main avenues still seen at Apamea (p168) or Palmyra (p208). It was four
times its present width and planted with a
seemingly endless row of columns that supported a canvas street covering.

The street is busiest at the western end,
where it's largely devoted to shops selling
textiles and clothes. There are several old
khans in this area, their gates still locked
at night. On the north side are the pretty
Khan az-Zeit (Map p114) and, some 300m
further north, **Khan Jakmak** (Map p114); on
the south is **Khan Süleiman Pasha** (Map p114),
built in 1732, with a central courtyard that
was formerly roofed by two domes.

South of the western stretch of Straight
St are several old Damascene houses (see
below) and twisting narrow alleyways that
are worth exploring.

OLD DAMASCENE HOUSES
Unseen behind the high walls within the
Old City are hundreds of delightful houses
built around courtyards and featuring their
own elaborate decoration (see Damascene
House Decoder, opposite). Unfortunately,
many of these treasures are in a sad state
of disrepair, but a loop off Straight St takes
in several examples, all of which have benefited from renovation.

Just a few steps away from Khan Süleiman
Pasha, **Beit al-Aqqad** (Map p114; ☎ 223 8038; www
.damaskus.dk in Danish; 8-10 Souq as-Souf; 9am-3pm
Sat-Wed, 9am-1pm Thu) was formerly the home
of a wealthy family of textile merchants. It
now houses the Danish Institute in Damascus. Visitors are welcome to come in and
look at the courtyard, which is graced by
a massive expanse of gorgeous inlaid-stone
decoration.

Head south down Sharia Hassan Kharet
and take the first left for **Beit as-Sibai** (Map
pp86-7; Sharia al-Qabbani; 8am-2pm Sun-Thu), built
between 1769 and 1774, and beautifully restored. This splendid building is the sort of
place you could imagine living in. In fact,
for a time during the 1990s it served as the
residence of the German ambassador. Now
it's mostly used as a set for historical TV

DAMASCENE HOUSE DECODER

The wonderful courtyard houses of Damascus were built on variations of the same basic theme, and architectural elements are common through them all. Here's how to tell your 'ataba from your qa'a.

- Dihliz – the entrance court or corridor that prevents the main courtyard from being seen by visitors. The dihliz was often plain and neglected, at worst filthy, to deter looters.

- Courtyards – every Damascene house has at least one, some modest, others grand, featuring marble and stone banding, geometric decoration and mosaic paving. They had birds singing in cages, and were always fragrant with citrus trees and cascades of jasmine. The most extravagant houses had up to three courtyards: the first, the salaamlik, was the public courtyard for entertaining guests; the second, the haramlik, was the private courtyard reserved for women and family; and the third was the khadamlik, for the servants.

- Fountains – a trickling water fountain made from decorative stone or marble mosaic, often filled with floating rose petals, is a cooling feature of every courtyard.

- Liwan – facing north for maximum coolness, with high ceilings to catch the breeze and circulate the cool air, the enormous, arched alcove dominating the courtyard is the liwan or summer room. The main room for entertaining in warm weather, it's generally elaborately decorated, with intricately painted ceilings, cushioned banquettes and carpeted floor.

- Qa'a – facing the liwan from across the courtyard, the raised qa'a or reception room is the main indoor entertainment area, with even more ornate decoration, carved ceilings, elaborate glass chandeliers, and carved wood or mother-of-pearl inlaid divans covered with cushions.

- 'Ataba – the threshold or first part of the qa'a, often at ground level, featuring a small fountain and a decorative niche for holding water jugs and nargileh pipes.

- Ajami – the technique of decorating wooden panels with a raised, elaborately painted pattern, gilding and lacquer.

- Muqarnas – highly decorated, painted wooden ceilings featuring boxed-in beams; they are reminiscent of Oriental carpets.

- Hammam – the wealthiest houses would have a marble-floored hammam or steam bath with stone fountain off the haramlik.

If you're keen to learn more, pick up a copy of Brigid Keenan's coffee-table book Damascus: Hidden Treasures of the Old City (2001).

dramas and as an atmospheric venue for ministerial functions. Visitors are welcome to wander around.

Walk on past Beit as-Sibai and turn right at the T-junction for **Beit Nizam** (Map pp86-7; Sharia nasif Pasha; 8am-2pm Sun-Thu), another breathtakingly beautiful 18th-century house, although in this case executed on a far grander scale. It has been organised around two large courtyards, the one to the rear coloured by orange trees and rose bushes. In the mid-19th century it served as the French consulate. Like Beit as-Sibai, it's often used as a set for film and TV productions.

A five-minute walk east through the back alleys brings you to **Dahdah Palace** (Map pp86-7; 9 Sharia ash-Shalla; 9.30am-2pm & 4-6pm Mon-Sat,

to 7pm in summer), an 18th-century residence owned by the Dahdah family. Ring the bell for an informal guided tour by the charming Mrs Dahdah and her daughter (both of whom speak excellent English) of the graceful courtyard, fragrant with jasmine and lemon trees, the liwan (summer room), and the reception room with its exquisite niche. They also sell antiques (see p114).

From Dahdah Palace, backtrack to Sharia al-Amin, turn right then left onto Straight St, then turn right for **Maktab Anbar** (Map pp86-7; Sharia Qasr ath-Thaqafa; 8am-6pm Sun-Thu). Built in 1867 by a Jewish trader – who, legend has it, travelled to India and returned with a hat full of diamonds – the extravagant palace was seized in 1890 when he couldn't pay his taxes, and was turned into a women's boarding school. These days it houses the architects responsible for the preservation and renovation of the Old City. There are three splendid courtyards featuring exquisite decoration and lush gardens.

From Maktab Anbar continue north and take the first left after the mosque; 50m along on the right is **Beit Jabri** (Map pp86-7; ☎ 544 3200; www.jabrihouse.com; 14 Sharia as-Sawwaf; ⊗ 9.30am-12.30am). Its courtyard is home to a hugely popular café (see p108), which is a lovely place to linger for a while. After you order, take the steps up to the beautifully restored qa'a (reception room) at the far end of the courtyard.

CHRISTIAN QUARTER

No longer gated, the **Christian Quarter** (Map pp86-7) begins where a small **Roman arch** stands on a patch of grass beside Straight St. It's all that remains of what was probably a grand triple arch, which once marked an important intersection. Occupying the northeastern part of the Old City, the quarter is home to numerous churches representing various denominations, including Syrian Orthodox, Greek Orthodox, Armenian, Greek Catholic, Syrian Catholic and Maronite. The wealth and education of the city's Christians is reflected in a thriving commercial atmosphere and a lively dining and drinking scene.

Chapel of Ananias   كنيسة حنانيا

In the far northeast corner of the Christian quarter, the **Chapel of Ananias** (Map pp86-7; Sharia Hanania; ⊗ 9am-1pm & 3-6pm Wed-Mon) is

housed in a cellar that was reputedly the house of Ananias, an early Christian disciple (see Biblical Damascus, below). To find the chapel, take Sharia Hanania, the last street on the left before Bab ash-Sharqi; it's at the far northern end in a crypt below the house.

Sharia Hanania is a lovely little street that's home to souvenir and antique shops, restaurants and bars.

St Paul's Chapel   كنيسة مار بولس

The Old City gate, **Bab Kisan** (Map pp86-7), purportedly marks the spot where the disciples lowered St Paul out of a window in a basket one night, so that he could flee from the Jews, having angered them after preaching in the synagogues (see Biblical Damascus, below). Beside the gate, sealed since at least the 18th century, is **St Paul's Chapel** (Map pp86-7), dedicated to the saint. Follow the driveway up to the new convent on the left and push open the heavy wooden doors into the back of Bab Kisan, which now contains the small chapel.

Central Damascus

The modern city may be short on sights and bereft of beauty but it's bustling and lively, with a vibrant social life, and definitely warrants some of your time. Start with a visit to the National Museum and its neighbour, Takiyya as-Süleimaniyya. The backstreets of Souq Saroujah are also worth a wander, as is the atmospheric old neighbourhood on the upper slopes of Salihiyya (the lower slopes of Jebel Qassioun).

BIBLICAL DAMASCUS

Christianity has been on the scene in Damascus since early in the 1st century. Saul of Tarsus, who had been the scourge of Christians in Jerusalem, was riding to Damascus on the instructions of the Jewish high priests in order to arrest Christians living there. En route he was blinded by a vision of God near the village of Darayya outside Damascus. He was led into the city to the home of a Christian named Judas. There he was cured of his blindness by Ananias, who had also received a vision: 'Arise, and go into the street which is called Straight…' (Acts 9:11). Converted, Saul of Tarsus became Paul the Apostle, and was baptised in the Barada River (not recommended today); he later spread the word of God throughout the Roman Empire.

His conversion outraged the Damascene Jews and when he began preaching around town he was forced to flee the city: 'And through a window in a basket was I let down by the wall, and escaped' (2 Corinthians 11:33). The houses of Ananias and Judas, and the 'window' of St Paul, are all commemorated in Damascus and held in reverence by the city's Christian communities. You can visit both the Chapel of Ananias (above) and St Paul's Chapel (above).

AL-MERJEH المرجه

Writing in 1875, Isabel Burton, wife of the British consul, describes the 'green' **Al-Merjeh** (Map pp82–3) as looking like a 'village common'. By the end of the 19th century it was the hub of Damascus, a small park housing the city's best hotels, and a terminus for trams. Damascus was the first city in the Ottoman Empire to possess electric trams, with six lines converging here, and the power supplied by a waterfall on the Barada River. Another century on and the trams were gone. Al-Merjeh is now a traffic island with a tiny patch of grass at the centre. It's also known as Saahat ash-Shohada or Martyrs' Sq. The martyrs referred to were victims of the French bombardments in 1925. The column at the centre has nothing to do with martyrs; instead, it commemorates the opening of the first telegraph link in the Middle East – the line from Damascus to Medina. The surrounding streets are busy with cheap eateries, pastry shops and budget hotels.

HEJAZ TRAIN STATION محطة الحجاز

A little south and west of Al-Merjeh, the grand **Hejaz train station** (Map pp82–3), completed in 1917, was the northern terminus of the Hejaz Railway, built to ferry pilgrims to Medina (see The Hejaz Railway, p395). Compared with the transport palaces of Europe the station is a provincial affair, but the interior has a beautiful decorated ceiling.

The actual platforms of the station are closed – a much-delayed project was to see the station expanded to include a high-rise hotel, shopping mall and underground railway – and all trains now leave from Khaddam station. There is a pleasant bar-café, a steam locomotive dating from 1908, and a public water fountain erected at the same time as the station.

SOUQ SAROUJAH سوق ساروجه

A charming, laid-back neighbourhood of narrow alleys lined with small shops and punctuated by medieval tombs and mosques, **Souq Saroujah** (Saddlers' Bazaar; Map pp82–3) is a fascinating place for a stroll.

In medieval times the areas immediately outside the city walls were developed as burial places for the dead; you can still see

this today, with large areas of cemeteries lying to the south of the old cities of both Damascus and Aleppo. Occasionally, however, the needs of the living would overwhelm those of the dead. Such was the case with the area now known as Souq Saroujah. During the Ayyubid era the fields just north of the Barada River became a favoured location for the tombs and mausoleums of nobles, and for several hundred years this site served as an exclusive burial ground. As the city expanded under the Ottomans, and space within the city walls was at a premium, the cemeteries became built over with the houses of well-off Turkish civil servants and military officers.

Unfortunately, the needs of the living are pressing once again, and many of the fine old houses have been demolished in the name of redevelopment. Of the handful that remain, **Beit al-Haramein** and **Beit al-Rabie** now serve as backpackers' hotels (see p103), while the venerable **Beit Shami** is now the Historical Museum of Damascus.

Historical Museum of Damascus

متحف تاريخ دمشق

The **historical museum** (Map pp86-7; Sharia ath-Thawra; adult/student S£75/5; 8am-2pm Sat-Thu) is in an attractive old house with eight richly decorated rooms of a central courtyard. A couple of rooms hold displays of photos and diagrams relating to old Damascus, and there is a superb large-scale model of the Old City, but it's the rooms themselves, decorated in typical Damascene fashion with inlaid marble, carved wood and painted ceilings, that are of greatest interest.

The museum is off Sharia ath-Thawra, where the flyover comes down north of Sharia Souq Saroujah, beside two tall modern buildings. It's on Ministry of the Interior property and visitors have to pass through a guarded gate to reach the arched entrance.

NATIONAL MUSEUM المتحف الوطني

The most important of Syria's museums is the **National Museum** (Map pp82-3; Sharia Shoukri al-Quwatli; adult/student S£150/10; 9am-6pm Wed-Mon Apr-Sep, 9am-4pm Wed-Mon Oct-Mar), and you'll get more out of Syria's archaeological sites if you take in the museum before and after your visits to the sites.

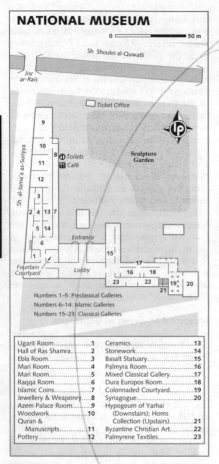

NATIONAL MUSEUM

0 ————————— 50 m

Numbers 1–5: Preclassical Galleries
Numbers 6–14: Islamic Galleries
Numbers 15–23: Classical Galleries

Ugarit Room.....................1	Ceramics...............................13
Hall of Ras Shamra..........2	Stonework.............................14
Ebla Room.......................3	Basalt Statuary......................15
Mari Room.......................4	Palmyra Room.......................16
Mari Room.......................5	Mixed Classical Gallery..........17
Raqqa Room.....................6	Dura Europos Room...............18
Islamic Coins...................7	Colonnaded Courtyard..........19
Jewellery & Weaponry....8	Synagogue............................20
Azem Palace Room.........9	Hypogeum of Yarhai
Woodwork.....................10	(Downstairs); Homs
Quran &	Collection (Upstairs)...........21
Manuscripts..............11	Byzantine Christian Art.........22
Pottery..........................12	Palmyrene Textiles................23

The **lobby** is devoted to Qasr al-Heir al-Gharbi, with large black-and-white photos of the palace with its façade still *in situ*. Upstairs is an airy gallery displaying a series of finely carved stone screens removed from the Qasr.

Preclassical Galleries

The **Ugarit Room** (1; see map) is devoted to finds from Ugarit (p149) and contains stone tablets inscribed with what is believed to be one of the world's earliest alphabets, along with beautiful bronze figurines. The **Hall of Ras Shamra** (2) contains finds from ancient Syria, including more from Ugarit and other sites. It leads into the **Ebla Room** (3), and on to two **Mari Rooms** (4 & 5), devoted to artefacts from the Mesopotamian city (p223) in the southeast of Syria, near the border with Iraq. The distinctive statuettes in here, with their feather skirts and lively black eyes, date to the 2nd millennium BC, making them roughly the same age as the Great Pyramids of Giza.

Islamic Galleries

The first room of the Islamic galleries, the **Raqqa Room** (6), contains artefacts, pottery and stucco panels recovered from the old Abbasid city (p216) destroyed by Mongols in 1260. A staircase leads up to the **Modern Art Galleries**, which were closed at the time of research, while the long corridor (7) running north begins with carved wooden fragments of a ceiling found at Qasr al-Heir al-Gharbi, goes on to **Islamic coins** and then leads to **jewellery and weaponry** (8), where some heavy jewellery pieces and wonderfully ornate weaponry are displayed. They embody the two traits for which the Mamluk dynasty was renowned: artistry and violence.

Off the far end is **woodwork** (10), where a large room is devoted to the intricate style of woodwork that developed throughout the Islamic era as a result of the religious ban on figurative representations. This room is dominated by two great cenotaphs: the one nearest the entrance, decorated with a beautiful star motif, dates from 1250; while the second dates from 1265 and comes from the Khaled ibn al-Walid Mosque in Homs (see p157). Other objects here include domestic furniture from some of the old houses of Damascus.

Purchase your ticket at the gate then stroll through the shady **sculpture garden**, which is best appreciated after seeing the museum proper.

Enter through the main gate of Qasr al-Heir al-Gharbi, a desert palace west of Palmyra dating from AD 688, the time of the Umayyad caliph Hisham. The gate was transported to Damascus stone by stone and reconstructed as part of the museum façade.

Within the museum, the exhibits are presented thematically and grouped into preclassical, classical and Islamic sections. Exhibits are labelled in English, Arabic and French, but *The Concise Guide: National Museum of Damascus* is also available at the gift shop and is well worth buying.

North of the woodwork room is the **Azem Palace Room** (9), which is a reconstruction of an original room from Azem Palace (p92) in the Old City.

The remaining rooms of the Islamic galleries are devoted to the **Quran and manuscripts** (11), **pottery** (12), **ceramics** (13) and **stonework** (14).

Classical Galleries

The classical galleries make up the whole east wing, with the first room containing a large collection of **basalt statuary** (15), executed in the black stone typical of the Hauran region. There's also an excellent mosaic here, recovered from Lattakia, which depicts the Orontes River in the form of a god.

The busts in the **Palmyra Room** (16) are representations of the dead. They would have fitted like seals into the pigeonhole-like chambers in which bodies were stored. To see how this worked, pass through the **Dura Europos Room** (18), which contains jewellery and ceramics from this Roman site on the Euphrates (p222), and down the stairs to the **Hypogeum of Yarhai** (21), which is an extraordinary reconstruction of an underground burial chamber from Palmyra's Valley of the Tombs (p209). Seeing this helps make sense of Palmyra's funerary towers,

and some of the museum exhibits there (which is where this reconstruction truly belongs).

Beside the staircase down to the hypogeum is a staircase that goes up to the **Homs Collection** (21 upstairs). Alongside some exquisite gold jewellery, there are coins depicting Venetian doges (chief magistrates), the Roman emperor, Philip the Arab and Alexander the Great.

The other attraction worth seeing is the **synagogue** (20), across a colonnaded courtyard. Dating from the 2nd century, it was discovered at Dura Europos, from where it was removed and reconstructed here. Other than its age, the most interesting features are the beautiful floor-to-ceiling wall frescoes. Executed in a colourful naive style, they depict scenes from Old Testament events, from the crowning of King Solomon through to the reign of David, the story of Moses and the flight from Egypt. This is a real oddity in that depictions of the human form go against Talmudic traditions.

While the frescoes are faded (hence the low light in the room), the fact that they've survived at all is because the synagogue lay buried under sand for centuries until its discovery in the 1930s.

DAMASCUS' ART SCENE

With a burgeoning contemporary art scene that's as vibrant as that of Cairo, Beirut and Dubai, a tour of Damascus' art galleries is a great way to while away a few hours. Art fans should check *What's On Syria* for details of more galleries and the latest shows, as many exhibitions are held in some of Damascus' old houses. Here's a taste of the city's best:

- **Atassi Gallery** (Map p80; ☎ 332 1720; www.atassigallery.com; 35 Sharia ar-Rawdah, off Sharia al-Jala'a; 10am-2pm & 6-9pm Sat-Thu) Damascus' premier gallery has a lively programme of regularly changing exhibitions, featuring some of the Middle East's most respected modern artists, from renowned Aleppan sculptor Abdel Rahman Mouakket to mixed media by Baghdadi-born Ali Talib.
- **Ayyam Gallery** (off Map p80; ☎ 544 5794; www.ayyamgallery.com; Samawi Bldg, Mezzeh West Villas, 30 Chile St; 10am-10pm Sat-Thu) In a chic, sleek art space designed by Syria's revered architect Ghiath Machnok, this is one of the region's most exciting galleries, showing engaging work by Syrian artists such as Abdulla Murad, Safwan Dahoul, Mounzer Kamnakache, Yousset Abdelke and Fadi Yazigi.
- **Art House** (off Map p80; ☎ 662 8112; behind the Children's Hospital, Mezzeh; 10am-9pm) This small gallery in the atmospheric lobby of the Art House hotel (p105) hosts regular art shows alongside a programme of music recitals and concerts. There's also a lovely terrace café for lunch.
- **Galerie Abdal** (Map pp86-7; ☎ 544 5794; Sharia Shaweesh; 10am-1am) A café with an exhibition space above that hosts regularly changing shows (see also p110).

TAKIYYA AS-SÜLEIMANIYYA التكية السليمانية
Lying immediately east of the National Museum, **Takiyya as-Süleimaniyya** (Map pp82–3) was built over six years, beginning in 1554, to a design by the Ottoman Empire's most brilliant architect, Sinan. A favourite of Sultan Süleyman the Magnificent, Sinan would later create the splendid Süleymaniye Mosque that dominates Istanbul's skyline.

The Takiyya (an Ottoman term for a Sufi hostel) is a more modest affair than the Istanbul mosque, blending local Syrian styles (the alternating Mamluk-era black-and-white banding and honeycomb-style stonework over the main entrance) with typically Turkish features (the high central dome and pencil-shaped minarets). It has two parts: the mosque to the south, and an arcaded courtyard with rooms that would have housed pilgrims. The former hostel area is now the Army Museum (see below).

Under the patronage of Süleyman's successor, Selim II, the Takiyya compound was extended with the addition of a small madrassa. Built around a central courtyard and fountain, the madrassa now serves as Artisanat, an appealing handicraft market, where the former students' cells are now shops and ateliers (see p114).

ARMY MUSEUM المتحف الحربي
The **Army Museum** (Map pp82-3; Sharia Shoukri al-Quwatli; adult/student S£5/3; ☽ 8am-2pm Wed-Mon) has a fascinating collection of military hardware from the Bronze Age to the near present.

Exhibits range from flint arrowheads to a pile of the twisted remains of planes shot down in the 1973 war with Israel.

Salihiyya الصالحيه
Salihiyya (Map p98) sprawls along the lower slopes of Jebel Qassioun, taking in the upper part of the modern city centre, as well as a ramshackle old quarter of small shops, atmospheric souqs and Islamic monuments on the lower part of the mountain.

The old quarter, also known as Al-Charkassyeh, first developed in the 12th century, when Nureddin settled Arab refugees here who had fled the Crusader massacres in Jerusalem in 1099. What developed in the subsequent four centuries was a dense neighbourhood of mosques, mausoleums and madrassas, 70 in total, representing a significant portion of the city's 250 official monuments. Strung out along Sharia Madares Assad al-Din, popularly known as Souq al-Joumma, few of the buildings can be seen from inside but just strolling by the domes and decorated portals makes for a wonderful one- or two-hour walk. It's now a lively souq street, so don't be surprised to see men riding donkeys or hear traditional street criers selling their goods.

The reason few buildings can be visited is that while they're ancient enough to warrant preservation orders, many of the monuments are being put into service (due to the pressing needs of locals), albeit rarely for the purposes intended. The small

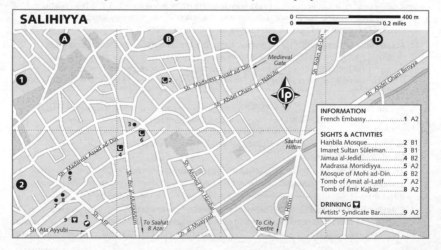

THE CRIES OF DAMASCUS

As you stroll the Old City's ancient alleys, at some point you'll come across a man leading a donkey or horse – his bridle prettily decorated with colourful ribbons and pompoms – pulling a cart from which its owner sells fresh fruit and vegetables, water or gas bottles. He'll periodically call out in Arabic as he moves through the streets, announcing his arrival and that he has something to sell. In the old days these salesmen were everywhere, each specialising in something and calling out some clever cry or witty sales pitch. The apricot seller would yell out 'I am the seller of sweetness and tenderness'; the cucumber trader might cry 'Who has got a pool to have these fish swim in?' (as locals kept the cucumber in their fountains to keep cool for salads); while the knife seller would call out 'Who wants to kill his mother-in-law?'

14th-century **Tomb of Emir Kajkar** serves as a Christian centre; the neighbouring **Tomb of Amat al-Latif** (1243) harbours a human-rights organisation; while **Madrassa Morsidiyya**, complete with the only surviving example of a square 13th-century minaret in Damascus, is a kindergarten. Across the street a 14th-century tomb, with elaborate carved-stone decoration around the doorway, is now somebody's home, judging by the satellite dish on the dome.

There are one or two hidden gems worth investigating. Tucked down narrow Sharia al-Nawa'eer, the 14th-century **Jamaa al-Jedid** (New Mosque) contains the tomb of Ismat al-Din Khatun, wife of first Nureddin and then his successor Saladin. The richly decorated burial chamber is worth a look.

Back on Souq al-Joumma, just a short distance east and facing a small square, is the modest **Mosque of Mohi al-Din**, with a beautiful late-Mamluk minaret. This is very much a community mosque, with men dozing in the shade of the prayer hall, but it's also a popular pilgrimage site – buried here is the body of Sheikh Mohi al-Din al-Arabi (who died in 1240), a great Sufi mystic whose writings are supposed to have greatly influenced Dante. The tomb is downstairs, off to the left-hand side of the entrance courtyard; only men are allowed in. The claustrophobic chamber is filled with a cenotaph, enclosed in silver casing and illuminated by fluorescent green light.

Leaving the mosque, **Imaret Sultan Süleiman**, another building designed by Sinan (the architect behind Takiyya as-Süleimaniyya), is across the main street. Historian Ross Burns, in *Monuments of Syria: A Historical Guide,* suggests the **Hanbila Mosque** is worth a visit for the Crusader columns in the courtyard; however, it's often locked.

To reach Salihiyya, walk north from Saahat 8 Azar (8 March Sq), also known as Saahat Arnous, in Central Damascus, along the bustling shopping street of Sharia Jamal Abdel Nasser. Cross Saahat al-Jasr al-Abiyad (Al-Jasr Sq), and continue up Sharia Afif until you get to Sharia Madares Assad al-Din (Souq al-Joumma). If taking a taxi, it's best to say Al-Jasr Sq, as drivers don't know where to take you if you say 'Salihiyya'; they will probably drop you on Sharia al-Hamra or Sharia Jamal Abdel Nasser.

Greater Damascus
JEBEL QASSIOUN   جبل قاسيون
That bare rocky rise northwest of the city, **Jebel Qassioun** (Mt Qassioun; 1200m; Map p80) provides a useful orientation tool. It's from the top of this mount that Mohammed is said to have looked down on Damascus and made the observation that opened this chapter. The distinctly urban view today is hardly one of paradise, but it looks stunning at dusk, when the city lights up. There is no public transport to the popular viewing points, so hire a taxi and negotiate for the driver to wait.

TISHREEN (OCTOBER) WAR PANORAMA
بانوراما حرب تشرين
Created with the help of the North Koreans, this **memorial** (Sharia 6 Tishreen; adult/student S£150/15; ☼ 9am-9pm Wed-Mon) to the 1973 war with Israel is quite extraordinary. The tour takes in paintings of various historical battles, a film, the moving panoramic painting, a 3D mural and diorama depicting the Israeli devastation of the town, and a room filled with portraits of former president Hafez al-Assad. You'll gain a great insight into the battle over the Golan Heights and the fighting in and around the town of

DAMASCUS

RICHARD BURTON, RENAISSANCE MAN

Adventurer, scholar, master of a couple of dozen languages or so, and translator of *The Thousand and One Nights* and *Karma Sutra*, Sir Richard Francis Burton (1821–90) was one of Britain's most fascinating and controversial explorers. His disdain for authority and keen interest in sexuality (not welcome in those prudish times) may have impeded the attainment of higher posts in both his military and diplomatic careers, but his thirst for knowledge of languages and cultures saw him lead an extraordinary life.

Having undertaken diverse challenges, from travelling to Mecca disguised as a pilgrim for the hajj to searching for the source of the river Nile, Burton took up the post of British consul to Syria in 1869. Although the consulate building was in the city, Burton and his wife Isabel chose to live in Salihiyya (p98), which at that time was a Kurdish village of 15,000 inhabitants, separated from the city by fields of orchards. Their house, as described in Isabel's letters, was flanked on one side by a mosque and on the other by a hammam, and had a rooftop terrace where the Burtons would entertain guests.

Being the colourful, unconventional character that he was, Burton lost no time in making enemies while trying to ease tensions between the Christian, Muslim and Jewish populations. After only two years in his post, the foreign office in London felt compelled to remove him following numerous petitions of complaint, thus ending what he would later refer to as the two happiest years of his life. Indeed, his love of Arab culture is reflected in his tomb in Surrey – it's in the shape of a Bedouin tent.

For more on Burton's intriguing life, check out *The Devil Drives: A Life of Sir Richard Burton* by Fawn McKay Brodie and *A Rage to Live: A Biography of Richard and Isabel Burton* by Mary S Lovell.

Quneitra, which isn't otherwise possible; it's definitely worth seeing if you're planning a visit to Quneitra (p130).

The panorama is located about 2km northeast of the centre, on the road to the Harasta bus terminal; take a Harasta microbus and ask to be let out when you spot the plaza on the opposite side of the highway filled with captured Israeli jeeps, tanks and fighter planes.

SAYYIDA ZEINAB MOSQUE

جامع السيدة زينب

This splendid Iranian-built mosque on the site of the burial place of Sayyida Zeinab, granddaughter of Mohammed, is about 10km south of the city centre, in a neighbourhood that is popular with Iranian pilgrims and is now home to most of the city's Iraqi refugees. Stylistically, the mosque is similar to that of Sayyida Ruqqaya in the Old City, with a glistening gold onion-shaped dome, intricately decorated blue tiles covering its façade and two freestanding minarets.

Women will have to don a cloak, available at the entrance, before entering, and men should wear trousers and a long-sleeved shirt. The main entrances to the sanctuary are on the northern and southern sides, and non-Muslims may stroll the courtyard that surrounds the central **mausoleum** as well as take a peek at the glittering interior, lined with mirrored tiles and dripping with chandeliers, although they can not actually enter the mausoleum. Their eyes brimming with tears, the Muslim faithful kiss and stroke the silver grate surrounding the tomb of Zeinab, a much-venerated descendant of the Prophet.

To get here, take a microbus for Karajat as-Sitt (S£5) from Sharia Fahkri al-Baroudi in the city centre; at Karajat as-Sitt change to a different microbus for the mosque (S£5). A return taxi from the city centre should cost S£500.

ACTIVITIES

If you're a male and visit only one hammam in Damascus, make it busy, men-only **Hammam Nureddin** (Map p114; ☎ 222 9513; Souq al-Bzouriyya; ⏱ 9am-midnight), accessed from the spice souq that runs between the Umayyad Mosque and Straight St. Founded in the mid-12th century, it is one of the grandest and oldest functioning hammams in the country. It has an excellent heated steam room, and the full deal of massage, bath and sauna with towel, soap and tea costs S£500 (bath only is S£200).

Hammam az-Zahariyya (Map p114; 🕐 8am-midnight Tue-Sun & 5pm-midnight Mon men, 9am-5pm Mon women), next to the madrassa of the same name, just north of Umayyad Mosque, has been in use since the 12th century. It's clean and well looked after, and a scrub, sauna, massage and tea costs S£560.

Opposite Beit al-Mamlouka hotel near Bab Touma, local favourite **Hammam Bakri** (Map pp86-7; ☎ 542 6606; Sharia Qanayet al-Hattab; 🕐 10am-5pm women, 5pm-midnight men, closed Fri) charges about S£300 for a scrub and massage. Charging similar prices, **Hammam al-Qaimariyya** (Zuqqaq Hammam; Map pp86-7; 🕐 7am-noon & 5pm-midnight men, noon-5pm women), north of Sharia al-Qaimariyya and 300m east of Umayyad Mosque, is also popular with locals.

WALKING TOUR

Wandering the historic Old City streets is the most wonderful thing to do in Damascus.

For something different (most people enter by Souq al-Hamidiyya), begin your tour at the Bab al-Jabiye end of Souq Medhat Pasha. This will take you directly into the hustle and bustle of this ancient road and centre of commerce known as **Straight**

WALK FACTS

Start Bab al-Jabiye
End Souq al-Hamidiyya
Duration two hours to half a day

St (**1**; p92). As you make your way along this exotic street you'll pass scores of tiny stores selling textiles, *jalabiyya* (robes), *kufeyya* (chequered scarves worn by Arabs), coffee, olive oil and spices. Notice the tattooed faces of the Bedouin ladies shopping, and the dignified faces in the framed portraits hanging at the back of most stores – a sign of respect to past family members, who ran these small businesses decades before. If you look up you will see bullet holes caused by planes at the end of the French mandate.

When you reach the end of the covered part of the souq, take a slight detour into the spice souq on your left, and head to **Al Ghraoui Confiseur Chocolatier (2)**, 'purveyors to Queen Victoria', for a retro box of chocolates. If you're in the mood for some peace and tranquillity before you push on, slip into the beautiful **Azem Palace (3**; p92) to enjoy the glorious courtyard garden. Return to Straight St and continue, passing the small shops selling wooden spoons and plastics, pots and pans, and sweets and nuts. You're likely to be offered a taste of pistachios or cashews – don't hesitate to try before you buy.

You'll soon notice antique shops and some second-hand stores selling engraved brass and copperware, wooden mother-of-pearl inlaid furniture, boxes and backgammon boards, carpets and kilims, coloured Oriental lamps, and other old Damascene delights. More interesting and original

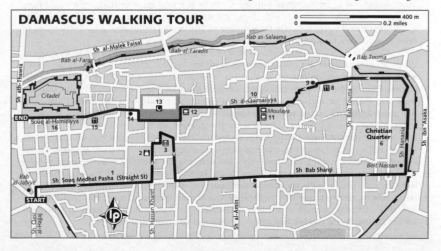

DAMASCUS WALKING TOUR

souvenirs can be found here and further along Straight St in the direction of Bab ash-Sharqi, than can be found in Souq al-Hamidiyya. Drag yourself away from the great shopping to note the **Roman arch** (**4**; p94), evidence that this was the main street in Roman and Greek times.

Once you arrive almost at **Bab ash-Sharqi** (**5**; p85), turn left into Sharia Hanania and the **Christian Quarter** (**6**; p94). There are even more shops here, but there are also some historic sites worth a look, including the courtyard of the fine old Beit Nassan. Stroll this characterful residential street until you arrive at busy **Sharia Bab Touma** (**7**). Cross the street, continuing past **Elissar** (**8**; p107), until

you arrive at **Hammam Bakri** (**9**; p101). Turn left into the narrow alley **Sharia al-Qaimariyya** (**10**), one of the Old City's liveliest arteries. It's lined with ateliers, art galleries, CD shops, hole-in-the-wall bakeries, carpet shops and renovated cafés, and you could spend hours dawdling along here.

Stop for lunch or a coffee and nargileh with young Damascenes at **Galerie Abdal** (**11**; p110) or **Moulaya** next door. Otherwise, continue along this charming lane to its prettiest part, shaded with vines, where you'll find two of the city's most atmospheric old coffeehouses. Stop at **Al-Nawfara** (**12**; p110) to get your caffeine fix, while being entertained by

---

DIALLING IN YOUR DIALECT IN DAMASCUS

With agreeable living expenses, a wonderful historic city to explore and friendly locals ready to engage with you, Damascus is becoming *the* destination to learn Arabic in the Middle East. Learning Arabic takes serious dedication and students often commit to living and learning in Damascus for over a year. This is one language where an immersive experience is really beneficial.

An introductory one-month intensive university course (around S£16,000) is popular, followed by tailored, private classes (around S£500 per hour) that help students expand their language skills. Most students find the going tough, because there is both classical Arabic and modern Arabic. Maj Greitz, a Swedish student who has been living in Damascus for six months, says, 'Arabic is in a totally different league [to learning other languages]. There is the alphabet, the new sounds and learning 'two' languages at the same time, and it's an incredibly hard language to get a grip on. At one stage though, there was a feeling of magic, when I started to learn how to read and write, when I could actually put words together on paper. It was pure magic!'

Students generally rent a room in a house with other students or with a local family. If you stay with a local family and they don't speak your native language, it can be trying if you've just arrived and your spoken Arabic isn't up to carrying a conversation, as Maj discovered: 'They were super nice people, but it was a big effort every time I wanted to ask for something or for some other reason had to communicate with them. I think at a later stage of studying it would have been more useful for me to stay with them.' But sharing with other students has its challenges as well, because it's very tempting for everyone to just speak English after a hard day trying to think in a different language, robbing you of valuable Arabic practice time.

Students are flocking to Damascus to study for a variety of reasons. Maj has been active in the plight of the Palestinians and outspoken against the invasion of Iraq, and plans to work here, if possible, after finishing her law degree. Maria Fernandez Coll, a long-time Arabic-language student from Spain, came to study Arabic because she was studying translation and saw that there was a need for Arabic translators. Chiara Chierici from Italy, who has studied Arabic for two years, simply fell in love with the language.

Regardless of what path you take to learn, the students we spoke to all had the same final advice – just get out there and try to speak Arabic! Chiara offers her advice: 'Don't be shy, go around and watch the people around you, sit in a tea shop and take your time.' Maj says, 'I think I would have tried to get a basic level in spoken Arabic faster, and then talked to more people, without being scared of making mistakes.' Maria says, 'You have to seize the opportunity to learn from the people in the street and spend your time with them. It was the biggest challenge, being able to communicate with the local people in their own language. I was studying for a long time and now I'm more or less able to do it. It is the best part of the learning, when you start practising it and you see that people understand you more and more'.

the dying art of the *hakawati* (traditional storyteller) – see The End of the Story? (p109).

Take a left turn and follow the walls of **Umayyad Mosque** (**13**; p88), but save your visit to this exquisite building for another day, when you aren't too tired to appreciate it (unless you're looking for some well-earned peace and tranquillity). Pass under the **western temple gate** (**14**; p88), stopping for the best ice cream in town at **Bekdach** (**15**; p107), and perhaps one last spot of shopping in the magnificent **Souq al-Hamidiyya** (**16**; p113).

COURSES

Studying Arabic in Damascus is phenomenally popular. Courses are offered at the following centres.

British Council (Map p80; ☎ 333 0631; fax 332 1467; www.britishcouncil.org/syria; Sharia Karim al-Khalil, off Sharia Maysaloun; ☺ language courses 9am-8pm Sun-Thu, 10am-5pm Sat) offers regular, intensive courses in both Modern Standard Arabic (MSA) and Syrian Colloquial Arabic (SCA), at three different levels.

Damascus University (Map p80; ☎ 212 9864; Arabic Language Department, Faculty of Letters) offers six Arabic courses in one academic year, with each course lasting two months, and a one-month introductory course. Each class is five days a week, 3½ hours a day.

DAMASCUS FOR CHILDREN

As elsewhere in the Middle East, Syrians love children. Even the very best restaurants in Damascus are accommodating when it comes to children, but a must (for kids of all ages) is an ice cream from **Bekdach** (p107) in Souq al-Hamidiyya.

In the souqs, urban-dwelling youngsters should enjoy the shopping experience – especially seeing sweets sold off a cart. Children will enjoy the garden area of the **National Museum** (p95), although the exhibits inside are not geared towards children. Boys and girls with a bent for the aeronautical will like looking at the old propeller and jet-powered aircraft at the **Army Museum** (p98). The rest of the time, though, you'll find yourself explaining the significance of the sights, certainly enough to keep any adult busy.

All the five-star hotels boast kid-friendly facilities, including baby-sitting.

TOURS

The best way to see Damascus is on foot – perhaps with a taxi back to your lodgings after a long day's walk. All hotels across all budget categories operate myriad tours; prices range from a minimum of S£250 per person in a shared minibus if organised through a budget hotel, to up to US$100 a day with private driver if organised through a four- or five-star hotel. Several travel agencies around the Cham Palace offer half-day and one-day excursions around Damascus and to destinations outside the city such as Palmyra and Bosra; however, you're better off organising tours or a private driver through your hotel.

FESTIVALS & EVENTS

International Flower Show Held in Damascus every May.

Jazz Festival Held in July in the citadel.

Silk Road Festival Held in late September, it celebrates Syria's long cultural history with events held in Aleppo, Damascus and Palmyra.

Damascus International Film Festival Held in November and December every year, showing an eclectic range of films, including many pan-Arab productions. There's sometimes also a theatre festival held at the same time.

SLEEPING

There's plenty of accommodation across all price brackets in Damascus, with some characterful new accommodation in the Old City. It's best to book in advance, though, as the good places fill up fast. Where room rates are specified in US dollars, the hotel expects payment in same. Credit cards are not accepted for budget and midrange options.

Budget

The bulk of the cheap hotels are found around Al-Merjeh, with the best budget hostels in Souq Saroujah, centred on atmospheric Sharia Bahsa, a little lane north off Sharia Shoukri al-Quwatli. Here you'll find Ghazal Hotel, Al-Haramein and Al-Rabie, Damascus' most popular backpacker places.

Al-Haramein Hotel (Map pp82-3; ☎ 231 9489; fax 231 4299; Sharia Bahsa; roof mattress S£200, s/d S£400/700) In a ramshackle old house on a leafy alley, Al-Haramein was once the long-standing backpacker favourite. Amenities are basic, but the hotel is somewhat redeemed with friendly reception staff, a long list of services, and public spaces that encourage chilling out. This place is still one of the budget travellers' favourites in Damascus, so book in advance to secure a room.

Al-Rabie Hotel (Map pp82-3; ☎ 231 8374; fax 231 1875; Sharia Bahsa; roof mattress S£200, s/d with shared showers S£450/700, d with shower S£1000) The reigning backpackers' favourite, Al-Rabie offers travellers a tranquil, leafy courtyard retreat from the bustling streets of Damascus, as well as simple, clean accommodation and friendly hosts who know what visitors want and can seemingly fulfil your every wish.

Al-Rais (Map pp82-3; ☎ 221 4252, 245 8039; Sharia as-Sandjakdar; s/d S£500/1000) One block east and south of Al-Merjeh, this one's very popular with visiting female Arabs and little or no English is spoken. The clean, simple rooms are light and bright, and come with a fan and a small TV.

Balkiss Hotel (Map pp82-3; ☎ 222 2506; fax 245 3734; Al-Merjeh; s/d S£500/1000; ⊠) This centrally located hotel, close to Al-Merjeh in the neighbourhood of the same name, is good value and an excellent choice for male travellers. The reasonably clean rooms are fitted out well for this price, with fridge, air-conditioning and fan, satellite TV and alarming tiger-skin bed covers, which could take your mind off the not-so-great private bathrooms. The clientele is predominantly Arab and Iranian.

Ghazal Hotel (Map pp82-3; ☎ 231 3736; www .ghazalhotel.com; Sharia Souq Saroujah; dm/s/d/tw S£300/ 600/1000/1000; ⊠) A welcome addition to the Souq Saroujah accommodation scene, this budget hotel owned by three friendly brothers is a relaxing, if somewhat offbeat, place to stay in this popular area of Damascus. Externally resembling a beach shack, it's an endearingly homely affair, with a suitably languorous feel. Double and twin rooms have new beds, spotlessly clean sheets, and hot water.

Sultan Hotel (Map pp82-3; ☎ 222 5768; fax 224 0372; Sharia Mousalam al-Baroudi; s/d/tr US$23/31/39; ⊠) The kitsch Arabian Nights–style common areas and a long list of services (eg organising tours and drivers, book exchange, laundry service, airport transfers) are the big attractions at this travellers' favourite just west of Hejaz train station. You certainly don't come here for the spartan rooms; while spotlessly clean, they come with little more than a fan and air-conditioning.

Midrange

The city's midrange options offer good value for money compared with Beirut, for instance.

Afamia Hotel (Map pp82-3; ☎ 222 8963; www .afamiahotel.com; Sharia Omar ben Abi Rabia; s/d/tr from US$30/35/45; ⊠ ⊡) After a recent renovation the Afamia is arguably Damascus' best value midrange hotel. The unrenovated 'Classic' rooms come with satellite TV, fridge, air-conditioning and hairdryer, but for US$5 extra the renovated 'Executive' rooms have the same amenities plus swish new carpets, curtains, lamp shades and bedspreads, new bathrooms, flat-screen TVs and complimentary ADSL internet.

Orient Palace Hotel (Map pp82-3; ☎ 223 1351; fax 221 1512; Saahat Hejaz; s/d US$28/40; ⊠) Opposite the old Hejaz train station, the splendid Orient Palace Hotel has been around since the 1920s, and depending on your level of enthusiasm for faded grandeur, it either retains plenty of period charm or resembles an early-20th-century medical institution. Rooms are big, and although a bit fusty, they're clean and most have balconies. These days the hotel fills quickly with Iranian tour groups.

City Hotel (Map pp82-3; ☎ 221 9375; fax 245 3817; off Sharia Omar ben Abi Rabia; s/d/tr US$30/40/45; ⊠) Also known as the Hotel al-Medina, this recently renovated and centrally located hotel offers decent comfort levels at a respectable price. The rooms come with fridge, satellite TV and hairdryer, and are decorated with inlaid mirrors, quilted brocade bedspreads and small desks. The hotel is fantastically popular with Iranian tour groups, so book ahead.

Al-Faradis Hotel (Map pp82-3; ☎ 224 6546; fax 224 7009; Al-Merjeh; s/d from US$62/67; ⊠) This comfortable four-star business hotel is in an excellent location, perfect for shopping the souqs as well as the odd pilgrimage – the hotel does a roaring trade hosting tour groups from Iran, here to explore the mosques of Damascus. The rooms are spacious, comfortable and well equipped, if a tad old-fashioned, and have fascinating views of the city.

Dar al-Yasmin (Map pp86-7; ☎ 544 3380; www .daralyasmin.com; Bab Touma; s/d/tr US$85/100/125; ⊠) In a restored old Damascene house with grey granite and white striped walls, traditional décor, and elegant courtyards with trickling fountains, this is an attractive boutique hotel in the Old City. The 18 rooms are set around two appealing courtyards, the first of which is quieter despite being above reception (rooms on the 1st floor are best), and the hotel also boasts its own small hammam with sauna and massage.

Top End

Damascus has benefited from a spate of elegant new boutique hotel openings in the Old City in recent years, which are a wonderful way to begin or end a Syrian sojourn. Prices listed do not include taxes, which add another 10%, and all hotels accept major credit cards.

Beit al-Mamlouka (Map pp86-7; ☎ 543 0445; www .almamlouka.com; opposite Hammam Bakri, near Bab Touma; d from US$135; ☒ ☐) Occupying a splendid 17th-century house on a busy narrow alley in the Christian Quarter, this intimate boutique hotel is a gem. Rooms are beautifully decorated with rich brocades, heavy drapes and Oriental chandeliers. We love the impressive attention to detail, from the fine decorative painting on the walls to the TV and air-conditioning cleverly hidden away.

Cham Palace (Map pp82-3; ☎ 223 2300; www .chamhotels.com; Sharia Maysaloun; s US$150-210, d US$160-240; ☒ ☐ ☒) One of the better hotels in the national chain, this one has a wonderfully chintzy lobby – worth a look even if you're not staying – but many of the 400 rooms are small and it's worth checking a couple out before setting your bags down.

our pick Hotel Talisman (Map pp86-7; ☎ 541 5379; www.hoteltalisman.net; 116 Tal Sharia al-Hijara; d/ste from US$175/225; ☒ ☐ ☒) In an elegant, restored Jewish palace down a dusty alley in the crumbling Al-Jdeida quarter of Damascus' Old City, the Talisman offers up a true *The Thousand and One Nights* experience. The spacious rooms are individually decorated with mother-of-pearl inlaid furniture, coloured glass chandeliers and carpets, along with mod cons like flat-screen TVs and DVD players. Rooms are set around two courtyards, one featuring an elegant *liwan* and a swimming pool, stunningly lit at night by Oriental lanterns. The second courtyard is smaller and more serene, with potted fruit trees. A wonderful property.

Art House (off Map p80; ☎ 662 8112-15; www .arthousedamascus.com; behind the Children's Hospital, Mezzeh; d from US$250; ☒ ☐ ☒) In an exquisitely restored old stone mill, this elegant

---

BEHIND CLOSED DOORS

Reforms by the young president of Syria, Bashar al-Assad, may not have been as wide-ranging as many might have hoped, but there is certainly a feeling of optimism in the capital. Culture and tourism are high on the agenda and Damascus has responded with a flurry of art gallery and hotel openings (including the long-awaited Four Seasons). In the Old City the changes might not be readily apparent – apart from a more lively café scene – but behind the high walls and heavy doors, a revolution is occurring.

May Mamarbachi, owner of the boutique hotel Beit al-Mamlouka, meticulously restored this elegant 17th-century home over three years, all the while earning herself a PhD in Islamic Architecture. At the Hotel Talisman – with only a 'Hand of Fatima' doorknocker to distinguish it from the other houses in the street – a Jewish palace now home to 17 rooms of Ottoman-era opulence. Outside the Old City, Art House is a project by the same entrepreneur as the Hotel Talisman. Here architect and manager Ghiath Machnok has converted an old mill into a unique property where artists and musicians meet, play and display – it's almost an artists' retreat as much as a hotel.

Back in the Old City, Beit al-Mamlouka and Hotel Talisman will soon be joined by several new properties. Mamdouh Akbik, owner-manager of the Afamia Hotel and member of the Chamber of Tourism, is one of many developers spreading blueprints out in the courtyards of run-down or derelict Damascene properties. Skilled craftsmen who can do *ajami* (the technique of intricately painting, gilding and lacquering wooden panels) and other old techniques are in high demand. Regulations regarding restoration are exacting, but Mamdouh, currently restoring a 150-year-old house to create an intimate hotel, says that while the Municipality and Antiquities regulations are tough, it's all going to be worth it, because 'we don't want the Old Town to lose its charm, its sense of normality, of community'. Mamdouh tells us that we won't recognise the ancient centre in another year – but you'll need to knock on the right door to see the changes.

boutique sleep is much more than a hotel. With regular art exhibitions, musical concerts and tai-chi classes, and a relaxing creekside location, Art House has become a destination in itself for artists and musicians. The public spaces are dramatic, with bare stone walls and high ceilings, particularly the grand lobby-cum-gallery reached via a sweeping staircase. The individually decorated spacious rooms are each inspired and named after a different artist.

Four Seasons Hotel Damascus (Map pp82-3; ☎ 339 1000; www.fourseasons.com; Sharia Shukri al-Quatli; d from US$265; ✴ ▢ ▨) Situated near the National Museum and close to the chic shopping and cafés of the new town, this plush piece of paradise in dusty downtown Damascus has been a huge success since opening. The spacious, comfortable rooms are richly decorated with all the creature comforts you expect from a luxury hotel, the food is fabulous and the faultless service, easily the best in Syria, is memorable.

EATING

There are restaurants scattered all over Damascus. The best in terms of quality and service are in the modern city, the most atmospheric are in the Old City, and there are cheap eateries all over.

Restaurants

Most Damascus restaurants open around noon for lunch and serve throughout the day until after midnight or when the last diners are ready to leave – which, because locals don't dine until 10pm or later, could be close to 2am. While reservations aren't necessary, it doesn't hurt to phone ahead – get your hotel to book for you and you'll get better service. Most restaurants have menus in English and Arabic but won't automatically give you a menu with prices, or the menu may have prices for meals but not for alcohol. Press the waiter for a menu with prices if you want one. Good restaurants serve complimentary fruit platters for dessert.

OLD CITY

Abu al-Azz (Map p114; ☎ 221 8174; Souq al-Hamidiyya; lunch S£300, dinner S£500; ✴ 9am-late) This place is popular with locals as much as tourists – Arab families pack the place over summer. Look for the sign 'Rest. Al Ezz Al Shamieh Hall', then pass through the bustling ground-floor

bakery and up a narrow staircase to two floors of dining; the upper level is the most atmospheric. Expect mezze, salads and kebabs, live Oriental music all day, and whirling dervishes in the evening from around 10.30pm. No alcohol served.

Al-Khawali (Map p114; ☎ 222 5808; off Straight St, cnr Maazanet al-Shahim; meal per person S£400; ✴ noon-2am) Devotees swear the Syrian cuisine served here is some of the best in the city. Try the *jedy bzeit* (lamb with lemon sauce), *shish taouk* (marinated chicken on skewers) served in pottery Turkish-style, or the chef's special chicken and thyme. It's off Straight St, in a beautifully renovated old Damascene house. No alcohol or credit cards.

Oxygen (Map pp86-7; ☎ 544 4396; Bab Touma; meal per person S£400; ✴ noon-2am) This eatery-cum-bar has a dance-club vibe, especially late at night when the big-screen TV blares. The Syrian and French food offers no surprises but it's good for groups, especially if you want to stay on and drink for a while after dinner.

Arabesque (Map pp86-7; ☎ 543 3999; Sharia al-Kineesa; meal per person S£500; ✴ noon-late) Dress up a little for this elegant, cosy local favourite serving up the usual Syrian and French cuisine. There's a decent wine selection but no credit cards are accepted.

Casablanca (Map pp86-7; ☎ 541 7598; Sharia Hanania; meal per person S£500; ✴ 1pm-1am) While Damascenes dress up on weekend nights, when cheesy live piano music is on offer, management is forgiving of travellers dropping by this elegant local favourite in casual gear. The French-heavy menu also features delicious Syrian standards such as mezze mixed grills. Alcohol is served and credit cards are accepted.

Leila's Restaurant & Terrace (Map pp86-7; ☎ 544 5900; Souq al-Abbabiyya, opposite east minaret of Umayyad Mosque; meal per person S£500; ✴ 11am-2am) This al fresco rooftop restaurant overlooking Umayyad Mosque has the most magical setting in Damascus, especially for sunset drinks – the fresh mint lemonade (S£75) is thirst-quenching – or later for dinner when the city lights twinkle. The menu features delicious Arabic mezze (S£50 to S£150) – try the eggplant *kibbeh* (cracked-wheat croquettes) – and succulent grills. Alcohol is served, but it's not on the menu – ask the waiter what is available.

Old Town (Map pp86-7; ☎ 542 8088; off Sharia Bab Sharqi; meal per person S£500; ☒ noon-late) Expensive cars are often parked outside this long-established restaurant in an elegant covered courtyard. Italian is served up alongside Arabic and French. Unfortunately service can be dreadful. Alcohol is served, but Old Town doesn't take credit cards.

Aldar Restaurant (Map pp86-7; ☎ 544 5900; off Sharia Bab Sharqi, beside Assieh School; meal per person S£700; ☒ 11am-2am) In a chic conversion of an old Damascene building, stylishly blending old and new, Aldar dishes up some of the tastiest Syrian cuisine in the city, with creative touches added to classics. For starters, don't miss the tasty, cheese *borek* (filled pastry) and the spicy *sojok* meatballs with a green pepper, onion and tomato sauce (S£150). Book a table for the live jazz on Tuesday night. Alcohol served, credit cards accepted.

Elissar (Map pp86-7; ☎ 542 4300; Sharia ad-Dawamneh, near Bab Touma; meal per person S£800; ☒ noon-late) The atmosphere in the lovely courtyard of this old Damascene favourite, with fairy lights and trickling fountain, surpasses the quality of food and service these days (both of which are hit and miss). However, it's popular with the diplomatic crowd, who garner more attention than most patrons. When the Syrian and French dishes are good they're great. Alcohol served, no credit cards.

CENTRAL DAMASCUS

The cheaper eateries are around the Al-Merjeh area (no alcohol, no credit cards), while the more stylish midrange places are in the new town to the north, and usually serve alcohol and take cards.

Al-Arabi (Map pp82-3; Al-Merjeh; meal per person S£150) Situated on a pedestrianised street off the southeastern corner of Al-Merjeh, Al-Arabi consists of two adjacent cheap restaurants, one more casual, the other a little fancier with a separate family section. Perhaps only for the culinary adventurous, specialities include sheep testicles (S£95 for 200g), sheep-brain salad with potatoes (S£90), and the local favourite, fried sheep brain with two fried eggs (S£90).

Al-Sehhi (Map pp82-3; ☎ 221 1555; Sharia al-Abed, off Sharia 29 Mai; meal per person S£150; ☒ noon-midnight) This modest family restaurant confines itself to the basics – mezze, grilled meats, and very good *fatta* (an oven-baked

bread dish soaked in tahini and spread with chickpeas, minced meat or chicken; S£70). There's a separate 'family area' for women diners. No alcohol or cards.

Al-Kamal (Map pp82-3; ☎ 222 1494; Sharia 29 Mai; meal per person S£200; ☒ 11am-midnight) Located near the main tourist office, this place resembles a Parisian bistro. Regulars come for the good-value French *plats du jour* and home-style Syrian dishes, including *kabsa* (spiced rice with chicken or lamb).

Gemini (Map pp82-3; ☎ 311 2070; Sharia al-Amar Izzedin al-Jazzari, off Sharia Maysaloun; meal per person S£700; ☒ noon-2am) This ever-popular eatery sees affluent groups of friends and families filling its tables for long leisurely meals. It's very Western, with a menu embracing Tex-Mex, French and Italian (from nachos and fajitas to pastas and veal escalope), good glasses of white wine, and Norah Jones on the stereo. Alcohol is served and credit cards are accepted.

our pick Al-Hallabi (Map pp82-3; ☎ 339 1000; Four Seasons Hotel Damascus; meal per person S£900; ☒ noon-4pm & 7pm-2am) This is the city's best restaurant, serving up refined Aleppan cuisine in opulent surroundings. Don't miss classics like *kibbeh safarjalieh* (*kibbeh* with quince and pomegranate sauce), or one of Chef Mohammed's own inventions such as *shahba hommos* (hummus with *mouhamara* – a spicy capsicum dip). There's excellent service and a superb wine list, and credit cards are accepted.

ABU ROUMANA

La Casa (Map p80; ☎ 333 1288; Sharia Abdul Malek; meal per person S£240; ☒ 9am-1am) Popular with middle-class Damascenes, who hang out here for hours playing backgammon and smoking sheesha, this is one of the few places where you'll see local girls drinking nonalcoholic beer. The menu features sandwiches (S£160) and pastas (S£240), but the big fresh salads are the local dish of choice (S£150 to S£300). No alcohol or credit cards.

Quick Eats
OLD CITY

Bekdach (Map p114; Souq al-Hamidiyya; ice creams S£50; ☒ 9am-late) A purveyor of scrumptious ice creams made with *sahlab* (like semolina powder). The generous servings of creamy ice cream are topped with crushed pistachio nuts. A souq shopping must.

DAMASCUS

Beit Jabri (Map pp86–7; ☎ 544 3200; www.jabri house.com; 14 Sharia as-Sawwaf; mezze S£40-125, juices S£60-125, sheesha S£120; ☺ 9.30am-12.30am) Popular with locals and tourists alike, this casual café in the lovely courtyard of a splendid old Damascene house (see p94) serves up Syrian standards like mezze and kebabs, alongside international dishes such as 'beef stricanof'. Locals mainly come for the sheesha and coffee, but the fresh juices are delicious.

Bab Sharqi (Map pp86–7; Sharia Bab Sharqi; pizzas S£80-150, pasta S£130; ☺ 11am-midnight) It's hard to get a table out the front of this excellent pizzeria-cum-takeaway place, especially on a summer evening, when students linger over cheap cold beers (S£60), bottles of Syrian wine (S£350), Italian-style pizzas and delicious *toshka* (Armenian toasted meat and cheese sandwiches; S£150).

Art Café Ninar (Map pp86–7; ☎ 542 2257; Sharia Bab Sharqi; pizzas S£150; ☺ 10.30am-2am) Don't be surprised if you see local artists sitting at the wooden tables painting and sketching, or a poet jotting down lines of verse in a notebook. Damascus' bohemian set flocks to this casual eatery in a big stone building, for the art exhibitions, excellent pizza and cheap beer. Be a local and drop by late.

On leafy Sharia al-Qaimariyya, east of Umayyad Mosque, near Al-Nawfara coffeehouse, are a couple of excellent **felafel and shwarma stalls** (Map pp86–7) that do delicious shwarma and enormous felafel and salad sandwiches for around S£50. There are more **shwarma and felafel places** (Map p114) in the covered shopping lane (specialising in Qurans, prayer beads and kids' toys) that runs north off the main drag of Souq al-Hamidiyya. And if you turn left at the end of this lane you'll come to two more popular places, **Shwarma Majed** (Map p114) and **Castello Fast Food** (Map p114), the latter good for a Western hamburger.

CENTRAL DAMASCUS

Al-Masri (Map pp82–3; ☎ 333 7095; Sharia Said al-Jabri; mezze S£30, mains S£100; ☺ 7.30am-5pm) 'The Egyptian' is popular with local office workers, with a menu featuring the kind of home-cooked fare you'd find in Cairo's backstreets, along with local favourites such as *shakshouka* (fried egg and mince meat; S£90) and *shish taouk* (S£90).

Pizza Roma (Map pp82–3; ☎ 213 3046; Sharia Odai bin ar-Roqaa, off Sharia Maysaloun; pizzas S£65-270, ☺ 11am-late) You can eat in or take away from this casual pizzeria west of Cham Palace, where the speciality is American-style deep-pan pizza and pasta (S£80). No alcohol or credit cards.

Pit Stop Café (Map pp82–3; ☎ 333 7095; Sharia al-Amar Izzedin al-Jazzari, off Sharia Maysaloun; meal per person S£300; ☺ 9am-2am) This buzzy modern eatery below Gemini serves up delicious cheesy pizzas, crepes and salads.

Downtown (Map pp82–3; ☎ 332 2321; Sharia al-Amar Izzedin al-Jazzari, off Sharia Maysaloun; meal per person S£450; ☺ 10am-1am) You're more likely to hear French being spoken than Arabic at this hip contemporary café. It has Scandinavian-style décor (think chocolate wood and clean lines) and the most decadently delicious sandwiches, salads and fresh juices in Damascus. Try the caviar *en croute* sandwich with cucumber, dill, caviar, cream cheese and a boiled egg (S£500), and the strawberry and blackberry juice (S£155).

Of the many pastry shops on the southern side of Al-Merjeh, one of the best is **Abu Rashid** (Map pp82–3), down the pedestrian lane on the southeastern corner of the square and up the top of the steps. It does delicious *kibbeh*, cheese or meat *borek*, and *ouzi sarrar*, a samosa-like pastry of rice, meat, peas and spices.

Around Al-Merjeh you'll find cheap shwarma and felafel eateries and excellent fresh juice (S£50) stands, right on the square. If you're staying near the post office, then **Al-Santir** (Map pp82–3) is a perennially popular place doing Western-style toasted sandwiches.

AL-MIDAN JAZMATI

You'll see few tourists in this old Damascus neighbourhood southwest of the Old City. Its main artery, Sharia al-Midan, is a 24-hour street but it's most atmospheric late at night, when locals head here for the hot chicken, shwarma and Arabic pastries. It's quite a scene, with the outdoor tables crammed with people tucking into the tasty takeaway and cars slowly cruising by taking in the action. Scores of shops line the street – it's a Middle Eastern gourmet delight, with white cheeses, olives, pickles and delicious sweets – and you'll notice prices are considerably cheaper here than in the rest of Damascus. Tucked down the laneways are some of Damascus' most historic mosques.

Anas Chicken (off Map p80; ☎ 212 1111; Al-Midan; shwarma S£60; ☒ 24hr) Locals swear this is the best eatery on the street. Its speciality is succulent roasted chicken with thick, hot, freshly fried potato crisps, and there are also tangy chicken shwarmas.

Self-Catering

There's a decent **fruit and vegetable market** between Al-Merjeh and Sharia Shoukri al-Quwatli (Map pp82–3), and another on Sharia al-Amin in the Old City (Map pp86–7).

For piping-hot, freshly baked bread, hit the no-name bakery on Sharia al-Qaimariyya near the CD shops; locals line up here every evening for the city's best croissants for their breakfast the next day. There are several hole-in-the-wall bakeries at the northern end of Sharia Bahsa in Souq Saroujah.

DRINKING
Coffeehouses & Cafés

Coffee in Damascus ranges from the traditional, short black Turkish coffee and light cardamom-scented Bedouin coffee, to good

---

THE END OF THE STORY?

In one of the tales in *The Thousand and One Nights,* a king commissions a merchant to seek out the most marvellous story ever. The merchant sends out his slaves on the quest and at last success is achieved – a slave hears a wondrous story told in Damascus by an old man who tells stories every day, seated on his storyteller's throne.

Jump forward several hundred years or so, and in Damascus today there is still an old man who tells stories every day, seated on his version of a storyteller's throne. His name is Abu Shady and he's the last of the Syrian *hakawati* (professional storytellers).

Hakawati were a common feature of Middle Eastern city street life as far back as the 12th century. With the spread of coffee drinking during Ottoman times, the storytellers moved off the street and into the coffeehouses. As with many Arab traditions, the art of public storytelling has largely failed to survive the 20th century, supplanted in the coffeehouses first by radio, then by television. According to Abu Shady, the last professional storyteller in Syria went into retirement in the 1970s. As a boy, Abu Shady went with his father to watch the *hakawati* perform at the coffeehouses, and fell in love with stories.

'It was my habit to read too much,' he tells us. 'When I was young I would run away from my job at the library to read books.' Abu Shady trained as a tailor but he would read every moment he could – Jean Paul Sartre, Victor Hugo, Maxim Gorky, Khalil Gibran…

When the last *hakawati* decided to retire and stop performing at Al-Nawfara coffeehouse, its owner, Ahmed al-Rabat, told Abu Shady 'You're the only one who can tell stories like him. You have to take over.' Because Abu Shady respected him like a father, he did, and in the 1970s revived the profession of storyteller.

Since then Abu Shady has been appearing nightly at Al-Nawfara in the lee of Umayyad Mosque. Costumed in baggy trousers and waistcoat with a tarboosh on his head, he recounts nightly from his volumes of handwritten tales. These include the legendary exploits of Sultan Beybars and Antar ibn Shadad, both Islamic heroes and – as Abu Shady tells it – regular doers of fantastic feats, sorcery and cunning roguery. He also invents his own stories, incorporating current events from articles he reads in the paper, such as incidents from the current war in Iraq or the situation in Palestine. The assembled listeners know the stories, but it's Abu Shady's delivery that they come for: he interjects with jokes and comments, works the audience, punctuates the words with waves of his sword, and smashes it down on a copper-top table for startling emphasis. The audience responds with oohs and aahs, cheering and interjecting comments of their own. Sadly, the numbers present are small these days. Abu Shady says that nobody has the time any more to listen to stories.

We ask Abu Shady what the future is for the *hakawati*. He admits with a smile and glint in his eye that his son is learning to tell stories, but he tells us 'It's up to him…' It's clear he's secretly hoping the young man will take over. Like us, Abu Shady doesn't want to see the final chapter close on the era of the storyteller.

You can see Abu Shady perform nightly at Al-Nawfara coffeehouse (p110), from around 7pm, give or take an hour or two.

Italian espresso and every conceivable kind of Starbucks-inspired mochaccino you can imagine. It could cost anything from S£50 at a traditional coffeehouse to S£125 for a fancy frappé at a contemporary café. Nargileh or sheesha pipe ranges from S£100 to S£150.

OLD CITY

Galerie Abdal (Map pp86-7; ☎ 544 5794; Sharia Shaweesh; ⏰ 9.30am-12.30am) A loud and lively vibe and regular art exhibitions have made this a long-standing favourite with artists and students, and it's very female-friendly. With a similar feel and attracting a similar crowd, Moulaya next door is another arty place that's perennially popular.

Beit Jabri (Map pp86-7; ☎ 544 3200; 14 Sharia as-Sawwaf; ⏰ 9.30am-late) Locals drop by for coffee, nargileh and conversation in the pretty courtyard of this elegant old house.

Narcissus (Map pp86-7; ☎ 543 1205; Sharia al-Amin; ⏰ 10am-late) Groups of young Damascenes head to this big old Damascene house in the evenings to smoke nargileh and snack on Arabic mezze.

Al-Nawfara (Map pp86-7; ☎ 472 900; Sharia al-Qaimariyya; ⏰ 8am-late) Nestled in the shadow of the Umayyad Mosque's eastern wall, 'The Fountain' is the most atmospheric of Damascus' traditional coffeehouses. This is where you can watch Abu Shady, the last of the *hakawati* (professional storytellers). Every evening around 7pm (give or take an hour or two), Abu Shady takes the chair to tell his version of fables and folk tales, and while his performance is in Arabic, it's enthralling – see The End of the Story? (p109) for more. If you can't find a table here, head across the lane to Ash-Shams, which occupies a former hammam.

Tche Tche (Map p114; ☎ 221 6339; Sharia Madhat Pasha, cnr Al Dakkakeen; ⏰ 10am-2am) Locals climb the stairs of this stylish sheesha café for the aromatic nargileh, long coffee menu and Middle Eastern pop music.

CENTRAL DAMASCUS

In Central Damascus you'll find a number of simple, old-fashioned coffeehouses, noisy with the staccato clacking of dominoes and backgammon counters. They're frequented mainly by males who sit around puffing nargileh, and women won't always feel comfortable. The rooftop coffeehouse Ash-Sharq al-Awsat (Map pp82–3), be-

tween the blue-tiled Iranian cultural centre and Shoukri al-Quwatli flyover, sees the occasional budget traveller dropping by.

The downtown shopping district of Salihiyya has a number of stylish contemporary cafés, particularly in the streets around the chic shopping street of Sharia Hafez Ibrahim. Frequented by young Damascenes, these cafés are a great place to meet locals, and women will feel as comfortable here as they would in any European city.

Inhouse Coffee (Map pp82-3; ☎ 333 6039; Sharia Hafez Ibrahim; coffees S£80-150; ⏰ 7am-1am) This funky café with its lime-and-black décor is always busy with local hipsters smoking, chatting and checking their email on their PowerBooks. It serves excellent espresso and myriad variations of macchiato, latte and decaf coffees. Try the iced spiced chai latte or spicy espresso with cinnamon on top. There are happy hours between 4pm and 5pm and between 9pm and midnight, when you get 50% off coffee and food – ideal if you're on a budget and hanging out for good coffee. There's also complimentary wireless internet.

ABU ROUMANA

Salé Sucré (Map p80; ☎ 333 7315; Sharia al-Rawda; sandwiches S£125, cakes S£60; ⏰ 8am-late) Affluent Damascenes, old and young, love this charming café-bakery. It's the place to head if you're craving good coffee and European café staples such as crusty French baguettes, quiches and German-style grain breads. The tangy citron tarts are sublime.

Bars

Although some restaurants in Damascus serve alcohol, there are few dedicated bars. The best place to head is the Old City, around Bab Touma and Bab Sharqi, which is nightlife central for Damascus. No alcohol is served in the Muslim neighbourhoods, so the action focuses on the Christian Quarter. Things don't kick off until around midnight, and Thursday and Saturday are the big nights.

OLD CITY

Bar Saloon (Map pp86-7; 148 Sharia Bab Sharqi; ⏰ noon-2am Mon-Sat) This endearingly dingy little liquor store–cum-bar is frequented by a motley crew of bohemian types, elderly locals, foreign Arabic students and travellers,

---

GAY & LESBIAN DAMASCUS

Just as President Ahmadinejad of Iran asserted that his country had no homosexuals while giving a speech at Columbia University, Syria officially boasts similar statistics. In a nation where every man and woman is expected to get married (to a member of the opposite sex, of course), Damascus isn't about to host an ironically themed Gay Pride march down Straight St.

That said, cruising among gay men does occur, notably in the souqs, the hammams and the area around Cham Palace. But as always in Middle Eastern countries, discretion is advised as homosexual acts are illegal and can land you in prison. While behaviour that is interpreted as being 'homosexual' in nature can also land you in prison, overall the secret police are far more interested in political subversion than in those wishing to make a dent in Syria's 100% heterosexual statistics.

---

all engaged in heated debate of some sort. Visitors might feel they've encroached on some sort of clique, but it's less exclusive than first appearances suggest and the beer's cheap.

Piano Bar (Map pp86-7; Sharia Hanania; ☿ noon-midnight) This old-fashioned bar-restaurant is stuck in a bit of a time warp, but it's worth dropping in to check out the spectacle of Syrian karaoke.

Oxygen (Map pp86-7; ☎ 544 4396; Bab Touma; ☿ noon-late) This funky lounge bar with eclectic décor and art on the walls is a long-standing favourite with young affluent Damascenes. It has a strict door policy, so dress up. Things don't heat up until very late.

CENTRAL DAMASCUS
There are several bars located in the modern city centre.

Artists' Syndicate Bar (Map p98; Sallat ar-Rawak al-Arabi, Sharia at-Tantawi; ☿ 5pm-midnight) This al fresco garden bar-cum-restaurant in residential Salihiyya may not be the most exciting place for a drink, but it's one of the few places in this area and is mildly intriguing.

Jet Set (Map pp82-3; ☎ 223 2300; Cham Palace, Sharia Maysaloun; ☿ 6pm-3am) Damascus' swankiest bar-cum-club sees a moneyed young set heading here late for the latest hits spun by local DJs.

XO Bar (Map pp82-3; ☎ 339 1000; Four Seasons Hotel Damascus; ☿ noon-2am) This elegant, low-lit, gentlemen's club–style bar, with plush sofas and Orientalist paintings on the wall, is ideal for whispered conversations – of romantic couples, local politicians and businessmen, and journalists and peacekeepers just back from Iraq. Travellers head here for a cocktail before or after dinner at Al-Hallabi (p107).

Liquor Stores

Damascus has no shortage of liquor stores selling beer, arak, spirits, and Syrian and Lebanese wine, in the Christian Quarter of the Old City and the modern town. A central liquor shop is **Elias Hayek** (Map pp82-3; Sharia Ramy; ☿ 10am-8pm Sat-Thu), on a side street running south off Al-Merjeh.

ENTERTAINMENT
Cinemas

Cinema de Cham (Map pp82-3; Cham Palace, Sharia Maysaloun; tickets S£150) Home to the Damascus International Film Festival, this excellent cinema screens everything from European art house to Hollywood blockbusters and the occasional Middle East film subtitled in English. Check *What's On Syria* to find out what's showing or just drop by the cinema.

Pubs & Nightclubs

Marmar (Map pp86-7; ☎ 544 6425; Sharia Dawamneh, near Bab Touma; ☿ 9pm-late) Tucked down a tiny passageway signed by a pink neon calligraphic squiggle, this pub is one of Damascus' best for DJs and live music. On weekends it pounds and heaves with a sweaty, young, bohemian crowd of locals and foreigners, while midweek sees the occasional film screened on its walls.

Domino (Map pp86-7; ☎ 543 1120; Saahat Bab Touma; ☿ 11am-late) A sheesha café serving light food by day and a casual bar in the early evening, Domino curtains off its windows and becomes a full-blown dance club after 11pm. It's one of the Old City's hottest night spots.

Popular spots for DJs and live bands on weekends, and films midweek, are **Le Serail Pub** (Map pp86-7; ☎ 373 7061; off Sharia Bab Sharqi, near Bab Sharqi, follow the graffiti-like painted 'pub' signs; ⊗ 9.30pm-very late) and **Back Door** (Map p80; ☎ 444 6255; Barada Club, Sharia Masr; cover charge S£500; ⊗ 9.30pm-very late). Back Door's DJs spin an eclectic selection of sounds, from hip-hop to Oriental lounge, and it also hosts the occasional live performance of *tarab*, an intense, improvisational form of Middle East music; reserve a table for Thursday night and don't arrive before midnight.

Theatre, Music, Opera & Ballet
Dar Al-Assad for Arts and Culture (Map p80; ☎ 245 6165/6144; www.daralassad.sy, www.opera-syria.org; Saahat Umawiyeen, Sharia Shoukri al-Quwatli; tickets S£80-150; ⊗ Dec-Jun) This is home to the superb Opera Theatre, Drama Theatre and Multi-Purpose Hall, all venues for nearly nightly performances of world-class opera, drama, classical music, and even folk music and pop concerts. Don't miss a performance by the acclaimed National Symphony Orchestra. You can pick up a programme from Dar Al-Assad, check the website, or see *What's On Syria* for more details. Tickets are dirt-cheap for such high-quality performances.

Art House (off Map p80; ☎ 662 8112; behind the Children's Hospital, Mezzeh; ⊗ 7-11pm) A welcome new venue, this boutique hotel–cum–art space hosts classical-music recitals (along with jazz concerts) and an excellent summer music festival.

All of the foreign cultural centres host performances of classical music, opera and ballet. Most notable is the **Centre Culturel Français de Damas** (Map pp82–3; ☎ 231 6192; fax 231 6194; www.ccf-damas.org; off Sharia Yousef al-Azmeh; ⊗ 8.30am-9pm Mon-Sat), which offers a vibrant programme of concerts and cultural events, from piano recitals to jazz (local and foreign) and mixed-media happenings with video installations. Its summer music festivals, held in atmospheric Old City locations, feature everything from Oriental jazz to the well-regarded Women's Orchestra of Oriental Music. Check café noticeboards and the centre's website, or phone for information.

Traditional Dance & Music
Abu al-Azz (Map p114; ☎ 221 8174; Souq al-Hamidiyya; ⊗ 9am-late) A three-piece band plays Oriental music at this Old City restaurant throughout the day and whirling dervishes perform around 10pm.

Umayyad Palace Restaurant (Map pp86-7; ☎ 222 0826; opposite Umayyad Mosque; lunch/dinner S£350/600 +

10% tax; ⊗ 12.30-5pm & 7.30pm-midnight) This restaurant offers a meal and floorshow package that includes a band and dervishes, but if you go on a night when there isn't a tour group, the performance is half-hearted and disinterested at best. You're better off heading to one of the many Old City restaurants and cafés that feature an *oud* (Arabian lute) player in the evenings.

Similar in style to Beit Jabri, and just across the lane, the fairy-lit **Beit Geddi** (Map pp86-7; ☎ 543 1607; Sharia as-Sawwaf; mezze S£35-100; ⊗ 9am-1am) has a musician playing the *oud* from around 8pm on Friday and Saturday nights, while at **Takaya** (Map pp86-7; ☎ 545 0770; Sharia Qasr ath-Thaqafeh; mezze S£60-125; ⊗ 9am-1am) the *oud* player strums Oriental classics from around 9pm most nights.

SHOPPING
Damascus is arguably home to the Middle East's best and most authentic shopping, most of which can be found in the rambling medieval souqs that spread through much of the northwestern quarter of the Old City (see Shopping the Damascus Souq, p115). Scores of antique, carpet and handicraft stores are dotted around the souqs, in the lanes surrounding Umayyad Mosque, along Sharia al-Qaimariyya, and in the Christian Quarter near Bab Sharqi on Sharia Hanania, which is the well-trodden tourist route up to the Chapel of Ananias. Straight St, in particular, is lined with small family-run businesses that specialise in one particular type of product, such as finely engraved brass- and copper-ware, handcrafted wooden mother-of-pearl inlaid furniture, richly decorated brocade, colourful handmade Oriental carpets, and even dazzling swords – although sadly the long tradition of Damascene steel is now reduced to one or two practitioners making ceremonial pieces. The selection tends to be better on Straight St than at the emporiums in the souqs, and prices are also more negotiable.

In Central Damascus, the place to head for gold jewellery, handcrafted *ouds*, and wooden inlaid boxes and backgammon sets is Handicrafts Lane, a small shaded alleyway adjoining the Takiyya as-Süleimaniyya complex, just south of Sharia Shoukri al-Quwatli. Off the lane is a Turkish madrassa, now Artisinat, a handicraft market where the former student cells are now occupied by traders and

APPRECIATING THE ARTISANS

As you wander the narrow alleys of the Old City, you'll hear the beating of brass and copper and the sounds of sawing and hammering, and smell wood chips, fresh paint or furniture polish. Follow your nose and ears and you'll find a tiny workshop where artisans and artists sit patiently carving elaborate wood decoration, creating mother-of-pearl inlaid mosaics, engraving intricate patterns on brass goods, or simply painting and sculpting. These are some of the best ateliers for seeing handcrafted goods made using traditional techniques:

- **Oriental Center Arts** (Map pp82-3; ☎ 222 2700; Artisanat; ⏰ 9am-8pm) Saeed Zozoul creates exquisite furniture, mirror frames, picture frames, and decorative panels and ceilings for old Damascene houses by shaping raised patterns using gypsum and plaster, painting them colourfully, then carefully applying gold leaf to embellish them further. Each piece takes about four days and can be made to order in five.
- **Radwan al-Taweel** (Map pp82-3; ☎ 221 5493; Artisanat; ⏰ 9am-8pm) Sixty-year-old Radwan has been engraving intricate arabesque patterns on copper and brass coffee pots, tea sets, lamps and trays since his grandfather taught him as a child. He takes about two days to decorate a large tray. Ask and he'll happily show you his well-used tools of the trade and his techniques. Radwan is very proud of the recycled brass shells, remnants from the war with Israel, that he engraves to produce umbrella/walking-stick holders – particularly the one he designed for Gadaffi.
- **Hassab al-Kazaz & Sons** (Map pp82-3; ☎ 222 4830; Artisanat; ⏰ 9am-8pm) These beautiful, bold-coloured glass chandeliers, lamps, vases and decorative objects are hand-blown. Ask and they'll take you to the workshop out the back where they're made.
- **Ibrahim Tawil** (Map pp82-3; ☎ 09-8899 3789; Artisanat; ⏰ 10am-8pm) Great-nephew of the famous *oud* (Arabian lute) maker Hanna Nahaat, Anton (Tony) Ibrahim Tawil makes beautiful *ouds* in this dusty workshop. Expect to pay from S£3000 for a quality instrument suitable for learners.
- **Deeb Balah** (Map pp86-7; Sharia al-Qaimariyya; ⏰ 10am-9pm) Deaf sandal-maker Deeb handcrafts simple leather sandals and Turkish-style slippers with colourful brocade patterns. He helpfully reads lips in English, so you can order a size or style to suit (from US$20 to US$35).
- **Mahmoud Shahin** (Map pp86-7; ☎ 541 3324; Sharia al-Qaimariyya; ⏰ 10am-8pm) Palestinian philosopher-writer-artist Mahmoud (see Mahmoud Shahin, p116) can be found most days in his tiny atelier drinking Turkish coffee and smoking cigarettes while he paints his small, striking paintings of veiled ladies, sensual shapes of women and other, often surreal, scenes.

craftspeople who are happy to demonstrate their skills at engraving and painting. The whole complex is lovely and certainly worth a look. For tips on getting the best deal, see The Art of Bargaining, p235.

The main commercial downtown shopping area is situated north of the Cham Palace, on Sharia al-Hamra, in the surrounding streets, and on pedestrianised Sharia Salihiyya, which are all jam-packed with cheap clothes, lingerie and shoe shops. Sharia Hafez Ibrahim is the place to head for chic fashion boutiques.

Antiques & Handicrafts

Bustling **Souq al-Hamidiyya** (Map p114) is not only a wonderful place to shop for the atmosphere, but it also has some of the city's best antique and craft shops. **Tony Stephan's** at No 156 is renowned for the finest quality at the best prices, with a wide range of beautiful textiles, splendid mother-of-pearl inlaid furniture, old Bedouin jewellery, and intricately engraved copper- and brassware. The quality is unsurpassed, so if you only have time to shop at one store, make it this one.

George Dabdoub (Map p114), on the small square in front of the entrance to Azem Palace, sells jewellery, brass, icons, brocade and carpets. The courteous staff and fair prices make this an easy place to shop.

Atmospheric **Azem Ecole** (Map p114) is situated in an elegant old madrassa and has some stunning stuff, including Bedouin jewellery, silk brocades and brass. Staff can be a little pushy and prices a little high; it's best for those who've honed their bargaining skills.

For inlaid wooden boxes, chests and backgammon boards, visit **Khalil Haddad** (Map pp86-7; 115 Sharia Bab Sharqi; ☿ 10am-8pm Mon-Sat), who fronts the actual workshop in which this exquisite work is produced. There are also many other workshops along Sharia Bab Sharqi and the surrounding streets with similar quality handicrafts.

Dahdah Palace (Map pp86-7; 9 Sharia ash-Shalla; ☿ 9.30am-2pm & 4-6pm Mon-Sat, to 7pm in summer) has a room full of old 'finds', including coins, figurines and tiles recovered from demolished Damascene houses. See also p93.

Brocade, Textiles & Traditional Garments

Damascus' famous brocade and silk textiles, in the form of shawls, throws, cushion covers and bedspreads, make wonderful souvenirs and gifts. Quality is assured at **Tony Stephan's** (Map p114), **Azem Ecole** (Map p114), Artisinat (handicraft market; Map pp82–3) off Handicrafts Lane and **Sharia al-Qaimariyya** (Map pp86–7). These are also great spots to find traditional black Palestinian dresses with red embroidered cross-stitch patterns.

A wonderful one-of-a-kind store, the not-for-profit **Anat** (Map pp86-7; ☎ 542 7878; Sharia Bab Sharqi, near Bab Sharqi; ☿ 10am-8pm winter, 10am-2pm & 5-10pm summer) is the place to shop for original gifts and souvenirs handmade in a workshop

SHOPPING THE DAMASCUS SOUQ

The Damascus souq (Map p114) is not as strictly ordered as its Aleppo counterpart, with few areas devoted strictly to a single type of goods. The main covered market, **Souq al-Hamidiyya**, starts with glitzy souvenir shops and ends with prayer beads and Qurans. In between, the majority of stores sell clothing of some description, typically poor quality, if not outright trash. But trashy can be fun – there are dress shops to make a drag queen swoon, while some of the lingerie has to be seen to be believed.

Alleyways to the north are more routinely domestic – toiletries, household items, toys, school books and stationery. The south is more colourful, particularly narrow, sloping **Souq Khayyatin** (Tailors' Souq), filled with cubbyhole traders dealing in bolts of fine cloth and richly coloured garments, from the practical (scarves and pants) to the peacock (belly-dancing outfits and wedding dresses).

The most aromatic and enchanting passage is **Souq al-Bzouriyya** (Seed Bazaar), which is the covered area running south from Umayyad Mosque. This mixes jewellery with perfumes, spices, nuts and sweets, all illuminated in the evening by glowing chandeliers. It's an alluring place in which to linger and examine little curiosities, such as the glazed-fruit shop and, just around the corner, Dr Mounif Aidi's herbal remedies. Al-Bzouriyya gives way to **Souq al-Attarine**, actually a stretch of Sharia Medhat Pasha (Straight St), which is devoted to spices and coffee.

In the souq, spice and food shops open as early as 7am, and most other shops open around 9am or 10am. Shops start to close at around 6pm, and by 7pm nearly all the shutters are down. Most of the souq stays closed all day Friday, although the shops and businesses in the Christian Quarter close on Sunday instead.

---

in the Palestinian refugee camp from embroidered textiles produced by women in villages all over Syria. Traditional Syrian and Palestinian embroidery techniques are employed to create contemporary items, including coin and cosmetic purses and hand and shoulder bags (in hundreds of sizes), cushion covers, slippers and clothes. The profits from the sale of these exquisite products are shared among the women.

For red-and-white (Bedouin) and black-and-white (Palestinian) *kufeyya* (chequered scarves), *dishdashas* (men's white dress), tarbooshes (traditional red hats) and wooden canes, head to the covered **Souq Medhat Pasha** (the area around Sharia Souq Medhat Pasha, the western end of Straight St; Map p114) and **Souq al-Khayyatin** (Map p114).

Carpets & Rugs

At the western end of Souq al-Hamidiyya there are several excellent rug and carpet traders, although prices tend to be higher here, and better bargains can be found on **Sharia al-Qaimariyya** (Map pp86–7) and the eastern end of **Straight St** (Map pp86–7), in the area around the Roman arch. There are several shops with good selections, including **Bel Oriental Carpets** (Map pp86–7) and **George Dabdoub** (Map p114).

Music
CDS

You'll find a dozen tiny CD stores on lively **Sharia al-Qaimariyya** (Map pp86–7) specialising in contemporary Arabic music, from lounge and trance to folk music and jazz. CDs cost around S£200. You'll see some selling for as little as S£25; avoid buying these, as they're pirated and Syria musicians struggle enough as it is. Look out for Lena Chamamyan, Kulna Sawa, Itar Shameh and InsaniT.

Abdel Razek Mousali (Map pp82-3; Sharia Bur Said, south of Saahat Yousef al-Azmeh) This is the city's best music store, with an extensive selection of music, from the giants of the Arab world (Umm Kolthum, Fairouz, Farid al-Atrache and Abdel Halim Hafez) to jazz, classical and contemporary Arabic music.

MUSICAL INSTRUMENTS

The beloved *oud* (Arabian lute) is a difficult instrument to master, and Western-trained musicians will find the different styles of tuning and playing bewildering at first, but it's a wonderful souvenir for musicians. Head to the workshop of **Ibrahim Tawil** (see Appreciating the Artisans, p113), great-nephew of the famous *oud* maker Hanna Nahaat. There is another workshop on Sharia Bahsa in Souq Saroujah selling

DAMASCUS

MAHMOUD SHAHIN: PHILOSOPHER, POET, PAINTER

Amid the carpet- and trinket-sellers along pretty, cobbled Sharia al-Qaimariyya, writer, philosopher and now artist Mahmoud Shahin sits quietly in his little atelier and paints. His works, often colourful, thought-provoking, dense and detailed, hang on the walls, while books he has written sit on a shelf, waiting for the occasional customer who takes an interest in this Jerusalem-born artist's unique take on life and wants to read more. Seemingly content now that he's replaced the pen with a brush (he didn't do this until 1995, when he was 51), he's free to pursue subjects such as the devil, heaven and hell – subjects that attract the censors if tackled in written form. And there's plenty of personal history to propel his paintings as well. Mahmoud grew up in the countryside until 1967, when his father's land was lost to Israel. Israel and Jerusalem feature in some of his works, but he doesn't want to return; instead, he listens to what is going on and directs those thoughts into his paintings.

---

ouds, but the quality is poorer here. At the entrance to Souq al-Hamidiyya, **Nabeel Fouad Salka** (Map p114; Souq al-Hamidiyya, shop no 25; 8am-8pm) sells high-quality *ouds*, along with mother-of-pearl decorated drums and other instruments.

GETTING THERE & AWAY

See the Getting Around section of the Transport chapter (p390) for information on transport options between Damascus and the rest of the country.

Air

The **Damascus international airport** (543 0201/9) is located 26km southeast of the city centre. There's a money exchange and a couple of ATMs in Arrivals, although the ATMs are not always in operation. The departure tax is S£200.

From Damascus, SyrianAir flies several times daily to and from Aleppo (from S£1200, one hour), and far less frequently to Deir ez-Zur (from S£1400, one hour), Qamishle (from S£1600, 80 minutes) and Lattakia (from S£1000, 45 minutes); frequency of services to the last three destinations can vary dramatically according to season and demand. Return fares are double the single fare.

For the main carriers that fly to Damascus, see p390.

AIRLINE OFFICES

You'll find many airlines have their offices on Sharia Maysaloun and Sharia Fardous, one block to the south of Maysaloun (Map pp82–3). Their opening hours are typically 9am to 6pm Sunday to Thursday (closed Friday).

There are several **SyrianAir** (central sales & reservations 00963 11 168, airport 00963 11 169; www.syriaair.com) offices in Damascus, but the **main office** (Map pp82-3; 245 0098; Sharia Said al-Jabri), across from Hejaz train station, is the best, with staff who speak English. It's more convenient to check timetables and buy tickets online.

Bus

You will find two main bus stations in the city of Damascus.

Harasta terminal (Karajat Harasta), 6km northwest of the city centre, is for departures to northern destinations. To get here, take a microbus from Al-Merjeh or the eastern end of Shoukri al-Quwatli for S£10, or a taxi for around S£80.

The new **Al-Samariyeh terminal** (Mezzeh West) has replaced the old Baramke terminal. Just opened at the time of research, it was a massive new car park with covered waiting areas and poor signage. It's on the far western outskirts of the city. This is where you catch buses going to southern destinations such as Bosra, Der'a and Suweida, and buses and service taxis to Beirut and Amman, along with some international services to Jordan, Lebanon, Egypt and the Gulf.

In addition, there are several other microbus and minibus stations serving regional destinations (for details, see opposite).

For a description of the various kinds of buses, see p399 in the Transport chapter.

NORTH OF DAMASCUS

All the big private bus companies run Luxury Pullmans from Harasta terminal. Prices are similar and destinations include

Aleppo (one way VIP/non-VIP S£230/150, five hours), Deir ez-Zur (S£200, seven hours), Hama (S£90, 2½ hours), Homs (S£75, two hours), Lattakia (S£120, 4½ hours), Palmyra (S£150, four hours) and Tartus (S£110, 3½ hours).

The touts can be annoying: as soon as you've cleared the security checks at the entrance, expect to have your sleeves tugged by guys wanting to lead you to their office. Ignore them and make a beeline for one of the two most reputable companies, Kadmous or Al-Ahliah. Booking in advance is rarely necessary and you'll never have to wait more than an hour or two to get a seat on your bus of choice, but if you feel more secure booking in advance head to the handily placed Kadmous ticket office (Map pp82–3), in the arcade by Victoria Bridge.

SOUTH OF DAMASCUS

A number of bus companies head south, but Damas Tours (Map p80) is the best, running good buses with air-con out of the new Al-Samariyeh terminal to Bosra (S£80, two hours, every two hours from 8am until 10pm) and Suweida (S£60, one hour 40 minutes, approximately every hour from 8am until 8.35pm). Al-Muhib also runs buses south at exactly the same times as Damas Tours and for the same price. Der'a (S£60, one hour 20 minutes) is serviced by Al-Soukor and Al-Wassim.

LEBANON, JORDAN & EGYPT

From Al-Samariyeh terminal, private bus companies have frequent services to Beirut (S£200, 4½ hours), departing every hour or so between 7.30am and 6.30pm, plus several buses daily to Amman (S£400, five to seven hours depending on border formalities – although some travellers have reported formalities taking so long as to extend the full trip to eight to 10 hours). Service taxi is considerably faster; for details, see p118.

Services to Egypt (from US$50 including ferry fare from Aqaba to Nuweiba, around 30 hours) vary dramatically depending on the season, with few services in winter and many more in summer.

TURKEY

Buses to Istanbul (S£2000, 30 hours) and other Turkish destinations, such as Antakya (S£450) and Ankara (S£1600), all depart

from the Harasta terminal. If you can't get a direct bus, take a bus to Aleppo, from where half a dozen buses run regular services across the border. This is also a cheaper option for those on a tight budget.

Car & Motorcycle

If you are travelling independently by car or motorcycle, see p400 for more information. Travellers are increasingly hiring cars for the convenience it brings. A popular option is to also hire a driver for a day (see p401 for details). For car-rental options try the following:

Budget (Map pp82-3; ☎ 499 9999; opposite Four Seasons Hotel Damascus)

Europcar Saahat Umawiyeen (Map p80; ☎ 222 9300; Sheraton Damascus Hotel & Towers); Sharia Shoukri al-Quwatli (Map p80; ☎ 222 9200; Le Meridien Damas)

Hertz (Map pp82-3; ☎ 223 2300; www.hertz.com; Cham Palace)

Microbus & Minibus

It's easier and more comfortable to use Pullman buses, but there are a few destinations where a microbus or minibus is the only option, including Quneitra, Zabadani and the Barada Gorge, Dumeir, Seidnayya, Maalula, An-Nabk and other destinations to the immediate north of Damascus.

The main microbus station is Bab Mousala garage (Karajat Bab Mousala, also known as Karajat Der'a; Map p80), in the neighbourhood of Bab Mousala about 1km south of the Old City. From here there are services for the Hauran region, including Suweida, Shahba and Der'a (for Bosra and the Jordanian border).

There are microbuses to Bab Mousala from a stop on Sharia Fakhri al-Baroudi (one block south and east of the Hejaz train station), although it's simplest to take a taxi, which should cost about S£50 from the city centre.

There are further minibus/microbus stations in the northeast of the city: Abbasseen garage (Karajat Abbasseen; Map p80) and Maalula garage (Karajat Maalula; Map p80) are located about 200m south of the Abbasseen stadium and just east of Saahat Abbasseen. These are where you come to catch transport to destinations to the immediate north of Damascus. Again, the easiest way of getting here from the city centre is by taxi (S£50).

Service Taxi

The main service-taxi station is at the new **Al-Samariyeh terminal** (Mezzeh West) on the far western outskirts of the city. Taxis leave throughout the day and night for Amman (S£400, five to seven hours, although sometimes longer depending on border formalities) and Irbid (S£250, 3½ to five hours) in Jordan, and Baalbek (S£300, 2½ hours) and Beirut (S£300, from four hours, depending on border formalities) in Lebanon.

Train

One of the landmarks of Central Damascus, Hejaz train station (Map pp82–3) is currently closed for extensive (and repeatedly delayed) redevelopment into a shopping mall, hotel and transport hub. All services go from **Khaddam train station** (☎ 888 8678), about 5km southwest of the centre. Take a taxi here for around S£50 from Al-Merjeh. There are several services a day via Homs and Hama to Aleppo, on clean new trains, including an overnight service (1st/2nd class S£300/250, six hours). Tickets for trains can be bought at both the Khaddam and Hejaz stations, providing you can find someone on duty.

The Damascus to Amman train service stopped running in 2006, although there are indications it may resume at some stage in the future.

GETTING AROUND
To/From the Airport

For a taxi from the airport to the city, buy a ticket from the official taxi desk in Arrivals for S£700. For £800 you can travel with Star Taxis, in new, clean, air-conditioned cars.

There's a Karnak airport bus service (S£50, 30 to 50 minutes, half-hourly between 6am and midnight) that runs from the airport forecourt (outside Arrivals/Departures) to the new Al-Samariyeh bus station (off Map p80) on the western outskirts of Mezzeh. It's more convenient to take a taxi directly to your hotel.

Bicycle

There's a group of about four or five bicycle repairs and spares shops lined up along Sharia Khaled ibn Walid, about 500m due south of the main post office. Don't expect to find any esoteric parts for your monoshocked mountain bike though.

Microbus

Damascus is compact and easy to get around on foot, but microbuses can be a handy way to travel the longer distances for those on a very tight budget.

While microbuses are popular with Arabic students living in Damascus, travellers without any Arabic might have difficulty locating the right bus, as route names are posted in Arabic only on the front of the bus.

Fares range from S£5 to S£10, paid on the bus. While the buses run set routes and there are fixed stops, drivers are flexible and will generally pick up and set down anywhere.

The main central terminal is at Jisr ar-Rais (Map pp82–3), the flyover west of the National Museum.

From here you can get microbuses to Bab Touma, Muhajireen, Mezzeh, Saahat Abbasid (or Abbasseen garage for Seidnayya and Maalula) and Harasta terminal, the northeastern bus station. The latter two can also be picked up along Sharia Shoukri al-Quwatli.

Microbuses for Bab Mousala garage leave from another station on Sharia Fakhri al-Baroudi (Map pp82–3), as do others that take you to the microbus for Sayyida Zeinab Mosque.

Taxi

While there appear to be thousands of yellow Damascus taxis motoring down every street, finding one with a working meter is increasingly rare – unless you use the new **Star Taxi** (☎ 9207), with good drivers and vehicles, meters that work and services to the airport, Jordan and Lebanon. The fare for a city-centre ride starts at around S£25 (although can be as low as S£15 if you find a driver willing to use a meter) and can rise to around S£50 for a cross-town fare. State your destination or a well-known nearby landmark and negotiate a price before getting in.

Note that it's extremely difficult to find an empty taxi around 4pm to 6pm (rush hour) on working days and throughout the evenings when people are heading out or home from shopping. Allow an hour to get to any of the bus terminals during rush hour.

Around Damascus & the Hauran

ضواحي دمشق وحوران

Heading south from Damascus towards the Jordanian border is a region of fertile agricultural land, rolling hills and fruit orchards that gives way to harsh, rocky basalt plains (known as the Hauran) straddling the Syria–Jordan border.

The black rock gives the villages and towns a peculiar, brooding quality that is best appreciated at Bosra. With its impressive Roman remains and one of the world's best-preserved Roman theatres, it's one of Syria's highlights and a must-do day trip from Damascus. The intriguing Druze towns of Suweida, Shahba and Qanawat can be visited on the same trip. Suweida has a well-regarded museum while the ruins of Shahba and Qanawat are worth a wander.

For those with an interest in Middle Eastern politics and history, a visit to the ghost town of Quneitra, within the UN-monitored Golan Heights, is a moving experience. The Israelis captured the town during the Six Day War of 1967, and deliberately destroyed it on their withdrawal.

There are several places of interest to the northeast of Damascus, off the Damascus–Aleppo Hwy (Hwy 5), including a number of predominantly Christian towns and villages and a handful of remote monasteries. To the west is the Barada Gorge, incised into the Jebel Libnan ash-Sharqiyya (Anti-Lebanon Range). Half the fun of a visit to the gorge is getting there via the snail-paced, narrow-gauge steam train. The other half is watching the locals at leisure, especially on a Friday, when picnicking families make the most of the Syrian weekend.

AROUND DAMASCUS & THE HAURAN

HIGHLIGHTS

- Relive the time when ancient **Bosra** (p125) was the capital of the Roman province of Arabia with a ramble around its remarkably well-preserved citadel and theatre
- Discover why magical little **Maalula** (p121) is Syria's most enchanting village
- Get monastic for a night or two at the remote hilltop monastery of **Mar Musa** (p123)
- Marvel at beautiful 4th-century mosaics at the impressive **Suweida museum** (p129)
- Sit back and enjoy the snail's pace of a journey on the jolly steam train to the locals' favourite picnic spot, **Barada Gorge** (p125)
- Be moved by the senseless destruction at the ghost town of **Quneitra** (p130) in the UN-patrolled demilitarised zone of the Golan Heights

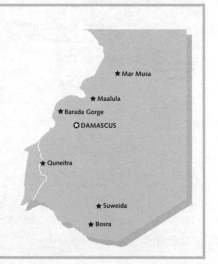

★ Mar Musa

★ Maalula

★ Barada Gorge

✪ DAMASCUS

★ Quneitra

★ Suweida

★ Bosra

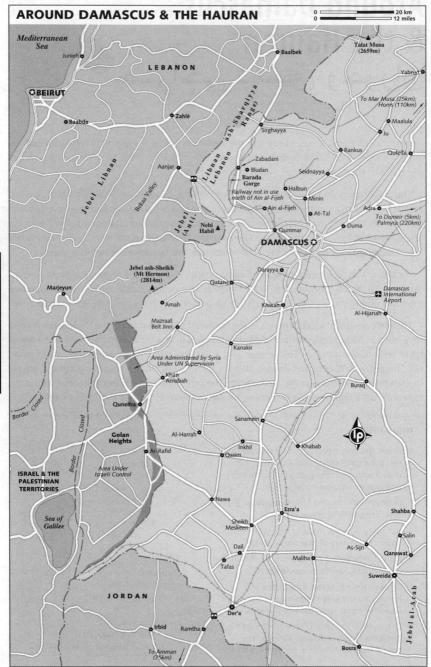

DUMEIR   الضمير
☎ 011

The restored **Roman temple** at Dumeir, a dusty little village some 40km northeast of Damascus on the Palmyra road, was dedicated in AD 245 to Zeus Hypsistos (the 'supreme' Zeus, or Zeus Baal Shamayin in Syria), during the reign of the Hauran-born emperor Philip the Arab. The temple was built on the site of a Nabataean altar, and there's evidence that the building's purpose was changed during construction. It may have been intended as a staging post at the intersection of two key caravan routes, a sacred compound, or simply a public fountain. Whatever the case, the temple is impressive. The great traveller Gertrude Bell said it reminded her of Baalbek (p354) in Lebanon.

The rectangular structure sits in a pit, the result of excavations and reconstruction work. Inside you'll find Greek inscriptions and carved reliefs. If you're coming from Damascus, the temple is off to the right of the main road just before you enter Dumeir. If the caretaker isn't around, someone will fetch him to let you in – tip him around S£50.

Getting There & Away

There are regular microbuses to Dumeir (S£20, 45 minutes) from the Abbasseen garage in northeastern Damascus.

SEIDNAYYA   صيدنايا
☎ 011

Perched spectacularly on an enormous rocky outcrop, the Greek Orthodox **Convent of Our Lady of Seidnayya** could easily be mistaken for a Crusader castle at first glance, particularly at night when it's splendidly lit. In fact, the convent stands on the site of one of the most important places of Christian pilgrimage in the Middle East, due to the presence of a portrait of the Virgin Mary purportedly painted by St Luke. All manner of miracles have been attributed to this icon, to the extent that, at the time of the Crusades, the Christians considered Seidnayya second in importance only to Jerusalem. Veneration of the icon is fervent, and it's fascinating to witness Muslim pilgrims as well as Christians.

One legend has it that the Byzantine emperor Justinian ordered the building of the convent in AD 546 on his way to Jerusalem, while another story has Audixa, wife of Emperor Tandosius, secluding herself here in AD 434 after a fight with her husband, and presenting the revered icon to the convent. What is known is that it was built on the site of an earlier Greek shrine and rebuilt following earthquakes. Medieval masonry is evident in the lower walls, but most of the structure dates from the 19th century.

Ascend the four flights of stairs, duck through the low wooden doorway, and admire the beautiful mosaics on your left before proceeding to the courtyard. The main chapel, on your right, is crammed with modern icons and other testimonies of faith from the convent's visitors. The pilgrimage shrine containing the famed relic is to the right of this chapel, in a small dark room. Remove your shoes and ensure you're modestly dressed; long skirts or trousers, long-sleeved shirts and a headscarf (for women) are appreciated.

After visiting the chapels, head to the roof – there are wonderful views over the town to the plains beyond.

The **Feast of Our Lady of Seidnayya** is held on 8 September each year, and the spectacle is worth attending if you're in the area. The main celebrations begin on the night of the 7th, and both Christian and Muslim pilgrims attend from the Middle East and beyond.

The town itself dates back to the 6th century BC and is scenically situated in the heart of the Jebel Libnan ash-Sharqiyya. It's modern and unremarkable, though, with little of interest beyond the convent, warranting no more than a half-day excursion. It's possible to combine Seidnayya with a visit to Maalula, although public transport between the two is infrequent.

Getting There & Away

Travellers generally visit Seidnayya on a day trip from Damascus. There are regular microbuses to Seidnayya (S£25, 40 minutes) from the Maalula garage in northeastern Damascus.

MAALULA   معلول
☎ 011 / pop 5000

In a narrow valley in the foothills of Jebel Libnan ash-Sharqiyya, Maalula is an enchanting little village in which yellow-stone and silvery-blue-painted fairytale houses are stacked up against a sheer cliff. There are few sights to see, but it's a pleasant place to explore for an hour or two.

If arriving by minibus, alight at the main village intersection, where there's a traffic island and the road splits. Head right up the hill, and at the top head right again; the road switches back, climbing steeply to the small **Convent of St Thecla** (Deir Mar Teqla), tucked snugly against the cliff. From here there are pretty views of the village.

The convent was established near one of the holiest Christian shrines, the Shrine of St Thecla. Thecla was a pupil of St Paul and one of the earliest Christian martyrs – see The Acts of Paul & Thecla, opposite, for more about her life. As one legend has it, after being cornered against the cliff at Maalula by soldiers sent to execute her, Thecla prayed to God, lightning stuck the cliff and a cleft appeared in the rock face, facilitating her flight.

The convent itself, a sanctuary for nuns and orphans, is of minor interest, but ahead lies the legendary escape route, **St Thecla Gap**. Cut through the rock by run-off from the plateau above the village, this narrow, steep-sided ravine resembles a mini version of the famed *siq* (gorge) at Petra. There are a few shrines within its walls, though electricity lines, graffiti and litter mar the experience.

At the end of the canyon, head to the left and follow the road for picturesque views of the village and valley, and the Byzantine **Monastery and Church of St Sergius** (Deir Mar Sarkis, also known as the Convent of Sts Serge and Bacchus). Built in AD 325, it's one of the oldest churches in the world. According to legend, Sergius (Sarkis) was a Roman legionary who, after converting to Christianity and refusing to make sacrifices to the god Jupiter, was executed.

The impressive low wooden doorway leading into the monastery is over 2000 years old; however, the highlight is the small church itself, which still incorporates features of the pagan temple that previously stood here. Note the hole in the circular altar, there to release the blood spilt from pagan sacrifices.

The splendid collection of icons includes some 17th-century gems, including several by icon-painting icon 'Michael the Crete'.

The hillside south of the church is riddled with small caverns that archaeologists believe were inhabited by prehistoric man some 50,000 to 60,000 years ago. More recently, they were used as underground places of worship and burial in the years before AD 313, when Constantine permitted religious freedom. This road loops back to the village, where it's possible to catch a minibus back to Damascus.

THE LANGUAGE OF THE CHRIST

The mainly Greek Catholic village of Maalula is one of the last remaining places where Aramaic, the language of Jesus Christ, is still spoken. Aramaic was once widely spoken in the Middle East and is one of the oldest continually spoken languages in the world, reaching its zenith around 500 BC. It bears similarities to both Arabic and Hebrew. The number of speakers was steadily dwindling until recently, but now interest in keeping the language alive has increased dramatically.

At the peaceful St Ephrem's Clerical Seminary, in Seidnayya, pilgrims are coming from all over the world to study religion in Aramaic while learning the language. According to the priests there, the students know how important the preservation of the language is, and also want to hear the words of the bible in the same language that Christ spoke them.

In Maalula's Monastery and Church of St Sergius, Aramaic is proudly alive and well. More than 5000 local worshippers all speak Aramaic. Until recently it was mainly used as an oral language, despite having a written form. However, the Syrian Government recently established an Institute for Aramaic, and new texts and language-learning materials are being written in the ancient language.

So was the Aramaic spoken in Mel Gibson's epic, The Passion of the Christ, accurate? Maalula's locals say that the first time they saw the film, they were so moved they didn't pay attention. On a second viewing, however, they realised they could barely understand a word of the dialect that Mel had used...

THE ACTS OF PAUL & THECLA

A saint in most Christian religions, we know about St Thecla and her miraculous escapades through the apocryphal writings of St Paul. While there are plenty of other versions of the story, this is the version apparently told by St Paul himself.

Thecla, a young girl who was engaged to be married, heard St Paul's 'discourse on virginity' and decided from that point on to follow God and the teachings of the apostle. Thecla's mother, and of course her fiancé, were furious and both St Paul and Thecla were to be punished. Thecla was to be burnt at the stake, but a wild storm put out the fire and she escaped. Later, after being sentenced to be devoured by wild animals for pushing away the advances of a nobleman, she survived by having a lioness fight to the death for her. While escaping would-be captors yet again, at Maalula, Thecla reached a dead end; however, lightning struck a wall of rock, splitting it open and allowing her safe passage. As she ran through the passage it closed behind her, effectively locking her captors out.

Thecla lived the rest of her pious life in a cave at this spot, and was soon seen as a 'female apostle' and a little bit of an early feminist icon. After her death her followers considered her a martyr. You can walk Thecla's path through the gorge, but don't try her other miraculous feats!

Sleeping & Eating

As Maalula is an easy half-day trip from Damascus, there's no need to stay overnight unless you want to attend the Festival of the Cross (13 September) or the St Thecla Festival (24 September).

Maaloula Hotel (☎ 777 0250; maaloula@scs-net .org; s/d US$95/111; ☒) This comfortable four-star offers clean, spacious rooms, and full amenities include a good restaurant serving Syrian and European food, and a coffee shop and bar.

Convent of St Thecla It's also possible to stay overnight in simple rooms at the convent. There are no fixed rates; make a generous donation instead.

La Grotta (☎ 777 0909) Adjacent to the Monastery and Church of St Sergius, this sparkling clean café in a light-filled stone building serves up excellent pizza, sandwiches, ice cream, cold beer and drinks. There's also a pleasant sun terrace.

There are a few snack places in the centre of town near the convent.

Getting There & Away

From Damascus, minibuses (S£25, one hour) depart from Maalula garage. In Maalula, buses stop at the main intersection in the village centre, just downhill from the Convent of St Thecla.

To proceed to Mar Musa, grab a Damascus-bound minibus and ask to be let off on the Damascus–Aleppo Hwy (a 10-minute ride away); there, flag down any bus or minibus going north to Homs or Aleppo

and ask to be let off at Nebek. From Nebek you will need to negotiate with a driver (around S£300 each way) to take you to the monastery.

MAR MUSA   مار موسى

At the ancient **Monastery of Mar Musa** (☎ 011-742 0403; www.deirmarmusa.org; admission by donation), also known as the Monastery of St Moses the Abyssian or Deir Mar Musa el-Habashi, it's very much like the last 1500 years never happened. A throwback to the 6th-century heyday of Byzantine Christianity, when the arid alienating landscape provided shelter for thousands of tiny, isolated, self-sustaining and pious communities, Mar Musa is one of the very few monasteries to survive.

Perched high on the edge of a cliff, facing east over a vast, barren plain, Mar Musa is well and truly off the beaten track. It's over 17km from the nearest town, the last stretch involving a sweaty 20-minute walk along a steep-sided rocky gorge.

According to legend, the monastery was founded in the 6th century AD by Moses (or Musa), the son of the King of Abyssinia (modern-day Ethiopia and Eritrea), who chose monastic life over the throne. The church was built in the 11th century, according to Arabic inscriptions on the walls. By this time the monastery was the seat of a local bishopric, flourishing into the 15th century, then gradually declining until it was finally abandoned in the 1830s. An Italian former Jesuit rediscovered it in the 1980s and, with the help of the local community

MEDITATIONS ON MAR MUSA *Terry Carter*

Along a dusty, almost deserted road about 60km from Damascus we passed a utility truck. Instead of the usual sheep or goats in the back, there was a lone backpacker in his early twenties – telltale white iPod earphones firmly in place – accompanied by several bales of hay. He smiled as we drove past, making our way to Mar Musa, another 20km or so away.

As we pulled up we were stunned by the dramatic setting, and even more stunned by the hike that lay ahead of us, up to one of the most fascinating monasteries in the world. By the look on our driver's face when he saw the path, we could tell that this was one sight our torpid friend would not be leaving the car for.

It seems odd that an Italian priest perched 1320m above sea level in a half-ruined monastery could have an impact on world peace. But people tend to forget that Syria is the home of a number of religions and subdivisions of religions, making it a fascinating country for those of an ecumenical bent. Father Paolo came to remote Mar Musa in the early 1980s. The brilliant frescoes of the church had barely a roof over them and the rest of the monastery was in ruins. With EU funding and massive amounts of hard work, the monastery and small church have been restored, and more work is going on to create separate women's lodgings at this mountainside retreat.

Mar Musa attracts backpackers, religious scholars and intellectuals, those looking to promote religious harmony, and those that just want to get away from it all. When we arrived there were just three women and seven men in residence – mainly Syrians, here for a long-term stay. As we chatted and sipped tea, aromas from the hearty lunch being prepared wafted over to the communal table where it would be served. From here the view down to the plains was stunning and worth every torturous, sweat-soaked step to get up here.

The monastery offers several ways for you to give something back if you stay here, from helping with studies on sustainable development of agricultural activities, to building new accommodation or simply cooking and cleaning. The knowledge that you take away from the experience – that people of different religions and cultures can live together in harmony – is what keeps Father Paolo here.

As we drove away, the backpacker we had seen before was walking alone on the stark road that leads towards the monastery. He had already put away his iPod. We didn't envy the hike he had before him, but we did the experience that he'd have.

and foreign funding, undertook to renovate the place and have it reconsecrated (see Meditations on Mar Musa, above).

A highlight of a visit here and the pride of the monastery is its ancient church, which contains several layers of beautiful frescoes, dating to the 11th, 12th and 13th centuries. Note the fresco of St Simeon, who appears to be in a cage on top of his pillar.

Since 1991 the monastery has been home to a small group of monks, nuns and novices, who numbered ten at the time of writing. As well as being mixed sex, Mar Musa is doubly unconventional in that it is also ecumenical, with both Syrian Catholics and Syrian Orthodox Christians represented within the community.

Visitors are made very welcome and it's possible to stay here. Basic accommodation and simple meals are free (bring your own sleeping bag; check the website for more information), but guests must take an active part in the community's life, praying and meditating with the monks, and helping out with cooking, cleaning and other manual work. Telephone or email if you're coming in a group, or would like to stay longer than one night.

Getting There & Away

To get to Mar Musa from Damascus, take a microbus from Abbasseen garage to Nebek (النبك; S£30, 50 minutes), 80km northeast of Damascus on the road to Homs and Aleppo, or take a bus from the Harasta terminal. Coming from Maalula on a Homs or Aleppo bus, you'll be dropped off on the highway at the Nebek turn-off, a 2km walk from town, but you have a good chance of getting a ride in. A taxi from Damascus or Homs will cost S£1500 return.

Once in Nebek, you should be able to negotiate a driver for the 17.5km to Mar Musa (S£300 return, 30 minutes); make sure to arrange for the driver to wait or return to pick you up, as the phone at Mar Musa doesn't always work. Once dropped off, you must walk the last 1.5km (about 20 minutes) along a steep winding path.

BARADA GORGE   وادي بردى

The Barada River flows into Damascus from the west, winding down from the magnificent Jebel Libnan ash-Sharqiyya and through low foothills to reach the city. The valley through which the Barada flows is splendid, with the river's fertile, green banks making a dramatic contrast to the rocky red mountains around it. Damascenes flock here on Fridays and throughout summer for riverside picnics. For the traveller, the main attraction is the trip through the magnificent Barada Gorge (Wadi Barada) on the narrow-gauge train called 'the Zabadani Flyer', so named because the main destination was once **Zabadani** (الزبداني), only 50km from Damascus but a rollicking three- to four-hour journey by train.

These days the train only goes as far as leafy **Ain al-Fijeh** (عين الفيجه), with its charming two-storey train station, but it's still fun. The antiquated wooden carriages are generally loaded with a wonderful cross-section of Syrian people – from elderly veiled women with children and grandchildren in tow, to groups of flirty teenage couples – all hauled by a groaning, wheezing old Swiss-built steam train. According to local legend, west of Ain al-Fijeh, on the mountain of Nebi Habil, is the site where Cain buried Abel after killing him.

Pretty Zabadani, situated on a fertile plain of fruit orchards, is still the Barada's most popular destination. Its 1200m altitude means it's considerably cooler than the capital. The hills here are clustered with holiday homes and the main street lined with restaurants and cafés. Downhill from the station is the older part of the village, with an old mosque and Catholic church. Wealthy Damascenes prefer the smaller, more exclusive getaway spot of **Bludan** (بلودان), some 7 km east of Zabadani.

Getting There & Away
The Zabadani Flyer leaves from Khaddam train station in Damascus at 7am on Friday (S£30), going as far as Ain al-Fijeh and returning to Damascus around 4pm.

EZRA'A   ازرع
☎ 015
Tiny Ezra'a has two of Syria's oldest still-functioning churches, the Basilica of St George and, just nearby, the Church of St Elias.

The Greek Orthodox **Basilica of St George** (Kineeset Mar Jirjis) stands on the site of an earlier pagan temple, as suggested by an inscription, dated AD 515, above the west entrance (to the left of the current entrance), which reads:

What once was a lodging place for demons has become a house of God; where idols once were sacrificed, there are now choirs of angels; where God was provoked to wrath, now He is propitiated.

The basilica's excellent state of preservation can be explained by the fact that it is believed to be the burial place of St George. (For more on St George and Syria, see p136.) There are no fixed opening times; if the church is locked, ask the locals for the caretaker or priest.

The 6th-century Melchite Greek Catholic **Church of St Elias** is also well preserved. It was one of the first churches anywhere to be built in the shape of a cross, a style that would later become popular.

If you have your own wheels, Ezra'a can be easily squeezed into a day trip to the Hauran region.

Getting There & Away
Minibuses to Ezra'a (S£25, 1½ hours) depart when full from the Bab Mousala garage in Damascus, dropping you off in central Ezra'a; the churches are 3km to the north. If you're lucky you might find a taxi or a ride, otherwise you'll need to walk.

BOSRA   بصره
☎ 015
The brooding black basalt town of Bosra (or Bosra ash-Sham), with its impressive, imposing citadel and one of the best-preserved Roman theatres in existence, is a must-do experience. The Nabataean capital in the 1st century BC and the capital of the Roman Province of Arabia from AD 106, Bosra has multiple layers of architectural history, making it one of Syria's most

engaging sights. As there is little else to see in town, a day trip from Damascus leaves ample time for most travellers to take in everything at a leisurely pace.

History

Bosra was mentioned in Egyptian records as early as 1300 BC, but it was not until the Nabataean kingdom relocated here from Petra, and Rome crowned it capital of the Province of Arabia, that its importance was secured. The fertile land surrounding the city, and the 1st-century construction of a road linking it with Damascus in the north and Amman in the south, ensured Bosra would become an important centre of trade and a key stop on caravan and pilgrimage routes throughout the Middle Ages.

During the Byzantine period, Bosra became a bishopric then archbishopric, and during the 6th century the largest cathedral in the region was built here, becoming one of the greatest in the East. Before the town's fall to the Muslims in 634, the young Prophet Mohammed, passing through with his merchant uncle's caravans, encountered a wise

priest named Bahira who, during theological discussions with Mohammed, revealed to him his future vocation as the Prophet.

An impressive example of Arab military architecture, the citadel was built in the 11th century and strengthened further by Saladin in the 12th century, enabling it to withstand both Crusader and Mongol attacks.

Today Bosra's friendly inhabitants live among the ruins of the old town.

Orientation & Information

The ruins and modern town lie just to the north of the main east–west road between Der'a and Suweida. Al-Muhib buses drop off outside their office 100m short of the citadel; Damas Tours buses and microbuses from Der'a pass the citadel and drop off 400m further along the road. Money can be changed at the Bosra Cham Palace hotel.

Sights

CITADEL & THEATRE

The **citadel** (adult/student S£150/10; ☺ 9am-8pm Jul-Aug, to 7pm Sep-Oct, to 4pm Nov-Jun) is a unique

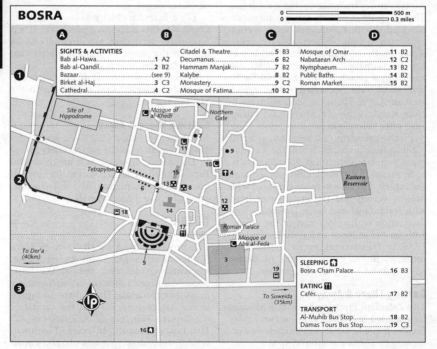

BOSRA

SIGHTS & ACTIVITIES		
Bab al-Hawa......................1 A2	Citadel & Theatre................5 B3	Mosque of Omar...............11 B2
Bab al-Qandil...................2 B2	Decumanus........................6 B2	Nabataean Arch.................12 C2
Bazaar.........................(see 9)	Hammam Manjak...............7 B2	Nymphaeum.......................13 B2
Birket al-Haj...................3 C3	Kalybe...............................8 B2	Public Baths......................14 B2
Cathedral.......................4 C2	Monastery.........................9 C2	Roman Market...................15 B2
	Mosque of Fatima.............10 B2	

Site of Hippodrome

Mosque of al-Khedr

Northern Gate

Tetrapylon

Eastern Reservoir

To Der'a (40km)

Roman Palace

Mosque of Abu al-Feda

To Suweida (35km)

SLEEPING 🏠	
Bosra Cham Palace.....................16 B3	

EATING 🍴	
Cafés..17 B2	

TRANSPORT	
Al-Muhib Bus Stop.......................18 B2	
Damas Tours Bus Stop................19 C3	

construction that began life as a classical Roman theatre and later had its impressive Arab fortifications grafted on. It's a wonderful experience to be lost within the dark, cavernous fortress halls, only to pass through a sunlit opening to find yourself looking down onto a vast terraced hillside of stone seating.

Buried under sand and long obscured by more recent buildings, including ramshackle residents' houses, the theatre's full glory was only laid bare in the 20th century. Built early in the 2nd century AD, it accommodated 9000 people (6000 seated and 3000 standing) and followed the conventions of Roman theatre design. The stage is backed by rows of Corinthian columns and originally had a façade of white marble, decorated with statues, and a wooden roof, while the rest of the theatre was covered by a retractable cloth shading. During performances perfumed water was sprayed into the air, a fragrant mist descending soothingly upon the spectators.

The citadel was built around the theatre in stages. The first walls were built during the Umayyad and Seljuk periods, with further additions made by the Ayyubids in 1200, following Crusader attacks in 1140 and 1183. The Ayyubids strengthened the fortifications by constructing more towers, resulting in the ring of eight towers connected by thick walls, encircling the theatre like a protective jacket.

The southwest tower contains a museum of popular culture and tradition, with scenes of Arab life depicted using mannequins and various exhibits of clothing and utensils. It's often closed, so ask at the ticket desk as you enter.

The theatre blossoms into life for the **Bosra Festival** (August to September; held every odd-numbered year and there is talk to make it an annual event), when it becomes an impressive venue for drama and concerts.

OLD TOWN
The remains of the old Roman town lie north of the theatre, covering around 1 sq km. The best approach is to walk around the north side of the citadel and then bear right for the Bab al-Qandil. As the site is unbounded, there is no admission fee or opening hours.

The **Bab al-Qandil** (Gate of the Lantern) is a monumental arch, with one great central arch flanked by two smaller arches. Dating from the early 3rd century, an inscription on one pillar states that it was erected in memory of the Third Legion, which was garrisoned here.

The gate marks an intersection with the old town's main east–west street, the colonnaded **decumanus**, which has been excavated to reveal its cobbled surface and parallel rows of column bases. At the western end of the decumanus rises the **Bab al-Hawa** (Gate of the Wind), a plain, single-arched structure that's flanked by the remains of the Roman-era city walls.

Returning east, the large dilapidated structure off to the right (south) is what remains of the **public baths**. Though the building is in a bad state, it is possible to get some sense of how it functioned. You enter off the decumanus into a large octagonal room that would have served as the changing hall; from here you pass into the *frigidarium* (cold room), which leads to a *tepidarium* (warm room) with a *caldarium* (hot room) either side.

Almost opposite the baths are four enormous Corinthian columns set at an angle to the decumanus – this is what's left of the **nymphaeum**, or public water fountain. On the side of the street heading north you can see another column and lintel incorporated into a modern house. It is believed that this is what remains of a **kalybe**, an open-air shrine for the display of statuary.

This street leads north, past the remains of a long rectangular **Roman market** with a paved plaza, to the **Mosque of Omar** (known by locals as Jami al-Arus), still in use today. According to local legend, it was built by (and named for) Caliph Omar, under whose leadership Syria was conquered in 636, making it one of the earliest mosques in the world. However, more recently archaeologists have identified it with Caliph Yazid II, placing its construction around 720. Further restoration of the mosque by the Ayyubids took place in the 12th or 13th centuries.

Nearly opposite the mosque, the **Hammam Manjak** was only fully revealed in the early 1990s. Built in 1372 under the Mamluks, this bathhouse served the passing pilgrim trade, and archaeologists consider it a masterpiece of medieval architectural engineering.

Head back south and bear left for the small **Mosque of Fatima**, notable for a square minaret separate from the main building. Built by the Fatimids in the 11th century, it was named after the Prophet's daughter. North of the mosque is Bosra's oldest **monastery**, thought to have been built in the 4th century. Locals believe this is where Mohammed met the priest Bahira. The façade has been rebuilt but the walls and apse are original. The square in front of the monastery is a makeshift **bazaar** where a couple of stalls sell dusty antiques and bric-a-brac.

South of the monastery lie the ruins of the **cathedral** (c 512), considered another masterpiece of early Christian architecture. It represents one of the earliest attempts to surmount a square base with a circular dome and was rebuilt a number of times before abandonment. Only the nave and two antechambers are still standing.

Continuing south, this small street intersects with the eastern end of the decumanus, marked by a **Nabataean arch**. Marking the edge of the Roman city, the gate was also probably the entrance to a Nabataean residence, thought to be the home of the Christian bishop. Beyond this is a massive Roman reservoir, 120m by 150m, which goes by the name of **Birket al-Haj** (Pool of the Pilgrimage), a reference to the era when Bosra was a stopover for pilgrims heading to Mecca.

Sleeping & Eating

Bosra Cham Palace (☎ 790 881/2/3; www.chamhotels .com; s/d US$110/130; ✖ 🖳 ⛱) A few hundred metres south of the theatre, this comfortable five-star is Bosra's only accommodation, boasting two decent restaurants, a bar and a café. Reservations are essential during the Bosra Festival.

There are several decent yet unremarkable cafés in the square beside the citadel/theatre, and a couple of cheap felafel and grilled chicken places on Sharia Ghasasena, near where the Damas Tours bus stops.

Getting There & Away

Damas Tours and Al-Muhib both run frequent, direct bus services between Bosra and the new Al-Samariyeh bus station in Damascus (S£60, two hours). Return buses leave every two hours, from 6am to 6pm, but it's wise to double-check departure times

at the bus company office when you arrive, and buy your return ticket in advance. Allow at least two hours for a quick look, half a day for a more leisurely visit. There are no buses from Bosra to Suweida.

SHAHBA   شهبا
☎ 016 / pop 22,000

Shahba, 90km south of Damascus, was founded as Philipopolis by the Hauran's most famous son, Emperor Philip of Rome. Construction of Philipopolis began in AD 244, the year of Philip's accession, and it was laid out in a classic Roman grid pattern oriented to the cardinal points of the compass, with four great gates in the surrounding walls. Unfortunately, building was halted abruptly when Philip was murdered five years into his reign. The town thrived for another century – as the magnificent 4th-century mosaics in Suweida's museum testify – but it was later abandoned. It only came to life again in the 19th century when settled by the Druze, who still comprise most of the population today.

The road from Damascus slowly climbs from the plain below up towards Shahba, entering via the partially reconstructed Roman north gate and proceeding down the modern main street, following the ancient town's cardo maximus (main north–south street). A roundabout at the town centre lies at the intersection with the Roman-era east–west decumanus. Ruins are everywhere and all the sights of interest are no more than a few minutes' walk away.

If you head right along the partly intact cobbled decumanus, past four **columns** on the right (the remains of a temple portico), you'll see a number of buildings of interest on the left, arranged around a large open space that was once the **forum** of Roman Philipopolis. The best-preserved of these buildings, on the south side of the square, appears to have been a family **shrine** dedicated to Philip's father, Julius Marinus. A set of stairs in the southeast corner gives access to the roof for a view over the site. The impressive structure on the western side of the forum, consisting of a series of niches arranged in a semicircle, is the remains of a palace facade. Just behind the shrine lies a modest **theatre**, with fish sculpted on the walls of the vaulted passages that lead to the seats.

Follow the street in front of the theatre 400m west to reach the remains of the town's **Roman baths** and, on the opposite side of the street, a small **museum** (adult/student S£75/15; 9am-6pm Wed-Mon Mar-Nov, 9am-4pm Wed-Mon Dec-Feb) with some fine 4th-century mosaics.

Getting There & Away
Suweida-bound buses pass through Shahba, which is 20km to the north, so the best way to visit both places is to hop off in Shahba, take a look around, then hop on one of the frequent microbuses heading south to Suweida (S£5, 15 minutes) that stop on the main street. Otherwise, minibuses from Damascus (S£25, 1¼ hours) run direct to Shahba from the Bab Mousala garage.

SUWEIDA السويدا
☎ 016 / 62,000
Capital of the Hauran, Suweida has a place in the hearts of many Syrians for two reasons: it's the centre of the viticulture industry (Syria's best wine and arak come from here) and the birthplace of Farid al-Atrache, a giant of the golden age of Arab music (see Farid al-Atrache, p72). For the casual visitor, however, anything of interest in this largely Druze town has been swept away by modern expansion. The town centre is unremarkable and the main reason to visit is Suweida's impressive museum. There is little else to keep you overnight, and it's an easy day trip from Damascus.

Orientation & Information
The main bus station is on the northern edge of town, a little over a kilometre from the centre, and just west of a large roundabout with a bronze relief of Basel al-Assad on horseback as its centrepiece. The museum is east of the roundabout (follow the road uphill for a kilometre) in an imposing grey modern building on the left.

To get to the town centre from the bus station or museum, walk due south to central Saahat Assad (Assad Sq), which resembles a large parking lot. It is distinguished by a prominent statue of the ex-president; nearby is another of Sultan Basel al-Attrache, hero of the 1925 revolution. The square is home to the minibus station, a good produce market selling delicious, fresh, locally grown fruit, and a modest shopping area. There's a branch of the **Commercial Bank of**

Syria (9am-2.30pm Sat-Thu) one block east of Saahat Assad that will change cash.

Sights
The French helped to build and curate Suweida's **museum** (adult/student S£150/15; 9am-6pm Apr-Sep, to 4pm Oct-Mar, closed Tue), housing an impressive archaeological collection covering the Hauran history from the Stone Age to the Roman era. There's prehistoric pottery, an extensive array of basalt statuary, and a kitschy-cool popular-tradition section. The highlight is the stunning 4th-century mosaics from Shahba. Descriptions are in Arabic and French only.

Suweida is graced by enormous, creamy stone **villas**, set among lush gardens with fruit trees. They were built with foreign remittances from Venezuela, Brazil and Argentina, second homes to Syrian expatriates from Suweida.

The only other points of interest are the old Ottoman-era **Governor's Residence** and an **arch with columns** that was once the old city gate, but is now stranded on a roundabout on the Der'a road.

Eating
There are numerous eateries in the town centre, including **Al-Amir** (Sharia 29 Mai), which serves decent Syrian fare, and **Asrar** (Sharia Hafez al-Assad), which does shwarma, grilled chicken and kebabs.

Getting There & Away
Luxury buses run frequently throughout the day between Damascus (from the new Al-Samariyeh bus station) and Suweida (S£40, 1¾ hours); in Suweida catch them from the main bus station. A minibus from Damascus (from the Bab Mousala garage) takes 1¾ hours and costs S£25.

QANAWAT قناوات
☎ 016
The village of Qanawat was a member of the Roman-inspired Decapolis, a politico-economic alliance of cities in the region that included such major centres as Jerash, Philadelphia (Amman) and Gadara (Umm Qais) in Jordan. While Qanawat flourished during the time of Trajan (AD 98–117), it declined with the arrival of Islam and was all but abandoned before being resettled by Druze in the 19th century.

Today it's a small agricultural hamlet of low black-stone buildings, many constructed from blocks from the ancient structures. Famed for its abundant and delicious fruit – try the mouth-watering mulberries or apricots – the area is beautiful in spring and early summer, when the fruit falls from the trees and the fields are carpeted with wildflowers.

Qanawat is a short minibus ride northeast of Suweida. Hop out at the *al-muderiyya* (town hall), a small, single-storey building with an entrance gate surmounted by the colours of the Syrian flag. Beside the town hall, a road is signposted 'To the ruins'. It runs up beside the picturesque gorge of Wadi al-Ghar, and from the road you can see the ruins of a **theatre** and a **nymphaeum**.

At the top of the hill is an open square with Qanawat's most interesting monument, the **Saray** (Palace; adult/student S£75/10; 9am-6pm Apr-Sep, to 4pm Oct-Mar, closed Tue), a ramshackle complex of temples. The most intact building is Roman, dating from the second half of the 2nd century AD. It was later converted into a Byzantine basilica when the area was given over to Christian worship. On entering the basilica you'll see recessed niches to the right; once a shrine, each niche probably held a small statue. The second area, with two rows of columns, is dominated by a monumental gateway on the north side. The pretty reliefs of grapevines you see are evidence of the region's centuries-old connection with viticulture.

As you leave the Saray, turn left to see the fine underground **cistern**, now minus its roof covering so you can see the rows of stone arches. Beyond are the remains of yet another **temple**, possibly dedicated to Zeus.

Return to the town hall for the minibus back to Suweida, but first take a quick stroll 200m south, where off to the right (west) are seven columns standing atop an almost square platform, the remains of the **Helios temple**. Today it's hemmed in by fertile farmers' gardens.

Getting There & Away

Minibuses regularly depart from Suweida's bus station for Qanawat (S£5, 10 minutes), more frequently in the morning, less so in the afternoon.

GOLAN HEIGHTS
مرتفعات الجولان

The Golan Heights in the southwest of the country mark the border between Syria and Israel and the Palestinian Territories. Originally Syrian territory, the Golan was lost to the Israelis in the Six Day War of 1967. After the Yom Kippur War of 1973, a delicate truce was negotiated between Israel and Syria by then–US secretary of state Henry Kissinger, which saw Syria regain some 450 sq km of lost territory. A complicated demilitarised buffer zone, supervised by UN forces, was also established, varying in width from a few hundred metres to a couple of kilometres.

In 1981 the Israeli government upped the stakes by formally annexing part of the Golan and moving in settlers. In Israeli eyes the heights are an indispensable shield against potential Syrian attack. The Syrians, of course, see things differently.

Syria's position is straightforward – Israel must completely withdraw from all of the Golan Heights before Syria will contemplate peace. This approach has been met by an equally intransigent response from Israel. It's hard to see the Golan Heights stalemate being broken any time soon.

While travel through the Golan Heights is not allowed, you can visit the town of Quneitra.

QUNEITRA   القنيطرة

It's been 30 years since a shot has been fired in Quneitra, once the area's administrative capital, but the ruins of this destroyed town serve as a bitter daily reminder of the conflict. Before the Israelis withdrew from the town after the 1973 ceasefire, they evacuated the 37,000 Arabs here and systematically destroyed Quneitra, removing anything that could be unscrewed, unbolted or wrenched from its position. Everything from windows to light fittings was sold to Israeli contractors, and the stripped buildings were pulled apart with tractors and bulldozers.

Quneitra today is a ghost town. The rubble of demolished houses lies next to the empty shells of mosques and churches rising among strangely peaceful scenes of

CROSSING INTO JORDAN

If you are looking for the best way to get between Damascus and Amman, then stick with the regular twice-daily direct bus, which goes by the alternative border crossing at Nasib/Jabir, southeast of Der'a. True, you could maybe knock a dollar or two off the fare by doing it yourself in a combination of minibuses and service taxis, but the inconvenience renders the exercise uneconomical and frustrating. However, if you are down in the Hauran already and don't want to double back to Damascus, crossing the border independently is straightforward enough, although it can involve a bit of hiking. Service taxis shuttle directly between the bus stations in Der'a and Ramtha (on the Jordanian side), and cost S£150 or JD2 per person.

Otherwise, you need to hitch or walk. Try to get a local bus from the Der'a bus station (on the outskirts of town) into the centre of Der'a, to save yourself the first 3km of walking. From there, head south on the Jordan road (signposted) and hitch or walk the 4km to the Syrian checkpoint. Once through formalities here, it's another 3km or so to the Jordanian checkpoint. The soldiers here may not allow you to walk the last kilometre or so to the immigration post, but are friendly and will flag down a car or bus for you. From Ramtha, minibuses go on to Mafraq, Irbid and Zarqa, from where you can proceed to Amman.

There is no departure tax and a Jordanian visa can be picked up on the spot at the border post for JD10 (approximately US$15).

devastation. The main street's once-prosperous banks and shops are lifeless, and the pockmarked hospital is the centrepiece for what has become something of a propaganda exhibit demonstrating the Israelis' senseless aggressiveness.

Quneitra is under Syrian control within a UN-patrolled demilitarised zone. There's a UN checkpoint in the town and barbed wire marking the border between Syrian territory and Israeli-occupied land. From a viewpoint near the checkpoint you can easily make out Israeli communication and observation posts on the other side. Much of the area is riddled with land mines.

Before visiting Quneitra, it's worth paying a visit to the Tishreen (October) War Panorama in Damascus (p99).

Entry Permits

To visit Quneitra you must obtain a permit from the **Ministry of the Interior** (Map p80; ☉ 8am-2pm Sun-Thu), off Saahat Adnan al-Malki in Abu Roumana, the embassy district of Damascus. To reach the building from the square, head west uphill with the steep grassy park on your right. Take the flight of stairs in front of you. The Ministry is in the unsigned, four-storey building second from the left (number 15). Hand your passport to the guys in the portable white guard box–cum-office. You won't be allowed inside so you need to patiently wait the 15 to 20 minutes it will take to get your permit. You have the option of getting the pass for that particular day or for the following day – it's best to arrive before 9am and get it for that day.

Getting There & Away

Official advice is to visit Quneitra from Damascus with your own car or with a driver and car (from US$60). There are a few reasons for this. Firstly, the Syrian intelligence officers who guide you around the site don't like doing it on foot (it's a large site and they have to do it several times a day) and have been known to turn visitors on foot away at the checkpoint. Secondly, when you get your permit, you'll be required to provide your car registration number, and the name and identification card of your driver if you have one. Thirdly, if you don't speak Arabic, an English-speaking driver will be a great help, as the officers don't speak English – they're just there to make sure you don't wander off into any minefields. When you arrive at the checkpoint you'll be asked for your permit and presented with your 'tour guide'; tip him generously at the end of your visit.

The Coast & Mountains
الساحل السوري والجبال

Syria's 183km-long Mediterranean coastline is dominated by the rugged 250km-long Jebel Ansariyya mountain range that runs along its entire length. Squeezed between the highland and the sea is a narrow coastal strip that widens towards the south, where the country is extremely fertile and agriculturally rich.

The port city of Lattakia (Al-Lathqiyya), with its beach resorts, and the ruined ancient city of Ugarit (Ras Shamra) lie in the north. Boasting a large population of Alawites and Christians, lively Lattakia is one of Syria's most vibrant cities, with a buzzing restaurant and café scene, and a bustling souq and shopping area. It's also one of the country's friendliest cities, making a stay here lots of fun.

From here roads lead north to Turkey, east across the mountains to Aleppo, and south to Tartus, a secondary port that preserves remnants of its medieval Crusader past in its ramshackle old town and on the tiny island of Arwad.

The mountains behind Lattakia contain thick forests, which are easy on the eyes after the often-featureless interior. Travellers who have spent time in the cities will find the air considerably fresher, too. Following excessive clearing of the forests for timber in the past, the government has laid aside sections for preservation.

Of most interest to travellers is that much of this area was in Crusader hands for centuries. They left behind a chain of spectacular hilltop eyries and precipitously located castles, the undisputed king of which is the stalwart Qala'at al-Hosn (Krak des Chevaliers).

HIGHLIGHTS

- Marvel at **Qala'at al-Hosn** (Krak des Chevaliers; opposite), possibly the finest Crusader castle in the world, as you mosey around its majestic ruins

- Kick back for a couple of days in the lively port town of **Lattakia** (p144), with its tree-lined boulevards, excellent restaurants, buzzing cafés and bustling shopping streets

- Speculate on how the temple of **Hosn Suleiman** (p142) was constructed so high up in the picturesque mountains

- Appreciate why TE Lawrence thought **Qala'at Salah ad-Din** (p151) was the most awe-inspiring example of castle building

- Roam the ramshackle old quarter of **Tartus** (p137), a low-key port town and a pleasant place to unwind for a couple of days

Qala'at Salah ad-Din ★

★ Lattakia

Hosn Suleiman ★

★ Tartus

Qala'at al-Hosn (Krak des Chevaliers) ★

QALA'AT AL-HOSN (KRAK DES CHEVALIERS)

قلعة الحصن

☎ 031

Author Paul Theroux described Qala'at al-Hosn as the epitome of the dream castle of childhood fantasies of jousts and armour and pennants. TE Lawrence simply called it 'the finest castle in the world'. Take their word for it: the remarkably well-preserved Qala'at al-Hosn (Krak des Chevaliers) is one of Syria's unmissable attractions. Impervious to the onslaught of time, it cannot have looked a great deal different 800 years ago, and such is its size and state of completeness that you could easily spend several hours absorbed in exploring it. A torch is handy for some of the darker passages and rooms.

The castle is easily visited by public transport as a day trip from Tartus or Hama. However, visiting by car allows for exploring the surrounding countryside and hilltop resort towns, which is highly recommended. Anybody passing through en route to Homs, Tartus or elsewhere can leave bags and packs at the ticket office.

History

The castle addresses the only significant break in the Jebel Ansariyya. Anyone who held this breach, known as the Homs Gap, between the southern end of the range and the northern outreaches of the Jebel Libnan ash-Sharqiyya (Anti-Lebanon Range), was virtually assured authority over inland Syria by controlling the flow of goods and people from the ports through to the interior.

The first fortress that is known to have existed on this site was built by the emir of Homs in 1031. He was briefly displaced in 1099 by the hordes of the First Crusade passing through on its way to Jerusalem, and was then given the complete push some 11 years later when the Christian knights, now established in the Holy City, began to extend their gains throughout the region. Around the middle of the 12th century the elite Knights Hospitaller replaced the First Crusaders and expanded Qala'at al-Hosn into its present form.

The knights built well and, despite repeated attacks and sieges, the fortress was never truly breached. When the Mamluk sultan Beybars marched on the castle in 1271, the knights at Qala'at al-Hosn were

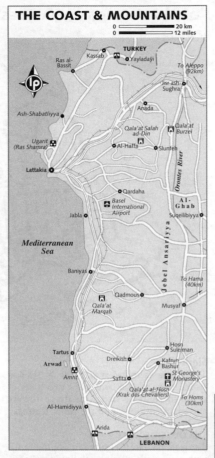

THE COAST & MOUNTAINS

a last outpost. Jerusalem had been lost and the Christians were retreating. Numbers in the castle, built to hold a garrison of 2000, were depleted to around 200. Surrounded by the armies of Islam and with no hope of reprieve, the Crusaders departed after a month, having negotiated safe conduct to head to Tripoli.

Beybars garrisoned the castle with his Mamluk troops and further strengthened the defences. Today it is possible to distinguish the Frankish aspects of the castle, with their Gothic and Romanesque building styles, and those of the Arabs – there are some beautiful Islamic geometric designs carved into structures on the upper levels of the main complex.

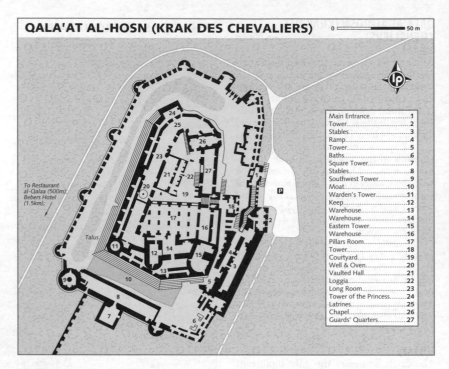

QALA'AT AL-HOSN (KRAK DES CHEVALIERS)   0 ——— 50 m

Sights

The **castle** (adult/student S£150/10; ☼ 9am-6pm Apr-Oct, to 4pm Nov-Mar) comprises two distinct parts: the outside wall with its 13 towers and main entrance; and the inner fortress.

THE OUTSIDE WALL

The **main entrance** (1) leads to a sloping ramp with steps wide enough to allow the garrison's horses to be ridden two abreast. The first **tower** (2) on the left was a guard room and, next to it, the **long hall** (3) served as stables – it's now a dark storeroom filled with building equipment. The ramp eventually emerges in a more open area where the passage doubles back on itself to lead up into the inner fortress, as well as continuing on ahead to exit via another **tower** (5), which gives access out into the moat area. As you emerge look back at the outer face of the doorway to see, carved into the stone, representations of two lions facing each other, possibly symbols of the English Crusader king, Richard I 'the Lion-Heart'.

The **moat** (10) here is usually full of stagnant water. When the castle was occupied, this water was used to fill the **baths** (6), which you can get down to by a couple of dogleg staircases over in the corner to your left. These stairs lead into a tight complex of rooms and those familiar with hammams will recognise the layout: there's a central chamber with a stone fountain; off it are private washrooms, a couple of which still contain stone basins. This was a Mamluk or later addition.

The cavernous room on the southern edge of the moat measures 60m by 9m and the roof is formed of one single vault – quite an impressive feat in stone. It was most likely used as **stables** (8). On exiting the western end of the hall two sets of stairs (these are quite decrepit, so be careful of your footing) give access to the battlements above. From up here it is possible to gain access to each of the three towers that punctuate the southern wall. The **square tower** (7) bore the brunt of the 1271 attack and was later rebuilt by Beybars. The **southwest tower** (9) was also rebuilt; its central pillar, which supports the upper levels of the construction, bears an inscription in Arabic recording

Beybars' full title, which translates as 'the Manifest King, Pillar of the World and the Faith, Father of the Victory'.

Walking around between the two walls from the southwest tower, you reach the **Tower of the Princess** (24) in the northwestern corner, unusual in that it is wider than it is deep. On the façade are three rows of triple-pointed arches. A large projecting gallery, from where rocks were hurled at assailants, is concealed in the face. The eastern face of this tower has a rear gate opening onto the moat.

Continue walking clockwise to reach a flight of steps leading up into the inner fortress.

GETTING THERE & AWAY

Take the Al-Hamidiyya microbus (الحميدية; S£10) from Sharia 6 Tishreen near the train station in Tartus and ask to be let off at 'al-athaar' or 'the ruins'. You'll be dropped at the track leading to Amrit, from where it's a 2.5km walk, half of it through shaded pine forest and the rest through orchards, corn and cacti. You'll pass an army post (the firing ranges are a little disconcerting) and some 200m further on, immediately after passing some communications towers, you'll see the temple remains in the distance on the left – take the dirt track to your left. Continue along the paved road, take the next dirt track on your left, and this will bring you to the meghazils.

To get back to Tartus, return to the main road and flag down a microbus – most stop opposite the service station.

THE INNER FORTRESS

The steps lead up into an open, central **courtyard** (19). On the western side is a **loggia** (22), or portico, with a Gothic façade of seven arches, two of which are open doorways. The other five arches are windows, each subdivided by a delicate pillar with an acanthus-leaf capital. It's a surprisingly delicate structure to find in such massively brutal surrounds.

Beyond the loggia is a large **vaulted hall** (21), which was probably a reception room, and beyond this is a 120m **long room** (23) running the length of the western wall. At the northern end is what were the **latrines** (25), used until very recently judging by the smell, while towards the south of the hall

are the remains of a **well and oven** (20), the latter measuring more than 5m in diameter. This area probably doubled as a storage area and granary, stockpiled with provisions against sieges.

The **pillars room** (17) has five rows of heavy squat pillars and is vaulted with fist-sized stones. It may have been used as a refectory. Several nearby rooms were **warehouses** (13, 14 and 16). In one are the remains of massive pottery oil jars and in another there's an oil mill, more oil jars and a well.

Back in the courtyard, the **chapel** (26) has a nave of three bays of vaults. It was converted to a mosque after the Muslim conquest and the minbar (pulpit) still remains. The staircase that obstructs the main door is a later addition and leads to the upper floors of the fortress.

The upper floor of the Tower of the Princess is a **café** with tea, coffee, cold drinks and snacks. There are also toilets up here. From the café you can make your way over to the round tower in the southwest corner known as the **Warden's Tower** (11); this was where the Grand Master of the Hospitallers had his quarters. From the tower's roof are some magnificent views; on a clear day you can make out the solitary pale figure of Safita's keep to the west.

Sleeping & Eating

Given that Qala'at al-Hosn is only just over an hour from Tartus, Homs or even Hama, most people visit on a day trip; hence accommodation choices are limited. However, a stay here is relaxing and having time to view the castle from different vantage points and at different hours is as enjoyable as exploring the structure itself.

Bebers Hotel (☎ 734 1201; akrmbibars@mail .sy; s/d/tr US$25/30/35) This would be the best hotel near the castle even if it didn't have spectacular views of the citadel. The light-filled rooms are clean and comfortable and all come with private bathrooms, fridge and satellite TV. All rooms possess stunning views from balconies or windows that look directly across a valley to the castle, as the crow flies just a few hundred metres away. Rooms 101 and 212 have the best views. The hotel is a 20-minute walk from the main castle entrance. Meals (US$5) are available.

Francis Hotel (☎ 730 946/7/8; www.francishotel
.net; Wadi Nassarah, Amar; ste US$60-90; ✖ ☒) A
ten-minute drive from Qala'at al-Hosn,
this enormous hotel-apartment complex
is situated on a hillside overlooking Amar.
The spacious, well-equipped suites come
with kitchenettes and big balconies with
breathtaking views. There's an enormous
swimming pool, restaurant and bar. Reception staff speak English.

Restaurant al-Qalaa (☎ 734 0493; meal per person
S£300) This restaurant is in a lone, white,
two-storey building immediately west of
the castle, on the next hilltop. It's worth
dining here for the views alone. The menu
features typical Syrian fare, including grilled
chicken and mezze.

Getting There & Away

Qala'at al-Hosn lies some 10km north
of the Homs–Tartus highway and can be
visited on a day trip from either town.
Coming from Damascus or Hama, it's
necessary to change buses in Homs. Buses
from Homs to Qala'at al-Hosn (S£30, 1½
hours) leave every hour on the hour; the
last bus returning to Homs departs from
the castle at 5.30pm in summer or 2.30pm
in winter. The Cairo and Riad hotels in
Hama run organised tours to the castle
(see p164).

From Tartus, catch a Homs microbus.
You'll be dropped off on the main highway at the turn-off for the castle, where
there's usually a microbus (S£60) waiting
to take people up the hill. To return, catch
the microbus back down to the junction on
the Homs–Tartus highway and flag down a
passing microbus to Tartus.

AROUND QALA'AT AL-HOSN

☎ 031

The landscape surrounding Qala'at al-Hosn
is beautiful – low, rolling, emerald-green
hills, shaded with foliage. The high altitude
cools the temperature, and the small villages and towns that dot the hilltops, such
as **Amar**, **Dreikish**, **Mashtu Helu** and **Safita**, are
popular summer resorts, not just with na-
tive Syrians but with thousands of Syrian
expats returning annually for vacations.
Other than the keep at Safita (p142), the
area's main sight is St George's Monastery,
located in a valley a few kilometres northwest of Qala'at al-Hosn. As there's no way

of getting around by public transport, the
only way to see this attractive area is to hire
a car or sign up for an organised tour.

St George's Monastery دير مار جرجس

St George is one of the most popular Christian saints in the Middle East, where in Arabic he's known as Mar Jirjis. Traditionally
he's thought to have been a Palestinian con-
script in the Roman army who was executed
in the 3rd century AD for tearing up a copy
of the Emperor Diocletian's decree forbid-
ding the practise of Christianity. Legends
about him grew from the 6th century onwards and these stories were likely carried
back to Europe by returning Crusaders. In
1348 England's Edward III made George
patron of the Knights of the Garter. Long
before then, there were churches dedicated
to him throughout the Middle East, and the
first church on this particular site was built
possibly as early as the 6th century.

The **monastery** (Deir Mar Jirjis; ✖ 6am-8pm) of
today is fully functioning, and takes the
form of a modern, large, walled compound
at the bottom of a valley, with the guardian Qala'at al-Hosn clearly visible high on
a hilltop just a few kilometres away. The
priest or a guide will greet you and show
you the 'New Church', dating from 1857,
adorned with a fine carved-wood iconostasis depicting various scenes from the life
of Christ and topped by a row of wooden
birds about to take flight, along with beautiful icons from the Jerusalem school. The
13th-century 'Old Church', accessed across
a lower, sunken courtyard, has a smaller,
even more intricate iconostasis, which is
over 300 years old and depicts scenes from
the life of St George. A further 'Old Monastery' dating back to the 6th century was
recently opened to visitors.

To get here, take the road from the highway towards Nasira; 4km after the turn-off
for Hosn and Qala'at al-Hosn take a fork
to the left. If you don't have transport you
could arrange to go by taxi from Qala'at
al-Hosn; there and back, plus an hour or so
waiting time, should cost around S£300.

SLEEPING & EATING

Although there's plenty of accommodation scattered around the valley, it's highly
seasonal; from mid-June to mid-September
you need to book well in advance.

Al-Fahd Hotel (☎ 730 822, 730 559; Al-Mishtaia; d with breakfast US$20; 🗪) Around 2km from the monastery, on the main road, this modest place has simple, clean rooms with private bathrooms, and balconies with brilliant views across the valley to Qala'at al-Hosn.

Al-Wadi Hotel (☎ 773 0456; www.alwadihotel.com; Al-Mishtaia; s/d US$60/75; 🖳 🗪) Next door to Al-Fahd, this excellent hotel with traditional décor – Oriental lamps, kilims and crafts – has loads of character and a ski-lodge feel about it, with its big lobby and fireplace. The comfortable rooms are spacious yet cosy, with minibar and satellite TV, and balconies have spectacular views. The swimming pool is enormous and also has valley and castle vistas.

There are no eating options here other than the hotels.

TARTUS

طرطوس

☎ 043 / pop 93,000

Tartus, Syria's second port, is a small, scruffy town that is unlikely to set pulses racing, but which makes for a pleasant overnight visit. The town's principal attraction is the compact remnants of the Old City (known to the Crusaders as Tortosa), a fascinating little warren. There's also the once-fortified island of Arwad, which lies a few kilometres offshore and is reached by boat or water taxi. Syrians love Tartus for its beaches, but visitors brave enough to pick through the junk on the sand and go for a dip should note the occasional dribble of sewage into the sea.

History

Tartus is thought to have been established by the Phoenicians as a service town for the island of Arados (Arwad) and given the name Antarados (meaning 'Anti-Arados' or 'Opposite Arados'). It wasn't until the time of the Byzantines that Antarados became important – it's said that the emperor Constantine preferred the Christian community on the mainland to the island pagans, and the town became known as Constantina. With the Byzantine empire's collapse, the town passed into the hands of the Arabs, from whom it was wrested in 1099 by the Crusaders.

Under the new moniker of Tortosa, the town was strategically important for the Crusaders' sea links with Europe. They turned Tortosa into a fortified stronghold and built a cathedral in honour of the Virgin Mary, who had long been associated with this site. In 1152, after Muslim forces had briefly taken Tortosa, control of the town was given to the elite Knights Templar.

In 1188 Saladin led another Muslim assault and forced the Crusader knights to fall back to the main fortified keep, the town's last defence. This they held, and eventually the Muslims withdrew. The Knights Templar set about refortifying the town and defending the approaches with a series of castles. These precautions enabled them to hold Tortosa against a further two major attacks by the Mamluks, but eventually, as the remaining Crusader strongholds in the Holy Lands fell, the knights retreated to Arwad. There they maintained a garrison for 12 years before finally departing for Cyprus.

The town languished – hence its modest size – and only began to flourish once Syria gained independence. With the subsequent partitioning off of Lebanon and the handing over of the Antakya region to Turkey, Syria found itself with only one functioning port (Lattakia), making it necessary to revive Tartus.

Orientation

The heart of town is the area around Sharia al-Wahda, stretching between the roundabout with the clock tower at its eastern end and the fishing harbour at its western end. Just to the north is the Old City; south are the town's few shopping streets. The Kadmous bus station is around 500m north of the clock-tower roundabout. Microbuses and trains halt out on the main highway, Sharia 6 Tishreen, which marks the eastern edge of town – from here it's a 15- to 20-minute walk to the centre. The commercial port is north of the town.

Information

Commercial Bank of Syria (cnr Sharia Khaled ibn al-Walid & Sharia al-Orouba; ☺ 8am-noon Sat-Thu) On the northeast side of the Old City.

Immigration office (☺ 8am-2pm Sat-Thu) Just south of Sharia Jamal Abdel Nasser, one block east of the park (it's well signposted). Visa extensions (less than one hour to process) require two photos and two completed forms, along with S£30 for an excise stamp.

Internet Centre (☎ 315 906; Sharia ath-Thawra; per hr S£50; ☺ 10am-10pm) As you walk down Sharia

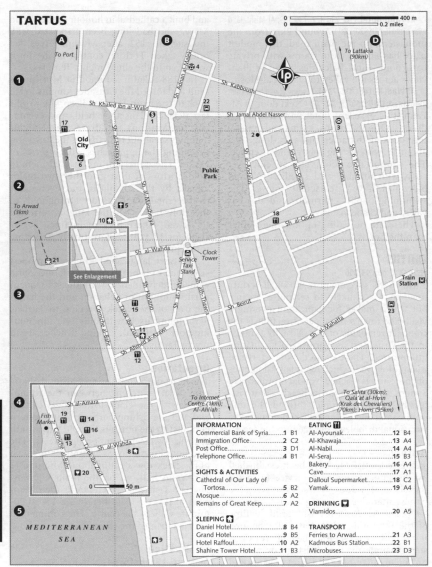

TARTUS

INFORMATION
Commercial Bank of Syria........1 B1
Immigration Office..................2 C2
Post Office...............................3 D1
Telephone Office.....................4 B1

SIGHTS & ACTIVITIES
Cathedral of Our Lady of
  Tortosa.................................5 B2
Mosque.....................................6 A2
Remains of Great Keep...........7 A2

SLEEPING
Daniel Hotel.............................8 B4
Grand Hotel.............................9 B5
Hotel Raffoul.........................10 A2
Shahine Tower Hotel............11 B3

EATING
Al-Ayounak...........................12 B4
Al-Khawaja............................13 A4
Al-Nabil.................................14 A4
Al-Seraj.................................15 B3
Bakery...................................16 A4
Cave......................................17 A1
Dallour Supermarket............18 C2
Yamak....................................19 A4

DRINKING
Viamidos...............................20 A5

TRANSPORT
Ferries to Arwad...................21 A3
Kadmous Bus Station...........22 B1
Microbuses............................23 D3

ath-Thawra, it's on the left-hand side about 1.5km south of the clock-tower roundabout; just look for a blue Ericsson sign.

Post office (cnr Sharia Jamal Abdel Nasser & Sharia 6 Tishreen; ☼ 8am-8pm Sat-Thu, to 2pm Fri) About a 15 minute walk from the centre of town.

Telephone office (Sharia Adnan al-Maleki; ☼ 24hr Sat-Thu, to 8pm Fri) Just north of the Sharia Khaled ibn

al-Walid and Sharia ath-Thawra junction. There are also a couple of card phones at the post office.

Sights
OLD CITY

The Old City is in essence the Crusader fortress of Tortosa, which over the centuries since the (un)holy knights departed has been occupied by local inhabitants. It's a compact area, tightly wrapped around by Sharia al-Khandek (which follows the course of the **old walls**, still visible in parts) on three sides and the seafront Corniche on the fourth. Between Sharia al-Khandek and Sharia al-Horreyya, a deep and wide grassy ditch remains as evidence of a **moat**.

The best impression of the fortifications is gained from the Corniche: you can pick out the bulky mass of the former **great keep**, or donjon, into which the Crusaders retreated when Saladin laid siege to the town in the 12th century. Much rebuilt and remodelled, it now forms part of a local municipal centre.

From the Corniche a short access road runs up to a ragged square – what would have been the castle's **courtyard**. The edges are blurred by a ramshackle assortment of newer structures, but it all blends with an admirable degree of unintentional harmony with the old broken stonework. It's worth exploring the narrow, snaking passageways off the square for the architectural surprises: a road north exits through a wonderfully muscular medieval gate, while a short flight of steps in the northeast corner leads to an arched passageway and then to the remains of a splendid vaulted hall, now half-open to the sky and sadly used as an unofficial garbage tip.

A mosque, several shops and a couple of coffeehouses around the square buzz with locals going about their business, adding to its modest charm.

CATHEDRAL OF OUR LADY OF TORTOSA
كاتدرائية طرطوس

Part cathedral, part fortress, Our Lady of Tortosa was constructed by the Crusaders in the 12th century, although a chapel dedicated to the Virgin Mary possibly existed on this site as early as the 4th century AD. Rebuilding on the existing consecrated site meant that the Crusader cathedral stood outside the walled enclave and hence was designed with its own defence in mind. This is particularly true of the rear of the building, which resembles a great keep complete with arrow slits. The only decorative elements are the five arched windows on the main façade (which were finished shortly before the Mamluks took over the

city in 1291) and the rebuilt doorway. It's a splendid piece of Crusader construction.

The interior is more recognisably ecclesiastic, with soaring arches and graceful vaulting, and is home to a tiny **archaeological museum** (adult/student S£150/10; 9am-6pm Apr-Sep, to 4pm Oct-Mar, closed Tue). There are some fascinating items on display, including exquisite jewellery, statuary and pottery from sites such as Ugarit (Ras Shamra), Arwad and Amrit, and there's good labelling in English.

ARWAD
أرواد

This small island, 3km southwest of Tartus, would be a gem if only it weren't so filthy. As it is, its walls are covered in graffiti and its streets often sprinkled with garbage. However, the boat ride out, skipping between the tankers, is good fun.

Founded by the Canaanites and at one stage occupied by the Egyptians, the island has a long and eventful history. In Phoenician times it was a prosperous and powerful maritime state, with colonies on the mainland at Amrit, Baniyas and Jabla. It gradually declined in the 1st millennium BC and was of little importance by the time it became part of the Roman Empire. During the Crusades it assumed strategic importance and in 1302 was the last Frankish outpost to fall to the Muslims.

Today there are no cars or wide streets, only a maze of narrow lanes that jog and jink between tightly packed buildings. It's densely populated by inhabitants who commute to the mainland via water taxi each day to work, although plenty are employed in the boat-building that goes on at two sites on the island, on the north and south tips. At any given time there are several timber skeletons of boats in various stages of construction. Otherwise, there's little else of interest.

Little is left of the island's defensive walls (just a stretch on the western side of the island), but two forts remain. The one that you see off to the right as you come into the harbour is closed to the public, but there's another on the island's highest point that houses a small **museum** (adult/student S£150/10; 9am-6pm Apr-Sep, to 4pm Oct-Mar, closed Tue). Sections of the museum were closed at the time of research, but the few exhibits we viewed were labelled in English. The views are fascinating. To find the museum just head directly inland and uphill from the harbour, past the souvenir shops selling sunhats, shell necklaces and trinkets, and you'll arrive at it eventually – the whole island only measures 800m by 500m.

To get to Arwad, take either a small water taxi (S£50) or larger passenger boat (S£100) from the port; they leave when full. You have to show your passport to the officials at the desk near the souvenir and snack shops, and once again when you buy your ticket on Arwad for the return journey.

Sleeping

Decent accommodation is thin on the ground in Tartus.

Hotel Raffoul (☎ 220 616, 220 097; Saahat Manchieh; beds per person S£200) Across from the cathedral, this hotel has only 10 rooms, but it's good value. Two of the rooms have private bathrooms; the rest share facilities. It's quiet and very well looked after. Before climbing the stairs, go to the grocer's store on the nearby corner and check in with the owner.

Daniel Hotel (☎ 312 757; fax 316 555; Sharia al-Wahda; s/d/tr S£300/600/900) The rooms here are basic but clean with large beds (with crisp, white sheets) and fans. The managers are helpful, speak English and offer free tea and coffee.

Grand Hotel (☎ 317 797; fax 315 683; Corniche al-Bahr; s/d US$25/30; 🕃) An old-style four-star, the Grand has plenty of character and is well maintained. Rooms have satellite TV, fridge and stunning sea views across the new Corniche, making the rate a bargain. The downside is that it's about 1km from the centre and surrounded by ramshackle houses and concrete shells of half-finished buildings. Breakfast is S£150 extra.

Shahine Tower Hotel (☎ 329 100; fax 315 290; Sharia Tarek ibn Ziad; s/d US$92/98; 🕃) Tartus' only luxury accommodation, the Shahine has 14 floors of plush rooms and lots of marble and brass in the lobby. It's popular with wealthy Syrians and tour groups. Credit cards are accepted.

Eating
RESTAURANTS
The local speciality, unsurprisingly, is fish, which is sold by weight. About the cheapest place to eat fish is the no-frills Al-Nabil (right), but a variety of eateries line the waterfront.

Al-Khawaja (☎ 213 900; Corniche al-Bahr; meal per person S£500; 🕃 noon-late) Tartus' best restaurant, Al-Khawaja has a casual downstairs eatery and a more refined upstairs restaurant that's popular with big families. The seafood and Syrian staples are all deliciously fresh – the *fatoush* salad (a tangy green salad with a mixture of dried wild thyme and sesame seeds and fried Arabic bread; S£30) and fried *kibbeh* (cracked-wheat croquettes; S£15) were some of the best we've had. Lebanese wine (S£600 a bottle), beer and arak are offered.

Yamak (☎ 328 755; Sharia al-Amara; meal per person S£500; 🕃 11am-2am) Up on the 4th floor of the nondescript Chamber of Commerce & Industry building opposite the fishing harbour, Yamak is another excellent restaurant. Choose your seafood from the iced display of the day's catch. The (cheaper) Syrian food is also good and alcohol is served.

Cave (☎ 220 408; Corniche al-Bahr; meal per person S£500; 🕃 noon-late) Occupying a vaulted hall burrowed into the sea wall of the Old City, the Cave has atmosphere and its grilled seafood is good.

CAFÉS & QUICK EATS
Snack places specialising in felafel, shwarma and grilled chicken are clustered around the clock tower and Sharia al-Wahda, and south down Sharia ath-Thawra. There's also a cluster of cheap-eats places along Sharia Ahmed al-Azawi, 500m south of Sharia al-Wahda.

Al-Ayounak (☎ 326 086; 7 Sharia Ahmed al-Azawi; pizzas from S£100; 🕃 noon-midnight) This small snack bar at the seafront end of the street specialises in pizzas.

Al-Seraj (off Sharia Tarek ibn Ziad; meal per person S£150; 🕃 11am-late Sat-Thu) Signposted in Arabic only (السرج), this place is worth searching out for its friendly service, clean surrounds and very decent, cheaply priced local fare, as well as pizzas.

Al-Nabil (Sharia al-Amara; meal per person S£175) One block back from the fishing harbour (just round the corner from the Daniel Hotel) and open seemingly all hours, Al-Nabil specialises in fried and grilled fish but also does chicken and kebabs.

SELF-CATERING
The small **Dalloul supermarket** (Sharia al-Quds) just east of the public park has groceries and toiletries. For freshly baked bread, rolls and

croissants, there's a small bakery next to Al-Nabil restaurant. A liquor store a couple of doors from the Daniel Hotel sells beer.

Drinking

The best bet for an evening in Tartus would be to settle into one of the coffeehouses along the seafront just north of the fishing harbour; the preferred choice is vibrant Viamidos.

Viamidos (☎ 094-667 887; Corniche al-Bahr; beer S£65; ☯ 24hr) This big, stylish, new café is the hit of the string of cafés on the waterfront and one of the few in Syria to serve excellent coffee alongside decent wines by the glass. Crowded with flirty young couples and groups of friends in the evenings, it's people-watching perfection. It's also very female friendly, attracting plenty of local girls sharing nargileh. The food is great too, with everything from pastas (S£145) and pizza (S£110) to big fresh salads (S£180).

Getting There & Away
BUS
Kadmous (Sharia Jamal Abdel Nasser) has a station just off the big roundabout north of the park. Buses depart hourly for Damascus (S£120, four hours), and there are frequent services to Aleppo (S£120, four hours), Hama (S£70, 1½ hours) and Homs (S£70, one hour). Small buses go to Lattakia (S£40, one hour) and Baniyas (S£15, 30 minutes) every 15 to 20 minutes.

Al-Ahliah (Sharia ath-Thawra) is south of the centre; destinations and fares are similar to those of Kadmous, although departures are less frequent.

MICROBUS
Microbuses depart from the main highway, Sharia 6 Tishreen, in front of the train station. Destinations include Lattakia (S£40, one hour), Baniyas (S£20, 30 minutes), Homs (S£35, one hour), Safita (S£15, 30 minutes) and Al-Hamidiyya (for Amrit; S£10, 15 minutes).

TRAIN
At the time of research, infrequent trains ran between Tartus and Lattakia. However, that was all set to change, with the government announcing a long-term plan to inject funds into the national railways and make greater use of its trains.

Getting Around
Everything in the centre is accessible by foot. If you don't want to walk, a local taxi should cost no more than S£30 to take you anywhere around town.

AROUND TARTUS
Tartus is a good base from which to explore the beautiful mountainous hinterland and several interesting sites.

Closest to town is Amrit, although as with many of Syria's preclassical sites, this is really one for the keen amateur archaeologist. Alternatively, head inland and into the hills.

The local transport hub up here is Safita, an attractive hilltop town with an impressive Crusader keep. From Safita you can push on to Hosn Suleiman – there isn't that much there but the scenery along the way is stunning. Tartus is also a convenient base for day trips to the castles of Qala'at Marqab to the north, on the way to Lattakia, and to Qala'at al-Hosn, on the road to Homs. It takes about an hour to get to either of these places.

Amrit   عمريت
Two remarkably odd-looking monuments, erected as long ago as the 6th century BC, dominate the mysterious ancient site of Amrit, 8km south of Tartus. The so-called **meghazils** (spindles) stand in what was once a necropolis and, although origins of this settlement are still a mystery, it appears that Phoenicians from Arwad made the area a kind of satellite or religious zone. The taller of the monuments has four lions carved in a Persian style around the base. Both towers stand above underground funeral chambers (take a torch) and betray a curious mix of Hellenistic, Persian and even Egyptian influences in their decoration.

About 1km to the north you will find the remains of a **temple** built to serve a cult centred on the springs here. The main feature is a deep basin cut out of the rock, which once would have formed an artificial lake. The water that filled the basin came from the nearby spring and was considered to have curative powers. Just 50m to the north you can make out the shape of a small stadium.

Known to the Greeks as Marathos and conquered by Alexander the Great in 333 BC, Amrit had fallen by the wayside by the time it was incorporated into the Roman Empire.

Safita   صافيتا
☎ 043 / pop 33,000

This restful mountain town is a lovely place to while away an hour or two. With the feel of an Italian or Greek Byzantine mountain village, it has narrow twisting alleys, old stone buildings, and lanes shaded by grape-vines. Dominated by a striking Crusader-era **keep** (admission S£100; 🕑 9am-1pm & 3-6pm summer, 9am-1pm & 2-4pm winter), all that remains of the once-powerful 'Castel Blanc', Safita would be a lovely place to spend a few days if it had decent accommodation.

Originally built in the early 12th century as part of the outlying defences of Tartus, the castle was rebuilt and strengthened after damage sustained in an attack by the Ayyubid ruler Nureddin (Nur ad-Din). It was garrisoned by the Knights Templar until 1271, when they were driven out by Beybars, who shortly after went on to take Qala'at al-Hosn.

From the very chaotic central town in-tersection, where most microbuses drop off their passengers, take the road leading uphill to the west. After about 500m the keep is visible ahead. Continue until you see a cobbled lane off to the right and follow it under the arched gate of what remains of the castle's defensive perimeter. If the site is closed, go to the little shop and the shopkeeper will let you in.

At 27m high, the keep is the largest of all surviving Crusader towers. It consists of just one single lower floor and one great upper floor (plus a subfloor passage that leads to a cistern for water storage). The lower level was a grand church with an ele-gant barrel-vaulted ceiling and an apse in the east wall. Only the arrow slits in the walls betray the room's military function. The church still operates, serving the local Syrian Orthodox community.

Stairs in the southwest corner lead to the upper level, which consists of a large hall divided by massive trunklike stone pillars (note the absence of corresponding pillars in the church below – no wonder the walls are so thick). This upper room probably served as a dormitory for the knights, who lived in monastic conditions.

Another flight of steps leads you up to the roof and spectacular views. It's some-times possible to make out Qala'at al-Hosn (the two were thus linked in the Crusaders'

chain of communications) to the southeast, and the snowcapped peaks of northern Lebanon to the south.

GETTING THERE & AWAY
From Tartus, the microbus for Safita (S£15, 30 minutes) departs from just south of the traffic circle in front of the train station. From Safita, microbuses for Hosn Suleiman (S£25, 40 minutes) depart from Sharia Maysaloun, 100m south of the town's main intersection.

Hosn Suleiman   حصن سليمان
A worthwhile excursion north of Safita in-volves journeying 25km along some of the highest mountain ridges of the Jebel An-sariyya to arrive at a remarkable testament to thousands of years of religious fervour. Outside the village of Hosn Suleiman are par-tial temple walls constructed of huge stone blocks, some of them as large as 5m by 3m. Built high in the mountains, days from any-where and at a time when travel was by foot or on horse, these walls are quite enigmatic.

Although evidence suggests the site has been home to temples of one religious per-suasion or another since the Persian oc-cupation of the Levant, what you can see today was erected mainly under Roman domination in the 2nd century AD.

Four gates permit entry to a large rectan-gular enclosure. A partially collapsed cella, which is the focal point of worship and of-ferings in the temple, rises from the centre of the site. The gates preserve the most in-tact decoration, with columns, niches and inscriptions (the clearest of these can be observed above the east gate). The east and west gates both display the same sculptural adornments: the figure of a bearded man stands above the lintel, while the same area on the inside is dominated by figures de-picting two youths and a lion's head. As you pass through each gate, look up to see the outspread wings of an eagle.

Across the road are the less extensive ruins of what appears to be another temple compound, but little is known about its his-tory or function.

GETTING THERE & AWAY
Hosn Suleiman is best visited with your own vehicle. Microbuses (S£25) run at irregular intervals from Safita, taking about 40 min-utes; tell the driver you want to go to Hosn

Suleiman. To get back to Safita, stand on the road and flag down any passing public transport – or any transport at all.

QALA'AT MARQAB   قلعة مرقب

After Qala'at al-Hosn and Qala'at Salah ad-Din, probably the third most impressive of Syria's Crusader castles is the brooding **Qala'at Marqab** (adult/student S£150/10; ☻ 9am-6pm daily Apr-Sep, 9am-4pm Wed-Mon Oct-Mar), built from black basalt rock. It's not as complete as Qala'at al-Hosn or as strikingly located as Qala'at Salah ad-Din, but set out on a spur it does command almost limitless views across the Mediterranean to the west and over the valleys dropping away to the east and south.

The original castle was a Muslim stronghold, founded possibly as late as 1062. During the early 12th century it passed into Crusader hands and was part of the principality of Antioch before being sold in 1168 to the Knights Hospitaller. It was the Hospitallers who gave the castle its present shape, concentrating their fortifications on the southern flank where the gentler slopes made the site most vulnerable. Their work was well done (according to TE Lawrence, Marqab combined 'all the best of the Latin fortifications of the Middle Ages in the East') and the castle stood up to two major assaults in the 13th century. Saladin, who in 1188 successfully captured the nearby castle that now bears his name, did not even bother with Marqab but just marched right by, preferring to concentrate on easier targets.

Historians suspect that its eventual fall in 1285 to the Mamluk sultan Qalaun (successor to Beybars) was due to a lack of manpower for the extensive defences. Qalaun brought down Marqab by 'mining': his soldiers dug under the foundations of the castle walls and towers, propping up the tunnels with wooden beams. By lighting a fire and burning the beams, they collapsed the tunnels and brought down the defences above them. Following the surrender of the Crusaders, the Mamluks repaired the castle – you can identify their handiwork in the telltale white bands of the south tower – and continued to use it until they lost power to the Ottomans, who had little use for castles and kept it as a prison.

At the time of research the castle was undergoing major restoration that was due to be completed during 2008.

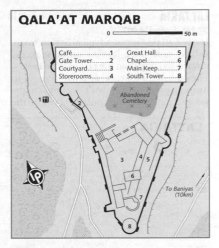

Touring the Castle

The exterior walls and towers are the most impressive elements of the castle. The entrance is through the square **gate tower** (2) in the west wall. After entering, turn right and walk down between the inner and outer walls, then up the short flight of stairs on the left to what was the inner **courtyard** (3) and the focus of activity in the castle. Across from where you enter the courtyard is a Gothic-style **chapel** (6) with two fine doorways, above which are lots of birds tweeting in nests.

Keep heading south past the chapel to the three-storey semicylindrical **main keep** (7). An internal staircase leads up to the roof, from where you can clearly make out the castle's concentric plan (echoing Qala'at al-Hosn) and enjoy some superb views of the coast. To the north and east are the barely distinguishable remnants of **storerooms** (4) and possibly dining and living quarters.

There is a **café** (1) outside the entrance to the castle, with spectacular views of the coast and olive groves and greenhouses down below.

Getting There & Away

Take a microbus (S£10) from Baniyas for Zaoube – these go by the castle. Services are infrequent so when it comes to returning you may want to catch a ride with some locals if you're in a hurry. Baniyas is reached by microbus from Tartus (S£20, 30 minutes) or Lattakia (S£25, 45 minutes).

LATTAKIA

أللاذقية

☎ 041 / pop 354,000

Lively Lattakia is not a typical Syrian town. A busy port since Roman times, it is less inward-looking than the rest of the country. The odd sign in Greek, and many more in Russian, point to the town's openness to the sea and its traffic with outsiders, while the

results of this foreign exchange can be seen in wide, tree-lined boulevards and vibrant cafés (as opposed to the more traditional Arabic coffeehouses).

Lattakia is one of the wealthiest and least conservative cities in the country, due to its many families with expatriate relatives working overseas, and the influx of money

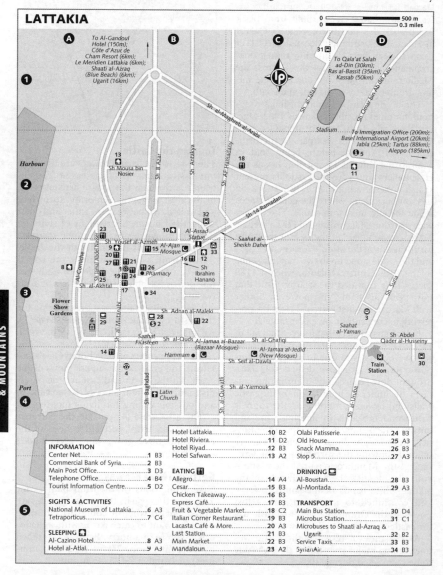

that came its way when local boy Hafez al-Assad ruled the roost. As a result Lattakia has some excellent restaurants and almost as many chic bar-cafés as the capital. Its inhabitants have always been snappy dressers – here the headscarf gives way to tight jeans and low-cut tops.

A stretch of coast has also been earmarked for massive redevelopment, with Gulf money being invested to establish luxurious five-star resorts, shopping centres and marina developments.

Its comparative liberalism and wealth aside, Lattakia has no real attractions, however it is a great place to spend a couple of days and makes a comfortable base for visits to the ruins of Ugarit and Qala'at Salah ad-Din.

History

Lattakia's history dates back to at least 1000 BC, when it was a small Phoenician fishing village. Alexander the Great passed through in 333 BC, shortly after his renowned victory over the Persians at Issus, but Lattakia didn't become a settlement of importance until the arrival of the Seleucids, the dynasty founded by one of Alexander's generals in the 4th century BC. They gave the town its name, 'Laodicea', in honour of the mother of Seleucus I. During Roman times Mark Antony granted the town its autonomy, and in the 2nd century AD it briefly served as the capital of the Roman province of Syria.

A string of serious earthquakes during the 5th and 6th centuries were precursors of troubles to come. Lattakia was badly battered by the Crusader wars, changing hands several times between the armies of the Christians and the Muslims, and it was sacked and pillaged by both.

Lattakia stagnated under the subsequent rule of the Ottomans as other Levantine ports were preferred, and its harbour silted up. Rebellions by the local Alawites against the ruling administration gave the town little chance of regaining its former prosperity. Only when Hafez al-Assad came to power did the fortunes of the town change. There was plenty of local redevelopment, including the largely redundant 'Olympic' stadium and international airport. Equally bizarre was the decision to site the new port terminal on the city-centre seafront,

UP IN SMOKE

Unless your father packed a pipe, you may be unaware that Lattakia is known for its pipe tobacco. But it's not just any tobacco, it's 'smoked' tobacco. The 'Syrian Lattakia' blend, as it's known, is made by smoking the leaves over different woods (such as oak) and herbs before cutting. The technique was apparently discovered after a bumper crop one year in the 1880s, when surplus tobacco was stored in the rafters of farmhouses during winter. When wood was burnt for heating, it gave the tobacco a unique smoky flavour. For many connoisseurs of the leaf, it's the Holy Grail – akin to a hand-rolled Cuban cigar – but because of its strong flavour it's generally only used in small amounts, mixed with other tobaccos to make a blend. These days, the technique has greatly disappeared from Syria and most of the tobacco that's labelled 'Syrian Lattakia' is manufactured in Cyprus – much to the disgust of those with leather elbow patches...

effectively placing an immense physical and visual concrete barrier between the town and the Mediterranean Sea, to which Lattakia has traditionally owed its character.

Orientation

The main north–south street is Sharia Baghdad, home to the main bank, shops and a smattering of cafés and coffeehouses. The other main street is the downmarket Sharia 14 Ramadan, which comes off the northern end of Sharia Baghdad and then runs northeast for 1.5km to the tourist information centre.

Partway along, 14 Ramadan widens out to accommodate a central strip of ornamental fountains and a statue of Al-Assad, a traffic-snarled area hazardous to pedestrians known as Saahat al-Sheikh Daher (Sheikh Daher Sq). Many of the cheap hotels and eateries are clustered around here.

The train and bus stations are almost 2km east of the centre. From either of these transport terminals it takes about 20 to 25 minutes to walk to Saahat al-Sheikh Daher; a taxi will cost S£25.

Information

Center Net (☎ 465 310; Sharia al-Mutanabi; S£50 per 30min; ☼ 11am-11pm) Extremely well located among the cafés and restaurants of the 'American Quarter'. Muna, who runs the place, is super friendly and helpful.

Commercial Bank of Syria (Sharia Baghdad; ☼ 8.30am-1.30pm & 5-8pm Sat-Thu) Has an ATM and may reluctantly change travellers cheques. There is no shortage of ATMs in town.

Immigration office (Saahat Jumhuriyya; ☼ 8am-2pm Sat-Thu) Some distance from the centre on the far side of a large traffic roundabout. You need six passport photos; after much shuffling between desks you will get your extension issued within an hour or so.

Main post office (☼ 8am-6pm Sat-Thu) Some distance from the centre, just north of the train station in a little alley off Sharia Suria.

Telephone office (Sharia Seif al-Dawla; ☼ 8am-10.30pm) Just west of Sharia Baghdad. You can also make cheap international phone calls from Center Net.

Tourist Information Centre (☎ 416 926; Sharia 14 Ramadan; ☼ 8am-8pm Sat-Thu) Located in the foyer of a municipal building at the eastern end of town. The friendly staff speak English but other than a map there's little information.

Sights & Activities

Lattakia has precious little to show for its 3000 or so years of history. More or less the only existing monument is a right-angled **tetraporticus**, a grouping of four columns, which is all that's left of a Roman gateway that once marked the eastern end of the 2nd-century-AD main street. It's on Sharia Bur Said, a short walk southwest of the train station.

Neither is there much remaining to represent the city's medieval Islamic heritage. The oldest parts are off and around Sharia al-Quds; plenty of historic fragments can be found down the various side alleys. Just east of the Ugarit cinema, keep an eye out for a stone-vaulted passageway, down which are a couple of doorways and windows with some splendid carved stonework. The area just beyond here, around the old fruit and vegetable market, is worth exploring, although the squeamish might want to avoid the butchers' passageways.

The **National Museum of Lattakia** (Sharia Jamal Abdel Nasser; adult/student S£150/10; ☼ 8am-6pm Apr-Sep, to 4pm Oct-Mar, closed Tue), near the waterfront, is housed in what was once an old khan, or travellers' inn, and is worth a quick visit, if just to admire the handsome

building. It contains some inscribed tablets from Ugarit, beautiful jewellery, coins and figurines, ceramics and pottery, and a Crusader-era chain-mail suit and swords.

BEACHES

Six kilometres north of town, **Shaati al-Azraq** (Blue Beach) is Syria's premier coastal resort. While there are a few small stretches of sand in the area, access to the best stretches of beach is controlled by the Le Meridien and Cham hotels; each charges around S£400 per person for nonguests to use the beach and hotel swimming pool. Both hotels also hire out pedal boats, jet skis and sailboards. To get to Shaati al-Azraq take a waiting microbus (S£15) from behind the large white school building on Saahat al-Sheikh Daher.

Sleeping

BUDGET

Hotel Lattakia (☎ 479 527; Sharia Yousef al-Azmeh; dm/d S£150/250) Tucked away down a narrow alley north of Al-Ajan Mosque, the Lattakia can be tricky to locate; it's best to ask locals for directions. It has a variety of rooms, from dorms to doubles, with or without private bathroom.

Hotel al-Atlal (☎ 476 121; Sharia Yousef al-Azmeh; beds per person S£250) This simple, quiet, family-run establishment, in the heart of the action, is more like a European pension than a hotel. It has freshly laundered sheets, and a pleasant common area with satellite TV and a fridge stocked with soft drinks. Shower facilities are shared but clean.

Hotel Safwan (☎ 478 602; safwanhotel@go.com; Sharia Mousa bin Nosier; s/d/tr S£300/500/700; ✹) Just a little north of the centre, close to the seafront, the Safwan is a bit shabby albeit clean. Rooms come with TV and air-con or fan, and guests have access to a kitchen and fridge. Friendly manager Mohammed, a self-confessed Tintin fan, is helpful and speaks English.

Hotel Riyad (☎ 479 778; fax 476 315; Sharia 14 Ramadan; s/d US$17/21; ✹) This shabby but clean two-star has a good location, right on the main square. Some rooms have air-con but some only have a fan for the same price. Front-facing rooms have balconies that look onto the action below.

Al-Gandoul Hotel (☎ 477 681; Al-Corniche; s/d/tr US$20/26/32) The best option in this price range, this place was undergoing renovation at the time of research. Despite the grotty elevator, the simply furnished rooms (with TV) were clean, although hopefully the renovations involve replacing the dirty, rust-ridden fridges.

MIDRANGE

Al-Cazino Hotel (☎ 461 140; www.alcazino.com; Al-Corniche; s/d/tr US$50/60/70; ☒) This fine hotel, in an elegant old sandstone building dating to 1923, oozes atmosphere with its grand staircase and warren of halls. Unfortunately the modern, simple rooms don't carry through the character and style of the public spaces, but they're clean and spacious. The front terrace café is a lovely spot for a drink in the evening. Prices drop by US$10 in the low season.

Hotel Riviera (☎ 211 806, 216 311; riviera@net .sy; Sharia 14 Ramadan; s/d US$66/77, incl breakfast; ☒) Opposite the Tourist Information Centre, this smart hotel is one of the city's best. A modern three-star with traditional décor, its comfortable rooms have air-con, satellite TV and fridge. Staff are extremely professional and friendly. The only downside is the slightly out-of-the-action location. Major credit cards are accepted.

TOP END

Lattakia's two luxury hotels are 6km north of the centre at Shaati al-Azraq, which is inconvenient for hanging out in town. They're largely patronised by holidaying Syrians and foreigners on package tours.

Côte d'Azur de Cham Resort (☎ 428 700; www .chamhotels.com; Shaati al-Azraq; d with garden/sea view US$140/180; ☒ ☒) The more attractive of Lattakia's two five-stars, this resort comes with a surprisingly sexy swathe of cream sand beach complete with curvy palm trees. The hotel is ornate, with lots of marble and brass, rooms are spacious and plush, and the facilities are excellent, including cafés and restaurants, ATM, internet café, liquor store etc. Out-of-season rates (October to April) can be significantly cheaper. Major credit cards are accepted.

Le Meridien Lattakia (☎ 428 736; www.lemeri dien.com; Shaati al-Azraq; s/d US$170/215; ☒ ☐ ☒) With its 70s-style décor, this hotel isn't really up to scratch as far as Le Meridien properties usually go. While you won't mind the retro décor in the lobby and bars

(it's almost groovy), the charm fades in the rooms – unless you go for the superior-floor rooms, which have new carpets, a bigger TV, minibar and big balcony. The swimming pool and beachside terraces are pleasant. Major credit cards are accepted.

Eating

RESTAURANTS

Most of the restaurants and cafés are in and around Sharia al-Mutanabi, which is known as the 'American Quarter' because of all its Western-style eateries. There are a few restaurants along Sharia Baghdad and a couple of seafood places along Al-Corniche. Most don't accept credit cards.

Italian Corner Restaurant (☎ 477 207; cnr Sharia al-Mutanabi & Sharia al-Akhtal; meal per person S£300; ☻ 10am-midnight) This rustic trattoria, complete with checked tablecloths and waiters in red checked shirts, serves up tasty Italian pastas (S£130) along with crepes (S£110), burgers (S£100) and steaks (£S230). The big glass windows provide good people-watching opportunities and the place hums late at night.

Last Station (☎ 468 871; 20 Sharia al-Mutanabi; meal per person S£300; ☻ 11am-11pm) Popular with local families, this old-fashioned place does tasty food at very reasonable prices. Expect everything from Syrian mezze (S£50) to pizza (S£100). Alcohol is served.

Cesar (☎ 475 403; Sharia 8 Azar; meal per person S£300; ☻ 11am-late) Located in the narrow alley running along the south side of Al-Ajan Mosque, connecting with Sharia 8 Azar, Cesar does good mezze and grilled meats, along with a few Continental dishes such as escalopes and pastas.

Allegro (☎ 458 000; Sharia al-Mutanabi; meal per person S£350; ☻ 11am-midnight) Lattakia's hippest restaurant is in a sleek contemporary space, with lots of chocolate wood and concealed lighting, that wouldn't be out of place in Beirut. It's a great spot for lunch, when it buzzes with noisy groups of locals enjoying the delicious food – a mix of Asian, Mexican, Italian and French that's served up on big white plates. The speciality is the Chateaubriand (S£275). Alcohol is served.

our pick Old House (☎ 461 013; Sharia Jamal Abdel Nasser; meal per person S£500; ☻ noon-late) This is one of Syria's most atmospheric restaurants. The interior of Old House has been decorated to look like the courtyard of an old house, with Mamluk-style banding on the walls, intricately patterned tiled floors, and traditional textiles for curtains. Devoted locals of all ages, but particularly Lattakia's old-timers, come for the rich Syrian specialities – the fried *kibbeh* and the *sojouk* (spicy Armenian sausages) are some of the best we've ever had. Service is welcoming and accommodating, and alcohol is served.

Mandaloun (☎ 454 400; Sharia al-Merkan; meal per person S£500; ☽ 1-11.30pm) Dress up for this elegant restaurant with stone walls and vaulted ceilings, where you'll be dining with Lattakia's affluent cigar-smoking power set. The French and Oriental cuisine is superb – try the tasty pink lentil soup or hearty traditional French onion soup (both S£60), and the melt-in-your-mouth filet mignon (S£350). We can even recommend the fish – and we don't say that often in Syria. There are excellent Lebanese wines on the menu and the service is superlative.

CAFÉS & QUICK EATS

Olabi Patisserie (☎ 094-657 765, 041 3005; Sharia Yousef Shahour, off Sharia Baghdad; ☽ 7am-midnight) Follow your nose to this old-fashioned café-cum-patisserie – you can smell the freshly roasted coffee (espresso, cappuccino etc) a block away. Olabi bakes the city's best cakes, sweets and croissants, and does delicious crepes. A coffee and a cake costs around S£150. There's free wireless internet access and during summer they also serve on the terrace across the road.

Express Café (☎ 456 200; 22 Sharia al-Mutanabi; dishes S£80-150; ☽ 9am-midnight) This gleaming diner-style cafeteria does excellent burgers (S£55), crepes (S£90) and pizza (S£125). The menu is in English. Pull up a seat at a window table for some people-watching on a weekend night, when Lattakia's teens flirt with each other on the street corner outside.

Lacasta Café & More (☎ 475 744; Sharia al-Mutanabi; meal per person S£250; ☽ noon-3am) Lattakia's multitasking locals sip excellent espresso coffee (S£50) as they puff on nargileh (S£100) and tuck into delicious cakes, crepes and desserts at this stylish café with white leather sofas and enormous glass windows. Sweets are prominent, but the friendly staff also serve up sandwiches and mezze, along with beer and alcoholic cocktails.

Stop 5 (☎ 477 919; 27 Sharia al-Mutanabi; ☽ noon-late) Looking like Mike Brady's den with its wood-panelled walls and chocolate vinyl seats, this casual eatery serves up great pizzas (S£100), burgers (S£100) and steaks (S£180), along with local and imported beers (S£50/90) and local and imported wine by the glass (S£40/80).

Snack Mamma (☎ 416 929; Sharia 8 Azar; ☽ 11am-late) With its mirrored walls, wood panelling and hanging beads, this tiny Italian trattoria has an endearingly retro feel to it. Locals love the home-style spaghetti bolognaise (S£100), which flies out the door, and terrific pizzas (S£125). Beer (S£55) is served.

Cheap eats can be found around the Saahat al-Sheikh Daher area, where you'll find fast-food places specialising in felafel, kebabs and shwarma. There's a good spit-rotisserie **chicken takeaway** (S£150 for a whole chicken plus salad, hummus and bread) next door to the Hotel Riyad.

SELF-CATERING

There's a small **fruit and vegetable market** (off Sharia 14 Ramadan) just north of the big white high school on Sharia 14 Ramadan. The **main market** (Sharia al-Ghafiqi) is just east of the Ugarit cinema. For bread and other groceries, there are a few little places down Sharia Ibrahim Hanano, off Sharia 14 Ramadan.

Drinking

Al-Boustan (Sharia Baghdad) is a simple coffee shop where old men sip thick, Turkish-style coffee at the pavement tables, while **Al-Montada** (Sharia Adnan al-Maleki) is more of a men's club, where the old guys puff on nargileh as they play chess and cards. Both are open almost all the time.

Women might feel more comfortable at café-restaurants such as Stop 5, Lacasta Café & More and Last Station, where you can have a drink without eating. It's also acceptable at the more casual of the other restaurants to just have a light snack to accompany your drinks.

Getting There & Away

AIR

Lattakia's Basel International Airport lies about 25km south of town, close to Jabla. Ordinarily, there are several flights a week to Damascus (S£1000, 45 minutes), with flights increasing during summer, when the airport gets busy with European charter flights. A taxi to the airport from Lattakia will cost about S£350.

SyrianAir (☎ 476 863; 8 Sharia Baghdad) has an office in the town centre.

BUS

The **main bus station** (Sharia Abdel Qader al-Husseiny) is about 200m east of the train station. At least a dozen companies have their offices here, including Al-Ahliah and Kadmous, and between them they offer frequent services to Damascus (S£120, 4½ hours), Aleppo (S£100, 3½ hours) and Tartus (S£35, one hour). There are a few services going to Antakya (S£250), and then on to Ankara and Istanbul (about S£2000, 17 hours) in Turkey.

MICROBUS

Lattakia's sprawling, dusty **microbus station** (Sharia al-Jalaa) is about 1km north of the centre beside a sports stadium. From here a confusion of services depart frequently for Baniyas (S£20, 45 minutes), Tartus (S£40, one hour), Homs (S£65, two hours), Al-Haffa (for Qala'at Salah ad-Din; S£25, 45 minutes) and Kassab (for the Turkish border; S£25, 1½ hours).

Microbuses for Ugarit (Ras Shamra; S£15) and Shaati al-Azraq (Blue Beach; S£15) depart from an alley at the side of the big white school on Saahat al-Sheikh Daher.

TRAIN

The station is 1.5km east of the town centre on Saahat al-Yaman. There are four trains a day between Lattakia and Aleppo (1st class express/1st class/2nd class S£120/80/50, 2½ or 3½ hours), and this is the rare occasion when we recommend taking the train over the bus. The trains are new, refreshments are served and even movies are offered. Not that you'll want to watch them – the scenery is beautiful. The track winds its way through the mountains, rattling through tunnels and across bridges high over valleys below. The trains go via Homs and Hama.

SERVICE TAXI

Service taxis used to go to Beirut and Tripoli in Lebanon from Sharia 14 Ramadan, outside the Hotel Kaoukab as-Sharq; however, these services were suspended after the border

---

TO TURKEY ON THE CHEAP

The cheapest way to get to Turkey starts at the microbus station in Lattakia. Take a service for Kassab (around S£25). You actually want to be dropped off 2km before the mountain village, where the road passes within 50m of the border – ask the driver for 'Turkiyya'. Once across the border you'll have to haggle with any taxi driver you find (pay no more than a few dollars) or try to hitch. You want to be taken on to Yayladagvi, from where you can pick up a *dolmus* (minibus) for Antakya and onward connections. A hassle-free but more expensive option is to go with **Al-Hassan** (☎ 352 021), which runs a daily minibus service to Antakya (S£500), departing at 7.30am.

---

was closed during the troubles in 2007. Until the border reopens, it's best to head to Damascus and travel from there. In the event that the border reopens, service taxis generally depart when full and the one-way fare to Beirut should be around US$25 per person, although the fare has been known to be higher during tensions.

AROUND LATTAKIA

It's an easy half-day trip to the fascinating ruins of Ugarit, which are worth a couple of hours of wandering, and the splendid Qala'at Salah ad-Din, also worthy of a few hours' exploration. You can do both in a full day. If you have to choose, we'd recommend Qala'at Salah ad-Din, as much for its beautiful location as for the extraordinary fortifications.

The scenery around this fertile region is lovely, with fruit orchards and high cypress hedges, and in season you'll encounter fruit stalls along the road selling apples and oranges.

Ugarit (Ras Shamra)   رأس شمره

The birthplace of one of the world's earliest alphabets and once the most important city on the Mediterranean coast, Ugarit was also the world's first international port. Evidence suggests that a settlement on this site was trading with Cyprus and Mesopotamia as far back as the 3rd millennium BC. Ugarit was at its peak around 2000 to 1800 BC, when it enjoyed a healthy trade

---

THE GOLDEN AGE OF UGARIT

Until a worker ploughing a farm near the coast adjacent to Lattakia struck an ancient tomb, the site of Ugarit was unknown. This exciting and important discovery in 1928 led to the excavation of the site the next year by a French team led by Claude FA Schaeffer. What he found was astonishing.

The oldest finds at Ugarit date back to 6000 BC. Findings that date from around 1450 BC to 1200 BC reveal a sophisticated and cosmopolitan metropolis with palaces, temples and libraries with clay tablets bearing inscriptions. These clay tablets, representing a Semitic language – and one of the first alphabets in the world – became a celebrated finding. The site also revealed vast Mycenaean, Cypriot, Egyptian and Mesopotamian influences in the artefacts, a result of trade both by sea and by land.

---

providing the Egyptian pharaohs with timber and exporting the city's trademark bronze-work to the Minoans of Crete. With the immense wealth accrued from trade, the city's royal palace was developed into one of the most imposing and famous edifices in western Asia. Ugarit's wealth was matched by its learning and innovation. For instance, the palace had a piped water system and drainage, as did the houses of the well-to-do.

The most significant achievement, however, was the development of the Ugaritic alphabet. Tablets discovered here are inscribed with what is thought to be one of the world's earliest alphabets. Prior to the one developed at Ugarit the two known systems of writing were hieroglyphics (developed by the Egyptians) and cuneiform (from Mesopotamia), both of which involved hundreds of pictograms that represented complete words or syllables. Ugaritic is a greatly simplified system of 30 symbols, each of which represents one sound. Some of the tablets discovered list these 30 letters in alphabetical order, providing a key for archaeologists to decipher the unearthed texts. These include stock accounts, commercial records, diplomatic correspondence and descriptions of gods and religion. Taken together the texts are a fantastically important source of information on early life in Syria and the eastern Mediterranean region.

Ugarit's fall was swift and occurred around 1200 BC at the hands of the Philistines. The city never recovered; the invasions heralded the beginning of the Iron Age, and Ugarit was forever left behind.

SIGHTS
Ugarit (adult/student S£150/15; ☺ 9am-6pm Apr-Sep, to 4pm Oct-Mar) was built in stone and, although

the buildings are long gone, the foundations and the lower courses of some walls are visible. Significant artefacts turned up by the digs (since the 1920s) have been removed to museums in Lattakia, Aleppo and Damascus, as well as to the Louvre in Paris. In short, what you'll see here goes only a little way to giving the visitor an understanding of Ugarit's significance.

On the right of the track up to the ruins is the original city entrance, today looking more like a large drainage outlet. Once

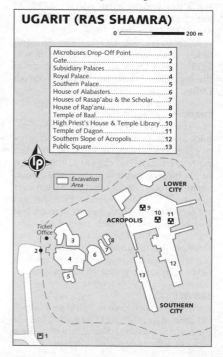

UGARIT (RAS SHAMRA)

0 ――――――――― 200 m

Microbuses Drop-Off Point....................1
Gate...2
Subsidiary Palaces...............................3
Royal Palace.......................................4
Southern Palace..................................5
House of Alabasters.............................6
Houses of Rasap'abu & the Scholar........7
House of Rap'anu................................8
Temple of Baal....................................9
High Priest's House & Temple Library...10
Temple of Dagon...............................11
Southern Slope of Acropolis.................12
Public Square....................................13

inside, you can gain an impression of the
layout of the place from the low hill in the
northeastern quarter of the site that once
served as Ugarit's **acropolis**. What you see
stretched out below is a massive jumble
of blocks with poorly defined streets and
buildings. Among the ruins are vaulted
tombs, wells and water channels.

Two temples dominated the acropolis: one was dedicated to the storm god,
Baal, the supreme deity for the Canaanites,
Phoenicians and Aramaeans; the other to
Dagon, the father of Baal and the god associated with crop fertility. What little remains of the **Temple of Baal** (9) is found to
the northwest of the acropolis, while the
Temple of Dagon (11), of which only some
of the foundations can be made out, is to
the east.

Ugarit's **royal palace** (4) and related buildings were in the west of the city, a short
way south of the tourist entrance. Presenting itself now as something of a labyrinth,
the palace's main entrance is in the northwestern corner, marked by the bases of
two pillars. Inside, the rooms are loosely
organised around a series of courtyards. It
was in storerooms of the palace that a good
many of the precious Ugaritic archives were
unearthed. The area between the palace and
the acropolis was given over largely to private housing.

The Mediterranean Sea is just visible
through the trees to the west. It has receded
100m or so since Ugarit's heyday. Don't try
to walk directly through to the water as this
is a military area. If you follow the road
back a bit, you'll find some quiet stretches
of water and beach.

GETTING THERE & AWAY
From Lattakia, local microbuses make the
6km trip to Ugarit (ask for Ras Shamra)
every hour or so from a back alley behind
Saahat al-Sheikh Daher. Ask the driver
where to get off for 'al-athaar' (the ruins).
Coming back, you can flag down any passing microbus, or it's easy enough to hitch.

Qala'at Salah ad-Din   قلعة صلاح الدين
Although it is much less celebrated than
Qala'at al-Hosn, TE Lawrence was moved
to write of Qala'at Salah ad-Din, 'It was I
think the most sensational thing in castle
building I have seen'.

To Lawrence, the castle was Saône (Say-
hun in Arabic), which is the name that the
Crusaders knew it by, after Robert of Saône,
one of the original Crusader builders. The
name Qala'at Salah ad-Din was only officially adopted in 1957.

Qala'at Salah ad-Din is a sensational
place fundamentally because of its setting –
the castle is perched on top of a heavily
wooded ridge with near-precipitous sides
dropping away to surrounding ravines.

Approaching from the nearby village of
Al-Haffa, you'll first see the castle from
the top of the ridge to the north. The
road then slithers down in a tight coil
of switchbacks, crossing a stream at the
bottom before winding its way back upwards. Nearing the top, the road turns
sharply to enter a flat-bottomed, narrow
canyon with sheer vertical sides; the castle sits up on the right, its heavy walls
smoothly continuing the line of the rock
face to form one towering cliff of stone.
Incredibly, the canyon is man-made – the
Crusaders laboriously hacked a huge volume of stone out of the hillside to separate the castle from the main spine of
the ridge. In the middle of the canyon,
they left a solitary freestanding needle of
stone 28m high, resembling a Pharaonic
obelisk, which provided support for a
drawbridge.

The fortifications were begun by the Byzantines in the latter part of the 10th century. The site was chosen for its proximity
to, and control of, the main route between
Lattakia and Aleppo, and for its command
of the coastal hinterland plains. The Crusaders took over in the early 12th century
and the construction of the castle as you
see it today was carried out some time before 1188, the year in which the Crusaders'
building efforts were shown to be in vain.
After a siege of only two days the armies of
Saladin breached the walls and the Western
knights were squeezed out of yet another of
their strongholds.

Unlike many other strategic sites, control
of which seesawed between the Crusaders
and the Muslims, this one stayed in the
hands of the Islamic armies. As its importance declined, the castle was abandoned.
A small village occupied the lower courts
at some point, but its remoteness eventually
led to its desertion too.

SIGHTS

The **castle** (adult/student S£300/15; ⏰ 9am-6pm Apr-Oct, to 4pm Nov-Mar, closed Tue) is approached up a flight of concrete steps on the south side, which climb towards a **gate tower** (7) where entry tickets are purchased. After passing through the tower into the castle's interior, a right turn leads to the inner courtyard area of the upper castle. The two **towers** (8 and 9) in the southern wall are both relatively intact, and it's possible to climb the internal staircase in each up to the 1st floor and roof for fine views of the surrounding countryside.

To the left of the furthest of the towers, a doorway leads to a flight of steps descending into the square sunken space of a former **water cistern** (10); a doorway from the cistern links to an adjacent large, low, pillared hall that served as **stables** (11). Incredibly, the damp space still smells of horses. From the stables it's possible to access two of the three small **semicircular towers** (15) of the eastern wall; these were originally built by the Byzantines and later strengthened by the Crusaders.

North of the stables is the largest and most heavily fortified of the castle's towers, the **keep** (12), or donjon, with 5m-thick walls. It was always assumed that any attack would come from along the ridge to the east. In fact, when the attack came, Saladin split his forces: half occupied the defences here as expected, but a second force bombarded the northern walls with catapults from the hilltop across the valley.

The missiles breached the walls of the lower courtyard and the Crusaders, who were undermanned, were unable to stop the Muslims streaming in. An intact staircase gives access to the roof of the keep, and vertigo-inducing views down into the defile.

The ruins to the north of the keep include the **postern gate** (13), from where the drawbridge was lowered onto the **rock needle** (14). A metal gantry protrudes from the unsealed gateway so the nerveless can step out and peer directly down into the defile.

The most prominent structure in this part of the castle is the **palace and baths complex** (5), easily identifiable by its high, typically Islamic entrance, decorated with stone stalactites and carved geometric patterning. This dates back to the Ayyubid period (1169–1260). Inside is a reception hall with *iwans* (vaulted halls), and beyond that the main room of the baths with a star-patterned floor around a central fountain.

From the palace a path leads north to a modest doorway that, if you step through, gives way to the dizzying spectacle of a cathedral-sized **sunken cistern** (4), which is still partially filled with water. Follow the same path west, passing the remains of the original **Byzantine citadel** (3) up to the right, to the **Tower of the Daughters** (1), which today serves as a small café. From here you can look down on the lower courtyard of the western castle, which is completely ruined and overgrown, and inaccessible. Complete the circuit by returning to the gate tower.

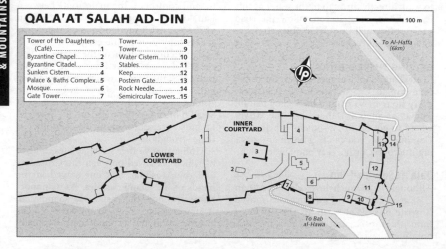

QALA'AT SALAH AD-DIN

Tower of the Daughters (Café)...........................1	Tower.......................8
Byzantine Chapel.............2	Tower.......................9
Byzantine Citadel.............3	Water Cistern...........10
Sunken Cistern................4	Stables.....................11
Palace & Baths Complex...5	Keep........................12
Mosque...........................6	Postern Gate............13
Gate Tower.....................7	Rock Needle.............14
	Semicircular Towers...15

To Al-Haffa (6km)

INNER COURTYARD

LOWER COURTYARD

0 — 100 m

To Bab al-Hawa

ASSAD'S RESTING PLACE *Terry Carter*

The driver we hired for our visit to the mausoleum of the late president Hafez al-Assad and his son became more open as we approached Qardaha, the birthplace of the dynasty: 'Look at how much money they've spent here, and while the people are poor!' He shook his head at each painting and reference to the former president and his 'martyred' son. Even the modern streetlights and white-painted fences, which we had not seen anywhere else, made him upset. 'In Islam, a good Muslim is buried simply, without fanfare,' he continued. 'Look at this waste!'

When we arrived at the mausoleum, it was apparent that some important people were arriving at the same time to show their respects. The gun-toting guards were at first hesitant to let us in, but we *salaam alaykum*-ed every one of them and every black-suit-wearing official we came across. Our driver, who had been criticising Assad just minutes ago, quickly found renewed respect for the former leader. He went in and prayed with the visitors, paying his respects with new-found devotion to the divisive leader.

Hafez al-Assad might not be able to reach out from the grave, but his legacy is a culture of fear that isn't disappearing fast.

GETTING THERE & AWAY

From Lattakia, take a microbus to the village of Al-Haffa (الحفه; S£20, 45 minutes); they depart from the far right-hand side (as you come from town) of the vast microbus lot. From Al-Haffa the castle is a gruelling 6km walk uphill and downhill – keep on heading east out of the village then follow the signs. The best bet is to haggle with a taxi driver at Al-Haffa; there are usually several cabs loitering where the microbuses stop. The local price is S£20 per person – a good test of your negotiating skills. The microbus drivers at the microbus station in Lattakia will drive you to the castle and back for S£200, which isn't a bad deal for a group of four.

Qardaha   القرداحة

Known to all Syrians as the birthplace of Hafez al-Assad, Syria's first president, Qardaha is now equally famed as the former president's last place of rest. Following his death in June 2000, his body was interred in this small hilltop town in a purpose-built **mausoleum** also containing the grave of his eldest son, Basil, 'the martyr' whose car accident saw him predecease his father by six years.

Indications of the hallowed nature of Qardaha are apparent from the approach along an expansive and well-maintained four-lane highway that runs from the coast up to the village. Soon after entering the town, you'll see the mausoleum off to the left – look for a red-tiled pagoda-like roof on a large villa.

The domed mausoleum is an Islamic star in plan, but otherwise the décor is restrained, with intricate floral decoration and verses from the Quran. Internally, it's a vast space, heavy with incense, but empty apart from the two graves. The one belonging to Hafez, a low benchlike cenotaph lying in a sunken section of floor, is in the centre. Basil occupies a similar grave off to one side, covered in a green cloth. It's moving in its simplicity.

There's nothing else to see in town. To return to Lattakia, walk east along the main road; after 400m the way widens and you'll come to a large statue of guess who with four dopey lions at his feet. Microbuses back to the coast depart from diagonally opposite the statue.

GETTING THERE & AWAY

Services for Qardaha (S£15, 35 minutes) depart from Lattakia's vast microbus station.

Orontes Valley

وادي العاصي

Bordered by the coastal strip to the west and the scorched desert to the east, the Orontes Valley provides a distinctively different experience from Aleppo to the north and Damascus to the south. While Syrians try to break land-speed records between the aforementioned cities, there are enough attractions in the region to make this more than just a blur outside a bus window.

Homs, Syria's third-largest city, and Hama, its fourth, are attractive stops on the journey north. Homs has a lovely restored souq, a relaxed Christian quarter and friendly locals. Hama is famed for its large *norias* (water wheels) and riverside parks. It's most active in summer, when the wheels groan with the flow of the Orontes River, known as Nahr al-Aasi (Rebel River) due to the fact that it flows from south to north – the opposite of most rivers in the region.

The striking Roman ruins of Apamea are well worth visiting for the colonnaded grace of the cardo maximus, both longer and wider than Palmyra's. Careful restoration over the last few decades has turned this once-shapeless site into an evocative one. Far less complex in structure are the intriguing beehive houses found at Sarouj and Twalid Dabaghein, which are still used as dwellings. These conical mud-brick structures are an arresting sight.

While the castle of Musyaf is suitably imposing, its connection with one of Islam's most fascinating sects, the Assassins, is the highlight. Members of this radical, mystical group were known for their ability to infiltrate their enemy and kill its leader, giving rise to the English word 'assassin'.

HIGHLIGHTS

- Explore **Apamea** (p167), Syria's second-most impressive archaeological site after Palmyra and definitely one for fans of colonnades

- Shop for gold, spices and sheesha pipes and watch artisans at work in the restored souq of **Homs** (p156)

- Adjust your ears to the torturous sounds of the groaning old *norias* of **Hama** (p162)

- Enjoy the glorious views over **Al-Ghab** (p166), Syria's most fertile farming valley, from Jebel Ansariyya

- Investigate the intriguing **beehive houses** (p171), still used as dwellings, in Twalid Dabaghein and Sarouj

- Climb the stairs of the Byzantine church at **Qasr ibn Wardan** (p169) to see a Martian landscape

★ Apamea
★ Al-Ghab
★ Qasr ibn Wardan
★ Twalid Dabaghein & Sarouj
★ Hama
★ Homs

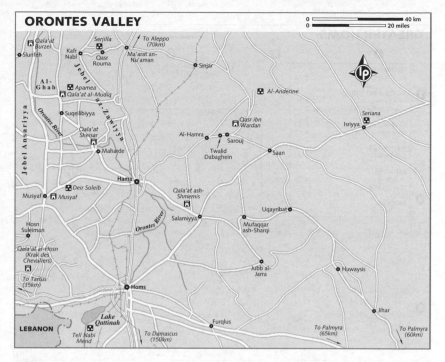

HOMS   حمص

☎ 031 / pop 823,000

With a history stretching back to the 1st
millennium BC, Homs, Syria's third-largest
city, at one time gave birth to a dynasty of
Roman emperors, and under the Byzantines
was an important centre of Christianity.
These days, its Christian neighbourhood is
one of Syria's most welcoming and relaxed,
and Homs' citizens are some of the country's
friendliest. That, combined with the city's
myriad leafy parks and gardens, sprawling
al fresco coffee shops, outdoor corn-on-the-
cob stands and restored souq where artisans
still work, make Homs a wonderful place to
kick back for a couple of days.

History

Digs at the tell (artificial mound) to the
south of the centre of the modern city indicate there were settlements in preclassical
times. However, Homs only gained importance during the Roman era. Formerly
known as Emesa, the town benefited from
close ties with Palmyra, 125km to the east.

Its regional importance was further enhanced around AD 187, when Julia Domna,
daughter of an Emesan high priest, married
a Roman garrison commander, Septimius
Severus, who six years later would become
emperor of Rome. They founded a Syro-
Roman dynasty that spanned four emperors
(reigning from 211 to 235). Unfortunately
it was a dynasty most noted for its rapid
decline into depravity. Most notorious of
all was Elagabalus, whose four-year reign
of chaos was abruptly terminated when
he was assassinated by his own Praetorian
guards, seeking to restore some order to
the empire.

Under the Byzantines, Homs became an
important centre of Christianity, and it still
has a very large Christian population. After
falling to a Muslim army led by the general
Khaled ibn al-Walid (revered as the warrior
who brought Islam to Syria) in 636, Homs
became an equally fervent centre of Islam.

Orientation

Central Homs lies either side of the main
east–west axis of Sharia Shoukri al-Quwatli,
a short but wide strip of road punctuated
at either end by a large roundabout; the
one at the western end is distinguished by

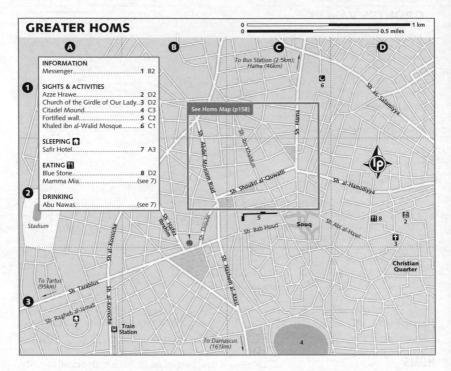

GREATER HOMS

INFORMATION
Messenger..............................1 B2

SIGHTS & ACTIVITIES
Azze Hrawe............................2 D2
Church of the Girdle of Our Lady..3 D2
Citadel Mound.......................4 C3
Fortified wall..........................5 C2
Khaled ibn al-Walid Mosque........6 C1

SLEEPING
Safir Hotel.............................7 A3

EATING
Blue Stone.............................8 D2
Mamma Mia..........................(see 7)

DRINKING
Abu Nawas...........................(see 7)

a clock tower. Cheap accommodation and eats are found in the side streets south of Sharia Shoukri al-Quwatli. The old city and souq lie southeast. The main bus station is around 2.5km northeast of town.

Information

Commercial Bank of Syria (Map p158; 8am-12.30pm Sat-Thu) There's no shortage of ATMs in Homs.

Foreign-exchange booth (Map p158; 8am-7pm) Grudgingly cashes travellers cheques; shuts for a few hours in the early afternoon for lunch.

Immigration office (Map p158; Sharia ibn Khaldun; 8.30am-2pm Sat-Thu) For visa renewals; it's on the 3rd floor of an administration building just north of Sharia Shoukri al-Quwatli. On the ground floor are photo studios that do passport photos.

Messenger (Map p156; ☎ 221 2336; Sharia Tarablus; per hr S£50; 24hr) This excellent internet café has plenty of terminals and offers 50% off the rate after midnight.

Post office (Map p158; Sharia Abdel Moniem Riad; 6am-5.30pm Sat-Thu) About 200m north of the clock-tower roundabout.

Telephone office (Map p158; Sharia Shoukri al-Quwatli; 8am-8pm Sat-Thu, to 1pm Fri) Just east of the

clock-tower roundabout; there are several card phones inside and cards are available from the counter.

Sights

OLD CITY & SOUQ   المدينة القديمة والسوق
Little remains of the old city of Homs. Its walls and gates were largely demolished in the Ottoman era, although there is a short section of **fortified wall** (Map p156) with a circular corner tower just south of Sharia Shoukri al-Quwatli. Half a kilometre to the south a large earthen mound marks the site where a **citadel** (Map p156) once stood.

A little way south of the roundabout at the eastern end of Sharia Shoukri al-Quwatli and tucked down a laneway is the unassuming 20th-century façade of the **An-Nuri Mosque** (Jamaa an-Nuri, also known as Jamaa al-Kebir; Map p158), which is actually much older than first appearances might suggest. Just north of the prayer hall, the mosque court-yard contains a curious long, low platform, with an ancient capital embedded in its western end.

A few steps from the mosque is Homs' restored old **souq** (Map p156), which buzzes in the evenings when the whole city seemingly comes out to shop. With its grey stones, vaulted ceilings and elegant white lamp posts, it's one of Syria's most attractive souqs. The artisans, carpenters, cobblers, metalworkers and knife-sharpeners sitting cross-legged on the floors of their workshops make it all the more fascinating, and it's an easy place to while away a couple of hours. Great buys include gold, sheesha pipes, spices and clothes.

CHRISTIAN QUARTER

From the souq, head east along Sharia Abi al-Hawl to explore the old Christian Quarter (Map p156). Along this street numerous expanses of black-and-white-banded stonework mark out buildings from the Mamluk era, all still in use as shops and dwellings. Encouragingly, there are plenty of signs of renovation and reconstruction.

Continue due east, straight over the crossroad, until you see a small gateway topped by a cross – this leads through a grey stone wall to the **Church of the Girdle of Our Lady** (Kineesat al-Zunnar; Map p156; Sharia Qasr ash-Sheikh). In 1953 the patriarch of Antioch, Ignatius Aphraim, declared a delicate strip of woven wool and silk, found in the church six months earlier, to be a girdle worn by the Virgin Mary. The story is that it had survived intact since the ascension of Mary into heaven, preserved in one container or another in a church on this spot. The church is an attractive little grey-stone building with a red pantile roof, and is still an active centre for Syrian Orthodox worship.

From the church follow the road that heads off to the north, taking the first right for the **Azze Hrawe** (Map p156; Sharia Omar al-Mokhtar; 8am-2pm Sat-Thu), a Mamluk-era residence of impressive size. It was being restored at the time of research and should soon open to the public as a National Folklore Museum. There's a beautiful big courtyard with a fountain and a *liwan* (summer room) featuring exquisite carved-wood decoration. Don't hesitate to knock on the door if it's closed; nobody minds you snooping around.

MUSEUM

In the big Department of Antiquities building on the main street, Homs' **museum** (Map p158; Sharia Shoukri al-Quwatli; adult/student S£150/10; 8am-4pm Apr-Oct, to 3pm Nov-Mar, closed Fri) con-tains a rather modest collection of artefacts, from prehistoric to early Islamic, unearthed in the region. Labelling is in Arabic only.

KHALED IBN AL-WALID MOSQUE

جامع خالد إبن الوليد

Built as recently as the first decade of the 20th century, Homs' best-known monument, Khaled ibn al-Walid Mosque (Map p156), is an attractive example of a Turkish-style mosque. The black-and-white Mamluk-style stone banding in the courtyard is particularly striking. Inside the prayer hall, over in one corner, is the domed mausoleum of Khaled ibn al-Walid, the military strategist and hero who conquered Syria for Islam in AD 636 (see Khaled ibn al-Walid, below).

You can enter the mosque if dressed modestly. Women have to borrow a *yishmak* (as they call the *abeyya,* or woman's cloak, here), cover their hair and also must enter through the small side door on the right to see the marble tomb. Do not enter during prayer.

The mosque is in a small park off Sharia Hama, 500m north of Sharia Shoukri al-Quwatli.

KHALED IBN AL-WALID

One of the great generals of Islam, this Homs hero (glorified at the mosque that bears his name) initially fought against the Prophet Mohammed before converting to Islam between 627 and 629 and playing a major role in its expansion. He joined forces with the Prophet for the invasion of Mecca in 629 and went on to greater victories after the death of Mohammed in 632. Khaled was the key leader in taking Syria for Islam in 633–634; in 635 Damascus surrendered. At the Battle of Yarmuk in 636 a last-ditch counterattack by Emperor Heraclius' army resulted in it being routed; 50,000 Byzantine troops were slaughtered.

Khaled ibn al-Walid's military achievements are legendary – he won more than 100 battles without loss while usually outnumbered – and his tactics, including the use of the pincer movement to surround enemy troops, have been studied by military planners throughout history. To his disappointment he died in his own bed in Homs instead of in a fierce battlefield scrap, in 642.

ORONTES VALLEY

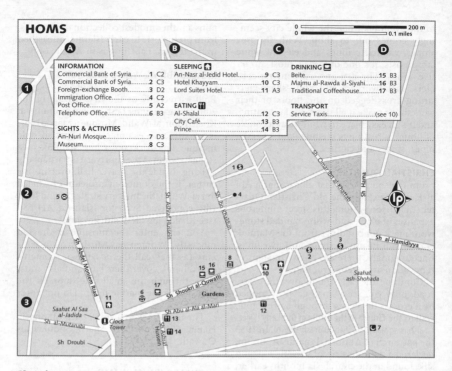

HOMS

INFORMATION	
Commercial Bank of Syria.........1	C2
Commercial Bank of Syria.........2	C3
Foreign-exchange Booth.........3	D2
Immigration Office.........4	C2
Post Office.........5	A2
Telephone Office.........6	B3

SIGHTS & ACTIVITIES
An-Nuri Mosque.........7 D3
Museum.........8 C3

SLEEPING	
An-Nasr al-Jedid Hotel.........9	C3
Hotel Khayyam.........10	C3
Lord Suites Hotel.........11	A3

EATING
Al-Shalal.........12 C3
City Café.........13 B3
Prince.........14 B3

DRINKING
Beite.........15 B3
Majmu al-Rawda al-Siyahi.......16 B3
Traditional Coffeehouse.........17 B3

TRANSPORT
Service Taxis.........(see 10)

Sleeping

There are several budget hotels on and around Sharia Shoukri al-Quwatli but they're a grim bunch; it's better to upgrade to Lords or Safir.

An-Nasr al-Jedid Hotel (Map p158; ☎ 227 423; Sharia Shoukri al-Quwatli; s/d/tr/q S£205/375/440/560) In a beautiful hundred-year-old building with high ceilings, this place has enormous rooms with balconies, decorative windows, and a big common area with a massive picture window looking onto the main-street action below. With a little renovation it could become Homs' backpacker favourite. For now, it's a passable budget place with clean sheets and hot water (showers S£50), although it's a little grubby and the showers are a bit too close to the squat toilets for our liking. Still, it's Homs' best budget hotel.

Hotel Khayyam (Map p158; off Sharia Shoukri al-Quwatli; s/d/tr/q S£225/450/625/800) If you can't get into An-Nasr al-Jedid, try this place on the side street next door as a last resort. Communal toilets are of the squat variety, and showers cost S£35.

Lord Suites Hotel (Map p158; ☎ 247 4008; www.lordsuiteshotel.com; mh@mail.sy; Saahat Al Saa al-Jadida; s/d/tr US$50/70/100; ❄) Apart from the science experiments in the soap dispensers, this is a spotlessly clean, modern place and an excellent midrange choice. The rooms, which are actually one-, two- and three-bedroom suites, are enormous, with a separate living area, making them an excellent choice for families and friends who want to bunk down together. There's a big buffet breakfast (included), and rooms come with fridge and satellite TV. Ask about discounts in winter.

Safir Hotel (Map p156; ☎ 211 2400; www.safirhotels.com; Sharia Ragheb al-Jamali; s/d/f US$136/152/190; ❄ ☒) This excellent five-star has plush, comfortable, well-equipped rooms, a massive swimming pool and tennis courts, a handful of good restaurants, cafés and bars, and a bookshop with a small selection of titles on Syria and the Middle East. It's popular with tour groups so book ahead. Credit cards are accepted. It's 1km southwest of the centre or a brief S£25 taxi ride.

Eating

Blue Stone (Map p156; ☎ 245 9999; cnr Sharias al-Jibawi & Qasr ash-Sheikh; meal per person S£300; ⊙ 9am-late) In a big grey stone building with huge picture windows looking out onto the street, this is the most happening bar-café-restaurant in the Christian Quarter. It positively hums in the evenings with the chatter of flirty young couples gazing into each other's eyes, same-sex groups of friends comparing rings (girls) and ring tones (boys), and families tucking into pizzas, pastas and big bowls of salad. While there's a full bar, sheesha is the intoxicant of choice.

Mamma Mia (Map p156; ☎ 211 2400; Safir Hotel, Sharia Ragheb al-Jamali; meal per person S£350; ⊙ noon-midnight) This is one of Safir Hotel's two restaurants. In a cheery trattoria, it dishes up generous servings of hearty Italian to a predominantly local crowd. The pizzas (from S£100) and pastas (S£250 to S£450) are both excellent.

Prince (Map p158; Sharia Ashraf Hussein; chicken & chips S£150; ⊙ 9am-midnight) is a basic snack joint serving up bigger-than-usual shwarmas, grilled chicken and other street-food standards, as well as fresh fruit juices. Next door, **City Cafe** (Map p158; ☎ 239 755; Sharia Ashraf Hussein; ⊙ 24hr) serves up similar fare. Around the corner there are a few more cheap takeaway places doing kebabs, hot chickens, felafel, hummus and salad, the best of which is **Al-Shalal** (Map p158; Sharia Abu al-Ala al-Mari; ⊙ 24hr), where locals line up for succulent shwarmas and juices.

Drinking

Majmu al-Rawda al-Siyahi (Map p158; Sharia Shoukri al-Quwatli; ⊙ 10am-late) This big, shady, garden café (whose name means something along the lines of 'Tourist Garden Association') is on the north side of the main street, close to the clock tower. Having a coffee here is a must just to take in the vibe, especially during summer evenings when the place is packed with locals.

Beite (Map p158; ☎ 234 032; Sharia Shoukri al-Quwatli; ⊙ 9am-late) Next door to Majmu al-Rawda al-Siyahi, this is a chic, new, two-storey café. The name translates to 'my home'; you have to press the buzzer beside the massive wooden door to enter. Its covered rooftop terrace is where Homs's affluent set meet.

Traditional coffeehouse (Map p158; Sharia Shoukri al-Quwatli; ⊙ 8am-late) A little down the road from the cafés above, and in complete contrast, is this coffeehouse. It's in a big, old, atmospheric stone building and is largely frequented by backgammon-playing old men.

Abu Nawas (Map p156; ☎ 211 2400; Safir Hotel, Sharia Ragheb al-Jamali; ⊙ 9am-late) If you're heading to Mamma Mia at the Safir Hotel, you can also get a drink in this bar, which is 1970s retro and fairly low-key.

Getting There & Away

BUS

There are two bus stations: the new 'hop-hop' minibus station, about 8km south of the city centre on the Damascus road; and the main 'luxury' bus station (Karajat Pullman), which is about 2.5km northeast of the city on the Hama road. To get between town and the main bus station costs around S£30; between town and the microbus station costs up to S£50.

At the main bus station you'll find all the usual private companies, including Al-Ahliah and Kadmous. From here there are frequent departures to Damascus (S£80, two hours), Aleppo (S£90, 3 hours) and Tartus (S£45, one hour). There are buses to Hama from here but it's more convenient to catch a minibus.

MINIBUS

Bright, new minibuses flit in and out of the new 'hop-hop' bus station, most of them going to Hama (S£25, 45 minutes). They depart as soon as they're full and you can generally turn up at any time, climb straight in, and expect to be away in less than 10 minutes.

TRAIN

The **train station** (Map p156; Sharia al-Korniche) is a 20-minute walk from the centre, so it's best to take a taxi (S£30) if you have heavy luggage and it's hot. There are around four departures each day on sleek new trains, heading south to Damascus (1st/2nd class S£120/60) and north to Aleppo (S£120/60).

Getting Around

To get into town from the main bus station costs around S£30; from the microbus station around S£50.

Expect to pay no more than S£25 to travel within the city.

HAMA   حماه

☎ 033 / pop 495,000

Hama is one of Syria's most attractive towns, with the Orontes River flowing through the city centre, its banks lined with trees and gardens and the ancient wooden *norias* (water wheels) groaning. While there isn't an awful lot to see, the peaceful atmosphere and tiny but charming old town make it a pleasant enough place to spend a couple of days. It's also a good base for excursions to some of the worthwhile sites further north up the Orontes Valley or further afield, such as Qala'at al-Hosn (Krak des Chevaliers; p133) or the Dead Cities (p198).

History

Excavations on the city's central tell have revealed that the locale was settled as long ago as the Neolithic Age. There are historical references to an Aramaean kingdom of Hamah (or Hamath), which traded with Israel during the reigns of biblical David and Solomon (1000–922 BC). Occupied later by the Assyrians, Hama joined Damascus in a revolt against their foreign conquerors in 853 BC, defeating the troops of Shalmenaser. Under Sargon II the Assyrians wreaked their revenge, and in 720 BC the city was razed and its citizens deported. By the time of the Seleucids, the Greek dynasty established by one of Alexander's generals, the town had been renewed and rechristened Epiphania after the ruler Antiochus IV Epiphanes (r 175–164 BC). It remained an important Roman and Byzantine centre until its capture by the Arabs in AD 637.

The town prospered under the Ayyubids, the dynasty founded by Saladin, but was often fought over by rival dynasties in Damascus and Aleppo, which it lay between.

The most recent chapter in Hama's history has been one of the country's saddest. It was here in 1982 that the repressive nature of Hafez al-Assad's regime was most brutally demonstrated. The details of what happened that bloody February are hazy at best, but it appears that about 8000 government troops were moved in to quash a rebellion by armed members of the then-outlawed Muslim Brotherhood. Fighting lasted three weeks and the level of destruction was immense. Only those who knew the city before this calamity can fully measure the damage. As recently as 1955, travel writer Robin Fedden wrote in his book, *Syria: An Historical Appreciation*, that Hama was 'extraordinarily unspoilt with houses that overhung the water and an extensive old town in which modern buildings barely intrude'; this is no longer the case. The heart of the old town was completely razed.

MASSACRE IN HAMA

The massacre in Hama in 1982 is one of the darkest events of modern Syrian history. The story goes back to the 1930s, when Syrian students joined the Egyptian Muslim Brotherhood, which called for a return to the Quran and what they considered to be the true word of Mohammed. In Syria they were opposed to the ruling Ba'ath party, which after 1970 was dominated by the Assad dynasty, whose Alawite religion the Muslim Brotherhood opposed.

Tensions kept escalating and on 7 July 1980 the Brotherhood attempted to assassinate Hafez al-Assad. After the failed attempt, the government passed a law making membership of the Muslim Brotherhood punishable by death. In late January 1982 the Muslim Brotherhood declared Hama a 'liberated city' after removing Ba'athists and government officials from their homes and workplaces, with at least a couple of dozen casualties. On 2 February 1982 the government struck back, with intensive shelling of the city followed by a warning that anyone left in the city would be declared a rebel. In the fighting that followed, between 10,000 and 25,000 people were killed, out of a total population of 350,000, and mosques, churches and archaeological sites were damaged and destroyed.

The massacre achieved the result that Assad wanted – the Muslim Brotherhood was smashed, with many of its leaders in exile and eventually gaining political asylum in other countries. While support for the methods of the Muslim Brotherhood was not great before the massacre, Assad earned himself many enemies after the event and the rest of his reign was tainted by his brutal response to the uprising.

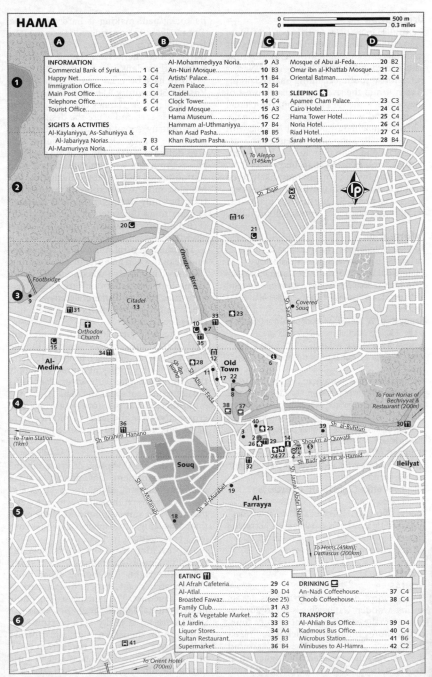

HAMA

0 — 500 m
0 — 0.3 miles

INFORMATION	
Commercial Bank of Syria	1 C4
Happy Net	2 C4
Immigration Office	3 C4
Main Post Office	4 C4
Telephone Office	5 C4
Tourist Office	6 C4

SIGHTS & ACTIVITIES	
Al-Kaylaniyya, As-Sahuniyya & Al-Jabariyya Norias	7 B3
Al-Mamuriyya Noria	8 C4

Al-Mohammediyya Noria	9 A3
An-Nuri Mosque	10 B3
Artists' Palace	11 B4
Azem Palace	12 B4
Citadel	13 B3
Clock Tower	14 C4
Grand Mosque	15 A3
Hama Museum	16 C2
Hammam al-Uthmaniyya	17 B4
Khan Asad Pasha	18 B5
Khan Rustum Pasha	19 C5

Mosque of Abu al-Feda	20 B2
Omar ibn al-Khattab Mosque	21 C2
Oriental Batman	22 C4

SLEEPING	
Apamee Cham Palace	23 C3
Cairo Hotel	24 C4
Hama Tower Hotel	25 C4
Noria Hotel	26 C4
Riad Hotel	27 C4
Sarah Hotel	28 B4

To Aleppo (145km)

Sh Zigar

To Four Norias of Bechrryyat & Restaurant (200m)

Orontes River

Footbridge

Citadel 13

Orthodox Church

Al-Medina

Sh Said al-A'as

Covered Souq

Old Town

Sh Ibn Rushed

Sh Abu al-Feda

To Train Station (1km)

Sh Ibrahim Hanano

Sh al-Buhturi

Sh al-Murabet

Souq

Sh al-Murabet

Al-Farrayya

Sh Shoukri al-Quwatli

Sh Badr ad-Din al-Hamid

Ileilyat

Sh Jamal Abdel Nasser

To Homs (45km); Damascus (200m)

To Orient Hotel (700m)

EATING	
Al Afrah Cafeteria	29 C4
Al-Attal	30 D4
Broasted Fawaz	(see 25)
Family Club	31 A3
Fruit & Vegetable Market	32 C5
Le Jardin	33 B3
Liquor Stores	34 A4
Sultan Restaurant	35 B3
Supermarket	36 B4

DRINKING	
An-Nadi Coffeehouse	37 C4
Choob Coffeehouse	38 C4

TRANSPORT	
Al-Ahliah Bus Office	39 D4
Kadmous Bus Office	40 C4
Microbus Station	41 B6
Minibuses to Al-Hamra	42 C2

ORONTES VALLEY

Orientation

Central Hama sticks to the switchbacks of the southern bank of the Orontes River. Its main drag, Sharia Shoukri al-Quwatli, runs east–west, while Sharia Jamal Abdel Nasser runs north–south, becoming Sharia Said al-A'as north of the river. Immediately west of the centre is the 'old town' and the citadel mound, and west of this is the traditionally Christian neighbourhood of Al-Medina with its two main shopping streets Sharia al-Mutanabi and Sharia Ibn Rushd. It's all very compact and easy to get around on foot.

Arriving by bus, you are most likely to be dropped off on Sharia al-Buhturi, the riverside street, one block north of the main cluster of hotels on Sharia Shoukri al-Quwatli.

Information

Ad-Diah (3 Sharia Abdel Alwani) Hama has Easycomm card phones; buy phonecards at this telecoms shop.
Commercial Bank of Syria (Sharia Shoukri al-Quwatli; ◷ 8.30am-12.30pm Sat-Thu) This main branch, just east of the clock tower, has an ATM. There are other ATMs all over Hama.
Happy Net (☎ 216 057; off Sharia Shoukri al-Quwatli; per hr S£50; ◷ 24hr) Internet access; in an arcade between Sharia Shoukri al-Quwatli and the Hama Tower Hotel. The Cairo and Riad hotels also offer internet access to guests.
Immigration office (Sharia Ziqar; ◷ 8am-2pm Sat-Thu) On the northern edge of town, near the museum, in a two-storey modern building with the word 'Passport' in English in massive letters above the main entrance. You need four photos and S£50; the whole process takes less than an hour.
Main post office (Sharia Shoukri al-Quwatli; ◷ 8am-5pm Sat-Thu) Centrally located, beside the clock tower on the main junction in town.
Telephone office (Sharia Shoukri al-Quwatli) Just behind the post office.
Tourist office (☎ 511 033; Sharia Said al-A'as; ◷ 8am-2pm Sat-Thu) In a small building in the gardens, just north of the river. The staff here don't have anything much to tell you and didn't even have maps when we visited.

Sights

NORIAS النواعير

Hama's most distinctive attractions are its *norias*, wooden water wheels up to 20m in diameter (the equivalent in height of a four- or five-storey building), which have graced the town for centuries. The land around the Orontes is considerably higher than the river itself, which is deeply incised into

its rocky bed, making it hard to irrigate. The *norias* were constructed to scoop water from the river and deposit it into aqueducts, which then channelled it to nearby fields and gardens.

There have been *norias* in Hama since at least the 5th century AD, as attested by a mosaic displayed in Hama's new museum, but the wheels seen today are the design of the 13th-century Ayyubids, who built around 30 of the things. Of these, 17 *norias* survive, dotted along the course of the river as it passes through town, although all have been reconditioned and/or rebuilt during the late Mamluk and Ottoman times. The *norias* still turn, but only during spring and summer; at other times the waters of the river are diverted into more modern irrigation schemes elsewhere, reducing water supplies.

The most central *norias* are right in the middle of town in an attractive park setting. The most impressive wheels, however, are about 1km upstream, and are collectively known as the **Four Norias of Bechriyyat**. They are arranged as two pairs on a weir that spans the river.

In the opposite direction, about 1km west of the centre, is the largest of the *norias*, known as **Al-Mohammediyya**. It dates from the 14th century and used to supply the Grand Mosque with water. Part of its old aqueduct still spans the road. Beside the *noria* there is a small stone footbridge that crosses the river and leads to another bit of parkland and an open-air coffeehouse.

OLD TOWN المدينة القديمة

Most of the old town was destroyed in the 1982 bombardment, leaving only a small surviving remnant edging the west bank of the river, between the new town centre and the citadel. In sum, it amounts to little more than a twisting, atmospheric alley that runs for a few hundred metres.

Approaching from the south, pass the riverside Choob coffeehouse, then swing off to the right, just before what looks like an arched gate but is in fact part of an old aqueduct. The lane passes the oddly named **Oriental Batman** (☎ 224 957; ◷ 9am-9pm Sat-Thu, 3-9pm Fri), a junky antique-cum-bric-a-brac shop, then turns north just before **Al-Mamuriyya**, a *noria* that dates from 1453. Sticking with the alley, pass the historic **Hammam al-Uthmaniyya** (bath & sauna S£150, massage

S£100; ☺ men 8am-noon & 7pm-midnight, women noon-6pm), which is spotlessly clean and popular with the locals. Virtually next door, the so-called **Artists' Palace** (Ateliers des Peintures; ☺ 9am-10pm) occupies a former khan, or travellers' inn; the old storerooms are now used as makeshift studio and exhibition spaces for local artists, some of whose work is for sale. The khan doesn't really compare with those seen in Damascus and Aleppo, but a little further is a much more noteworthy monument, the Azem Palace.

Ross Burns, historian and author of the sage *Monuments of Syria,* regards the **Azem Palace** (Beit al-Azem; adult/student S£150/10; ☺ 9.30am-2.30pm Wed-Mon) as 'one of the loveliest Ottoman residential buildings in Syria'. It's the former residence of the governor Asaad Pasha al-Azem, who ruled the town from 1742. The palace has strong echoes of the more grandiose building of the same name in Damascus, which is hardly surprising as the latter was also built by Al-Azem after he was transferred to the capital. Burns singles out the *haramlik* (family or women's quarters), the area to the right of the entrance, as being particularly noteworthy.

A short distance north of Azem Palace is the splendid riverside **An-Nuri Mosque**, built by the Muslim commander Nureddin, uncle of Saladin, in the late 12th century. If you cross the bridge beside the mosque, you have a very picturesque view of the river and three *norias,* which are, from east to west, **Al-Kaylaniyya, As-Sahuniyya** and **Al-Jabariyya**.

CITADEL & GRAND MOSQUE
القلعة والجامع الكبير

The term 'citadel' is a bit of a misnomer, because it refers to what used to be rather than what is. What the locals call Al-Qalaa, or 'the castle', is actually no more than a great earthen mound, or tell. Danish archaeologists who carried out extensive work on the tell who found evidence of continuous settlement since Neolithic times, particularly during the Iron Age. Sadly, apart from a few unrecognisable fragments, nothing remains as all the stone was long ago carted off for use in other buildings. The area has been landscaped and developed into a picnic and recreation area, with a small café; it's popular with locals, particularly on Fridays and public holidays.

Looking north from the tell, just over the river, you'll see the small **Mosque of Abu al-Feda**, resting place of the 14th-century soldier-turned-poet of that name, who was also a noted historian, astronomer and botanist. His treatise on geography was a major resource for European cartographers from the Renaissance onwards. He was elevated to become emir of Hama in 1320. During his rule, Abu al-Feda commissioned his own mosque and tomb beside the Orontes in what he wrote was 'one of the most delectable of spots'.

About 400m southwest of the citadel is the **Grand Mosque** (Sharia al-Hassanein; ☺ sunrise-sunset), which, after being almost completely destroyed in the fighting of 1982, has since been faithfully restored. It was originally built by the Umayyads in the 8th century, along the lines of their great mosque in Damascus. It had a similar history, having been converted from a church that itself had stood on the site of a pagan temple.

HAMA MUSEUM
متحف حماة الاثري

Hama's excellent regional **museum** (Sharia Ziqar; adult/student S£150/10; ☺ 9am-4pm Nov-Mar, to 6pm Apr-Oct, closed Tue), located about 1km from the centre, is housed on the ground floor of a striking sandstone building. Each room is devoted to a particular era, including Neolithic and Palaeolithic, the Iron Age, Roman and Islamic. There's some interesting material on finds at the citadel mound, including a splendid 2.5m-high, 10-tonne black basalt lion that once guarded the entrance to an Iron Age palace. Other stand-out items are some intricate 8th-century bronze and gold-leaf figurines with blue lapis eyes; an exquisitely rendered 3rd-century mosaic, depicting a group of young women playing music and dancing; and a fragment of a 5th-century Byzantine mosaic, recovered from Apamea, that depicts a *noria*.

To get to the museum, walk north along Sharia Said al-A'as and take the first left after the large **Omar ibn al-Khattab Mosque**, completed in 2001.

SOUQ
السوق

Hama was never a great trading centre and today its main **souq** (off Sharia al-Murabet) is modest, with hardly any of the great commercial khans that fill the old cities of Aleppo and Damascus. The two noteworthy khans that Hama does possess have long since been pressed into other uses: **Khan Rustum Pasha** (1556), just south of the town centre on Sharia al-Murabet, is an orphanage (although it's occasionally open to the public as an exhibition space); while **Khan Asad Pasha** (1751), also on Sharia al-Murabet but further south, is now a local Ba'ath Party branch.

Tours

The Cairo and Riad hotels in Hama run excursions with negotiable itineraries to places that would be hard to get to in one journey using public transport. Popular options are full-day trips involving two or three locations, such as Apamea, Musyaf and Qala'at al-Hosn (Krak des Chevaliers; S£2300); four of the Dead Cities (S£1500); the Dead Cities, Ebla, Qala'at Samaan and Aleppo (S£3500); or the beehive houses and Qasr ibn Wardan (S£1100). It's also possible to hire a car and driver and put together your own itinerary. Expect to pay between US$70 to US$100 for the day; ask your hotel to organise a driver.

Sleeping

BUDGET

Cairo Hotel (☎ 222 280; cairohot@scs-net.org; Sharia Shoukri al-Quwatli; dm/s/d/tr/q S£175/350/500/650/750; ✸ ▣) This backpacker favourite near the clock tower has clean dorms and rooms with fridge, satellite TV and private bathrooms. In summer you can crash on a mattress on the roof for S£100. Air-conditioning is S£50 extra, breakfast S£100 and internet access S£75 for an hour. Staff are welcoming, speak English, and can arrange trips around the region (see above).

Riad Hotel (☎ 239 512; riadhotel@scs-net.org; Sharia Shoukri al-Quwatli; dm/s/d/tr/q S£175/350/500/600/750; ✸ ▣) Similar in many respects to the Cairo, and equally as popular with backpackers, this is another decent budget option. All rooms have fridges and TVs and the back rooms have great balconies. There's a good communal kitchen and a pleasant dining area. As at the Cairo, the staff are friendly and can arrange tours (see above).

Hama Tower Hotel (☎ 226 864; fax 521 523; off Sharia Shoukri al-Quwatli; s/d/tr US$25/30/35; ✸) It's hard to beat the central location and spectacular views at this good option occupying the top floors of a tower block overlook-

ing the river. Rooms are simple yet spotlessly clean and come with fridge and TV. Breakfast is delicious although the stunning views are distracting. There's an all-day coffee shop and staff can order in dinner if you fancy eating on your balcony. Discounts are offered off-season.

MIDRANGE

Noria Hotel (☎ 512 414; www.noria-hotel.com; Sharia Shoukri al-Quwatli; s/d/tr/q US$25/35/47/55; ✸ ▣) This large, modern three-star has a smart reception area with – refreshingly – women at the counter. The spacious rooms have air-con, fridge and satellite TV, and were being renovated at the time of research; the plush new rooms were to include internet access. Guests can take advantage of the tours organised out of the Cairo Hotel.

Sarah Hotel (☎ 515 941; Sharia Abu al-Feda; s/d US$27/35; ✸) In a picturesque area in Hama's tiny old quarter, the simple rooms here are looking a little worn around the edges, but there's a café-restaurant on premises and the location is unbeatable.

Orient Hotel (☎ 225 599; www.orienthouse-sy.com; Sharia al-Jalaa; d/ste US$60/75; ✸) In a splendid, restored 18th-century building, with beautifully decorated ceilings, Oriental lamps and a big central light-filled courtyard, this is Hama's most atmospheric accommodation. There is a new extension so ask for one of the rooms in the Ottoman-era building. Rooms are well equipped with TV and fridge, and there's a restaurant on site. The only downside is the location, at least a 20-minute walk from the centre; take a taxi.

TOP END

Apamee Cham Palace (☎ 525 335; www.chamhotels .com; Sharia abi Nawas; s/d/tr US$110/130/150 plus tax; ✸ ✸) This elegant tower has plush, comfortable rooms with all the mod cons you'd expect from a five-star. Located on the river, it's a lovely walk from here to the town centre through the old quarter. The lobby is disquietingly empty unless there's a tour group staying, but you won't spend much time there anyway.

Eating

Dining in Hama is limited to some pleasant waterside terrace restaurants and a few takeaway places specialising in delicious succulent hot chickens.

RESTAURANTS

Le Jardin (☎ 525 335; Sharia abi Nawas; meal per person S£300; 🕒 10am-late) Overlooking the splendid An-Nuri Mosque, river and water wheels, and serving alcohol (beer S£95), this leafy, terrace café-restaurant is a wonderful place to while away a few hours puffing on a nargileh (S£100) as you take in the atmosphere. Local families love it here, and on weekends fill their tables with plates of mezze (S£60) and kebabs (S£100). It's part of the Apamee Cham Palace; credit cards are accepted.

Al-Atlal (☎ 222 234; Sharia al-Buhturi; meal per person S£300; 🕒 9am-1am) On a tree-shaded terrace beside the river, this casual restaurant serves up the usual mezze and meaty grills, as well as hamburgers and pizza. It's the first place on the left as you walk east from the centre along Sharia al-Buhturi. No alcohol is served; credit cards aren't accepted.

Sultan Restaurant (☎ 235 104; meal per person S£300; 🕒 8am-2am) This café-restaurant in a lovely waterside stone building was closed for renovation at the time of research, but the owners assured us that opening was imminent. To get here, pass through the low, vaulted tunnel beside the An-Nuri Mosque.

Four Norias (Sharia al-Buhturi; meal per person S£400; 🕒 9am-late) On the banks of the river beside the *norias*, around 500m east of the centre, this large open-air terrace restaurant is popular with groups and families and gets lively on summer evenings. There's a long list of mezze and kebabs, and costumed boys serving nargileh. No alcohol; no cards accepted.

Family Club (Nadi al-Aili; Sharia Kawakili, Al-Medina; meal per person S£450; 🕒 6pm-late) At the rear of a building a block north of the Orthodox Church, this church club welcomes anybody to its open-air terrace restaurant on the 1st floor. The food is good – it's the usual Syrian staples.

QUICK EATS

In the couple of blocks along Sharia Shoukri al-Quwatli and its side streets, there are a number of cheap felafel, shwarma, kebab and chicken restaurants. Go to any that seem to be doing the most business with the locals. A long-standing favourite is **Broasted Fawaz** (☎ 223 884; same block as Hama Tower Hotel; meal per person S£200; 🕒 8am-late), for its deliciously succulent hot chickens and freshly fried hot potato crisps with garlic sauce.

> ### SWEET HAMA
>
> Although you can find it elsewhere in Syria (and Lebanon, especially Tripoli), a Hama speciality worth trying is *halawat al-jibn* – a soft cheese-based, doughy delicacy, drenched in honey or syrup and topped with pistachios, and often served with ice cream. It's made by taking raw cheese and reducing the salt content by soaking, then melting, stirring and stretching the cheese to make dough. This dough is rolled out and cut, with each piece then filled with *kashta*, a creamy dessert filling, and rolled to form a cylinder. The result is sweet, delicious, filling and quite irresistible. It's easy to find in Hama, as a lot of places around Sharia Shoukri al-Quwatli sell it – a few sell nothing else but this decadent treat.

Almost anytime you can pick up dessert at **Al Afrah Cafeteria** (Sharia Shoukri al-Quwatli), an ornate, old-fashioned, marble-fronted café on the next block where locals line up for the sweets with sugar syrup.

SELF-CATERING

For fruit there is a good little **market** just off the western end of Sharia Shoukri al-Quwatli, while for groceries there's a Western-style **supermarket** (cnr Sharia Ibrahim Hanano & Sharia Al-Mutanabi), which, though small, is decent and well stocked. You can get takeaway beer at a couple of **liquor stores** at the northern end of Sharia al-Mutanabi, near the citadel.

Drinking

The open-air **Choob coffeehouse** is set in a garden of shady eucalyptus trees and has views of the river and *norias*. There is also another open-air coffeehouse, **An-Nadi**, next to the big city-centre *noria* and facing the Choob across the river; a third is by Al-Mohammediyya *noria*, west of the citadel. Open from early until very late, all are frequented predominantly by men, so some women may not feel comfortable here.

Getting There & Away

BUS

The main bus companies, Al-Ahliah and Kadmous, have their offices in the town centre on Sharia al-Buhturi, and the buses stop out front.

Al-Ahliah has the greatest number of departures and the times are posted inside the office in English. It has frequent services to Damascus (S£90, 2½ hours), Aleppo (S£80, 2½ hours), Homs (S£30, 45 minutes), Tartus (S£80, two hours), Lattakia (S£100, three hours), Idlib (S£50, one hour) and Raqqa (S£145, five hours). Note that if you're travelling to Homs, departures by microbus are far more frequent.

For roughly the same prices, Kadmous, facing the river west of the main bridge, has several buses a day to Damascus and more frequent departures to Aleppo, Lattakia, Tartus, and Palmyra (S£85, three hours), which continues on to Deir ez-Zur.

There are no direct services to Qala'at al-Hosn (Krak des Chevaliers) from Hama; you have to change at Homs.

MICROBUS & MINIBUS
The main microbus station is a 15-minute walk from the centre of town, at the southwestern end of Sharia al-Murabet in a dusty lot at the junction with the main Damascus road. From here there are regular departures to Homs (S£25, 45 minutes), Musyaf (S£25, 45 minutes), Salamiyya (S£20, 40 minutes) and Suqeilibiyya (for Apamea; S£25, 40 minutes).

The minibus station is a further 200m left and along the Damascus road. Services depart from here for Homs (S£15), Salamiyya (S£20), Suqeilibiyya (S£15) and Musyaf (S£15).

For minibuses to Al-Hamra (for Qasr ibn Wardan; S£20) there's a separate station north of the river on Sharia al-Arkam. Head up Sharia Said al-A'as, past the tourist office, and take either the third or fourth street on your right (you won't miss it); it's about a 10-minute walk from the centre.

TRAIN
The train station is just under 2km from central Hama. There are around four daily departures on sleek new trains to Damascus (1st/2nd class S£120/60, around two hours) and the same number in the opposite direction to Aleppo (1st/2nd class S£120/60, around two hours).

Getting Around
Hama's centre is compact and it's easy to get around on foot. Local buses may come in handy for getting to and from the bus and train stations, both of which are uncomfortably far from the town centre; they leave from Sharia al-Buhturi beside the bridge. You pay the S£2 fare on the bus. Alternatively, a yellow taxi will cost around S£30 to either minibus station or the train station.

AROUND HAMA
There are three main excursions to make from Hama around the Orontes Valley. You can travel north to the Roman-era ruins of Apamea, west into the hills to the Assassins' castle of Musyaf, or east out to the Byzantine ruins of Qasr ibn Wardan. Each of these trips takes about half a day but could be extended by adding in extras, such as stopping off at Qala'at Sheisar on the way to Apamea, or swinging past Qala'at ash-Shmemis (قلعة الشميمس) on the way back from Qasr ibn Wardan.

Hama also makes a good base for visiting Qala'at al-Hosn (Krak des Chevaliers), via a change of bus at Homs, while the Dead Cities are only 60km to the north and easily reached by microbus.

All these trips can be done fairly easily through a combination of public transport and hitching, or alternatively you could take advantage of the organised tours offered by some of Hama's hotels (see p164).

Al-Ghab   الغاب
From Hama the Orontes River flows northwest for 50km and then into Al-Ghab plain, a vast, green, agriculturally rich valley stretching between Jebel Ansariyya to the west and Jebel az-Zawiyya to the east. As you drive through here, expect to see trucks piled unimaginably high with produce, sacks of potatoes, wheat and bales of hay, along with colourfully painted pickups with farm workers in the back – men with red-and-white *gutras* (headcloths) and women in headscarves and big straw hats.

It's said that in ancient times the pharaoh Thutmose III came here to hunt elephants, and a thousand years later Hannibal was here teaching the Syrians how to use elephants in war. Under the Seleucids the plain must have been as rich and fertile as it is now, as it supported large cities such as Apamea, but as the population dwindled the untended land degenerated into a swamp. In recent times, with World Bank help, this low-lying area of some 40 sq km has been drained and criss-crossed with irrigation ditches, returning it to its former status as one of the most fertile areas in Syria.

Qala'at Burzei   برزاي قلعة

One for completists only, at Qala'at Burzei you will find the minimal remains of a once sizable Crusader castle. The castle was built in the 12th century but fell to Saladin not long after, in 1188. The most intact part of the ruins is the watchtower that guarded the eastern approach, and you can also pick out the keep on the far western side. It's a bit of a scramble to get up to the ruins, so wear decent footwear.

The site is about 4km north of the turn-off for Slunfeh on the Jisr ash-Shughur road (No 56) and is accessed by a side road off to the west.

Apamea   أفاميا

Apamea (Afamia in Arabic) would be con-sidered one of the unmissable highlights of Syria, if it weren't for the unsurpassable mag-nificence of Palmyra. As it stands, the ruinous site is like a condensed version of Zenobia's pink sandstone desert city, but built in grey granite and transposed to a high, wild, grassy moor overlooking Al-Ghab plain.

The site has no set opening hours as it's unfenced and there's nothing to stop anyone wandering across it at any time. However, an admission fee (adult/student

S£150/10) for the site is payable at the ticket office, and ticket officials occasionally pa-trol the site.

The site lies about 1km north of the main road; the turn-off is marked by a long, low, old grey-stone building housing a museum devoted to mosaics, which is also worth a visit.

Once at the site, expect annoying guys to follow you around on foot and on motorbikes in an attempt to sell you fake 'antique' coins and postcards. Don't encourage them: ignore them completely and they'll go away. If you act nice, they won't leave you alone. There's a sweet old man at the end of the site near the cafeteria who sells soft drinks, water and post-cards – buy something from him instead.

HISTORY

Founded early in the 3rd century BC by Seleucus I, a former general in the army of Alexander the Great, Apamea became an important trading post and one of the four key settlements of the empire to which Se-leucus gave his name. It was connected by road to another key Seleucid town, Lattakia (Laodicea), which served it as a port. Se-leucus had great skills as a diplomat: while Laodicea was named after his mother, he also took due care to keep things sweet with his Persian wife, Afamia, by naming this settlement after her.

As a result of the rich pasture of Al-Ghab, Apamea was renowned for its horses. Ac-cording to Greek historian Strabo, the city

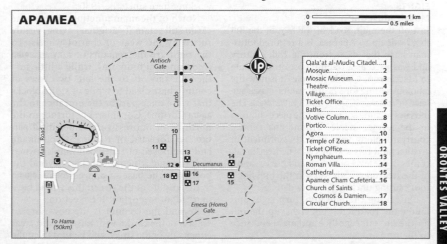

APAMEA

Qala'at al-Mudiq Citadel	1
Mosque	2
Mosaic Museum	3
Theatre	4
Village	5
Ticket Office	6
Baths	7
Votive Column	8
Portico	9
Agora	10
Temple of Zeus	11
Ticket Office	12
Nymphaeum	13
Roman Villa	14
Cathedral	15
Apamee Cham Cafeteria	16
Church of Saints Cosmos & Damien	17
Circular Church	18

0   1 km
0   0.5 miles

Antioch Gate
Cardo
Main Road
Decumanus
Emesa (Homs) Gate
To Hama (50km)

ORONTES VALLEY

had some 30,000 mares and 3000 stallions, as well as 500 war elephants.

Apamea was seized by the general Pompey for the Romans in 64 BC, and only entered into its true golden era in the 2nd century AD, when much of the city was rebuilt after a severe earthquake in AD 115.

In its heyday, Apamea boasted a population of about 500,000 and was notable enough to be visited by Mark Antony, accompanied by Cleopatra, on his return from staging a campaign against the Armenians on the Euphrates River. Prosperity continued into the Byzantine period, but the city was sacked by the Persians in AD 53 and again in 612. Barely a quarter of a century later, Syria was seized by the Muslims and Apamea fell into decline. It assumed importance during the Crusades when the Norman commander, Tancred, took possession of the city in 1106. The occupation was short-lived, however, and Nureddin won the city back 43 years later. Eight years on, the city was all but flattened in a devastating earthquake.

The site was not abandoned completely: a nearby hilltop that had served as an acropolis under the Seleucids and Romans became a citadel under the Mamluks. It sheltered a small village, which later became a popular stopover for pilgrims on their way south to Mecca. The village, which takes its name Qala'at al-Mudiq from the citadel, has long since outgrown its fortified walls and now tumbles down the hillside to the main road.

SIGHTS
Mosaic Museum

Just off the main road, at the foot of the hill that leads up to Apamea, is a restored Ottoman khan that dates from the 18th century and was used as a trading post on the route to Mecca from Constantinople. It is now the fabulous setting for a heartbreaking **mosaic museum** (adult/student S£75/5; ☻ 8am-3pm Wed-Mon). The mosaics include some very fine pieces housed in the former stables around the central courtyard, along with an odd assortment of architectural bits and pieces. The heartbreak comes in the level of neglect and preservation of the treasures, with leaks in the building's roof causing unchecked water damage.

On exiting the museum, turn right and follow the road left, then right, up the hill for the site's ticket office and main entrance to the ruins.

Theatre

Part way between the museum and the site proper, and off to the right, is a hollow filled with the barest vestiges of what was a 2nd-century-AD theatre. After serving as a convenient quarry for the neighbouring village for centuries, the remains are less than impressive, yet archaeologists believe that this may once have been the largest theatre in the eastern Roman Empire, bigger even than the one at Bosra.

Cardo

The main feature of the ruins of Apamea is the north–south cardo (main street), marked out along much of its length by parallel colonnades. Several lesser decumani (east–west cross-streets) intersected the cardo, and the main surviving decumanus now serves as the modern access road to the site – you'll walk or ride up it from the main highway. The junction of the cardo and decumanus is the main entry point for the site.

At 2km Apamea's cardo is longer than the one at Palmyra. Many of its columns, originally erected in the 2nd century AD, bear unusual carved designs and some have twisted fluting, a feature unique to Apamea. Visitors to this site as recently as 50 years ago would have seen nothing of this; in what's termed 'reconstructive archaeology', the columns have been recovered from where they once lay, scattered and overgrown with weeds, and have been re-erected by a Belgian team that has been working here since the 1930s.

North of the main junction, parts of the cardo still retain its original paving, visibly rutted by the wear of chariot wheels. To the right are the remains of a **nymphaeum** (monumental fountain), while a little further on and off to the left, two rows of column bases lead to a pile of stone blocks that were once part of the entrance to the **agora** (forum). Considerably further to the north is an impressive and beautiful **portico**, set forward of the main colonnade and composed of taller columns crowned by a triangular pediment. Just beyond the portico is the base of a large **votive column** in the middle of the street: this would have marked an important intersection.

Beyond the column is the best-restored section of the cardo, with raised paved areas either side of the street, and behind them the lower portions of facades that would most likely have been shops – it's possible to gain a clear impression here of how the cardo must have looked in its heyday. The northernmost end of the cardo is marked by the recently restored **Antioch Gate**, beyond which once stretched the ancient city's necropolis.

Decumanus   دوكومانوس

About 400m east from the main junction and café area, there are the remains of a **Roman villa** with an impressive entrance and colonnaded courtyard. Across the way is a **cathedral** from about the 5th century.

Qala'at al-Mudiq Citadel   القلعة

The citadel of Qala'at al-Mudiq, which sits atop a spur just west of the ruins of Apamea, is, typically, more impressive from the outside. It dates from the 13th century and occupies what had been the acropolis of the ancient city. Inside is a tumbledown village with colourfully painted doors, many painted with the palm tree scene representing paradise that indicates the occupants have done the hajj.

It's worth visiting for the views out over Al-Ghab, and of the theatre and ruins. You can walk up to the citadel or, if you have a car, drive up and park in the central square.

Take the narrow dirt path to the right, where you can ask at the house at the end of the lane (with a green door) if you can see the view – it's worth it, as it's spectacular. They're used to visitors and don't mind, but a tip is in order.

Expect to be hounded by scruffy but sweet little children and mangy dogs along the way; you might even score an invitation to tea from a local.

GETTING THERE & AWAY

Microbuses (S£25, 40 minutes) and minibuses (S£15, 40 minutes) regularly run the 45km from Hama to the village of Suqeilibiyya, where it's necessary to change to a microbus for Qala'at al-Mudiq (S£15, 10 minutes).

The whole trip takes about an hour, except on Friday, when you can wait ages for a connection. You need to tell the driver to let you off at the museum – 'al-mathaf'. See p164 for information about organised tours from Hama.

Musyaf   مصيف

The solid castle of **Musyaf** (adult/student S£75/5; 8am-6pm Apr-Oct, to 4pm Nov-Mar, closed Tue) sits in the foothills of Jebel Ansariyya, about 40km west of Hama. On the way here you'll pass through magnificent mountain scenery dotted with granite and limestone rock formations and thick with pine forests, olive groves and flowering shrubs. Shepherds herd their flocks along the road and will give you a wave as you pass. The air is fresher and the temperature a couple of degrees cooler than down in the valley. It's worth visiting for the journey alone.

Musyaf was an important and well-preserved Ismaili fortress. The outer walls are intact and suitably imposing, especially when viewed against the mountain backdrop. And there are the colourful historical associations.

It's not known when the first fortifications were erected on this site, but there was definitely a castle of some sort here in 1103 because it was seized by the Crusaders. They didn't have enough manpower to garrison it and by 1140–41 it had passed into the hands of the mysterious Ismaili sect, more dramatically known as the Assassins (see The Assassins, p170).

The entrance to the castle is via a long flight of stairs at the south, which leads up into the main keep. Opening hours can be a bit hit-and-miss: if the caretaker is not around when you arrive, someone will be loitering around the foot of the stairs and can call him.

GETTING THERE & AWAY

Minibuses to/from Hama and Homs cost S£15 and S£20 respectively; microbuses cost S£25 and S£30. Avoid making the journey on Friday, when services are greatly reduced. Musyaf is also conveniently visited en route to Qala'at al-Hosn (Krak des Chevaliers) as part of an organised tour with one of the Hama hotels (see p164).

Qasr ibn Wardan   ورادان إبن قصر

A splendid sandstone palace about 60km northeast of Hama, **Qasr ibn Wardan** (adult/student S£75/5; 8am-6pm Apr-Oct, to 4pm Nov-Mar, closed Tue) lies on a road that goes to nowhere. There's little out here but hard-baked earth and dust, but it's a fascinating journey all the same – in the space of little more than an hour you pass from the comforting surrounds of urban Hama to a landscape that in parts resembles Mars. On the way you'll pass through farmland where whole families work the fields alongside each other, and rocky landscapes dotted with brown Bedouin goat-hair tents and Bedouin herding their flocks of sheep.

Erected by the Byzantine emperor Justinian in the 6th century (it was completed in AD 564) as part of a defensive line that included Rasafa and Halabiyya on the Euphrates, Qasr ibn Wardan was a combined military base, palace and church. Its appearance, however, would seem to belie any defensive function; rather than a frontier outpost it looks more like a modestly grand public building that would be more at home on some city square. One theory for this is that Qasr ibn Wardan was a base from which to consolidate control over the local Bedouin population, and as such it was meant to impress upon the nomads the strength and status of their would-be overlords.

The palace, assumed to have been home to the local governor, is the building closer to the road and the caretaker will usually open this up first. There are no set opening hours. The best-preserved part is the south façade, constructed of broad bands of black basalt and yellow brick, through which you enter into a hall with rooms off to either side. Many of the stones lying around are carved with symbols and you can pick out a jar, some scales, a sheep and a fish. In the courtyard two large stones are carved with a sundial and a calendar. On the north side of the courtyard are the former stables, while on the east side, to the right as you enter, is a small bath complex.

The church is architecturally similar in style to the palace but smaller. Its basic form is a square, and it was once capped by a large dome (long since disappeared) and ringed by galleries on three sides. The fourth side is rounded off by a semicircular and half-domed apse that's common to many early Byzantine churches. Stairs in the northwestern corner lead to an upper gallery, which originally would have been reserved for women.

Admission is payable at a small ticket office within the entrance, to the kind caretaker, Mohammed al-Khudr, who has worked here for 10 years. Don't be surprised if he follows you around and offers you tea – he doesn't have too many visitors.

THE ASSASSINS

The group known today as the 'Assassins' were actually Nizari Ismailis, a Shiite Muslim sect. Shrouded in mystery and myriad theories, this small sect had a mountain stronghold at Alamut, in Iran, where one of the myths – or legends – of the Assassins was born. The devotees of the sect were trained to kill up close and personal, with the likely outcome being their own death. According to the explorer Marco Polo, the use of hashish and the promise of a garden of paradise in the afterlife were tools to control the behaviour of the followers of the sect. One theory has it that this is how the word 'assassin' came about – as a derivative of the full Arabic word for hashish.

In Syria the Assassins were notable for their control of the castle at Musyaf. As Shiites they were at war with the ruling Sunni Ayyubid dynasty and, lacking numbers, their preferred method of attack was carefully planned assassinations – they were always concerned with taking out their target with as little collateral damage as possible. As their exploits became well known, the sect found having an insider place a dagger and a note next to the bed of a sleeping enemy was enough to achieve their aims. In fact, legend has it that after a couple of assassination attempts on his life, Saladin (who was laying siege to their stronghold at Musyaf) spotted a figure leaving his heavily guarded tent, having left a note and a dagger at the foot of his bed. Regardless of the status of the legend, Saladin ceased his attacks – as did the Assassins.

The Assassins did take out some notable figures in history: Raymond II of Tripoli in 1152 and Conrad de Montferrat, king of Jerusalem, in 1192. But by 1273, Mamluk Sultan Beybars had not only all but finished off the Crusader presence in the Levant, he had also made certain to take out the Ismaili fortresses as well. For more on this fascinating topic, *The Assassin Legends: Myths of the Isma'ilis*, by Farhad Daftary, as well as Bernard Lewis' *The Assassins*, are essential reading.

BEEHIVE HOUSES

'They are like no other villages save those that appear in illustrations to Central African travel books.' So wrote Middle Eastern adventurer Gertrude Bell after encountering Syrian beehive houses. She was right. These structures are the ultimate in simplicity – whitewashed, conical, mud-brick structures of one chamber, accessed by a single small opening. But they're also well adapted to the climate: the thickness of the walls and lack of windows mean that the darkened interior remains a constant temperature, equally impervious to the heat of summer days and the cold of winter nights.

Although the appearance and building method of the beehive houses has changed little since Bell's time, there are far fewer of the structures these days and less enigmatic concrete boxes have taken over. Those that still exist are mostly used for storage of hay and fodder rather than as family dwellings. You'll see them east of Aleppo on the dusty plains as you head out to the Euphrates, and in the arid areas east of Hama, where in villages like Sarouj and Twalid Dabaghein people still inhabit these intriguing dwellings.

AROUND QASR IBN WARDAN

Between Qasr ibn Wardan and the village of Al-Hamra lie the hamlets of **Sarouj** (سروج) and **Twalid Dabaghein** (دباغين توالد) with their curious beehive houses – see Beehive Houses, above. Beyond Qasr ibn Wardan, a further 25km of rough road leads northeast to **Al-Anderine** (العندرين), another Byzantine settlement of which precious little remains today. The defensive settlement was dominated by a cathedral, but only a few pillars still stand.

GETTING THERE & AWAY

Although public transport doesn't go all the way out to Qasr ibn Wardan, it is still relatively easy to get there under your own steam if you're happy to get a lift with locals. Take a minibus from Hama to Al-Hamra (S£20, 45 minutes). From Al-Hamra you have to hitch the remaining 20km; although there's not much traffic going this way, whatever there is will most likely stop and take you on. You shouldn't have to wait much longer than 20 minutes or so for a ride out and about the same for the ride back.

While catching a ride with locals is not unusual in Syria, locals no longer recommend that single women travellers hitch in this area, since a young Canadian backpacker sadly went missing in 2007. It's worth noting that the young woman was the first foreigner ever to disappear in Syria, and it's not yet clear if she even disappeared on the way here.

Sarouj and Twalid Dabaghein are 50km and 53km from Hama respectively. The Cairo and Riad hotels in Hama both include a visit to the beehive houses as part of their organised trips out to Qasr ibn Wardan (see p164). You can also hire a car and driver or a taxi for around S£600.

Isriyya
أثريا

Only the main temple remains of the ancient desert settlement of **Seriana**, located at the town of Isriyya. Apart from a missing roof, the temple, dating from the 3rd century AD, is largely in one piece.

The stone employed is the same as that used in much of the construction in Palmyra. Seriana was in fact an important way station in the imperial Roman road network, with highways to Palmyra, Chalcis, Rasafa and Homs (ancient Emesa) all meeting here.

GETTING THERE & AWAY

Getting to Isriyya can be a bit trying. Buses and microbuses regularly ply their trade between Hama and Salamiyya (السلمية), but this part of the trip is best done with a driver or hire car. From Homs you could hire a service taxi for about S£600 one way. Otherwise, you could take a microbus the first 45km northeast to Saan (S£15). From there you have another 45km of road to travel, and may still be obliged to deal with a service taxi for the remainder of the trip.

Aleppo

حلب

While Damascus was always the 'holy' city, the seat of rulers and wary of foreigners, Aleppo (or Halab as it is known), Syria's second city, has been one of commerce since Roman times. While both cities claim the title of 'oldest continually inhabited city in the world', it's in Aleppo that the legacy of history feels more immediate.

Aleppo today retains that air of an Arabian bazaar city, with people going about business as they have done for centuries. The streets speak a rhythm of sounds – from horse-drawn carts over cobblestones to the more frenetic pace of donkey-riding couriers, still the fastest way through the atmospheric, labyrinthine souq that's fragrant with olive soap, exotic spices, roasting coffee and succulent grilled shwarma.

While Aleppo may not bustle as it did when it was a key stop on the Silk Road, the relative lack of big investment has actually done the city a favour. The World Heritage–listed Old City was saved from irreparable damage by not succumbing to modernisation. Today it is without doubt a fragile treasure, but a new breed of local investors and entrepreneurs have been wisely spending money to immaculately restore some old city treasures. A plan is in place to restore all of the historic buildings in the Old City – still a thriving centre with more than 100,000 residents. This new wave of preservation has brought boutique hotels and restaurants and has not only saved some classic buildings, but has also given the visitor a real feel for the city as it once was.

HIGHLIGHTS

- Haggle beside the locals in **Aleppo's souq** (p191), arguably the most vibrant and authentic in the whole Middle East

- Lose yourself in the labyrinthine alleys of charming **Al-Jdeida** (p181)

- Live like a pasha for a night at one of Aleppo's Arabian Nights–style **boutique hotels** (p187) and try to stop yourself extending your booking

- Explore **Qala'at Samaan** (p195), the hilltop remains of a sumptuous Byzantine cathedral dedicated to an ascetic who lived his life on top of a pillar

- Tiptoe around the **Dead Cities** (p198), the eerie shells of abandoned ancient towns and villages scattered across the landscape

- Savour Aleppo's deliciously complex cuisine at beautiful **Beit Sissi** (p189)

Qala'at
Samaan
★

★ Aleppo

Dead
Cities
★

■ AREA CODE: 021	■ POPULATION: 2 MILLION

HISTORY

Aleppo vies with Damascus for the title of the world's oldest continually inhabited city. In fact, a handful of other Middle Eastern towns make this claim too, but texts from the ancient kingdom of Mari on the Euphrates River indicate that Aleppo was already the centre of a powerful state as long ago as the 18th century BC, and the site may have been continuously inhabited for the past 8000 years. Its pre-eminent role in Syria came to an end with the Hittite invasions of the 17th and 16th centuries BC, and the city appears to have fallen into obscurity thereafter.

During the reign of the Seleucids, who arrived in the wake of Alexander the Great's campaign, Aleppo was given the name Beroia, and with the fall of Palmyra to the Romans became the major commercial link between the Mediterranean and Asia. The town was destroyed by the Persians in AD 611 and fell easily to the Muslims during their invasion in 637. The Byzantines overwhelmed the town in 961 and again in 968 but they could not take the Citadel.

Three disastrous earthquakes also shook the town in the 10th century and Nureddin (Nur ad-Din) subsequently rebuilt the town and fortress. In 1124 the Crusaders under Baldwin laid siege to the town.

After raids by the Mongols in 1260 and 1401, in which Aleppo was all but emptied of its population, the city finally came into the Ottoman Turkish orbit in 1516. It prospered greatly until an earthquake in 1822 killed over 60% of the inhabitants and wrecked many buildings, including the Citadel.

As long as four centuries ago European merchants – particularly French, English and those of the various city-states of Italy – had established themselves here. However, the flood of cheap goods from Europe in the wake of the Industrial Revolution, and the increasing use of alternative trading routes, slowly killed off a lot of Aleppo's trade and manufacturing. Today the major local industries are silk-weaving and cotton-printing. Products from the surrounding area include wool, hides, dried fruits and, particularly, pistachios, for which Aleppo is justly famous.

ORIENTATION

There are two distinct parts to central Aleppo: the New City, with the bulk of the places to stay and eat; and the Old City, with its many sights.

The New City centre lies south of the large public park, focused on the vast public plaza of Saahat Saad Allah al-Jabri. West of this square is the modern commercial centre – seen by very few visitors – while east is the main travellers area, bounded by Sharia al-Baron, Sharia al-Quwatli, Sharia Bab al-Faraj and Sharia al-Maari. In this tightly hemmed quadrilateral are myriad budget hotels and eateries. Sharia al-Baron is home to many travel agents, airline offices, banks and cinemas.

The Old City lies southeast of the New City, a 10-minute walk away. The two are separated by a couple of drab, wide avenues (Sharia al-Mutanabi and Sharia Bab Antakya) that feel more Murmansk than Middle East. The heart of the Old City is the compress of streets that make up the city's famed souq. Its main thoroughfares run east–west, slipping by the south face of the Great Mosque and terminating at the massive earthen mound of the Citadel. To the north of the Old City is the Christian-Armenian quarter Al-Jdeida, an area with its own distinct character and charm, and a buffer between old and new Aleppo.

ALEPPO AND THE SILK ROAD

Aleppo, Palmyra and Damascus were all notable stops on the Silk Road linking China to the Middle East and Europe. The Silk Road didn't only carry goods for sale: the road (actually a route that had several variations) transported knowledge, ideas and religions along its path. From before the birth of Christ through to the late Middle Ages, the route included Aleppo, which became a commercial hub due to its strategic position between the Mediterranean and the Euphrates. As the Roman Empire declined, the route became less travelled, but after the Mongol invasion it was revived and Aleppo prospered once again as a market city during the Ottoman Empire. To this day Aleppo attracts travellers and traders from the Middle East and Africa to its souq.

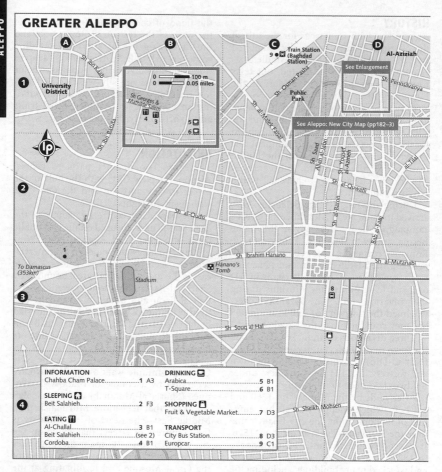

GREATER ALEPPO

INFORMATION			DRINKING 🍺		
Chahba Cham Palace	1	A3	Arabica	5	B1
			T-Square	6	B1
SLEEPING 🛏					
Beit Salahieh	2	F3	SHOPPING 🛍		
			Fruit & Vegetable Market	7	D3
EATING 🍴					
Al-Challal	3	B1	TRANSPORT		
Beit Salahieh	(see 2)		City Bus Station	8	D3
Cordoba	4	B1	Europcar	9	C1

INFORMATION
Bookshops
Chahba Cham Palace (Map pp174-5; Sharia al-Qudsi)
The best bookshop in Aleppo is at this hotel. It has a reasonable selection of books about Syria and the Arab world, some locally produced guidebooks, and a handful of novels in both English and French. There's also a limited range of international newspapers available. It's a S£50 taxi ride out there.
Librairie Said (Map pp182-3; cnr Sharia Qostaki al-Homsi & Sharia Litani) Has a small selection of dusty old novels as well as the odd Syria coffee-table book.

Internet Access
Aleppo has few internet cafés. You're more likely to find wireless internet access in the modern cafés in the New City, as young Aleppans prefer to use their own laptops.

Concord Internet Café (Map pp182-3; Sharia al-Quwatli; per 30min S£50; ⏰ 9am-11pm) Above a pastry café.

Medical Services
There are pharmacies all over Aleppo, with several congregated around the junction of Sharia al-Quwatli and Sharia Bab al-Faraj.
Dr Farid Megarbaneh (☎ 221 1218) This doctor, who speaks excellent English and French, is recommended.

Money
There are ATMs all over Aleppo, so leave the travellers cheques at home – you'll be hard-pressed to find a bank that will change them.
Commercial Bank of Syria (Map pp182-3; Sharia Yousef al-Azmeh; ⏰ 8.30am-1.30pm Sat-Thu) It's marked

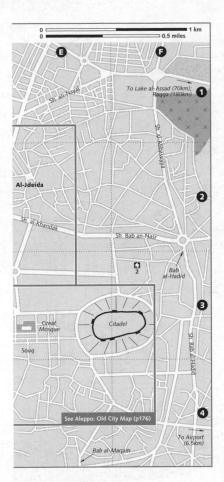

by a big sign in English but the entrance is hidden at the back of an arcade.

Exchange office (Map pp182-3; cnr Sharia al-Quwatli & Sharia Bab al-Faraj; 9am-7.30pm) Convenient but doesn't accept travellers cheques.

Post

DHL (Map pp182-3; ☎ 444 0322; off Sharia al-Quwatli; 9.30am-9pm)

Main post office (Map pp182-3; Saahat Saad Allah al-Jabri; 8am-5pm) On the southwest side of the main square. The parcels office is around the corner to the left of the main entrance.

Telephone

Telephone office (Map pp182-3; Saahat Saad Allah al-Jabri; 8am-10pm) At the post office.

Tourist Information

Automobile & Touring Club Syria (☎ 224 7272) Look out for the publications, brochures and maps produced by this organisation, available from some hotels, cafés and museums.

Tourist office (Map pp182-3; ☎ 212 1228, 223 0000; Sharia al-Baron; 8.30am-8pm Sun-Fri, 9am-2pm Sat) In the gardens opposite the National Museum. There's little information; the best you'll get is a free map.

Visa Extensions

Immigration office (Map p176; Sharia al-Qala'a; 8am-1.30pm Sat-Thu) On the 1st floor of the government building just north of the Citadel. Bring four passport photos and then fill out forms in quadruplicate. The processing takes around 1½ hours and there's a fee of S£25. Extensions of up to two months are possible. Get your photos done at one of the shacks on the road across from the office.

SIGHTS
Old City
المدينة القديمة

At one time walled and entered only by one of eight gates, the Old City has long since burst its seams and now has few definable edges. Exploring its seemingly infinite number of alleys and cul-de-sacs could occupy the better part of a week, depending on how inquisitive you are. We recommend visiting at least twice: once on a busy weekday to experience the all-out five-senses assault of the souq, and a second time on a Friday when, with all the shops closed, the lanes are silent and empty. Relieved of the need to keep flattening yourself against the wall to let the overladen donkeys and little minivans squeeze by, you're free to appreciate architectural details.

Begin your exploration of the Old City at Bab Antakya, one of only two remaining city gates, which is on the street of the same name about 500m south of Amir Palace Hotel. From here the sight descriptions below follow a route eastward. The area is just as easily approached from the north via the Great Mosque or from the east starting at the Citadel.

BAB ANTAKYA
باب أنطاكية

The 13th-century Bab Antakya (Antioch Gate; Map p176), the western gate of the old walled city, is all but completely hidden by the swarm of busy workshops surrounding it, but you definitely get a sense of 'entering' as you pass under its great stone portal and through the defensively doglegged vaulted

ALEPPO: OLD CITY

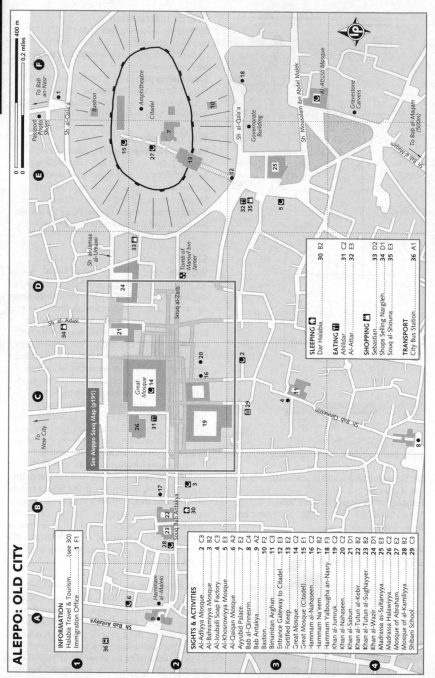

INFORMATION
Halabia Travel & Tourism.............(see 30)
Immigration Office...................................**1** F1

SIGHTS & ACTIVITIES
Al-Adliyya Mosque............................**2** C3
Al-Bahramiyya Mosque....................**3** B2
Al-Joubaili Soap Factory..................**4** C3
Al-Khosrowiyya Mosque...................**5** E3
Al-Qaiqan Mosque.............................**6** A2
Ayyubid Palace...................................**7** E2
Bab al-Qinnesrin...............................**8** C4
Bab Antakya.......................................**9** A2
Bastion...**10** F2
Bimaristan Arghan............................**11** C3
Entrance Gateway to Citadel...........**12** E3
Fortified Keep....................................**13** E2
Great Mosque....................................**14** C2
Great Mosque (Citadel)....................**15** E1
Hammam al-Nahaseen......................**16** C2
Hammam Na'eem................................**17** B2
Hammam Yalbougha an-Nasry........**18** F3
Khan al-Jumruk..................................**19** C2
Khan al-Nahaseen.............................**20** C2
Khan al-Sabun....................................**21** D1
Khan al-Tutun al-Kebir......................**22** B2
Khan al-Tutun al-Sughayyer............**23** B2
Khan al-Wazir.....................................**24** D1
Madrassa as-Sultaniyya....................**25** E3
Madrassa Halawiyya..........................**26** C2
Mosque of Abraham..........................**27** E2
Mosque of al-Kamiliyya....................**28** B2
Shibani School....................................**29** C3

SLEEPING 🛏
Dar Halabia...**30** B2

EATING 🍴
Ahildar...**31** C2
Al-Attar..**32** E3

SHOPPING 🛍
Sebastian...**33** D2
Shops Selling Nargileh......................**34** D1
Souq al-Shouna..................................**35** E3

TRANSPORT
City Bus Station..................................**36** A1

lonelyplanet.com ALEPPO •• Sights 177

ALEPPO

KEEPING IT REAL

More damage was done in the 20th century to the precious historic fabric of our urban spaces than at any other time in history, according to Anthony M Tung in *Preserving the World's Great Cities* (2001). Tung blames concrete and steel, industrialisation and the automobile, but in these respects Aleppo has been lucky. The city enjoyed its greatest period of prosperity under the Mamluks and early Ottomans, when cash from commerce furnished it with the grandest of architecture, but Aleppo was well into decline by the end of the 19th century and languished in the 20th century, subsequently missing out on many of the most destructive aspects of modernism. As a consequence, few cities anywhere in the world have a medieval heritage as rich as Aleppo's.

Unfortunately, misguided planning in the 1950s ploughed major new roads through the Old City, causing considerable damage, compounded by the new building construction that went with them. Since then, Aleppo's Old City has been listed by Unesco as a World Heritage Site – keeping company with monuments such as the Great Wall of China, the Pyramids and Machu Picchu. More significantly, it has been the subject of an ongoing rehabilitation programme managed by the municipality in conjunction with the German government (via the offices of the German Agency for Technical Cooperation or GTZ – see www.gtz-aleppo.org). There are 240 classified historical monuments in the Old City and a strategy for the restoration and rehabilitation of all of them. Tourism is part of the plan, but a balance between this, the privacy of the residents and the preservation of authenticity is paramount. The aim is to nurture local communities and businesses and create more community spaces in the hope that the Old City will survive as a historic but living entity, and not become just another open-air museum piece.

The Old City has more than 100,000 residents. About one third of its houses currently require urgent structural repairs while another third need maintenance or rehabilitation. Financial and technical help has been made available for residents to achieve this. Traffic management and renewal of the water supply and sewer networks are also underway. While much more funding is needed, at least there is a plan in place to preserve what is one of the real gems of the Middle East.

passageway. Once through here you emerge onto Souq Bab Antakya, the bazaar's bustling main thoroughfare, which runs due east to halt abruptly at the foot of the Citadel, some 1.5km away.

Until the development of the New City in the 19th century, this was Aleppo's main street, tracing the route of the decumanus, the principal thoroughfare of the Roman city of Beroia. A great triumphal arch is thought to have stood on the site of Bab Antakya and part of its remains were used in the construction of nearby **Mosque of al-Kamiliyya** (Map p176), 200m ahead on your left. First, take a quick detour left, immediately after the gate, up a flight of stone steps beside a hammam (often flagged by towels drying outside), to a street that follows the line of the old city ramparts. In addition to fascinating views, there's the little **Al-Qaiqan Mosque** (Crows' Mosque; Map p176) with its doorway flanked by basalt Byzantine columns, a façade studded with column segments, and a block inscribed with Hittite script embedded in the south wall.

KHAN AL-JUMRUK & OTHERS
خان الجمرك و غيره

Beyond Al-Kamiliyya mosque, a corrugated-iron roof blots out the sunlight and the souq proper starts. To the left are entranceways to two adjacent khans, or travellers' inns, **Khan al-Tutun Sughayyer** (Map p176) and **Khan al-Tutun Kebir** (Map p176), the little and big khans of Tutun, although in fact they're both fairly modest in scale. A few steps along on the right is **Al-Bahramiyya Mosque** (Map p176), built in early Ottoman style in the late 16th century. From here on, virtually every building is a khan and there are a few in particular worth investigating.

At the point at which the street again becomes spanned by stone vaulting, slip off to the right, then take an immediate left to reach the great gateway of the magnificent **Khan al-Jumruk** (Map p176). Completed in 1574, this is the largest and most impressive of Aleppo's khans. At one time it housed the consulates and trade missions of the English, Dutch and French, in addition to 344 shops. Its days as a European enclave

ALEPPO'S TOP HISTORIC HOUSES

Aleppo has an embarrassment of riches when it comes to traditional houses. While they all look like fortresses from the exterior, a peek inside reveals an oasis of calm. All are in the Al-Jdeida quarter (Map pp182–3).

- Beit Kebbeh
- Beit Sader
- Beit Mariana Marrache
- Beit Balit
- Beit Basil
- Beit Dallal
- Beit Wakil
- Beit Altounji
- Beit Ghazzali
- Beit Ashiqbash (Museum of Popular Tradition)

are now long gone but the khan is still in use, serving as a cloth market. The decoration on the interior façade of the gateway is splendid.

Next to Al-Jumruk (but entered from the east side) is the much smaller **Khan al-Nahaseen** (Khan of the Coppersmiths; Map p176), dating from the first half of the 16th century. Until the 19th century, rooms on the 1st floor housed the Venetian consul, and during the 20th century they were the residence of the Belgian consul, Adolphe Poche, and his family. Madam Jenny Poche, descended from the last of the Venetian consuls, maintains the property, which may well qualify as the oldest continuously inhabited house in Aleppo. Its rooms are filled with a beguiling variety of collections gathered by family members over the centuries, including archaeological finds, antiquities, mosaics and precious early photography, and there's a fine library where Madam Poche's father once waltzed with Agatha Christie. Visitors (no large groups) are welcomed only by appointment; phone the current Belgian consulate (☎ 362 2666).

SOUQ السوق

Not as extensive as Cairo's Khan al-Khalili or as grand as Istanbul's Grand Bazaar, Aleppo's souq (Map p191) is nonetheless one of the most atmospheric in the Middle East. Its appeal derives largely from the fact that it's still the main centre of local commerce. If an Aleppan housewife needs some braid for her curtains, a taxi driver needs a new seat cover, or the school kids need backpacks, it's to the souq that they all come. Little seems to have changed here in hundreds of years, and while recent years have seen an increase in tourism, the local trade has yet to be displaced by sightseers.

Parts of the souq date from the 13th century, but the bulk of what stands today belongs to the Ottoman era (largely 16th- to 19th-century). A walk through the souq could take all day, particularly if you accept invitations by the stall owners to stop for tea. For tips on what to buy where, including a detailed map, see Shopping (p191).

GREAT MOSQUE الجامع الكبير

On the northern edge of the souq is the Great Mosque (Al-Jamaa al-Kebir; Map p176), or Umayyad Mosque, the younger sibling (by 10 years) of the Umayyad Mosque in Damascus. It's also known as Al-Jamaa Zacharia after Prophet Zacharia, the father of St John the Baptist. Started by Caliph Al-Walid (r AD 705–15), who earlier founded the Umayyad Mosque in Damascus, the work was completed by his successor Caliph Suleiman (r AD 715–17). However, aside from the plan, nothing survives of the original mosque as the building has been destroyed and rebuilt countless times.

Miraculously, the mosque's freestanding **minaret** has managed to survive in exactly its original form, as built from 1090 to 1092, although it does have a pronounced lean as a result of an earthquake. Standing 45m high, it's majestic, rising up through five distinct levels, adorned with blind arches, to a wooden canopy over a muezzin's gallery from where the call to prayer was announced.

While it's not possible to climb the minaret, visitors are allowed inside the mosque. There's no admission fee but footwear must be removed and women must hire an *abeyya* (hooded cloak) to wear for S£50. Entrance is directly into the courtyard, the floor of which is decorated by black-and-white marble geometric patterns. Under a strong sun, the reflected light is so harsh it hurts the eyes, while the hot marble scorches shoeless feet.

Inside the prayer hall is a fine 15th-century carved *minbar* (pulpit). Behind the grille to the left of this is supposedly the head of Zacharia. The padlocks fastened to the grille are placed here temporarily by locals who believe that a few days soaking up the *baraka* (blessings) from the tomb will give them strength.

MADRASSA HALAWIYYA   المدرسة الحلوية
Opposite the western entrance of the mosque, this former theological college (Map p176) was built in 1245 and stands on the site of what was once the 6th-century Cathedral of St Helen. The prayer hall opposite the entrance incorporates all that remains of the cathedral, which is a semi-circular row of six columns with intricately decorated, acanthus-leaved capitals. For several hundred years the cathedral and the Great Mosque (built in the cathedral's gardens) stood next to each other, serving their respective faiths, which worshipped side by side in harmony. The cathedral was only seized by the Muslims in 1124 in response to atrocities committed by the Crusaders.

AROUND THE GREAT MOSQUE
The souq is at its most atmospheric immediately south and east of the Great Mosque. This is where you'll find gold and silver, carpets and kilims (see p191).

Away from the shopping temptations, there are another couple of khans well worth your time. In the block east of the Great Mosque is the early-16th-century **Khan al-Sabun** (Soap Khan; Map p176), largely obscured by a clutter of shops but with a distinctive, richly decorated Mamluk façade, considered to be one of the best examples of Mamluk architecture in the city. Internally it's one of the prettiest of khans, with vine-hung trelliswork and the brightly hued wares of carpet sellers draped over the balconies.

The 17th-century **Khan al-Wazir** (Minister's Khan; Map p176), a block further east, also has a beautifully decorated gateway. It's one of the grandest such structures in Aleppo and largely unaltered by modern development.

BAB AL-QINNESRIN   باب قنسرين
Sharia Bab Qinnesrin is the southern continuation of Souq an-Nahaseen (Coppersmiths' Souq, which unfortunately no

longer houses coppersmiths), and it runs down to Bab al-Qinnesrin, the surviving southern Old City gate. It's been a prime beneficiary of the attentions of the GTZ and the Old City rehabilitation project (see Keeping It Real, p177). It only stretches for a little over 500m, but in that stretch there's quite a lot to see.

The Rehabilitation of the Old City of Aleppo, a permanent exhibition in the splendid 16th-century **Shibani School** (Map p176; ☎ 331 9270; Al Jaloum quarter; ☒ 9am-4pm Wed-Mon), illustrates the work underway to make the city more liveable. The guide Mustapha may even take you to the rooftop to enjoy the spectacular views.

You'll find towards the bottom of Souq al-Nahaseen, just before it becomes Sharia Bab Qinnesrin, a short passageway leading to **Al-Adliyya Mosque** (Map p176), built in 1555 and one of the city's major Ottoman-era mosques. It's worth a quick look inside for the fine tiling. To the south, the street doglegs round the jutting corner of a small khan, now used by shoe wholesalers, beyond which noses are set twitching by the fragrant smells emanating from **Al-Joubaili Soap Factory** (Map p176), ages old and still producing soaps the traditional way using olive oil and bay laurel.

Directly across the street, behind railings, is the splendid **Bimaristan Arghan** (Map p176), one of the most enchanting buildings in the whole of Aleppo. Dating from the 14th century, it was converted from a house into an asylum, a role it continued to perform until the 20th century. The main entrance gives access to a beautifully kept courtyard with a central pool overhung by greenery. Diagonally across, a doorway leads through to a series of tight passages, one of which terminates in a small, octagonal, domed courtyard. Off this are 11 small cells; these are where the dangerous patients were confined.

Continuing south, you reach the huge, wonderfully preserved and tunnel-like **Bab al-Qinnesrin** (Map p176), which, like Bab Antakya, incorporates a defensive dogleg.

CITADEL   القلعة
Rising up on a high mound at the eastern end of the souq, the **Citadel** (Map p176; ☎ 362 4010; adult/student S£150/10; ☒ 9am-6pm Wed-Mon summer, to 4pm winter) is Aleppo's most famous and most

spectacular landmark. Dominating the city, it has long been the heart of its defences.

The mound it stands upon is not, as it first seems, artificial: it's a natural feature that originally served as a place of worship, as evidenced by two basalt lions unearthed and identified as belonging to a 10th-century-BC temple.

It's thought the first fortifications were erected at the time of the Seleucids (364–333 BC), but everything seen today dates from much later. The Citadel served as a power base for the Muslims during the 12th-century Crusades, when the moat, 20m deep and 30m wide, was dug and the lower two-thirds of the mound were encased in a stone glacis. Much rebuilding and strengthening occurred during Mamluk rule from 1250 to 1517 and it's largely their work that survives.

Touring the Citadel

To enter, cross the moat by a stepped bridge on the south side. Any attacking forces would have been dangerously exposed on the bridge as they confronted the massive **fortified keep**, from which defenders could rain down arrows and pour boiling oil through the row of machicolations. The **bastion**, off to the right, was added in the 14th century to allow for flanking fire on the bridge.

The first great gate was set to the right rather than dead in front of the bridge to prevent charges with a battering ram. Note the beautiful calligraphy and entwined dragons above the gate and the door decorated with horseshoes. Once through the gate, a succession of five right-angle turns and three sets of steel-plated doors formed a formidable barrier to any would-be aggressors. Some of the doors still remain; one is decorated with a pair of lions, echoing the millennia-old use of lions as guardians against evil, as seen in the National Museum.

Take the path north. On the right is a series of doorways, one of which has steps leading down to two sunken chambers that served as a cistern and prison. Beyond is a set of stairs doubling back to lead up to the remains of an **Ayyubid Palace** dating from the 13th century. The most striking remains are of a soaring entrance portal with stalactite stone decoration. To the rear of the palace is a recently renovated Mamluk-era hammam.

A path from the hammam leads back towards the fortified keep and its heavily restored throne room, with a magnificent, intricately decorated wooden ceiling.

Back on the main path, off to the left is the small 12th-century **Mosque of Abraham**, attributed to Nureddin and one of several legendary burial places for the head of John the Baptist.

DIY ALEPPO

Yep. Keep that guidebook closed and just wander. Aleppo is one of the best cities in the Middle East (perhaps in the world) to just let your curiosity guide you. We'll give you some starting points first, of course:

- Northeast of the Citadel via the Bayada quarter to Bab al-Hadid – this ramshackle area sees few foreigners exploring its fascinating streets. Follow the main thoroughfare past Souq al-Haddadin (Blacksmiths' Market) with diversions through the mazelike Bayada quarter to imposing Bab al-Hadid. Along the way you'll pass some of Aleppo's oldest madrassas, mosques, hammams and palaces. There's been little renovation and no signs exist, so look out for fine architectural details and peak through doors and windows when you can.

- Bab al-Hadid to Al-Jdeida – instead of taking the main route along Sharias Bab al-Hadid and Bab al-Nasr to Al-Jdeida, take the backstreets through the living breathing lanes of this old neighbourhood. People are focused on their everyday life, so you'll be pleasantly ignored, but while it's easy to get lost in the tangle of streets, rest assured someone will point you in the right direction if you can't find your way.

- Northwest of the Citadel via the Farafra quarter to Bab al-Nasr – another old area ignored by tourists, who tend to stick to the main roads en route between the Old City and Al-Jdeida, these dusty streets are home to dilapidated khans, mosques, the Masbanat al-Zanabili (two 19th-century soap-making factories), hammams, palaces and even a synagogue.

At the northern end of the path, opposite what is now a café, is the 13th-century **great mosque**, a rather grandiose title for a building of such humble dimensions. The café is housed in an Ottoman-era barracks, and it's from here that you are gifted with extraordinary views over the collage of roofs, domes and minarets.

SOUTH OF THE CITADEL

Opposite the Citadel entrance is the Ayyubid **Madrassa as-Sultaniyya** (Map p176). The prayer hall has a striking mihrab (niche indicating the direction of Mecca) with eye-catching ornamentation achieved through multicoloured marble inlays. Unfortunately this part of the building is often locked. Also here is the **mausoleum of Al-Malek az-Zaher Ghazi**, a son of Saladin (Salah ad-Din), and one-time occupant of the Citadel.

Across the road to the west is a low, multidomed mosque set in gardens. Known as **Al-Khosrowiyya Mosque** (Map p176), it's notable for being one of the earliest works of the famed Turkish architect Sinan, dating to 1537. It still serves as the main place of worship for the neighbourhood and each Friday streams of men and young boys make a beeline here to assume their places for noon prayers.

To the east of Madrassa as-Sultaniyya is Hammam Yalbougha an-Nasry (p185).

Al-Jdeida ﺍﻟﺠﺪﻳﺪﺓ

Al-Jdeida quarter is the most charming part of Aleppo. It's a well-maintained warren of narrow, stone-flagged lanes with walls like canyons. The façades that line the alleys are blank because the buildings all look inwards onto central courtyards. Every so often one of the studded wooden doors with their clenched fists for knockers will open and passers-by can get a glimpse inside.

Much of the architecture dates from the Ottoman era, making the quarter younger than the Old City (hence its name Al-Jdeida, 'the new'), but it's equally fascinating. It developed as an area for Christian refugees (largely Maronite and Armenians), who became prosperous traders.

The quarter has been undergoing something of a rebirth in recent years. With the backing of an enlightened city mayor, private investors have been encouraged to purchase and renovate properties in the quarter and convert them to commercial usage. As a result there are myriad boutique hotels occupying former merchants' mansions and an ever-growing number of restaurants and bars sprouting in striped-stone courtyards and cellars.

AROUND SAAHAT AL-HATAB
ﺳﺎﺣﺔ ﺍﻟﺤﻄﺐ ﻭﺣﻮﺍﻟﻴﻬﺎ

If there's a heart to Al-Jdeida, then it's Saahat al-Hatab (Hatab Sq) in the oldest area of Salibeh, lined with shops selling oriental jewellery. To the north is **Sharaf Mosque** (Map pp182–3), one of the neighbourhood's earliest monuments, built in the reign of the Mamluk sultan Qaitbey (r 1468–96). At the western corner, just the other side of Orient House Antiques (p192), a stylised sculpture of two robed women marks the turn for Sharia al-Sissi. Along here on the right, **Beit Sissi** (Sissi House; Map pp182–3) is a 17th-century residence that was one of the first of the area's many historic houses to be restored; it's now a renowned restaurant (p189). About 50m further on the left, **Beit Wakil** (Map pp182–3) is two 18th-century houses lovingly transformed into a stunning boutique hotel and courtyard restaurant (p189).

Backtrack across Saahat al-Hatab and make a beeline south along Sharia al-Kayyali. On the right is a door with a plaque announcing **Beit Ghazzali** (Map pp182–3). This is the largest house in the quarter. It was built in the 17th century and served as an Armenian school for much of the 20th century. It's now owned by the city council and is undergoing restoration until its fate is decided. Some of the walls have fine painted decoration and there's a splendid private hammam.

MUSEUM OF POPULAR TRADITION
ﻣﺘﺤﻒ ﺍﻟﺘﻘﺎﻟﻴﺪ ﺍﻟﺸﻌﺒﻴﺔ

A little further down from Beit Ghazzali is yet another house, Beit Ajiqbash (built 1757), now a home for the **Museum of Popular Tradition** (Map pp182-3; ☎ 333 6111; Sharia Haret al-Yasmin; adult/student S£75/5; ☑ 8am-2pm Wed-Mon), with fascinating artefacts relating to everyday life in bygone times. The splendid architecture and intricate decoration make this a must-visit.

ALEPPO

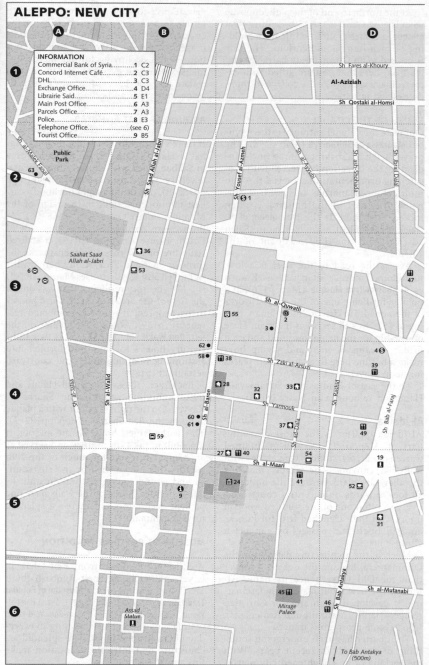

ALEPPO: NEW CITY

INFORMATION

Commercial Bank of Syria	1 C2
Concord Internet Café	2 C3
DHL	3 C3
Exchange Office	4 D4
Librairie Said	5 E1
Main Post Office	6 A3
Parcels Office	7 A3
Police	8 E3
Telephone Office	(see 6)
Tourist Office	9 B5

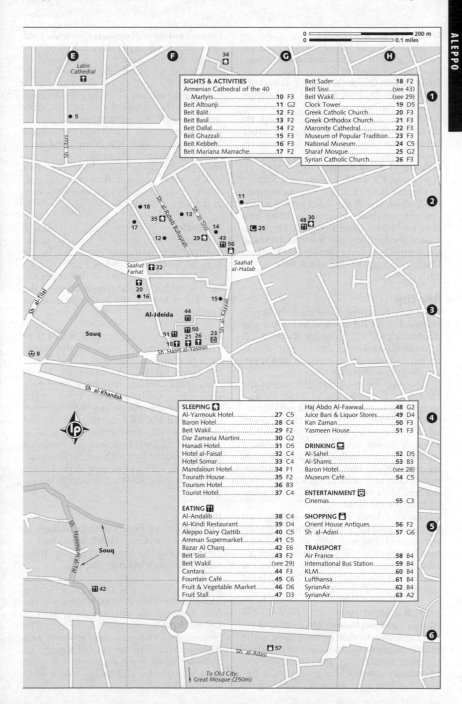

0   200 m
0   0.1 miles

SIGHTS & ACTIVITIES
Armenian Cathedral of the 40
Martyrs...................................**10** F3
Beit Altounji.............................**11** G2
Beit Balit..................................**12** F2
Beit Basil..................................**13** F2
Beit Dallal.................................**14** F2
Beit Ghazzali............................**15** F3
Beit Kebbeh..............................**16** F3
Beit Mariana Marrache..............**17** F2

Beit Sader.................................**18** F2
Beit Sissi.................................(see 43)
Beit Wakil...............................(see 29)
Clock Tower..............................**19** D5
Greek Catholic Church...............**20** F3
Greek Orthodox Church.............**21** F3
Maronite Cathedral...................**22** F3
Museum of Popular Tradition....**23** F3
National Museum......................**24** C5
Sharaf Mosque..........................**25** G2
Syrian Catholic Church..............**26** F3

SLEEPING
Al-Yarmouk Hotel......................**27** C5
Baron Hotel...............................**28** C4
Beit Wakil.................................**29** F2
Dar Zamaria Martini..................**30** G2
Hanadi Hotel.............................**31** D5
Hotel al-Faisal...........................**32** C4
Hotel Somar..............................**33** C4
Mandaloun Hotel......................**34** F1
Tourath House...........................**35** F2
Tourism Hotel...........................**36** B3
Tourist Hotel.............................**37** C4

EATING
Al-Andalib.................................**38** C4
Al-Kindi Restaurant...................**39** D4
Aleppo Dairy Qattib..................**40** C5
Amman Supermarket.................**41** C5
Bazar Al Charq..........................**42** E6
Beit Sissi...................................**43** F2
Beit Wakil...............................(see 29)
Cantara.....................................**44** F3
Fountain Café............................**45** C6
Fruit & Vegetable Market..........**46** D6
Fruit Stall.................................**47** D3

Haj Abdo Al-Fawwal..................**48** G2
Juice Bars & Liquor Stores.........**49** D4
Kan Zaman...............................**50** F3
Yasmeen House.........................**51** F3

DRINKING
Al-Sahel....................................**52** D5
Al-Shams..................................**53** B3
Baron Hotel.............................(see 28)
Museum Café............................**54** C5

ENTERTAINMENT
Cinemas....................................**55** C3

SHOPPING
Orient House Antiques...............**56** F2
Sh al-Adasi...............................**57** G6

TRANSPORT
Air France.................................**58** B4
International Bus Station............**59** B4
KLM..**60** B4
Lufthansa..................................**61** B4
SyrianAir...................................**62** B4
SyrianAir...................................**63** A2

Latin
Cathedral

Sh al-Tilani

Sharaf Mosque

Saahat
Farhat

Saahat
al-Hatab

Al-Jdeida

Sh al-Tilani

Souq

Sh Haret al-Yasmin

Sh al-Khandak

Sh al-Rahib Buhayrah

Sh al-Sissi

Sh al-Kayali

Souq

Sh Hamman al-Tal

Souq

To Old City;
Great Mosque (250m)

Sh al-Adasi

CHURCHES & CATHEDRALS

Al-Jdeida is home to five major churches, each aligned to a different denomination. Immediately west of the museum is the **Syrian Catholic Church** (Mar Assia al-Hakim; Map pp182–3), built in 1625 and happy to admit visitors who come knocking. Next stop is the 19th-century **Greek Orthodox Church** (Map pp182–3) and further beyond that, still on Haret al-Yasmin, is the entrance to the 17th-century **Armenian Cathedral of the 40 Martyrs** (Map pp182–3). If possible, it's worth visiting on a Sunday to observe the Armenian mass performed here, which is still pervaded with a sensuous aura of ritual. It starts at 10am and lasts two hours. North of these three, on Saahat Farhat, are the **Maronite Cathedral** (Map pp182–3) and a smaller **Greek Catholic Church** (Map pp182–3), which date to the 19th century.

New City

Most visitors' experience of modern Aleppo is limited to the Bab al-Faraj area, a low-rise neighbourhood of cubbyhole shops, small businesses, *mekaniki* (car repair workshops) and, east of the baroque **clock tower**, the swish new Sheraton hotel.

However, the most pleasant part of the New City is northwest of here, in and around the upmarket **Al-Aziziah** neighbourhood, developed during the 19th century and home to Aleppo's moneyed families, most of whom are Christian. The busy streets are lined with splendid mansions, modern fashion boutiques, lively contemporary cafés and swish new restaurants, and the area has a real buzz about it that other parts of Aleppo lack.

There's a large **public park**, prettily laid out with pathways meandering through well-tended greenery and an impressive fountain entrance off Sharia Saad Allah al-Jabri. If you're through with walking for the day this is a great place to bring a book and picnic.

NATIONAL MUSEUM   المتحف الوطني

Aleppo's **National Museum** (Map pp182–3; ☎ 212 2400/1; adult/student S£75/10; ☽ 9am-5.30pm), in the middle of town opposite the tourist office, is rather nondescript apart from the extraordinary colonnade of giant granite figures that fronts the entrance. Standing on the backs of stylised creatures are wide-eyed characters, replicas of pillars that once supported the 9th-century-BC temple-palace complex at Tell Halaf, near the border with Turkey in the northeast of the country.

From the entrance hall the exhibits were displayed chronologically in an anticlockwise direction, but at the time of research the museum was undergoing extensive 'renovation', which was being conducted with scant concern for safety and little respect for the artefacts. We hope your visit will be more pleasant than our last one. Below is the route through exhibit rooms at the time of research.

Tell Brak   تل براك

Tell Brak, 45km north of Hassake in far northeastern Syria, was excavated by Sir Max Mallowan, husband of Agatha Christie. Most of the exhibits in this room are finds from his digs, although many of the best pieces went to the British Museum in London.

Mari   ماري (تل الحريري)

This room contains some of the museum's best pieces, unearthed at Tell Hariri, the site of the 3rd-millennium-BC city of Mari (p223), on the Euphrates River near the present-day Iraqi border. Look for the tableaux of delicate carved-shell figurines of a general and his fettered prisoners and chariots, which attest to the high level of artistry at this early time, and the wonderful greened bronze lion with a doleful expression. Along with a twin, now in the Louvre in Paris, it was discovered flanking a temple doorway.

Hama   حماه

The exhibits of finds from excavations in 1931–38 at the Hama citadel, dating back to 1000 BC, were no longer on display at the time of research but may reappear.

Ugarit   اوغاريت (رأس شمره)

Many of the finds display evidence of the links between the one-time busy port of Ugarit (Ras Shamra; p149) and Egypt. The bronze Egyptian figures were probably gifts from a pharaoh to the king of Ugarit. An alabaster vessel bears the name of Ramses II in hieroglyphs, and there's also a limestone obelisk.

Tell Halaf تل حلف
This hall is dominated by figures similar to the replicas at the museum entrance; however, these are millennia old. The figures are believed to represent gods and a goddess; the central one is thought to be Haddad, the weather god, symbolically linked to the bull (on which he stands). The colossi were originally flanked by two wide-eyed sphinxes; a replica of one is here. The large panels are plaster casts of originals that once adorned Tell Halaf's palace walls – the originals were destroyed during WWII in a bombing raid on a German museum.

Tell Arslan Tash تل ارسلان طاش
The astonishing collection of ivory carving was discovered in the remains of a palace at Tell Arslan Tash, an Aramaean city (ancient name Hadatu) in the northeast of the country, excavated by the French in 1928. They are not Syrian in origin and have been identified as coming from Phoenicia, and are dated to the 9th century BC. There is a series depicting the birth of the god Horus from a lotus flower, which is similar to an alabaster carving of Tutankhamen emerging from a lotus on display in the Egyptian Museum in Cairo.

Tell Ahmar تل احمر
Tell Ahmar is the site of another ancient Aramaean city, and is near what is now the Syrian-Turkish border, 20km south of the crossing point of Jarablos. The wall paintings displayed in this room were removed from the remains of a palace excavated by the French in the 1920s and date from around the 8th century BC.

ACTIVITIES
Originally constructed in 1491, **Hammam Yalbougha an-Nasry** (Map p176; ☎ 362 3154; near Citadel entrance) was one of Syria's finest working bathhouses and something of a city showpiece, yet was closed for maintenance when we visited with no opening date fixed. If you can manage to get in to take a look around, there's a splendid sun clock inside the dome above reception. If it is operational again, don't leave Aleppo without having a massage and scrub here.

The renovated, men-only **Hammam al-Nahaseen** (Map p176; hammam only S£300, complete massage & scrub S£500), in the heart of the souq just south of the Great Mosque, is open long hours and is still a local favourite despite increasingly attracting tourists.

Hammam Na'eem (Map p176; hammam only S£350, complete massage & scrub S£425), also known as Hammam al-Jedida, is a quiet, clean, friendly, men-only place north of the main souq street. To find it, coming from Bab Antakya along Souq Bab Antakya, take the first left after the start of the corrugated-iron roofing and it's just ahead on the right.

TOURS
Halabia Travel & Tourism (Map p176; ☎ 224 8497; www.halabia-tours.com) Run by the friendly and knowledgeable Abdel Hay Kaddar. They can organise visas and meet you at the Turkish, Jordanian and Lebanese borders. A variety of tours are on offer.

Tahhan Tourism (☎ 263 5178) Offers a variety of tours in and around Aleppo, from Qala'at Samaan (US$55) to Qala'at al-Hosn (Krak des Chevaliers; US$80), in new air-conditioned vehicles with multilingual tour guides.

SLEEPING
The accommodation scene in Aleppo has improved at the top end, with a slew of new boutique hotels. The midrange options are a little limited but Aleppo's good-value boutique hotels are a good excuse to spend a couple of nights in higher-priced digs. Good, clean budget lodgings are thin on the ground and the handful of recommended places fill up fast. Book in advance.

Budget
Hanadi Hotel (Map pp182-3; ☎ 223 8113; Bab al-Faraj; s/d/tr S£350/1000/1500; ✺) Once you get past the shock of the Barbie-esque colour scheme (think pink), this excellent budget hotel has the makings of a backpacker favourite. It has the friendliest multilingual reception staff in Aleppo, pleasant rooms facing an enormous shady sun terrace, and a long list of services. It's well located 100m south of the clock tower.

Tourist Hotel (Map pp182-3; ☎ 221 6583; Sharia ad-Dala; s/d/tr without bathroom S£400/700/900, d/tr with bathroom S£800/1200) Aleppo's best budget option is more akin to a homely European-style pension than a hotel. The staff are warm, friendly and multilingual, the décor is delightfully old-fashioned and the place is immaculate. Some rooms have shared bathrooms; others have private bathrooms. Booking in advance is essential. Breakfast is S£100.

Hotel Somar (Map pp182-3; ☎ 211 3198, 212 5925; Sharia ad-Dala; s/d/tr US$13/19/23, without bathroom US$11/16/21; ✖) A rather old-fashioned but well-kept little hotel; the walls had been freshly painted when we visited. The simple rooms open onto a couple of leafy covered courtyards dripping with vines. Satellite TV and air-conditioning/heating cost US$1 extra.

Al-Yarmouk Hotel (Map pp182-3; ☎ 211 6154, 211 6155; fax 211 6156; Sharia al-Maari; s/d/tr S£600/1000/1400; ✖) The Yarmouk may not see too many Western tourists – it mainly hosts Arab and Russian traders – but the chain-smoking English- and Russian-speaking staff are welcoming and it's a decent fallback if the other budget places are full. Having benefited from a makeover, each of the hotel's three floors has been painted a different colour, so take your pick from glossy lavender, pink and lemon. Rooms with bathrooms come with fridges, TVs, clean sheets and towels.

Tourism Hotel (Map pp182-3; ☎ 225 1602/3/4/5; fax 225 1606; Saahat Saad Allah al-Jabri; s/d/tr US$20/25/30) This retro 1970s-style hotel, opposite the main square in the New City, is a time-machine trip. But go beyond the wood panelling, kitsch chandeliers and tinted mirrors of the lobby, and you get clean modern rooms that represent the best-value sleeps in Aleppo. The spacious, comfortable rooms have small balconies, spotless private bathrooms, satellite TV, air-conditioning and fridges – all for a remarkable price.

Midrange

Hotel al-Faisal (Map pp182-3; ☎ 211 4434, 211 2618; fax 221 2573; Sharia Yarmouk; s/d/tr US$30/35/40; ✖) With more than a touch of Oriental chintz and grandma-approved décor, this three-star is popular with European tour groups. The rooms have recently been refreshed with a splash of pastel paint, new carpets and floral duvets, and they're extremely clean. Breakfast is filling and there are fascinating views from the breakfast room. The staff are multilingual and helpful. It's a safe choice.

Dar Halabia (Map p176; ☎ 332 3344, 224 8497; www.halabia-tours.com; Sharia Lisan ad-Din al-Khatib; s/d/tr US$34/48/60; ✖) Enchantingly situated in an 18th-century stone house a short stroll from Bab Antakya, Dar Halabia is a pleasant retreat and still the only hotel in Aleppo's Old City – for now at least. Spread over two levels, rooms face a sunny plant-filled courtyard – a wonderful spot to chill on a starry evening. All rooms are individually decorated with traditional décor (some more atmospheric than others) and it's good value – if a little quiet at night.

Baron Hotel (Map pp182-3; ☎ 221 0880/1; www.the-hotel-baron.com; 8 Sharia al-Baron; s/d/ste US$44.40/55.50/88.80; ✖) Aleppo's legendary Baron is a museum piece – see The Baron Hotel, below. But just like Syria's museums, it's suffering from a combination of neglect and indifference. Even with a 'renovation', which appears to have been little more than a lick or two of paint and upgraded bath-

---

THE BARON HOTEL

Built at a time when travel invariably involved three-week sea voyages, a set of garden-shed-sized trunks to be carried by porters, and a letter of introduction to the local consul, the Baron Hotel (above) belongs to a very different era. When it went up (1909–11), the hotel was on the outskirts of town 'in gardens considered dangerous to venture into after dark', and from the terrace guests could shoot ducks on the neighbouring swamp.

The Baron quickly became known as one of the premier hotels of the Middle East, helped by the fact that Aleppo was still a busy trading centre and staging post for travellers. The Near Eastern extension of the *Orient Express* used to terminate in Aleppo, and the rich and famous travelling on it generally ended up staying in the Baron. The old leather-bound visitors book turns up names such as aviators Charles Lindbergh, Amy Johnson and Charles Kingsford-Smith, as well as TE Lawrence (see Lawrence of Arabia, p188), Theodore Roosevelt and Agatha Christie, who wrote the first part of *Murder on the Orient Express* while staying here. Kept securely stashed in the safe, the visitors book sadly isn't available for viewing, but you can see a copy of Lawrence's bar bill displayed in the lounge.

Today, however, it's fair to say that the poorly maintained hotel trades heavily on its history and the nostalgia for an era when travel to the Middle East was a far more exotic affair – that alone makes it worth a toast in the bar.

rooms, it's still hard to justify the room rate given the austere facilities and woeful breakfasts. Those looking for a place to have a decent kip should look elsewhere. History buffs shouldn't stay anywhere else. The atmospheric bar is worth a visit.

Tourath House (Map pp182-3; ☎ 211 8838/48/58; www.tourathhouse.com; Sharia al-Raheb Buhayrah; s/d US$50/70; ✷) This tiny boutique hotel, located in a splendid 260-year-old stone residence, has some of the friendliest and most professional young staff in Aleppo. There is a beautiful courtyard with an attractive *liwan* (summer room) and decorative ceiling that has been turned into a traditional *majlis* (reception room). The rooms, while boasting mother-of-pearl inlaid furniture and wooden shutters, are rather austere, but compared to some of the other Al-Jdeida sleeps, it's great value.

Beit Salahieh (Map pp174-5; ☎ 332 2222; www .beitsalahieh.com; off Sharia al-Kawakibi, btwn Citadel & Bab Al-Hadid; s/d US$61/82; ✷) This attractive hotel, formerly known as Diwan Rasmy, is secreted away down a narrow stone-walled alleyway near the Citadel, in the Al-Jibelah quarter. Housed in a converted 15th-century palace, it features a grand central courtyard, sprawling rooftop terraces and covered arcades, beautifully lit by Oriental lamps at night. While there are four traditionally decorated suites, the remaining rooms were unwisely renovated in a bland modern style, but these were soon to be transformed. While the location is fine for daytime exploration, at night the area is very quiet.

Mandaloun Hotel (Map pp182-3; ☎ 228 3008, 219 944; www.mandalounhotel.com; Sharia al-Tilal Hazazeh (Old Fire Station St); s/d US$67/78; ✷) Travellers love the Mandaloun, a beautiful courtyard hotel in Al-Aziziah that provides oodles of atmosphere without producing a massive bill when you leave. It's a dramatic three-storey property, and all rooms face the exquisite light-filled centre courtyard. Rooms feature intricately carved wooden shutters and are decorated in a simple but elegant style with wrought-iron beds, local textiles and tiny tables. Air-conditioning/heating, satellite TV and minibar are provided.

Top End

ourpick **Beit Wakil** (Map pp182-3; ☎ 211 8169, 211 7083; www.beitwakil.com; Sharia as-Sissi; s/d/ste US$77.70/111/144.30; ✷) Nestled in the stone-walled lanes of the old Al-Jdeida quarter in a painstakingly restored 18th-century merchant's residence, Beit Wakil was one of Aleppo's first boutique hotels. With its high vaulted ceilings, elegant courtyards, intricately carved stone and Mamluk-era horizontal stripes, it's wonderfully authentic. The tranquil vine-filled courtyard with bubbling fountain is a wonderful spot for a drink, and the restaurant is probably Aleppo's best after Beit Sissi. The suite is worth the extra cash.

Dar Zamaria Martini (Map pp182-3; ☎ 363 6100; www.darzamaria.com;off Saahat al-Hattab; d US$110; ✷) This captivating hotel in Al-Jdeida now sprawls across several grand courtyard houses dating from the 17th and 18th centuries, leveraging off the success of the original, more intimate property. While the renovations are wonderful, the hotel lacks the simple elegance of Beit Wakil, although the rooms are significantly more comfortable. There are pretty plant-filled courtyards and beautiful spacious rooms decorated with inlaid furniture, traditional textiles and Oriental carpets. While the rooftop restaurant does a roaring trade, service could be improved – the same goes for the hotel.

EATING

Known for its richness and use of spices, Aleppan cuisine is distinctive within Syria and, in turn, the Middle East. Dining here is a real pleasure. Although street-food joints are ubiquitous, the good restaurants are mostly concentrated in Al-Jdeida and Al-Aziziah. Crammed together on Sharia Georges and Mathilde Salem in Al-Aziziah are half a dozen restaurants and cafés with pavement tables occupied by young Aleppans sipping imported beer and toying with their mobile phones, while inside groups of bejewelled women chatter and pick at mezze.

Most Aleppo restaurants, unless otherwise stated, open around 11am for lunch and serve through until well after midnight – usually until the last diners are ready to leave, which can be 2am or even 3am. Remember, locals dine late and most places don't get busy until 10pm or later. Reservations are rarely necessary, except where noted.

Old City

There are few decent restaurants in the Old City and its immediate surrounds.

ALEPPO

LAWRENCE OF ARABIA

Has there ever been a movie that gives such a strong sense of a man as David Lean's 1962 movie *Lawrence of Arabia*? The Orientalist fantasies, the emotive soundtrack by Maurice Jarre – it's a true epic. But was the man as immense as the film that he inspired?

Born in 1888 into a wealthy English family, Thomas Edward Lawrence (or TE Lawrence as he's more commonly known) studied archaeology, gaining a keen interest in Crusader castles that saw him set out on a three-month tour of Syria in 1909, covering more than 1600km. On foot. He then studied Arabic in Byblos, Lebanon, and worked on excavations in Syria between 1911 and 1914 and then at the Hittite settlement at Carchemish on the Turkish side of the border on the Euphrates River.

With the outbreak of WWI, Lawrence became an intelligence agent in Cairo. Highly regarded in this capacity, he adopted an attitude that was both unobtrusive and nonconformist. In 1915, as a specialist on Middle Eastern military and political issues, he recorded his ideas on the Arab question and these were taken into consideration by British intelligence. Supporting the cause of the Arab revolt and manifesting his own hostility towards French politics in Syria, Colonel Lawrence favoured the creation of a Sunni and Arab state and in 1916 went to Arabia to shore up the support of the dissident Arabs. Working behind Turkish lines, Lawrence and the Arabs became more of an irritant than an outright fighting force, but their successful guerrilla incursions – in no small part due to Lawrence's brilliance as a tactician – cost the Turks precious resources.

In November of 1917, Lawrence was captured and claimed he was flogged for rebuffing the sexual advances of a Turkish commandant. This was meant to have occurred at Der'a, which most travellers pass through on the way to the ruins at Bosra. While his version of events is disputed by several of Lawrence's biographers, it's clear that whatever occurred had a long-lasting psychological effect on him.

It was the desert revolt of October 1918, however, that etched Lawrence's name into legend. At the side of Emir Faisal, whom he made the hero of the Arab revolt, and of the English General Allenby, Lawrence conquered Aqaba. He then entered Damascus in triumph, marking the final defeat of the Ottoman forces. But due to infighting by the Arabs and a cynical reneging of promises by the English and the French through the Sykes-Picot Agreement, a chance of Arab unity was lost. A disillusioned Lawrence turned down the honours of the Order of the Bath and the Distinguished Service Order in the presence of King George V – who apparently was holding the awards at the time.

In 1921, following the conference in Cairo in which both Lawrence and Churchill participated, Lawrence was sent to Transjordan to help Emir Abdullah – the great-grandfather of the current King Abdullah II of Jordan – to formulate the foundations of the new state. Nevertheless, he later left this position and enrolled with the Royal Air Force (RAF) in 1922, under the assumed name of Ross, first as a pilot, then as a mechanic under yet another assumed name. During this time he worked on his memoir, *The Seven Pillars of Wisdom*. He left the RAF in February 1935, aged 46, and despite looking forward to writing more, all that he achieved at such an early age weighed heavily on him. Lawrence, who had already lived enough life for several men, wasn't to see old age. He died in May 1935 in a motorcycle accident.

Beit Salahieh (Map pp174-5; ☎ 332 2222; www .beitsalahieh.com; off Sharia al-Kawakibi, btwn Citadel & Bab Al-Hadid) As Diwan Rasmy, this boutique hotel had a well-regarded restaurant with stunning Citadel views. At the time of our visit its reincarnation, Beit Salahieh, had not yet reopened the restaurant.

Al-Attar (Map p176; ☎ 333 9033; Sharia al-Qala'a; ☻ 9am-late) One of several sheesha cafés in a row facing the Citadel, Al-Attar's touts are the least annoying and its food is the

freshest. On offer are mezze (S£50), grills – try the *shish taouk* (marinated chicken grilled on skewers) with chips (S£150) – and fresh juices (S£50).

Ahlildar (Map p176; ☎ 333 0841; Souq ibn al-Khashab, opposite Grand Mosque exit; ☻ 8.30am-10pm) In an elegant, restored old house with a somewhat disconcerting flat-screen TV decorating the downstairs wall, Ahlildar is the only eatery in the souq serving full meals, everything from mezze (S£35 to

S£150) and kebabs (S£150) to French dishes like cordon bleu (S£225).

There are several felafel sellers in the souq, in the area immediately south of the Great Mosque, along with a couple of fresh juice stalls.

Al-Jdeida
RESTAURANTS
Cantara (Map pp182-3; ☎ 225 3355; just off Sharia al-Kayyali; pizzas S£160-260, pastas S£200; ☉ noon-midnight) A courtyard restaurant, although not in the same league as Beit Wakil or Beit Sissi, Cantara offers an Italian-influenced menu with plenty of pastas and pizzas made in a proper stone oven. Credit cards are accepted and they serve beer and wine.

Kan Zaman (Map pp182-3; ☎ 331 1299; Sharia al-Kayyali; meal per person S£600; ☉ noon-1am) Close to Cantara and across the lane from Yasmeen House, Kan Zaman's beautifully decorated rooms sprawl over several levels, with a couple of romantic nooks for couples. There's a long list of cold and hot mezze (S£35 to S£200), fresh salads (S£75 to S£150) and succulent grills (S£160 to S£250). Credit cards are accepted and alcohol is served.

our pick **Beit Sissi** (Map pp182-3; ☎ 213 007, 93-500 500; Sharia as-Sissi; meal per person S£700; ☉ noon-late) Splendidly set in a restored 17th-century house with dining in an elegant courtyard (or a cosy interior room in the colder months), Beit Sissi is Aleppo's finest restaurant. Expect Syrian, Aleppan and French cuisine of the highest quality. Don't miss the delicious green beans in olive oil, the tasty ratatouille aubergine, the *sujok* (spicy sausage rolled in Arabic bread, sliced into snail-like pieces and then fried – the best we've tasted!) and the signature dish, cherry kebab. There's a wonderful *oud* (lute) player most nights. Alcohol is served and credit cards are accepted.

Beit Wakil (Map pp182-3; ☎ 221 7169; Sharia as-Sissi; meal per person S£700; ☉ noon-late) Similar in quality and cuisine to Beit Sissi, and just across the alley, Beit Wakil also delights with some equally interesting and tasty dishes. The cherry kebab is a must, along with the *toshka* (Armenian toasted meat and cheese sandwiches). Alcohol is served and credit cards are accepted.

Yasmeen House (Map pp182-3; ☎ 222 4462/5562; Sharia al-Kayyali; meal per person S£800; ☉ from 8pm) With its white tablecloths, elegant Yasmeen

House (in another grand old courtyard house) seems a little more formal than the other restaurants, but its enormous round tables make it ideal for groups. Expect delicious Syrian and Arabic food. Wine is also served – try the excellent Lebanese Ksara.

QUICK EATS
Haj Abdo al-Fawwal (Map pp182-3; off Saahat al-Hatab) Opening early every morning, this is *the* best place to get Aleppan-style *foul* (fava bean soup), delicately seasoned with cumin, paprika, garlic, lemon juice and fresh parsley. Crowds gather around the tiny shop from 7am, bearing empty containers of every size and description, pushing and shoving their way to the front for their share of this aromatic dish. Don't leave Aleppo without trying some for yourself.

New City
RESTAURANTS
Al-Andalib (Map pp182-3; Sharia al-Baron; meal per person S£350; ☉ noon-late) This rooftop restaurant on the same block as the Baron Hotel is popular with travellers who eat early, around 6pm to 7pm. Later on, after 10pm, it tends to be locals only – mostly male, so women may feel uncomfortable. The menu includes kebabs, salads, fries, hummus and a *baba ghanoug* that's a purée of aubergines with tahini and olive oil. The food is fresh and beer is served.

Bazar Al Charq (Map pp182-3; ☎ 224 9120; btwn Sharia al-Mutanabi & Sharia Hammam al-Tal; meal per person S£400; ☉ 11am-late) Delicious food is served in a cavernous, atmospheric restaurant decorated to resemble a bazaar. The *toshka* (S£150) is particularly tasty and the succulent kebabs (S£200) are popular. No alcohol.

Al-Challal (Map pp174-5; ☎ 224 3344; Sharia Georges & Mathilde Salem; meal per person S£450; ☉ 9am-late) This modern eatery attracts an affluent (mainly male) Aleppan crowd. The menu combines mezze and Middle Eastern grills (S£220) with international dishes such as escalopes and steaks (S£250). Alcohol is served.

Cordoba (Map pp174-5; ☎ 224 0868; Sharia Georges & Mathilde Salem; meal per person S£450; ☉ 9am-late) This long-standing local favourite is easily the best restaurant on this strip, with some

ALEPPAN CUISINE

One of the delights of Aleppo is its unique cuisine. Primarily influenced by the exchange between Aleppan and Ottoman chefs, but also influenced by Armenians and Jewish settlers, it's more complex, richer and spicier than your classic Middle Eastern cuisine. Some dishes you must try are *mouhamara*, a traditional dip of walnuts, pomegranate molasses, toasted bread crumbs, olive oil, roasted peppers and spices; *sujok*, spicy sausage rolled in Arabic bread, sliced into snail-like pieces and then fried; and the famous cherry kebab, a lamb kebab with a tasty cherry sauce. Beit Sissi (p189) is a favourite for these dishes (and the Syrian president agrees). In Damascus, Al Hallabi (p107) at the Four Seasons Hotel might not be to everyone's budget, but the chef is Syria's best. He's from Aleppo, of course!

of the tastiest Aleppan food you'll find in Syria. There's no menu in English, but try the *toshka* and *maajouka* (meat, cheese, pistachios and peppers shaped into a patty). Beer and arak are served.

CAFÉS & QUICK EATS

Fountain Café (Map pp182-3; Mirage Palace Hotel, Sharia al-Mutanabi; ☺ 9am-midnight) This café offers a welcome air-con retreat from the heat and dust outside. Burgers and sandwiches (club, steak, chicken, ham; S£95 to S£160) are huge and delicious, and the iced milkshakes (S£70) are excellent. Head to the adjoining bar if you feel like a cold beer.

Al-Kindi Restaurant (Map pp182-3; Sharia Zaki al-Arsuzi; meal per person S£250) Just off Sharia Bab al-Faraj, this is one of a cluster of similar kebab restaurants, all of which offer reasonable food at budget prices. It has an extensive menu in English made up of myriad mezze and grilled kebabs and is open from early until very late.

In the block bounded by Sharia al-Maari, Sharia Bab al-Faraj, Sharia al-Quwatli and Sharia al-Baron are plenty of cheapies offering the usual fare – prices are more variable than the food so check before you sit down. There's a row of excellent late-opening **juice bars** (Map pp182-3) at the Bab al-Faraj end of Sharia Yarmouk.

SELF-CATERING

The **Amman supermarket** (Map pp182-3; Sharia al-Maari) is a good place for purchasing basics such as bread, cheese and biscuits, along with toiletries. For fresh food, there's a **fruit and vegetable market** (Map pp182-3; Sharia Bab Antakya) and an excellent **fruit stall** (Map pp182-3; Sharia Jbrail Dalal), 200m north of Bab al-Faraj.

Across the road from the National Museum, **Aleppo Dairy Qattib** (Map pp182-3) stocks a range of delicious cheeses, olives and pickles; look for the red-and-white mirrored 'happy cow' sign.

If you take an empty mineral-water bottle to the juice bars on Sharia Yarmouk, they'll fill it up for you to take away. Among the juice bars there are two **liquor stores** (Map pp182-3) where you can buy Al-Chark beer for S£50.

DRINKING

Aleppo is not a late-night city and there's not much going on beyond midnight. The best places for a drink are the restaurant-cafés of Al-Aziziah or the bar-restaurants in Al-Jdeida.

Cafés & Coffeehouses

The following venues are all open from very early until very late, and some don't close.

Arabica (Map pp174-5; Sharia Bin Silvania) In Al-Aziziah, Syria's Starbucks does delicious iced lattés (S£90) as well as providing a fascinating slice of life that you won't experience in the Old City, especially after 6pm, when the music goes up a few notches and Aleppo's *shebab* (youth) spill out on to the footpath. The café offers free wireless internet and if you don't have your own laptop they'll even lend you one.

T-Square (Map pp174-5; ☎ 460 6033/44; Sharia Bin Silvania) This funky contemporary café-eatery next door to Arabica is where Aleppo's hipsters hang out. It's a great place for meeting locals and people-watching. Like Arabica, the place buzzes in the evenings, when the tables are jammed and it's standing-room only on the pavement.

Museum Café (Map pp182-3; Sharia al-Maari) Male travellers will enjoy this simple coffeehouse in the city centre, but it's men-only so women will feel uncomfortable.

Al-Sahel (Map pp182-3; Sharia al-Maari) This upstairs coffeehouse is close to Bab al-Faraj and the clock tower. The place is grungy (in an old Aleppan sort of way) and the entrance is in the side street, through the reception of the Al-Sahel Hotel.

Al-Shams (Map pp182-3; Saahat Saad Allah al-Jabri) On the corner of the big main square, this men's coffee shop is a popular haunt of Aleppo's chess players.

Bars

Aleppo is Al-Chark territory, which is the less appealing of Syria's two local brews, and there's not exactly a wealth of venues in which to drink it. The atmospheric interior bar or the front terrace at the **Baron Hotel** (Map pp182-3; ☎ 221 0880/1; 8 Sharia al-Baron; beers S£100) is a must, at least once.

There are also a couple of underground cave bars at Beit Sissi (p189) and Beit Wakil (p189) in Al-Jdeida. The one at Beit Sissi is buried deep in former cellars, with goblin faces leering out of the rock walls, while the one at Beit Wakil has colourful décor. Beit Sissi also has a moody low-lit bar upstairs, with a piano player playing tunes in winter.

ENTERTAINMENT

There is no shortage of cinemas (Map pp182–3) along Sharia al-Baron and its northern extension Sharia Yousef al-Azmeh. Most of what they screen is martial arts, soft porn and trashy B-movies. More entertaining are the airbrushed posters outside advertising the movies. These slightly risqué posters, used to entice the almost exclusively male customers, generally depict the very scenes that have been removed by the censor.

SHOPPING

The best place to shop in Aleppo is without a doubt the souq. This is the place to shop for olive soap, textiles and traditional dress.

Shopping the Aleppo Souq

Aleppo's souq (Map p191) is significantly less touristy than the markets in Damascus, although the pressure to spend is still there. Great buys include textiles, brocade, gold, silver, carpets and olive soap.

Like any Middle Eastern souq, Aleppo's bazaar is broken down into the usual

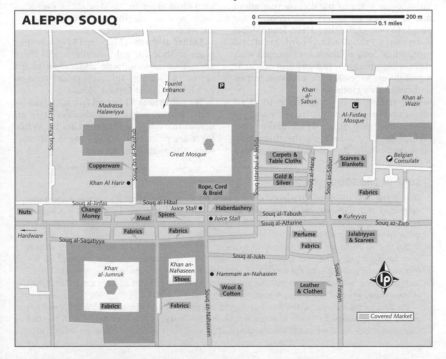

ALEPPO SOUQ

ALEPPO

TOP BUYS IN THE SOUQS

- aged olive soap
- Oriental carpets and kilims
- nargileh/sheesha water pipes
- mother-of-pearl inlaid backgammon sets
- brocades and other richly decorated textiles

---

demarcations – gold in one alley, spices in another, carpets in one spot, scarves across the way. The exception to this is bustling **Souq al-Attarine**, which sells everything: hardware, clothing, spices, perfumes and even meat.

South of Souq al-Attarine the laneways almost exclusively give way to fabrics, clothing and shoes. Textiles have always been an important component of Aleppo's trade and **Souq al-Jukh** still operates as a major wholesale cloth market.

North of Al-Attarine the souq is at its most dense. Squeezed around the Great Mosque are veins of parallel narrow alleys that in places are barely wide enough for people to pass each other. Here, **Souq al-Hibal** is devoted to shops selling cord, braid and rope, while **Souq al-Tabush** is crammed with stalls selling buttons, ribbons and all manner of things necessary for a woman to run up her family's clothes.

Souq az-Zarb is a good place to head for *jalabiyyas*, the cotton robes worn by women and men alike, which make great nightdresses, or a *keffiyeh*, the distinctive black-and-white or red-and-white head-dress worn by traditional Arabs in the Palestinian Territories, Jordan, Syria and the Gulf States.

Shops in the souq open from early in the morning until around 6pm Saturday to Thursday, while on Friday virtually the whole souq closes and is eerily deserted; many of the small passageways and khans are locked but it's still an atmospheric place for a wander. Shops owned by Christians close on Sunday and stay open on Friday.

Outside the Souq

Sebastian (Map p176; ☎ 332 3672; Sharia al-Qala'a; ☹ 8am-8pm Sat-Thu) On the fringes of the souq, this place stocks a small but superb range of high-quality textiles, tablecloths, inlaid backgammon boards and boxes. However, the speciality is rustic kilims, silk rugs and antique carpets, costing anything from US$50 to US$15,000. The multilingual owner, Mohammed, is highly knowledgeable, accepts credit cards and provides certificates, but most of all, he won't pressure you to get a sale.

Orient House Antiques (Map pp182-3; 1st fl, Saahat al-Hatab) Over in Al-Jdeida, the Beit Sissi store is a wonderful place to browse for antiques and bric-a-brac.

Saahat al-Hatab (Map pp182–3) is the place to shop for gold jewellery, and there are a few more antique and carpet shops across the square, although prices tend to be higher than at Orient House.

Souq al-Shouna (Map p176) is a handicrafts market behind the sheesha cafés on the southwestern side of the Citadel. While there are price tags, bargaining is still possible, although not required.

SOAP IN THE SOUQ

One of the best things about Aleppo's fantastic souq is the olive soap. It's unique, handmade, decorated and 100% natural, being made of 90% olives and 10% bay laurel. And if it's good enough for the great queens of the Middle East (Cleopatra, Nefertiti, Sheba and Zenobia) it's good enough to pack away as a souvenir.

But not all soaps are created equal. The oldest, highest-quality (and most expensive) soap is aged for eight years. The next quality down is aged for only three years and is best kept for the hair and body, while the cheapest soaps are only three months old and used just for your hands. So how do you tell? When cut in half the aged soaps have a brown rim and are a rich dark green in the centre, whereas the younger soaps are a light green all the way through.

Locals buy their soaps by the kilo but they're happy to sell less to tourists. While there are plenty of soap shops on Sharia al-Maari and Sharia Bab Antakya, the best dealer is in the Old City souq – look for Adel and Malek Kaymouz' olive-soap store in Souq Al-Attarine (Map p191).

For nargileh/sheesha pipes, mother-of-pearl inlaid wooden boxes and backgammon boards visit the shops on **Sharia al-Adasi** (Map p176), which is north of the main souq; walk east from the front of the Great Mosque and then head north (left) up the third lane.

Sharia Bab Antakya (Map p176) is the place to head for olive soap, and you'll find more soaps and hammam products in **Souq al-Sabun** (Map p191).

GETTING THERE & AWAY
Air
Aleppo has an international airport with connections to Turkey, Europe and other cities in the Middle East. **SyrianAir** (www.syria air.com; Reservations ☎ 224 1232, 222 0501; central office Map p182-3; Sharia al-Baron; head office Map p182-3; Saahat Saad Allah al-Jabri) has weekly flights to Istanbul and Cairo and several daily flights to Damascus (from S£1200, one hour). Other airline offices:

Air France (Map pp182-3; ☎ 223 2238; Sharia al-Baron)
KLM (Map pp182-3; ☎ 221 1074; Sharia al-Baron)
Lufthansa (Map pp182-3; ☎ 222 3005; Sharia al-Baron)

Those flying in should take a taxi from outside the airport terminal hall. It takes around 20 minutes to reach the city centre and will cost about S£500. A return taxi will cost a little less.

Bus
PULLMAN BUS STATION
Most buses stop at the **Pullman Bus Station** (Map pp174-5; Sharia Ibrahim Hanano), about 500m west of the National Museum, from where it's a ten-minute walk east to Sharia al-Baron and the bulk of the budget and mid-range hotels. If you're staying in Al-Jdeida, take a taxi for around S£30.

More than 30 private companies, including **Kadmous** (☎ 224 8837; www.alkadmous.com) and Al-Ahliah, have their sales shacks around the edge of the bus bays. It's easy to shop around but there's not much difference in prices. Destinations include Damascus (VIP/non-VIP S£230/150, five hours), Deir ez-Zur (S£150, five hours), Hama (S£90, 2½ hours), Homs (S£100, three hours), Lattakia (S£120, 3½ hours), Qamishle (S£180, eight hours), Raqqa (S£100, three hours) and Tartus (S£130, four hours). Departures are frequent so there's no need to book ahead.

CITY BUS STATION
South of Mirage Palace Hotel, this station (Map p176) is a vast area of dusty bus bays stretching over 500m and incorporating four stations serving local city buses, old battered regular intercity buses, intercity Pullmans, and minibuses that cover the region around Aleppo.

INTERNATIONAL BUS STATION
Little more than a parking lot, this station (Map pp182-3) has private companies running services to Turkey. It's immediately north of the tourist office and behind Sharia al-Baron. Between the handful of companies heading to Turkey (of which Etihad and Volcano come recommended), there are half a dozen daily services to Istanbul (about S£2000, 17 hours) and plenty more to Antakya (S£250, two to three hours). Note that sometimes the Istanbul service requires a change of bus at Antakya. From the same station you can also get buses to Amman (S£550, nine hours) in Jordan.

Car & Motorcycle
Europcar (Map pp174-5; ☎ 222 4854; fax 223 2302; http://car-rental.europcar.com; ◷ 8am-7pm) has an office at Baghdad Station but cars can be booked online. For details of average rental rates, see p401.

Service Taxi
Next to the Pullman bus station is a service taxi stand. Service taxis are an inexpensive and slightly faster way to travel, but can be more crammed than buses. Sample fares include Hama S£160, Homs S£180, and Damascus S£400.

Train
Aleppo's train station (Map pp174-5), known as Baghdad Station, is about 1.5km north of the centre in Al-Aziziah. To walk from here down to the vicinity of the budget hotel district takes about 25 minutes; head due south from the station, keeping the park on your right, until you reach a large open square (Saahat Saad Allah al-Jabri), at which point take a left down Sharia al-Quwatli.

Trains to Lattakia (1st class express/1st class/2nd class S£120/80/50, 2½ or 3½ hours) depart around four times a day, usually two in the morning and two in the afternoon. There are six return trains,

FROM ALEPPO TO HOLLYWOOD

The name Moustapha Akkad might not be familiar to you, but the *Halloween* series of movies would be. This Aleppan native, born in 1930, was a producer on every *Halloween* movie – all eight of them.

When Akkad decided he wanted to head to Hollywood, his father gave him a copy of the Quran and some cash. Later, armed with a master's degree, Akkad was mentored by film auteur Sam Peckinpah, famous for Westerns such as *The Wild Bunch*. But Akkad had his own epics that he wanted to bring to the big screen and in 1976 directed and produced his first feature, *Muhammad, Messenger of God*, released in the West as *The Message*. Given that Islam forbids images of the Prophet, Akkad made the movie without ever showing the subject of the film. He saw it as a way to help bridge the divide between the West and Islam.

In 1978 Akkad produced the first (and iconic) *Halloween* movie with director John Carpenter, and the franchise from this low-budget horror flick was born. In 1980 he directed his next epic, the now highly acclaimed *Lion of the Desert*, about the real-life Bedouin leader Omar Mukhtar. The film was controversial because of funding by Libya's Muammar Gaddafi.

In his films Akkad wanted to show the struggles and heroes of Islam, and his next project was to be the ultimate film about Saladin, to be filmed in Jordan. In a tragic twist worthy of an epic, Akkad and his daughter were killed in the 2005 Amman hotel bombings in Jordan. The Arab and Islamic worlds lost a great storyteller and a brilliant producer on that day.

including two additional evening services. Most travellers love this wonderfully scenic trip. Services to Damascus (1st class/2nd class/sleeper S£240/120/350, 4½ hours) via Homs and Hama operate four times a day on fast new trains: two early in the morning, one in the afternoon and one overnight.

Trains operate between Aleppo and Istanbul via Konya three times a week, with a sleeper service (by far the best and safest option) once a week. At the time of research trains departed Istanbul for Aleppo (single/twin berth sleeper $US40/60) on Sunday morning, arriving in Aleppo Monday afternoon, and departed Aleppo for Istanbul (single/twin berth sleeper S£5000/7000) on Tuesday morning, arriving in Istanbul Wednesday night.

There's also a weekly train to Tehran via Lake Van in Turkey, where passengers alight and ferry across the lake to meet the Iranian train. Check times and fares on www.tcdd.gov.tr.

GETTING AROUND

Everything in the city centre is accessible on foot. Buses to various parts of Aleppo depart from the City Bus Station behind Mirage Palace Hotel, off Sharia Bab Antakya, but you really won't need to use these. If you must, tickets (S£10) are bought from the driver.

An average across-town taxi ride should cost S£25 to S£50. Note that taxi drivers here are often more interested in getting the cash, regardless of whether they get you remotely near where you've asked them to go.

AROUND ALEPPO

There are worthwhile sites around Aleppo to warrant at least two or three days' exploring. A day spent around Qala'at Samaan and another among the Dead Cities to the south could turn out to be highlights of your trip. The fact that these sites are out of the way is half the appeal; however, good weather is a prerequisite, as to explore the sites you'll be out in open, exposed countryside, which quickly turns to mud underfoot in rain.

Although all of the sites around Aleppo are accessible by public transport, if you're short on time, hire a car and driver. While you could approach Aleppo's tourist office and be intercepted by a 'guide' offering his services before you get to within 100m of the door, be aware that many of these guys know little about the sites, speak little English, and probably don't even know the way. You'll waste precious time and are better off organising a driver through your hotel. The going rate is between US$70 and US$100 for a full day, depending on the distance and the price of petrol.

With such an arrangement you dictate your own itinerary. With a car you should be able to cover in a full day all the sites described in the North & West of Aleppo section (below), or all those described in South of Aleppo (p197).

NORTH & WEST OF ALEPPO

The half-dozen major sites north and west of Aleppo are scattered across Jebel Samaan in such a way that it's impossible to combine them all into one trip without your own car. Qala'at Samaan, the jewel of the collection, is fairly accessible by public transport, and from there it's possible to push on to Ain Dara and get back to Aleppo by minibus in one long, exhausting day. Alternatively, you could combine Qala'at Samaan with Qalb Lozeh, if you do a little backtracking. Cyrrhus is more problematic and requires cash and time; if you are planning on visiting the Dead Cities to the south then it's probably not worth the expense to duplicate the experience here.

Qala'at Samaan   قلعة سمعان

The ruined basilica of **Qala'at Samaan** (adult/student S£150/10; ⏱ 9am-6pm Apr-Sep, to 4pm Oct-Mar),

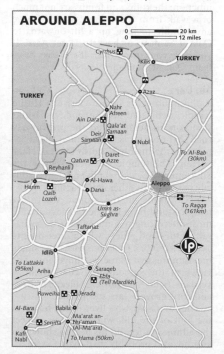
AROUND ALEPPO

also known as Saint Simeon, is the must-see site of the many archaeological ruins that dot the countryside north of Aleppo. Enough remains of the basilica to impress, with a glorious situation high on a rocky outcrop. The views are excellent. From Aleppo, it's an easy half-day trip; if you set off by 9am you'll be back by early afternoon.

The structure takes its name from a peculiar individual named Simeon. Born around AD 389–90, Simeon was the son of a shepherd who opted at a young age for life in a monastery. However, finding monastic life insufficiently ascetic, he retreated to a cave in the barren hills, where he lived under a regimen of self-imposed severity.

Word of this extremely pious individual got around and people began to visit to seek his blessing. Simeon apparently resented this invasion of his solitude so intensely that he was driven to erect a 3m-high pillar upon which he took up residence so that people couldn't touch him. Legend goes that as his tolerance of people decreased he erected ever higher pillars. In all he's said to have spent close to 40 years on top of his pillars, the last of which was 18m in height. There was a railing around the top, and an iron chain attached to the stone to stop him toppling off in the middle of the night.

Simeon would preach daily from his perch and shout answers to his audiences' questions; however, he refused to talk to women and even his mother was not allowed near the column.

Simeon's increasingly eccentric behaviour eventually drew pilgrims from as far as Britain and France, where he was known as Simon Stylites, a name derived from the Greek word for pillar, *stylos*. The notion of stylism caught on and Simeon inspired a fashion for pious pillar-top dwelling that spread all the way to central Europe, where it eventually faltered in the face of a colder climate.

When he died in 459, Simeon was possibly the most famous person in the 5th-century world. His body was buried in the great Christian centre of Antioch (present-day Antakya) and an enormous church was built around the famous pillar. The church had a unique design with four basilicas arranged in the shape of a cross, each opening onto a central octagonal yard covered by a dome. Beneath the dome stood the pillar. One basilica was used for worship and the other three housed the many pilgrims. Completed in around 491 after about 14 years of building, it was the largest church in the world at the time.

With the arrival of Islam in Syria, the Byzantine Christians were put on the defensive and the church complex was fortified, hence the name Qala'at (fortress). It eventually fell to the Islamic Fatimid dynasty in 1017 and was apparently never again used as a place of worship.

The church ruins are remarkably well preserved. The main Romanesque façade still stands, while behind it the arches of the octagonal yard are reasonably complete. There's plenty of ornamental carved stonework to admire, although Simeon's pillar is in a sad state and is nothing more than a boulder, reduced centuries ago by pilgrims chipping away at it for holy souvenirs.

The views of the barren hills to the west are stunning and the ruins of Deir Samaan can be seen down to the southwest at the foot of the hill.

DEIR SAMAAN   دير سمعان

Deir Samaan (Monastery of Simeon) began life as the small Greek agricultural village of Telanissos, but during the first part of the 5th century found itself being rapidly transformed by a steady influx of travellers, and their forerunners, pilgrims. As the antics of Simeon drew ever-larger crowds, so the village expanded to provide hostelries, churches and three monasteries to accommodate the pilgrims.

The basilica and Deir Samaan were connected by a processional way, Via Sacra. A monumental arch remains partway up the slope, marking the old route. In the village there are shells of two of the monasteries, a church and the bazaar; 150m south of the arch are two very impressive hostelries and a tomb chapel hewn out of rock and reached by a stone bridge.

Local people live among the ruins, having built their own dwellings from stone recycled from ancient Deir Samaan, but they don't mind if you wander around.

GETTING THERE & AWAY

Take a minibus from the City Bus Station in Aleppo to the village of Daret Azze (S£15, 50 minutes); they depart every half-hour or so. During the trip keep a lookout for the 5th-century Mushabbak basilica standing alone in fields off to the left, about two-thirds of the way along the route. From Daret Azze it's about 6km to Qala'at Samaan. The minibus driver may offer to take you the extra distance or you can negotiate with a local taxi driver (around S£100). If there isn't much traffic on the road, you won't have to wait long before a vehicle stops for you.

The last minibus from Daret Azze to Aleppo leaves at about 6pm.

Qatura   قطوره

About 2km west of Daret Azze on the road to Qala'at Samaan is the turn-off to Qatura. Follow this road off to the west and you'll come to more ruins, which include some Roman-era tombs cut into the rock. The last tomb on the road is carved with a reclining figure in much the same style as at Palmyra. You can also quite clearly make out Latin and Greek inscriptions.

To get here, when you pick up a lift out of Daret Azze ask to be let off at the Qatura junction; the ruins and tombs are not much of a walk from there. You shouldn't have any trouble picking up a lift onwards to Qala'at Samaan or back to Daret Azze. If you have your own driver, it's an easy drive from Qala'at Samaan.

Ain Dara   عين داره

A thousand years before Christ, a Hittite temple dedicated to the goddess Ishtar stood on an acropolis off the present-day road that now leads north from Qala'at Samaan to the mainly Kurdish town of Nahr Afreen. The temple was destroyed in the 8th century BC, was rebuilt and then gradually gave way to other constructions.

Excavations on the mound where the temple stood have revealed its layout and, most interestingly, some extraordinary basalt statues and reliefs, which litter the **site** (adult/student S£75/5; ☉ sunrise-sunset). The single most impressive statue is a huge lion. The views of the surrounding countryside – verdant fields, sunflowers, oleander trees and fruit groves – are spectacular.

The caretaker, who lives in the house at the foot of the hill, will greet you, collect the admission fee, do his best to show you around, and probably invite you for tea.

lonelyplanet.com   AROUND ALEPPO •• South of Aleppo   **197**

ALEPPO

GETTING THERE & AWAY

Ain Dara is around 18km north of Qala'at Samaan. You can probably get a ride from Deir Samaan towards Nahr Afreen (you want the road that goes through Deir Samaan, not the one that leads up to Qala'at Samaan) and get dropped off at the turn-off to Ain Dara, sometimes signed 'Tell Ain Dara'.

Alternatively, from Aleppo catch a minibus direct to Nahr Afreen (S£20) and from there take one of the irregular pick-ups to Ain Dara (S£15), which is 7km to the south. It will drop you at the turn-off just before the village; you can see the acropolis in the distance. Follow the road around (about 2km), or cut across the path and onion fields directly to the site.

Cyrrhus (Nebi Huri)   النبي هوري

In this wonderfully remote location, overlooking the Turkish border and deep in Kurdish territory, is the 3rd-century provincial town of Cyrrhus (Nebi Huri to the locals). The setting is bucolic – Kurdish families riding tractors out to work in the fields together, shepherds lying back on their elbows under the shade of trees, and donkeys grazing by the road. Little is left of the town today, but Cyrrhus once held a strategic position for troops of the Roman Empire and boasted a citadel, theatre and cathedral.

From the dusty town of Azaz the road takes you through pleasant countryside, dotted with wheat fields and olive groves, across two 3rd-century humpback Roman bridges on the Sabun River and past a Roman-era **mausoleum**. Preserved by local Muslims as a holy site, as evidenced by the ribbons you see tied to the bars for good luck, the pyramid-capped monument has survived well. The ground floor has been recycled as the tomb of a local Muslim prophet named Houri. From here, branch right off the road to Cyrrhus, which is just 200m further on.

The easiest structure to distinguish out of what is a fairly crumbling bunch of ruins is the **theatre**. Of the town walls, colonnaded street and basilica in the north of the town, not much remains, but scramble up through the ruins past the theatre to the Arab citadel at the top and you'll enjoy sweeping views across to the Turkish mountains.

GETTING THERE & AWAY

Minibuses run from Aleppo to Azaz (S£15, one hour), from where you'll have to bargain with one of the taxi drivers to take you the remaining 28km to the site, which takes about 30 minutes one way. This should cost around S£800 return. (Hitching is not recommended, as there is little traffic on this road.)

For a day trip from Aleppo covering Cyrrhus and Qala'at Samaan, hiring a driver and car is a good option. You can probably bargain down to US$70 or US$80 from the standard $US100 starting price for a decent car and English-speaking driver.

Qalb Lozeh   قلب لوزه

One of the very best-preserved examples of Syrian-Byzantine ecclesiastical architecture, the church of **Qalb Lozeh** (adult/student S£75/5; ☼ sunrise-sunset) predates Qala'at Samaan by perhaps only a couple of decades. It was built as a stop-off point for pilgrims en route to see Simeon on his pillar. The entrance to the church, flanked by two three-storey towers, its walls and the semicircular apse are almost completely intact. Even some stone slabs of the roof have been retained, but the once-impressive arch between the towers has been lost forever. The simple elegance of the structure, clean lines of the columns around the apse and classical decoration make this church an obvious precursor to the Romanesque style that would later dominate the breadth of European church-building. Expect to be met by the caretaker and his delightful children, who will try to sell you some embroidery; have your change ready.

GETTING THERE & AWAY

Qalb Lozeh lies 32km west off the main road from Aleppo to the Turkish border and Antakya. To get there, take a minibus from Aleppo to Harim, which is a small, attractive provincial town crowned by an Ayyubid castle. From Harim you'll need to negotiate a taxi.

SOUTH OF ALEPPO

Ebla, Ma'arat an-Nu'aman, Jerada and Ruweiha are all just off the main Aleppo–Hama highway, and while most are accessible by public transport, it would be difficult to visit them all this way in a single day. If you have a car and driver, seeing the lot is possible in one long day. These sites are equally easy to visit from Hama.

Ebla (Tell Mardikh)   تل مرديخ

Lying about 60km south of Aleppo, the ancient city of **Ebla** (Tell Mardikh; adult/student S£150/10; ☼ 8am-6pm Apr-Sep, to 4pm Oct-Mar) is of enormous fascination to archaeologists and historians, but less so to most visitors unless they possess a vivid imagination or have done their homework.

The Italian teams (there's plenty of Italian labelling on sights here) excavating the site since 1964 discovered Ebla was one of the most powerful city-states in Syria in the late 3rd millennium BC, but was sacked before the close of the millennium, probably by Sargon of Akkad or his grandson Naram-Sin (c 2250 BC). In its heyday, Ebla probably controlled most of northwestern Syria. It rose again for a relatively brief period from about 1900 BC to 1750 BC, before being destroyed in 1600 BC by Hittite invaders. Troops of the First Crusade passed by thousands of years later, when it was known as Mardic Hamlet.

In recent times, digs here have unearthed more than 15,000 clay tablets in a Sumerian dialect, providing a wealth of information on everything from economics to local administration, and dictionaries of other tongues. However, only a small portion of the cuneiform secrets has been unlocked.

The site lies over a rise about 1km beyond the village of Tell Mardikh. You buy your ticket outside the small, burgundy-coloured, multidomed **museum** (☼ 8am-6pm Wed-Mon Apr-Sep, to 4pm Wed-Mon Oct-Mar) dedicated to the story of the excavations, and then continue along the road and over the rise. The shallow remains of the city lie before you, dominated by the limestone tell that once formed the core of the city's fortress. It's forbidden to clamber over the site so stick to the trails around the edge of the excavations. It's best to head straight up the stairs to the highest (and often windiest) point of the site, from where there's a great view of the ruins and village below. The most interesting ruins are probably those labelled 'Palace G', just west of the acropolis, which display remains of a royal staircase, walls and columned halls.

GETTING THERE & AWAY

Take any Hama-bound minibus (S£20, one hour) or one of the less frequent ones to Ma'arat an-Nu'aman (ask for Al-Ma'ara), and ask to be let off at the Tell Mardikh turn-off. From there it's a 20-minute walk through the village of Tell Mardikh to the site. Follow the elegant, tall, white street lamps.

Ma'arat an-Nu'aman (Al-Ma'ara)
معرّة النعمان

This lively little market town has a past that's more interesting than the town itself. It was witness to a gruesome bit of history when the Crusaders' behaviour reached a new low. On 12 December 1098, under the command of Count Raymond of Toulouse, the Crusaders attacked the fortified Muslim town of Ma'arat an-Nu'aman, slaughtering thousands. But the horror was amplified by what followed: 'In Ma'ara our troops boiled pagan adults in cooking pots; they impaled children on spits and devoured them grilled', confessed one of the Crusader chroniclers.

The **Mosaic Museum** (adult/student S£150/10; ☼ 9am-6pm Wed-Mon Apr-Sep, to 4pm Wed-Mon Oct-Mar), housed in the 16th-century Khan Murad Pasha, displays mosaics from the floors of the more important or luxurious buildings and private houses of the clusters of 5th- and 6th-century Byzantine towns that are now collectively referred to as the Dead Cities. The museum is about 50m to the north of the bus station, on the right side of the square.

Further north and off to the right is the **Great Mosque**, whose 12th-century minaret was rebuilt after an earthquake in 1170. From the mosque, head to the right of the square and north for a few hundred metres – where the street opens out you'll see the sad remains of a medieval **Citadel**.

GETTING THERE & AWAY

There are frequent microbuses to Ma'arat an-Nu'aman (S£25, one hour) from Aleppo's City Bus Station. Lumbering big buses also do the run (S£15, one hour 20 minutes) from the Pullman station.

DEAD CITIES

The star attraction of the region around Aleppo is the Dead Cities, a series of ancient ghost towns scattered among the limestone hills that lie between the Aleppo–Hama highway in the east and the Orontes River in the west. They date from the time when this area was part of the hinterland of the great Byzantine Christian city of Antioch. There are reckoned to be some 600 separate sites, ranging from single monuments to nearly whole villages complete with houses, churches, mills, hammams and even wine presses. Taken together they represent a great archive in stone from which historians can put together a picture of life in antiquity.

The great mystery is why the towns were abandoned. Some of the sites, especially Serjilla, have an eerie quality, as though their occupants had just vanished. The latest theory is that these towns and villages were emptied by demographic shifts; trade routes changed and the people moved with them. However, the Dead Cities are inappropriately named: some form part of present-day villages, with people inhabiting the ancient ruins or incorporating oddments of antiquity into the structure of their homes.

The number of sites is overwhelming – we describe only a handful of the most interesting and easily accessible. If you have the inclination, you could spend weeks pottering around these fascinating sites, stumbling across Byzantine-era ghosts wherever you wander. Beware of the present-era wild dogs that inhabit some of these areas and keep a watchful eye when exploring.

Jerada & Ruweiha   جاراده ورويحة
Of these twin Dead Cities, Jerada is the closer to the Aleppo–Hama highway. The site is partially occupied, with some of the big old houses serving as barns for villagers, who have built their own dwellings on the northern fringes of the ruins. These ruins include the extensive remains of noble houses, a 5th-century Byzantine cathedral and a six-storey watchtower. Some of the simple geometric designs on column capitals and lintels are vaguely reminiscent of Visigothic decoration in Spain around the same time.

Follow the road for another 2.5km or so across a barren lunarlike landscape to reach the striking, scattered remains of Ruweiha. The most imposing building here is the 6th-century **Church of Bissos**. Its transverse arches are thought to be among the oldest

of their kind. Just outside, the domed mausoleum housing the body of Bissos (possibly a bishop) has since found its echo in similar designs throughout the Arab world. Few people live among the vast ruins now, although it's a popular weekend picnic spot.

Serjilla   سرجلا
Serjilla and Al-Bara are two of a cluster of five or more Dead Cities strung out on either side of a country lane that runs north from the green-domed mosque just outside Kafr Nabl. About 2km after the mosque you'll see a sign for **Shinshira** pointing off to your right. After a further 2km, off to the left, are the grey stone remnants of **Mahardiyya** buried within some olive groves. Both of these Dead Cities are worth exploring, but if you're pushed for time, skip them and look out instead for the signposted turn-off to Serjilla, to the right.

Serjilla (adult/student S£75/5) is undoubtedly the most eerie and evocative of the Dead Cities, especially in winter when the ruins might be shrouded in mist. Serjilla has the greatest number of semi-complete buildings, all of which sit in a natural basin in windswept and hilly moorland. Although deserted for about 15 centuries, the stone façades are clean and sharp-edged and the surrounding ground is covered with short grass. The neatness adds to the spooky air.

At Serjilla's centre is a small plaza flanked by a two-storey tavern and a large hammam. Now stripped of the mosaics that once decorated it, the latter building is quite austere. Next door lies an *andron* (men's meeting place), and further east a small church, along with substantial remnants of private houses and villas. As you clamber down narrow grassy lanes between high stone walls, punctuated by carefully carved windows and doors, you half expect a householder to step out on a quick errand to fetch something from the market.

Al-Bara   باره
Al-Bara is the most extensive of the Dead Cities. It's also the furthest north from Kafr Nabl; you continue on beyond the turn for Serjilla and past another small Dead City called **Bauda**.

Surrounded by rich arable land and occupying a strategic position on the north–south trade route between Antioch and

ALEPPO

Apamea, Al-Bara flourished from the 4th century onwards, becoming one of the most important centres of wine and olive-oil production in the region. Even when the trade routes shifted in the 7th century (which saw many neighbouring towns abandoned), Al-Bara prospered and grew. It boasted large villas, three monasteries and numerous churches – at least five can still be detected among ruins that cover 6 sq km.

The town weathered the coming of Islam and remained predominantly eastern Christian – and the seat of a bishopric subordinate to Antioch – until its occupation by the Latin Crusaders in the very last years of the 12th century.

It was from Al-Bara that the Crusaders set out to perpetrate their horrible cannibalistic episode at Ma'arat an-Nu'aman in 1098 (see p198). Twenty-five years later they were driven out and Al-Bara reverted to Muslim control.

As it stands today, there's no obvious route around the site; the land is densely covered by vegetation and you have to tramp through the undergrowth and groves of cherry, apricot and olive trees to discover the old buildings and ruins.

Don't miss the striking **pyramid tombs**, 200m apart, decorated with Corinthian pilasters and carved acanthus leaves, a very visible testament to the one-time wealth of the settlement. The larger of the two still holds five sealed, decorated sarcophagi. From the pyramids you can wander south past an underground tomb with three arches to a large, well-preserved **monastery**, or head north to find the ruins of the five **churches**.

Getting There & Away

If you don't have your own driver, take a microbus for Ma'arat an-Nu'aman (commonly referred to as Al-Ma'ara; S£20, one hour). For Jerada and Ruweiha ask to be let off at Babila, 7km before Al-Ma'ara, from where you can see the ruins over to the west, 3km away. If you start walking you're bound to be offered a lift before you get too far.

To get to Al-Bara, Serjilla and the other neighbouring Dead Cities, stay on the bus all the way into Al-Ma'ara, where you can catch a microbus for Kafr Nabl (S£10), some 10km away. From Kafr Nabl it's a further 6km to Al-Bara. If the microbus driver offers to take you on, you could offer him an additional S£10 per person. Otherwise walk out of the village, follow the main street, then after about 1.5km bear right at the large new mosque with the green dome; it won't be long before a passing car offers you a lift.

Palmyra to the Euphrates

تدمر إلى نهر لفرات

Palmyra, Syria's star attraction, is a sublime sprawling archaeological site, spectacularly set between a lush date palm oasis and a majestic mountain-topped castle, in the middle of a vast emptiness. The Orontes River is to the west and the Euphrates to the east. But the apparent emptiness of the landscape is deceptive.

While little could surpass the spectacle of the Palmyra ruins – particularly with a backdrop of the rising or setting sun – the desert of this northeastern region of Syria is dotted with other ancient sites of both archaeological significance and jaw-dropping beauty. Majestic Qala'at Najm dominates a rugged hill jutting into the awesome Euphrates River while the isolated Qasr Al-Heir Al-Sharqi is dramatically sited in a sparse, arid plain.

The vast desert is not only home to the splendours of past civilisations. For many Bedouin and other seminomadic people, life continues here as it has done for centuries, and while their method of transport may have changed – from camel to donkey to pick-up truck – the hospitality of these nomads living in an inhospitable environment has not. The chance to share a cup of tea with the Bedouin may well be a highlight of your visit to Syria.

The harsh, extreme northeast of the country is also home to about one million Kurds, a stateless people still struggling towards some day attaining their own homeland. It is here also that the cool green ribbon of the Euphrates, which provides welcome relief for the traveller, continues its journey before emptying into the Gulf after having travelled more than 2400km from its beginnings high in the mountains of eastern Anatolia in Turkey.

HIGHLIGHTS

- Rise early for sunrise and picture-perfect light at the sublime ruins of **Palmyra** (p202)
- Savour the splendid vistas of the awesome Euphrates River from **Qala'at Najm** (p216)
- Surround yourself with the azure waters of Lake al-Assad from the top of **Qala'at Ja'abar** (p214)
- Explore the striking ruins of **Rasafa** (p217), which rise dramatically from the featureless desert
- Chat to Bedouin shepherds on the road to remote **Qasr Al-Heir Al-Sharqi** (p213)
- Step back 5000 years and imagine the ancient civilisation of the Mesopotamians at **Mari** (p223)
- Enjoy ancient **Dura Europos** (p222) overlooking the Euphrates River

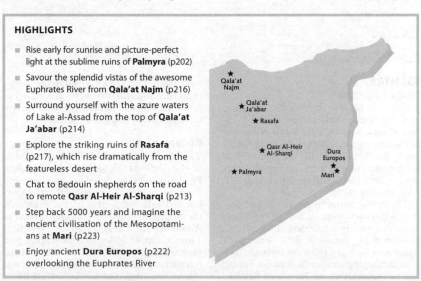

★ Qala'at Najm
★ Qala'at Ja'abar
★ Rasafa
★ Qasr Al-Heir Al-Sharqi
Dura Europos ★
★ Palmyra
Mari ★

PALMYRA TO THE EUPHRATES

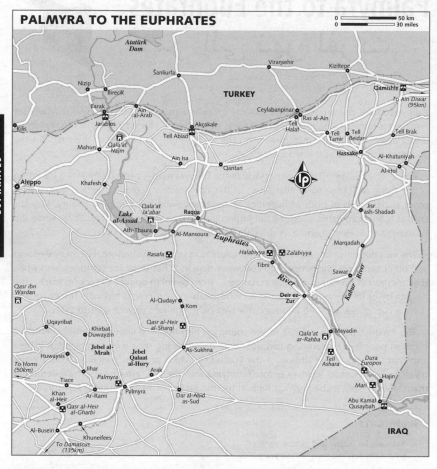

PALMYRA   تدمر

☎ 031 / pop 50,000

Palmyra is Syria's star tourist attraction and one of the world's most splendid historical sites. Known to the locals as Tadmor (its ancient Semitic name), Palmyra's intriguing history, along with the profusion of colonnades, temple remains and funerary towers, in a mesmerising desert oasis setting, renders visitors speechless.

The ruins, dating largely to the 2nd century AD, cover some 50 hectares and have been extensively excavated and restored. Nevertheless, archaeologists continually make new finds. In 1994, for instance, Belgian archaeologists stumbled across Roman tombs southeast of the Temple of Bel. The

new town has grown around the ruins, especially towards the west, and now has more than 40,000 inhabitants who survive on agriculture, trade and tourism.

History

Tadmor is mentioned in texts discovered at Mari dating back to the 2nd millennium BC. Early rulers included the Assyrians and Persians, before the settlement was incorporated into the realm of the Seleucids, the empire founded by a former general of Alexander the Great. From an early time Tadmor was an indispensable staging post for caravans travelling between the Mediterranean, Mesopotamia and Arabia. It was also an important link on the old Silk Route from China and India to Europe, with the city prospering greatly by levying heavy tolls on the caravans.

As the Romans expanded their frontiers during the 1st and early 2nd centuries AD to occupy the eastern Mediterranean shores, the Seleucid dynasty failed. Tadmor became stranded between the Latin realms to the west and those of the Parthians to the east. The oasis used this situation to its advantage, keeping the east–west trade routes open and taking the role of middleman between the two clashing superpowers. The influence of Rome grew, and the city they dubbed Palmyra (City of Palms) became a tributary of the empire and a buffer against rivals to the east. The Palmyrenes were permitted to retain considerable independence, profiting also from rerouted trade following the defeat of the Petra-based Nabataeans by Rome.

The emperor Hadrian visited in AD 129 and declared Palmyra a 'free city', allowing it to set and collect its own taxes. In 212, under the emperor Caracalla (himself born of a Syrian mother), Palmyra became a Roman colony. In this way, its citizens obtained equal rights with those of Rome and exemption from paying imperial taxes. Further wealth followed and Palmyra spent lavishly, enlarging its great colonnaded avenue and building more and larger temples.

As internal power struggles weakened Rome, the Palmyrenes strengthened their independence. A local noble, Odainat, defeated the army of one of Rome's long-standing rivals, the Sassanians, and proclaimed himself 'king'. In 256 the emperor Valerian bestowed upon Odainat the title of 'Corrector of the East' and put all Roman forces in the region under his command.

The most glorious episode in Palmyra's history – which also led to the city's subsequent rapid downfall – began when Odainat was assassinated in 267. His second wife, Zenobia, took over in the name of their young son, Vabalathus. Rome refused to recognise this arrangement, particularly as Zenobia was suspected of involvement in her husband's death. The emperor dispatched an army to deal with the rebel queen. Zenobia met the Roman force in battle and defeated it. She then led her army against the garrison at Bosra, then the capital of the Province of Arabia, and successfully invaded Egypt.

With all of Syria and Palestine and part of Egypt under her control, Zenobia declared her independence from Rome and had coins minted in Alexandria bearing her

THE PROBLEM WITH PALMYRA

Palmyra's economy is largely dependent on tourism, and many locals support large extended families with proceeds from operating the town's hotels, restaurants and shops. When tourist numbers plummeted after September 11, 2001, local businesses hit hard times and competition between them became fierce – and sometimes nasty. The restaurant business, for instance, is fiercely competitive and running down the competition is the local sport. Wherever you eat, expect to hear tales of horror about others. Just ignore it.

The hotel scene is just as combative, the major object of disaffection being Al-Faris Hotel, over a kilometre outside town. If you're arriving in Palmyra by bus, you may be 'encouraged' to alight at Al-Faris rather than at the official bus stop in town, but don't get off the bus unless you want to.

Those travellers who make it past Al-Faris and into town will no doubt encounter another competition-fuelled annoyance upon arrival – the hotel touts. These guys (often kids) will try to take you to one of the hotels in town paying them a commission. Be aware that if you turn up at a hotel with one of them, an extra 10% to 20% will be added to the quoted cost of a bed or room to cover his commission. And beware of the old 'That hotel is full/dirty/closed/a brothel' spiel about the hotel you've already booked; the touts will say anything to steer you towards a commission-paying place.

Some local business-people understand that this has created a poisonous atmosphere in the town and note that many visitors are choosing to take a day trip here instead of staying overnight; others take a shorter-term view and will do anything to get your business, regardless of the long-term effect on the town.

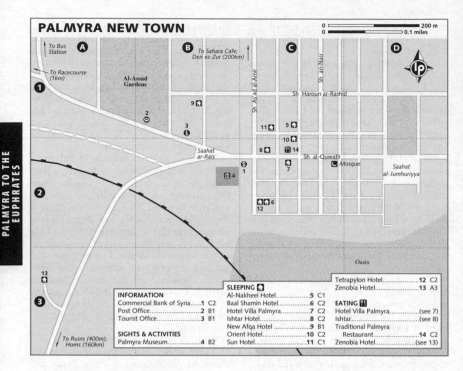

PALMYRA NEW TOWN

image and that of her son, who assumed the title of Augustus, or emperor.

Claiming to be descended from Cleopatra, Zenobia was, it seems, a woman of exceptional ability and ambition. Though she was headstrong and wilful, the 18th-century historian Edward Gibbon also said of her in his *Decline and Fall of the Roman Empire*:

> She equalled in beauty her ancestor Cleopatra and far surpassed that princess in chastity and valour. Zenobia was esteemed the most lovely as well as the most heroic of her sex. She was of dark complexion. Her teeth were of a pearly whiteness and her large black eyes sparkled with an uncommon fire, tempered by the most attractive sweetness. Her voice was strong and harmonious. Her manly understanding was strengthened and adorned by study.

The Roman emperor Aurelian, who had been prepared to negotiate, could not stomach such a show of open defiance. After defeating Zenobia's forces at Antioch and Emesa (Homs) in 271, he besieged Palmyra itself. Zenobia was defiant to the last and instead of accepting the generous surrender terms offered by Aurelian, made a dash on a camel through the encircling Roman forces. She headed for Persia to appeal for military aid, only to be captured by Roman cavalry at the Euphrates.

Zenobia was carted off to Rome in 272 as Aurelian's trophy and reputedly paraded in the streets, bound in gold chains. Later freed, she married a Roman senator and lived out her days in Tibur (now Tivoli), close to Rome.

Zenobia's defeat marked the end of Palmyra's prosperity. A further rebellion in 273, in which the Palmyrenes massacred a garrison of 600 Roman archers, elicited a brutal response and Aurelian's legionaries slaughtered large numbers and put the city to the torch. Palmyra never recovered. The emperor Diocletian (r 254–305) later fortified the broken city as one in a line of fortresses marking the eastern boundary of the Roman Empire, and Justinian further rebuilt the city's defences in the 6th century. The city survived primarily as a military outpost and the caravan traffic all but dropped away.

In 634 the city fell to a Muslim army led by Khaled ibn al-Walid, and from this time Palmyra all but fades from history. Architectural and archaeological evidence tells that the Arabs fortified the Temple of Bel, which became host to a small village, and a castle was built on a nearby hilltop, but the great city itself was largely abandoned. Its structures were devastated by earthquake and largely covered over by wind-blown sand and earth.

It wasn't until 1678 that Palmyra was 'rediscovered' by two English merchants resident in Aleppo. Few followed in their footsteps; the buried desert city was an often-dangerous five days' journey from civilisation. It took a 1751 expedition, which resulted in drawings and the first tentative excavations, to truly pique travellers' interest. Throughout the rest of the 18th and 19th centuries a steady flow of intrepid visitors made the expedition out from Aleppo or Damascus, although it wasn't until the early 20th century that the first scientific study began. The earliest surveys were carried out in the 1920s by the Germans. In 1929 the French took over.

Work intensified following WWII, and continues to this day.

Orientation

Modern Palmyra is laid out on a grid pattern. The main street is Sharia al-Quwatli, which runs east from the main square, Saahat ar-Rais, which is on the western edge of town. On the south side of this square is the museum.

The ancient site is just over 500m southwest of here along a road that crosses a reconstructed section of Zenobia's walls, which runs just behind the museum. The town is tiny and can be walked from end to end in 10 minutes.

Arriving buses drop off in one of three places: the Karnak office in the centre of town; the Sahara Cafe on the northern outskirts of town, from where a taxi will cost S£25; and near the new Palmyra bypass in the west of town, from where it's a 10-minute walk, straight on ahead, to the town centre. (See Getting There & Away, p213, for more details on buses.)

Information

Several hotels have set up computers in their foyers to allow guests to use the internet, such as the Ishtar Hotel (p211), and a new internet café was about to open at the time of research, Moon Light Internet Café.

CBS (Commercial Bank of Syria; Map p204; Saahat ar-Rais; ☿ 8am-8pm Sat-Thu) In front of the museum; there were plans for an ATM at the time of research.

Post Office (Map p204; Saahat ar-Rais; ☿ 8am-2pm) Also has a couple of cardphones in front of the main entrance, accessible 24 hours.

Tourist Office (Map p204; ☎ 591 0574; Saahat ar-Rais; ☿ 8am-2pm) Across from the museum; staff can organise guides and provide a map.

VISITING PALMYRA

Although visitors can no longer expect to enjoy the ruins in complete solitude, the flow of tourists is still often little more than a trickle. Added to which, the site is so vast that it is easy to lose yourself and imagine that you're a 19th-century adventurer stumbling across the fallen, half-buried city for the very first time. This is especially true at first light. For this reason, if no other, avoid visiting Palmyra as a day trip from Damascus or Hama because no matter how early you set off, you'll arrive too late to see the ruins at their best. The heat and the touts can get a little too much in the middle of the day as well.

The unhurried traveller could easily spend several days wandering around the main site, which spreads over a very large area, bounded by what have come to be known as Zenobia's walls. Then there are the funerary towers and underground tombs, as well as Qala'at ibn Maan, the Arab castle on the hill. A visit of less than two days sells the experience short for most travellers. It's also highly recommended that you see the site both at sunrise, when the early morning light infuses the stone with a rich pink hue, and again at sunset, ideally watching the sun drain from the ruins from the vantage point of the castle or the rocky outcrops to the south. During the rest of the day, find some shade and read a book.

Sights

PALMYRA MUSEUM متحف تدمر

Only the keenest of archaeologists would benefit from a visit to Palmyra's modest museum (Map p204; adult/student S£150/10; ☺ 8am-1pm & 4-6pm Apr-Sep, 8am-1pm & 2-4pm Oct-Mar, closed Tue). With its poor labelling, it adds little to the experience of Palmyra. There are a few highlights, however, including a large-scale model of the Temple of Bel that gives a good impression of how the complex would have looked in its original state, and some fascinating friezes depicting camel trains and cargo ships, attesting to the importance trade played in the wealth of Palmyra.

There are some dynamic mosaics found in nobles' houses east of the Temple of Bel, including one representing a scene from the Iliad in which Ulysses discovers Achilles disguised in women's clothes, concealed among the daughters of the king of Scyros (this scene is also portrayed in a fresco in the Hypogeum of the Three Brothers – see p210).

Other notable exhibits include a collection of coins depicting Zenobia and her son, discovered in 1991, and countless busts and reliefs that formed part of the panels used to seal the loculi in Palmyra's many funerary towers and hypogea (underground burial chambers; to see exactly how this worked, visit the Japanese Tomb, p210). The most outstanding piece in the collection is a 3m-high statue of the goddess Allat, associated with the Greek Athena, discovered in 1975 by Polish archaeologists.

THE RUINS

Set the alarm for an early start to beat the heat – from May through to September the sun can be merciless – and take plenty of water and a hat. Follow the road that runs south directly opposite the tourist office to reach the Temple of Bel and monumental arch, the latter being the best place from which to start exploring.

Depending on the heat and your energy levels, you may need to organise transport to visit Qala'at ibn Maan (the Arab castle), the Valley of the Tombs and the hypogea; most hotels are keen to oblige.

Although there is no admission fee to the main site, the museums, Temple of Bel, Qala'at ibn Maan and some of the tombs charge admission. The main site has no fixed opening times but paying attractions keep set hours.

THE GOOD THINGS IN LIFE AREN'T FREE...

Admission fees at Palmyra are a little steep for Syria; however, everything else is so inexpensive in Syria, there is really nothing to complain about! But you'll be surprised to learn that there have been fees to visit Palmyra for nearly 200 years.

The Middle East has always attracted intrepid female explorers and adventurers – Gertrude Bell, Lady Jane Digby and Freya Stark to name just three – but Lady Hester Stanhope was one of the more extreme examples. She was the niece of a British prime minister and, as such, a one-time resident of 10 Downing St. On the death of her beloved uncle and her removal from the centre of British politics, Lady Hester decided to travel abroad and find herself a new court. Along with her retinue she travelled in the Middle East, interfering in local affairs but winning the admiration of the Arabs, who regarded her as a queen.

One of her greatest moments of glory was, in 1813, riding into Palmyra on an Arab stallion at the head of her travelling procession. On this occasion she was hosting a fete for the local Bedouin, during which she ordered that a silver dollar be given to all present. To the grand sheikh of the Bedouin she presented a piece of paper, handwritten, on which she directed him to charge every traveller who visited the ruins a thousand piastres. 'This enormous tax,' wrote traveller John Carne in Letters from the East (1826), 'which it is impossible to escape, causes several travellers to leave Syria without seeing the finest ruin in the world'. One visitor who did attempt to evade the tax, reports Carne, had his hut set on fire by the Arabs.

At least the penniless traveller of today is able to visit a great deal of the site for free and finds cash admissions barring the way only to a few selected sections, such as the Temple of Bel. And if the traveller decides to give these sights a miss and hold back on the cash, the chances of having the hotel burned from under them are these days very slim.

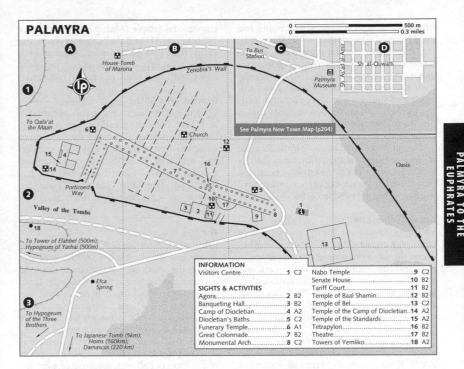

Temple of Bel   معبد بل

The single most impressive part of the ruins and the most complete structure is this **temple** (Map p207; adult/student S£150/10; ☼ 8am-6pm Apr-Sep, 8am-4pm Oct-Mar, closed Tue), also known as the Sanctuary of Bel. Although very little is known about Palmyra's deities, Bel is assumed to be the most important of the gods in the Palmyrene pantheon, the equivalent of the Greek Zeus or Roman Jupiter.

Raised on a slight tell (mound) indicating the existence of a pre-Classical settlement on this site, you enter the temple through the ticket office, just north of the main monumental entrance. The keeplike entrance was created by the Arabs when they converted the temple into a fortress; an inscription in a recessed arch dates the work to 1123–24.

The complex consists of two parts: a huge walled courtyard, or **temenos**, and, at its centre, the temple proper or cella. The courtyard was originally surrounded by a 15m-high wall, but only the northern side is original, dating from the 2nd or 3rd century AD; the rest is of Arab construction. A double colonnade used to run around three sides of the interior while the fourth (western) side had a single row of columns much taller than the others. Some of these can be seen to the right and left of the entrance.

Just to the left of the entrance inside the courtyard is a **sunken passage** that enters the temple from outside the wall and gradually slopes up to the level of the courtyard. This was probably used to bring sacrificial animals into the precincts. The podium of the **sacrificial altar** is on the left, and beside it are the foundations of a **banqueting hall**. The remains of another platform are to the right and this was possibly used for religious purification ceremonies.

The **cella** (Map p207) was completed in AD 32, a date given in a dedication inscribed on a pedestal found inside, and now exhibited in the Palmyra Museum. It's unusual in that the entrance is in one of the sides rather than at an end, and is offset from the centre. Inside is a single chamber with adytons (large niches) at either end. The adyton ceilings, carved from single slabs of stone, are magnificent: the northern ceiling has a cupola featuring seven busts of divinities and the 12 signs of the zodiac, while the southern ceiling has a circular pattern of acanthus leaves surrounded by a ring of geometric patterning all inset within a square frame, itself surrounded by an elaborate pattern of hexagonal coffers. The stepped ramp leading to the southern portico suggests that it may have contained a portable idol used in processions.

The earth-coloured building by the Temple of Bel was originally the residence of the Ottoman governor of Palmyra. It later became a prison, and at the time of research was about to open as the new **Visitors Centre** (🕑 8am-6pm).

Great Colonnade   الشارع الطويل
The spine of ancient Palmyra was a stately **colonnaded avenue** (Map p207) stretching between the city's main funerary temple in the west and the Temple of Bel in the east, and covering a distance of almost 1km. Unlike the typical Roman model, Palmyra's main avenue was far from straight, pivoting decisively at two points – a result of piecemeal growth and improvisation. Where the modern asphalted road slices across the ancient way is an imposing **monumental arch** (Map p207). Dating from the reign of Septimius Severus, when Palmyra was at its peak, the construction is actually two arches, joined like a hinge to swing the street through a 30° turn, aiming it at the Temple of Bel.

The section of street between the Bel temple and the arch has largely vanished, with just a few sparse columns to indicate the route the colonnades once took, but the section west of the arch is magnificent. This section lies at the heart of the ancient civic centre; it has been heavily restored and gives a very clear idea of how the city must have appeared in all its original splendour.

The street itself was never paved, probably to save damage from camel caravans, but flanking porticoes on either side were. Each of the massive columns that supported the porticoes has a small jutting platform about two-thirds of the way up, designed to hold the statue of some rich or famous Palmyrene who had helped pay for the construction of the street.

Nabo Temple   معبد نبو
The ruined area to the left immediately after passing through the arch is a small trapezoidal **temple** (Map p207) built in the 1st century AD and dedicated to Nabo, the Palmyrene god of destinies. All that's left are the temple podium, lower courses of the outer walls and some re-erected columns.

Diocletian's Baths   حمامات ديوكلسيان
On the north side of the great colonnaded way, four columns standing forward of the line of the portico announce the location of what was once a public bathhouse founded by Diocletian. These columns once carried a pediment over the entrance, but this has been lost. The **baths** (Map p207) survive only as trenches and as outlines scored in the baked earth.

Theatre
Palmyra's **theatre** (Map p207; adult/student S£150/10; 🕑 8am-6pm Apr-Sep, 8am-4pm Oct-Mar, closed Tue), lies on the south side of the street, accessed between two arches in the colonnade. Until the 1950s it was buried beneath sand but since then it has been extensively restored.

Beneath the platforms on many of the columns are inscriptions with names for the statues that once stood there: representations of prominent people including emperors, princes of Palmyra, magistrates, officials, high-ranking priests and caravan chiefs.

The freestanding stage façade of the theatre itself is designed along the lines of a palace entrance, complete with a royal door and smaller doors on either side. From the rear of the theatre, a pillared way once led south to a gate in the city walls dating from the era of Justinian. North of this pillared way are the substantial remains of the Tariff Court and agora (opposite).

Tetrapylon   التترابيل
Perhaps the most striking construction at Palmyra, the **Tetrapylon** (Map p207) marks the second pivot in the route of the colonnaded street. It consists of a square platform bearing at each corner a tight grouping of four columns. Each of the four groups of pillars supports 150,000kg of solid cornice. A pedestal at the centre of each quartet originally carried a statue. Only one of the 16 pillars is of the original pink granite (probably brought from Aswan in Egypt); the rest are a result of some rather hasty reconstruction carried out from the 1960s onwards by the Syrian Antiquities Department.

From here the main colonnaded street continues northwest, while smaller pillared transverse streets lead southwest to the agora and northeast to the Temple of Baal Shamin.

Agora   السوق العامة

The **agora** (Map p207) was the hub of Palmyrene life, the city's most important meeting space, used for public discussion and as a market where caravans unloaded their wares and engaged in the trade that brought the desert oasis its wealth. What remains today is a clearly defined courtyard measuring 84m by 71m. Many pillars survive to indicate that the central area was once enclosed by porticoes on all four sides and that the pillars carried statues. The dedications reveal that the portico on the north held statues of Palmyrene and Roman officials, the eastern one had senators, the western portico was for military officers, while on the south side, merchants and caravan leaders were honoured. Sadly, today no statues remain and most of the pillars are small stumps.

Adjoining the agora in the northwest corner are the remains of a small **banqueting hall** (Map p207) used by the rulers of Palmyra. South of the agora is another large, walled rectangular space, known as the **Tariff Court** (Map p207) because this is where the great tariff stele (now residing in the St Petersburg Hermitage) was found. The enormous stone tablet dates from AD 137 and bears the inscription 'Tariff of Palmyra', setting out the taxes payable on each commodity that passed through the city.

The small structure at the north end of the court, closest to the theatre, has a semicircular arrangement of tiered seating leading archaeologists to believe that it may have been the city's **Senate** (Map p207), or council building.

Temple of Baal Shamin   معبد بعلشمين

Dating from AD 17 and dedicated to the Phoenician god of storms and fertilising rains, this small shrine is all that remains of a much larger compound. It stands alone 200m north of the main colonnaded street, near the Zenobia Hotel, in what was a residential area of the ancient city. Baal Shamin was an import, like Bel, who only really gained popularity in Palmyra when Roman influence was at its height.

Although the temple gate is permanently padlocked, it is possible to peer inside. Fronting the **temple** (Map p207), the six columns of the vestibule have platforms for statues, and carry inscriptions. The column on the far left, dated AD 131, has an inscription in Greek and Palmyrene that praises the secretary of the city for his generosity during the imperial visit of 'the divine Hadrian' and for footing the bill for the temple's construction.

Funerary Temple

Beyond the Tetrapylon the main street continues for another 500m. This stretch has seen much less excavation and reconstruction than elsewhere and is still littered with tumbled columns and assorted blocks of masonry. The road ends at the impressive portico of a **funerary temple** (Map p207), dating from the 3rd century AD. The portico with its six columns stands as it was found but the walls are a relatively recent reconstruction. This was the main residential section of town and streets can be seen leading off to both sides. There is scattered masonry everywhere, in places literally heaped into small hillocks of statuary fragments and decorated friezes and panels.

Camp of Diocletian   مخيم ديوكلسيان

Southwest of the funerary temple, reached via a porticoed way, is an extensive complex known as **Diocletian's camp** (Map p207). Dating from the late 3rd or early 4th century AD, it comprises the remains of a monumental gateway, a tetrapylon and two temples; one of these, the **Temple of the Standards** (Map p207), dominates from an elevated position at the head of a flight of worn steps. The 'camp' was erected after the destruction of the city by Aurelian. The extent of the complex and the fact that it was built on top of, and incorporates, earlier structures of evident grandeur has led some historians to speculate that it occupies what had been the palace of Zenobia.

Behind the complex a section of fortified wall climbs a steep hill – from where there are excellent views of the site – then descends, edging around the southern edge of the city.

VALLEY OF THE TOMBS   وادي القبور

To the south of the city wall at the foot of low hills is a series of variously sized, freestanding, square-based towers. Known as the **Towers of Yemliko** (Map p207), they were constructed as multistorey burial chambers, stacked high with coffins posted in pigeonhole-like niches, or loculi, which were then sealed with a stone panel carved with a head and shoulders portrait of the deceased; you can see dozens of these stone portraits in the Palmyra Museum, and in the National Museum at Damascus (p95).

The tallest of the towers – at four storeys high – is the most interesting. It dates from AD 83 and although it is kept locked you can peer in through the barred entrance. There is also an interesting carved lintel above the doorway and an inscription further up identifying the family interred within. A rough path winds up behind the towers to the top of a rocky saddle for a wonderful view of the Palmyrene landscape.

Further west, deeper into the hills, are plenty more of these funerary towers, some totally dilapidated, others relatively complete. By far the best preserved is the **Tower of Elahbel** (adult/student S£75/5), which is situated about 500m west of the Yemliko group. Built in AD 103, it has four storeys and could purportedly accommodate up to 300 sarcophagi. It's possible to ascend an internal staircase to visit the upper storey tomb chambers and to get out onto the roof. Also here is the chamber that formerly housed the **Hypogeum of Yarhai**, dismantled and reconstructed in the National Museum.

To visit Elahbel it's necessary to buy a ticket at the Palmyra Museum and join an organised foray led by a caretaker; these depart at 8.30am, 10am, 11.30am and 4.00pm Wednesday to Monday and 9am and 11am Tuesday. From October to March the last visit is 2.30pm. At all other times the tomb is locked. The visit also includes the Hypogeum of the Three Brothers, which makes it worthwhile.

HYPOGEUM OF THE THREE BROTHERS
مدفن الاخوان الثلاثة

In addition to the funerary towers, Palmyra boasts a second, later type of tomb, the hypogeum, which was an underground burial chamber. As with the towers, this chamber was filled with loculi fitted with stone carved seals. The best of the 50 or more hypogea that have been discovered and excavated, apart from the Hypogeum of Yarhai, is the **Hypogeum of the Three Brothers**,

which lies just southwest of the Palmyra Cham Palace hotel.

The tomb dates from AD 160 to AD91. It is very modest in size but contains some beautiful frescoes, including portraits of the three brothers in oval frames. There are also three large sarcophagi topped by figures reclining on couches. You'll notice that these figures, like many in the Palmyra Museum, are headless; the official Palmyra guide suggests that this is because early tomb robbers found they could quite easily sell the stone heads.

The hypogeum can only be visited as part of an organised group, through the museum.

THE JAPANESE TOMB
Discovered in 1994 and opened to the public in 2000, this underground tomb takes its name from the nationality of the archaeological team responsible for its immaculate restoration. The tomb dates from AD 128 and is occupied by two brothers with the unlikely names of Bwlh and Bwrp. The entrance is richly decorated and gives way to a main gallery lined with a pigeonhole arrangement of loculi sealed with carved busts and decorated with an ornate frieze and painting of a family banqueting scene. Two side chambers contain sarcophagi topped by family sculptures. The ensemble is superb and helps make sense of all the miscellaneous bits of sculpture exhibited in the Palmyra Museum.

The tomb is in the Southeast Necropolis, which is several kilometres beyond the Palmyra Cham Palace. It's not attractive scenery to hike through, but if you do want to walk, continue on the road south of the hotel for 2km taking an immediate left after the petrol station, and the necropolis is a further 3km. The best way to get here is in a car, either by taxi or as part of an organised trip. Either way, check with the museum first that the tomb is open.

QALA'AT IBN MAAN
قلعة إبن معن

To the west of the ruins perched high on a hilltop, **Qala'at ibn Maan** ((Map p207; adult/ student S£150/10; 9am-dusk) is most notable as the prime viewing spot for overlooking the ruins of Palmyra. The castle is said to have been built in the 17th century by Fakhreddine (Fakhr ad-Din al-Maan II), the Lebanese warlord who challenged the Ottomans for control of the Syrian desert. However, it's also possible that some sort of fortifications existed up here well before then.

The castle is surrounded by a moat, and a footbridge allows access to the rooms and various levels within. However, it's not necessary to enter the castle to enjoy the views. The best time to go up is in the late afternoon, with the sun to the west, casting long shadows among the ruins below. To reach the castle on foot is quite a hike with a scramble up a steep zigzagging path to reach the summit. Approaching by car is easier and most of the hotels in town organise sunset trips up to the castle for around S£150.

Sleeping

There are far more beds than there are tourists in Palmyra and it's rarely hard to find a room, except during the Palmyra Festival. All the same, book in advance to avoid dealing with the touts: see The Problem with Palmyra, p203.

BUDGET

All of Palmyra's budget accommodation is located on or just off the main street, Sharia al-Quwatli.

Baal Shamin Hotel (Map p204; ☎ 5910 453; roof mattress S£100, dm/s/d S£125/200/300) The rooms here are spartan but they are also fairly clean, and chatty manager Mohammed Ahmed camps in the prettily decorated lobby and entertains guests with tea and coffee. Breakfast is S£50.

New Afqa Hotel (Map p204; ☎ 5791 0386; roof mattress S£100, s/d S£250/500) This is a fairly decent option: rooms are comfortable if a little spare, and there's a spacious reception with satellite TV and beer in the fridge.

Sun Hotel (Map p204; ☎ 5911 133; sunhotel-sy@ hotmail.com; roof mattress S£125, dm/s/d S£150/250/400) This cosy hotel with family room is more like a European pension with its homey feel – the owner, Mohammed Talla'a's mother even cooks (breakfast costs S£50). Rooms are clean with bathrooms and kilims on the floor.

Al-Nakheel Hotel (Map p204; ☎ /fax 5910 744; s/d US$10/15; ❄) Decorated like a traditional Bedouin tent, with kilims on the floors and walls, and cushions scattered everywhere, this small hotel has lots of character and is one of Palmyra's more attractive budget options. Some rooms have TV and air-con

and some don't, so let the hotel know when you book if mod cons are important. Breakfast is included in the price.

Ishtar Hotel (Map p204; ☎ 591 3073; www.ishtar hotel.net; Sharia al-Quwatli; s/d/tr US$17/25/35; ❄) With some of the most welcoming and accommodating staff in Palmyra, and spotlessly clean rooms, the Ishtar is Palmyra's best budget option. In addition, there's a great little restaurant and bar in the lobby – and cold beers at the ready when you return from the ruins.

MIDRANGE

Midrange hotel rates can drop very quickly into the budget range out-of-season, so don't hesitate to ask for a discount when booking.

Orient Hotel (Map p204; ☎ 5910 131; orienthotel@ hotmail.com; s/d US$30/40; ❄) This family-owned hotel with its farmhouse-scene paintings and frilly floral bedspreads is favoured by the tour companies, and rightly so – the rooms are spotlessly clean with gleaming en suites complete with fresh towels and toiletries, TV and fridge. Room rates include breakfast.

THE BEDOUIN

Mounted on a camel, swathed in robes and carrying a rifle for security and a coffee pot for hospitality, the archetypal Arab, as portrayed by Omar Sharif in *Lawrence of Arabia*, is no more. Certainly not in Syria, anyway. Although still known as Bedu, these days few of Syria's 100,000 Bedouin population could be regarded as desert wanderers. They used to make their living guiding caravans across the deserts and supplying camels and protection against bandits but the overland trade routes died with the coming of the aeroplane. The grazing lands of Syria have depleted as well and this has reduced the number of Bedouin involved in raising animals from Bedouin camps.

Those who still herd goats, sheep and, most romantically, camels (their frugal intake allowing the Bedouin to *really* roam), continue to wear traditional dress though. This can include, for men, a *kanjar* (dagger) – a symbol of dignity, but these days used for precious little else – while women tend to dress in colourful garb, or sometimes black robes, and occasionally sport facial tattooing and kohl around the eyes. Working in the often-searing sun day after day, the traditional dress is as much about keeping the sun off as it is about modesty.

While the battered pick-up truck might have replaced the camel as a means of transport for most, the black goat-hair tents (*beit ash-sha'ar*; literally 'house of hair') are still the preferred address. Camps you'll see on the way to Palmyra often house a dozen or so Bedouin – all members of an extended family.

One other constant of Bedouin traditional life remains their famed hospitality. Born of the codependency the nomads developed in order to survive in the desert, modern-day hospitality manifests itself in unmitigated generosity extended to strangers. Should you be fortunate enough to encounter the Bedouin (and many Palmyra hotels now offer trips out to Bedouin camps) you can expect to be invited into their tents and offered bitter black coffee, sweet tea and possibly even something to eat. Money is not expected in return so you should try to be a gracious guest and not take advantage of their hospitality.

The best encounters, rather than these prearranged and often awkward meet-and-greets, are ones where you come across Bedouins guiding their herd of sheep or goats in the most remote parts of Syria. We've met teenage boys who were learning English through books and TV and helped them with their pronunciation, an enigmatic young girl eagerly accepted our offer of a fresh bottle of water on a hot day, and we had a boy atop a donkey share some of our food – all encounters that linger long in our memories.

Hotel Villa Palmyra (Map p204; ☎ 5910 156; villapalmyra@mail.sy; Sharia al-Quwatli; s/d US$50/60; ⊠ ▣) Extensively renovated in 2007, this smart hotel has marble-tiled floors, comfortable, spacious and well-equipped rooms with fridge and TV, and very spiffy bathrooms. Many rooms, along with the top floor restaurant, have unsurpassable views over the oasis to the ruins. Breakfast is included in room rates and there's a business centre with internet access. Credit cards are accepted.

Tetrapylon Hotel (Map p204; ☎ 5917 170; www.tetrapylon.com; s/d US$70/80; ⊠) The plastic rainbow-coloured décor of this modern, new hotel may be reminiscent of a McDonalds or IKEA kid's playground, but the place is spotlessly clean and the rooms come with satellite TV and minibar. Rates include breakfast.

Zenobia Hotel (Map p204; ☎ 591 8123; cham-resa@net.sy; s/d US$70/80; ⊠) Built around 1900, renovated in 2007, and overlooking the ruins, the Zenobia has the most character of any of Palmyra's hotels. The comfortable, generously sized rooms are plush with kilims and Orientalist paintings on the walls, and mother-of-pearl inlaid wooden furniture. Book rooms 101 to 106 for views of the ruins. The hotel also has Palmyra's best restaurant (see opposite. Credit are cards accepted.

Eating

Certainly not celebrated for its dining opportunities, Palmyra's food scene is steadily improving with the opening of several new hotel restaurants.

Traditional Palmyra Restaurant (Map p204; ☎ 910 878; Saahat ar-Rais; dishes S£100-250; ⊠ 11am-late) This place focuses on Syrian food and does a decent Bedouin-style *mansaf* (rice dish), along with good mezze and kebabs.

Ishtar (Map p204; ☎ 591 3073; Sharia al-Quwatli; meal per person S£300; ☿ noon-11pm) In the lobby of the Ishtar hotel, this friendly restaurant hasn't been open for long but its home-cooked Syrian food is going down a treat. Expect a soup, mezze and grills for S£300, plus there's a daily chef's special.

Hotel Villa Palmyra (Map p204; ☎ 913 600; Sharia al-Quwatli; meal per person S£400; ☿ noon-11pm) Long considered one of Palmyra's best restaurants. At the time of our visit, the nameless restaurant at the Hotel Villa Palmyra had not yet reopened after extensive renovation. Its Arabic food had always been very good, alcohol was served, and the restaurant has spectacular views across to the ruins.

Zenobia Hotel (Map p204; ☎ 591 8123; meal per person S£400; ☿ 11am-late) Easily Palmyra's best restaurant, the Zenobia serves up delicious Syrian food on a shady terrace overlooking the ruins. The Zenobia soup with *kechk* ('cheese' made from fermented corn) and meat (S£125) is rich and tasty, the plate of six mezze absolutely delicious, and the mixed grilled meats succulent. This is one place where we recommend an early dinner, so you can enjoy the sunset over the ruins.

Entertainment

Once the sun goes down, there's very little to do in Palmyra. But before the light completely fades, it's worth taking a seat at the outdoor terrace at the Zenobia Hotel (above) to cool off with a chilled Barada beer (S£100) while watching the ruins turn a flaming pink. Back in town, the Ishtar Hotel (p211) and Hotel Villa Palmyra restaurant (above) both have cave-themed basement bars.

Getting There & Away

BUS

Palmyra's 'bus station' is on the edge of town, some 2km north of the museum (taxi S£25), at the Sahara Café. Buses depart more frequently for Damascus (S£125, three hours) and Deir ez-Zur (S£85, two hours), generally on the hour every hour from sunrise to sunset.

MINIBUS

Minibuses (S£40) for Homs (two hours) depart frequently throughout the day from

6am to sunset, from the eastern end of the main street at Saahat al-Jumhuriyya.

QASR AL-HEIR AL-SHARQI   قصر الحير الشرقي

Driving through the rocky moonlike landscape, the majestic East Wall Palace or **Qasr al-Heir al-Sharqi** (adult/student S£75/5) appears suddenly out of nowhere. One of the most isolated and startling monuments to Umayyad Muslim rule in the 8th century AD, the palace held a strategic position, commanding desert routes into Mesopotamia. As support from the nomadic Arab tribes (of which they themselves were a part) was one of the main Umayyad strengths, it is no coincidence that they made their presence felt in the desert steppes.

The palace complex and rich gardens, once supplied by an underground spring about 30km away, covered a rough square with 16km sides. Built by the Umayyad caliph Hisham abd al-Malek (r AD 724–43), the palace long outlived its founders. Haroun ar-Rashid, perhaps the best known ruler of the Abbasid dynasty that succeeded the Umayyad, made it one of his residences, and evidence suggests that it was only finally abandoned as late as the 14th century.

If you have any interest in archaeology, a visit to the palace, 120km northeast of Palmyra, makes an excellent excursion from the town. Once you arrive, simply begin your explorations; the friendly teenage Bedu caretakers will see you and come and collect the ticket money at their leisure; if it's a hot day, offer them a ride back to their home.

Sights

The partly restored walls of one of the main enclosures, with their mighty and defensive towers, are the most impressive remaining sign of what was once a sumptuous anomaly in the harsh desert. The ruins to the west belong to what may have been a **khan**. In the southeastern corner are remnants of a **mosque**; the column with stairs inside was a minaret. The remains of **baths** are to the north of the main walls. Traces of the old perimeter wall can just be made out to the south, bordering the best track leading here from the highway.

The castle had a counterpart southwest of Palmyra, **Qasr al-Heir al-Gharbi** (West Wall Palace), but little of interest remains at the site. Its impressive façade was dismantled and reconstructed at the National Museum in Damascus (p95).

Getting There & Away

The only way to get to Qasr al-Heir al-Sharqi is by private transport. Most of the hotels in Palmyra are more than happy to oblige with a car and driver, with most hotels charging around S£1500 to S£2000 for a half-day trip. Some of the hotels also offer the worthwhile combination of Qasr al-Heir ash-Sharqi and Rasafa (p217). If driving from Palmyra, set the trip meter to zero at the As-Suknah turn-off. The turn-off to the palace is on a dirt road exactly 38km from here, on the left.

LAKE AL-ASSAD   بحيرة الأسد

The glorious azure-coloured inland sea that is Lake al-Assad is Syria's pride and joy, and with good reason – a visit here is as invigorating as a trip to the seaside.

By the time the emerald green Euphrates enters Syria at Jarablos (once the capital of the Neo-Hittite empire) it is already a mighty river. To harness that power for irrigation and hydroelectricity production, one of the Assad regime's most ambitious plans, to dam the Euphrates, went into effect in the 1960s. Work began at Tabaqah in 1963 and the reservoir started to fill in 1973. Now that it's full, it stretches for some 60km, and the electricity produced was supposed to make the country self-sufficient.

The flow of the Euphrates, however, has been reduced by the construction of Ataturk Dam in Turkey, and Syria and Iraq are concerned that the Turks may at any time decide to regulate the flow for political reasons. The decision by Istanbul in late 1995 to proceed with construction of a further dam, the Birecik, has only served to heighten the two Arab countries' worst fears. The Turks deny all claims of having used their position to reduce the flow of the river, attributing any slowing down to natural causes.

The dormitory town of Ath-Thaura (the Revolution; الثورة) was built at Tabaqah to accommodate the dam workers and farmers who had to be relocated because of the rising water levels. Not only villages, but also some sites of both historical and ar-

chaeological importance, were inundated. With aid from Unesco and foreign missions, these were investigated, documented and, whenever possible, moved to higher ground. The 27m-high minaret of the Maskana Mosque and the 18m-high minaret from Abu Harayra were both segmented and then transported, the latter to the centre of Ath-Thaura.

Qala'at Ja'abar   قلعة جعبر

Appearing to rise out of the turquoise lake, **Qala'at Ja'abar** (adult/student S£150/10; ⏰ 8am-6pm Apr-Sep, 8am-4pm Oct-Mar) is as impressive from a distance as the water vistas are from atop the citadel.

Situated on the bank of Lake al-Assad, about 15km north of Ath-Thaura, the castle was built entirely of bricks in classic Mesopotamian style. Before the lake was dammed, the castle had rested on a rocky perch since before the arrival of Islam, had been rebuilt by Nureddin (Nur ad-Din) and altered by the Mamluks. It makes a spectacular backdrop for a day by the lake, and on Friday this is an extremely popular picnicking spot with locals. It is also an ideal place for a swim but women might feel more comfortable swimming from a hired boat, away from prying eyes.

If the citadel is locked, collect the key from the caretaker Abdullah at the restaurant on your right before the citadel. There's a pleasant leafy terrace at the restaurant where you can sit in the shade overlooking the lake, or down on the grass by the water, and have a feast of some 10 dishes including mezze, salad, fresh fish and chips (S£300) and sheesha. It's possible to camp here for S£150 with your own tent, or you can hire a big tent for S£3000. Abdullah will also rent you a boat (S£50 per person per hour) to cruise around the citadel to take photos and out to a small island in the lake where you can swim and sunbathe in privacy.

GETTING THERE & AWAY

Without your own car, Qala'at Ja'abar can be difficult to get to. It's necessary to go via Ath-Thaura, either coming from Raqqa (S£30 by microbus) or Aleppo (S£70 by bus). Raqqa is the much closer base; from Aleppo it can be a long and hassle-filled day. You can negotiate with a local driver in Ath-Thaura; expect to pay about S£500 return.

ASK THE ARCHAEOLOGIST

Canadian Greg Fisher is a doctoral student in archaeology and history at Oxford, specialising in the Roman Near East. A frequent visitor to Syria, he's studying the relationship between the Roman Empire and Arab confederations of 6th century Syria. Fresh from a research trip to the Roman ruins in Syria, Greg gives us his ruins rundown:

What makes Syria's ruins special? The sheer quantity and quality; Syria has ruins from many periods. The Roman and Byzantine remains are stunning, ranging from massive deserted cities overlooking the Euphrates, to tiny hidden churches with mosaics and inscriptions, to entire abandoned landscapes dotted with buildings. It's one of the best repositories of ancient architecture in the world.

What gets you excited when visiting ruins? Syrian archaeology is still in its infancy. Major studies only began in the 19th century and these are constantly reinterpreted as new evidence comes to light. There's always a chance you'll find something new. At Palmyra, you'll find bilingual inscriptions in situ or half-buried on columns in the sand. At Rasafa, some of the churches still have wall paintings. In other countries these artefacts have been stolen, put in museums or simply vanished. To find them here brings a sense of historical immediacy, which is exciting.

What should travellers not miss? Rasafa (p217), Zenobia (Halabiyya; p218) and Dura Europos (p222) are musts. Everyone heads to Palmyra – one of the most stunning sites in the ancient world – but if you visit Rasafa, you'll see exquisite architecture in an unparalleled setting, and you'll be alone. At Zenobia, you can climb the massive Roman walls and see for miles across the Euphrates flood plain and get to explore one of the world's most unique fortification designs. At Dura Europos, you can marvel at the tenacity of those who lived in this harsh environment, and try to imagine the horror they faced when it fell to the Persian army in the 3rd century.

Do archaeologists need good imaginations? Can you 'see' chariots charging down the Cardo Maximus? Absolutely! So often we're only left with what's underground. After doing something like calculating the height of the missing ceiling from the arch springers you dug up, a little imagination goes a long way. In Syria we're spoiled because of the quantity of sites that retain original features. When I first visited Rasafa, I sat outside the ornamental north gateway for half an hour, just feeling the heat beating down and listening to the wind. Imagination comes easily at times like that.

What are your thoughts on the state of Syria's sites? I'm worried about the threat from the environment (climate, earthquakes, etc) on remote sites. Even at Palmyra, a massive amount of work remains to be done and there are only limited resources available from international teams and the Syrian government. It's easy to see the physical decay of walls, artwork, etc, but the very richness of Syria's archaeological heritage makes it hard to prioritise. Conservation remains a priority, as does maintaining the physical security of artefacts, especially mosaics – too many end up on the black market for 'collectors'.

Thoughts on the state of preservation in the museums? The National Museum in Damascus has one of the world's most impressive ancient collections but it needs reorganisation and modernisation. Labelling is missing and the environment isn't kind on exhibits – the priceless Dura synagogue artwork probably isn't doing well without humidity and temperature control. Syria has an immensely rich cultural heritage that deserves to be looked after.

What are the most recent interesting discoveries? New mosaics and inscriptions often turn up but what's more interesting is the constant reinterpretation and reevaluation of this heartland of the Roman Empire, which is a result of the growth in excavation, analysis and research. Every season adds more to the puzzle.

What's the best bit about exploring Syria? The quality of the sites and the high probability that you will be the only person there.

What else is out there to be discovered? So much – a lot of the major sites remain unexcavated or partially excavated. There are many inscriptions out there that might help us understand the society and culture of the Near East better. Syrian archaeology has a long life yet.

If driving, from the centre of Ath-Thaura, you have to head out towards the north of town. You will have to show your passport at the police checkpoint on the way. The turn-off for the citadel is a few kilometres further on to the left, and from here it's about another 10km. You may be able to get a ride with a family on Friday when the dam is crowded with picnicking day-trippers. On other, quieter days, be prepared for long waits.

QALA'AT NAJM   قلعة نجم
Majestic Qala'at Najm, the northernmost castle on the Euphrates, has been splendidly restored and is a magical site to explore as much as it provides a superb vantage point for spectacular river vistas.

Originally built under Nureddin in the 12th century, it was later reconstructed under Saladin (Salah ad-Din) and commands a natural defence position over the Euphrates plain; the views across what was once a strategic crossing point are alone worth the effort of visiting.

Jassim, the caretaker, will let you in to the castle and give you a guided tour of the bakery and kitchen, sauna, palace and mosque. As there was no entrance fee at the time of research, a tip of S£100 is in order for his troubles.

The citadel is best visited with your own wheels or with a car and driver. It's possible, although difficult, to get close by public transport – take a bus to Ain al-Arab (عين العرب) from Aleppo's East Bus Station or City Bus Station (p193; S£40, two hours) and get off at the village of Haya Kebir. However, from Haya Kebir it's 15km to the castle, and getting a ride with a local is the only way. An early start is essential, as there's not a lot of traffic on this dead-end trail. The road passes through rolling wheat fields that form a cool green carpet in spring.

RAQQA   الرقة
☎ 022 / pop 187,000
Raqqa is a dusty town with little to detain a traveller, but in the 8th and 9th centuries AD, as the city known as Rafika, it was reputedly a glorious place that served as a summer residence of the legendary Abbasid caliph Haroun ar-Rashid (AD 786–809), of *The Thousand and One*

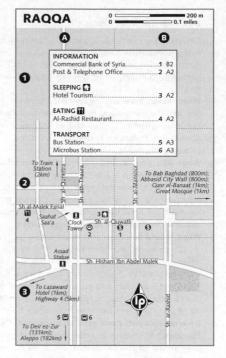

Nights fame (see The Thousand & One Nights, p68). The area around the city had been the site of numerous cities that had come and gone in the preceding millennia, including Nikephorion, founded by the Seleucids (sometimes attributed by legend to Alexander the Great). After the Mongol invasion in 1260, Rafika virtually ceased to exist.

Orientation & Information
The heart of town is a quiet square, Saahat Saa'a (Clock Square), with a clock tower at its centre. The site of the old city lies to the east, reached by following Sharia al-Quwatli. The central bus station is on Sharia Saa'a, 300m due south of the clock tower. There's a post and telephone office on the east side of Saahat Saa'a, and a local branch of the **CBS** (Commercial Bank of Syria; Sharia al-Quwatli) with an ATM.

Sights & Activities
Only a few scant remnants that barely hint at the city's glorious past remain. The partly restored, mid-12th-century **Bab Baghdad**

(Baghdad Gate) is about a 15-minute walk to the east of the clock tower. Built of mud-brick, it's relatively modest in scale and stands off to the side of the modern road. Running north from the gate is a heavily restored section of the old **Abbasid city wall**, punctuated at regular intervals by the bases of what were once more than 100 towers. After about 500m, there's a break in the walls for Sharia Tahseh (also known as Sharia Shbat); take the first left inside the walls and 200m down is the 9th-century **Qasr al-Banaat** (Maidens' Palace), with four high-arched *iwans* (vaulted halls) around a central courtyard.

Continue west along Sharia Tahseh; north of the first major intersection (with Sharia Seif ad-Dowla) are the remains of the **Great Mosque**, built during the reign of the Abbasid caliph Al-Mansur in the 8th century and reconstructed in 1165 by Nureddin.

Sleeping & Eating

The options are unappealing, and unless you must, avoid staying at Raqqa.

Hotel Tourism (☎ 220 725; Sharia al-Quwatli; s/d S£300/500) One block east of the clock tower, this place is depressingly gloomy with grimy rooms that were occupied by Iraqi refugees looking for work when we stopped by. The shared toilet facilities are particularly grim.

Lazaward Hotel (☎ 216 120-22; Sharia Saqr Quraysh; s/d US$24/34; ❄) Raqqa's best hotel is a three-star with dirty carpets, sticky furniture and a grotty bathroom. There's a decent rooftop **restaurant** serving Syrian food and beer with interesting views over town; breakfast (included in room rates) is surprisingly good, although service is excruciatingly slow.

Al-Rashid Restaurant (☎ 241 919; Sharia al-Malek Faisal; meal per person S£250; ✆ noon-midnight) Although this shabby school hall looks far from promising from the outside, the food is fine; expect mezze, chicken and kebabs.

Getting There & Away

BUS

Several bus companies operate from Raqqa's central bus station, including Kadmous, which has several daily services to Aleppo (S£90, 2½ hours), Damascus (S£190, six hours) and Deir ez-Zur (S£70, 2½ hours). If

the times of the Kadmous departures don't suit, try one of the other companies. Alternatively, take a microbus.

MICROBUS

The microbus station is across the road from the bus station. From here there are regular services west to Al-Mansoura (for Rasafa; S£20, 20 minutes), Ath-Thaura (for Qala'at Ja'abar; S£25), Aleppo (S£80) and Deir ez-Zur (S£65).

RASAFA   الرصافة

Striking Rasafa, an ancient, long-abandoned walled city, lies 25km south of the Euphrates highway, rising up out of the featureless desert. It's a fascinating place to explore, made all the more intriguing by its remote location. Bring a hat for protection against the sun as there is no shelter inside.

History

Raqqa was possibly inhabited in Assyrian times, and Diocletian established a fort here as part of a defensive line against the Sassanian Persians late in the 3rd century AD. A desert road led through Rasafa from the Euphrates south to Palmyra. About this time a cult to the local martyr St Sergius began to take hold. Sergius was a Roman soldier who converted to Christianity and was executed for refusing to perform sacrifices to Jupiter. By the 5th century Rasafa had become an important centre of Christian worship and an impressive basilica had been built.

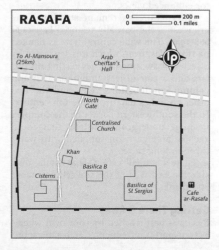

A century later the city was at the height of its prosperity. The Byzantine emperor Justinian (r AD 527–65) further fortified the growing settlement against the threat of Persian assault. Ultimately, this was to no avail as Rasafa capitulated to the eastern empire in 616.

Following the Muslim Arab invasion of Syria the city was occupied by Hisham abd al-Malek who pursued an energetic building policy, constructing a whole series of castles and palaces in Syria (including Qasr al-Heir ash-Sharqi, see p213); here in Rasafa he adorned the existing city with a palatial summer residence. Just seven years after Hisham's death, the palace and city were razed by the Baghdad-based Abbasids, fierce rivals of the Umayyads. The city remained occupied but with a much reduced population.

It was finally abandoned altogether when invading Mongols swept across northern Syria in the 13th century.

Sights

The walls, enclosing a quadrangle measuring 550m by 400m, are virtually all complete. The main entrance is by the **North Gate**. Once inside, you are confronted by the immensity of the place, mostly bare now save for the churches inside. Little excavation has yet been done and you should stroll around the defensive **perimeter walls** before exploring the site. At certain points it is possible to climb to the upper terrace for enhanced views.

Three churches remain standing. The grandest is the partially restored **Basilica of St Sergius**. The wide central nave is flanked by two aisles, from which it is separated by a series of sweeping arches resting on pillars and a pair of less ambitious arch and column combinations. This and the two other churches date from the 6th century. In the southwestern corner of the complex lie huge underground **cisterns** that could keep a large garrison supplied with water through long sieges.

There's a small café, **Café ar-Rasafa**, outside the east wall of the site selling snacks and drinks.

Getting There & Away

Rasafa is best reached by your own wheels as transport is infrequent. Catch a microbus

from Raqqa to Al-Mansoura (S£20, 20 minutes) then negotiate a driver (S£500 return) or wait for a lift to take you the 25km to the ruins. If you're impatient, you can ask one of the pick-up drivers lounging around here to take you there and back for an emperor's ransom – S£200 would not be unusual.

HALABIYYA   حلبيه

The captivating fortress of Halabiyya (also known as Zenobia) was founded by Queen Zenobia, the rebellious Palmyrene leader, in the years immediately preceding her fall in AD 272. It was later refortified during the reign of Justinian, and it is mainly these ruins that survive today.

The fortress town was part of the Byzantine Empire's eastern defensive line against the Persians (which failed in AD 610). The walls are largely intact, and there are remnants of the citadel, basilicas, baths, a forum, and the north and south gates. The present road follows the course of the old colonnaded street.

Lovers of castles could spend hours here exploring the walls; however, the lush Euphrates setting and views are equally as engaging for some.

Zalabiyya   زلبيه

Across the river and on a hill further south is the much less intact forward stronghold of the main fort, Zalabiyya. In summer, the Euphrates is sometimes passable between the town and the fort, which is what made Zalabiyya necessary. The views back to Zalabiyya from here are worth the effort of getting here. Along the way you'll pass friendly farmer families working the fields together.

Getting There & Away

Halabiyya and Zalabiyya are not easy to reach without your own transport. They're best visited with a car and driver and the drive here along the verdant flood plain of the Euphrates is rewarding. Halabiyya is the more interesting of the two, and at least the first stage of the journey is straightforward enough then Get a Deir ez-Zur bus from Raqqa and get out at the Halabiyya turn-off. Try to negotiate with a local to take you the rest of the way (around S£500 return) or undertake the 8.5km walk. To get to Zalabiyya, 4.5km from Halabiyya, head north, crossing the pontoon bridge and passing a train station en route. The hardest bit is getting back. If you're here in the afternoon, you might be able to get a ride with a passing truck.

DEIR EZ-ZUR   دير الزور

☎ 051 / pop 263,000

Deir ez-Zur ('Deir' to the locals) is a busy little market town by the Euphrates. On weekdays its streets are filled with colourfully dressed farmers from the surrounding countryside, in town to buy and sell produce at the small but thriving souq off the main square. While it became something of a boomtown in the early 1990s with the discovery of high-grade oil nearby, this didn't seem to affect the essential character of Deir ez-Zur.

The character of the town is heavily influenced by its distance from Damascus and its proximity to Iraq. The dialect spoken here is much rougher than the Syrian Arabic spoken elsewhere in the country and some of the vocabulary even differs – the standard Syrian greeting of *kifak* in Deir becomes *shlonak*.

Many travellers find themselves stopping over in Deir en route to the ancient sites of Mari and Dura Europos. Although there really isn't that much to see in town, it has a pleasant riverside setting and a wonderful fragrance of jasmine, and the pedestrianised shopping lane Sharia al-Maisat buzzes at night. Men far outnumber women here, more than any other Syrian

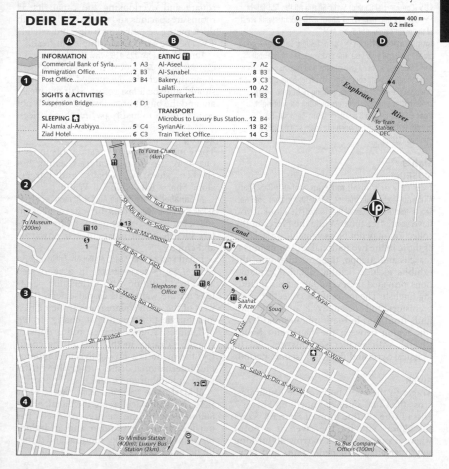

DEIR EZ-ZUR

0   400 m
0   0.2 miles

INFORMATION
Commercial Bank of Syria........... 1 A3
Immigration Office..................... 2 B3
Post Office................................ 3 B4

SIGHTS & ACTIVITIES
Suspension Bridge..................... 4 D1

SLEEPING
Al-Jamia al-Arabiyya.................. 5 C4
Ziad Hotel................................ 6 C3

EATING
Al-Aseel................................... 7 A2
Al-Sanabel............................... 8 B3
Bakery..................................... 9 C3
Lailati..................................... 10 A2
Supermarket........................... 11 B3

TRANSPORT
Microbus to Luxury Bus Station.. 12 B4
SyrianAir................................. 13 B2
Train Ticket Office.................... 14 C3

town, so females travelling solo may not always feel comfortable.

Orientation

The centre of town is the main square, Saahat 8 Azar, a scruffy, dusty place with the busy souq on its east side. The main north–south road, which runs from the canal through to the square, is bisected by the main east–west axis, which also runs through the square and is called Sharia Khaled ibn al-Walid to the east, and Sharia Ali ibn Abi Taleb to the west. The body of water flowing just north of the square is not the Euphrates but a canal. The river is a further 200m north.

Information

CBS (Commercial Bank of Syria; Sharia Ali ibn Abi Taleb; ⏲ 8am-12.30pm Sat-Thu) About a 10-minute walk west of the main square, it has an ATM.

Immigration Office (⏲ 8am-1.30pm Sat-Thu) A good place to extend your visa; the process takes only about half an hour. You need two photos and it costs S£25. To find the office, walk south from the telephone office, then diagonally across the square, turning right onto Sharia ar-Rashid; it's the low concrete building on your right.

Post Office (Sharia 8 Azar; ⏲ 8am-8pm Sat-Thu, to 1pm Fri) Halfway between the main square and the minibus station.

Sights

MUSEUM

Deir ez-Zur's small **museum** (Saahat ar-Rais, Sharia Ali ibn Abi Taleb; adult/student S£150/10; ⏲ 8am-6pm Apr-Sep, to 4pm Oct-Mar, closed Tue) is worth a look if you have some free time. While the pieces in the collection may not be as valuable or striking as those in the two national museums in Damascus and Aleppo, the presentation of the exhibits include helpful, detailed explanations provided in several languages including English. The focus of the collection is on prehistoric and ancient Syria, and important finds from digs in the Euphrates and Jezira (the region between the Tigris and Kabur Rivers), with smaller sections devoted to Classical Syria and the Arab Islamic period.

RIVER

To get to the main body of the Euphrates, cross the canal and head north up Sharia 7 Nissan (the continuation of Sharia 8 Azar) for 500m. You hit the river at a point where it's crossed by a narrow 400m-long **suspension bridge**, for pedestrians and bicy-

cle users only. It's an impressive structure, and a favourite place with the locals for an evening promenade. On the other side of the bridge is a small recreation ground where the local boys swim.

Sleeping

Al-Jamia al-Arabiyya (☎ 351 371; Sharia Khaled ibn al-Walid & Sharia Maysaloun; s/d S£325/400) Though it has shabby, spartan rooms the hotel is kept reasonably clean. Rooms are equipped with fans, basin and balcony. Toilets (squat) and showers are shared. The owner Nuredin speaks English.

Ziad Hotel (☎ 214 596; fax 211 923; Sharia Abu Bakr as-Siddiq; s/d US$25/35; ❄) This hotel will come as an absolute blessing! Just west of the main square and overlooking the canal, its 33 rooms are spacious and spotlessly clean, with thick mattresses, air-con, fridge and satellite TV. The free breakfast is simple but fresh.

Furat Cham (☎ 225 418; www.chamhotels.com; s/d US$160/190; ❄ ▨) Located 5km out of town along the river, the overpriced Furat Cham should only be a last resort. Staff are pleasant and the buffet breakfast is good, but not good enough to justify paying these prices.

Eating

There may not be many restaurants in Deir but there are myriad eateries selling hot chicken, shwarma, kebabs, and burgers along Sharia Khaled ibn al-Walid.

Al-Sanabel (Sharia Ali ibn Abi Taleb; meal per person S£150; ⏲ 11am-10pm) This dirt-cheap, neon-lit snack bar is west of the main square and offers succulent spit-roast chicken, shwarma and chips.

Lailati (☎ 229 648; Sharia Ali ibn Abi Taleb; meal per person S£250; ⏲ noon-midnight) In a renovated Art Deco building with Orientalist paintings on the walls, this casual eatery 400m west of the main square is easily Deir's best and buzziest. Attracting a chatty crowd of families, young couples and groups of women (a rarity in this part of the country) the menu is a mix of Syrian standards plus international dishes – everything from pizza to hamburgers – and it's all good.

Al-Aseel (Sharia Abu Bakr as-Siddiq; meal per person S£250) A small place beside the canal, about 800m west of the centre, Al-Aseel has outside seating in summer and an indoor restaurant for the colder months, and dishes up decent Syrian staples.

ENGAGING WITH THE EUPHRATES

The Euphrates (a combination of Greek words that translates to 'gentle current') is one of the world's great rivers, and its significance of predates Biblical times. But it is the mention of the river, known as 'Perath' in Hebrew and 'Al-Furat' in Arabic, in both the Book of Revelation and by the Prophet Mohammed that makes it most intriguing.

The river starts in northeast Turkey only 80km from its partner, the Tigris, and makes its way through Turkey, then Syria, meeting up with the Tigris in southern Iraq before heading into the Persian Gulf. The total length of the river is about 2800 kilometres and it's one of the four rivers that flow from the Garden of Eden, according to the Bible. Along with the Tigris, its water supply was important in the development of Mesopotamia – the world's earliest civilisation. The name Mesopotamia is Greek for 'between rivers', referring to the Euphrates and the Tigris.

While the Euphrates languidly flows through Syria, political tension flows through the countries that it services. Turkey, Syria, and Iraq all have a vested interest in the Euphrates for irrigation and the creation of hydroelectric power. The Southeast Anatolia Project in Turkey is the biggest development project ever in the country and involves the construction of 22 dams and 19 power plants, most of which are now completed. Syria has created the Tabaqah Dam on Lake Assad, which has doubled the amount of irrigated land in Syria.

The consequences of a severe drought would severely affect the livelihood of millions of people across Turkey, Syria and Iraq. However, would it be a catastrophe of Biblical proportions? The Book of Revelation in the New Testament of the Bible warns that when the river Euphrates runs dry, Armageddon follows. The Prophet Mohammed warned that the river will one day dry up, revealing unknown treasures that will cause widespread war. See it while you can.

DEC (☎ 220 469; meal per person S£350; ☉ 6pm-late) A large dining hall on the north bank of the river, this place fills up after 10pm and is particularly popular with groups and parties. Food is the standard mezze, and kebabs and beer are served. To get here, cross the suspension bridge; as you do so you'll see the restaurant's illuminated Viking ship sign off to the right.

There are also a couple of restaurants on the south bank of the Euphrates, north of the suspension bridge. Though their pleasant riverside settings compensate for the mediocre food, they're little more than open-air terraces; have a drink only and eat elsewhere.

SELF-CATERING

You'll find hole-in-the-wall bakeries on the main street where huge discs of flat bread (S£10) are pulled out of the clay ovens continually. There's a decent supermarket west of the main square and several grocery stores along Sharia Ali Ibn Abi Taleb.

Entertainment

There are a number of grubby coffee-houses on Ali Ibn Abi Taleb and a popular place at the junction of Sharia Khaled Ibn al-Walid Sharia Sobhi; both are filled most evenings with old men engrossed in high-volume games of cards, dominoes and backgammon.

Getting There & Away

AIR

The airport is about 7km east of town. The 'regular' flights between Deir ez-Zur and Damascus have been known to get cancelled – regularly (S£1400, one hour). A shuttle bus runs to the airport from the office of **SyrianAir** (☎ 221 801; Sharia al-Ma'amoun; ☉ 8.30am-12.30pm Sat-Thu).

BUS

The luxury bus station is 2km south of town, at the far end of Sharia 8 Azar. There's a local microbus service (S£10) to the airport from a stop about a five-minute walk south of the main square, on the right-hand side; otherwise a taxi (ask for 'al-karaj') will cost S£30. Several bus companies depart regularly for Damascus (S£200, seven hours) via Palmyra (S£75, two hours) and to Aleppo (S£145, five hours) via Raqqa (S£65, two hours). Kadmous, Al-Furat and Raja have town centre offices on Sharia Salah ad-Din al-Ayyubi, about 400m east of Sharia 8 Azar; otherwise, if you're flexible, you can just show up at the bus station and buy a ticket.

MINIBUS & MICROBUS

The minibus station is on Sharia 8 Azar about 1km south of the main square. From here there are regular departures for Raqqa (S£65, two hours), for Hassake in the northeast (S£80, 2½ hours) and south to Abu Kamal (S£60, two hours) for Mari and Dura Europos.

SOUTHEAST OF DEIR EZ-ZUR

Poplars, fir trees, oleanders, eucalypts and sunflowers, roadside markets selling produce fresh from the vegetable garden, old guys dozing behind pyramids of watermelons, women with water-containers balanced on their head crossing the highway… the route from Deir ez-Zur to Dura Europos is one of the most fascinating in Syria. It's as verdant as they come, because the road southeast follows the fertile Euphrates River flood plain. All the way down to the Iraqi border, the route is dotted with sites of archaeological interest. With a car, you could visit the lot and be back in Deir ez-Zur for dinner on the same day. With a very early start, it might just be possible to do the same with a combination of microbuses and catching rides with locals.

Dura Europos تل الصالحية

With extraordinary views over the Euphrates flood plain, the extensive, Hellenistic/Roman fortress city of **Dura Europos** (☎ caretaker 09 654 6597; adult/student S£75/5) is by far the most intriguing site to visit on the road from Deir ez-Zur to Abu Kamal.

Based on earlier settlements, the Seleucids founded Europos here in around 280 BC. The town also retained the ancient Assyrian name of Dura (wall or fort), and is now known to locals as Tell Salhiye. The desert plateau abruptly ends in a wall of cliffs dropping 90m into the Euphrates here, making this the ideal location for a defensive installation.

In 128 BC the city fell to the Parthians and remained in their hands (although under the growing influence of Palmyra) until the Romans succeeded in integrating it into their defensive system in AD 165. As the Persian threat to Roman preeminence grew, so too did the importance of Dura Europos. It is famous for its reputed religious tolerance, seemingly confirmed by the presence of a church, synagogue (now

DURA EUROPOS

0 — 200 m
0 — 0.1 miles

SIGHTS & ACTIVITIES

Agora	1	B4
Bath	2	B4
Bath & Amphitheatre	3	A3
Baths	4	A3
Christian Chapel	5	A4
Houses	6	B4
Houses	7	A3
Houses & Bath	8	A4
Khan	9	A4
Military Temple	10	B3
Mithraeum	11	A3
Palace of Dux Ripae	12	A3
Redoubt Palace	13	B4
Synagogue	14	A4
Temple of Adonis	15	A4
Temple of Aphlad	16	A4
Temple of Artemis	17	B4
Temple of Atargatis	18	B4
Temple of Azzanathkona (Praetorium)	19	A3
Temple of Bel	20	A3
Temple of the Two Gads	21	B4
Temple of Zeus Dolichenus	22	A3
Temple of Zeus Kyrios	23	A4
Temple of Zeus Megistos	24	B4
Temple of Zeus Theos	25	B3

in the National Museum in Damascus; see p95) and other Greek, Roman and Mesopotamian temples side by side.

The Sassanian Persians seized control of the site in 256, and from then on its fortunes declined. French and Syrian archaeologists continue to work on the site.

Bring plenty of water and a hat for protection against the sun. Phone the caretaker if he's not around to let you in.

SIGHTS
Touring the Ruins

The western wall stands out in the stony desert 1km east of the main road; its most imposing element is the **Palmyra Gate**. Just inside the Palmyra Gate and past some houses and a bath was a **Christian chapel** to the right, and a **synagogue** to the left. The road leading towards the river from the gate passed Roman **baths** on the right, a **khan** on the left and then the site of the Greek **agora**.

Opposite the agora are the sites (little remains) of three **temples** dedicated to Artemis, Atargatis and the Two Gads. The original Greek temple to Artemis was replaced by the Parthians with a building along more oriental lines, characterised by an internal courtyard surrounded by an assortment of irregular rooms. These were added to over the years, and even included what appears to have been a small theatre for religious gatherings. In the block next door, the temple dedicated to Atargatis was built along similar lines. Precious little remains of the temple of the Two Gads, where a variety of gods were worshipped.

At the northwestern end of the city the Romans installed themselves, building barracks, baths, a small **amphitheatre** and a couple of small **temples**, one to Zeus Dolichenus. West of the **new citadel**, which commands extraordinary views over the Euphrates Valley, the Romans placed their **Palace of Dux Ripae**, built around a colonnaded courtyard of which nothing much is left.

GETTING THERE & AWAY
Any microbus between Abu Kamal and Deir ez-Zur will drop you on the highway near the ruins – it takes 1½ hours to get here from Deir. Ask to be dropped off at Tell Salhiye and the site is clearly visible from the road about 1km distant.

Mari   تل الحريري

The ruins of **Mari** (Tell Hariri; adult/student S£75/5), an important Mesopotamian city dating back some 5000 years, are about 10km north of Abu Kamal. The mud-brick ruins are the single greatest key serving to unlock the door on the very ancient past of Mesopotamia – but to those without an archaeological or historical bent, they are not all that inspiring.

The most famous of Mari's ancient Syrian leaders, and about the last of its independent ones, was Zimri-Lim, who reigned in the 18th century BC and controlled the most important of the trade routes across Syria into Mesopotamia, making his city-state the object of several attacks. The Royal Palace of

Zimri-Lim was enormous, measuring 200m by 120m, and had more than 300 rooms. Today, sheltered from the elements by a modern protective roof, the palace remains the main point of interest of the whole site.

The Babylonians under Hammurabi finally destroyed the city in 1759 BC. Before this, Mari had not only been a major commercial centre but also an artistic hothouse, to which the many fragments of ceramics and wall paintings discovered since 1933 amply attest.

Large chunks of pottery still lie scattered about the place, but the most interesting discoveries are on display in the museums of Aleppo and Damascus, and in the Louvre. Excavations begun in 1933, financed largely by the French, revealed two palaces (including Zimri-Lim's) and five temples: a great many archives in Akkadian – some 25,000 clay tablets – were also discovered, providing valuable insights into the history and workings of this ancient city-state. Teams continue to work at the site.

Although attributed to Zimri-Lim, the **Royal Palace** had been around for hundreds of years by the time he came to the throne. Comprising a maze of almost 300 rooms disposed around two great courtyards, it was protected by earthen ramparts. Interpretations of what each room was used for vary. For instance, some say the room directly south of the central courtyard was a throne room; others say it was a sacred hall dedicated to a water goddess. It appears that the area to the northwest of the central courtyard served as the royal living quarters; the baths were located immediately to the right (directly north of the central courtyard).

Just to the southeast of the palace complex are several temples. A temple to Ishtar stood to the west of the palace.

GETTING THERE & AWAY
There is a microbus from Abu Kamal that goes right by Mari. It leaves from a side street east of the square and takes about half an hour by a circuitous route (S£15). Alternatively, if you are coming from Deir ez-Zur, buses will drop you at the turn-off from the highway (ask for Tell Hariri). From this same spot it is normally possible to catch a ride with a local or pick up a passing microbus for the return trip to Deir ez-Zur.

AGATHA & SIR MAX

Agatha Christie's husband was Sir Max Mallowan, a noted archaeologist who in the late 1930s excavated in northeastern Syria. Between 1934 and 1939, accompanied by his already famous crime-writing wife, he spent summer seasons at Chagar Bazar, 35km north of Hassake, where they had built a mud-brick house with a beehive dome. While at Chagar Bazar, Mallowan was also digging at Tell Brak, 30km to the east, where he unearthed the remains of the so-called 'Eye Temple', the finds from which are displayed in Aleppo's National Museum (p184). Christie spent her time here writing.

Surprisingly, given all the time she spent in the country, Syria did not find its way to a starring role in any of her more famous mysteries. Instead she dreamed up *Appointment With Death*, set around Petra, where she and Mallowan had visited on one of their journeys home; and *Murder on the Orient Express*, which opens in Aleppo but then unfolds aboard the train on which Christie frequently travelled between Europe and the Middle East. The Syrian desert also features in a short story 'The Gate of Baghdad' (published as part of *Parker Pyne Investigates*, 1934), and Aleppo cameos again in *Absent in the Spring* (1944), a novel written under the pseudonym Mary Westmacott.

Her time onsite did result, however, in a substantial and humorous autobiographical work called *Come, Tell Me How You Live* (1946). This is the tale of an archaeologist's wife, a lively account of hiring mouse-killing cats, disinterring corpses and constipation. Solving murders seems a breeze by comparison.

THE NORTHEAST

Bordered by Turkey and Iraq, there are no major monuments or must-see sites in this Kurdish region in the northeastern corner of the country. Only about one million of a total of some 20 million Kurds live in Syria. The rest are spread across southeastern Turkey, northern Iraq and northwestern Iran.

The area between the Kabur and Tigris Rivers, also known as the Jezira, is an increasingly rich agricultural zone, helped along by underground aquifers and the irrigation schemes born of the Lake al-Assad project on the Euphrates to the west.

The numerous tells dotted around the place are a sign that this area has been inhabited since the 3rd millennium BC, its mainstay being the wheat and cotton crops that still predominate. The tells are increasingly attracting archaeological teams, and although there is generally precious little for the uninitiated to see, you can visit the sites so long as you respect the teams' work. They are generally present in spring and summer. **Tell Brak**, 45km northeast of Hassake, was excavated under the direction of Max Mallowan (see Agatha & Sir Max, above).

Ras al-Ain رأس العين

There's not a lot to this Kurdish town on the Turkish border and you cannot cross into Turkey from here. In summer, the attraction is a restaurant in the main park (near the road to Hassake), where they set the tables in the shin-deep water from nearby sulphur springs and you cool your heels as you eat.

Of interest only to the most enthusiastic of archaeologists is **Tell Halaf**, 3km away, the site of an ancient northern Mesopotamian settlement discovered in 1899 by Baron Max von Oppenheim, a Prussian engineer overseeing the construction of the much-trumpeted Berlin–Baghdad railway. Although plenty more artefacts are said by locals to be buried here, you'll see nothing other than a bald artificial hill. The bulk of what was found went to Berlin and was destroyed in WWII. Replicas were made of some artefacts, which can be seen at Aleppo's National Museum (p184), including the giant basalt statues at the entrance.

GETTING THERE & AWAY

If you must, Ras al-Ain is best visited with your own wheels. The microbus from Hassake, about 75km away, takes about 1½ hours (S£55) and no public transport returns in the afternoon.

Qamishle القامشلي

This characterless Kurdish stronghold is situated at a crossing point on the Turkish border in the northeast. The town has had a troubled and violent past and tensions periodically run high between the Kurds and Turkish and Kurds and Syrians.

There's nothing to see in Qamishle and the town rarely sees travellers passing through. The border is mainly used by Iraqi refugees crossing to renew their visas. As a result there are long lines and infuriatingly long waits; some travellers have reported waiting all day.

The Turkish border is about 1km from the town centre; you have to walk across the border. Once on the Turkish side, it's a further five minutes' walk into Nusaybin, where it's possible to pick up a *dolmus* (minibus) for onward travel. The crossing is officially open from 9am to 3pm.

SLEEPING & EATING
Hotels here are full of male refugees and Kurdish workers. Many appear to be operating as brothels. The only accommodation in town we can recommend is the **Hotel Semiramis** (☎ 421 185; s/d/tr US$15/22/24), 100m south of the bus station. The basic rooms are fairly clean and the manager is friendly.

Across from the Chahba Hotel there's a nondescript **restaurant** (meals around S£200), where you can get *foul* (fava bean soup), mezze and kebabs.

GETTING THERE & AWAY
Air
The airport is 2km south of town, although we're not sure why anyone would want to fly here. Take a taxi or any Hassake-bound bus. The SyrianAir office is just off the main street, two blocks south of the Semiramis. At the time of research there were weekly flights to and from Damascus.

Bus
Buses operate from Qamishle to major destinations, including Damascus (S£350, 10 hours) and Aleppo (S£180, six to eight hours), departing from a station on Sharia Zaki al-Arsuzi, the street running beside the river.

Syria Directory

CONTENTS

ACCOMMODATION

Throughout this book we've listed accommodation prices for Syria using both the Syrian pound (S£) and US dollars (US$)

BOOK ACCOMMODATION ONLINE

For more accommodation reviews and recommendations by Lonely Planet authors, check out the online booking service at www.lonelyplanet.com. You'll find the true, insider lowdown on the best places to stay. Reviews are thorough and independent. Best of all, you can book online.

PRACTICALITIES

Electricity

- You'll need the European **two-round-pin plug** to connect to the region's electricity supply (220VAC, 50Hz).

Newspapers & Magazines

- Syria's only English-language daily newspaper is the government-owned **Syria Times** (www.syriatimes.tishreen.info)

- **Syria Today** (www.syria-today.com) is the country's first independently produced English-language magazine and covers economic, political and social development.

Radio

- In Damascus you can listen to the **BBC World Service** on AM 1323.

Weights & Measures

- Syria uses the **metric system**. Basic conversion charts are given on the inside front cover of this book.

---

as quoted by hotels and hostels. Note that in some top-end hotels they will insist that you pay with US dollars.

Throughout this book we have divided accommodation into budget, midrange and top-end categories; the corresponding price ranges are detailed below.

A budget double room will cost under S£1785 (US$35), a midrange hotel room S£1785 to S£5100 (US$35 to US$100), and top-end hotels over S£5100 (US$100).

Rooms in cheap hotels are often let on a share basis and will have two to four beds. If you want the room to yourself you may have to pay for all beds, or an intermediate sum – try to bargain.

It's worth knowing that during the low season (December to March) and outside the peak holiday seasons (around major religious festivals, such as Eid al-Adha), big discounts are frequently available in Syrian hotels and it's always worth asking about special offers. Prices in some midrange and top-end hotels also go up by as much as 40% during the Islamic religious holidays due to an influx of Gulf Arabs; see Holidays (p231) for more details. In Damascus, note that religious tourism (mainly from Iran) sees some decent budget and midrange hotels booked up well in advance.

For more details on planning your trip see Itineraries (p17.

Camping
Official camping opportunities in Syria are limited – apart from camping on the roof of a backpacker hostel. If you do decide to camp 'freelance', especially in remote areas, be aware that temperatures can drop quite low in the winter months, wild dogs can cause you some concerns and the locals will think you're nuts.

Hotels
BUDGET
The quality of budget hotel options across Syria is uneven. Some cities have numerous budget lodgings, such as Aleppo, while others that probably should be on the tourist trail have limited options. Considering this, it's worth planning day trips to sights from places such as Damascus, Aleppo, Homs and Palmyra.

One of the biggest drawbacks with budget accommodation in Syria is that rooms often open onto common rooms with blaring TVs, or overlook busy streets. One word: earplugs! Another drawback is bathroom and toilet facilities that are either inadequate or inoperable. During the hotter months, if there isn't a ceiling fan, you should be able to borrow a floor-standing fan.

MIDRANGE
Some properties in Syria that should be charging budget rates just scrape into the midrange level – but because they offer decent facilities or service they are worth reviewing. As it stands, midrange hotels vary wildly in terms of facilities; some extras to look for include air-con, satellite TV and a fridge (handy if you're self-catering).

TOP END
The top end of Syria's accommodation has improved in both Damascus and Aleppo, with both new boutique and five-star properties having opened their doors. Top-end

POPULATION DATA
The population data in this book is based on the best resource material available, but due to the fluctuation of population numbers in both Syria and Lebanon, the figures may not be accurate at the time of your visit. The figures will, however, will be enough to tell you if a destination is a village or a metropolis.

hotels generally have air-con, satellite TV, minibar, and a restaurant or hotel bar. Many have health clubs and swimming pools. International chain hotels tend to have better facilities and staff.

The countrywide chain of state-owned five-stars, the Cham Palaces (pronounced 'sham') get the tour buses, but are of little interest to independent travellers. The notable exception is the Cham Palace in Damascus (p105).

Credit cards are accepted at all top-end hotels.

Rental Accommodation
The best way to find long-term rental apartments in Syria is to ask around. Foreign students living in Damascus recommend **House of Damascus** (www.houseofdamascus.com) for finding rooms to rent.

ACTIVITIES
Cycling
The big cities of Syria are filled with anarchic traffic, poor surfaces and high noise levels, but away from urban areas the mountains and deserts are excellent for cycle touring. In particular, the Dead Cities (p198) and the areas around Palmyra (p201) and Qala'at al-Hosn (Krak des Chevaliers; see p136) are super for cycling.

If you decide to bring your own bicycle, remember that as well as being reckless, Syrian drivers are not used to bicycles. Be extremely careful and don't assume that you have been spotted. Also keep in mind that bicycle shops are almost nonexistent outside the capital cities, so you need to bring everything you are likely to need, including spare spokes, chain, cables, tubes and tyres. On the flipside, you'll be warmly welcomed wherever you go – and will probably have trouble getting away each morning! A well-written blog on what to expect is Travelling Two (http://travellingtwo.com).

Trekking

There are wonderful trekking opportunities in Syria, but currently little in the way of organised trips. The Dead Cities (p198) and the areas around Palmyra (p201) and Qala'at al-Hosn (Krak des Chevaliers; see p136) are fantastic for trekking. For an organised trip, you could try **Jasmin Tours** (www.jasmintours.com); see p398 for more information.

Water Sports

Your best bet for water sports is Lattakia, where the Shaati al-Azraq (Blue Beach; p146) passes for Syria's premier coastal resort. Access to the best stretches of beach is controlled by Le Meridien and Cham hotels (see p147). Both chains hire out pedal boats, jet skis and sailboards.

BUSINESS HOURS

Government offices are generally open 8am to 2pm Saturday to Thursday, give or take an hour, and embassies and consulates are closed Saturday. Other offices and shops keep similar hours in the morning and often open again 4pm to 6pm. Most restaurants but only a few small traders will open on Friday.

Banks generally follow the government office hours, but there are quite a few exceptions; some branches keep their doors open 9am to noon, while some exchange booths are open until 7pm.

Post offices close at 8pm in Damascus and Aleppo (open on Fridays, too); in smaller cities, post offices close at 2pm. Telephone offices have much longer hours.

OPEN SESAME

Where possible, we've indicated throughout this book opening times of places of interest. However, often the reality on the ground is that site opening hours are at the whim of the ticket office or guardian. If you ask around, 'the man with the keys' can often be located and will be willing to open up. However, all opening hours must be prefaced, therefore, with a hopeful *in sha' Allah* (God-willing).

Principal museums and monuments are open 9am to 6pm in summer, and to 4pm from October to the end of March, while others are generally open 8am to 2pm. Most are closed Tuesdays.

CHILDREN

Children are much loved and fussed over in the Middle East and bringing yours along will open doors and guarantee new friends. For babies and toddlers, major brands of disposable nappies, wet wipes and jars of baby foods are easily available at pharmacies, where the selection is usually greater than at supermarkets. It's a good idea to bring your own powdered formula milk from home, as you might not be able to find a familiar brand. Bottled water is reliable and available everywhere, while hotels and restaurants will usually be happy to provide boiled water for babies' bottles, as well as running bottles and dummies through their dishwasher or boiling them for sterilisation.

If your kids aren't used to the heat, it's a good idea to avoid travel at the height of summer (July and August), when it can become very humid near the Mediterranean coast and dry and dusty elsewhere. Likewise, if they're not keen on shivering in the evenings, it's best not to travel in the middle of winter (late December to early February), when higher altitudes will be snowy and many budget accommodation options might get rather chilly, with unreliable hot water. To cope with the summer rays, sunhats and maximum protection sun block are an absolute must. For winter, bring plenty of cold-weather clothes. See When to Go in the Getting Started in Syria chapter (p62) and the Getting Started in Lebanon chapter (p243) for details on the best times to visit.

Eating out with children in Syria and Lebanon can be a real pleasure, and there are few restaurants – even at the very top end of the price scale – that won't be happy to see small patrons at their tables. Most will be happy to provide child-size portions or simple dishes if your kids aren't keen on the local cuisine, and many restaurants – except the most basic – have highchairs available.

There are also plenty of international fast-food chains, especially in Beirut, vending pizzas, burgers, sandwiches and the like, for when the familiar is the only thing that will do.

The larger chain hotels in both countries are used to catering for families. Cots can be booked in these hotels, and babysitting facilities are often available. Even if you have several small children with you, you'll normally not be required to pay extra, and rollaway beds – or even just an extra mattress on the floor – can accommodate children too big for a cot.

Most top-end hotels also have interconnecting rooms available for families with older kids.

It's a good idea to visit your local doctor or pharmacist before you leave home, and stock up on rehydration salts, fever-reducing medicine and other simple essentials, to counter any minor disasters along the road. A potential worry is the high incidence of diarrhoea and stomach problems that travellers experience in the Middle East.

For more detailed advice on health matters when travelling with children in the region, see p410.

For more comprehensive advice on travelling with children, see Lonely Planet's *Travel with Children* by Cathy Lanigan.

Sights & Activities

The open spaces of tourist sights can provide ample opportunities for children to expend some of that boundless energy.

Outside of Damascus, the hotels and beaches of Lattakia (p146) are notable for water-based children's activities.

See also Damascus for Children (p103) for other details on keeping the kids entertained.

CLIMATE

Temperatures range widely from blistering summer highs to snow-laden winter lows. During summer proper (June to August) daily highs average around 35°C on the coast and inland. However, head east into the desert and that rises to an average 40°C and highs of 46°C are not uncommon. In Damascus, the winter (December to February) daily average temperature might be 10°C, although it can get colder and snow is not uncommon.

You certainly get snow on the higher peaks and it's even been known to fall as far east as Palmyra.

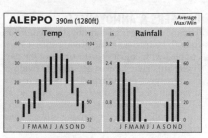

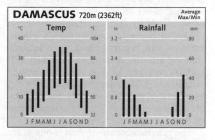

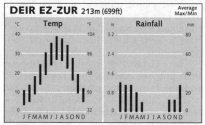

COURSES

Language courses are the most popular courses given in both countries, but given that Arabic is difficult to learn, these courses are generally geared to those intending to live and study in Syria (see Dialling in Your Dialect in Damascus, p102). For details on courses in Damascus, see p103.

CUSTOMS

Customs officials are now very used to seeing laptops and digital cameras entering the country, but it pays not to look like a journalist or photojournalist – so leave that flak jacket in your bag.

The duty-free allowance is 200 cigarettes and 570ml of spirits.

Don't bring in firearms or ammunition and please, no live, frozen or stuffed birds. Just so you know.

DANGERS & ANNOYANCES

The main danger and annoyance (common to both countries) is the driving style. Chaos coupled with courtesy is the order of the day. If you are driving, relax, get into the swing of it and expect the unexpected. If you have a driver and he's (it's always a 'he') placed all his faith in Allah, shots of coffee, cigarettes and a policy of never driving slower than 160km per hour, ask him to slow down (or say 'shway shway', slowly, slowly). As a pedestrian, never relax – you're the last thing most drivers are thinking about.

Despite being depicted by the US administration and Western media as a terrorist training ground, Syria is an extremely safe country to travel in. You can walk around virtually anywhere, day or night without any problems. Syrians are friendly and hospitable and if someone invites you to their village or home you should accept their offer.

The general absence of theft is one of the most refreshing things about travelling in Syria. This is no excuse for inviting trouble through carelessness, but at least you don't have to keep a hawk-like watch over your belongings.

There is, however, another kind of petty theft in Syria, overcharging. Few travellers completely avoid the odd petty rip-off, but you can minimise it by asking at your hotels how much things should cost that you want to buy, or how much that taxi should cost. While it is annoying, when put in perspective, the amount is usually petty unless you're a committed shoestringer.

DISCOUNT CARDS

There are no discount cards available for seniors in Syria.

Student Cards

Student cards get huge reductions on archaeological site and museum fees which, after accommodation, are the major expense when travelling in Syria. The standard admission fee is S£150 (about US$3.25) but with a student card this drops to S£10 (US$0.22). Ticket officials are often fussy about which kinds of cards they will accept. Student IDs issued by your college or university have a good chance of being rebuffed; you really need an International Student Identification Card (ISIC), or something similar that carries a photo and signature.

EMBASSIES & CONSULATES

It's important to realise what your own embassy – the embassy of the country of which you are a citizen – can and can't do to help you if you get into trouble. Generally speaking, it won't be much help in emergencies if the trouble you're in is remotely your own fault.

Remember that you are bound by the laws of the country you are in. Your embassy will not be sympathetic if you end up in jail after committing a crime locally, even if such actions are legal in your own country.

In genuine emergencies you might get some assistance, but only if other channels have been exhausted. For example, if you need to get home urgently, a free ticket home is unlikely – the embassy would expect you to have insurance.

If you have all your money and documents stolen, it might assist with getting a new passport, but a loan for onward travel is out of the question.

Embassies & Consulates in Syria

Note: at present the Canadian embassy provides consular services to Australian citizens in case of emergency, while citizens from Ireland and New Zealand are looked after by the UK. All the following countries are represented in Damascus.

Belgium (Map p80; ☎ 011-6139 9931; fax 6139 9977; www.diplomatie.be/damascus/; No 10 Al Salaam St, Mezzé East)

Canada (off Map p80; ☎ 011-611 6692; fax 611 4000; www.damascus.gc.ca; Lot 12, Autostraad al-Mezze) About 4km west of city centre.

Egypt (Map pp82-3; ☎ 011-333 3561; fax 333 7961; Sharia al-Jalaa, Abu Roumana)

France (Map p98; ☎ 011-330 0200; fax 339 0260; www.ambafrance-sy.org; Sharia Ata Ayyubi, Salihiyya)

Germany (Map p80; ☎ 011-332 3800/1; fax 332 3812; 53 Sharia Ibrahim Hanano)

Jordan (Map pp82-3; ☎ 011-333 4642; fax 333 6741; Sharia al-Jalaa, Abu Roumana)

Netherlands (Map p80; ☎ 011-333 6871, fax 333 9369; Sharia al-Jalaa, Abu Roumana)

Turkey (Map p80; ☎ 011-333 1411; 58 Sharia Ziad bin Abi Soufian)

UK (Map p80; ☎ 011-373 9241/2/3/7; fax 373 1600; www.fco.gov.uk; 11 Sharia Mohammed Kurd Ali, Malki) Note that you need to make an appointment.

USA (Map p80; ☎ 011-3391 4444; fax 3391 3999; http://damascus.usembassy.gov/; 2 Sharia al-Mansour, Abu Roumana)

FESTIVALS & EVENTS
April & May
Spring Flower Festival Held in Hama during the last two weeks of April; expect lots of colour, people promenading through into the early hours of the morning, temporary markets, and the sluices open so that the fast-flowing Orontes gets the huge waterwheels turning.

Palmyra Festival Held around the end of April or early May, this popular annual folk festival has desert ruins as its venue, with horse and camel racing during the day and music and dance performances in the ancient theatre (part of the civic centre) by night. For more information, see Palmyra Festival (p211).

International Flower Show Held in Damascus every May.

July
Cotton Festival Held in Aleppo, this festival celebrates the cotton harvest.

September
Bosra Festival Held every odd-numbered year, it's a festival of music and theatre, noteworthy for the chance of being part of an audience in the town's spectacular Roman theatre-cum-citadel.

Silk Road Festival Held in late September, it celebrates Syria's long cultural history with events in Aleppo, Damascus and Palmyra.

Suweida Apple & Vine Festival Held in late September, this festival celebrates the annual harvest.

November & December
Damascus International Film Festival Held annually, it shows an eclectic range of films, including many pan-Arab productions. There's also a theatre festival.

GAY & LESBIAN TRAVELLERS
Homosexuality is prohibited in Syria and conviction can result in imprisonment. In fact, the public position is that homosexuality doesn't exist in Syria, but of course it's no less prevalent than anywhere else in the world. However, discretion is advised.

That said, in his travelogue *Cleopatra's Wedding Present* (2003), the late Robert Tewdwr Moss describes a few months in Syria during which time he was anything but discreet about his homosexuality, and neither were many Syrians he met.

HOLIDAYS
Islamic Religious Holidays
All Islamic holidays throughout the region are celebrated within the framework of the Muslim calendar, while secular activities are planned according to the Christian system.

The Muslim year is based on the lunar cycle and is divided into 12 lunar months, each with 29 or 30 days. Consequently, the Muslim year is 10 or 11 days shorter than the Christian solar year, and the Muslim festivals shuffle along the Western calendar, completing the cycle in roughly 33 years.

Year zero in the Muslim calendar was when Mohammed and his followers fled from Mecca to Medina (AD 622 in the Christian calendar). This Hejira, or migration, is taken to mark the start of the new Muslim era, much as Christ's birth marks year zero in the Christian calendar.

Eid al-Adha Also known as Eid al-Kebir, the 'great feast', this marks the time of the hajj, the pilgrimage to Mecca. The hajj culminates in the ritual slaughter of a lamb (in commemoration of Ibrahim's sacrifice) at Mina. This marks the end of the pilgrimage and the beginning of Eid al-Adha, or Feast of Sacrifice.

Ras as-Sana Islamic New Year's Day (literally 'head of the year'). This day is celebrated on the first day of the Hejira calendar year, 1 Moharram. The whole country has the day off but celebrations are low-key.

Ashura This is the day of public mourning observed by the Shiites on 10 Moharram. It commemorates the assassination of Imam Hussein ibn Ali, grandson of the Prophet Mohammed, which led to the permanent schism between Sunnis and Shiites.

Moulid an-Nabi Feast celebrating the birthday of the Prophet Mohammed on 12 Rabi' al-Awal. One of the major holidays of the year – the streets are a feast of lights. For a long time this was not celebrated at all in the Arab world.

ISLAMIC HOLIDAYS

Hejira Year	New Year	Prophet's Birthday	Ramadan	Eid al-Fitr	Eid al-Adha
1429	10 Jan 08	20 Mar 08	2 Sep 08	2 Oct 08	9 Dec 08
1430	29 Dec 08	9 Mar 09	22 Aug 09	21 Sep 09	28 Nov 09
1431	18 Dec 09	26 Feb 10	11 Aug 10	10 Sep 10	12 Nov 10
1432	7 Dec 10	15 Feb 11	1 Aug 11	30 Aug 11	6 Nov 11
1433	26 Nov 11	5 Feb 12	20 Jul 12	19 Aug 12	26 Oct 12

Ramadan The ninth month of the Muslim calendar, the month in which the Quran was first revealed. From dawn until dusk, Muslims are expected to abstain from eating, drinking, smoking and sexual activity. Non-Muslims are not expected to observe the fast, but eating, drinking and smoking in public is prohibited. Given this, and the fact that people get a little grumpy near the end of the month, it can be an awkward time to visit, but the night-time activities when the fast is broken are fascinating.

Eid al-Fitr A three-day feast (often longer) that marks the end of Ramadan. Similar in nature to Eid al-Adha. Generally, everything shuts down during this holiday.

Public Holidays

The Islamic holidays (and Christian Easter) change each year. Below are the fixed public holidays. Most holidays are either religious (Islamic and Christian) or celebrations of important dates in the formation of modern Syria.

New Year's Day (1 January) Official national holiday but many businesses stay open.

Orthodox Christmas (7 January) A fairly low-key affair and only Orthodox businesses are closed for the day.

Commemoration of the Revolution (8 March) Celebrates the coming to power of the Arab Ba'ath Socialist Party.

Easter (March/April) Different dates each year. The most important date on the Christian calendar.

Commemoration of the Evacuation (17 April) Celebrates the end of French occupation in Syria.

May Day (1 May) Official national holiday.

Martyrs' Day (6 May) Celebrates all political martyrs who died for Syria.

INSURANCE

Whichever way you're travelling, make sure you take out a comprehensive travel insurance policy that covers you for medical expenses and luggage theft or loss, and for cancellation of (or delays in) your travel arrangements. Ticket loss should also be included, but make sure you have a separate record of all the details, or better still, a photocopy of the ticket.

Some policies specifically exclude dangerous activities, which can include scuba diving, motorcycling, snow sports and even trekking. If you plan on doing any of these things, make sure you get a policy that covers it.

For information on insurance matters relating to cars, see p401. The international student travel policies handled by **STA Travel** (www.statravel.com) and other student travel organisations are usually good value.

INTERNET ACCESS

Since President Bashar al-Assad opened the internet flood gates, online activity has bloomed like a Damascene rose and every major town has at least two or three internet cafés. To date there are only a few national Internet Service Providers (ISPs) and costs are typically S£100 (US$2) per hour. If you're lugging a laptop then you can get connected in some of the better hotels via an Ethernet (network) cable, but modem connections are still the most common. Hotels promising wi-fi can't always deliver and while wi-fi-enabled cafés have sprung up, generally you're on your own if there is a connection problem. Note that if you're carrying any electrical items that are plugged into a wall socket, power surges pose a real risk to your equipment in Syria, so it's a good idea to pack a portable surge protector.

LEGAL MATTERS

Travellers should have few opportunities to get to know the legal system personally – a good thing in Syria; we hear the food's not so great. Carrying any kind of narcotics (including marijuana/hash) is a foolish undertaking. If you are caught in possession in Syria, you could well wind up doing a heavy jail sentence. If you do cross the law in any way, your embassy can do little more than contact your relatives and recommend local lawyers.

MAPS

A good map is that produced by Freytag & Berndt, distinguished by a red-and-green cover. It shows the country at a scale of 1:800,000 and also carries decent city plans of Damascus and Aleppo. It's difficult to get hold of in Syria. Another sheet map published by GEO Projects, at a scale of 1:1,000,000, also has decent city plans of Damascus at 1:15,000 and Aleppo at 1:12,500 on the reverse side. Tourist offices throughout Syria have free city and regional maps, which are also good.

MONEY

The official currency is the Syrian pound (S£), also called the *lira*. There are 100 piastres (*qirsh*) to a pound but this is redundant because the smallest coin you'll find is S£1. Other coins come in denominations of two, five, 10 and 25. Notes come in denominations of 50, 100, 200, 500 and 1000.

Common exchange rates are listed on the inside front cover. For information about costs for your trip, see p63.

ATMs

There is a growing number of ATMs across Syria, especially in Damascus and Aleppo. Cash advances are officially not possible as the Commercial Bank of Syria (CBS) has no links with international credit-card companies. However, a few individual entrepreneurs carry out transactions via Jordanian or Lebanese banks. Bear in mind that the rate they offer may not be too great. If you do need a cash advance, ask at any shop displaying a Visa or Amex sign and chances are you'll be pointed in the right direction.

Black Market

We thought the days of someone whispering 'change money?' in your ear were over, but it still exists. Given that banks offer the same rates, it's inexplicable. Out of banking hours, hotel receptions are often willing to change cash or travellers cheques at the going bank rates.

Cash

Bring as much in cash dollars as you're comfortable with. Many midrange hotels only take US$ (ie no local currency), although some will take US$ travellers cheques at a push. Don't forget that if you're flying out, you'll have to pay the departure tax of S£200, so keep just enough tucked away.

Credit Cards

Major credit cards such as Visa, Master-Card, Diners Club and Amex are accepted by top-end hotels and the swishest restaurants and shops, particularly those that trade with travellers. Credit cards are also handy for buying air tickets (as the only alternative is hard currency) and for most reputable car-rental companies (it will save you having to leave a large cash deposit).

Moneychangers

The banking system in Syria was state-owned until 2004 and its public face is the Commercial Bank of Syria (CBS), with at least one branch in every major town. The majority of branches will change cash and travellers cheques in most major currencies. Each branch has its own quirks: generally speaking, the smaller the town, the smaller the hassle.

There are also a number of officially sanctioned private exchange offices. These change cash, and sometimes travellers cheques, at official bank rates but generally don't charge commission. The other advantage is that whereas banks usually close for the day at 12.30pm or 2pm, the exchange offices are often open until 7pm.

Tipping

Waiters in better restaurants generally expect a tip, and some will help themselves by short-changing you a little, but otherwise a standard 10% of the bill is a good benchmark. Other services are also carried out with a view to being tipped – everything from having your luggage taken to your room to having doors opened for you. In most cases a tip of S£25 is considered fair. Guides and drivers will expect a tip, although in our experience, services delivered rarely warrant one.

Travellers Cheques

Cash is definitely king in Syria and given that there are now ATMs in the major tourist destinations, cash withdrawals and credit cards are the preferred means of payment. Waiting in line in banks getting travellers cheques cashed is not our preferred way of spending a morning in Syria. Some branches of the CBS will charge a minimum one-off commission of S£25 per transaction, whether you change one or several cheques. A couple of US$50 or €50 notes tucked away somewhere are much more useful at a pinch.

PHOTOGRAPHY & VIDEO

Both Syria and Lebanon are photogenic countries with dramatic landscapes and clear Mediterranean light. Dust is a problem in both countries and it is a good idea to keep your equipment wrapped in a plastic bag, even inside a camera bag. Take a soft lens brush and some camera wipes for lens cleaning. A dedicated flash is definitely useful if you want to photograph the dark interiors of churches and mosques, or to help make portraits in the sun.

The best times to shoot are in the morning until 10am and the afternoon between 4pm and sunset. During the middle of the day the harsh sunlight plays havoc with getting a nicely exposed shot.

Photographic Supplies
In Damascus and Aleppo there's a number of specialist photo shops that sell memory cards and spare batteries. Canon and Nikon are best represented.

Restrictions
Be very careful when taking photos of anything other than tourist sites. It is forbidden to photograph bridges, train stations, anything military, airports and any other public works. If you accidentally shoot something sensitive and you're spotted by officials, offer to delete it.

As a matter of courtesy, don't photograph people without asking their permission first. Unless there are signs indicating otherwise, photography is usually allowed inside archaeological sites.

POST
The Syrian postal service is slow but dependable. Letters mailed from the main cities take about a week to reach Europe and anything up to a month to Australia or the USA. Stamps for postcards to the UK, Europe, Australia and the USA cost S£18. You can also buy *tawaabi* (stamps) from most tobacconists, as well as at post offices.

The **poste restante counter** (8am-5pm, closed Fri) in the **central post office** (Map pp82-3; Sharia Said al-Jabri) in Damascus is more or less reliable. Take your passport as identification and be prepared to pay a S£10 pick-up fee.

SHOPPING
While Syria finally has some High Street shopping and you can buy most of the popular brands you'll find anywhere in the world, it's much more fun to head to the souqs. Every town and village has a souq of some sort, although by far the best are in Damascus and Aleppo.

Carpets, rugs and kilims are best found in the markets of Damascus and Aleppo. You can find gold shops scattered about the bigger cities of Syria, but they are at their most concentrated in parts of the Damascus and Aleppo souqs. As a rule, gold is sold by weight, and all pieces should have a hallmark guaranteeing quality. Silver is the most common material used by Bedouin women to make up their often striking jewellery.

For centuries Damascus was, along with Toledo in Spain, one of the greatest centres for the production of quality swords. Tamerlane forcefully transferred the Damascene sword-makers to Samarkand in the 15th century, but something of the tradition stuck. Several shops in Damascus still produce them for sale as souvenirs.

From Morocco to Baghdad you will find much the same sorts of engraved brass and chased copper objects for sale. Most common are the very large decorative trays and tabletops, but other items typical of the Middle East include Arabic coffeepots and even complete coffee sets with small cups (the little traditional cups without handles should preferably be ceramic). Incense-burners and teapots are also popular buys.

A local speciality is *ad-dahiri* (the ancient art of brass and copper engraving and gold and silver inlaying), which in the past was the preserve of Damascene Jews. They've all left, but others carry on the work.

Quite a few souq stalls sell either *ouds* (Arabic lutes) or *darbukkas,* the standard Middle Eastern–style drum. The latter can go quite cheaply, and even the *ouds* are hardly expensive at around US$40 for a typical tourist model, but a decent playable one starts at around US$100.

Damascus, in particular, is known for its textiles, and has been since antiquity. This has to be one of the best places in the world to look for tablecloths and the like. They are generally made of fine cotton and handsomely adorned with silk. The heavy Damascene tablecloths are just about the most beautiful things to buy in Syria. Made from fine lustrous cotton they come in deep reds, burgundies, azure blues and emerald greens, patterned with geometric or paisley-style designs. The best have traditionally been made in Damascus, but these are becoming much more difficult to find as far fewer are produced these days.

Brocade is another speciality, and the Bedouin-style vests on sale in some of the more reputable shops in the Damascus souqs are very popular. Good ones will go for around US$15. Along the same line are

---

THE ART OF BARGAINING

Almost all prices are negotiable in the souq: there is no 'recommended retail price'. Bargaining is a process – no, a ritual – to establish how much the customer is willing to pay. It can be a hassle, but *always* keep your cool and remember it's a game, not a fight.

The first rule is never to show too much interest in the item you want to buy. Secondly, don't buy the first item that takes your fancy. Wander around and price things, but don't make it obvious; otherwise, when you return to the first shop the vendor will know it's because they are the cheapest.

Decide how much you would be happy paying and then express a casual interest in buying. The vendor will state their price, grossly inflated, doubly so if it's a foreigner doing the buying. Respond with a figure somewhat lower than the one you have fixed in your mind. So the bargaining begins. The shopkeeper will inevitably huff about how absurd your offer is and then tell you the 'lowest' price. If it is still not low enough, be insistent and keep smiling. Tea or coffee might be served as part of the bargaining ritual but accepting it doesn't place you under any obligation to buy. If you still can't get your price, then walk away. This often has the effect of closing the sale in your favour. If not, there are many more shops in the souq.

If you do get your price or lower, never feel guilty. No vendor, no matter what they say, *ever* sells below cost.

---

jalabiyyas, the long and loose robes that you'll see many men and women getting around in. The men's version tends to be fairly sober in colouring, while this kind of women's clothing can be almost blindingly gaudy.

A popular buy with foreigners are woodwork items. They range from simple jewellery boxes to elaborate chess sets and backgammon boards. The better-quality items tend to be of walnut and inlaid with mother-of-pearl. If the mother-of-pearl gives off a strong rainbow-colour effect, you can be almost sure it is the real deal and not cheap plastic. The actual woodwork on many of these items tends to be a little haphazard, even on the better-quality items, so inspect the joints and inlay carefully.

The ubiquitous nargileh (water pipe) are about as vivid a reminder of a visit to the Middle East as one can imagine. Some of the smaller, simpler ones can start from as low as US$10 to US$20, but ornate ones will cost considerably more. Remember to buy a supply of charcoal and flavoured tobacco to get you going (apple flavour is a safe choice) if you intend to smoke up a storm when you return home. However, this has to be the most awkward souvenir to cart around with you – and its chances of surviving the post are not good. Buy it on the last day.

Another simple idea (and much easier to carry around) is a *kufeyya* (the traditional Arab headcloth) and *iqal* (the black

cord used to keep it on your head) so characteristic of the region. Be aware that the quality of *kufeyya* varies considerably, with some being very bare strips of white cotton and others densely sewn in red or black patterns. Compare before you buy. Even the quality of the *iqal* can vary. A good set should not cost more than about US$5 to US$10.

SMOKING

Syrian men love to smoke. Syrian women love to smoke nargileh. While this is generalising a little, you find smoking ubiquitous throughout Syria. While you might find nonsmoking rooms available in top-end hotels in Damascus, you'll have little luck anywhere else. In restaurants those who are irritated by cigarette smoke won't find this aspect of Syria appealing.

SOLO TRAVELLERS

Solo travellers generally have no problems travelling in Syria and Lebanon – apart from continually answering the obvious question, why *are* you alone? In the Middle East family and friends are essential to a happy life, and many people you meet won't understand why you are travelling alone. There are advantages; touts will leave you alone if there are groups to chase and travellers with outgoing personalities will find it easy to strike up a conversation in a café.

If you're travelling solo and want to make friends, plenty of young Syrians and Lebanese are keen to practise their high school or university English. Cafés are great places to meet young locals and get an insight into their lives; they'll probably invite you back to their place for more coffee, tea and conversation.

To meet other travellers, the best thing to do is to stay at *the* backpacker hang-outs in each town and we've mentioned these in the reviews. This is also a great way to do day trips – often people are happy to have an extra person on board to share the cost and you will occasionally find it hard to get on tours as a solo traveller.

Women travelling on their own should exercise a degree of caution; see Women Travellers (p238) for more information.

TELEPHONE

The country code for dialling Syria is ☎ 963, followed by the local area code (minus the zero), then the subscriber number. Local area codes are given at the start of each city or town section. The international access code (to call abroad from Syria) is ☎ 00. Reverse-charge calls cannot be made from Syria; to get the operator dial ☎ 143/144.

Mobile Phones

Depending on your operator, travellers from most countries can use their mobile Global System for Mobile (GSM) phones in Syria. Coverage is not complete across the country, but it's reliable in most cities. Check with your GSM service company for details as to whether they have an agreement with one of the operators in Syria. The best SIM card to buy to use in your mobile phone while in Syria is the Syriatel 'Ya Hala' SIM card, as **Syriatel** (www.syriatel.com) has the best coverage across Syria. At the time of writing, the SIM cost S£650, and the validity of the card (in terms of length of activation) depends on the amount of recharge units you feed the phone. For instance, a S£300 card gives you 16 days and a S£1000 card gives you 60 days of activation. You will need your passport and the cards are available at mobile-phone shops everywhere throughout the country and at the arrivals hall at Damascus International Airport.

PhoneCards

Calling from Damascus, Aleppo and Hama is straightforward – you just use one of the direct-dial Easycomm card phones dotted about town (plentiful in Damascus, less so in Aleppo and Hama). Phonecards are bought from shops – just ask at the nearest shop, no matter what kind of shop it is, and if they don't have them, they'll point you to someone who does. The cards come in denominations of S£200 (local and national calls only), S£350, S£500 and S£1000. For cheaper rates to Australia call from 2pm to 7pm; to the USA from 3am to 8am; and to Europe from 1am to 7am.

Elsewhere in the country, international calls have to be made from card phones located inside or just outside the local telephone office.

TIME

Both Syria and Lebanon are two hours ahead of GMT/UTC in winter (October to March) and three hours ahead in summer (April to September), when daylight saving is used. For more on international timing, see the map of the world time zones (p434).

One important thing to bear in mind regarding time is that Syrians and Lebanese always seem to have plenty of it – something that should take five minutes will invariably take an hour. Trying to speed things up will only lead to frustration. Take it philosophically and don't try to fight it – a bit of patience goes a long way here.

TOILETS

Travellers who have experienced some Middle Eastern toilets need not fear – Syrian and Lebanese toilets are generally very clean. You will find a mixture of Western-style upright toilets and the squat hole-in-the-floor variety, although the latter are becoming less common. In both Syria and Lebanon you are almost always close enough to a decent hotel or restaurant that will let you use their facilities. Remember toilet paper is not always available so *always* carry a small tissue pack.

TRAVELLERS WITH DISABILITIES

Generally speaking, scant regard is paid to the needs of disabled travellers in Syria. Steps, high kerbs and other assorted obstacles abound, streets are often badly rutted and uneven, roads are made virtually uncrossable by heavy traffic, while many doorways are low and narrow. Ramps and specially equipped lodgings and toilets are an extreme rarity. You will have to plan your trip carefully and will probably be obliged to restrict yourself to luxury-level hotels and private, hired transport.

VISAS

All foreigners entering Syria must obtain visas from Syrian consulates abroad, but if there is no Syrian representation in your home country, then *in theory* you should be able to get a visa at the border or on arrival at the airport (for details on obtaining visas at the border see the following section). Some travel companies (tourism operators) in Syria claim to be able to organise your visa by faxing them copies of your passports and associated documents.

The easiest and surest way to get your visa is to apply for it in your home country. Try to avoid applying in a country that is not your own or where you don't hold residency as the Syrians look poorly on this – they will ask you for a letter of recommendation from your own embassy (which is often an expensive and time-consuming proposition); at worst they'll turn you down flat. In fact, US citizens must get their visas at home, as US embassies abroad have a policy of not issuing letters of recommendation – however, amusingly, they will issue a letter stating that they don't issues letters of recommendation. If your home country doesn't have a Syrian embassy or consulate, then there's no problem with you applying anywhere else – but be aware of your own countries' restrictions in issuing letters of recommendation. While there are plenty of reports of visitors getting visas without a letter, or in countries where they shouldn't be able to (in theory), it's always better to plan ahead.

At most embassies and consulates you can apply in person or by post and the visa takes from four days to two weeks to issue. There are rarely any problems with getting the visa; however, if there is any evidence of a visit to Israel and the Palestinian Territories in your passport, your application will be refused (for more details regarding passports and visiting Israel and the Palestinian Territories, see p390). There are two

types of visa issued – single- and multiple-entry – but both are valid only for 15 days inside Syria and must be used within three months of the date of issue (six months for multiple-entry visas). Don't be misled by the words on the visa stating a validity of three months – this simply means the visa is valid *for presentation* for three months. Once in Syria it is easy to get your visa extended in the major cities and some towns. Offices where this can be done are noted in the text.

Visas at the Border

The official line is that if there is no Syrian representation in your country, you are entitled to be issued a visa on arrival at the border, airport or port. Conversely, there are multiple Syrian consulates in Australia but there have been plenty of emails from Aussie travellers who managed to get a visa at the Turkey–Syria border with no problems. It's a situation that seems largely governed by the whim of the individual immigration official. Because of this, our advice is get your visa in advance. If that's not possible in your own country then consider picking up the visa en route on your travels. Note that some people have been reporting waits of up to eight hours at the border for faxes from Damascus to get entry visas.

Getting Your Visa in the Middle East

In Jordan, the Syrian embassy in Amman issues visas only to nationals and residents of Jordan and to nationals of countries that have no Syrian representation. So, if you are from a country such as the UK, the USA or France, which has a Syrian embassy, then officially you cannot get a Syrian visa in Jordan. In Egypt, the Syrian embassy in Cairo issues visas to *all nationalities* on the same or next day, depending on how early in the morning you lodge your application. For Australians and Canadians the visa is free, Americans pay around US$34, UK citizens pay about US$60 and most other nationalities pay around US$54; note these prices are approximate and readers have reported paying different amounts.

In Turkey, you can get Syrian visas in both Ankara and Istanbul without too much of a problem. Australians and Canadians pay nothing, while New Zealanders pay about US$6. German, French and US citizens pay

SYRIA DIRECTORY

more, while Brits take all the prizes, paying about US$60. Nonresidents in Turkey need a letter of recommendation from their embassy, for which they may be charged. UK citizens, for example, have to pay around UK£35 for this service. Visas in Turkey take one working day to issue. Note that the Syrian consulate in Istanbul is only open for applications from 9.30am to 11am, and for pick-up from 2pm to 2.30pm the next working day.

We've had reports that visas issued in Cairo and Turkey are only valid for presentation within one month; ask for more details when collecting.

Visa Costs

The cost of visas varies according to nationality and where you get them. There seems to be little rhyme or reason in deciding which nationalities pay what, except in the case of UK passport-holders, who always pay a lot. New Zealanders need to apply to Melbourne or Sydney as there's no Syrian representation in New Zealand (the same costs apply).

Visa Extensions

If your stay in Syria is going to be more than 15 days you have to get a visa extension while in the country. This is done at an immigration office, which you'll find in all main towns and cities. The length of extension appears to depend on a combination of what you're willing to ask for and the mood of the official you deal with – it's usually one month. You can get more than one extension.

Extensions are usually only granted on the 14th or 15th day of your stay, so if you apply earlier expect to be knocked back. If, as occasionally happens, you are allowed to extend your visa earlier than this, check that the extension is from the last day of your visa or previous extension and not from the day of your application.

The specifics vary from place to place but there are always several forms to fill in, in French, usually containing questions repeated several times in slightly different ways. You need from three to six passport photos. The cost is never more than US$1. Processing time varies from on-the-spot to come back the following day. Damascus and Aleppo are about the most tedious places to extend your visa, while small towns like Deir ez-Zur or Tartus are the most straightforward.

WOMEN TRAVELLERS

As a woman traveller in Syria you can expect little verbal harassment and virtually none if you're with a male companion. The banter is usually inane proposals of marriage or even declarations of undying love, but harassment can also take the form of leering and sometimes of being followed.

If you are being harassed, and if you're in a crowded area, a decent, loud 'halas!' (which means 'enough') should attract enough attention to embarrass the perpetrator. Otherwise, the best bet is to simply ignore it (see also Tips for Women Travellers, opposite).

VISAS

country	single-entry visa	multiple-entry visa
Australia	A$35* A$75**	A$45* A$100**
Canada	US$56	US$108
France	€26	€49
Germany	€30	€49
Ireland	UK£37	UK£70
UK	UK£37	UK£57***
USA	US$61****	

* If applying in the Melbourne consular office.
** If applying in the Sydney consular office.
*** British citizens looking for a multiple-entry visa should be aware that visas are not currently issued at a point of entry into Lebanon.
**** In the USA the visa cost is the same for single or 'double' entry. The latter allows you to enter twice – useful if you wish to enter Lebanon and return to Syria. Note that the cost includes a US$16 visa fee and a US$45 nonrefundable application fee.

TIPS FOR WOMEN TRAVELLERS

There are a number of things that you can do to lessen the likelihood of harassment, but top of the list is to dress modestly. Other helpful tips:

- Wear a wedding band. Generally, Middle Eastern males have more respect for a married woman.
- If you are unmarried but travelling in male company say you are married rather than girl-friend/boyfriend or just friends.
- Don't say that you are travelling alone or just in the company of another female friend – always say that you are with a group.
- Avoid direct eye contact with local men; wearing dark sunglasses can help.
- On public transport, sit next to a woman if possible.
- Be very careful about behaving in a flirtatious or suggestive manner; it could create more problems than you bargained for.
- If you need help for any reason (directions etc), ask a woman first.
- If dining alone, be aware that some places are almost strictly male preserves, such as the local coffeehouse.
- It is perfectly acceptable for a woman to go straight to the front of a queue or to ask to be served first before any men that may be waiting.
- Women should not get into an unlicensed service taxi if there are no other passengers, especially at night.
- Don't respond to any obnoxious comments – act as if you didn't hear them. If they persist, an easy Arabic word to remember is *'Halas!'* ('Enough!'), best recited in a loud, but firm voice. This should attract enough attention for local onlookers to scold the perpetrator(s).
- Going to the nearest public place, such as the lobby of a hotel, usually works in getting rid of any 'admirers'. If they still persist, however, then ask the receptionist to call the police. This will definitely frighten them off.

While Syria is a very safe country for female travellers, the disappearance of a solo female traveller who was staying in Hama in 2007 serves to highlight the dangers of travelling alone in any country.

The majority of Syrians are conservative about dress. The female traveller wearing shorts and a tight T-shirt on the street is, in some people's eyes, confirmation of the worst views held of Western women.

As hot as it gets in Syria you'll have fewer hassles if you don't dress for hot weather in the same way you might at home. Baggy T-shirts and loose cotton trousers or long skirts will protect your skin from the sun and from unwanted comments.

Unfortunately, although dressing conservatively should reduce the incidence of such harassment, it by no means guarantees you'll be left alone.

Some activities, such as sitting in coffee-houses, are usually seen as a male preserve and although it's OK for Western women to enter, in some places the stares may cause discomfort. Many restaurants have a 'family area' set aside for women and if you are travelling without male company you might feel more comfortable in these sections. As a rule, mixed foreign groups have no problem wherever they sit, including coffeehouses and bars.

Staying in budget hotels can sometimes be problematic if you're alone. You may have to take a room for yourself if there are no other travellers to share with.

WORK

Unless you are working for a multinational and get a posting, possibilities for working in Syria are are severely limited. About the only work available might be as a language teacher. The **American Language Center** (ALC; ☎ 011-332 7236) is probably the best place to try your luck, followed by the

British Council (Map p80; ☎ 011-333 0631, fax 332 1467; www.britishcouncil.org/syria; Sharia Karim al-Khalil, off Sharia Maysaloun; ☺ 9am-8pm Sun-Thu, 10am-5pm Sat), both of which are in Damascus.

Because the British Council is smaller and tends to recruit directly from the UK rather than locally, the ALC should be your first port of call. The ALC prefers people with a Bachelor's degree and some form of teaching experience. A Certificate in English Language Teaching to Adults (Celta), or second language qualification, knowledge of Arabic, postgraduate studies and prior experience in teaching improve your chances.

Native French-speaking travellers could try their luck at the **Centre Culturel Français** (Map pp82-3; ☎ 011-231 6181; fax 231 6194; off Sharia Yousef al-Azmeh, Bahsa; ☺ 8.30am-9pm Mon-Sat) in Damascus.

Lebanon

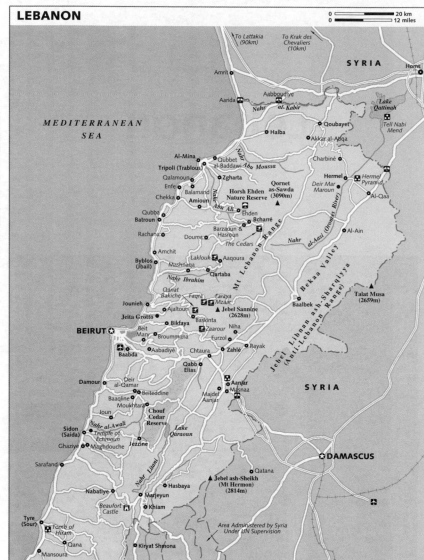

LEBANON

0   20 km
0   12 miles

MEDITERRANEAN
SEA

SYRIA

Homs

To Lattakia
(90km)

To Krak des
Chevaliers
(10km)

Amrit

Aabboudiye

Aarida

Nahr al-Kabir

Lake
Qattinah

Tell Nabi
Mend

Halba

Qoubayet

Akkar al-Atiqa

Al-Mina

Charbiné

Qubbet
al-Baddawi

Nahr Abu Moussa

Tripoli (Trablous)

Hermel

Hermel
Pyramid

Qalamoun

Zgharta

Deir Mar
Maroun

Enfe

Balamand

Horsh Ehden
Nature Reserve

Qornet
as-Sawda
(3090m)

Al-Qaa

Chekka

Amioun

Abu Ali

Ehden

Qubba

Batroun

Bcharré

Rachana

Barzaoun &
Hasroun

Douma

The Cedars

Nahr al-Aasi (Orontes River)

Al-Ain

Amchit

Laklouk

Aaqoura

Byblos
(Jbail)

Mashnaqa

Qartaba

Nahr Ibrahim

Bekaa Valley

Qanat
Bakiche

Faqra

Faraya
Mzaar

Talat Musa
(2659m)

Jounieh

Ajaltoun

Jebel Sannine
(2628m)

Baalbek

Jeita Grotto

Baskinta

Bikfaya

Niha

Beit
Mary

Zaarour

Eurzol

BEIRUT

Broummana

Rayak

Aabadiyé

Chtaura

Zahlé

Baabda

Qabb
Elias

Damour

Deir
al-Qamar

Aanjar

SYRIA

Beiteddine

Masnaa

Baaqline

Majdel
Aanjar

Moukhtara

Joun

Chouf
Cedar
Reserve

Sidon
(Saida)

Nahr al-Awali

Temple of
Echmoun

Lake
Qaraoun

Ghaziye

Maghdouche

Jezzine

Sarafand

Nahr Litani

Qatana

DAMASCUS

Jebel ash-Sheikh
(Mt Hermon)
(2814m)

Nabatiye

Hasbaya

Marjeyun

Beaufort
Castle

Khiam

Tyre
(Sour)

Tomb of
Hiram

Qana

Mansoura

Kiryat Shmona

Area Administered by Syria
Under UN Supervision

Bint
Jbayl

Quneitra

Nahariya

Golan
Heights

ISRAEL & THE
PALESTINIAN
TERRITORIES

Jordan River

Sea of
Galilee

Ezra'a

To Haifa (25km);
Tel Aviv (116km);
Jerusalem (180km)

To Jerusalem
(150km)

To Der'a (23km);
Ramtha (45km);
Amman (115km)

Sheikh Meskeen

Mt Lebanon Range

Jebel Libnan ash-Sharqiyya
(Anti-Lebanon Range)

Getting Started in Lebanon

Lebanon is the perfect destination for experiencing a rich variety of sights, sounds, cuisines and cultural edifices within an incredibly compact area. It plays host to ancient cities, world-class nightclubs, Mediterranean beaches, labyrinthine medieval souqs and stunning mountain landscapes – all accessible, traffic permitting, in just a few hours from the capital, Beirut.

If you're visiting for more than a few days, or combining your visit with travel in Syria, see our suggested itineraries (p17). If truly off-the-beaten-track is what you require or you're short on time, it's a good idea to rent a car, since public transportation outside the main cities can be patchy and time consuming.

For such a small and generally built-up country, it's remarkably easy to get away from it all. Trekking parts of the burgeoning Lebanon Mountain Trail (p338), which takes you along the gorgeous Qadisha Valley floor, will ensure that the only buildings you'll see are ancient rock-cut churches, and the only people a sprinkling of hermit monks and goatherds.

Though Lebanon is not a particularly budget-friendly destination, with a little care it's easy to enjoy the country whatever the thickness of your wallet.

With youth hostelling and home-stays gradually gaining popularity, a tighter budget may actually help you to get beneath the skin of the country far better than two weeks of top-end hotels and glittering shopping malls. But, if you can stretch to it, a few killer cocktails at one of Beirut's glitziest clubs is a great way to start or end a Lebanese sojourn in the city's inimitable style.

WHEN TO GO

The best time of year to visit Lebanon depends entirely on what you're intending to do there. If you want to experience the most spectacular hiking, the perfect time to visit is during spring (March to May).

By May, the weather may already be warm enough for a dip in the Mediterranean, and you'll be able to live the Lebanese cliché of taking to the mountain slopes in the morning and swimming on the coast in the afternoon.

HOW MUCH?

Postcard LL700

Newspaper LL2000

Average museum admission LL5000

Bottle of local wine LL10,000

One-minute phone call to UK LL3000

LONELY PLANET INDEX

Litre of petrol LL1300

Litre of bottled water LL600

Bottle of beer in bar/restaurant LL3000

Souvenir T-shirt LL8000

Shwarma LL3000

DON'T LEAVE HOME WITHOUT...

- Checking the latest travel advisory warnings (see Staying Safe, p244)
- Getting a new passport if your current one contains an Israeli stamp.
- Checking the current visa status for Lebanon (see p388).
- Packing something chic if you're planning a night out in Beirut.
- Throwing in your hiking boots if you intend to get off the beaten track into Lebanon's stunning wilderness.

STAYING SAFE

Though its recent history has included several lengthy periods of relative calm, Lebanon's chequered religious, political and social fabric has frequently caused tensions to flare suddenly and violently.

Many countries, including the UK, Australia and the USA, currently include Lebanon on their list of countries to which all but essential travel should be avoided. Most specifically, foreign offices advise against travel south of the Nahr Litani (Litani River) and into Palestinian refugee camps, and suggest avoiding all public demonstrations.

Despite the bleak warnings, however, if you opt to travel to Lebanon you'll find warm, welcoming people eager to help travellers, and you'll quickly feel safe and at home.

Nevertheless, it's important to take some precautions, since circumstances can change extremely rapidly: in summer 2006, for example, many travellers suddenly found themselves stranded after Israel's attacks on the country shut down the international airport and rendered the main highway to the Syrian border impassable. Most crucially, when in Lebanon, keep your eye on the news.

Furthermore, try to avoid driving at night (largely due to Lebanon's hair-raising, headlight-free driving) and take local advice when travelling in the south. If you're planning on visiting any Palestinian refugee camps, make sure you take a reliable local companion. Recent threats against UN Interim Forces in Lebanon (Unifil) troops have led some to warn against visiting restaurants or other establishments frequented by Unifil staff in Tyre.

Likewise, it makes sense to avoid public demonstrations, which can often become heated and unpredictable. It may pay to talk with your embassy in Lebanon if you're in any doubt as to your safety.

Finally, theft is a minor problem, but random crime is far lower than in most Western cities. There has been a spate of motor-scooter bag snatchings, particularly in Beirut, but, as in any large city, you only need exercise normal precautions.

Aside from these sensible measures, relax and enjoy all that Lebanon has to offer – before the tourist masses finally come pouring back.

See Climate (p383) for more information.

To accompany your pre-departure research, pick up a copy of the groovy CD compilation *Music For An Arabian Night/Holiday In Beirut* by Ron Goodwin & his Orchestra.

The next best time for hiking is during autumn, though if it's action you're seeking, beware that it can be extremely quiet: many summer tourist spots will have wound down for the season, while the ski resorts are still oiling their ski lifts.

The onset of Ramadan probably won't affect your travel plans too dramatically in Lebanon, since most towns contain a mixture of Christians and Muslims.

Sun seekers will be happy any time between June and September, when the beach clubs of Beirut see almost 24-hour action and barely a cloud intrudes on a sweltering summer sky. Soaring temperatures, however, can make things a bit sticky, while interiors will be very hot and arid. For advice on avoiding sun stroke or dehydration, see the Health chapter (p409).

Summer is also prime festival season, a time to indulge in music performances beneath the stars. Prices rise quite steeply during these periods, when flocks of expat Lebanese descend on the country.

Winter is best to visit if you're intending on hitting the slopes, when trendy ski resorts like Faraya Mzaar (p299) and the Cedars (p342) gear up for business, the ski season usually stretching from early December to early April.

The Christmas period is festive countrywide, with Lebanon's Christians putting up their fairy lights and celebrating in churches. You should ensure, though, that your hotel room has some sort of heating and reliable hot water; otherwise, you could be in for some chilly mornings.

COSTS & MONEY

Lebanon's restaurant and hotel prices are roughly equivalent to North America and large parts of Europe. Beirut is full of fine restaurants, where a meal for two will easily tally up to US$100, and top-end hotel rooms go for over US$250 per night.

It is, however, perfectly possible to travel the country on a tight budget. Beirut has several budget hotel options, with dorm rooms for US$7 per person per night, and public transport is cheap and cheerful – if time-consuming – even to the more rural parts of Lebanon. Moreover, street food is good value and delicious, with a shwarma coming in at around US$2 and a strong cup of coffee at less than US$1.

For the most freedom on the road, it's probably best to aim for somewhere in between. Lebanon's midrange hotels represent good value, especially out of high season as rates drop dramatically. Renting a small car will mean you can see more of the country in much less time. Meals consisting of mezze will rarely cost more than US$10 per person, meaning you should still have change in your wallet for a cold local Almaza beer or two.

Ya Libnan (www.yalib nan.com) and the Daily Star (www.dailystar.com .lb) are both good online sources of up-to-date information on Lebanon.

TRAVEL LITERATURE

There are few contemporary travel books dealing specifically with Lebanon; *The Hills of Adonis: A Journey in Lebanon* (1990) by Colin Thubron is one of the best. Also well worth reading are William Dalrymple's *From the Holy Mountain: A Journey in the Shadow of Byzantium* (1997)

TRAVELLING SUSTAINABLY IN LEBANON

In the summer of 2006, the war between Israel and Hezbollah saw a large-scale environmental crisis hit Lebanon (see Oil Spill Lebanon, p259), damaging the natural and human world alike. Add to this a prolonged civil war, during which little attention was paid to vanishing natural resources, the Lebanese penchant for huntin', shootin' and fishin', a rash of uncontrolled building countrywide and a propensity for driving gas-guzzling monsters, and a somewhat disheartening picture emerges of Lebanon's current situation. Moreover, recent travails have left much of the country's population struggling financially: as the rich in Beirut get richer, the poor in many other parts of the country get poorer.

There are, however, many simple ways to have a positive impact while visiting the country.

- When visiting nature reserves, engage the services of one of the park's guides where possible, whose fee goes towards preserving and enhancing the area.

- Share the wealth among the lesser-known businesses: limiting your use of international chains will ensure a better distribution of tourist income and guarantee you a more interesting experience.

- Don't stick solely to our Eating recommendations: this is only a selection of what's on offer, and you'll quickly discover your own favourites if you venture where your tastebuds take you.

- Consider hiking with one of Lebanon's many trekking groups (see p382) who have valuable insights into low-impact tourism and often strive to help disadvantaged local communities.

- If you're renting a car, try to team up with other travellers to split the cost: you're reducing the environmental impact substantially if you can cram four travellers into a Fiat Punto.

- Look for recycling points for your plastic mineral-water bottles, which bob with the tide in alarming numbers along the Beirut sea shore.

- Take a registered guide to show you around ancient historical sites. In recent years, work has been sporadic for these invaluable sources of local knowledge.

- Peruse the eco-friendly links included in Lebanon's Environment chapter (p258).

TOP PICKS

LEBANON
Beirut •Damascus

BEST OF THE FESTIVALS

Lebanon's festivals are among the country's highlights for visitors. See individual chapter listings for more information.

- Al Bustan Festival (www.albustanfestival .com) February-March (p295)
- Beirut International Platform of Dance Festival (www.maqamat.org) April-May (p281)
- Souq el-Bargout, Beirut; May/June & November/December (p290)
- Byblos International Festival (www.byblos festival.org) June-July (p311)
- Baalbek Festival (www.baalbeck.org.lb) July & August (p354)
- Beiteddine Festival (www.beiteddine.org) July & August (p322)
- Beirut International Film Festival (www.beirutfilmfoundation.org) October (p281)
- Beirut Marathon (www.beirutmarathon.org) November (p281)
- Docudays: Beirut International Documentary Festival (www.docudays.net) November/December (p253)

MUST-SEE MOVIES

Lebanon's film industry, though small and frequently struggling, has turned out some treasures. Here's a selection to get you in the Middle Eastern mood. See p253 for more on Lebanese film.

- *Towards the Unknown* (1957) Director: Georges Nasser
- *The Broken Wings* (1962) Director: Yousef Malouf
- *Bint el-Haress* (1967) Director: Henry Barakat
- *The Little Wars* (1982) Director: Maroun Baghdadi
- *West Beirut* (1998) Director: Ziad Duweyri
- *In the Shadows of the City* (2000) Director: Jean Chamoun
- *Harab Libnan* (2001) Director: Omar al-Issawi
- *Bosta* (2005) Director: Philippe Aractingi
- *Giallo* (2005) Director: Antoine Waked
- *Caramel* (2007) Director: Nadine Labaki

TOP READS

A selection of stories – some fact, some fiction – together illustrate the many paradoxes that make up today's Lebanon. For more details on Lebanese literature, see p253.

- *The Prophet* (1923) Kahlil Gibran
- *Memory for Forgetfulness: August, Beirut 1982* (1982) Mahmoud Darwish
- *Death in Beirut* (1976) Tawfiq Yusuf Awwad
- *Sitt Marie Rose: A Novel* (1982) Etel Adnan
- *Beirut Blues* (1994) Hanan al-Shayk
- *The Rock of Tanios* (1994) Amin Maalouf
- *The Stone of Laughter* (1998) Hoda Barakat
- *Pity the Nation: Lebanon at War* (2001) Robert Fisk
- *Bliss Street* (2004) Kristin Kenway
- *Lebanon: A House Divided* (2006) Sandra Mackey

and Robert D Kaplan's *Eastward to Tartary: Travels in the Balkans, the Middle East and the Caucasus* (2000), both with chapters on travels in Lebanon.

A great vintage starting point is Mark Twain's wry *The Innocents Abroad* (1869) chronicling his journey across the Middle East in 1867.

Another good book depicting a Lebanon long-gone is the biography of colourful Lady Hester Stanhope (see also The Antics of Lady Hester, p371), *Lady Hester, Queen of the East* (2006) by Lorna Gibb.

Jean Said Makdisi's *Beirut Fragments: A War Memoir* (1990) and *Teta, Mother and Me* (2004) illustrate the difficult and dangerous day-to-day life of one woman and her family during the civil war, chronicled by Edward Said's sister. Thomas Friedman's *From Beirut to Jerusalem* (1995) also contains a grimly humorous account of life in Beirut during the difficult and dramatic war years.

For a lighter look at Lebanese life, get a hold of *Life's Like That! Your Guide to the Lebanese* (2004) and its sequel *Life's Even More Like That* (2006) by Michael Karam, Peter Grimsditch and Maya Fldawi, with painfully accurate caricatures of Lebanese characters, from dog-walking Filipino maids to Hummer drivers, ladies who lunch, and frazzled foreign correspondents. It's a must-have companion to people-watching at Beirut's cafés.

A good window into Lebanon's environmental issues is Green Line (www.greenline.org.lb), one of the country's most active environmental protection organisations.

INTERNET RESOURCES

Lebanon's Ministry of Tourism (www.destinationlebanon.gov.lb) An excellent resource from the Ministry, including maps, downloadable brochures, e-cards, and a themed trip planner.

Discover Lebanon (www.discoverlebanon.com) Photos, listings, maps and forums.

Lebanon Panorama (www.lebanonpanorama.com) Panoramic 360-degree views of Lebanon.

Lonely Planet (www.lonelyplanet.com.au) Succinct summaries on travelling to Lebanon, Thorn Tree bulletin board, accommodation listings and links to the most useful travel resources elsewhere on the web.

Lebanon's Culture

THE NATIONAL PSYCHE

Like its neighbour Syria, hospitality in Lebanon is spelt with a capital 'H' and despite its multiple setbacks and political upheavals, Lebanon remains one of the friendliest places in the world to visit. Beirut, in particular, welcomes visitors with open arms. Instead of being intimidated by heavily armed soldiers perched atop tanks on street corners, you'll soon find that even a simple smile will generally get you a 'welcome' and an enthusiastic wave. Moreover, the Lebanese diaspora is so widespread that no matter where you come from, almost everyone you meet will likely have a sibling, cousin or uncle living in your country – a link that will win you instant friends.

Most Lebanese share three distinct characteristics: an immense pride in their country and its diversity (you'll probably hear the phrase 'Lebanon has 18 official religions' more times than you can count), a reluctance to talk about the civil war – which most people would simply prefer to forget – and an overriding optimism that 'everything's going to be all right', with the good times just around the corner. While each of these things may seem a little paradoxical to a first-time visitor, you'll soon realise that each is essential to keeping the troubled country soldiering on, no matter how bad life gets.

Though politics, unemployment and corruption are hot topics, guaranteed to ignite lengthy and animated discussion, the Lebanese certainly don't let these aspects of their culture get them down. The Lebanese like to savour life, and most important is enjoying the good times with family and friends.

Spend a little time getting to know some locals and they'll soon consider you both.

LIFESTYLE

It's hard to generalise about a country that has traditionally experienced – and continues to experience – sharply delineated differences in generation, income and religion. While party-central Beirut seems, on the surface at least, no different from any European capital city, venture just a few dozen miles north or south and you'll find people in traditional villages living and farming almost exactly as they did a century ago. Add to this a substantial Palestinian population almost entirely cut off from the mainstream – and rarely referred to in conversation by the Lebanese themselves – and a complex picture begins to emerge.

One lifestyle factor that cuts across all boundaries is the crucial importance of family life in Lebanon. Extended families often live in close proximity, their social lives tightly bound together, and many children live at home until married, either to save money for their own home or simply because they prefer it that way. Social life, too, is both close-knit and gregarious: everyone within a small community tends to know everyone else, usually knowing as much about others' lives and business as they do about their own.

Marriage is the second factor of utmost importance throughout Lebanon and members of all religions tend to marry young. For women to remain unmarried into their 30s is rare and often raises eyebrows, though a man still single at 30, like anywhere in the Middle East, is thought to be waiting for the right girl. There's generally an expectation that people

Emily Nasrallah's *Flight Against Time* touches the subject of emigration from a slightly different perspective, telling the tale of rural parents whose children have left for new lives overseas.

Lebanon's 18 official sects are Muslim (Shiite, Alawite, Ismaili and Sunni), Christian (Maronite, Greek Orthodox & Catholic, Armenian Catholic, Gregorian, Syrian Orthodox, Jacobite, Nestorian, Chaldean, Copt, Evangelical and Roman Catholic), Druze and Jewish.

will marry within their religion; however, like many social expectations, this is slowly changing. Since Lebanon currently only legally recognises civil marriages contracted overseas, many mixed-religion couples opt for marriage in Cyprus or Greece, if one half of the couple (usually the woman) doesn't choose to convert.

For young Lebanese, Christians – both male and female – usually have far greater social freedom than Muslims or members of other religions, evident in Beirut's profusion of largely Christian-populated bars and clubs. But while these freedoms may at first appear similar to their counterparts in the West, there is a limit to what is deemed acceptable behaviour.

Drinking heavily, sleeping around or taking drugs is frowned upon in Lebanese society – not that you'd necessarily know it on a night out on Beirut's Rue Monot.

Christian and Muslim women in Lebanon are nowadays increasingly accepted into most professions. Particularly in Beirut you'll see a profusion of Filipino, Thai and Indian housemaids – recognisable by their frilly pink gingham aprons – who work full-time to cook, clean and look after the children while the mother of the house is out at work.

A university education is highly valued in Lebanon and for those who are not from a wealthy family this usually involves juggling a part-time job of at least 20 hours a week alongside attending classes. Many study with a view to emigrating overseas, lured by the promise of higher salaries, a phenomenon commonly known as Lebanon's 'brain drain': see The Brain Drain, below.

THE BRAIN DRAIN

A favourite Lebanese topic, which you'll likely encounter several times on your travels, is the country's 'brain drain'. Current unofficial estimates suggest that one in three educated Lebanese citizens would like to live abroad, while a recent study by the Beirut Research and Development Centre (BRDC) found that 22% of the Lebanese population is actively working on ways to leave the country. Another survey of university students showed that as many as 60% are hoping to leave Lebanon following graduation, to work abroad.

There are a number of reasons why so many of Lebanon's bright young things are disappearing elsewhere, not the least the climate of fear that has lingered after the Israel–Hezbollah war of summer 2006. Terrorist attacks on Lebanese politicians, in which civilians are sometimes caught up, have also sent young Lebanese, especially those with dual nationality and thus an easy 'escape route', in pursuit of jobs overseas. Most popular tend to be the burgeoning Gulf states, which have the advantage of high salaries and being fairly close to home, with the USA, Canada and Europe all coming in close behind.

The second major reason for the mass exit is that salaries in Lebanon are often simply too low to make for a comfortable, viable living. 'I've got a great job, a car, a high salary,' explains Mirvat Melki, a software engineer originally from Beirut, on leave from a lucrative position in Ghana. 'All the things I could never dream of having here in Lebanon, even though I'm pretty highly qualified. I earn about 10 times as much, per month, there as I would do here – if I could get a job at all.' Melki says that those who have managed to acquire good jobs – often through family connections – hold tight to them and are reluctant to relinquish the security and move on. Many younger, educated people, he continues, are afraid for the country's future. 'Politics aren't safe; taxes are high; economics are bad. It cost me US$100,000 to go to university. In Lebanon, I'd have to work for a million years to pay that back. I miss home, but under these conditions, what choice do I have?' Perhaps one day, he says, he'll come home – but until then, like so many young Lebanese professionals, he's enjoying the financial freedom of a life overseas too much to really consider it.

POPULATION

Lebanon's population of just over four million people is boosted by its Palestinian refugees, the UN Relief and Works Agency (UNRWA) putting the total registered refugees at 408,438.

The population is urban-based, with around 90% of people living in the main cities, and Beirut being the most populated (over 1.5 million), followed by Tripoli, Sidon and Tyre. The population growth rate is around 1.2%, with an average of 1.88 children per household, both figures very low for the Middle East. Lebanon has a youthful population, and more than a quarter is under 14 years of age.

Lebanon hosts 18 'official' religious groups, along with small populations of Baha'is, Mormons, Buddhists and Hindus; Muslims are estimated at around 60% of the population. Before the civil war, unofficial statistics put the ratio closer to 50:50, Muslim to Christian; the shift is attributed to the mass emigration of Christians during and after the civil war, and higher birth rates among Muslims.

An interesting *International Herald Tribune* article on sectarian strife within Lebanon's soccer community can be found at www.iht.com/articles /2007/10/24/sports /CUP.php.

SPORT

Though sport doesn't play as dominant a part on Lebanon's cultural scene as it does, for example, in many European countries, there's nevertheless a loyal football (soccer) following, which remains a male-dominated pastime for participants and fans alike. Basketball is also a popular spectator sport, and Lebanon has hosted several regional championships. The Asian Athletics Championships, scheduled for Lebanon in 2007, were moved at the last minute due to the unstable political climate, a factor which continues to hamper sports participation on an international level.

The most popular nonprofessional sports in Lebanon are probably skiing and hiking, with paragliding and potholing also becoming increasingly popular. During the summer months, the usual range of water sports is practised along the coast, though there's as much strutting and preening as serious swimming going on at most of Lebanon's beaches. See p381 if you're keen to participate in Lebanon's outdoor pursuits, or individual destination chapters for beach club and ski listings.

MULTICULTURALISM

Lebanon is made up of a patchwork of religious and cultural groups, many having settled in Lebanon to escape persecution in other countries. These include the Armenians, who arrived en masse in Lebanon in 1915 to escape massacre at the hands of the Ottomans; a large Armenian community today exists in the small town of Aanjar (p351) in the Bekaa Valley. While Armenians have largely managed to integrate into mainstream Lebanese society, one group still largely outside it is the Palestinian refugees, who have no real rights in Lebanon. Only a tiny proportion have been granted citizenship, possibly due to Lebanon's belief that granting citizenship to Palestinians gives the Israelis more justification for never allowing right of return, and unless you take a trip out to a refugee camp their presence as a cultural force in Lebanon is almost nonexistent. See The Displaced and the Dispossessed (p34) for more on the Palestinians of Lebanon.

WOMEN IN LEBANON

Lebanon's women today hold a complicated and contradictory place in a society which, though in many ways is more liberal than its Arab neighbours, is nevertheless far from gender-equal.

NAYLA MOAWAD

Though women may, in many spheres of Lebanese life, appear to be enjoying more freedom than ever before, one area in which they remain under-represented is politics. With only a handful of female MPs currently holding office – less, indeed, than in Syria or Jordan – one who has made it her business is Lebanon's first female minister, Nayla Moawad, Minister for Social Affairs, who in 2004 announced her candidacy for the since frequently postponed presidential elections.

Born in 1940 in the small mountain town of Bcharré, 13 years before Lebanese women were granted the vote, Moawad trained as a journalist, reading English at Cambridge University. It wasn't until the assassination in 1989 of her husband, René Moawad, just days after he became president of Lebanon, that she decided to continue his legacy by entering politics herself. In doing so, she became the first woman in post–civil war Lebanon to venture into the political arena, likening her mission to that of a soldier, passing the torch from comrade to comrade.

Having been a member of the Lebanese National Assembly since 1991, Moawad has served as an advocate for women's rights and democracy, setting up the René Moawad Foundation in 1990, dedicated to promoting social and rural development; she is also president of the Centre for Research and Education on Democracy. Inspiring a new generation of powerful female figures, including Sunni MP Bahia Hariri, sister of assassinated former Prime Minister Rafiq Hariri, Moawad believes that the participation of women in Lebanon's politics isn't a matter of religion, sect or background, but simply a matter of conviction, courage – and time.

One of the most crucial hurdles for women's equality in Lebanon lies in the sectarian judicial system. Religious, rather than civil, courts govern personal status matters including divorce, inheritance and marriage. This essentially means that women are not only not equal to men, but also not equal to each other: since 1959, for example, Christian women have been entitled to the same inheritance as male heirs, whereas Muslim women still usually only receive half. Amnesty International also points out that there is little protection under current civil law against female-targeted violence in the family; some religious courts may rule, for instance, that a physically abused woman is obliged to return to her spouse.

Nevertheless, with around 50% of university graduates nowadays being female and women comprising well over a quarter of the labour force, it's clear that the place of women in Lebanese society is changing – if all too slowly. Throw in a new generation of prominent and empowered female singers, actors, writers and journalists, and most Lebanese women would argue that such change has already successfully begun.

For more on the work of the René Moawad Foundation, go to the foundation's website at www.rmf.org.lb.

MEDIA

In its 2006 Press Freedom Index, **Reporters Without Borders** (www.rsf.org) ranked Lebanon 107th of 168 listings, with the highest level of press freedom being enjoyed by Finland and the lowest being North Korea. Lebanon came somewhere between Sierra Leone and Cambodia, having fallen substantially over the last five years from 56th place to its current ranking largely due to the volatile political climate. Reporters Without Borders asserts that Lebanon's media 'is some of the freest and most experienced in the Arab world', but recent factors have undermined such positive statements. Dangers exist to journalists, as they do the rest of the population, as an indirect result of everyday risks associated with living with political instability. In 2006 a 23-year-old photojournalist and a technician for the Lebanese Broadcasting Corporation (LBC) were both killed by Israeli air strikes. Those in the media must also negotiate a landscape of potential consequences, including harassment or even assassination, for stating unpopular views. The murders of prominent anti-Syrian journalists Gibran Tueni and

TO BOLDLY GO...

Soon after the assassination of former Prime Minister Rafiq Hariri on Valentine's Day 2005, a pair of Lebanese media professionals got together to discuss what they perceived as a gap in independent news coverage of the ensuing turmoil in Lebanon. One was 28 years old, an IT expert with a background in building innovative websites; the other, aged 60, a seasoned journalist in retirement, with the urge to fill that gap.

The result was *Ya Libnan* (www.yalibnan.com), an English-language Lebanese news site that now provides arguably the best, most diverse, and unquestionably the most exciting up-to-date account of Lebanon's fast-paced cultural, political and security situation. The site offers writers the option of anonymity, though many opt to nevertheless print their by-lines. The founders have no illusions about freedom of the press, aware that some writers are wary to express views or perspectives in a climate in which assassinations and harassment of journalists have both occurred. By allowing its writers the choice, the Ya Libnan team believe they're able to access the widest possible pool of writers, and the greatest cross-section of independent viewpoints.

'We were frustrated with the perspectives coming from the various Lebanese news outlets,' explains the younger of *Ya Libnan*'s cofounders, who himself prefers to remain anonymous. 'Most media organisations are owned or tied to politicians, so you end up with heavily weighted news. We couldn't get our hands on any independent news out of Lebanon, and decided to start a blog about it.'

The blog proved so successful that it quickly ballooned, harnessing the power of fellow bloggers to create what the founders call a 'mass collaboration portal, delivering news in a professional format'.

'All our writers are volunteers,' the younger cofounder explains, 'over 100 writers from many different countries, with some sort of connection to Lebanon. They come from all kinds of backgrounds and ages, providing a whole host of perspectives. That's why there's not really a consistent style on the site; it changes quite a lot. And since they're all volunteers, there are no agendas, either political or financial.'

And they don't seem to be afraid of telling it like it is – in any arena. When Cirque du Soleil came to town in the summer of 2006, *Ya Libnan* was at pains not to flatter what it deemed a lacklustre performance; the result was an icy review, in contrast to glowing praise in the mass media. The site's sole agenda, it appears, is to make the world aware of Lebanon and of the diversity it encompasses. Currently, its top readerships are the USA, Lebanon, Canada and Australia, with more than one million unique users in 2006 alone. 'Unfortunately,' grins the cofounder, 'when Lebanon hits its biggest crises, our news ratings pick up. When we have a nice quiet summer, our site doesn't get viewed so much.'

And if, after a few weeks glued to its coverage, you feel the need to support its worthy aims, you can either contribute, or purchase a few items from *Ya Libnan*'s own line in pro-Lebanon wares. Its bumper stickers, coffee mugs and badges all proclaim the message you'll hear time and again while on the road in Lebanon: 'Druze, Muslim, Christian: LEBANESE.'

Samir Kassir in 2005 have significantly fuelled these fears. The founders of online news site *Ya Libnan* (see To Boldly Go..., above) offer their writers the option of anonymity, therefore hopefully allowing freedom of speech and opinion while ensuring author safety.

Lebanon's TV fare is far from unbiased, with each of the most popular commercial stations – Future TV (a favourite of Sunni Muslims), LBC (largely targeting Maronite Christians), news channel NBN and New TV – having their own clear agenda and political allegiances. Lebanon also allows elected politicians to have active ownership of media outlets. Much of what's shown on each, though, is the standard televisual fare of sitcoms, American movies, local soap operas and Mexican telenovelas.

Similarly, many newspapers have one slant or another. But *An Nahar*, an Arabic daily, the *Daily Star* in English and *L'Orient-Le Jour* in French are three titles that largely defy the party line and are well worth keeping an eye on for news, commentary and analysis. See p269 for more on Lebanon's print publications.

ARTS
Literature

Though Beirut was the publishing powerhouse of the Middle East for most of the 20th century, like most cultural activities it suffered during the war and much of its recent literary content has been shaped by this drawn-out and horrific event. Even today, a great deal of Lebanon's literary output remains concerned with themes drawn from these 15 years of hardship.

The Arab Book Fair in Beirut has been held every year since 1956 for around 10 days in spring.

Modern Lebanese writers fall into two distinct groups: those who stayed on to write about the conflict from personal 'frontline' experience, often known as the 'Beirut decentrists', and those who sought safety elsewhere or were born overseas of Lebanese parents. Of those who remained in Lebanon, Emily Nasrallah is a leading figure, and her novel *Flight Against Time* is highly regarded. Those who work overseas include the younger London-based Tony Hanania, born in 1964, whose book *Unreal City* is the story of a young scion from a feudal family who leaves for England, returns to war-torn Lebanon and falls in with Hezbollah fighters as he searches for meaning amid anarchy. Amin Maalouf, who relocated to Paris at the outbreak of the civil war, is another notable name. His most enchanting book, *The Rock of Tanios*, set in a Lebanese village where the sheikh's son disappears after rebelling against the system, is considered by many to be his masterpiece.

Of those authors most widely available in translation, Lebanon's two major figures are Elias Khoury, who lives in Lebanon, and feminist author Hanan al-Shaykh, who's based in London. Al-Shaykh's *The Story of Zahra* is a harrowing account of the civil war, while her *Beirut Blues* is a series of long, rambling letters that contrast Beirut's cosmopolitan past with its war-torn present. Elias Khoury has published 10 novels, many available in translation, and serves as editor for the weekly cultural supplement of *An Nahar*. His 1998 novel *Gate of the Sun* has achieved particular international acclaim. For some reading recommendations, see p246.

Poet Khalil Gibran (1883–1931; see p341) remains the celestial light in Lebanon's poetry scene, though modern poetry, too, has been thriving in Lebanon since the 1950s, with many poets from other Arab countries flocking to Beirut to take advantage of its thriving, and relatively liberal, scene. Interestingly, today many young poets are emerging from the largely Shiite south, a movement known as Shu'ara al-Janub (Poets from the South), for whom poetry seems to be a means to express the frustrations and despair of life in that particularly war-ravaged region.

An in-depth account of Lebanese literature, for the serious scholar, is provided by Elise Salem in *Constructing Lebanon: A Century of Literary Narratives*.

Cinema

Though Lebanese cinema has never been able to compete with the Bollywood-scale production of Cairo's slush and schlock, it has nevertheless survived the raw years and is appearing back on the scene with vigour and verve. **Docudays** (www.docudays.com), Beirut's annual documentary festival, is highly regarded internationally, and attracts a global crowd and jury, while there are several film academies in the city churning out young hopefuls.

In 2007 two Lebanese directors, Nadine Labaki and Danielle Arbid, made it to the prestigious Cannes Film Festival with their respective films *Caramel* and *Un Homme Perdu*. *Un Homme Perdu* tells the story of a French photographer who meets a mysterious, solitary figure who disappeared from Lebanon 17 years earlier. *Caramel*, meanwhile, is the tale of five Lebanese women, each from a different religious background and generation group, who meet at a Beirut beauty salon, using the caramel of the title to wax their legs. Labaki herself – a notable music video director – plays Layal, a salon worker having an affair with a married man. The film also deals with interreligious marriage and lesbianism, among other themes.

The greatest of the past cinematic stars was undoubtedly Georges Nasser, whose tragic 1958 *Ila Ayn (Whither?)* is a classic of Lebanese cinema, and became the first film to represent Lebanon at Cannes. Later, in Lebanon's heady 1960s, state intervention in the Egyptian film industry drove many Egyptian moviemakers into exile, causing levels of production to increase dramatically in Lebanon from a handful per year in 1965 to about 200 films in 1975. This meant, however, that Lebanese cinema became an industry driven by expatriates, and it wasn't until the 1970s that a number of talented Lebanese directors emerged, including Maroun Baghdadi, whose 1975 movie *Beirut Oh Beirut* was one of several film responses to the outbreak of the civil war. Baghdadi died an untimely death in 1993, aged just 43, after falling down an elevator shaft.

The civil war temporarily brought Lebanon's film industry to a virtual halt, with most filmmakers forced to work outside the country, seldom having their films shown within its boundaries. Baghdadi continued to work (winning an award at Cannes) and, ironically, many critics believe that Lebanese cinema actually produced some of its best work under highly restricted circumstances in response to the tragic war.

By 1992 the film industry was once again finding its feet, with the controversial (and initially banned) *Tornado*, directed by Samir Habchi, again dealing with the civil war. It tells the story of a young Lebanese student on a visit home from the Soviet Union, who finds himself actively involved in the conflict. In 1998, *West Beirut*, directed by LA-based Ziad Doueiri (a former cameraman for Quentin Tarantino) won international critical acclaim. The lyrical, funny film tells the semiautobiographical story of a teenager living in West Beirut during the first year of the civil war. The same year, Palestinian filmmaker Mai Masri made a highly acclaimed award-winning documentary, *Children of Shatila*, which looks at the history of the notorious refugee camp as seen through the eyes of children. Look out for her new documentary, *33 Days*, filmed under Israeli bombardment in the summer of 2007, and, at the other end of the genre spectrum, for Michel Kammoun's first film *Falafel*, a romantic comedy involving a young man on his perilous way to a Beirut party.

Music

Much of the music popular in Lebanon is equally renowned in Syria; for more, see p71. In both countries, music is rarely far away wherever you are, with strains of both traditional songstresses and contemporary rap and lounge wafting from every passing car or bullet-riddled apartment building. Beirut's music production industry is flourishing – some say almost rivalling Cairo's – and, hand in hand, its music video industry is blossoming.

Lebanon's two most famous female vocalists are the living legend Fairouz and the younger Najwa Karam, known as the 'sun of Lebanese song'. Fairouz has enjoyed star status since her first recording in Damascus in the 1950s, and later became an icon for Lebanon during the civil war

Arab Film Distribution (www.arabfilm.com) sells DVDs and VHS copies of new and remastered Lebanese movies and documentaries, and ship internationally.

The Beirut Film Foundation (www.beirut filmfoundation.org) works on several projects to keep Lebanese cinema alive, including the restoration of old film prints.

(which she sat out in Paris). Her concert in downtown Beirut following the end of the fighting attracted 40,000 people and provided a potent symbol of reunification.

Now in her 70s, she still performs several concerts annually, composing new songs with her son Ziad, a renowned experimental jazz performer.

Najwa Karam has created an international audience for traditional Lebanese music, rising to stardom during the 1990s and proving her worth with a sell-out world tour in 1996. With more than 16 albums under her belt, including the 2001 *Nedmaneh,* which sold four million copies worldwide, she remains a driving force on the Lebanese music scene.

Current hot names in mainstream pop include Nancy Ajram, whose brand of cute, sassy Lebanese pop sees albums frequently selling into the millions, as well as songstress Haifa, and all female outfit The 4 Cats with catchy tunes and raunchy videos along much the same lines. More good, solid pop is presented from a male perspective by Fadl Shakir.

A popular musician who marries classical Arabic music with contemporary sounds is Marcel Khalife, from Amchit, near Byblos. An *oud* (lute) player with a cult following, Khalife has many songs with a controversial political side, such as his composition for the dead of the Sabra and Shatila refugee camps.

On the dance floors and in the laid-back bars of Beirut's Rue Monot and Rue Gouraud, contemporary fusions of oriental trip-hop, lounge, drum and bass, and traditional Arabic music, for both the dance floors and chilling out, have dominated sound systems for the last few years. Said Mrad's best-selling 2001 album *Orient Back Beats/2001 Nights* comprises techno and dance remixes of traditional Arab songs, while the Beirut-based REG Project – featuring Ralph Khoury, Elie Barbar and Guy Manoukian – specialises in Arab deep house and lounge. You'll hear these sounds, along with traditional belly-dancing tunes remixed to an electronic beat to enrapture a new generation of listeners, almost anywhere you stop off for a strong drink, and a dance, or two.

If you're looking for driving music, some radio channels to tune into are:

88.0 Nostalgie: Easy listening in French and English

99.9 Fame FM: Dance music

105.5 Radio One: Rock, pop and dance

LOOKING FOR LIVE MUSIC

Across Lebanon you'll be presented with plenty of opportunities to experience the country's many forms of live music, if you know where to look. In Beirut, your best points of reference are newspaper and magazine listings (p269) along with flyers and posters, which you'll find largely on the streets of Hamra (p271) and at the Virgin Megastore (p267) on the Place des Martyrs. Along with one-off concerts, several Beirut venues offer reliable live music options almost every night of the week. Try the Blue Note (p288) for live jazz, the Gemmayzeh Café (p288) for traditional Lebanese sounds and Bar Louie (p286) for funky small live outfits.

Outside the capital, it may be more difficult to track down live music, though during the summer months you're likely to stumble across small local festivals with great local music performances in a variety of shapes and sizes. Across the country, there are also a few notable places to head to for evening drinks and tunes. The Cafés du Bardouni in Zahlé (p350) usually have live performances in the summer months, while up north, the cafés in Ehden's central square or at the source of the Mar Sarkis Spring (p339) are good choices. Up the coast from Beirut, the Citadelle Café (p311) at Byblos has nice live performances on Friday nights, and down south the Al-Midane Café (p320) at Deir al-Qamar has great live music at the atmospheric town square on summer weekends.

On top of all this, there are, of course, Lebanon's many larger music festivals; see p246 for a list of the best.

Architecture

For information about Baalbek's spectacular remains, see p354; for traces of the Romans in Beirut, see p276; and for details on the Umayyad ruins at Aanjar, see p351.

For further information on B 018 and Bernard Khoury's more recent architectural projects, go to the projects section of www.bernard khoury.com.

Much of Lebanon's less-ancient heritage architecture has been damaged over the last century by the combined effects of war and redevelopment, but there remain a substantial number of examples of the country's traditional architecture dotted about the country. Beirut's beautiful old Arabic-Italian crossbreed buildings can still be seen on the Ain al-Mreisse Corniche (p273), in the backstreets of Achrafiye (p276) and Gemmayzeh (p278) and near the American University of Beirut (AUB) in Hamra and Ras Beirut (p271).

In contrast, most buildings constructed since the 1960s are fairly miserable, weather-beaten concrete blocks ranging in design from spartan to '70s space-age, although there are some modernist gems, particularly in Achrafiye. In Downtown (Beirut Central District; p274) many of the buildings were too damaged by the war to be saved, and masterly reconstruction has been accomplished in the 'spirit' of the original.

In regional Lebanon, styles vary. To the north, Tripoli's old city (p329) contains a wealth of medieval and Islamic architecture, while a fine collection of 18th-century merchants' houses can be seen in the small town of Amchit (p312), north of Byblos. Deir al-Qamar (p317), in the southern Chouf Mountains, is a well-preserved village, with some beautiful 18th- and 19th-century villas and palaces. Beiteddine Palace (p320), also in the Chouf Mountains, is a melange of Italian and traditional Arab architecture, although it is more remarkable for its lavish interiors than any architectural innovation.

Interior designers are doing wonderful work in Lebanon today. For the most part thoughtful, playful and stylish, it's often a shame that many places are either private residences or clubs that don't last long enough for people to pay a visit. One notable exception is the nightclub B 018 (p289) designed by Bernard Khoury. Situated on the former Green Line, the club pays homage to the past at a site that was formerly a quarantine zone, a refugee camp and the site of an appalling massacre during the war – and is worth a visit as much for its appearance as its sizzling tunes and funky crowd.

Painting, Visual Arts & Photography

For a Beirut-based photographic archive of the Arab world, go to the Arab Image Foundation at www.fai.org.lb.

Lebanon's first art school, the Académie Libanaise des Beaux-Arts, was established in 1937, and 20 years later AUB established its Department of Fine Arts. The two institutions have nurtured a growing artistic community. In the 1950s and 1960s a number of galleries opened to showcase the country's art, while the private Sursock Museum (p276), in Achrafiye, also began to show new artists. By the 1960s a group of artists and scholars, headed by Janine Rubeiz, had formed Dar el-Fan (Place of Art), providing a vibrant forum for artists to gather and discuss their work.

Like most of Lebanon's cultural output, the visual arts suffered during the civil war, but the scene reestablished itself with vigour soon afterwards and today there's a thriving artistic community in Beirut. Apart from the earlier William Blake–style paintings of poet Khalil Gibran, famous 20th-century artists include the painters Hassan Jouni, Moustafa Farroukh and Mohammad Rawas. Better-known contemporary painters include Marwan Rechmaoui, Bassam Kahwaji, Amin al-Basha, Helen Khal and Etel Adnan (who, like Gibran, is also a writer).

Many galleries exhibit sculpture as well as painting. Contemporary figures to look out for include Rudy Rahmé, Camille Allam, and Catalan-born Ana Corbero who draws inspiration from her life in Lebanon, while a permanent sculpture display can be seen at the workshop and galleries at the home of the Basbous brothers in the village of Rachana (p313), to the north of Beirut. Their larger works line the streets nearby and attract many visitors, especially on weekends. Another contemporary famous name is abstract painter Salwa Zeidan, whose works are in many major private collections worldwide and whose exhibitions regularly travel the globe.

The photography and visual arts scene is the most vibrant and cutting-edge of all the arts in the region, and can be experienced at local galleries such as Espace SD (p278).

The best other places to experience the current Lebanese visual arts scene in all its forms are the numerous small galleries around Hamra and Gemmayzeh and in the studios of Saifi Village (p289); we have also listed some of Beirut's current best galleries (p278). Check newspaper and magazine listings for upcoming gallery openings (see p269); Beirut's cultural centres (p268) also put on regular shows.

Beirut's Espace SD gallery website features info on the exhibitions and artists at www.espacesd.com.

Theatre & Dance

Most theatre in Lebanon is based in Beirut, where prominent, established and esteemed Lebanese playwrights such as Roger Assaf, Jalal Khoury and the late Issam Mahfouz inspire and encourage younger artists – though lack of funding remains a perennial problem – and a revitalised Lebanese theatre scene is gradually emerging.

The Théâtre de Beyrouth (p289) in Ain al-Mreisse (Minet al-Hosn) puts on high-quality performances (often experimental works) by young actors and playwrights. It also hosts foreign productions and is a good place to find quality English- or French-language theatre. Al-Medina Theatre (p289) is a performance venue based in West Beirut, which shows plays, primarily in Arabic, while in Achrafiye, Monnot Theatre (p289) tends to show French-language productions. The AUB campus has a theatre, which sometimes performs plays in English, although the quality of the productions varies wildly.

For more on the dance troupe Caracalla, go to www.caracalladance.com.

As in Syria, both raqs sharki (belly dancing) and *dabke,* the traditional Levantine folk dance widely known as Lebanon's national dance, are popular. For more on these, see p73. Caracalla, meanwhile, is the closest thing Lebanon has to a national dance troupe. Founded by Abdel-Halim Caracalla, the choreographer of the Baalbek Festival in the 1960s, the group's performances are inspired by oriental dance, but combine opera, dance and theatre. With colourful costumes and musicals based on diverse sources, from Shakespeare to modern Lebanese literature, they can be seen at some of Lebanon's summer festivals, and at the Monnot Theatre in Achrafiye.

Lebanon's Environment

If you enter Lebanon via Beirut, the first thing you'll notice is that the country appears to pay its natural surroundings very little regard. Beirut's streets, though quite clean, are littered with recyclable material due to the city's lack of recycling facilities. The streets are rarely leafy and there is a dearth of city parks. With Beirutis driving close to 1.5 million cars within the compact city limits, you'll also notice the air pollution, especially in the summer months when the smog hanging over the city can seem to have the consistency of soup. Beirut's coastline, too, could do with some improvement. Empty water bottles, plastic bags and other nonbiodegradable refuse scatter its rock pools, and the public beaches to the south of Beirut aren't recommended for swimming due to water pollution and yet more rubbish floating in on the tide.

Drive north along the coast and the picture becomes even bleaker. Decades of unfettered building work have created an almost unbroken strip of unattractive development extending from Beirut at least as far as Byblos, with only a short break in the sprawl before building up again on the outskirts of Tripoli. This stretch of development teeters up the mountain slopes away from the coast, making for a welcome break for both eyes and lungs when it finally thins out towards Lebanon's central mountain ranges.

Historically, it's unsurprising that the environment hasn't been top of the country's agenda. A 15-year civil war, combined with social turbulence and economic woes before, during and after, has meant that energies and financial resources have, consequently, been channelled elsewhere.

The absence of basic services during the war also meant that solid waste was dumped throughout the country. Although the worst of these excesses were cleaned up with the creation of massive landfill sites, there continues to be a lack of general environmental awareness and adequate waste disposal. As late as the mid-1990s Lebanon still did not have a single functioning wastewater treatment plant, and raw sewage was pouring out to sea. A number of treatment plants have since been rehabilitated and new ones built, but offshore water quality remains a concern.

The biggest recent environmental crisis to hit Lebanon, however, occurred during the 2006 Israel–Hezbollah war, when Israeli aircraft bombed the coastal power plant at Jiyyeh, south of Beirut. An estimated 15,000 tonnes of fuel oil spilled into the sea, threatening wildlife, marine life and delicate ecosystems, as well as the livelihoods of local fishermen (see Oil Spill Lebanon opposite).

But despite this gloomy picture, there are plenty of signs that Lebanon's environment is becoming of greater concern on both a public and governmental level. Tapping into the country's ecotourism potential – since large areas of Lebanon thankfully remain unravaged by pollution or building work – government agencies are realising there's actually profit to be had in protecting Lebanon's greatest, most diverse resource. See The Lebanon Mountain Trail (p338) and Trekking (p382) for more information and listings of just a few of the many ecotrekking operations to choose from if you're planning on hiking around the country's scenic treasures. Paradoxically, one area that has suffered the least damage is the south of the country, since massive numbers of land mines, cluster bomblets and other unexploded ordnance have left the area largely undeveloped and unspoilt, though sadly as out-of-bounds to visitors as ever.

For updates on Lebanon's environmental situation, look at the UN Environment Programme reports at www.unep.org/Lebanon/.

OIL SPILL LEBANON

The Jiyyeh oil spill of summer 2006, which saw thousands of tonnes of fuel oil pour into the sea, constitutes the biggest environmental crisis ever to hit the Eastern Mediterranean basin. The spill extended 120km along Lebanon's shoreline and reached as far north as the Syrian coast.

Within a week, volunteer groups and environmental agencies had flocked in to assess the damage and begin clean-up operations, with groups of volunteers working around the clock to contain and collect the oil. It was, however, too late for much of the oil, which had sunk to the seabed causing damage to marine ecosystems.

Environmentalists contend that the damage has not ended there. With beaches thick with residue, endangered green turtle hatchlings were in some places unable to make it from the beach to the sea. In other coastal locations, distress to the marine balance has led to a scarcity of the foods that rare migrating birds usually feed on along Lebanon's shores.

A year after the crisis, a report published by Greenline (www.greenline.org.lb), one of Lebanon's biggest volunteer-based environmental organisations, contended that the country's shores remained severely polluted. The report went on to say that international agencies differed in their opinion on the spill's long-term effects. While the UN Environment Programme (UNEP) stated that damage was moderate and the effects not long-lasting, the UN Development Programme (UNDP) assessed the damage as severe and long-term.

Either way, clean-up efforts and independent environmental assessments continue and are likely to do so for some time. For the latest on Lebanon's seas in the aftermath, visit Oil Spill Lebanon at www.oilspilllebanon.org.

It's promising that dozens of NGOs and volunteer groups have sprung up independently, to push for greater care of Lebanon's natural wonders. Some of the best and most widely known are listed throughout this chapter. There are also campaigns underway to promote awareness of the dangers of pesticide use. Some restaurants in Beirut are now trying to use organic produce (see p290 for Souq el-Tayeb, Beirut's first organic farmers market), and farmers are being taught about alternatives to chemical pesticides and fertilisers.

While there is undoubtedly a long way to go, ongoing improvements to existing nature reserves, such as the Tyre Beach Nature Reserve (p376) and Aamiq Marsh (p261), and the creation of new forest areas such as the recently opened Horsh Beirut (p280), show signs that all is not lost in Lebanon's battle to keep its countryside as green as its cedar-tree emblem, regardless of the political or social situation of the moment.

THE LAND

Roughly half the size of Wales, Lebanon is one of the world's smallest countries. Within its borders, though, lie several incredibly diverse geographical regions, and considerably more greenery than in any other country in the Middle East.

First, there is the narrow coastal strip, alternating between sandy beaches and rocky outcrops forming natural ports, on which the major cities are situated. Inland, the 'backbone' formed by the Mt Lebanon Range rises steeply with a dramatic set of peaks and ridges; the highest peak, Qornet as-Sawda, reaches over 3000m, and is located southeast of Tripoli. South of Beirut are the beautiful Chouf Mountains, which become progressively lower in altitude as you head south. This is an area particularly abundant in waterfalls, due to a layer of nonporous rock that forces water to the surface in large enough quantities to produce large springs at elevations of up to 1500m. The result is that you'll spot crops being cultivated at unusually high altitudes when travelling in the area.

The Lebanese Ministry of the Environment has details of its activities and press releases available at www.moe.gov.lb.

To the east the Mt Lebanon Range gives way steeply to the Bekaa Valley, 150km from end to end. Although low in comparison with the mountain peaks, it's still 1000m above sea level. Flanked by mountains, the Bekaa Valley lies in a rain shadow and is considerably more arid than the rest of the country; nevertheless, it is the major agricultural area, especially noted for its high-quality wines – along with its less visible crops of cannabis. Further east again, and forming a natural border with Syria, the Jebel Libnan ash-Sharqiyya (Anti-Lebanon Range) rises in a sheer arid massif from the plain.

WILDLIFE
Animals
Slowly, it seems, the Lebanese are being weaned off their addiction to hunting, shooting or spearing anything wild that dares step, swim or glide within its diminutive borders. Over the last few years, increasingly strict hunting bans have been put in place, resulting in once-prolific indigenous species beginning to repopulate the country's reserves. Wolves, wild boar, ibexes and gazelles may remain endangered species in Lebanon, but they have once again been sighted in the glorious Chouf Cedar Reserve (p323), along with wild cats, porcupines and badgers.

One group of creatures that has, in general, been less affected by Lebanon's troubled past are the vast numbers of migrating birds that pass through its airspace on paths between Africa and Europe or Asia. Some 135 species of bird have been observed off the Lebanese coast, while further out at the Palm Islands Reserve (p333), over 300 have been seen. A variety of nesting birds make their homes on the islands, including the mistle thrush, tern, broad-billed sandpiper, osprey and various types of finch, while endangered turtle species come ashore to lay their eggs. The Bekaa Valley is another extremely important migratory stop for millions of birds, including storks (which pass through every April), hoopoes, red-rumped swallows, buzzards, golden eagles and kestrels – so if birds are your thing, all you'll need is a pair of binoculars and a notebook to be in ornithological heaven.

Plants
In spite of widespread deforestation before, during and after the war, Lebanon remains the most densely wooded of all the Middle Eastern countries. Many varieties of pine, including Aleppo pine, flourish on the mountains, in addition to juniper, oak, beech and cypress. In spring there is an abundance of wildflowers on the hills and mountains, including the indigenous Lebanon violet.

That said, the most famous flora of all in Lebanon – the cedar tree – is now found on only a few mountaintop sites, notably at Bcharré and near Barouk in the Chouf Mountains. These lonely groves are all that remain of the once-great cedar forests; however, there are some sites where new trees are being planted. It will take centuries before new forests look anything like their predecessors. For information on Lebanon's cedar trees, see p324.

NATIONAL PARKS & RESERVES
Lebanon's national parks and reserves are well worth visiting and supporting. Home to diverse flora and fauna, most have a 'Friends Association', offering both environmental and practical information for visitors, and can organise a guide to accompany you on walks. Recently, several small new reserves have been created – albeit with tiny budgets and

The Society for the Protection of Nature in Lebanon (www.spnlb .org) is a dynamic organisation, committed to conserving Lebanon's wildlife in all its forms.

The Association for Forests, Development and Conservation (www.afdc .org.lb) runs reforestation, firefighting and ecotourism programmes, as well as an ecolodge 7km from the Chouf Cedar Reserve.

A wealth of information on Chouf Cedar Reserve's work, programmes and visitor information can be found on their website at www.shoufcedar.org.

extremely long-term goals in mind – showing that signs bode well for Lebanon's natural future.

Chouf Cedar Reserve

Lebanon's largest nature reserve, Chouf Cedar Reserve (p323) covers over 50,000 hectares – an astonishing 5% of the country's entire area. Established in 1996, it's well managed and easy to visit, boasting six cedar forests, including three that contain old-growth cedars, and a huge variety of flora and fauna, including a number of endangered species.

Horsh Ehden's website can be found at www .horshehden.org.

Horsh Ehden Forest Nature Reserve

Just 3km from the summer resort of Ehden, this small reserve (p339) comprises a unique natural habitat supporting rare indigenous trees and plants, including the Cicilian fir, the Lebanon violet and the Ehden milk vetch along with dozens of rare birds and butterflies.

More information on the conservation of Aamiq Marsh can be found at http:// en.arocha.org/lebanon/.

Palm Islands Reserve

A series of islands lying 5km off the coast of Tripoli, the Palm Islands Reserve (p333) covers 5 sq km of land and sea and form an important nesting place for marine birds as well as turtles and Mediterranean monk seals.

Aamiq Marsh

Aamiq Marsh (p354), halfway between Chtaura and Lake Qaraoun, is Lebanon's last major wetland. The area is a haven for migrating and aquatic birds, but was in a perilous state until a Christian nature conservation organisation began working with locals to improve the area.

Beirut بيروت

What Beirut is depends entirely on where you are. If you're gazing at the beautifully recon-structed colonial relics and mosques of central Beirut's Downtown, the city is a triumph of rejuvenation over disaster. If you're in the young, vibrant neighbourhoods of Gemmayzeh or Achrafiye, Beirut is about living for the moment: partying, eating and drinking as if there's no tomorrow. If you're standing in the shadow of buildings still peppered with bullet holes, or walking the Green Line with an elderly resident, it's a city of bitter memories and a dark past. If you're with Beirut's Armenians, Beirut is about salvation; if you're with its handful of Jews, it's about hiding your true identity. Here you'll find the freest gay scene in the Arab Middle East, yet homosexuality is still illegal. If you're in one of Beirut's southern refugee camps, Beirut is about sorrow and displacement; other southern districts are considered a base for paramilitary operations and south Beirut is home to infamous Hezbollah secretary general, Hassan Nasrallah. For some, it's a city of fear; for others, freedom.

Throw in maniacal drivers, air pollution from old, smoking Mercedes taxis, world-class universities, bars to rival Soho and coffee thicker than mud, political demonstrations, and swimming pools awash with more silicone than Miami. Add people so friendly you'll swear it can't be true, a political situation existing on a knife-edge, internationally renowned museums and gallery openings that continue in the face of explosions, assassinations and power cuts, and you'll find that you've never experienced a capital city quite so alive and kicking – despite its frequent volatility.

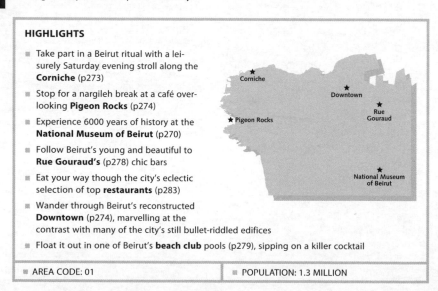

HIGHLIGHTS

- Take part in a Beirut ritual with a lei-surely Saturday evening stroll along the **Corniche** (p273)

- Stop for a nargileh break at a café over-looking **Pigeon Rocks** (p274)

- Experience 6000 years of history at the **National Museum of Beirut** (p270)

- Follow Beirut's young and beautiful to **Rue Gouraud's** (p278) chic bars

- Eat your way though the city's eclectic selection of top **restaurants** (p283)

- Wander through Beirut's reconstructed **Downtown** (p274), marvelling at the contrast with many of the city's still bullet-riddled edifices

- Float it out in one of Beirut's **beach club** pools (p279), sipping on a killer cocktail

- Corniche
- Downtown
- Rue Gouraud
- Pigeon Rocks
- National Museum of Beirut

■ AREA CODE: 01	■ POPULATION: 1.3 MILLION

HISTORY

For most outsiders, Beirut's history begins and ends with its bloody civil war, waged for 15 years along the infamous Green Line that cut the city in two, with Muslims to the west and Christians to the east. But its story stretches back much further than its modern strife, and the city's surface today conceals a fascinating, though often barely visible, ancient history.

The earliest traces of habitation in Beirut date from the Stone Age when the area now occupied by the city was in fact two islands in the delta of the Beirut River. Later, when the river silted up, the area became one land mass. Excavations in the Downtown area have revealed a Canaanite site dating from 1900 BC, with an entrance gate of dressed stone, and, nearby, the remains of Phoenician canals.

The city's name is probably a derivative of the Arabic for 'well' or 'spring' (modern Arabic still uses the word *bir* for well). The first historical reference to Beirut dates from the 14th century BC, when it is mentioned in cuneiform tablets discovered at Tell al-Amarna, Egypt, in the form of letters from the Canaanite king of Beirut begging the pharaoh Amenhotep IV for assistance in repelling Hittite invaders.

In Phoenician times, Beirut appears to have been overshadowed by Sidon, Tyre and Byblos, but after Alexander the Great's conquest it starts to be mentioned in Hellenistic sources, and excavations have revealed an extensive Hellenistic city upon which the later Roman grid was based. It wasn't until the Roman period, however, that the city really came into its own, both as a commercial port and military base, with large public buildings and monuments swiftly erected, along with a series of baths, a theatre and a number of markets. Evidence of both the baths and the main public square, the Cardo Maximus, are still visible today in modern Beirut.

By the 3rd century AD, the city had found particular fame and prestige through its School of Law, one of the main Roman centres of jurisprudence, which rivalled those of Athens, Alexandria and Caesarea. It was actually here that the basis of the famous Justinian Code, upon which the Western legal system drew inspiration, was established. The city's importance as a trading hub and centre of learning continued as the Roman Empire gave way to the Byzantine; its commercial enterprises flourished around the silk trade, and Beirut became the seat of a bishopric. But then, in 551, a devastating earthquake, combined with a tidal wave, almost destroyed the city, killing a vast number of citizens. The School of Law was quickly evacuated and moved to

BEIRUT

SPIRITS AGAINST BULLDOZERS

While wandering Downtown Beirut, you'll doubtless come across the immense building site known as the Souqs Project, a vast new leisure complex now scheduled to open sometime in 2008, incorporating shops, restaurants and office units. Standing on the opposite side of the road to view construction work going on over the fence, you should spot one incongruous little old dome among the profusion of glass and steel. This is the remains of a *zawiya*, or hospice and religious school, built by 16th-century mystic and scholar, Mohammed ibn Iraq al-Dimashqi; it's the only Mamluk building still standing in Beirut, and one with a curious tale attached.

The Souqs Project stands on the site of Beirut's historic main souqs, destroyed during the civil war. In 1992, the rubble was first cleared by archaeologists who worked against the clock to investigate the area before it was built over by developers. A bulldozer clearing an area in what had been Souq Tawile was scooping up debris when it came up against a small, domed building. The machine suddenly stopped. The driver, wanting to finish his job, started the machine up again, but when he tried to move the controls, his hand was suddenly paralysed. Later, when he moved away from the site, the paralysis disappeared.

News quickly spread of the 'miracle' that saved the building and crowds visited the shrine, with reports circulating of miraculous healing among the ill who had prayed there. Muslim religious authorities erected a protective wall around the *zawiya*, announcing that it would not be demolished. Thus, when the Souqs Project finally opens its doors for business, you'll see the mystical *zawiya* standing proud amid yet another Beirut shrine to shopping.

Sidon, and the calamity marked a decline of the city that was to last for centuries.

In 635, the city fell to Muslim Arab conquerors, who seized it without much effort, and their rule went uninterrupted until 1110 when, after a long siege, the city fell into the Crusader hands of Baldwin I of Boulogne, and a Latin bishopric was established.

Beirut remained in Crusader hands for 77 years, during which time the Crusaders built the succinctly titled Church of St John the Baptist of the Knights Hospitallers, on the site of an ancient temple (now the Al-Omari Mosque). In 1187 Saladin (Salah ad-Din) managed to wrest the city back into Muslim hands, but was only able to hold on to it for six years before Amoury, King of Cyprus, besieged the city and Muslim forces fled. Next, under the rule of Jean I of Ibelin, the city's influence grew and spread throughout the Latin East, but the Crusaders lost the city again, this time for good, in July 1291, when the Muslim Mamluks took possession.

The Mamluks remained in control of Beirut until they were ousted from the city by the Ottoman army in 1516. Once part of the powerful Ottoman Empire, the city was granted semiautonomy in return for taxes paid to the sultan. One of its emirs, Fakhreddine (Fakhr ad-Din al-Maan II), established what was in effect an independent kingdom for himself and made Beirut his favourite residence, becoming the first ruler to unite most of the territory encompassed by modern Lebanon under one authority. Fakhreddine's keen business sense led him to trade with the European powers, most notably the Venetians, basing his trading empire around silk, and Beirut began to recover economically and regain some of its former prestige.

The 18th century, though, would present mixed fortunes for the city. Emir Bashir Shihab II (1788–1840) injected it with new vigour, renewing prosperity and stability, but in 1832 entered into an alliance with Ibrahim Pasha, son of the rebellious Mohammed Ali of Egypt. Mohammed Ali's threat to the Ottoman Empire, and by extension to the balance of power in Europe, alarmed the British and in 1840 the city was bombarded and subsequently recaptured for the Ottomans, and Emir Bashir was sent into exile.

The population of Beirut at that time was only 45,000, but a booming silk trade and the influx of Maronites fleeing massacres in the Chouf Mountains and Damascus led numbers to double during the following 20 years. This was the start of the commercial boom that transformed Beirut from a backwater into a commercial powerhouse, and also marked the beginning of European meddling in Lebanon. The massacres of the Maronites resulted in the arrival of French troops in Beirut, while ties with Europe steadily grew in the coming decades. In 1866 Syrian and American missionaries founded the Syrian Protestant College, now known as the American University of Beirut (AUB; see p271), which soon became – and remains today – one of the most prestigious universities in the Middle East.

During WWI, Beirut suffered a blockade by the Allies, which was intended to starve out the Turks. This, combined with a series of natural disasters, resulted in widespread famine, followed by plague, which killed more than a quarter of the population. A revolt broke out against the Turks and resulted in the mass hanging of the rebel leaders in what became known as the Place des Martyrs (Martyrs' Sq).

WWI ended Turkish rule and on 8 October 1918 the British army, including a French detachment, arrived in Beirut; on 25 April 1920 the League of Nations granted a French mandate over Lebanon (and Syria), and Beirut became the capital of the state of Greater Lebanon.

During WWII Beirut was occupied by the Allies and, thanks to its port, became an important supply centre. In 1946 the French left the city and, following Lebanon's first civil war in 1958, Beirut managed to reinvent itself as one of the main commercial and banking centres of the Middle East. The 1948 Arab-Israeli War and then the 1967 Six Day War saw huge numbers of Palestinian refugees settle in refugee camps south of Beirut, where, despite massacres and intense poverty, they remain today. Nevertheless, the 1960s were truly swinging in Beirut, with international superstars arriving to putter on its waters on private yachts and party the night away in its seafront hotels. This would be short-lived, though, and all hopes of a glorious Beiruti 'Paris of the East' effectively died with the coming of the civil war in 1975.

GREATER BEIRUT

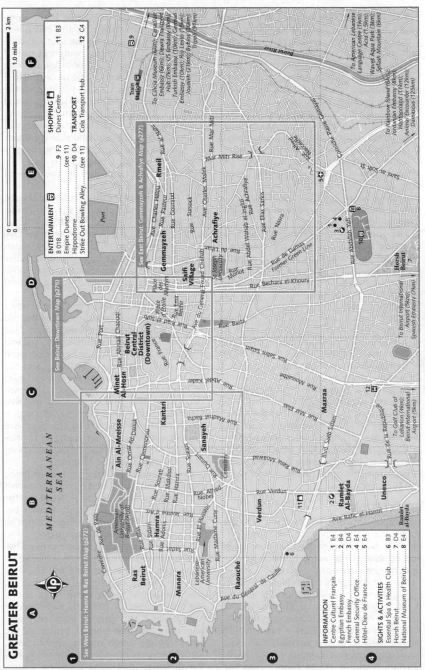

The civil war saw Beirut transformed into a bloody, terrifying epicentre of anarchy. The city was ruled, area by area, by militias loyal to one of various factions; the infamous Green Line tore the city into Christian and Muslim halves, while massacres, hostage-takings and suicide bombings soon became commonplace.

Continual intercommunal fighting between militias, combined with shelling from Israeli fighter planes, soon devastated the city, leaving tens of thousands of human casualties and a shattered economy. By 1991, the end of the civil war saw the Green Line dismantled and the arduous task of rebuilding began, but the scars are still evident in the old bullet holes that pockmark many buildings.

The post-war government faced a daunting task in repairing the country's destroyed infrastructure, but did so with spirit and panache, the jewel in the crown being the reconstruction of the Beirut Central District, or Downtown (see Solidere's Struggles, p276).

Recent events have cast a dark shadow over the city's troubled modern history. The Israel–Hezbollah offensive of 2006, though causing little damage to the centre of Beirut, devastated some southern suburbs, and deflated the hopes of many Beirutis for a prosperous, forward-looking future. Meanwhile, the resulting economic downturn, combined with a spate of killings of anti-Syrian MPs (most notably former prime minister Rafiq Hariri in 2005) and the erection of a Hezbollah 'tent city' in the city centre, have led many Beirutis to believe that plenty of storms are still to be weathered.

ORIENTATION

Geographically, Beirut is an easy city to get about. It's manageable, for the most part, on foot, with enough landmarks to keep you orientated on jaunts between its distinct neighbourhoods.

Most midrange accommodation, cheap eats and internet cafés are located around the university district of Hamra, to the northwest of the city. Hamra's main streets – Rue Hamra and Rue Bliss – run roughly parallel and from east to west, Rue Bliss bordering the vast campus of the AUB. Directly to the north of Hamra runs the seafront Corniche, or Ave de Paris, along which are some of Beirut's top-end hotels and best beach clubs. To the south, the affluent district of Verdun comprises one of Beirut's wealthiest neighbourhoods, with designer clothes shops lining its central Rue Verdun. East from Hamra, you'll reach the busy Rue Fakhr ed-Dine, which marks the eastern boundary of the immaculately restored Beirut Central District, also known as Downtown. An unmistakable landmark on Rue Fakhr ed-Dine, useful for navigating, is the shell of the Holiday Inn (see p282), which stands beside the swanky InterContinental Phoenicia.

At the centre of the immaculately restored Downtown is the circular Place d'Étoile, also known as Nejmeh Sq, which is lined with pavement cafés. Just east again is Place des Martyrs. A good landmark by which to get your bearings here is the immense Mohammed Al-Amin Mosque, which looks very much like Istanbul's Blue Mosque, especially at night.

The eastern edge of Place des Martyrs is marked by the broad, chaotic Rue de Damas, once the path of the Green Line that sliced Beirut in two during the civil war years. This road marks the border between traditionally Muslim West Beirut and the Christian East, and forms the western edge of the trendy, atmospheric Gemmayzeh neighbourhood that is centred on Rue Gouraud. South from Gemmayzeh, with a rough boundary marked by the busy Ave Charles Malek, is another young and popular area, Achrafiye, whose action focuses on clubbers' paradise, Rue Monot.

To the south of Achrafiye, further down Rue de Damas, you'll find the Cola transport hub, the National Museum of Beirut and the hippodrome race course, and, further on, the infamous Palestinian refugee camps of Sabra, Shatila and Burj al-Barajnah.

Something important to bear in mind before you take to Beirut's streets is that street signs aren't easy to navigate by. The blue street signs, located on corner buildings, rarely show the street name itself, showing only the sector (suburb) name, sector number and rue (street) number. Compounding this, numbered buildings are rare and some streets are entirely unnamed, while others are often locally known by different names than those given on a map.

BEIRUT IN...

Two Days

Start your day with a strong coffee and a pastry on **Rue Bliss** (p271) with the AUB students. Then head for the must-see **National Museum of Beirut** (p270) before working your way back along the former Green Line to **Gemmayzeh** (p278) for lunch at **Le Chef** (p283).

Late afternoon, take a stroll along the **Corniche** (p273), timing it for a sunset drink and a nargileh overlooking **Pigeon Rocks** (p274), then take to the night sky on the Ferris wheel at **Lunapark** (p273). Next, return to your hotel room to primp and preen in time for dinner in **Achrafiye** (p284), then wander over to **Rue Monot** (p276) for some serious clubbing action.

Clothes shoppers should start day two by heading to the **ABC Mall** (p290) or **Rue Verdun** (p271) to browse the designer rails, or check out the high-street names on Rue Hamra. For more unusual shopping, stroll around **Saifi Village** (p289), before checking out the gorgeous, though controversial, reconstructed **Downtown** (p274). For a night of live tunes, head either to the **Blue Note** (p288) or **Bar Louis** (p286) for smooth jazz, or the **Gemmayzeh Café** (p288) to hear live *oud* (lute) music.

Four Days

Follow the two-day itinerary, then on day three head to **Baalbek** (p354) for the superlative Roman ruins, stopping for lunch at Zahlé's picturesque **Cafés de Bardouni** (p350) and visiting the **Ksara Winery** (p351) on the way back. On day four, take a trip to the ancient site of **Byblos** (p306) for the ruins, the fossils (p310) or just for lunch at the **Byblos Fishing Club** (p312). Stop off on the way back at the **Jeita grotto** (p303) or Jounieh's soaring **téléférique** (p304) for under- or over-ground thrills.

Buildings themselves are frequently only identified by their function (eg the British Bank Building).

The best thing to do, therefore, is take a decent map with you (see Maps below) and check every few streets that you're heading the right way, aided by the landmarks you spot en route.

Maps

If you're planning on doing a lot of wandering in Beirut, an invaluable aid is the English-language *Zawarib Beirut*, Beirut's equivalent to a UK *A–Z* street map, which covers 100 sq km of the city and its suburbs. It's available at most bookshops and hotels and costs LL15,000 or US$10, after which you're more-or-less guaranteed not to put a foot wrong in Beirut ever again. Just remember that names here are listed in their English, rather than their French form (eg Damascus Blvd instead of Rue de Damas).

Another decent city map, albeit in a more unwieldy fold-out form, is provided on the reverse of the countrywide road map *Lebanon Tourist Map* published by **Paravision** (www.paravision.org), again widely available at Beirut bookshops for LL12,000.

INFORMATION
Bookshops

Beirut has a good selection of foreign language bookshops. The best place to browse is Rue Bliss in Hamra, where lovely, dusty shops stock new and used titles, as well as maps, postcards and the innovative 'postcardigital' series. These are CD-rom postcards containing glorious photos and enough interesting tidbits to assuage the fears of even the most worried relative back home.

Books & Pens (Map p272; ☎ 741 975; Rue Jeanne d'Arc, Hamra; ☿ 8am-10pm Mon-Fri, 8am-8pm Sat) This bookshop stocks extensive art supplies and stationery, as well as international newspapers and magazines.

Librairie Antoine Hamra (Map p272; ☎ 341 470; Rue Hamra); Achrafiye (Map p277; ☎ 331 811; Ave Elias Sarkis) A reliable chain with travel titles, a broad selection of nonfiction and illustrated tomes and a wide range of books for children.

Naufal Booksellers (Map p272; ☎ 354 898; Rue Sourati, Hamra) Stockist of all things Lebanese, from maps to cookery books; a great place with helpful staff, to spend an hour or two browsing and planning your onward journey.

Virgin Megastore (Map p275; ☎ 999 666; Opera Bldg, Place des Martyrs, Downtown; ☿ 9am-11pm Mon-Sat) A failsafe option for fiction, new releases, maps and coffee-table titles. Also a good place to browse for Lebanese music, and pick up tickets to the slew of Lebanese summer festivals.

BEIRUT

Cultural Centres

The cultural centres listed below are very active in Beirut, often staging art and photography exhibitions, film festivals, plays and musical events highlighting work from their respective countries. Check the press, the relevant websites or phone them to find out what's on.

British Council (Map p272; ☎ 428 900; www.british council.org/lebanon; Berytech Bldg, opp French Embassy) Events include exhibitions, theatre productions and film screenings.

Centre Culturel Français (Map p265; ☎ 420 230; Espace Des Lettres, Rue de Damas) Near the National Museum of Beirut.

Goethe Institut (Map p272; ☎ 740 524; www.goethe .de/beirut; Gideon Bldg, Rue Bliss, Manara)

Instituto Cervantes (Map p275; ☎ 970 253; www .cervantes.es; Rue al-Maarad, Downtown)

Italian Cultural Institute (Map p272; ☎ 749 801; www.iicbeirut.org; 2nd fl, Najjar Bldg, Rue de Rome)

Emergency

Ambulance (Red Cross) (☎ 140)
Civil Defense (☎ 125)
Doctors at Home (☎ 444 400/401) A medical call-out service for emergencies, it charges LL50,000 for a daytime visit and LL60,000 at night. It's open 24 hours.
Fire Brigade (☎ 175)
Internal Security Forces (☎ 112)
Police (☎ 160)
Tourist Police (☎ 350 901, 343 286, 343 209)

Immigration Office

Visa extensions can be obtained from the **General Security Office** (Map p265; ☎ 1717 for visa, work permit & residency permit information in English, Arabic & French; www.general-security.gov.lb; Rue de Damas; ⊗ 8am-1pm Mon-Thu, 8-10am Fri, 8am-noon Sat), just north of the National Museum. For more information, see Visa Extensions (p389) in the Lebanon Directory.

Internet Access

You'll have no problem finding reliable internet access in Beirut, though many internet cafés are as noisy and smoke-filled as the city's bars. The biggest concentration is in the vicinity of the AUB campus (p271) and, just like the bars, opening times are flexible, with many staying open beyond midnight.

If you have a wireless-enabled laptop, you'll find there are many 'hotspots' throughout the city, though most require a prepaid card. One of the most popular services is **IDM** (www

.idm.net.lb/wifi), which offers access via pre-paid scratch cards. Costs range from $US5 for one hour to $US40 for one week unlimited use, and cards are available in bookshops, cafés, hotels and computer equipment shops. Some cafés also have their own individual paid wireless services; Starbucks, on Rue Hamra, sells its own cards for prices equivalent to those of IDM.

All the internet cafés listed below have roughly equivalent prices – around LL3000 per hour – and all are open early in the morning until midnight, if not substantially later.

Momento Internet Café (Map p272; ☎ 811 815; Rue Labban, Hamra)

PC Club (Map p272; ☎ 745 338; Rue Sidani, Hamra) A popular student hangout that rarely shuts its doors.

Santa Computer (Map p277; ☎ 446 275; Rue Gouraud, Gemmayzeh) Handy to the Gouraud restaurant area.

Virgin Café (Map p275; ☎ 999 777; Opera Bldg, Downtown) Situated on the 4th floor of the Virgin Megastore, this is one of the only internet cafés currently operating in Downtown.

Web Café (Map p272; ☎ 348 881; Rue Makhoul, Hamra) Surf the internet with chilled musical accompaniment and an ice-cold beer.

Internet Resources

Beirut Spring (www.beirutspring.com) A popular blog dealing with Lebanese society, written by 29-year-old Lebanese Mustapha, now living abroad.

Blogging Beirut (www.bloggingbeirut.com) Featured by many newspapers across the world, this blog is also home to the famous 'I Heart Beirut' bumper stickers.

Cyberia (www.thisiscyberia.com) One of Lebanon's main internet service providers (ISPs) and its 'portal' website is a good resource for an up-to-date weather check, and movie listings across Beirut; it also has a useful telephone directory listing everything from art galleries to universities.

Daleel (www.thedaleel.com) A useful internet directory with links to a vast range of services, groups and activities in Beirut and beyond.

Terranet (www.terra.net.lb) Another good ISP site offering movie listings, news and a travel booking service for onward flights.

Buy Lebanese (www.buylebanese.com) Really a resource for when you get back home, this popular shopping site will send those sweets, nargilehs, Beirut T-shirts or pickled cucumbers you forgot to buy, direct to over 50 countries.

Laundry

Self-service laundrettes aren't exactly two-a-penny in Beirut, so most travellers either have their laundry cleaned at the hotel, or pack the travel wash and do it, in the time-honoured fashion, in the shower. Beirut's budget hotels can usually arrange for a load to be done for about US$3 per 4-5kg; the more expensive hotels charge this just for one shirt or pair of jeans.

The best exception to the rule is the cheerful **Laundromatic** (Map p272; ☎ 03-376 187; Rue Sidani; load under/over 4.5kg incl detergent LL4000/5500, dryer per 10 min LL2000; ☖ 9am-7pm Mon-Sat), which proclaims itself to be the 'first coin-operated launderette in Lebanon' and where washing and ironing services are also available.

Media
Beirut's two foreign-language newspaper options are the *Daily Star* (www.dailystar.com; LL2000) in English and *L'Orient-Le Jour* (www.lorientlejour.com; LL2000) in French. Online, the best source of up-to-date independent journalism is **Ya Libnan** (www.yalibnan.com). See the Media section in the Culture chapter (p251) for an overview of Lebanon's press.

Though its publishing run is often interrupted, the monthly *Time Out Beirut* (www.timeoutbeirut.com) is another great source of up-to-date 'what's on' listings. The *Guide* (LL5000) is a glossy monthly that reviews the latest hotspots, as well as detailing events, concerts, exhibitions and activities for kids. It can be quite hard to find, and only the larger bookshops seem to stock it. Librairie Antoine (see Bookshops, p267) is a good bet. *Agenda Culturel* (LL3000) offers the same information, in French, but is published every two weeks and covers the whole country.

Medical Services
Beirut boasts several good hospitals, with facilities to rival any major European city.
American University of Beirut Hospital (Map p272; ☎ 350 000, 354 911; Rue Sourati) Considered one of the best hospitals in the Middle East, with English and French spoken.
Clemenceau Medical Center (Map p272; ☎ 372 888; Rue Clemenceau) Affiliated with John Hopkins International.
Hôtel-Dieu de France (Map p265; ☎ 615 300; www.hdf.usj.edu.lb; Rue Alfred Naccache, Achrafiye)
Rizk (Map p277; ☎ 200 800; Rue Zahar, Achrafiye)
St George's Greek Hospital (Map p277; ☎ 585 700; Rue Rmeil, Achrafiye) Known locally as 'Roum'.

Money
You'll barely be able to walk 10 yards without spotting an ATM in Beirut, most of which dispense both US dollars and Lebanese lira. If you're looking for moneychangers, there are plenty dotted all along Rue Hamra.
Amex (☎ 977 800) If your Amex card is lost, stolen or damaged while in Lebanon, call the American Express representative office who'll give you details of how to replace it.
Amir Exchange (Map p272; ☎ 341 265; Rue Hamra, Hamra; ☖ 8am-8pm Mon-Sat) One of the few places you can change travellers' cheques, preferably in US$, it charges US$2 to US$3 per US$100. Bring your passport and original purchaser's receipt.
Sogetour (Map p272; ☎ 747 111; Ground fl, Block A, Gefinor Center, Rue Maamari, Hamra; ☖ 8.30am-4pm Mon-Fri, 8.30am-1pm Sat) The best place in Beirut to exchange Amex travellers cheques in US dollars. It charges a 2% commission.

Pharmacies
Berty Pharmacy (Map p277 ☎ 200 767, 322 266; Nazlet el-Salameh, Sassine Sq, Achrafiye; ☖ to 11.30pm Mon-Sat, to 10pm Sun) A well stocked pharmacy.
Mazen Pharmacy (☎ 313 362; Blvd Saeb Salam, Mazraa; ☖ 24hr) It offers a free delivery service between 8am and midnight; you simply telephone your order through and pay on delivery. The pharmacist speaks English and French and can advise you on what drugs you may need.
Wardieh Pharmacy (Map p272; ☎ 343 679, 751 345; Wardieh Sq, Rue Sourati, Hamra) Another pharmacy offering free 24-hour home delivery.

Post
Though there are plenty of yellow tin post boxes scattered about Beirut, it's best to send letters direct from the post office to make sure you get the postage cost correct. Most of Beirut's post offices are open 8am to 5pm Monday to Friday and 8am to 1.30pm Saturday. For details of courier services, see Post (p387) in the Lebanon Directory.

Handy post office branches:
Libanpost Achrafiye (Map p277; ☎ 321 657; Ogero Bldg, Sassine Sq, Achrafiye); Gemmayzeh (Map p277; ☎ 442 902; Zighbi Bldg, Rue Gouraud, Gemmayzeh); Hamra (Map p272; ☎ 344 706; Matta Bldg, Rue Makdissi, Hamra)

Telephone & Fax
For details of how to make phone calls or send faxes, see Telephone & Fax (p387) in the Lebanon Directory.

Tourist Information
Tourist Information Office (Map p272; ☎ 343 073; www.destinationlebanon.gov.lb; Ground fl, Ministry of Tourism Bldg, 550 Rue Banque du Liban, Hamra; ☖ 8am-

1.30pm & 2-4.30pm Mon-Thu, 8.30am-3pm Fri, 8am-1pm Sat) Though it may look closed when you pass its big windows on Rue Hamra, it probably isn't: enter by the back door, accessible through the covered car park. Staff are extremely helpful, with a range of free brochures available in different languages and a selection of larger, illustrated books to sit down and browse through. The office may also have LCC bus route maps available for free: just ask at the counter.

Tourist Police Office (Map p272; ☎ 752 428; fax 343 504; Rue Banque du Liban, Hamra; ☼ 24hr) Located on the opposite side of the covered arcade from the Tourist Information Office, head here for complaints, problems or if you've been robbed.

Travel Agencies

There are travel agents all over Beirut but two reliable options are listed below.

Campus Travel (Map p272; ☎ 744 588; www.campus -travel.net; Maktabi Bldg, Rue Makhoul, Hamra) Travel agency focusing on student travel. Arranges skiing trips, tours in Lebanon and to neighbouring countries, such as Syria and Jordan.

Tania Travel (Map p272; ☎ 739 682; www.tania travel.com; 1st fl, Shames Bldg, Rue Sidani, Hamra) Located opposite Jeanne d'Arc theatre, this agency offers tours to Aanjar, Baalbek, Bcharré, Beiteddine, Byblos, the Cedars, Deir al-Qamar, Sidon, Tyre and day trips to Damascus.

Visa Extensions

See Visa Extensions (p389) for details of how to extend your one-month visa and make it valid for three months.

DANGERS & ANNOYANCES

The most obvious hazard in Beirut is the traffic, especially for pedestrians: parents with children may balk at the sight of a dual carriageway turned six-lane highway with no pedestrian crossing in sight. Moreover, look out for potholes, broken paving stones and loose electrical wiring on Beirut's pavements. This is especially problematic at night as some areas of the city have poor or no street lighting.

Theft in Beirut is not a great problem, but it pays to be vigilant with your bags at busy places. It is also advisable to keep your bag on your non-curb-side shoulder when walking the streets, since there have been reports of handbag robberies by thieves riding motor scooters.

At the time of writing, much of Downtown was heavily guarded by armed police, along with tanks, machine guns and rolls of barbed wire. While this shouldn't discourage you from wandering its pristine streets, prepare to have your bag checked at many Downtown intersections and carry your passport, in case you're asked for ID.

Despite a strong police presence and no tangible threat to visitors, it's a good idea to stay away from the Hezbollah 'tent city', which currently extends from the south of Place des Martyrs to the northern end of Rue Monot.

For more on safety information, see Staying Safe, p244.

SIGHTS
National Museum of Beirut

المتحف الوطني

Once situated on a strategically important intersection of the former Green Line, this must-see **museum** (Map p265; ☎ 612 295/7; www .beirutnationalmuseum.com; cnr Rue de Damas & Ave Abdal-lah Yafi; adult/student & child LL5000/1000; ☼ 9am-5pm Tue-Sun except some public holidays) has an impressive collection of archaeological artefacts, statuettes and sarcophagi. Every hour, between 9am and 4pm, the museum screens *Revival*, a fascinating short documentary on how staff saved the collection from the destruction of the civil war and subsequently restored the museum to its former glory.

The easiest way to get to the museum is to either take a 15-minute walk from Sodeco Sq along Rue de Damas (part of the former Green Line), or hail a service taxi and ask for Musee or the Hippodrome.

Inside, the exhibits are organised from prehistory to the Mamluk period, and it takes a couple of hours to view them at a leisurely pace. Nearly all exhibits are labelled in English, Arabic and French. A floor plan is included in the admission fee, but for more detailed information, invest in a museum guide (LL15,000) from the gift shop.

Highlights of the museum's collection include a Neolithic pebble idol from Byblos, possibly dating back as far as 9000 BC, one of the earliest representations of the human form found in Lebanon; the famous gilded bronze Phoenician statuettes, also from Byblos; a series of beautiful, cute white marble baby boy statues from Echmoun, offered to the gods in thanks for healing children; and a collection of Byzantine gold jewellery, found in a jar beneath a Beirut house.

Hamra & Ras Beirut

During the dark days of Lebanon's civil war, the adjacent districts of Hamra and Ras Beirut (Map p272) – home to Beirut's three universities – were the hub of the city's intellectual activity, the intelligentsia clustering around cafés such as the Wimpy whose names live on in Beirut's history, though not their physical presences. Nowadays, these districts are less cool than Achrafiye or Gemmayzeh, but both Hamra and Ras Beirut nevertheless host a handful of good hotels and a plethora of cheap eateries, filled with students. Hamra in particular is a great hub for shopping, particularly for books, and has a lively but down-to-earth 24-hour vibe centred on **Rue Bliss**, courtesy of its student population.

Slightly further south from Hamra and Ras Beirut is the affluent, largely Muslim, district of Verdun, where lunching ladies flit all day between the glittering storefronts of Gucci, Armani and Hugo Boss. If label shopping's your thing, join them trailing along the **Rue Verdun** – preferably with a little handbag-sized dog if you can borrow one – and salivate at the temptations on display.

Just off the eastern end of Rue Hamra is the **University of Lebanon campus**, with its 19th-century buildings and very attractive grounds. This is also the location of the **Sanayeh Public Garden**, one of the city's few public parks and a nice place for a stroll beneath the mature, leafy trees.

AMERICAN UNIVERSITY OF BEIRUT

The American University of Beirut (AUB; Map p272) is one of the Middle East's most prestigious educational institutes, and its campus and the surrounding Ras Beirut and Hamra areas are a hive of activity during semesters. The university is privately owned, nonsectarian and teaches all classes in English – hence the local students wandering around the Hamra district conversing in English as often as Arabic. Both the museum and the campus grounds are open to the public and are definitely worth a look.

Spread over 28 hectares, the beautiful, tree-shaded campus runs from Rue Bliss down to the sea and even has its own beach club for the summer months (see p279). But the stately charms of the campus did not save it from the ugliness of the civil war, with various kidnappings and murders of university staff, including the ninth president of the university, Dr Malcolm Kerr, who was assassinated outside his College Hall office in 1984. Today it's tranquil, green and filled with milling students; check out the What's On section of the university's website (www.aub.edu) to sample a taste of campus life.

THE LOOTING OF LEBANON

Amid the chaos of Lebanon's civil war, it wasn't only banks that robbers targeted to drain their coffers. The country's archaeological treasures, too, were subject to a degree of pillage not seen since waves of 18th- and 19th-century European colonists hauled off the region's treasures to stock their museums.

Militias stole from Department of Antiquities storerooms, ransacked archaeological sites and bulldozed entire cemeteries and ancient settlements in their search for treasure, destroying layer upon layer of historical evidence that can never be replaced. Even sarcophagi at the National Museum of Beirut were smashed in the hope of finding treasure inside. The thieves were frequently aided by unscrupulous middlemen and Western art dealers, who turned a blind eye to the provenance of the artefacts.

Many of the museum's treasures, however, were saved from looters by the diligence of its staff and it retains an impressive collection, frequently bolstered by new finds under the auspices of the Directorate General of Antiquities. It seems, though, that less attention is being paid to the city's open-air relics, as new condos and office blocks rise around them. Wander to the Cardo Maximus and you'll see rubbish, upturned plastic chairs and boxes of unlabelled remnants scattered about the majestic pillars.

A collection of articles, including an excellent piece by Robert Fisk chronicling the looting of Lebanon, can be found at http://phoenicia.org/feature.html.

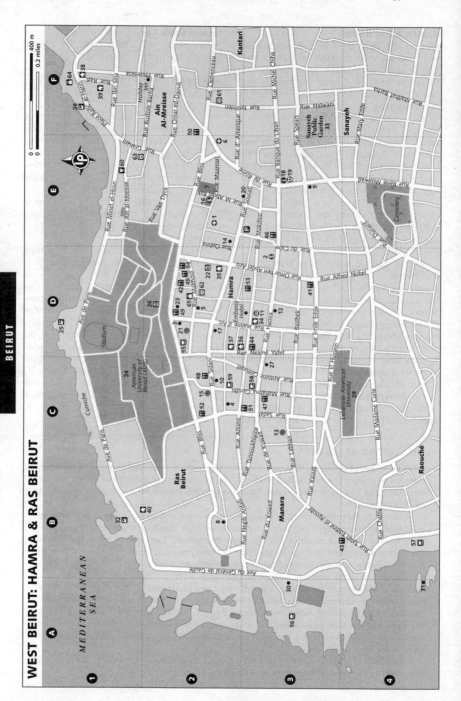

WEST BEIRUT: HAMRA & RAS BEIRUT

AUB Museum

This **museum** (Map p272; ☎ 340549; http://ddc.aub.edu .lb/projects/museum/; AUB campus; admission free; 9am-5pm Mon-Fri except university & public holidays) was founded in 1868 and is one of the oldest in the Middle East. On permanent display is its collection of Lebanese and Middle Eastern artefacts including weapons, tools, flints, figurines, pottery and jewellery, along with a fine collection of Phoenician glass and Arab coins dating from as early as the 5th century BC.

The AUB Museum runs monthly lectures throughout the year, hosts temporary exhibitions and children's activities, and is involved in ongoing excavations in Lebanon and Syria.

Corniche

The Corniche (seafront; Map p272) is a favourite promenade spot, especially late in the afternoon and on weekends. Families, couples and groups of dressed-up young people saunter along its length, stopping to greet friends or to have a coffee-and-nargileh break at one of the cafés along the route. While many locals say the Corniche starts at Ras Beirut on Ave de Paris in the east and ends at the St George Yacht Motor Club (p279) in Ain al-Mreisse to the west, others say it encompasses the entire waterfront area around to Pigeon Rocks (p274) to the south.

You'll see a great cross-section of Beiruti life on your walk, from backgammon-playing old men to teenagers dressed to impress, particularly on a Saturday night, when people bring their own plastic chairs and set up temporary camp to watch the world go by. Just north of Pigeon Rocks, you'll spot the sparkling, squealing attractions of the **Lunapark** amusement park, whose Ferris wheel is a favourite with adults and kids alike.

Pole fishing from the Corniche is a popular pastime, especially near the steps that lead down to the front of the Corniche wall, though you'll probably wonder whether they ever catch anything big enough to be worth the effort. You'll probably also be tempted by vendors with their handcarts of hot nuts, corn and *ka'ik,* the handbag-shaped circular bread that's hooped around their carts. You'll also hear the clinking of coffee cups from wandering coffee vendors.

You are sure to encounter the BYO nargileh culture, which entails parking your car near a bench on the Corniche, cranking the music up and lighting up your own hookah pipe to share among your closest friends. If you're visiting during the summer months, just before you reach the **AUB Beach** (p279) you will also see the teenagers risking life and limb diving off the Corniche and landing in the sea between the rock formations.

BEIRUT

GETTING INVOLVED

For those visitors to Lebanon keen to contribute their time and skills to volunteering with a Lebanese charitable organisation or NGO, or visiting or volunteering on projects specifically at a Palestinian refugee camp, it can be very hard to find initial information.

A few good web-based starting points for investigating these possibilities are the following:

- **Association for Volunteer Services Lebanon** (www.avs.org.lb) A good first point of contact for those interested in volunteering in any capacity in Lebanon

- **Caritas Liban** (www.caritas.org.lb) A church-based aid organisation, running social and healthcare projects across Lebanon

- **Canadian-Palestinian Educational Exchange** (CEPAL; www.cepal.ca) Sends Canadian volunteers to work on various summer projects in the Burj al-Barajnah and Shatila refugee camps near Beirut, and in Wavel camp near Baalbek

- **Daleel** (www.thedaleel.com) Internet guide with many links to charities and other organisations

- **Lebanese Association of SOS Children's Villages** (www.sos.org.lb) Part of the SOS global network

- **LebCare** (www.lebcare.org) A charity founded in 2006 in response to the Israel–Hezbollah War, helping refugees and others in need

- **Palestinian Human Rights Organisation** (PHRO; www.palhumanrights.org) Offers information on all aspects of Palestinian refugee life in Lebanon

Pigeon Rocks

These natural offshore rock arches (Map p265) are the most famous, and indeed one of the only, natural features of Beirut. The stretch of the Corniche directly in front of the rocks is an excellent vantage point, but far more interesting is to take one of the tracks down to the lower cliffs. One track starts from the southern side of the rocks and, after a steep 100m, you find yourself down on the lower level of chalk cliffs. Almost immediately, you can completely forget you are in the city. The way across the rocks is quite rugged and sensible shoes are a good idea, although you see local women teetering precariously across the cliffs in high heels.

There are a number of inlets and caves in the cliffs. During summer, small boats take people around the rocks and to the caves for a small fee.

Downtown

Beirut's glittering centrepiece, once the original Paris of the Middle East, was an area where, for many years, the rattle of sniper fire echoed through husks of once grand old buildings centred around the **Place d'Étoile**. Think Paris, post-apocalypse, and you'll have a good idea of how

Downtown (Map p275) – also known as the Beirut Central District or Solidere – looked in the early 1990s, after a decade and a half of civil war. Now, in better years, you could almost say it's touristy. It's the cleanest, most pedestrianised and least congested part of the city, but does, as most Beirutis will tell you, lack just a little soul. One major criticism of this area is that no provision was made for a festival hall, world class museum or opera building – it's comprised largely of offices, government buildings, investment banks and pricey boutiques. To make up for this creative dearth, the **Saifi Village** (p289) has sprung up in the residential district just behind Place des Martyrs. It is filled with a burgeoning selection of small galleries, boutiques and one-off designer craft shops.

Downtown is also the site of the impressive **Mohammed al-Amin mosque** (Map p275), in which former prime minister Rafiq Hariri is buried – it looks like a younger sibling of Istanbul's Blue Mosque. To its north, **Place des Martyrs** (Map p275) has been the location of some of the largest ever Lebanese public gatherings, notably the 14 March demonstration held on the one-month anniversary of the murder of Hariri, which

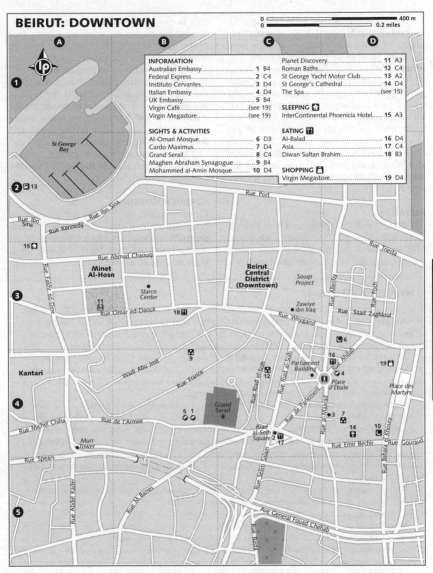

BEIRUT: DOWNTOWN

0	400 m
0	0.2 miles

INFORMATION
Australian Embassy..................... 1 B4
Federal Express........................ 2 C4
Instituto Cervantes.................... 3 D4
Italian Embassy........................ 4 D4
UK Embassy............................ 5 B4
Virgin Café.........................(see 19)
Virgin Megastore...................(see 19)

SIGHTS & ACTIVITIES
Al-Omari Mosque....................... 6 D3
Cardo Maximus......................... 7 D4
Grand Serail.......................... 8 C4
Maghen Abraham Synagogue.......... 9 B4
Mohammed al-Amin Mosque......... 10 D4

Planet Discovery...................... 11 A3
Roman Baths........................... 12 C4
St George Yacht Motor Club........... 13 A2
St George's Cathedral................. 14 D4
The Spa...........................(see 15)

SLEEPING
InterContinental Phoenicia Hotel...... 15 A3

EATING
Al-Balad............................. 16 D4
Asia................................. 17 C4
Diwan Sultan Brahim.................. 18 B3

SHOPPING
Virgin Megastore..................... 19 D4

brought 1 million Lebanese – a quarter of the country's population – to the streets, resulting in the final withdrawal of Syrian troops from Lebanon (see p40).

To the northeast of Place des Martyrs, don't miss the **Al-Omari Mosque** (Map p275), originally built in the 12th century by the Crusaders as the Church of St John the

Baptist of the Knights Hospitallers, and converted by the Mamluks into a mosque in 1291. **St George's Cathedral** (Map p275; ☎ 561 980; services 7.15am & 6.30pm Mon-Thu & Sat, 9am & 11am Sun), beside the Mohammed al-Amin Mosque, is also worth a visit, being a Maronite church dating back to the Crusades. Other important sites not to miss are the magnificently restored **Roman baths** (Map p275); the **cardo maximus** (Map p275), evocative remains of a Roman-era market area; and the **Grand Serail** (Map p275), a majestic Ottoman-era building that has been restored to its former grandeur and now houses government offices. The roads around the Grand Serail, however, are largely blocked off at present in a tangle of tanks and razor-wire, so you may not be able to get as close as you'd like. Just to the north of the Grand Serail, between Rue France and Wadi Abou Jmil, is the remains of the **Maghen Abraham Synagogue** (see The Jews of Beirut, p278).

Achrafiye

An attractive district of former East Beirut, Achrafiye (Map p277) is lined with beautiful old stately buildings and built upon the site of a Roman City of the Dead; it's still largely a Christian preserve, characterised by its small, winding streets that make their way up the hill that springs from Downtown and Gemmayzeh. Though slowly being eclipsed in funkiness by Gemmayzeh, it remains one of the coolest spots for nightlife, packed in around the famous **Rue Monot**, which continues to dominate the clubbing scene. But aside from the booze and the bling, Achrafiye is tree-lined and tranquil (during daylight hours, at any rate) and boasts cute galleries, a theatre, antique shops, churches, the **ABC Mall** (p290) and the fabulous Sursock Museum.

SURSOCK MUSEUM

Lit up at night, so that the full glory of its colourful stained glass is on show, the **museum** (Musée Nicholas Ibrahim Sursock; Map p277; ☎ 334 133; Rue Sursock, Achrafiye; ⊙ call for opening hrs) is truly an extraordinary sight.

SOLIDERE'S STRUGGLES

Repairing the catastrophic damage to Beirut's Downtown, or Beirut Central District (BCD), was one of the greatest challenges facing the government in the aftermath of the civil war. Redevelopment had a symbolic as well as a practical purpose: by re-creating the area associated with Lebanon's past prosperity the country was signalling that it was once again open for business.

In 1994 the Lebanese parliament, headed by Prime Minister Rafiq Hariri, formed the Lebanese Company for the Development and Reconstruction of the BCD, known as Solidere (www.solidere .com.lb), a joint stock company in which pre-existing property owners were majority shareholders and whose shares traded on the Beirut stock exchange.

But though widely credited as having made the most important mark on Beirut's renewal – with the flawless Downtown district a testament to its efforts – Solidere has not been without its share of troubles and controversy. First came the problems establishing to whom preexisting property belonged. In one case, there were 4700 claimants to a single plot of land in the souq area. The solution was to give everyone with some sort of legal claim shares in Solidere equal to the value of their property holding. Altogether the value of the claimants' shares was some US\$1.7 billion.

Next, Solidere had to cooperate with archaeologists, handing over the excavation of archaeological sites as they were uncovered; many archaeologists feel, however, that Solidere failed to give proper weight to historical concerns.

In exchange for restoring infrastructure and more than 200 buildings from the Ottoman and French Mandate periods, Solidere itself received 1650 real-estate lots, worth around US\$1.17 billion, in addition to investment from the state and private investors. Many say that the company grossly underestimated land values when distributing shares to property owners, pulling off a massive land grab, as well as generating a huge profit, at their expense. Others criticised the project's largest stakeholder, Prime Minister Hariri, as having had a conflict of interest between the project and his political position.

Most recently, the St George Hotel and Yacht Motor Club launched a campaign known as 'STOP Solidere' (you'll see the massive banner on the side of the derelict St George Hotel). The hotel's owners claim that long-awaited rebuilding of their landmark hotel is in dispute, following Solidere's claims to the entire waterfront of St George Bay. See the hotel's protest page, www .stgeorges-hotel.com, for more on the hotel's side of the story.

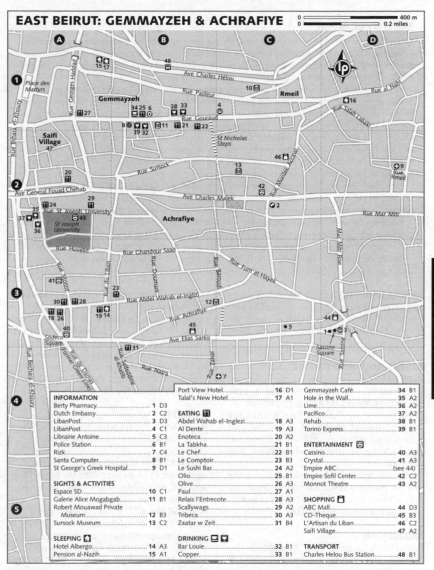

EAST BEIRUT: GEMMAYZEH & ACHRAFIYE

0 — 400 m
0 — 0.2 miles

INFORMATION				EATING				Gemmayzeh Café	34	B1
Berty Pharmacy	1	D3		Abdel Wahab el-Inglezi	18	A3		Hole in the Wall	35	A2
Dutch Embassy	2	C2		Al Dente	19	A3		Lime	36	A2
LibanPost	3	D3		Enoteca	20	A2		Pacifico	37	A2
LibanPost	4	C1		La Tabkha	21	B1		Rehab	38	B1
Librairie Antoine	5	C3		Le Chef	22	B1		Torino Express	39	B1
Police Station	6	B1		Le Comptoir	23	B3				
Rizk	7	C4		Le Sushi Bar	24	A2		ENTERTAINMENT		
Santa Computer	8	B1		Olio	25	B1		Cassino	40	A3
St George's Greek Hospital	9	D1		Olive	26	A3		Crystal	41	A3
				Paul	27	A1		Empire ABC	(see 44)	
SIGHTS & ACTIVITIES				Relais l'Entrecote	28	A3		Empire Sofil Center	42	C2
Espace SD	10	C1		Scallywags	29	A2		Monnot Theatre	43	A2
Galerie Alice Mogabgab	11	B1		Tribeca	30	A3				
Robert Mouawad Private				Zaatar w Zeit	31	B4		SHOPPING		
Museum	12	B3						ABC Mall	44	D3
Sursock Museum	13	C2		DRINKING				CD-Theque	45	B3
				Bar Louie	32	B1		L'Artisan du Liban	46	C2
SLEEPING				Copper	33	B1		Saifi Village	47	A2
Hotel Albergo	14	A3								
Pension al-Nazih	15	A1						TRANSPORT		
Port View Hotel	16	D1						Charles Helou Bus Station	48	B1
Talal's New Hotel	17	A1								

Owned by the Sursock family, one of the country's most illustrious dynasties, the extraordinary and magnificent Lebanese-Italian architectural style of the building itself often overshadows the temporary exhibitions. The location of the museum, in a wonderful street of luxurious modern apartment blocks and beautiful Ottoman-and French Mandate–era mansions, makes a walk around the neighbourhood mandatory. The interior of the museum is equally grand with vast marble floors and wood panelling. Some of the rooms are decorated in the oriental style and the main hall has a collection of 19th-century Turkish silver as well as a gigantic 7th-century Abbasid jar. The former

BEIRUT

THE JEWS OF BEIRUT

Tucked away to the north of the Grand Serail are the remains of the once grand **Maghen Abraham synagogue** (Map p275), which in the early 20th century served a thriving Jewish Beirut community. Though desperately in need of rebuilding, you can still make out the stars of David and Hebrew inscriptions adorning the synagogue's surviving walls.

This is not the only evidence of Lebanon's once open and active Jewish community. In Deir al-Qamar, the now disused synagogue remains intact; in Beirut and elsewhere there are several overgrown Jewish cemeteries. But today, most of Lebanon's Jews prefer to keep their religious identity closely guarded and no accurate figures on exactly how many Jews remain in Beirut, or elsewhere in the country, are available. Some sources say there are as few as 40; others, as many as 1500. Either way, for a city that once contained 16 synagogues, Beirut displays little evidence that the once 14,000-strong Jewish community of Lebanon, whose roots can be traced back in the area as far as 1000 BC, ever existed at all.

One man, however, is attempting to redress this balance. Aaron-Micael Beydoun, a 21-year-old Muslim Lebanese American, is the founder of the website/blog/research project The Jews of Lebanon (www.thejewsoflebanon.org). His aim, he says, is to remind the Lebanese public that coexistence between religious groups has been, and should continue to be, one of Lebanon's strongest features. With plans to launch an appeal to renovate the Maghen Abraham synagogue, and a commitment to bring the story of Lebanon's Jews to the attention of the world, Beydoun is determined to give a face and voice to this forgotten and maligned Lebanese community.

study of Nicholas Ibrahim Sursock features his portrait by Kees Van Dongen and houses a small collection of icons. Call or check the press to find out if exhibitions are scheduled during your visit.

ROBERT MOUAWAD PRIVATE MUSEUM

This **museum** (Map p277; ☎ 980 970; www.rmpm .info; cnr Rue Achrafiye & Rue Baroudi; ☼ 9am-5pm Tue-Sun) is housed in Pharaon Palace, once the home of Robert Mouawad, a jeweller and collector of gorgeous objets d'art, including clocks, porcelain, jewellery, icons and watches.

Like the Sursock Museum just down the road, it makes a beautiful respite from the city, with the palace itself every bit as sumptuous as the items on display.

Gemmayzeh

Fast rivalling Achrafiye for its nightlife, dynamism and pulling power, Gemmayzeh (Map p277) still has a rough-and-ready edge, making it fun to hang out in its numerous hole-in-the-wall bars, though, like everywhere in Beirut, it's developing fast. Saved from suffering as much damage as Downtown or Achrafiye during the civil war, it's got a satisfyingly authentic feel, with streets filled with lovely old buildings, boutiques and plenty of artists in residence.

From Gemmayzeh's main street **Rue Gouraud**, where most of the bars and cafés are congregated, a pleasant walk up to Achrafiye takes you up the steep **St Nicholas Steps** to Sursock St. Just beyond the steps on the opposite side of Rue Gouraud, should the urge suddenly take you, is a pet shop offering photos of customers, draped lavishly with its giant python, for LL10,000.

Galleries

Beirut's vibrant art scene ensures that there are many galleries. Check local listings for exhibitions.

Agial Art Gallery (Map p272; ☎ 345 213,; www .agialart.com; 63 Rue Omar ben-Abdel Aziz, Hamra) Close to the AUB, this is a shopfront gallery that specialises in showcasing the work of local artists.

Espace SD (Map p277; ☎ 563 114; www.espacesd .com; Ave Charles Hélou, Achrafiye) Set over three levels, it exhibits contemporary Lebanese and international artists, in addition to furniture design, fashion and accessories.

Galerie Alice Mogabgab (Map p277; ☎ 210 424; Rue Gouraud, Gemmayzeh) Specialises in modern art, including works by artists from abroad.

Cilicia Museum

The gorgeous collection of Armenian religious and cultural artefacts at this **museum** (off Map p265; ☎ 04-410 001; www.cathcil.org; Antelias; ☼ 10am-5pm Tue-Sat, 10am-1pm Sun) is one of Beirut's best-kept secrets. And secrets play a major role in the history of this museum, as most of the collection was smuggled out of what was known as Turkish Armenia in 1915, by monks from the Monastery of Sis in Cilicia. Given just several days to flee the genocide by the Turks, the monks removed as much of their treasure as they could and began their dangerous overland journey, eventually arriving in Aleppo (Syria). In 1930 they finally settled in Antelias, just north of Beirut.

To get to the museum, take the LCC bus 6, or any minibus going north to Jounieh and Byblos via the highway, and get off near the green-coloured footbridge over the southbound highway at Antelias. From here you should be able to spot the spires of the cathedral. You can also take the LCC bus 2 that finishes its route at Antelias. Get off at the last stop and walk towards the water from where you'll spot the entrance. The museum is at the left rear of the courtyard. Call in advance to arrange an extremely worthwhile guided tour, during which you'll learn not only about the items on display, but also about the often tragic history of the Armenian diaspora.

ACTIVITIES
Beach Clubs
Swimming is one of the most popular activities for Beirutis in summer. Shun the poorly maintained public beach at Ramlet al-Bayda, south of Raouché, and splash out on a day at one of Beirut's excellent beach clubs. While they're 'beach' clubs in the loosest sense of the word – there's no sand – there are pools, loungers, good food and cocktails galore, usually enveloped in a thick aura of exclusivity. Designer bikinis, mobile phones and unnaturally sculpted bodies are the norm and the experience is as much about seeing and being seen as it is about taking a dip. Most are open from 8am to 8pm, or later for drinks and dancing; only the Riviera and the St George are open all year round (though it's not much fun to swim outdoors in December anyway).

AUB Beach (Map p272; Corniche; admission AUB students LL3500 , guests LL10,000) Though scruffier than the rest, this university beach has a great atmosphere in the summer, and admits nonstudents.

Riviera Beach Club (Map p272; ☎ 373 210; Ras Beirut; admission LL20,000) Belonging to the upmarket Riviera Beirut Hotel and therefore free to guests, you'll officially need to take out membership if you're not staying at the hotel – but if it's a quiet day, you'll probably be allowed in for the regular admission fee. Facilities include a marina, a good lap pool and a nice fish restaurant.

St George Yacht Motor Club (Map p275; ☎ 356 350; Ain al-Mreisse; admission Mon Fri LL15,000, Sat & Sun LL20,000) The swishest of the beach clubs in the centre of town, the St George is a recently renovated version of what was *the* club of the 1960s. It has a marina, a nice pool, jet skis, restaurants and grass on which to stretch out, along with a pleasant children's playground.

La Plage (Map p272; ☎ 366 222; Ain el-Mreisseh; admission LL20,000; 9am-7pm May-Oct) A small, cool beach bar with great seafood and typically bronzed and beautiful bodies arranged around the pool, hidden at the eastern end of the Cornice.

Golf
The **Golf Club of Lebanon** (off Map p265; ☎ 822 470; www.golfclub.org.lb; in Ouzai, just north of the international airport), set in 50 picturesque hectares, is Lebanon's only championship level 18-hole course. The club also has tennis and squash courts, swimming pool and billiard tables on offer, and allows visitors onto its greens for US$35 on weekdays and US$50 on weekends, plus optional equipment rental and caddy fee.

Health Clubs & Spas
Beirutis are buff, and keep themselves so by submitting themselves to a whole host of pumping and perking procedures. Most gyms only admit members for one month or more, but hotel health clubs are an exception to the rule. Try the **Essential Spa & Health Club** (Map p265; ☎ 869 666; Mövenpick Hotel & Resort, Ave Général de Gaulle), **Gym 20** (Map p272; ☎ 745 755; Crowne Plaza Hotel, Rue Hamra) or, for pampering, the best of the bunch, **The Spa** (Map p275; ☎ 369 100; InterContinental Phoenicia Hotel, Rue Fakhr ed-Dine, Minet al-Hosn).

COURSES
American Language Center (Map p272; ☎ 366 002, 03-602 871; 1st fl, Choueiry Bldg, Rue Bliss, Hamra) Offers monthly, colloquial (spoken) Arabic courses for beginners, intermediates and advanced students over a period of a month (25 hours).

American Lebanese Language Center (off Map p265; ☎ 489 166/500 978; www.allcs.edu.lb; Confidence Center Bldg, Sin el-Fih) Provides two- to three-month courses in spoken Lebanese Arabic, along with modern standard Arabic, Chinese and European languages. Courses operate around four or five times per year.

BEIRUT

Lebanese-American University Continuing Education Program (Map p272; ☎ 867 618-20; www.lau.edu .lb; LAU Campus, Beirut) Offers tailor-made Arabic courses for beginners, intermediate and advanced learners, in small groups.

BEIRUT FOR CHILDREN

Though Beirut may not strike you as a child-friendly city at first sight – with its suicidal traffic, lack of pushchair-navigable footpaths and open potholes – there's actually a lot to keep younger visitors happily entertained for a couple of days. Beirutis coddle their kids, so you'll find they'll be made a fuss of in restaurants, taxis or even just out on the street.

Some great activities for children include the flashing rides and Ferris wheel at **Lunapark** (p273), on Beirut's Corniche, while older children will appreciate the wonders of the **National Museum of Beirut** (p270). The **St George Yacht Club** (p279) and **Riviera beach club** (p279) have children's pools in operation during the summer months.

To let off steam somewhere a little greener, the **Sanayeh Public Garden** (Map p272) has bike hire and paved paths perfect for in-line skating, while the 40,000-sq-metre pine forest on the edge of Beirut at **Horsh Beirut** (Map p265), newly opened to the public, is a cool, deliciously green respite from the city with a playground for children.

If you and your kids are feeling intrepid, you can hire bikes from **Beirut-by-Bike** (☎ 03-435 534; per hour/day LL4000/15,000). Downtown is officially a cyclist-friendly no-car zone on Sundays, but in practice is currently safe to cycle throughout the week, since military roadblocks have rendered it largely out of bounds to cars. Meanwhile, the pavement along the Corniche makes a good place to cycle if you're adept at dodging pedestrians. Nearby, there's the **Strike Out Bowling Alley** (Map p265; ☎ 785 310-2; Dunes Centre, Rue Verdun, Verdun; ☽ 1-11.30pm) for hitting the lanes.

One of the more educationally stimulating activities on offer is at **Planet Discovery** (Map p275; ☎ 980 650/660; Rue Omar ed-Daouk, near Starco bldg; adult & child LL5000; ☽ 9am-3pm Mon-Thu, 10am-7.30pm Fri & Sat, closed Sun), an interactive science museum especially designed for three- to 15-year-olds. Adults will be unable to resist the soap bubble display, where bubbles big enough to encase their young charges can be blown. Puppet shows are also held at 4pm and 5pm most Fridays and Saturdays, which cost an additional LL5000 on top of the entry fee. Six-month-olds to 12-year-olds, meanwhile, will be in seventh heaven at **Rainbow Island** (off Map p265; ☎ 05-956 444/5; www.rainbowislandjunior.com; Faubourg St Jean, cnr Damascus Hwy & Presidential Palace Rd, Hazmieh; toddlers LL8000, older children LL11,000-17,000; ☽ 10am-8pm), a vast indoor playground with learning activities, computer games and arts and crafts.

Lebanon's water parks do brisk trade throughout the summer months: try **Waves Aqua Park** (off Map p265; ☎ 04-533 555, 03-727 571/9; Mar Roukos, Metn); **Splash Mountain** (off Map p265; ☎ 04-531 166-8; www.splashmountainlb .com; Beit Mery; ☽ 10am-6pm), which also incorporates Putt Putt mini-golf course; or **Rio Lento** (☎ 04-915 656; www.riolento.com; Nahr al-Kalb; adult/child US$11/13.50; 9am-6pm, early Jun-end Sep) home to some particularly scary water slides including the near-vertical 'Kamikaze.'

Lebanon's largest theme park is **Habtoorland** (off Map p265; ☎ 05-768 888; www.habtoorland .com; adult/child US$15/10) at Jamhour, 15 minutes drive from Beirut just off the Beirut–Damascus Hwy, including scream-inducing rides and roller coasters with a loose Phoenician theme. All of these parks are within an hour of Beirut, traffic permitting.

If you or your kids are animal-lovers, don't miss **Animal Encounter** (off Map p265; ☎ 05-558 724, 03-667 355; www.animalencounter.org; Ras el-Jabal Rd, Aley; ☽ 11am-6pm Sat & Sun) 17km from Beirut, a well-known and respected refuge for unwanted, impounded or abandoned domestic and wild animals.

TOURS

Beirut is easily managed without taking an organised tour, particularly if you follow the suggestions in Beirut In… (p267). If time is important, contact the travel agencies listed (p270) for more information about tours around Beirut and further afield.

FESTIVALS & EVENTS

Given the size of the country, any festival in Lebanon is easily accessible from Beirut. Bookings are advisable and tickets for most concerts can be purchased at the Virgin Megastore (p267) and often online from the festival site. For a list of Lebanon's festivals and event highlights, see p246.

Beirut International Film Festival (www.beirutfilm foundation.org) Held in October, this festival showcases films from Lebanon and the Middle East, and aims to encourage coproductions between Arab and international communities.

Beirut International Marathon (www.beirutmara thon.org) Held each autumn, this is an incredibly popular event attracting international athletes. Only over-17s can run the full marathon itself, but there's a 5km mini-marathon for nine- to 17-year-olds, a wheelchair full- and mini-marathon, and a 10km fun run for anyone over nine.

Beirut International Platform of Dance (www.maqamat.org) The festival, which runs annually between April and May, showcases the region's best contemporary dance ensembles, along with a scattering of international names, and is organised and run by Maqamat, a contemporary dance troupe based in Beirut.

Docudays (www.docudays.net) The Beirut International Documentary Festival, held each November or December, enjoys a world-class reputation, with filmmakers from across the globe flocking in to attend.

Souq el-Bargout A fun, twice-yearly, citywide flea market. See p290 for more details.

SLEEPING
Budget
Cheap accommodation isn't plentiful in Beirut and the places listed here are currently the best on offer. Each year, however, Lonely Planet receives dozens of emails from disgruntled and dismayed travellers who have booked rooms or airport transfers, only to find no preordered taxi or even no room awaiting them when they arrive. To prevent this, try to reconfirm your booking by phone 48 to 24 hours before arrival, and take with you a print-out of any email correspondence regarding arrival dates and room or airport transfer prices.

Talal's New Hotel (Map p277; ☎ 562 567; ZSAL72 TNH@yahoo.com; Ave Charles Hélou, Gemmayzeh; dm/s/d/ tr with air-con & TV US$7/16/20/24; ☒ ☐) A popular, friendly place not far from Place des Martyrs and Gemmayzeh, offering comfortable beds at bargain-basement prices. The rooms are basic but clean, the atmosphere livelier than nearby Pension al-Nazih, and drinks from the fridge are signed for using the 'honesty system'. There's a communal kitchen, laundry facilities (US$3 for 5kg) and internet access (first 15 minutes free, LL1000 per hour after that). If it's full in summer, the obliging owner/manager will try to find you some space on the roof. There's a reliable airport pick-up service available for US$15.

Pension al-Nazih (Map p277; ☎ 564 868, 03-475 136; www.pensionalnazih.com; Ave Charles Hélou; d US$25, s/d without bathroom US$10/15; ☒ ☐) A few steps away from Talal's, Pension al-Nazih is a clean, quiet budget option. On our most recent visit, the hotel's 10 rooms were occupied with satisfied travellers, though the owner appeared to be a compulsive spraycan user: fly spray, air freshener – you name it, he'll try to blast it so keep your expensive perfume well away. Breakfast costs US$3 extra; airport pick-up can be arranged for US$20.

Regis Hotel (Map p272; ☎ 361 845; Rue Razi, Ain al-Mreisse; s/d US$28/34; ☒) Though the street on which it stands might seem a bit bleak, the Regis is a fine, basic hotel for those looking for more privacy than a dorm room, and with great proximity to the Corniche and its beach clubs. Its 20 large, reasonably clean rooms have air-con or fan, plus a fridge and TV, and five (rooms 101, 201, 301, 401 and 402) have a decent sea view. Triple rooms cost the same as a double; decent discounts can be had on stays of several nights and for stays from October to May. Airport pick-up is available for $15 and staff can arrange laundry services for a small sum.

Midrange
Beirut's midrange accommodation options are generally located in the Hamra and Ras Beirut areas. Many of these hotels can be noisy, so opt for a back room wherever possible. Prices can drop significantly out of season (up to 40% for some hotels) and the rates quoted here are standard rack rates – it's always worth asking about discounts for stays longer than a couple of nights.

Port View Hotel (Map p277; ☎ 567 500; www.portviewhotel.com; Rue Gouraud, Gemmayzeh; s/d US$40/50; ☒ ☐) A better option than the budget offerings, this small, relaxed place has basic, good-value rooms within easy walking distance of Rue Gouraud's bars and restaurants. But the Port View's most attractive feature is its manager, whose extensive knowledge of the city can make your stay extra special.

ourpick L'Hote Libanais (☎ 03-513 766; www.hotelibanais.com; Zico House,174 Rue Spears; s/d US$40/60) A cause for celebration on the Beirut accommodation front, this is a new and exciting

THE HOLIDAY INN

Probably the most visible and painful monument to the civil war is the Holiday Inn, rising like a massive tombstone behind the swish InterContinental Phoenicia.

Opened only shortly before the war, the hotel quickly became a prime sniper position. In turn, it attracted firepower of all calibres, which left it in its current bullet-riddled state. Designed to withstand an earthquake, the building is apparently still structurally sound but remains derelict, with shreds of curtain still flapping at its windows and pigeons its only long-term guests.

way to explore Beirut and beyond. Lebanese families, famed for their hospitality, invite you into their homes, where you'll sleep, eat and generally be made to feel like part of the family. It's an absolutely unique way to experience the country, and get a glimpse into the life of the real Beirut. The company also offers similar B&B accommodation the length and breadth of the country, from Tripoli to Tyre, with discounts available for multiple-night stays. It's best to email or telephone the company's extremely helpful staff to discuss your requirements and arrange your stay.

Cedarland Hotel (Map p272; ☎ 340 233/4; www.cedarlandhotel.com; Rue Omar ben Abdel Aziz, Hamra; s/d/ste US$42/49/53; ✖ ▣) While it's adjacent to a particularly bustling Hamra intersection, it's spotlessly clean, if a little tired-looking and beige. Breakfast is US$5 extra per person, but with Hamra's numerous cafés just a short walk away, it's easy enough to pick up breakfast elsewhere. It offers good discounts for long-term stays.

Casa d'Or (Map p272; ☎ 746 400; www.casadorhotel.com; Rue Jeanne d'Arc, Hamra; s/d/ste US$60/70/90; ✖ ▣) One of Beirut's best midrange hotels, the Casa d'Or is a modern addition to the Hamra sleeping scene. Warm and welcoming, with a wide variety of bright, clean rooms and suites, it comes highly recommended by Lonely Planet travellers. Wireless internet is available in the lobby and restaurant and there are good low-season discounts.

Mayflower Hotel (Map p272; ☎ 340 680; www.mayflowerbeirut.com; Rue Neamé Yafet, Hamra; s/d/ste US$80/94/150; ✖ ▣ ☎) A comfortable, old-fashioned Hamra institution, with spot-

lessly clean rooms and the added bonus of a small pool, the Mayflower recently hit the headlines by filing a lawsuit against UK newspaper the *Independent*, after journalist Robert Fisk suggested that some hotel guests were involved with armed Lebanese militias. Militant or not, to really soak up some civil war history, imbibe a few beers at the hotel's Duke of Wellington bar. Prices drop by 40% during the low season.

Marble Tower Hotel (Map p272; ☎ 354 586, 346 260; marble@marbletower.com.lb; Rue Makdissi, Hamra; s/d/ste LL130,000/149,000/290,000; ✖) Located smack-bang in the centre of Hamra this is a long-standing favourite for many travellers familiar with Beirut. Its well-worn though spotlessly clean rooms can be a bit noisy but the service is excellent, the price includes breakfast, the beds are comfortable and the suites are great value.

Top End

If you're going to splash out on accommodation somewhere in Lebanon, Beirut is the place to do it. The normal slew of quality, though quite bland, five-star hotels compete for action around the Corniche, but there are also a few notable exceptions worth exploring if you've just come up trumps at the Casino de Liban.

Riviera Hotel (Map p272; ☎ 373 210; www.rivierahotel.com.lb; Ave de Paris, Ras Beirut; s/d/ste with sea views US$130/150/200; ✖ ▣ ☎) Though its rooms are looking a little dated, the Riviera is a friendly, comfortable hotel with great sea views. Its biggest draw-card is one of the best (and most lively) beach clubs (p279) in Beirut, reachable by a tunnel under the road so that you don't have to risk life and limb to Corniche traffic. Breakfast can get a little repetitive if you're staying for a few days, and you might consider skipping it and heading instead for a café in Hamra, just up the hill.

Palm Beach Hotel (Map p272; ☎ 372 000; www.palmbeachbeirut.com; cnr Place Rafic al-Hariri & Rue Phoenicia; d/ste US$160/280; ✖ ▣ ☎) The Palm Beach is a great choice, with plush, comfortable rooms, friendly desk staff and a good central location. With a sumptuous rooftop bar and pool commanding panoramic views over the city, the Palm Beach manages to be luxurious and individual, without the hefty price tag attached to Beirut's topmost hotels.

Hotel Albergo (Map p277; ☎ 339 797; www.alber gobeirut.com; 137 Rue Abdel Wahab el-Inglizi, Achrafiye; d US$255, ste US$325-1400; ✕ ☐ ⍗) This hotel is a sybaritic dream, with 33 rooms of individual and effortless opulence, themed in Oriental, European, Colonial and Mediterranean styles. Located on a terrific Achrafiye street, close to some of Beirut's most stylish eating establishments, it's also home to exquisite Italian gastronomic delights at its restaurant Al Dente (p284) just next door. The rooftop pool and bar complete the picture, with service so attentive your request will have been met before you've had time to utter it.

InterContinental Phoenicia Hotel (Map p275; ☎ 369 100; www.ichotelsgroup.com; Rue Fakhr ed-Dine, Minet al-Hosn; d US$275-540, ste from US$990; ✕ ☐ ⍗) Beirut's most prestigious pre–civil war hotel has been redeveloped in a rather glitzy style with acres of marble and plenty of swags and tails. It has the best amenities in town and has once again become the favourite of Beirut's moneyed set. At the time of writing, however, around 30 MPs were cloistered in its topmost floors under heavy security in advance of the presidential elections, making it less pleasant for other guests, who had to undergo rigorous security checks just to get to their highly pricey rooms.

EATING

Beirutis love their food in all its forms – fast, filling or fancy. Wherever you turn in the city, you'll be just footsteps away from something delicious. Currently, the unstable economic climate means, sadly, that restaurants open and close with alarming alacrity. We recommend that rather than sticking rigidly to our suggestions below, you pick an area of the city and simply wander. It won't be long before you'll discover your own culinary gems, since Beirut's restaurants rarely disappoint.

Restaurants
HAMRA & AROUND

Pasta di Casa (Map p272; ☎ 366 909, 363 368; Ashkar Bldg, just off Rue Clemenceau, Hamra; mains around LL9000; ⍋ noon-midnight) An unpretentious local Italian place, just a short walk from most Hamra and Corniche accommodation options. Friendly staff and huge bowls of home-made pasta – one portion alongside a starter or salad is big enough to share unless you're ravenous – make it a wel-

coming place to which it's easy to return again…and again…and again. It only has 10 tables, doesn't accept credit cards and gets very busy after about 9pm.

Walimat Wardeh (Map p272; ☎ 752 320; Rue Makdissi; mains around LL10,000; ⍋ midday-3pm, 8pm-midnight) This simple, stylish place hidden away in Hamra is well worth seeking out. It's reasonably priced, with good brunches, Lebanese specialities on a changing chalked-up menu, tango music on Thursday nights and an unpretentious, laid-back local crowd.

Blue Elephant (Map p272; ☎ 788 488; Searock Hotel, Rue Salah Eddine el-Ayoubi, Raouche; mains from LL15,000; ⍋ 7pm-2am) OK, so it's a little overdone with its profusion of bamboo, screechy Thai soundtrack and indoor waterfalls, but the Blue Elephant, housed in the Searock Hotel on a road just above Lunapark, is nevertheless an excellent place to go for an upscale Thai fix. The sweet corn cookies and green curries are particularly tasty, and there's a decent vegetarian menu – but watch out for the over-attentive waiters who will replenish your every sip and spoonful, no matter how much you protest.

GEMMAYZEH

Gemmayzeh's fast-developing culinary scene revolves around Rue Gouraud, particularly the section between Ave de Damas and the St Nicholas steps. Busiest after 9pm, when scores of well-heeled and well-groomed 20- and 30-somethings take to the streets, it's a fab place to stroll and sample multiple cuisines at chic small eateries.

Olio (Map p277; ☎ 563 939; Rue Gouraud; pizza LL9000-15,000; ⍋ noon-midnight Mon-Sat) Like many of the street's gems, this tiny place with a handful of tables fills up rapidly after 9pm. Locals flock for wood-fired pizzas, generous portions of pasta and hearty red wines. Try the fabulous bruschetta pomodoro to start and grab a table near the window to watch sleek new Ferraris roll by outside.

our pick Le Chef (Map p277; ☎ 445 373, 446 769; Rue Gouraud; 2-course meals around LL10,000; ⍋ 6am-6.30pm Mon-Sat) A Beirut institution that's a must for its low prices, charismatic head waiter and great old-world atmosphere. As the Rue Gouraud eating scene develops around it, this daytime 'workers' café' keeps faithfully dishing out huge platefuls of cheap and cheerful Arabic food, with a menu that changes daily and has unusual regional

BEIRUT

specials thrown in. If they have it, don't miss the allegedly aphrodisiac *moolookhiye* (fragrant rice with chicken, lamb and mallow; see also p47). Vegetarians will also find themselves well catered for, with tasty spinach pâté, soups and melt-in-the-mouth aubergine stew, served with rice.

La Tabkha (Map p277; ☎ 579 000; Rue Gouraud; mains around LL8000; ☒ lunch & dinner) A trendy Beirut chain serving contemporary versions of traditional French and Lebanese dishes in minimalist surroundings. The daily specials, chalked up on the board, are a great lunchtime option, as is the Lebanese mezze buffet. There's a second, equally yummy, branch on Rue Mahatma Gandhi in Hamra (Map p272).

ACHRAFIYE

Achrafiye does trendy dining largely at the high end of the price scale, with a slightly older and more sedate crowd than on Rue Gouraud in Gemmayzeh. For a simpler lunch, see Cheap Eats (below).

Abdel Wahab el-Inglizi (Map p277; ☎ 200 550; Rue Abdel Wahab el-Inglizi; mezze around LL6500; ☒ noon-4pm, 7pm-1am) Set in a nice old Ottoman house, this place is a favourite with locals for its table-bending buffets. It is a great choice if you're hungry for high quality mezze and are a particular fan of hummus, of which there are numerous varieties – it won't leave you much room for dessert.

Scallywags (Map p277; ☎ 03-046 289; Rue St Joseph University; mains around $US10; ☒ 7pm-1am) A lovely, friendly fusion restaurant in a quaint and quiet Achrafiye street, this place is great for an intimate dinner, with a Mediterranean-ish menu that changes daily depending on what takes the chef's fancy. It's worth calling ahead to book, as there's only a handful of tables.

Olive (Map p277; ☎ 211 711; Rue Abdel Wahab el-Inglizi; mains around $10; ☒ 1pm-11pm) One of Beirut's few vegetarian restaurants, this great, laid-back place offers all-organic food in a beautiful French mandate–era building. With your meal, try the organic juices; afterwards, linger over a slice of home baked cake.

Relais l'Entrecote (Map p277; ☎ 332 087/8; Rue Abdel Wahab el-Inglizi; mains around LL18,000; ☒ midday-3pm, 7pm-midnight) If you're craving a piece of Paris, this is the place. Unbeatable for its steak frites, it's a fab spot for a hearty lunch washed down with a robust bottle of red wine. If you have any room left

afterwards, the chocolate fondant is highly recommended.

Al Dente (Map p277; ☎ 202 440; Rue Abdel Wahab el-Inglizi, Achrafiye; mains around LL28,000; ☒ 12.30-3pm & 8.30-11pm Mon-Fri, 8.30-11pm Sat) Attached to the Hotel Albergo (p282), this formal Italian restaurant's suitably lavish décor and lengthy wine list make it a favourite with Beirut businessmen and a fabulous place for a special occasion. The melt-in-the-mouth risottos are Italian cuisine at its very best, and well worth the high prices. Bookings are essential.

Le Sushi Bar (Map p277; ☎ 338 555; Abdel Wahab el-Inglizi; sushi around LL6000 per portion; ☒ noon-midnight) A highly chic, minimalist destination for sushi connoisseurs: if you like your sashimi extra special, served on ice, and accompanied by a glass of perfectly chilled champagne, this is a splash-out must.

DOWNTOWN

Aside from al-Balad, Downtown's dining options are largely top end, both in terms of price and dress code. Great for lavish nights out, they offer fabulous food and a glittering atmosphere.

Al-Balad (Map p275; ☎ 985 375; Rue Ahdab, Downtown; mezze around LL5000; ☒ noon-midnight) This place offers the tastiest, best-value Lebanese mezze in Downtown, and is especially popular with lunching business people. The spicy red hummus, in particular, is well worth a dip.

Diwan Sultan Brahim (Map p275; ☎ 989 989; near Starco Center, Minet el Hosn; mezze around LL5500; fish market price; ☒ noon-2pm & 7pm-midnight) If you're looking for fine fish, it's hard to beat the freshest catch in town. Select your own; the red mullet and deep-fried sardines (known as *bizri*) are house specialities. The excellent mezze are well known in Beirut, and it's a busy place, particularly on weekends, so be sure to book.

Asia (Map p275; ☎ 991 919; Capitol Bldg, Riad al-Solh Sq; mains from US$15; ☒ 7pm-1am) Beirutis love Asia as much for its expansive rooftop views across the city as for its pricey, but perfect, Asian fusion cuisine. Dress up, since the crowd's predictably glam, and book ahead for a decent table.

Cheap Eats

Every suburb has a multitude of stalls offering felafel, *manaeesh bi-zaatar* (a thyme and sesame-flavoured bread), kebabs, *foul* (fava beans), fresh juices, *fatayer bi-sbanikh* (spinach parcels) and shwarma; the best way to get a feel for where to eat is to wander around and choose the busy ones, as they are likely to be offering the freshest food. Prices are on a par: a felafel will cost around LL2500, a *manaeesh* (flat bread) LL2000, a kebab LL3000, a large fresh juice LL3000 and a shwarma LL3000.

Bliss House (Map p272; ☎ 756 555; Rue Bliss, Hamra; ☼ 7am-5am) This is one of the most popular takeaways in Beirut and is always packed with AUB students grabbing a quick snack. Its three shop fronts offer cheap and filling shwarma, kebabs, fresh juice and fruit cocktails topped with honey and nuts.

Japanese Please! (Map p272; ☎ 361 047; Rue Bliss, Hamra; sushi from LL2000 per portion; ☼ 11am-4pm & 7-11pm Mon-Sat) This tiny sushi bar is a welcome oddity among the fast-food franchises of Rue Bliss. Customers can take-away, eat at the bar, or take advantage of the free delivery service. Reasonable prices, with great teriyaki and tempura.

Marrouche (Map p272; ☎ 743 185/6; Rue Sidani, Hamra; ☼ 24hr) Specialises in very tasty *shish tawouq* (marinated grilled chicken on skewers) and chicken shwarma.

Kabab-ji (Map p272; ☎ 351 346; Rue Hamra, Hamra; ☼ 8am-2am) A long-standing branch of the Lebanon-wide chain. It's a little more stylish than most kebab shops and an extremely popular place to sit and sample fresh and delicious kebabs and grills.

Barbar (Map p272; ☎ 379 778/9; Rue Spears, Hamra; ☼ 24hr) The granddaddy of them all, this phenomenally popular chain sells *manaeesh*, shwarma, pastries, mezze, kebabs, ice cream and fresh juice. Join the hordes of people gobbling their snacks on the street in front, or organise to have food delivered to your hotel or apartment.

Zaatar w Zeit (Map p277; ☎ 614 302; Rue Nasra, Sodeco, Achrafiye; ☼ 24hr) This branch is busiest late at night when patrons from the nearby clubs flock here to re-energise over cheap and delicious *manaeesh* with a multitude of toppings. There is another branch on Rue Bliss (Map p272) that is equally popular, with AUB students there at all hours.

Mino (Map p272; ☎ 365 632; Rue Bliss, Hamra; ☼ 11am-late) This tiny shwarma stand really sells only four things – meat and chicken shwarma in two sizes. But what it does, it does well, and it beats waiting at Bliss House when it's packed with students.

Paul (Map p277; ☎ 570 170; Rue Gouraud, Gemmayzeh; ☼ 8am-11pm) A chain café but a good one nonetheless, this bakery stocks excellent breakfast pastries for around LL3000, generous sandwiches, quiches and *café au lait* so good you'd swear you were in Paris.

Taj al-Moulouk (Map p272; ☎ 370 096; Rue Bliss, Ras Beirut; ☼ 5.30am-1.30am) Great Turkish coffee and an amazing array of glistening pastries, for around LL1500 per portion, make this old-fashioned patisserie an essential pit

BEIRUT

HUBBLE, BUBBLE, TOIL & TROUBLE

Step into a Rue Bliss café after 9pm and you'll likely enter the sweet-smelling, hazy world of the nargileh. Nargileh smoking has never been so popular with the city's teenagers and it's estimated that 80% of 13- to 15-year-old smokers smoke nargilehs rather than cigarettes, since their parents are less likely to disapprove.

The nargileh (or hubble-bubble, hookah or water pipe), which passes the smoke through cooling liquid, first emerged in Turkey in the 16th century, with *objet d'art* pipes bearing coloured glass bases and heavily decorated beaten shafts of silver or gold.

Though it might feel less abrasive than cigarette smoking, there's growing concern that Lebanon's nargilehs may be damaging its youthful population. A study undertaken by the AUB and World Health Organisation showed that 60% of Lebanese teenagers are smokers. Most think that the nargileh is less addictive than cigarettes, but nargileh smoke can actually be more harmful since a pipe takes on average eight times longer to smoke than a cigarette. One seasoned nargileh smoker may, in one session, therefore be inhaling the equivalent of 100 cigarettes.

Still, it's worth a try at least once while in Beirut. The nargileh's tobacco and molasses mix (called sheesha or shisha in Arabic) is commonly flavoured with apple, strawberry, melon, cherry or mixed fruit: when you order your first, just choose your flavour and the waiter will help you get started, periodically checking that the coals are still burning. And however bad it might be for your health, it's important to take a puff now and then, just to keep the coals hot.

stop. It's take-away only, unless you transport your sticky purchases to its ice cream parlour two doors away.

Self-Catering

Beirut is packed with small neighbourhood grocery shops selling the basics, usually alongside a local greengrocer, with tempting piles of fruit and vegetables on display. If you're day-tripping outside Beirut you'll also often find fresh fruit and vegetables available at roadside stalls, along with jars of gorgeous olives and sometimes homemade cheese or bread. It's well worth slowing down to sample and support local rural economies by shopping at these smaller stores and stands.

But if a supermarket's what you need, the best Hamra has to offer are the **Consumers Co-op** (Map p272; Rue Makdissi, Hamra; 7am-11pm) and **Smith's** (Map p272; Rue Sadat; 6.30am-8.30pm Mon-Sat) which stocks many American brands. Look out for Charcuterie Bayoud (Map p272) a few doors up from the Co-op, which is as popular for its beer, wine and spirits as its meats. Excellent vintage Lebanese and imported wines can be sourced at Enoteca (Map p277) and **Le Comptoir** (Map p277) in Achrafiye. Gourmet picnic ingredients can be sourced at Souq el-Tayeb (see p290), the tantalising weekly Saturday Saifi Village organic farmers' market.

DRINKING
Bars

Beirut has an embarrassment of riches when it comes to bars. While this is great for patrons, for bar owners the competition is fierce and bars open, close, change names, venues, décor and style regularly.

With dinners booked from 9.30pm onwards, bar-hopping is a late-night pastime. Beirutis don't like waiting in line or being turned away from a bar or club, so generally they book a table or space at their favourite bar for straight after dinner. If you arrive early at one of the hottest bars, you'll probably get a space (and get to check out the ultrahip interior), but check that you won't be asked to move just as the night starts hotting up. Weekends are by far the most popular and many bars and clubs simply stay open until the patrons start to go home. For a drink in the afternoon or early evening, head to the cafés on the Corniche or in Hamra; at night, wander Achrafiye and Gemmayzeh.

Pacífico (Map p277; ☎ 204 446; Rue Monot, Achrafiye; local beers LL6000; 7pm-late) This Latin-themed bar is the long-standing number one with the local 30-something crowd. Happy hour is between 7pm and 8pm and it serves good Mexican food throughout the evening.

Lime (Map p277; ☎ 03-348 273; Rue Monot, Achrafiye; local beers LL5000; 7.30pm-late) A popular drinking spot with an outdoor terrace, it's another Rue Monot stalwart.

Hole in the Wall (Map p277; Rue Monot, Achrafiye; 7pm-late) For those wanting a break from cool interiors and guest DJs and needing a beer poured into a glass with a handle, this one's for you. It's a great little pub smack bang in the centre of Rue Monot, and it's a regular stop for expats.

Bar Louie (Map p277; ☎ 03-477 336; Rue Gouraud, Gemmayzeh; 11am-late) More laid-back than the majority of Beirut's bars, Bar Louie sports a friendly crowd and live music almost nightly. A couple of doors away, its equally diminutive 'shots bar' deals out some potent creations to get you in the partying mood, with welcoming barmen filled with tips on the current nightlife scene.

Torino Express (Map p277; ☎ 03-611 101; Rue Gouraud, Gemmayzeh; 8am-2am) One of the coolest, smallest bars in Beirut, it's a café by day, with great paninis and espressos, which transforms into a bar by night, with a DJ, glorious cocktails and a very cheerful crowd.

Also on Rue Gouraud, Copper and Rehab are two other good choices, both small, atmospheric and currently unbearably hip.

Cafés & Coffeehouses

If you really want to do as the locals do, you'll drink your coffee short, strong and at every available opportunity. On the Corniche on a Friday or Saturday night, it's almost obligatory to take a stroll to Uncle Deek (Map p272), where green T-shirted bus boys ferry tiny cups to drivers and pedestrians alike.

Al-Kahwa (Map p272; ☎ 362 232; Al-Kanater Bldg, Rue Bliss, Hamra; 10am-1am) Usually lost in a thick haze of nargileh smoke (apple nargilehs go for LL10,000), this is a popular hang-out with students from the AUB. Its friendly atmosphere and reasonably priced menu make it a reliable choice for breakfast, lunch or for dinner. An Arabic or cooked English breakfast comes in at LL6000, and there are also tasty jacket potatoes and quesadilla appetisers to munch on.

COFFEE, COFFEE EVERYWHERE

Coffee should be black as hell, strong as death, and sweet as love.

Turkish Proverb

Café culture in Beirut has changed dramatically in recent years, as Costa and Starbucks chains have put in an appearance, luring the young and hip away from the more traditional coffee haunts of old. But the oldies still remain, where you can sip strong black coffee from a tiny china cup, rather than a low-fat soya double iced mocchacino from a pint jug. Either way, though, coffee retains its pull over the Lebanese population, whose lives might grind to a halt if you took away their grindable beans.

The region's obsession with coffee is said to stem from 1526 when Ali, son of pious mystic Mohammed ibn Iraq al-Dimashqi, learned that his father had died in Mecca. The distraught son departed for Arabia immediately and spent almost 15 years in the holy city, where he adopted some of the local customs, including the drinking of coffee, then unheard of in Beirut. Unable to kick the habit, he returned to his home town with sacks of beans and is credited with single-handedly creating generations of caffeine addicts.

In old-fashioned Beirut coffeehouses today, the *café* on the menu is generally Turkish coffee brewed in a pot with a handle (generally called an *ibrik*). Sometimes this coffee is mistakenly called 'Arabic coffee', which has far more cardamom than its Turkish cousin. Sugar is added during the time of brewing, so tell the waiter how you'd like it: without sugar *(bidoon sukkar)*, a little sugar *(sukkar qaleel)*, medium *(maDbooTah)* or very sweet *(sukkar katheer)*. Remember not to gulp down the last mouthful or you'll be drinking mud, with that half-inch of coffee grounds still sitting in the bottom of the cup.

Whether it's from a street vendor clinking cups to attract customers, a roadside van with an espresso machine perched on the back, or a stylish café offering 10 different coffee blends, coffee is an integral part of Beiruti life. But beware that if you order a 'white coffee' *(ahweh baida)* it won't be a *café au lait*: in Lebanon, this means a cup of boiling water scented with orange-blossom water – nice, but not exactly the caffeine fix you might be craving.

Lina's (Map p272; ☎ 751 244; Rue Mahatma Gandhi, Hamra; ☯ 10am-11pm Mon-Sat) A large, laid-back corner spot for people-watching, Lina's is a comfy and reliable option for coffee and a light lunch, attracting young and old Beirutis alike. Good salads go for around LL8000; sandwiches are LL5000 to LL7000.

Al-Raouda (El Rawda; Map p272; ☎ 743 348; the Corniche, Manara; ☯ 8am-midnight) A waterfront favourite with local families (it has a small playground), this place is worth a stop for its good, strong coffee (LL1000) and nargilehs, and is packed on weekends. It's a little hard to find – walk down the lane right next to the Lunapark entrance and you'll spot the misspelt 'El Rawda' sign.

Bay Rock Café (Map p272; ☎ 796 700; Ave du Général de Gaulle, Raouché; ☯ 7am-2.30am) A fabulously situated café overlooking Pigeon Rocks. Meals, snacks, coffee and drinks are a bit pricey, but the outdoor terrace is a particularly attractive place to watch the sunset with a beer or a nargileh.

Tribeca (Map p277; ☎ 336 388; Rue Abdel Wahab el-Inglizi, Achrafiye; bagels LL5000-10,000; ☯ 8am-1am) A relaxed and friendly New York–style place to chow down on a bagel or big slice of chocolate fudge cake.

Ristretto (Map p272; ☎ 739 475; Rue Mahatma Gandhi, Hamra; ☯ 7am-8pm Mon-Sat) As its name implies, this small café serves good strong espresso shots. It also serves some of the best breakfast eggs and pancakes in town, and is an excellent place to cure that Rue Monot–induced hangover. Its lunch menu changes every day: if you're a homesick Brit, check if their Friday special is fish and chips with tartare sauce.

ENTERTAINMENT

Currently the best sources of 'what's on' information, including cinema listings, are the *Daily Star* newspaper and the monthly *Guide*; check out Media (p269) for more information.

Cinemas

Cinemas in Beirut tend to screen the same Hollywood movies that play worldwide, but Beirut's cultural centres (p268) frequently

BEIRUT

GAY & LESBIAN BEIRUT

Homosexuality is illegal in Lebanon, but there's a clandestine gay scene in Beirut – and it's clandestine for a very good reason. Any openly gay establishment is likely to be frequently raided and its patrons harassed. While Lebanon prides itself as one of the most liberal of Middle Eastern countries, its attitude towards sexuality (at least in law and on the surface of society) is decidedly heterocentric. All men and women in Lebanese society are expected to get married and have children and there is enormous pressure to comply. Being openly gay is rare – having an openly gay relationship even rarer – and you will be arrested if caught having sexual relations that are 'contradicting the laws of nature'.

There are signs, though, that there may be more acceptance forthcoming. Both Acid (opposite) and B 018 (opposite) nightclubs are very gay-friendly establishments, while Beirut's hammams and a number of cafés provide opportunities to meet. At clubs pay careful attention to the behaviour of other patrons and if people start dancing 'apart' suddenly, there's probably a very good reason – raids do occur.

Given this, as a gay visitor to Beirut, your best option is to make some contacts before you arrive. Your first point of contact could be **Helem** (☎ 745 092; www.helem.net; 1st fl, Yamout Bldg, 174 Rue Spears, Beirut), whose name stems from the Arabic acronym for Lebanese Protection for Lesbians, Gays, Bisexuals and Transgenders. The website offers a wealth of information and articles on gay and lesbian issues in Lebanon and further afield, while its offshoot, www.beirut .helem.net, offers a range of listings of gay-friendly cafés, restaurants, beach clubs, hammams and cruising areas. Helem also publishes a ground-breaking quarterly magazine, Barra (Arabic for 'Out'). Other useful gay and lesbian resources include the following sites:

- http://legal.20m.com
- www.bintelnas.org
- www.gaymiddleeast.com
- www.travelandtranscendence.com

organise screenings that showcase current independent, foreign, art house and classic films. There are also film festivals during the year, in particular the Mid East Film Festival Beirut and Docudays (p280). Three of the most convenient mainstream cinemas, all part of the Empire chain, are listed below.

Empire ABC (Map p265; ☎ 209 208; ABC Mall, Achrafiye)

Empire Dunes (Map p265; ☎ 792 123; Dunes Centre, Verdun)

Empire Sofil Center (Map p277; ☎ 328 806; Sofil Center, Ave Charles Malek, Achrafiye)

Live Music

Beirut isn't really filled with dedicated live-music venues, but the cultural centres (p268) and the Monnot Theatre (opposite) make up for this shortfall with programmes of local and visiting musicians. Festivals during the summer months (see p246) also offer extensive opportunities to see live performances; some cafés have musical guests, and posters advertising them often go up around

Hamra and Gemmayzeh. Bar Louie (p286) also has a wide variety of live music, usually with a performance every night some time around 10pm.

Blue Note (Map p272; ☎ 743 857; www.bluenote cafe.com; Rue Makhoul, Hamra; admission LL8000-20,000 depending on artist; ☺ 11am-2am) This is *the* place to hear live jazz. Generally Thursday, Friday and Saturday are the only nights when the music is live, and these are definitely the best nights to visit. There's a very good food menu if you want to dine first, but live jazz is the main course here. Aficionados should phone or check the website to see who's playing before booking as it sometimes books non-jazz acts.

Gemmayzeh Café (Map p277; ☎ 580 817; Rue Gouraud, Gemmayzeh; ☺ 8am-3am) This vast and beautiful Beirut institution, dating back to Ottoman times, is one of the best places to hear live Arabic music in Beirut. It generally consists of an *oud* (lute) player and singer, and you should make a booking for the live music and dinner – the café has a great mezze menu, but it's worth popping in here any time of day for a strong coffee and a quick round of backgammon. Note that there's no name on the outside of the café but, bigger and more imposing than all the other places on Rue Gouraud, it's hard to miss.

Nightclubs

A stay in Beirut is incomplete without devoting at least one evening to the art of Beiruti nightclubbing. Keep in mind that visiting one of the nightclubs listed is usually preceded by dinner generally finishing no earlier than 11pm, followed by a spot of bar-hopping; most clubs don't really get going until at least 1am.

Acid (off Map p265 ; ☎ 03-714 678; Sin el-Fil, south of the Sin el-Fil roundabout, next to Futuroscope Exhibition Hall; women free, men around US$20 incl open bar; ☺ 9pm-6am Fri-Sat) Loud and brash with pounding techno and a very gay-friendly scene, Acid is vast, friendly and the place to really let loose on the dance floor beneath an impressive laser display. Make sure you're ready for quite a night of it, as chances are you'll be dragged along to an after party when the club's doors finally close.

B 018 (☎ 03-800 018; Lot 317, La Quarantine; ☺ 9pm-7am) This venerable club is easily the most famous in town. Known for its particular décor as much as its music, it's situated underground in a car park a couple of kilometres east of Downtown. With its mock-horror baroque interior, complete with coffins for seats, B 018 is certainly memorable. Those suffering from claustrophobia needn't worry – the roof is always opened at some stage during the night. Its liberal reputation means that gays and lesbians will feel comfortable here. To get there, ask a taxi driver for the club or for the Forum de Beyrouth.

Cassino (Map p277; ☎ 656 777; cnr Sodeco Sq & Rue de Damas; admission free; ☺ 9pm-5am Thu-Sun) For something other than house, techno and commercial classics, head to Cassino, where the music's Arabic pop and, at least for part of the night, live. It's champagne and cigars all the way, so dress to the nines and book a table in advance if you want to make sure you'll make it past the doormen.

Crystal (Map p277; ☎ 332 523; Rue Monot, Achrafiye; admission free; ☺ 10pm-4am) Crystal is, without a doubt, Beirut's glitziest, glammest club. It's a great space with a good, fun atmosphere,

where the well-heeled clientele generally book a large table with friends (for dinner) and settle in for a night of dollar-flashing. If you want to join in, consider ordering the US$3000 salmazar of champagne and have it carried, spotlit, to your table – which it pays to book in advance.

Spectator Sports

Football (soccer) is by far the most popular spectator sport and Beirut's most popular teams are Beirut Nejmeh, Beirut Ansar and Olympic Beirut. If you want to catch a match, check the *Daily Star* for listings.

If you're into horseracing, the **Hippodrome** (Map p265; ☎ 632 515; admission LL5000-15,000; ☺ 11am-4pm Sun), just behind the National Museum of Beirut, is one of the only places in the Middle East where you can legally place a bet. Horse racing has always been wildly popular with the Lebanese; built by the Sursock family just after WWI, the Hippodrome was *the* place to go in the good old days. Go quickly, however, as the municipality, which owns the race track, is threatening to sell off the land to commercial concerns.

Theatre

There are several excellent theatres in Beirut that sometimes stage non-Arabic productions. Listings for what's on at individual theatres can be found in the local daily newspapers and in the *Guide* (see p269).

Al-Medina Theatre (Map p272; ☎ 371 962; cnr Rue Justinien & Rue Clemenceau, Kantari) Shows modern Lebanese plays in Arabic, French and sometimes English.

Monnot Theatre (Map p277; ☎ 320 762-4; next to St Joseph's Church, Rue St Joseph University, Achrafiye) Regular programme of French-language theatre, along with live music performances. Don't be fooled by the name. It's not on Monot St, but on the street next to the church.

Théâtre de Beyrouth (Map p272; ☎ 366 085; Rue Graham, Ain al-Mreisse) Small theatre hosting cutting-edge productions and performances from Lebanon and abroad, in Arabic, English and French.

SHOPPING

The key to good shopping in Beirut is to pick your district. If you're looking for one-off clothes, carpets, jewellery, antiques or other special bits and bobs, head to **Saifi Village** (Map p277; ☺ 10am-7pm Mon-Sat, late night shopping Thu), a beautifully restored arts quarter just off Place des Martyrs. Highlights include **Plum** (☎ 976 565; Rue Ariss Kanafani), which stocks young designers' creations; and **Ceramic Lounge** (☎ 03-129 781; Rue Mkhallissiye), a café where you can create your own customised painted pots, plates and mugs. On Saturdays, **Souq el-Tayeb** (☎ 03-340 198; www.soukeltayeb.com; Saifi Village car park; ◌ 9am-2pm Sat) sets up in the Saifi Village car park; it's Lebanon's first farmers market and a great place to pick up ingredients for a picnic or a home-cooked meal.

For High Street shopping and bookshop browsing, the university district of Hamra, where bookshops dot Rue Bliss and the small streets leading off it, is your best bet. If you're in the mood for a wander around a mall, the **ABC Mall** (Map p265; www.abc.com.lb; ☎ 212 888; Mar Mitr Rise; ◌ 10am-10pm) stocks brand names, a wide range of children's clothes and hosts several cafés and a cinema.

If you're heading to a particularly swanky nightclub, a stroll along Rue Verdun (Map p265) could be the perfect thing, lined with designer clothes shops and well-dressed locals sipping espressos, while Downtown, too, has its share of high-end boutiques. Scheduled to open in 2008, Downtown's Souqs Project promises to bring yet more high-end fashion and interior design stores into the city centre. For junk shops, Gemmayzeh's the place to explore; for antiques and souvenirs, Achrafiye.

Good quality Middle Eastern souvenirs – satin slippers, wooden boxes, backgammon sets and ceramics – can be found at **Artisans du Liban et d'Orient** (Map p272; ☎ 362 610; the Corniche, Ain al-Mreisse; ◌ 10am-6pm Mon-Sat) and at the worthy **L'Artisan du Liban** (Map p277; ☎ 580 618; Rue Montee Accawi, Achrafiye; ◌ 10am-6pm Mon-Sat), which supports Lebanese craftsmen in need.

Another great place to seek out original souvenirs is the **Oriental Art Centre** (Map p272; ☎ 349 942; Rue Makhoul, Hamra; ◌ 9am-1pm & 3.30pm-6pm Mon-Sat). Owned by the same old gentleman, in the same location, since 1955, it sells hand-tinted lithographs and vintage postcards, offering nostalgic, David Roberts-like visions of a long lost Middle East.

Cool books on Middle Eastern visual culture, photography and cultural studies can be found at **CD-Thèque** (Map p277; ☎ 746 078; Ave Elias Sarkis, Achrafiye) and at **Virgin Megastore** (Map p275; ☎ 999 666; Opera Bldg, Place des Martyrs, Downtown; ◌ 9am-11pm Mon-Sat), both of which stock an enormous range of excellent DVDs, videos and CDs from the region, in all genres and styles.

Finally, twice a year – usually in November or December and in May or June – Beirut hosts the **Souq el-Bargout**, a massive informal flea market, which consumes the city centre's streets each evening for about a fortnight. An evening of browsing and stopping to nibble snacks from its vendors is an unmissable experience if you're in town at this time.

GETTING THERE & AWAY

For information about getting to Syria from Beirut, see Travel Between Syria & Lebanon (p396). Buses, minibuses and service taxis to destinations north of Beirut leave from Charles Helou bus station (Map p277) and the Dawra (aka Dora) transport hub (7km northeast of town). To the south and southeast they leave from the Cola transport hub (Map p265) on the opposite side of town, south of Blvd Saeb Salam. See the relevant town and city sections for further details.

Air

Beirut has the only airport in the country, **Beirut Rafic Hariri International Airport** (BEY; ☎ 628 000; www.beirutairport.gov.lb). See p391.

AIRLINE OFFICES

Most airlines have their offices in the **Gefinor Center** (Map p272; Rue Maamari, Hamra). For details of major airlines flying to and from Beirut, see p391.

Bus & Microbus

Buses and microbuses travel between Beirut and Lebanon's major towns. There are three main bus hubs in Beirut:
Charles Helou bus station (Map p277) Just east of Downtown, for destinations north of Beirut (including Syria).
Cola transport hub (Map p265) This is in fact a confused intersection that is sometimes called Mazraa. It is generally for destinations south of Beirut.
Dawra transport hub Northeast of Beirut, and covering the same destinations as Charles Helou, it is usually a port of call on the way in and out of the city.

Charles Helou is the only formal bus station and is systematically divided into three signposted zones:
Zone A For buses to Syria.
Zone B For buses servicing Beirut (where the route starts or finishes at Charles Helou).
Zone C For express buses to Jounieh, Byblos and Tripoli.

Zones A and C have ticket offices where you can buy tickets for your journey.

Cola is not as well organised as Charles Helou, but if someone doesn't find you first (which is what usually happens) ask any driver where the next bus to your destination is leaving from. Buses usually have the destination displayed on the front window or above it in Arabic only. There are also a growing number of microbuses covering the same routes, which are slightly more expensive than regular buses, but a lot cheaper than service taxis. Microbuses are operated by individuals. The advantage is that they are small, comfortable and frequent, but you'd be taking your chances regarding the driver's ability. You pay for your ticket on the microbus, at either the start or the end of your journey.

Service Taxi & Taxi

Taxis to Syria depart from the Charles Helou and Cola bus stations and operate on the usual system of waiting until the vehicle fills up before leaving. They have an advantage over the buses in that you don't have to wait around too long to depart, but the disadvantage is that they can be a bit of a squash, especially on a long journey. If you want the taxi to yourself, you will have to pay for all five passenger seats. See Service Taxi & Taxi (p292) for more information.

GETTING AROUND
To/From the Airport

Beirut Rafic Hariri International Airport (off Map p265; ☎ 628 000; www.beirutairport.gov.lb) is approximately 5km south of Beirut city centre. It's possible to catch a bus into the city, but the airport isn't fantastically set up for such an arrangement. The airport bus stop, from which buses leave, is a 1km walk from the terminal – a hot walk, if you happen to arrive at midday in August.

The red-and-white LCC bus 1 will take you from the airport roundabout to Rue Sadat in Hamra, useful if you're staying in one of Hamra's numerous midrange hotels, or at one of the swankier places – including the Riviera and the Palm Beach – along the Corniche. Bus 5 will take you to the Charles Helou bus station hub. Fares are LL700.

The blue-and-white OCFTC buses 7 and 10 also stop at the airport roundabout; bus 10 goes to the Charles Helou bus station, and

bus 7 goes to Raouché, from where you can take bus 9 to Hamra. Fares are LL700. The buses operate between 5.30am and 6pm and all being well, the maximum wait should be 10 minutes. Service taxis can also be hailed from the highway – further on from the roundabout – and cost LL2000 per person.

If you can stretch to it, the best way to avoid hassle is to pre-arrange an airport pick-up with your hotel. Even Beirut's budget hostels offer this service, and will charge you substantially less than a normal taxi might, usually around US$15. If you don't have a pick-up arranged, most yellow taxi drivers will attempt to charge around US$25 for the trip, though with hard bargaining you may be able to drive them down to as little as US$10. Make sure you agree clearly on the price before you get into the cab.

Car & Motorcycle

For general information on hiring a car or motorcycle, see p403. Here's a selection of car-rental companies.

Advanced Car Rental (☎ 999 884/5; www.advanced carrent.com) This friendly local company offers substantial discounts on its published prices and comes highly recommended over some of the larger, more international firms. Extra services include free drop-off to any hotel in Beirut, and a free Advanced Car Rental CD, providing an in-car version of Arabic elevator music.

Avis (☎ 367 124; www.avis.com.lb)

Budget (☎ 740 741; www.budget-rental.com)

Lenacar–Europcar (☎ 480 480; www.lenacar.com)

Sixt (☎ 301 226; www.sixt.com.lb)

Thrifty Car Rental (☎ 510 100; www.thrifty.com.lb)

Public Transport

Beirut is well serviced by its network of buses. The red-and-white buses are run by the privately owned **Lebanese Commuting Company** (LCC; ☎ 744 174; www.lccworld.com) and the large blue-and-white OCFTC buses are government owned. Sometimes the tourist information office (see p269) has free LCC route maps available.

Buses operate on a 'hail-and-ride' system: wave to the driver and the bus will stop. The only official bus stops are where the bus starts and finishes. There are no timetables, but both companies run buses from roughly 5.30am to 9pm, with services departing roughly every 15 minutes.

Buses can be excruciatingly slow but are handy if you're on a time-rich, cash-poor stay. They're especially good value for trips to places such as Brummana (p296) and Beit Mery (p295).

The bus routes most useful to travellers are listed here. A short trip will almost always cost LL750, a longer trip LL1000.

LCC BUSES

1 Hamra–Khaldé Rue Sadat (Hamra), Rue Emile Eddé, Hotel Bristol, Rue Verdun, Cola roundabout, Airport roundabout, Kafaat, Khaldé

2 Hamra–Antelias Rue Sadat (Hamra), Rue Emile Eddé, Radio Lebanon, Sassine Sq, Borj Hammoud, Dawra, Antelias

5 Ain al-Mreisse–Hay as-Saloum Manara, Verdun, Yessoueiye, Airport roundabout, Hay as-Saloum

6 Cola–Byblos Antelias, Jounieh, Byblos (Jbail)

7 Museum–Bharssaf Museum, Beit Mery, Brummana, Baabdat, Bharssaf

15 Cola–Aley-Qmatiye Airport Bridge, Galerie Semaan, Hazmieh, Aleh, Qmatiye

OCFTC BUSES

1 Bain Militaire–Khaldé Bain Militaire, Unesco, Summerland, Khaldé

4 Dawra–Jounieh Dawra, Dbayé, Kaslik, Jounieh

5 Ministry of Information–Sérail Jdeideh Ministry of Information, Sodeco, Borj Hammoud, Sérail Jdeideh

7 Bain Militaire–Airport Bain Militaire, Summerland, Borj Brajné, Airport

8 Ain al-Mreisse–Sérail Jdeideh Ain al-Mreisse, Charles Helou, Dawra, Sérail Jdeideh

9 Bain Militaire–Sérail Jdeideh Bain Militaire, Rue Bliss, Rue Adbel Aziz, Rue Clemenceau, Rue Weygand, Tabaris Sq, Sassine Sq, Hayek roundabout, Sérail Jdeideh

10 Charles Helou–Airport Charles Helou, Shatila, Airport roundabout

15 Ain al-Mreisse–Nahr al-Mott Ain al-Mreisse, Raouché, Museum, Nahr al-Mott

16 Charles Helou–Cola Charles Helou, Downtown, Cola

23 Bain Militaire–Dawra Bain Militaire, Ain al-Mreisse, Charles Helou, Dawra

24 Museum–Hamra Museum, Barbir, Hamra

Service Taxi & Taxi

Service taxis are plentiful and cheap in Beirut. Most routes around the capital are covered and you can hail one at any point on the route. The only way to find out if the driver is going where you want is to hail him and ask. If the driver is not going where you want he'll (and it's nearly always a 'he') respond by driving off. If he's going in your direction the acknowledgment to get in may be as imperceptible as a head gesture.

You can get out at any point along their route by saying 'anzil huun' (I get out here), to the driver. Occasionally when the drivers have an empty car they will try and charge you a private taxi fare. To let him know that you want to take the taxi as a service taxi, be sure to ask him 'servees?' Taxis are usually an elderly Mercedes with red licence plates, generally with a taxi sign on the roof and smoke belching from both the interior and the exhaust. The fare for all routes in central Beirut is either LL1000 or LL1500, seemingly depending on the taxi. The fare to outlying suburbs is LL2000. Try and pay at the earliest opportunity during your trip. It's a good idea to keep a few LL1000 notes handy for these trips.

If you do wish to take a service taxi as a private taxi, make sure the driver understands exactly where you are going and negotiate a price before you get in. Most destinations in the centre of Beirut cost LL5000 to LL8000; however, it's not uncommon for drivers to ask for LL10,000, and grudgingly settle for LL7000. If you think the driver is asking too much, just wave him on and wait for another one.

You can also telephone for a taxi from a number of private hire firms. They charge a bit more, but are safer at night. Remember to ask the fare over the phone.

The following companies are considered most reliable:

Allo Taxi (☎ 366 661)

Lebanon Taxi (☎ 340 717-19)

Taxi Premiere (☎ 389 222) Based in Verdun, offers airport service and services to Syria and Jordan.

TV Taxi (☎ 862 489, 860 890)

Mt Lebanon & the Chouf Mountains

جبل لبنان وجبال الشوف

Mt Lebanon, the traditional stronghold of the Maronites, is the heartland of modern Lebanon, comprising several distinct areas that together stretch out to form a rough oval around Beirut, each home to a host of treasures easily accessible on day trips from the capital.

Directly to the east of Beirut, rising up into the mountains, are the Metn and Kesrouane districts. The Metn, closest to Beirut, is home to the relaxed, leafy summer-retreats of Brummana and Beit Mery, the latter host to a fabulous world-class winter festival. Further out, mountainous Kesrouane is a lunar landscape in summer and a skier's paradise, with four resorts to choose from, during the snowy winter months.

North from Beirut, the built-up coastal strip hides treasures sandwiched between concrete eyesores, from Jounieh's dubiously hedonistic 'super' nightclubs and gambling pleasures to the beautiful ancient port town of Byblos, from which the modern alphabet is believed to have derived. Inland you'll find the wild and rugged Adonis Valley and Jebel Tannourine, where the remote Afqa Grotto and Laklouk, yet another of Lebanon's ski resorts, beckon travellers.

To the south, the lush green Chouf Mountains, where springs and streams irrigate the region's plentiful crops of olives, apples and grapes, are the traditional home of Lebanon's Druze population. The mountains hold a cluster of delights, including one real and one not-so-real palace – Beiteddine and Moussa respectively – as well as the expansive Chouf Cedar Reserve and Deir al-Qamar, one of the prettiest small towns in Lebanon.

MT LEBANON & THE CHOUF MOUNTAINS

HIGHLIGHTS

- Absorb 7000 years of history at the ruins at **Byblos** (p306), followed by 40 years of history at the **Byblos Fishing Club** (p312)
- Remember how to tell your stalactites from your stalagmites at the spectacular **Jeita Grotto** (p303)
- Take a heart-stopping ride on Jounieh's **Téléférique** (p304)
- Hit the slopes and après-ski parties of wintertime **Faraya Mzaar** (p299)
- Gape at the incredible mosaics at **Beiteddine Palace** (p320)
- Get back to nature with a hike among the cedars at the **Chouf Cedar Reserve** (p323)

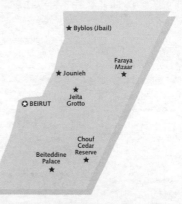

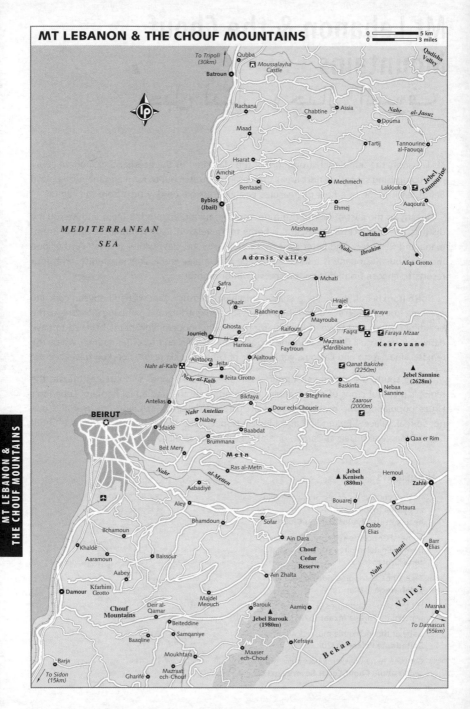

MT LEBANON & THE CHOUF MOUNTAINS

THE METN & KESROUANE
المتن وكسروان

The Metn, the mountainous area to the immediate east of Beirut, was the frontline between the Christians and the Druze during the civil war.

These days few traces of the fierce fighting remain and it has become a popular summer getaway for middle-class Beirutis escaping the stifling heat, pollution and humidity of the city.

Outside the summer months it can be very quiet – except at 4pm on weekdays when Brummana's high school gets out and floods of teenagers overrun its cafés, and at 1pm on weekends when flocks of day-tripping families stop off here for lunch. Brummana is the main resort area with plenty of accommodation and restaurants, while Beit Mery has Roman and Byzantine ruins and the famous Al Bustan festival. Both can be visited as an easy day trip from Beirut, keeping in mind that on the trip up and down the mountain you'll experience some of the most hair-raising driving in Lebanon.

The only thing that might slow your journey down, if you're with a rental car, is actually locating the two towns in the first place since there are few road signs leading the way out of Beirut. If in doubt, point yourself as due east as possible and stop frequently to ask directions.

Beyond the Metn is the Kesrouane *caza* (district), known almost exclusively today for its wide range of ski resorts. Historically, Shiites inhabited the Kesrouane but in the 13th and 14th centuries the area's Mamluk overlords settled Sunni Muslim Turkoman clans to police the territory.

It was from these Turkomans that the dominant Assaf dynasty emerged, and under the Ottomans the Assafs in turn encouraged Maronite emigration to the Kesrouane to keep the Shiites under control. This they did with such efficiency that by the 18th century most of the original Shiites had been driven out of the area and it became primarily Maronite. Nowadays, it's famed for its spectacular vistas and the flashy aprés-ski scenes of its popular winter resorts.

BEIT MERY   بيت مري
☎ 04

This popular summer retreat, its name meaning 'House of the Master' in Aramaic, is 17km from Beirut centre and 800m above sea level with wonderful views down to the sea on the west side and to the mountains on the east.

The original village has grown into a small town: many of the villas have been built in strategic positions to take advantage of the views, with little concern for aesthetics. Eclipsed in popularity by Brummana just up the road, its main pulling-power lies in its various ruins and in its wintertime festival (see below).

Sights
The **ruins** that remain here date from the Roman and Byzantine periods. Worth seeing in particular are the fine **mosaics** on the floor of the 5th century Byzantine church. The remains of a number of small **temples** surround the mosaics, including one dedicated to Juno built in the reign of Trajan (AD 98–117). There is also a fairly well-preserved public bath, where you can see the original hypocaust tiles that acted as the heating system.

Nearby is the Maronite monastery of **Deir al-Qalaa**, built in the 18th century on the remains of a Roman temple, which in turn was probably built on an earlier Phoenician temple. As at Baalbek (p354), the Roman temple was dedicated to Baal, known here as Baal Marqod. Heavily damaged in the civil war and occupied until 2005 by Syrian soldiers, the monastery is worth a visit, although reconstruction work is ongoing. Other than visiting these sites, there is little to do in Beit Mery except enjoy the views and stroll to Brummana and back for lunch, which is a pleasant enough way to pass a quiet afternoon.

Festivals & Events
The **Al Bustan Festival** (www.albustanfestival.com), with a varied programme of chamber, choral and orchestral music along with theatre and dance performances, usually begins in mid-February and runs for about a month. Most performances take place in the town's Emile Bustani auditorium and at the Hotel Al Bustan (p296). Check out the festival website for more information.

MT LEBANON & THE CHOUF MOUNTAINS

Sleeping & Eating

Hotel Al Bustan (☎ 972 980-82; www.albustanhotel
.com; s/d/ste from US$195/215/230; ✗ 🗔 ⚑) This
luxurious hotel is a lovely, comfortable
place to stay with excellent views, though
because of the price it's only really a worthwhile alternative to Beirut during the festival period, when it serves as a venue for
events. Breakfast costs US$12.

There are two well-regarded restaurants
within the Hotel Al Bustan, **Il Giardino** (2-course
meal per person US$25-30), an Italian trattoria, and
the popular French **Les Glycines** (3-course menu
per person US$37), as well as a good bar, the **Scot-
tish Bar**, recommended for its great views.

Tigre (meals around US$12) Near Deir al-Qalaa
and serving hearty traditional Lebanese
food, this place has breathtaking views
without a breathtaking price.

Getting There & Away

From Beirut you can catch a service taxi to
Beit Mery (LL2500) at Dawra bus station
or at the National Museum of Beirut. Taxis
stop on the main roundabout in the town
and you can easily walk around the whole
town from there. Two buses, OCFTC bus
17 or LCC bus 7, also head up here from
opposite the National Museum.

BRUMMANA   برمانا
☎ 04

Around 4km northeast of Beit Mery, though
almost connected to the former by a constant string of shops and cafés, the resort
town of Brummana has nothing as grand
as ancient monuments to distract you from
the serious pursuits of eating, drinking and
partying.

During summer the place is crowded to
bursting point and on weekends the traffic
can be horrendous. Things are particularly
busy during the national tennis tournament, held in August.

If visiting out of season, things are much
quieter – and many of the hotels considerably better value, especially midweek – but it
lacks the buzz of the busy summer months.

NOSTRADAMUS OR NOT?

One of the Metn's most famous exports of recent years is celebrity psychic Michel Hayek. Famous
throughout Lebanon and the Middle East for his yearly slew of predictions, usually doled out
on New Year's Eve in front of LBC channel TV-cameras and a large component of the Lebanese
general public, he spookily often seems to get it quite right.

Hayek, 40-year-old son of a butcher from a small Metn village, has been predicting the future
not only to TV audiences but also to private commercial firms – including solicitors, account-
ants and stockbrokers – across the globe, whose payrolls he has been on for almost a decade.
His first apparent glimpse into the future came in the '80s, when he successfully predicted the
Challenger space shuttle disaster (allegedly trying in vain to warn the American authorities about
the impending explosion) and realised he had a gift for sensing the signs and 'vibrations' foreshadowing future events.

In 1997, Hayek is said to have predicted the death of Princess Diana, and in 2005 predicted
that a 'large explosion' would disrupt Downtown Beirut; five weeks later, former prime minister
Rafiq Hariri was killed in the massive Downtown bomb blast outside the St. George Yacht Club.
He also apparently forecasted the 2005 assassination of Gibran Tueni, warning his wife not to let
him buy the car in which he was gunned down. He has, he says, for his troubles, been parodied
and derided in the Lebanese media.

Hayek, however, doesn't think he's endowed with a unique gift, believing that everyone has
the ability to sense the things that he does, if only they'd listen to their intuition. A sense of
foresight, he says, is just like a regular sense of sight.

Though many people trust unquestioningly in Hayek's predictions, his critics claim that his
predictions are often wrong, and sometimes so vague that they can't help be right in such a
turbulent country. Hayek himself acknowledges that he's not right all the time, but this hasn't
managed to dampen his phenomenal popularity. And his 'feelings' extend beyond the public
and political sphere: in 2007 his personal predictions included marriage to his girlfriend, a child
psychologist, to whom he proposed after just three dates, a sixth sense telling him that it was
the right thing to do.

Nonetheless, the views down to Beirut and the Mediterranean are even better than at Beit Mery.

Information

Internet access is available in the centre of Brummana, but the addresses change every summer and your best bet is to walk along the main street or ask at a hotel. Credit Libanais has an ATM in the main street and there are a couple of moneychangers there as well. Other banks have ATM machines inside. The **post office** (8am-5pm Mon-Fri, 8am-noon Sat) is on the main street.

Sleeping

Brummana is geared towards well-off Lebanese and Middle Eastern clients, with a distinct shortage of cheap and even midrange accommodation. Unless you fall in love with the town at first sight, it's probably better value to stay in Beirut and visit on a day trip.

Kanaan Hotel (☎ 960 025; fax 961 213; Rue Centrale; s/d low season US$35/40, high season US$40/60) One of the least pricey options in town, this place, located on the main road directly opposite Brummana High School, is small and open all year round. Its rooms are simple but all have attached bathrooms and balconies with views right down to the sea, while the lounge is decorated with old Lebanese objets d'art, oil paintings and chandeliers.

Garden Hotel (☎ 960 203; www.gardenhotellb.com; s/d/ste low season US$45/50/75, high season US$70/80/120; 🕸 🖳 🐼) A friendly family-run hotel near Printania Palace Hotel, it's especially good value in low season. The rooms are a little old-fashioned but are well appointed and the hotel has nice gardens and relaxing poolside setting.

Hotel Le Crillon (☎ 865 555; www.lecrillon.com; Rue Centrale; s/d/ste low season US$45/50/60, high season US$80/110/130; 🕸 🖳 🐼) This comfortable hotel has great views from most of its rooms, towards Jebel Sannine. Though the rooms aren't anywhere near as nice as the lobby or the grounds, it makes up for the shortfall with a pool, Jacuzzi and sauna and very friendly staff.

Printania Palace Hotel (☎ 862 000; www.printania .com; Chahine Achkar St; s/d low season US$80/90, high season US$150/160; 🕸 🖳 🐼) A large, old-fashioned and charming four-star hotel, with all the accoutrements you would expect for the price

tag. The rooms are large and pleasant, and there's a well-known French restaurant, as well as a Lebanese/Mediterranean restaurant serving a hearty Sunday buffet lunch.

Grand Hills Hotel & Spa Hotel (☎ 862 888; www .grandhillsvillage.com; deluxe d/grand deluxe d/ste US$247/297/345; 🕸 🖳 🐼) Part of Grand Hills Village, a swish residential compound set on a huge chunk of prime Brummana real-estate, this lavish place is owned by Robert Mouawad, a well-known international jeweller. The hotel exhibits the same attention to detail as one of his famous jewellery pieces, with the 118 rooms and suites exquisitely decorated in 25 different themes – all with great views. With a fabulous spa and its own botanical gardens, you'll find yourself wanting to sell your own jewellery to stay an extra night but before you do, it's worth checking the website for special multinight packages offering substantial discounts.

Eating & Drinking

Brummana has a great range of eating options in all price brackets. All those listed here are along the main road, where you'll also find the usual shwarma and felafel joints.

Crepaway (☎ 964 347; Rue Centrale; mains from LL5000; 11am-midnight) This chain outlet serves up decent burgers and pizza along with French-style crepes.

Manhattan (☎ 961 967; Rue Centrale; mains around LL7000; 8am-midnight) A popular American-style diner dishing up large plates of burgers, pizza and salads: look for the curiously familiar 'M' sign that will make you wonder how they haven't been sued yet.

Mounir (☎ 873 900; Rue Centrale; mezze LL4000-7000; 11am-midnight) With fabulous views towards the Mediterranean, wonderful mezze, seafood and grills, and a relaxing garden and children's playground, this is perfect for settling in for a long late lunch. Bookings are essential, especially if you want a table with a view in summer.

Taboo Pub (☎ 528 104; Rue Centrale; 6pm-late) On the corner just along from the police station, this is a popular place for a drink, with live music on weekend evenings.

Le Gargotier (☎ 960 952; Rue Centrale; meals per person US$20; noon-3pm & 7pm-midnight, closed Fri) and its sister restaurant **La Gargote** (☎ 960 096) further down the road past the high school, both serve good traditional French food in traditionally French surroundings.

MT LEBANON & THE CHOUF MOUNTAINS

Getting There & Away

Service taxis from the National Museum or Dawra charge LL2500 to Beit Mery or Brummana. Bus 7 LCC (LL750, 40 minutes) leaves from just east of the National Museum.

JEBEL SANNINE جبل صنّين

This impressive mountain (2628m) is worth climbing in the summer for the unparalleled views of Lebanon from its summit. There are actually two summits: the higher one is less interesting and it is the slightly lower peak that affords the spectacular views.

To make the climb, head for the village of **Baskinta**, which is east of Bikfaya. From there, continue 6km to the hamlet of **Nebaa Sannine**, where there is a spring that feeds **Wadi Sellet ash-Shakroub**, the starting point for the climb. It is best to make the climb from the most southerly slopes rather than tackling the slopes that overlook the hamlet. It is a moderately steep climb and should not take more than three hours. The last part of the climb is easier: there is a path that runs like a ledge around the top of the mountain.

From the top you can see Qornet as-Sawda, Lebanon's highest peak at 3090m, to the north, and Jebel ash-Sheikh (Mt Hermon; 2814m) to the south. The Bekaa Valley and the Anti-Lebanon Range are clearly visible to the east and in the foreground are Jebel Keniseh (880m) and Jebel Barouk (1980m).

To the west you can see the foothills of the Mt Lebanon Range slope all the way down to Beirut. Choose a clear, fine day to make this ascent; you'll need good strong shoes, plenty of water and to be reasonably fit.

Getting There & Away

Though difficult to do without your own transport, you could take a taxi to tiny Nebaa Sannine and arrange to be picked up there at a specific time and place. Failing that, you would have to make the walk back to the village of Baskinta, about 6km, and try your luck at picking up a service taxi from there.

It would be a wise idea to inform your hotel or friends of your plans and what time you expect to be back.

QANAT BAKICHE & ZAAROUR قناة بكيش والزعرور

Qanat Bakiche and Zaarour sit on the slopes of Jebel Sannine and are Lebanon's two smallest ski-resorts. Historians think Qanat Bakiche was named after Bacchus, to whom there are lots of shrines in the area.

Both are set in spectacular locations and were severely damaged during the civil war – Zaarour was destroyed twice. Though they have both recovered well, they are far more low-key than Lebanon's other ski locations.

Qanat Bakiche has uncrowded slopes and just one hotel, the basic but comfortable **Snow Land Hotel** (☎ 03-340 300; d US$75), which also offers equipment and lessons. More adventurous skiers and snowboarders will be happy to note that the resort has a snowcat for trips to the back country, as well as snowmobiles for hire.

Zaarour operates as a private club, with a good safety record and excellent opportunities for cross-country skiing. The best way to find out whether you can wheedle

---

SKI FACTS: QANAT BAKICHE & ZAAROUR

- **Altitude** Qanat Bakiche: 1904m to 2250m; Zaarour: 1651m to 2000m
- **Lifts** Qanat Bakiche has one beginner and two medium/advanced; Zaarour has three beginner, two medium and two advanced
- **Adult Day Pass** Qanat Bakiche: US$10 (Monday to Friday), US$18 (Saturday and Sunday); Zaarour: US$17 (Monday to Friday), US$27 (Saturday and Sunday)
- ☎ 03-340 300 in Qanat Bakiche; 04-310 010 in Zaarour
- **Opening hours** 8am to 3.30pm Monday to Friday, 8am to 4pm Saturday and Sunday

Since Zaarour operates as a private resort and Qanat Bakiche's slopes are fairly limited, these resorts don't seem the obvious choice for visitors compared to Faraya Mzaar or the Cedars. However, if you can gain access to Zaarour, or you don't mind the extra work to get the fresh stuff at Qanat Bakiche, both have awesome views and uncrowded slopes.

a day without a full club membership is to give the resort a call (☎ 04-310 010/1). Both resorts are difficult to reach without a car: the only practical way is to organise a taxi either from Beirut or from Faraya, though you'll probably have to bargain hard to make the trip worth your while.

FARAYA & FARAYA MZAAR (OUYOUN AL-SIMAAN)

فاريا وفاريا المزار (عيون السيمان)

☎ 09

Better known for the ski resort, Faraya Mzaar, lying 6km above it, Faraya itself is a sleepy village that only truly comes alive from December to March with the annual invasion of ski-toting Beirutis. Most skis, however, spend more time facing skyward in front of the cafés than racing down the well-groomed slopes, and aprés-ski activities start early in the afternoon and end late in the evening. But Faraya Mzaar has more to offer than just partying; with the fastest and most extensive lift system, decent annual snowfall and the best variety of slopes for all abilities, it's the biggest – and many say the best – resort in Lebanon, though perhaps not as picturesque as the Cedars further north.

The slopes themselves consist of three separate areas, Refuge, Jonction and Wardeh, and there are also a few cross-country skiing trails.

In the summer, Faraya Mzaar takes on a different character altogether, as the bleak mountainscapes become barren and lunar and the resort itself is devoid of almost all its trade. Unless you're using it as a base for hiking in the region, it's not the most exciting place to be and many of the bars and cafés are closed until the first snow flurries. For more information on the resort, see Ski Facts: Faraya Mzaar (this page).

Sights & Activities

The main attraction of the area, except for the snow, is its bleak natural beauty. On the road between Faraya and Faraya Mzaar it's worth stopping off at the famous **Faraya Natural Bridge** (Jisr al-Hajar). You'll spot it on the road between the village and the resort (marked the 'highway' route at the crossroads in the lower Faraya village). Otherwise look out for the restaurant **Au Pont Naturel** (☎ 341 134), which is open year

---

> ### SKI FACTS: FARAYA MZAAR
>
> - **Altitude** 1850m to 2465m
> - **Lifts** 18
> - **Adult Day Pass** US$25 to US$30 Monday to Friday, US$25 to US$50 Saturday and Sunday
> - ☎ 09-341 501
> - **Opening hours** 8am to 3.30pm Monday to Friday, 8am to 4pm Saturday and Sunday
>
> Faraya Mzaar is the best equipped and most popular ski resort in Lebanon and on a good weekend it looks like all of Beirut is on the slopes at once. Unfortunately, the Lebanese tend to ski like they drive - with the same disregard for the rules - so keep your eyes peeled for errant 'bipolar' traffic. Weekdays are far quieter (and less expensive) and after a good snowfall it can be a magical place to ski or snowboard.
>
> Many coming to the resort take the aprés-ski activities far more seriously than the skiing and the resort has a hard-partying reputation, though it's also family-friendly, with children's lessons available at its five beginner slopes. Adult passes are available either at the office opposite the Mzaar Intercontinental Hotel entrance, or at the base of the slopes near the ski lifts. There's free access to the slopes for children under five: take your tiny people's passports and a passport photo of each to the office opposite the Mzaar Intercontinental for their free pass.
>
> Ski and snowboard equipment can be rented from a number of places for between US$15 and US$20 per day, and there are rescue and Red Cross teams on hand.

round, with decent mezze, grills and great views of the bridge. You can take an interesting but steep walk down to the bridge itself, which, centuries ago, was thought to be a work of human construction, but it is in fact entirely a freak of nature.

If you're looking for ski equipment, you'll find plenty of shops on the road leading up to Faraya from the coast, while on the road from Faraya Mzaar to the slopes you'll see snowmobiles for hire. At the bottom of the slopes themselves are yet more ski equipment sales and rental points.

Sleeping

Most skiers stay in the purpose-built Faraya Mzaar ski village near the slopes, though there are also some good budget-conscious options in Faraya village, 6km below the ski resort. It's worthwhile checking, before choosing accommodation in Faraya village, whether your hotel offers free transport to the slopes, a handy way to avoid negotiating taxis if you haven't rented a car.

Much of Faraya Mzaar's accommodation consists of private apartments and chalets that are rented out for the entire ski season. Bookings are heaviest just before Christmas and it can be busy through to the end of March depending on snow conditions. Hotels are nearly always booked well in advance for the weekends but you can usually find somewhere to stay during the week. If you haven't booked months in advance, check with **Ski Leb** (www.skileb.com) for last-minute hotel vacancies.

FARAYA VILLAGE

Coin Vert Hotel (☎ /fax 720 812; s/d/tr US$30/40/50) This friendly, family-run hotel is on the main road of Faraya village just before the roundabout. It's a small, simple but clean one-star hotel that's open all year. It has a restaurant serving European and Lebanese dishes (with an average cost of US$10 for lunch or dinner) and a bar that's popular during the ski season. There's also a ski shop where you can rent equipment.

Tamer Land Hotel (☎ 321 268; s/d/ste US$45/60/75) Another friendly family-run hotel in the centre of the village (up past the roundabout), with a choice from around 50 regular rooms or 20 suites suitable for families. It's clean, welcoming and all rooms have a private bathroom and satellite TV. The hotel also has two restaurants and a pub.

FARAYA MZAAR

Auberge Suisse (☎ 953 841; d US$85; 🛏) One of the best places at the lower end of Faraya Mzaar's price scale, this place has been operating since the '70s, meaning the décor is just a little dated but perfectly fine for a place to lay a weary skier's head.

Merab (☎ 341 341; s & d from US$95; 🛏 💻) A small three-star hotel right in the middle of the resort, it has snug but nicely furnished rooms with minibar, central heating and room service.

Intercontinental Mzaar Lebanon Mountain Resort (☎ 340 100; s/d from US$259/297; 🛏 💻 🐕) This huge Intercontinental resort and spa is the most expensive hotel in Faraya. It has a superb location and all the usual five-star amenities, including equipment rental and Les Thermes du Mzaar, a luxury spa for serious pampering. With direct access to the slopes, excellent restaurants with everything from Argentinean steaks to Italian calzones and a scrumptious chocolate fondue at its Le Refuge restaurant, it offers the best winter experience in town.

Eating & Drinking

Faraya village's main street is lined with simple fast-food restaurants and seasonal cafés, all of which serve up decent food at reasonable prices. There are also a few small supermarkets where you can pick up basic provisions if you're self-catering in a chalet or visiting in summer and planning on picnicking.

Up at the resort itself are plenty of restaurants charging higher prices but serving more sophisticated food, with an emphasis on warming Alpine winter favourites such as fondue and raclette. The Intercontinental is especially noted for its wide range of upscale dining options and is also the place to head for post-exertion drinks.

Chez Mansour (☎ 341 000; mains LL8000) This good-value restaurant underneath the Merab hotel (left) is at the heart of the Faraya Mzaar resort. Less glitzy than many of the other offerings around here, it has reasonably priced, unpretentious food that matches its atmosphere.

Jisr al-Qamar (☎ 03-877 993; mezze LL2500-4000) Its name meaning 'Bridge of the Moon', this is a good Lebanese restaurant in Faraya village near the Coin Vert Hotel. Friendly and cosy in winter, with a roaring log fire in the middle of the restaurant, it's good value with the standard selection of mezze and grills. Expect to pay LL8000 and upwards for generous portions of grilled meats. There's also a little children's play area up the front.

Though the coolest place in town – in terms of nightlife, rather than temperatures – changes each season, there are currently three places in which to see and be seen. There's **Igloo** (☎ 640 067), a Rue Monot style bar/restaurant/club that really gets going towards midnight. You can't fail to spot the white igloo-shaped building in the heart of the resort.

Le Stars (☎ 340 100), housed in the Intercontinental Mzaar hotel (see opposite), is the second-best place to dance the snowy night away, attracting a wealthy but slightly less funky crowd.

L'Interdit (☎ 03-822 283) is another popular restaurant-nightclub with a dance floor surrounded by tables. The menu is mostly French and expensive (a drink will set you back US$10), but if you want to dance there's everything from techno to funk and soul.

Getting There & Away

You should be able to pick up a service taxi all the way to Faraya from Beirut's Dawra bus station, but only in the busy winter season when there are plenty of people coming and going. Since Faraya is not on the main route to anywhere else, in low season it's best to go by service taxi to Jounieh and get a taxi from there. If you haggle, you will probably get a taxi to take you for US$20 for the 30-minute ride from Jounieh. When you leave, you will either need to get the hotel to call a taxi for you or, if you are lucky, find one in the main street in the Faraya village on its way back to Jounieh or Beirut. The more expensive hotels offer transfers to and from Beirut.

FAQRA فقرا
☎ 09

Faqra, 6km before Faraya Mzaar on the main road up from Faraya to Faraya Mzaar, is one of the world's first private ski-resorts and you can only ski here if you stay at the swanky hotel, or are invited by a member who has one of the chalets within the grounds. The ski slopes are well run and maintained with good medical facilities; there are three lifts plus a baby lift and a reasonable ski area, though snow coverage is a little patchier than at Faraya Mzaar.

Like most of Lebanon's ski resorts, there's not much to recommend staying here in summer, though it makes an interesting day trip from Beirut or Byblos if you're touring the region for the scenery and ruins, and the resort itself runs a host of hiking, riding and adventure sport activities.

The main reason to come here, apart from skiing, is to see the **ruins** (☺ 8am-5pm)

set below a field of bizarre rock formations, a common sight in the area. Officially, there's an entrance charge of LL3000 but in practice there's often no-one there to collect payment, and the gates are open for you to wander around. For most of the year, you're likely to have the ruins entirely to yourself.

The ruins date from the Greek era, looking especially dramatic when covered with snow, and lie very picturesquely on the side of a hill overlooking the valley below. There is a heavily restored large temple with six Corinthian columns that feature widely on postcards of Lebanon. The temple is dedicated to Adonis, the 'very great god', and sits in the middle of a labyrinth of rocks. A rectangular court cut out of the rock precedes it and nearby are a couple of altars, one dedicated to Astarte (the great goddess of fertility), the other to Baal Qalach.

Just down the hill from here is another smaller temple that was originally dedicated to the Syrian goddess Atargatis, and later to Astarte. In the 4th century AD it was transformed into a church, and a Byzantine-style cross can still be seen on one of the fallen stones in what was the nave.

Surrounding the larger temple are some rock-cut tombs and to the north is a ruined cube-shaped base known as the **Claudius Tower**. According to an inscription above the entrance it was rebuilt by the Emperor Claudius in AD 43-44, but is likely to date back even further. It is thought to have been dedicated to Adonis. The base was originally covered with a step pyramid, perhaps like the one near Hermel (p361). Inside there are steps leading up to the roof and two altars, one of which has been restored with 12 tiny columns supporting its table top.

The only place to stay in Faqra is **L'Auberge de Faqra** (☎ 300 600; www.faqraclub.com; s/d from US$187/231; ❄ ▯ ▯), an ultrasmart hotel, which is part of the large sports and leisure development. Hotel guests can use facilities such as the swimming pool, and tennis and squash courts, although there is a small extra charge. The rooms and service are of a very high standard and there's a ski lift to the most challenging ski area right outside the door. The resort is open in the summer, with mountain biking, horse riding and a plethora of other outdoor activities on offer, but seems in comparison rather empty and forlorn, as if pining for the purr of chi-chi

Beirutis' Maseratis and the gentle clink of champagne flutes around its log fires.

On the main road to Faqra, around 1.5km past the ruins, **Chez Michel** (☎ 03-694 462; mezze around LL4000), an upmarket log-cabin style affair is on the left hand side just before Faqra Club. By far the most famous restaurant in the area, it serves great mezze and grills, and has an excellent Lebanese wine list. While it's officially open all year round, you may nevertheless find it closed during the nonskiing season; Saturday nights during the ski season usually end with some wild partying. If you can pull yourself away from the log fire, there are also fantastic views. Note that reservations are essential on winter weekends.

THE COAST

Heading north along Lebanon's coast, the division between Beirut and the coastal towns is almost completely blurred by concrete, billboards and breakneck traffic. But taking an exit from the motorway will reveal some great beach clubs, one of the world's most visually stunning sets of caves and one of Lebanon's most significant and picturesque ruins. Making the region even more tempting, the area's proximity to Beirut makes all its attractions a comfortable day trip from the capital.

NAHR AL-KALB   نهر الكلب

The mouth of Nahr al-Kalb (Dog River; the Lycus River of antiquity) is on the coast road, heading north between Beirut and Jounieh. Prior to the building of the huge highway that now crosses the river the steep-sided gorge was very difficult for armies to traverse, forcing them to cross in single file and leaving them vulnerable to attack. To give thanks for their successful crossing, conquering armies have historically left plaques or commemorative inscriptions (stelae) carved into the sides of the gorge, the oldest dating from Ramses II's reign of around 1298–1235 BC, along with some even earlier Assyrian carvings, and the most recent being those left by Christian militias during the civil war.

All of the stelae carved before 1920 are marked with Roman numerals, and except

for those of Nebuchadnezzar II, commemorating his 6th century BC campaigns in Mesopotamia and Lebanon, all run along the left bank, following the ancient courses of the steep roads carved along the slopes of the gorge.

Nebuchadnezzar's own (No I) are on the right (north) bank near the motorway junction, but are very eroded and not really worth the detour from the left bank. Listed below are the significant left bank inscriptions, which begin opposite the old, triple-arched Arab bridge.

Riverside Inscriptions

II A lengthy Arabic inscription lying almost at water level opposite the Arab bridge and commemorating its construction. It dates from the 14th century and was inscribed on behalf of Mamluk Sultan Seif ad-Din Barquq by the builder of the bridge, Saifi Itmish.

III A few metres downriver there is a Latin inscription from the Roman emperor Caracalla (Marcus Aurelius Antonius, AD 198–217) describing the achievements of the 3rd Gallic Legion. Just above the Roman inscription is a modern obelisk, which marks the French and Allied armies' arrival in Lebanon in 1942, while beyond it is another modern inscription commemorating the 1941 liberation of Lebanon and Syria from Vichy forces.

IV A French inscription marks the French invasion of Damascus on 25 July 1920 under General Gouraud. Not far from this is a plaque with Arabic script and the date 25/3/1979; next to this, another plaque with the engraving of a cedar tree and another Arabic inscription commemorates the withdrawal of French troops from Lebanon in 1946.

V The original stele showing an Egyptian pharaoh and the god Ptah has been covered by a later inscription by Emperor Napoleon III's army commemorating its 1860 expedition in the Chouf.

VI An Assyrian king, depicted wearing a crown with his right hand raised, is badly preserved.

VII Next to VI is another Assyrian figure, which is now almost impossible to make out.

VIII Further along, another Assyrian stele, which again is in a very bad state of preservation.

IX Above VI and VII, a commemoration of British-led 'Desert Mountain Corps' and its 1918 capture of Damascus, Homs and Aleppo.

X Right by the motorway, a British commemorative plaque dating from 1918 marks the achievements of the British 21st Battalion and the French Palestine Corps. Beside this, steps lead up the mountainside and over the motorway, leading to the other inscriptions.

XI A weathered Greek inscription.

XII Another very worn Greek inscription.

XIII About 30m further on, a stony path climbs sharply, just after some cedars carved into the rock by Phalange fighters. This next stele shows an Assyrian king in an attitude of prayer.

XIV Next to XIII is a rectangular tablet showing Pharaoh Ramses II of Egypt (1292–1225 BC) sacrificing a prisoner to the god Harmakhis.

XV A little higher and only a few metres away on a dead-end path is another inscription of an Assyrian king.

XVI About 25m further up the slope, you come to the road at the top. There you'll see a rectangular stele, which shows Ramses II again, this time sacrificing a prisoner to the sun god Amun by burning him to death.

XVII The last stele depicts, in cuneiform script, Assyrian king Esarhaddon's victory against Egypt in 671 BC.

Getting There & Away

Being so close to Beirut, Nahr al-Kalb is very easy to get to with a couple of hours to spare from either, or makes a great day trip combined with the Téléférique at Jounieh and the Jeita Grotto.

You can take a service taxi (LL2500) or a minibus heading to Jounieh from Beirut's Dawra or Charles Helou bus stations, and ask the driver to drop you off there. The river mouth is just to the right after exiting the long motorway tunnel on the highway and is easy to spot. When you leave, it's easy to flag down another service taxi or minibus going in either direction on the highway.

An alternative, if you're staying in Jounieh or Byblos, is to negotiate a return taxi fare for a day trip to both Nahr al-Kalb and Jeita Grotto. This should cost around LL25,000 from Jounieh, if you drive a hard bargain.

JEITA GROTTO   مغارة جعيتا

A stunning series of caverns, **Jeita Grotto** (☎ 09-220 840/3; www.jeitagrotto.com; adult/child under 12 LL18,150/10,075; 🕑 9am-6pm Tue-Fri, 9am-7pm Sat & Sun summer, 9am-5pm Tue-Sun winter, closed Mon except in Jul & Aug & for 4 weeks Jan & Feb) contains one of the world's most impressive agglomerations of stalactites and stalagmites and is one of the country's biggest tourist attractions. Stretching some 6km back into the mountains, these caves are the source of the Nahr al-Kalb and in winter the water levels rise high enough to flood the lower caverns. During the civil war, the caves were used as an ammunitions store, but they were cleared and reopened to the public in 1995.

The breathtaking upper cavern, home to some extraordinary stalactites and stalagmites, quickly opens up to reveal its astonishing size. The lower cavern, explored by a short boat ride, is beautifully lit, but is often closed in the winter because of high water levels. Regardless of what time of year you visit, however, the upper cavern is the highlight of the show.

Despite all sorts of unnecessary additions – including a toy train ride – the grotto is breathtaking for both adults and children. There is strictly no photography allowed inside the caves, and cameras must be placed in the lockers provided before you proceed into either cavern.

The road to the caves is the first turn on the right past Nahr al-Kalb, if you are heading north. You can catch a service taxi to Nahr al-Kalb and either walk from there (if you're fit – it's close to a one-hour uphill slog), or catch a taxi to take you up from the highway, since not many service taxis ply this road. It is about 5km from the highway to the grotto. A return trip to the caves from Nahr al-Kalb will set you back around US$12 to US$15. The turn-off to the grotto is, unusually, clearly signposted on the highway from both directions.

JOUNIEH   جونيه

☎ 09 / pop 103,227

Prior to the civil war, Jounieh, 21km north of Beirut, was a sleepy fishing village. But with Beirut sliced in half by the conflict, wealthy Christian Beirutis turned to Jounieh as a place to party their troubles away. The town now suffers from a split-personality: on the south side of town, the old Centre Ville clustered around the Rue Mina, retains its charm. But to the north, Rue Maameltein's weird, continuous strip of lurid bars and 'super' nightclubs with exotic dancers and prices as stiff as the drinks, have turned it into an imitation Middle Eastern Vegas in the worst possible way. Outside the centre, towards the mountainside, things get even worse, with gravity-defying high-rise buildings plonked up the steep mountainside.

Nowadays, Beirut is firmly back at the helm of nightclub action but Jounieh remains popular in summer with expat Lebanese returning for their holidays and visiting Gulf Arabs, particularly Saudis, intent on dipping their toes in the Med. There's not much to detain a traveller unless you're heading for the dizzy heights of the Téléférique or the blackjack table, or you're particularly intent on being danced at by a bored Eastern European girl.

Orientation

The town is roughly divided into three parts; viewed from the south they are Kaslik, Centre Ville and Maameltein. Kaslik, near the motorway, is home to designer clothing outlets, cinema complexes, fast-food outlets and some clubs.

Heading north, about 20 minutes' walk downhill towards the sea is Centre Ville, concentrated on Rue Mina. Here you'll find a large supermarket, banks, cafés, some carpet shops and the taxi stand. North of the municipality building, Rue Mina becomes Rue Maameltein and is the start of the Maameltein area, lurid home to some hotels, most of the 'super' nightclubs, the Téléférique station and the casino.

Information

Cell CD Internet, next to the Téléférique, and Café Net on Rue Mina both have good internet facilities (per hr LL2000) and are open daily till late.

The **post office** (7.30am-5pm Mon-Fri, 8am-1pm Sat) is opposite the municipality building.

Sights & Activities

There's really not much to do in Jounieh except have a meal, a stroll past the traditional houses on Rue Mina, a ride on the Téléférique and perhaps a flutter at the Casino du Liban.

If you fancy a swim, you can head to any of the resorts that surround the bay, where you'll pay between US$5 and US$10 depending on the facilities offered. Most also have windsurfing equipment and body boards for hire.

Once you have exhausted the above possibilities, it's time to take to the **Téléférique** (التلفريك; ☎ 936 075; www.teleferiquelb.com; adult/child aged 4-10 return ticket LL7500/3500; 10am-11pm Jun-Oct, 10am-7pm Nov-May, closed Mon, Christmas Day & Good Fri), a cable car travelling from the centre of town up to the dizzying heights of Harissa (opposite). This ride, dubbed the Terrorifique by some, takes about nine minutes with the second half of the trip living up

to its nickname as it climbs higher up the steep hillside. If *Vertigo* made you quiver, this is definitely one to avoid; if, on the other hand, you have *Rear Window* tendencies, you'll enjoy the bizarre views into people's living rooms as you ascend between huge apartment blocks.

Sleeping

Options are limited to only one hotel for those on a tight budget. Those looking for midrange accommodation should note that low-season rates are significantly lower, so it's worth asking for the best price.

Hotel St Joseph (☎ 931 189; Rue Mina; basic/large r US$20/25, discounts for several nights stay) Located in the old part of town, about 70m north of the municipality building, this increasingly shabby pension housed in a 150-year-old building was once the mayor's residence and is well positioned. It's basic, to say the least, but very friendly and its Anglo manageress (or 'dogsbody' as she prefers to call herself) will make it impossible not to feel at home. You're welcome to cook in the kitchen – or may be invited to join the feast if one of the owners are rustling something up. One American guest suggested they should use the hotel as a 'training centre for commandos' so you'll get the idea that there's not much luxury to be had.

La Medina Hotel (☎ 918 484, 03-274 011; www.lamedinahotel.com; Rue Maameltein; s/d US$65/90;) Opposite the Téléférique building, the hotel's rooms are clean – if decidedly pink – and its prices moderate compared to its neighbours, all year round.

Holiday Suites Hotel (☎ 933 907; www.holidaysuites.com; Rue Mina; s/d/ste US$65/75/95;) In a similar vein as La Medina, this hotel is friendly enough, with worn-looking but clean rooms overlooking the sea, pool and water sports facilities. Though it utilises a logo somewhat similar to a leading hotel chain, it's apparently unconnected,

Chateau Raphael (☎ 498 363; Rue Maameltein; ste from US$250;) At the very opposite end of the hotel spectrum, in every respect, from Hotel St Joseph is this ultracamp 'luxury boutique' suite hotel whose motto is 'Be a king in our kingdom'. Catering to spectacular Lebanese weddings and wealthy Gulf Arabs, its faux-palatial style is sure to please those with a big budget and a healthy penchant for all that glitters.

Eating

Jounieh has all the ubiquitous tiny felafel-type stalls, juice bars and cafés you'll require, while on Rue Mina there are a few swish bars serving up big plates of burgers and Tex-Mex along with good strong cocktails. If it's a bit of glitz you're looking for, then Rue Maameltein will satisfy with its abundance of steak and seafood restaurants, though Chez Sami stands out in a class of its own.

Sushi Bento (☎ 919 193; Rue Maameltein; noodle dishes from LL5500; ☺ 11am-11pm) Offers decent sushi (LL1500 to LL3000), sashimi and good-value set meals in the thick of the action.

Makhlouf (☎ 645 192; Rue Maameltein; mains LL11,000; ☺ 24hr) A branch of the immensely popular Lebanese chain, this is always packed with locals. It has a nice outdoor terrace overlooking the sea and is perfect for a sunset nargileh or a simple, inexpensive dinner: shwarma costs LL3500; a large fresh juice is LL3000.

Chez Sami (☎ 910 520; Rue Maameltein; mains around US$35; ☺ noon-midnight) Considered one of the best fish restaurants in the country, Chez Sami is set in a wonderful old stone house. It sports a very stylish interior, but it's the two outdoor terraces overlooking the beach that are the focus of attention. Besides the fresh fish – which you pick direct from the day's catch (500g of fish from LL25,000) – and excellent service, it's also famous for its mezze. The restaurant is no secret though, so book ahead.

Patisserie Rafaat Hallab (☎ 635 531; Rue Maameltein; cakes & ice creams LL1000-1500; ☺ 7am-midnight May-Sep) Satisfy urges for the sweet and sticky at this branch of the famous Tripoli sweet-makers, located directly opposite Chez Sami.

Entertainment

Jounieh was once famed for its nightlife. But these days, especially on Rue Maameltein, it largely consists of hotel discos and 'super' nightclubs with tacky floorshows and overpriced drinks.

There are, however, a few decent bars and late-night cafés sprinkled along the more tranquil Rue Mina. Since they open and close with great speed in the current uncertain climate, it's best to wander until you find one that takes your fancy.

Casino du Liban (☎ 853 222; www.cdl.com.lb; ☺ slot-machine area noon-5am, gaming rooms 8pm-4am) This is Jounieh's most famous nightspot. Overlooking the northern end of Jounieh bay, it opened in 1959 and was the symbol of Beirut's decadence in the 1960s. The rich and famous flocked here to see extravagant floorshows, hang around the gaming tables à la James Bond, and patronise the restaurants and bars. Those heady days of the '60s are long gone, but if you're a hardened gambler or don't mind throwing away money for the sake of kitsch or curiosity, it could be worth a visit to one of the 60 gaming tables or five restaurants. You'll need to be over 21 and wearing smart casual gear (no jeans or sports shoes) for the slot-machine area, and a suit and tie (men) and evening dress (women) for access to the main gaming rooms.

Getting There & Away

You can get from Beirut to Jounieh by LCC and OCFTC bus (see p291) for LL1500. Service taxis leave from Beirut's Dawra bus station and cost LL2000. If you catch a taxi that is going further north, you will be dropped off on the highway. Ask to be let out near the Téléférique, where there is a pedestrian bridge across the highway, which leads to the centre of town (about a five-minute walk). A private taxi from Jounieh to Hamra (Beirut) costs around LL22,000.

HARISSA   حريصا

High above Jounieh bay is the gigantic white-painted bronze statue of the **Virgin of Lebanon** with her arms outstretched, as she has stood since the end of the 19th century. Around her are churches and cathedrals of various denominations, including the modernist Notre Dame du Liban cathedral, which was designed to be reminiscent of a bird in flight.

During religious festivals, such as Easter, there are often rather colourful **religious parades** that attract the crowds. At other times, pilgrims climb the spiral staircase around the statue's base. Others just enjoy the fantastic view from the top. The usual way to reach Harissa is by the terrifying Téléférique – see opposite. If you can't face that and would rather take taxi from Jounieh, it should cost around LL7000 from the main taxi stand on Rue Mina.

BYBLOS (JBAIL)   بيبلوس (جبيل)

☎ 09 / pop 21,600

With its picturesque ancient fishing harbour, Roman remains, Crusader castle and beautifully restored souq, many visitors fall in love at first sight with Byblos. In existence before the great civilisations of the Middle East were even thought of, Byblos – known as Gebal in the Bible and, less romantically, as Giblet by the Crusaders – lays claim to being one of the world's oldest continually inhabited towns. It's also known as the birthplace of the modern alphabet. Its ancient name is thought to derive from the Greek *bublos*, meaning papyrus, since the town was once a Phoenician stopping-off place for papyrus shipments en route to Egypt. Although only around 40km from Beirut, the harbour, ruins and old town feel a world away and it's a must-see place on any visit to Lebanon, however long or short.

Back in the more glamorous days of the '60s, Byblos was a favourite watering hole for the crews of visiting private yachts, international celebrities, and the Mediterranean jet set. These days, however, visitors are lower-key and come for a wander around the ruins, a seaside seafood feast, and a lazy afternoon admiring the shimmering harbour. Don't miss, too, the amazing Mémoire du Temps fossil museum and shop (see Gone Fishing p310) in the heart of the old souqs.

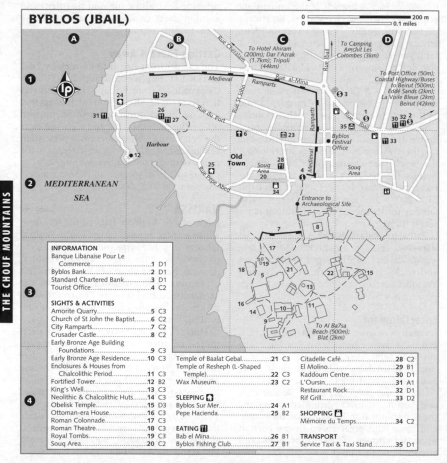

MT LEBANON &
THE CHOUF MOUNTAINS

BYBLOS (JBAIL)

MEDITERRANEAN SEA

Harbour

Old Town

Medieval Ramparts

Entrance to Archaeological Site

To Hotel Ahiram (200m); Dar l'Azrak (1.7km); Tripoli (44km)

To Camping Amchit Les Colombes (3km)

To Post Office (50m); Coastal Highway/Buses to Beirut (500m); Eddé Sands (2km); La Voile Bleue (2km); Beirut (42km)

To Al Ba7sa Beach (500m); Blat (2km)

0   200 m
0   0.1 miles

INFORMATION	
Banque Libanaise Pour Le Commerce	1 D1
Byblos Bank	2 D1
Standard Chartered Bank	3 D1
Tourist Office	4 C2

SIGHTS & ACTIVITIES	
Amorite Quarry	5 C3
Church of St John the Baptist	6 C2
City Ramparts	7 C3
Crusader Castle	8 C2
Early Bronze Age Building Foundations	9 C3
Early Bronze Age Residence	10 C3
Enclosures & Houses from Chalcolithic Period	11 C3
Fortified Tower	12 B2
King's Well	13 C3
Neolithic & Chalcolithic Huts	14 C3
Obelisk Temple	15 D3
Ottoman-era House	16 C3
Roman Colonnade	17 C3
Roman Theatre	18 C3
Royal Tombs	19 C3
Souq Area	20 C2

Temple of Baalat Gebal	21 C3
Temple of Resheph (L-Shaped Temple)	22 C3
Wax Museum	23 C2

SLEEPING	
Byblos Sur Mer	24 A1
Pepe Hacienda	25 B2

EATING	
Bab el Mina	26 B1
Byblos Fishing Club	27 B1

Citadelle Café	28 C2
El Molino	29 B1
Kaddoum Centre	30 D1
L'Oursin	31 A1
Restaurant Rock	32 D1
Rif Grill	33 D2

SHOPPING	
Mémoire du Temps	34 C2

TRANSPORT	
Service Taxi & Taxi Stand	35 D1

History

The earliest known occupation of Byblos dates from the 5th millennium BC, when the first settlers fished and tended their animals here. This was the era of early agriculture and the remains of cultivated grains have been found at a partially excavated site on the promontory, whose tools and primitive weapons are now at Beirut's National Museum (p270). Also found at the site are chalcolithic terracotta storage jars, dating from around the 4th millennium BC, inside which inhabitants used to bury their dead.

By the middle of the 3rd millennium BC, the city-state of Byblos had been colonised by the Phoenicians and become a significant religious centre. The temple of Baalat Gebal, probably built on the site of a sacred grotto, was famous throughout antiquity. Close links with Egypt encouraged the city's cultural and religious development, with its temple receiving generous offerings from several pharaohs. As Byblos flourished, it evolved its own personal hybrid style of art and architecture – part Egyptian, part Mesopotamian, and later showing some Mycenaean influences.

Around 2150 BC, however, the Amorites, a hardened Semitic-speaking people, invaded the city and ruined much of its well-ordered layout and prosperity. This is the period from which the underground royal tombs, and the Obelisk Temple dedicated to Resheph, god of burning and destructive fire, date.

The Amorite occupation ended in 1725 BC with another invasion, this time by the warlike Hyksos from western Asia, who arrived with horses and chariots, hurling javelins and carrying lances, all new to the people of this region. The Egyptians, also suffering from a Hyksos invasion, soon retaliated and from 1580 BC claimed the Phoenician coast. A long period of trade and development followed, during which the kings of Byblos were subservient to their Egyptian masters. Many Egyptian customs were adopted, with temples and burial chambers decorated in the Egyptian style.

The linear alphabet, perhaps the most significant achievement of the Phoenicians, was also developed during this period. Thought to have originated in Byblos, it was invented as a more practical way of recording trade transactions than the cuneiform script, and quickly spread throughout the civilised world.

The Egyptian-dominated period of prosperity, however, did not last and between 1100 and 725 BC Byblos was eclipsed by Tyre as the most important Phoenician city-state. It then became a pawn in the power struggle between the Greeks and Assyrians (725–612 BC), eventually being ruled by the Assyrians and then the Neo-Babylonians.

Following the conquest of Babylon by Cyrus the Great in 539 BC, Byblos was regenerated as a trading link to the east under the Persian Empire. During the Hellenistic period, unlike Tyre, the city voluntarily became an ally of Alexander and continued to flourish under its own royal dynasty.

When the Greek Empire waned and the Roman Empire waxed, Byblos concentrated its trading efforts to the west. From 63 BC onwards, the Roman Empire became a market for Phoenician goods and the city boasted lavish public architecture and suburban farming developments. Unfortunately, with an ironically modern twist, Byblos had sowed the seeds of its own downfall by not regulating the pace of deforestation – and now the very resource that had made this boom town wealthy was suddenly in short supply. But when the Roman Empire split into east and west in AD 395, Byblos allied itself to Constantinople and became increasingly important as a religious centre. Pagan religion gradually gave way to Christianity and the city became the seat of a bishopric under Emperor Diocletian, protected by the Eastern Roman Empire until the Islamic invasion in 636.

Under the Muslims the focus turned eastward and Byblos' sea port dwindled into insignificance along with the city's defences. Byblos, by now known as Jbail, was left vulnerable. During the Crusader offensive, which began in 1098, Jbail fell to Raymond de Saint-Gilles, Count of Tripoli. Despite resuming trade with Europe, the city never regained its former power. Subsequent struggles between Crusader and Muslim forces continued until August 1266 when Emir Najibi, lieutenant of the Mamluk sultan, Beybars, laid siege to the town.

The next few centuries were relatively uneventful; the Turks took control of the city in 1516 and Byblos passed into insignif-icance until Ernest Renan, a French histo-rian and philosopher, began to excavate the site in 1860. Excavations came to a stand-still during the civil war and are nowadays still slowly ongoing.

Orientation

Byblos is a compact city and it generally takes new arrivals just a few minutes to find their bearings. The medieval town, where most visitors spend their time, stretches north from the perimeter of the seaside ruins, flanked to the north by Rue al-Mina and to the west by the harbour, home to a string of good restaurants. The modern town, through which you'll arrive, is centred on Rue Jbail at the eastern end of Rue al-Mina, where the buses and taxis congregate and most of the fast-food outlets, money-changers and banks are located.

Information

Banque Libanaise pour le Commerce (Rue Jbail) Has an ATM.
Byblos Bank (Rue Jbail) Has an ATM.
Byblos Sur Mer (☎ 548 000; Byblos harbour) Money can be changed at this hotel.
Medical Emergency (☎ 140)
Police (☎ 112)
Post Office (☎ 540 003; ⏲ 7.30am-5pm Mon-Fri, 8am-1pm Sat) Turn into the street, off Rue Jbail, with Diab Brothers on the corner; it's 20m up the hill on your right, on the 2nd floor of the building.
Standard Chartered Bank (Rue Jbail) Has an ATM.
Tourist Office (☎ 540 325; ⏲ 8.30am-1pm Mar-Nov, closed Sun Dec-Feb) Located near the archaeological site entrance in the souq area, it has maps of the architectural site, but no town map.

Sights
THE RUINS

This ancient **site** (adult/student & child LL6000/1500; ⏲ 8.30am-6pm) is entered through the re-stored Crusader Castle and it's definitely worth taking a guide, who should cost be-tween LL10,000 and LL20,000 depending on how many people are in your group. If you have time before visiting the ruins, scour the souvenir shops in the souq for a copy of Bruce Conde's *Byways of Byblos* (US$3), published in the 1950s and a charming pocket guide to Byblos. Many of the artefacts originally located on the site are now housed at the National Museum of

Beirut (p270), so a visit there, either before or after visiting the ruins, is highly recom-mended to really complete the picture.

CRUSADER CASTLE

The most dominant monument at the ar-chaeological site is the castle built by the Franks in the 12th century and constructed out of monumental blocks, mostly pillaged from the Roman ruins and some the largest used in any construction in the Middle East (apart from one or two immense stones at Baalbek – see p359). The castle, measuring 49.5m by 44m, is bordered by a deep moat and you can spot Phoenician ramparts on either side of the entrance. Unless you're passionate about Frankish architecture, though, the best part of a castle visit is the commanding view of Byblos from the top of the ramparts, which gives you a clear idea of the layout of the ancient city. It's worth noting that because of the many layers con-tained in the small site, later monuments were moved and reconstructed in order to gain access to those underneath.

CITY RAMPARTS

The 25-m thick city ramparts, dating from the 3rd and 2nd millennia BC, curve around from the castle to the shore and on the op-posite side of the castle curve first west and then south, blocking access to the promon-tory where the original city was confined.

TEMPLE OF RESHEPH

This L-shaped 3rd-millennium-BC temple was burned and rebuilt during the Amor-ite occupation. The later temple, known as the Obelisk Temple, was moved to a nearby site so that Maurice Dunand, the resident archaeologist, could excavate the original structure beneath.

TEMPLE OF BAALAT GEBAL

This is the oldest temple at Byblos, dat-ing back to the 4th millennium BC, and was once its largest and most important. Dedicated to Aphrodite/Astarte during the Roman period, the colonnade of six stand-ing columns from around AD 300 are the vestiges of a colonnaded street that was built to approach it. Destroyed and rebuilt on several occasions, current excavated re-mains date from the 3rd millennium BC; numerous alabaster fragments of votive vases, many inscribed with the names of Old Kingdom pharaohs, were discovered here dating from this period and can now be seen in Beirut's National Museum.

OBELISK TEMPLE

The temple, rebuilt on its current site, consists of a forecourt and courtyard housing the slightly raised sanctuary. The cube-shaped base of an obelisk stands in the middle of the sanctuary and is thought to have been a representation of Resheph. In the courtyard is a collection of standing obelisks, including one built at the command of Abichemou, king of Byblos, at the end of the 19th century BC. The obelisks were thought to have originally been 'God boxes', where the gods were believed to live and would have been worshipped. Several votive offerings have been found here, including the famous bronze figurines now housed at Beirut's National Museum.

KING'S WELL

In the centre of the promontory is a deep depression, which is the site of the King's Well (Bir al-Malik). According to legend, Isis sat weeping here when she came to Byblos to search for Osiris. Originally a natural spring, the well supplied the city with water until the end of the Hellenistic era. By Roman times it was used only for religious rituals since the city's water came from the surrounding mountains and was transported through a network of earthenware pipes.

ROMAN THEATRE

This charming reconstruction of the original theatre is only one-third its original size and has been sited near the cliff edge, offering marvellous views across the ocean. First built in AD 218, its orchestra had a fine mosaic floor depicting Bacchus, now at the National Museum.

ROYAL TOMBS

Nine royal tombs are cut, uniquely, in vertical shafts deep down into the rock, dating from the 2nd millennium BC. The most important is that of King Hiram (1200 BC), who was a contemporary of Ramses II of Egypt and whose grave shaft was inscribed with early Phoenician script that said 'Warning here. Thy death is below'.

Hiram's sarcophagus is now a highlight of the National Museum. There are steps leading down into one of the tombs, and a tunnel leads to another containing a stone sarcophagus of a 19th-century-BC prince, Yp-Shemu-Abi.

EARLY SETTLEMENTS

To the south of the site are Neolithic (5th millennium BC) and Chalcolithic (4th millennium BC) enclosures, houses and huts, of which only the crushed limestone floors and low retaining walls remain. Throughout this area, large burial jars were found in which bodies were curled up into foetal positions. Dominating the ruins here is an **Ottoman-era house**, along with a reasonably well-preserved Early Bronze Age residence and building foundations.

THE MEDIEVAL TOWN
Church of St John the Baptist

In the centre of this Crusader town is the Romanesque-style Church of St John the Baptist, which was begun in 1115 but badly damaged by an earthquake in 1170. Ancient columns were used in the doorways, and the heavy buttressing on the western side is thought to have been an effort to prevent further damage. One of its most unusual architectural features is the open-air baptistry, which sits against the north wall, its arches and four supporting pillars topped by a dome.

The church sports an unusual layout, with apses facing northeast, but a sharp change in direction brings the northern half of the church back into its more conventional east–west alignment. Apparently, this is because a mistake in orientation was only discovered after the apses had been built and was corrected halfway through construction. The south portal is purely Romanesque, but the north doorway consists of an 18th-century Arab design.

To the west of the church is a single standing column and an overgrown mosaic floor, which are remnants of an earlier Byzantine church.

Wax Museum

Almost opposite the Church of St John is the kitsch **Wax Museum** (☎ 540 463; admission LL6000; ☯ 9am-5pm) containing 125 wax figures in 22 different tableaux representing the history of Byblos from earliest times. This place is only for real history buffs or true lovers of a waxen genre so popular throughout Lebanon that Madame Tussaud herself would feel quite at home.

Souq Area

Byblos's beautifully restored souq (market) houses a range of souvenir shops and small cafés. However, the highlight is without doubt **Mémoire Du Temps** (☎ 547 083; www.memory oftime.com; ⏰ 8.30am-5.30pm) where you can buy ancient fossilised fish remains, each with its own certificate of authenticity, for as little as US$10.

See Gone Fishing, below, for details of the shop's own provenance.

The Harbour

It seems hard to believe that this peaceful little harbour was once a nerve centre of world commerce, but it was from this small port that the cedar and other wood, for which Byblos was famous, was shipped to the capitals of the ancient world. Much later the Crusaders left their mark here, building defensive towers on either side of the harbour mouth. A chain between the towers could be raised to prevent boats from entering. The northern tower was restored in Mamluk times and is still in fairly good condition.

From the top you can look down and see the remains of ancient quays in the clear water below.

GONE FISHING

Tucked away in a narrow Byblos alleyway lies the workshop of friendly local palaeontologist Pierre Abi-Saad, along with his hundred-million-year-old catch of fishy history. Discovered 800m above sea level in a quarry owned by his family for three generations, the thousands of fossils so far discovered by the Abi-Saads constitute the only fish fossils ever found in the Middle East and are displayed at virtually every important natural history museum worldwide. Step into Pierre's workshop-turned-museum and you'll have a unique opportunity to see how fossils are discovered – and perhaps even get to wield a chisel yourself.

'More than 80% of the fossils we find,' grins Pierre as he chips away slowly at a chunk of limestone, 'are of fish that are now extinct. Many have never even been studied or named. Look.' He points enthusiastically around the room, highlighting ancestors of stingrays, examples of the most primitive eels yet discovered, coelacanths (the earliest fish ever to exist on earth), octopi, shrimps, squid, ancestors of swordfish, and, entertainingly, a fossil of a fish that had swallowed another fish – all gleaming, perfect representations of creatures that lived a mind-blowingly long time ago. 'Through these,' he whispers, gazing fondly at his incredible collection, 'we can see the evolution of life itself.'

Abi-Saad's dream is to one day establish a real museum of fossils in Byblos, to showcase his massive quantity of finds, which includes an almost 4m-long shark, the largest complete specimen in the world. At present, he says, barely 5% of his total collection is crammed onto the workshop's shelves. Until then, however, he's content to continue with his favourite part of the job, the excavation digs at the quarry itself. 'Sometimes you can work for weeks and not find anything; other times, you come across these incredible discoveries. I'm happy to spend 14 or 15 hours alone, just digging and discovering in the quarry.'

The quarry itself, which came into his grandfather's possession during French occupation when he worked as a mountain guide for holidaying soldiers and came across a crop of fossils by chance, is accessible to visitors who can join digs for free, mostly during cooler spring and autumn months.

Abi-Saad taps again at the piece of limestone, shards flying across the room. 'You have to learn to read the stone,' he explains. 'You have to learn how to feel it. It's an art that's transmitted to you as a child.' Hunting fossils, he continues, is much the same as conventional fishing. 'There's no detector you can use. But a good fisherman knows where to find the fish, though not how many he'll catch.' Another hard tap and the limestone chunk splits in two. 'It's my hobby, it's my passion and it's my job,' he smiles. 'There.' Slowly, Pierre Abi-Saad prizes the pieces apart to reveal a small, perfect image of a fish. 'You're the first one to see this creature for a hundred million years,' he says. 'If you're not careful, pretty soon you'll be hooked.'

Activities

SWIMMING

Just a five-minute walk south of the ruins is **Al ba7sa**, a free public beach with great views back to the archaeological site. Byblos also has several beach clubs to rival Beirut, situated around 2km south of town on the coastal road, which runs parallel between the motorway and the sea. Currently, the two hippest options are open 9am until the wee hours:

Eddé Sands (☎ 546 666; www.eddesands.com) Open year round, this is a huge, fantastic, luxurious treat, with its five pools, six restaurants, sandy beach, boutique hotel, open-air spa and sandy beach.

La Voile Bleue (☎ 796 060) Just south of Byblos, La Voile Bleue is another highly popular local choice for lazing the days and dancing the nights away. The club charges US$12 entry at weekends.

BOATING

A cluster of long motorboats in the harbour takes visitors on 15-minute rides (LL6000 per person) from spring until autumn.

Festivals & Events

The Byblos International Festival, held each summer since 2003 amid the spectacular archaeological site, is well worth attending if you're in town during July or August. It features music, theatre and dance acts, with both international names (Nouvelle Vague and Placebo have both played there) and local celebrated talent in attendance. For more information on the year's line-up, visit the festival website at www.byblosfestival.org.

Sleeping

Sadly, Byblos doesn't currently have much choice when it comes to hotels. In summer months, the Byblos Fishing Club (see p312) rents out small bungalows in its nearby Pepe Hacienda for US$20: call the Fishing Club in advance, or drop into the hacienda to check its availability. If you don't mind staying a little out of town, the nearby **King George Hotel** (☎ 547 048; Mar Elias St, Blat; s/d/tr US$30/40/50; 🔀) in Blat is a good-value option, a short 10-minute taxi ride from town.

Camping Amchit Les Colombes (☎ 622 401/2; camp sites US$3, 'tungalows' US$20, 3-4-person chalets US$30; 🔀) About 3km north of town, to the left hand side off Rue Jbail and down a hill, this camp site isn't an easy place to spot

from the road. If you do make it here, the camping's cheap and adequate and it's a quiet spot with views of the sea, though it's not particularly well-kept and the bizarre, claustrophobic tent-shaped bungalows, or 'tungalows,' are best avoided. Nevertheless, it has all the necessary amenities, including showers, toilets, kitchen with gas burners, and electrical points for caravans (220V), along with fairly forlorn fully furnished chalets. The camping ground is set on a wooded cliff top, with steps down to its own rocky beach and the chalets and 'tungalows' have fabulous views. It's at least a brisk 30-minute walk from Byblos; a service taxi costs LL1500.

Hotel Ahiram (☎ 540 440; www.ahiramhotel.com; s/d/tr US$50/65/75; 🔀) Quite recently renovated, this hotel just off Rue Cheralam is a reasonable, though unexceptional, choice and all rooms have air-con, balcony with sea views and bathrooms including a small bath. It does, however, have direct access to a pebbly beach. Prices include breakfast and are lower outside the summer season.

Byblos Sur Mer (☎ 548 000; Byblos Harbour; s/d/ste US$65/75/105; 🔀 🔀) This long-established hotel has comfortable, smallish rooms with wonderful views over Byblos harbour and its seafront swimming-pool area. There's no denying that its position is sensational and the staff are friendly, but the rooms are a little tired and overpriced. The hotel has its own restaurant on the 1st floor and operates the restaurant **L'Oursin** (🕙 Apr-Sep) across the road and by the sea.

Eating & Drinking

Citadelle Café (☎ 03-584 165; 🕙 7am-midnight) On a corner of the square just opposite the tourist office and the Notre Dame de la Porte gate (translated on street signs as the 'Gate's Lady'), this makes the perfect place for a big breakfast or cheap lunch. The hummus wraps are sensational, the coffee is strong, the beer cheap and there's live guitar music on Friday nights. André, the friendly owner, is knowledgeable and will be happy to answer all your questions on Byblos and around.

Bab El Mina (☎ 540 475; Byblos harbour; mezze from LL3500, mains around LL15,000; 🕙 11am-midnight) Next to the Fishing Club, this is a good option for fresh fish and mezze, with a 'fisherman's basket' for two for LL45,000.

PEPE THE PIRATE

Widely known as the Pirate of Byblos, Pepe Abed, who finally shuffled off this mortal coil in early 2007 aged 95, was for decades a Byblos tourist attraction in his own right. Born in Mexico to Lebanese parents, he worked as a jewellery designer and marine archaeologist, but was perhaps better known for his ability to throw a party, attracting the rich, famous and beautiful people of the pre-war jet set – including Marlon Brando, David Niven and Brigitte Bardot – to his bar, the Fishing Club, which opened in 1963.

Though the civil war saw Pepe back in Mexico while his local Lebanese businesses closed, he soon returned to Lebanon and once again worked designing jewellery, saving enough money to get the Fishing Club back on its feet. The beautiful people, however, never known for their long memories, didn't rematerialise, and while the Fishing Club remains an institution, it is now every bit as much museum as restaurant. Indeed the collection of artefacts (including Jacque Cousteau's hat) that Pepe collected over the years now forms the basis of the Pepe Abed Foundation.

These days, Pepe's son Roger – whose motto is 'Good things never end' – runs the joint, along with his own son, Pepe Junior, and Pepe's presence lives on, not only in his collection of artefacts but also in the mugs, stickers and ashtrays featuring his visage. Indeed, the Fishing Club restaurant remains as much an essential Byblos stop-off as ever.

El Molino (☎ 541 555; 2-course meal with 2 margaritas per person around LL35,000; ☺ noon-midnight Tue-Sun) For authentic Mexican food in a good, fun atmosphere, which possibly has something to do with the excellent margaritas, try El Molino. It gets very busy so you should book, especially for weekend nights when it's worth staying on late for yet more of those tequila-fuelled treats.

Byblos Fishing Club (☎ 540 213; Byblos harbour; 2-course meal per person US$25; ☺ 11am-midnight) This place is famed for the stream of film stars, politicians and beauty queens, who have passed through over the decades, as well as for its owner Pepe (see above) who, though gone, is certainly not forgotten. Loved by locals for its fresh fish – the restaurant has its own dedicated fleet of four fishermen – it's a piece of Byblos heritage. On a busy weekend in front of a glistening harbour, with a strong arak firmly in hand, you can almost imagine it's still the 1960s, that your speedboat's out the front, and Bardot and Brando are holding court at the next table. Back up the harbour road towards the souq, you'll see signs for the Pepe Hacienda, a nice summer option for a leisurely drink in the garden.

There is no shortage of small places selling shwarma sandwiches and felafels along Rue Jbail – the best being Restaurant Rock and **Ka**ddoum Centre – as well as the usual pizza and burger joints. **Rif Grill** (☎ 545 822; off Rue Jbail) is another good choice, serving salads for around LL4000 and burgers and pizza for LL6000 to LL8000.

Getting There & Around

The service-taxi stand in Byblos is near the Banque Libanaise pour le Commerce. A service taxi to/from Beirut (the hub in Beirut is Dawra) costs LL3000. You can also take an express bus heading for Tripoli from Charles Helou (LL1500, around 50 minutes) and ask the driver to stop at Jbail. The LCC bus No 6 (LL750, around one hour) and minibuses (LL1000) also leave from Dawra and travel regularly along the coast road between Beirut and Byblos, stopping on Rue Jbail. It's a scenic and pleasant trip – traffic permitting.

AMCHIT   عمشيت
☎ 09

The town of Amchit, 3km north of Byblos, is a well-preserved relic of Lebanon's past. Do not let your first impression of low-rise concrete chaos put you off: Amchit is famous for its collection of **traditional town houses**, which were built by wealthy silk merchants in the 19th century. They are now nearly all privately owned – some are fully restored, others are in need of work.

There are 88 old houses in total, which are now under a preservation order. The houses were constructed using the old stones of the area and you can often spot an ancient piece of carving being used as a lintel. The architecture is influenced by both the Oriental and Venetian styles, with double-arched mandolin windows and covered courtyards. This Italian influence was

due to the trade agreement between Lebanon and the Duke of Tuscany.

A service taxi from Byblos costs LL1500.
The highway dissects the town and the
town houses are on the upper part of the
town, away from the sea.

RACHANA   رشانا
About 17km north of Amchit is the turn-off
to Rachana, the 'Museum Village'. Situated
high on a hill it's easily recognised by the
wonderful **modern sculptures** lining the road.
This is the work of the Basbous brothers,
who have created an extraordinary artistic community in the village. Of the three
brothers – Michel, Alfred and Yusuf – only
Alfred is still alive, and he has a gallery in
the village where you can purchase some of
his works, starting at around US$500.

One of the highlights of the village is
Michel's house, which is built in organic
shapes, reminiscent of the work of Gaudi.
He used all manner of found materials,
such as the curved windscreen window.
There is also an outdoor sculpture park,
where entries in the annual sculpture sym-
posium (held annually during the last week
in August and first week in September) are
displayed.

To find the studios, turn left at the junction of the main street in Rachana, by a
small shop selling cold drinks. A few hundred metres along the road you will come to
a bend and Yusuf's house. Alfred's house is
a short distance around the corner.

The turn-off to Rachana is about 5km
south of Batroun at a Lebanese army post.
The village is a further 3km to the northeast. If you don't have your own transport,
you'll need to get a taxi from Byblos and
arrange for it to wait for you while you visit
the studios. The return trip will cost about
US$15 to US$20.

BATROUN   البترون
☎ 06 / pop 11,082
Batroun is a sweet, lively Maronite town
22km from Byblos and 56km north of Beirut. It makes a nice place to stop, though
with few tempting accommodation options,
it's sadly at present not a great base for
exploring the region.

Batroun was once the Graeco-Roman
town of Botrys, but was founded much earlier, and is mentioned in the Tell al-Amarna

tablets (Tell al-Amarna is the modern name
of Akhetaten, an ancient Egyptian city) as
a dependency of the king of Byblos. Called
Butron in medieval times, it fell under the
diocese of the County of Tripoli and was
famous for its vineyards.

Today, the main road, Rue Principe, is a
good place to find all necessary amenities,
including an ATM, bars, restaurants, shops
and pharmacies, as well as stalls and cafés
selling Batroun's famous lemonade, a sweet
blend of lemon juice, sugar and water that's
a delicious summer cooler.

Sights & Activities
Batroun's various sights are well signposted; the best way to enjoy them is by
wandering the tangle of old streets full of
well-preserved Ottoman-era stone houses
that run between Rue Principe and the sea.
Just behind the harbour, **St George's Orthodox
Church** was built in the late 18th century
and has 21 fine, painted panels and carved
wooden doves above the altar screen. Close
by is the larger **St Estaphan (Stephen) Church**,
also known as the fisherman's church. On
the sea itself, the **old harbour** has a small section of an extraordinary natural sea wall,
creating a pool on the land side. The Phoenicians reinforced this natural feature and
the remains of their harbour are visible.

Around 5km south of Batroun is **White
Beach**, with a string of pleasant beach cafés
set against an impossibly turquoise sea.
Although covered with fine white pebbles
(hence the name) rather than sand, it is
spotlessly clean and the water is crystal
clear. This stretch of beach is also known
as one of the best spots in Lebanon for
windsurfing and **surfing**; see p383 for Batroun
surfing details. On the way down towards
White Beach, following the old coastal road
that runs to the west of the highway, you'll
spot a number of other beach club–style
places for a dip and a seafood lunch, including trendy **Bonita Bay** (☎ 744 844) and **Pierre
and Friends** (☎ 03-352 930); the latter is also a
sailing club.

Sleeping & Eating
Unfortunately, there are no nice quaint
options in Batroun's old town itself and
accommodation is limited to dated, resort-
style complexes at the southern end of Batroun's piece of coast.

Aqualand (☎ 742 741; d US$90) Next door to San Stephano, this place offers pretty much the same sorts of facilities at slightly lower prices, though it's not quite as smart as its neighbour.

San Stephano Resort (☎ 740 366; www.san stephano.com; studio/ste US$125/170; ☒) This resort complex has a large swimming pool, a restaurant and a beach snack-bar. It also houses the popular Doppio nightclub. Well equipped as it is, it's a bit overpriced in high season, and in low season it's almost entirely deserted.

Le Marin (☎ 744 016, 03-328 628; mezze from LL4000, mains from LL9000; ☣ 11am-10pm) Just south of the harbour, this seafood restaurant is popular with locals and serves up tasty plates of mezze, too.

White Beach Restaurant (☎ 742 404; meal per person US$15-20; ☣ 10am-late) Beside the sea south of Batroun on White Beach itself, (p313) this is a very pleasant place offering traditional mezze and seafood meals.

You can find Batroun's lemonade speciality at the several juice shops and cafés along the main street. Close to the souq area, **Chez Hilmi** (☎ 740 507; lemonade LL2000; ☣ 7am-9.30pm) sells the original and best, along with great sweets.

Getting There & Away

As Batroun is a coastal town just off the highway, you can easily take a service taxi from Beirut or Byblos that's heading for Tripoli to drop you at the turn-off and walk the short way into town. The cost from Beirut should be LL5000. Alternatively, take the Tripoli bus from Beirut and get the driver to drop you off. The price will be the full fare to Tripoli, LL2500.

MOUSSALAYHA CASTLE قلعة المسيلحة

About 3km beyond Batroun, in the narrow valley at Ras ech-Chekka, is the attractive Moussalayha Castle, which used to defend the only land route between Beirut and Tripoli. Sadly, nowadays, the castle is dwarfed by the motorway that runs right next to it, though standing with your back to the traffic and your fingers in your ears, you can still appreciate its magic. It stands on a rocky outcrop and is built on the summit in such a way as to look like part of the living rock, its entrance at the top of a steep, rock-cut stairway.

Although the site is very ancient (it is probably the ancient Gigarta mentioned by Pliny), the castle probably dates to the 16th century. It seems that the site was abandoned until the present Moussalayha Castle was constructed. Beneath the castle runs a small river with an ancient stone bridge crossing it.

If you are using a service taxi heading for Tripoli, simply get it to drop you off at Moussalayha and then flag down another service taxi when you want to continue your journey (there are plenty of service taxis serving this route). The castle is within easy walking distance from the highway.

ADONIS VALLEY & JEBEL TANNOURINE

جبل تنّورين ووادي أدونيس

Famed for its romantic legends as much as for its dramatically bleak and beautiful scenery, the Adonis Valley is a deep, jagged slice forged in the coastal mountains by the Nahr Ibrahim (Adonis River) as it flows out to sea. The river's source, the Afqa Grotto, is at the head of the valley, and in ancient times its northern side was a pilgrimage route. Now the road is dotted with ancient remains as well as breathtaking views. To the north lie villages perched on the side of Jebel Tannourine and the ski resort of Laklouk. The entire area can be visited on a day trip from Beirut, but it's worth considering renting a car or a taxi for the day, since public transport to this region is virtually nonexistent.

AFQA GROTTO مغارة أفقا

This huge cavern, which in its isolation feels a little as though you've reached the ends of the earth, dominates the rocky mountainside at the head of the valley and is best seen after winter, when water roars down under a stone Roman bridge before snaking its way towards the sea. This is the sacred source of the Nahr Ibrahim where, mythology tells us, Adonis (or Tammuz to the Phoenicians) met his death, when gored by a wild boar while out hunting (see Lovers Forever, opposite). The grotto is also intertwined with the legendary love story

LOVERS FOREVER

According to Greek mythology, Adonis was the most beautiful baby in the world, the fruit of an incestuous union between King Cinyras and his daughter Myrrha (who was turned into the myrrh tree for her sins). The goddess Aphrodite (Venus, to the Romans) took the baby and left him in the care of Persephone, goddess of the underworld, who, enchanted by Adonis' beauty, refused to return the child. Zeus mediated between the two goddesses, coming up with something akin to a modern divorce settlement, which decreed that Adonis was to spend half the year with Aphrodite, and the other half in the underworld with Persephone.

Eventually, and rather inevitably in Greek mythology, Aphrodite and Adonis became lovers, incurring the wrath of Aphrodite's husband, Ares, who turned himself into a boar to attack Adonis at Afqa. Though Aphrodite tried in vain to heal his wounds, her lover bled to death in her arms. In the places where his blood hit the ground, red anemones sprang up. Despite the vicious attack, however, the decree of almighty Zeus remained in force and Adonis was permitted to return to his lover every six months. Each spring those same red anemones (*naaman* or 'darling' in Arabic – also an epithet for Adonis) return, symbolising his return to the world.

Apart from being a racy tale of incest, true love, jealousy, sex and murder worthy of a modern Arabic soap opera, the Adonis and Aphrodite myth symbolises those most ancient of themes: fertility and rebirth. In the myth's earlier Semitic form, Aphrodite was Astarte, the great goddess of fertility; her lover was Tammuz (called 'Adon' by his followers, transformed into Adonis by the Greeks), a god associated with vegetation who journeyed to the underworld each year. Astarte would follow to retrieve him, and while she was gone the world would become barren, reproduction would stop and life itself would be threatened. Followers of Adonis would spend seven days lamenting his death; then on the eighth day, in a practice echoed in Christianity, his rebirth was celebrated.

of Adonis and the goddess Aphrodite, since legend has it that here is where they exchanged their first kiss, and the Greek word for kiss, *aphaca*, would appear to reinforce the romantic connection.

The area is rife with ancient shrines and grottos dedicated to this tragic tale. Adonis' story has come to symbolise life, death and rebirth, the theme echoed in the stories of Osiris and Christ. Each spring the river runs red, and in antiquity this was believed to be the blood of Adonis. In reality, the force of the water flowing down the valley picks up ferruginous minerals from the soil and stains the water the colour of red wine.

After winter a torrent rages down from the grotto 200m above. When the flow isn't too strong, you can enter the cave by walking up a set of steps on the right-hand side of the bank of the river (steep but not too difficult). Inside, the cave is enormous and the freezing water surges out of an unseen underground source. When the flow of water slows in the summer it is possible to explore the extensive tunnels and caverns further into the mountain.

At the foot of the main fall is a Roman bridge. If you walk down beneath the bridge,

there is a café on a terrace, with soothing views of the water as it crashes and tumbles over the rocks (or, in summer and autumn, slowly trickles) to the river below.

On a raised plateau nearby, above the left bank and just below the village of Khirbet Afqa, are the ruinous remains of a **Roman temple** dedicated to Astarte. Its broken columns are made of granite from the famous Pharaonic-era quarries at Aswan in Egypt. The cost involved in bringing the stone hundreds of kilometres down the Nile, shipping it to the Lebanese coast and then dragging it up the valley must have been astronomical, and is a testament to the temple's importance as a pilgrimage site. In the foundations, on the riverside, is the entrance to a sort of tunnel that is thought to have carried water into a sacred pool in the temple, into which offerings may have been thrown, or in which devotees carried out their ablutions. Constantine destroyed the temple because of its licentious rites, but the power of legend has stayed. Both Christians and Shiite Muslims attribute healing powers to the place, and strips of cloth are still tied to the nearby fig tree in a ritual that dates back to antiquity.

Sleeping & Eating

La Reserve (☎ 01-498 775; www.lareserve.com.lb) Just after the turn-off to Afqa is this well-appointed camping ground and outdoor activities resort. It organises a huge range of activities, including rafting, caving, hiking and mountain biking (check out its website for more information and the prices of individual activities). Accommodation in canvas tents, sleeping up to four people, costs LL15,000 per adult and LL10,000 for children over three; younger children stay for free. Mattresses and pillows are provided but you will need your own sleeping bag.

The **café-restaurant** (meals per person US$6-8; ⓥ spring-summer) beneath the bridge is the only place to eat. It serves tea, coffee and cold drinks, including beer. Light meals and snacks of the kebab-and-chips variety are available quite cheaply.

Getting There & Away

Without a private car, the only way to get to Afqa is by taxi. It's not on a service taxi route, so this will cost around US$20 from Byblos. If you're driving, be aware that signposting to Afqa is particularly bad: if you get as far as Aaqoura on the road from the coast, you've gone too far and need to turn around and try again.

AAQOURA   العاقورة

Aaqoura is famous for its spectacular location, its devotion to Maronite Christianity and, in summer, its cherries. In autumn and winter, it becomes a strange and spooky place, as the mists and clouds descend all around and all that can be seen is the illuminated grotto at the top of the cliff. Although the town doesn't warrant a trip by itself, it's a nice stop on the road up to Laklouk.

Reputed to be one of the first villages in the area to convert to Christianity, Aaqoura has some 42 churches within its confines. The most famous is **Mar Butros** (St Peter), which sits in a grotto in the towering cliffs that surround the village and can be reached by steps carved out of the rock. The hollowed-out tombs inside the grotto may originally have been part of a Roman necropolis, but what is particularly noteworthy here are the faint traces of writing at the back of the cave. These are thought to be rare extant examples of a Chinese-influenced vertical Syriac script brought

back by Christian missionaries to China in the 7th century. Down in the village there are also the remains of a Roman road, which was part of the pilgrimage route that would lead devotees of the Adonis cult over the mountains and into the Bekaa Valley. Note that the mountains around Aaqoura were heavily mined during the civil war, and hiking without a local guide is still not advised.

LAKLOUK   اللقلوق

☎ 09

Laklouk might seem lacklustre compared to Faraya, but it remains a popular ski resort set in an attractive rocky location, 1920m above sea level, 28km east of Byblos. Family-oriented, with gentle to medium slopes and good cross-country skiing opportunities, it's a relaxed and low-key alternative to Faraya Mzaar, albeit with few accommodation and eating options outside the main resort hotel. In low season, however, there's little to detain a visitor, when the village's buildings seem unloved and unkempt without a soothing layer of white stuff. Bear in mind, also, that the ski resort is around 2km further north from what's signposted as the centre of Laklouk itself.

Sights & Activities

Further on from Laklouk are a couple of places worth visiting. About 2km from the resort on the Chatin–Balaa road are the unusual **Balaa rock formations**, which consist

---

SKI FACTS: LAKLOUK

- **Altitude** 1650m-1920m
- **Lifts** Nine
- **Adult Day Pass** US$12 (Monday to Friday), US$20 (Saturday and Sunday)
- **Opening hours** 8am to 3.30pm Monday to Friday, 8am to 4pm Saturday and Sunday
- ☎ 03-256 853

Laklouk in winter is a relaxed, family-friendly resort, with three chairlifts, three ski lifts and three baby lifts. It's also possible to do cross-country skiing and snowshoeing, and makes a good base for visiting the natural wonders of Balaa Gorge and the Afqa grotto.

of several houses or chapels carved into the rock. They are known as the 'bishop's house' and the landscape here, with its otherworldly shapes, is reminiscent of Cappadocia in Turkey.

Further along the same road, about 6km from Laklouk, is **Balaa Gorge**. There is a small turning on the left, if you are coming from Laklouk, and, after about 400m, the road ends. This is the beginning of the descent on foot to the gorge. The walk down is easy and takes about 15 minutes. At the bottom is an extraordinary natural rock formation – a rock bridge spans the chasm and a waterfall crashes down into a deep hole behind. It is well worth the effort to visit, but be warned: there are no fences or barriers and the drops are sheer. The return walk takes approximately 25 minutes.

Sleeping & Eating

Shangrila Hotel (☎ 03-256 853; www.laklouk resort.com; s/d/tr US$88/110/132; ⊠ ⊠) This pleasant, traditional hotel built in the 1950s is right in the centre of the resort and close to the ski lifts. It is open all year and in summer has a nice pool and can arrange archery, rock climbing, biking and tennis. The price incudes breakfast, and the restaurant serves a range of European and Lebanese dishes.

For cheap eats, there are a couple of simple snack places close to the slopes (only open in winter). Other than that you are limited to the hotel restaurants.

Getting There & Away

Laklouk isn't on any bus or service-taxi route, so use your own transport or take a taxi from Byblos (around US$30 one way).

DOUMA   دوما
☎ 09

If you're pottering about the Adonis Valley countryside, stop for a short walk around Douma, another traditional, very well-preserved red-roofed village, famous for being in the shape of a scorpion (seen from the hillside overlooking the village). About 22km northeast of Byblos, it is a quiet and peaceful place that is said to have been named after the wife of Roman Emperor Septimus Severus, who came here to escape the summer heat on the coast. Under the Ottomans it was famous for the production of swords and guns, a lucrative

business in always-troubled Lebanon, and this paid for the grand houses that can be seen around the village.

The main square has a **Roman sarcophagus** and there are two churches, while above the village is a series of Roman inscriptions dating from the reign of Hadrian.

There are no buses to Douma and very few service taxis from Byblos. You can take a service taxi to Batroun on the coast and pick up a taxi from there (about US$20), or from Byblos (around US$30).

THE CHOUF MOUNTAINS

DEIR AL-QAMAR   دير القمر
☎ 05

Without doubt one of Lebanon's prettiest villages, Deir al-Qamar is a treat for visitors, with an interesting history that supports many Lebanese citizens' belief in their tolerant religious roots, since it once hosted an active church, synagogue, mosque and Druze meeting hall on the central square. Nowadays, it's a sweet, sleepy place, especially enchanting at sunset when the bats flit overhead and the old buildings on the square are most like a fairytale setting.

Deir al-Qamar's roots lie in the Middle Ages when Fakhreddine, the Druze governor of Lebanon, extended his power throughout the region to cover an area roughly equivalent to modern Lebanon, succeeding in uniting into one what before had been a number of small fiefdoms (see p319). Due to water shortages at his first capital, he moved to nearby Deir al-Qamar, which is fed year-round by numerous springs. Over three centuries later, the village remains one of the best-preserved examples of 17th- and 18th-century provincial architecture in the country.

Sights
MOSQUE OF EMIR FAKHREDDINE MAAN
جامع الامير فخر الدين المعني

To the west of the fountain is the mosque of Fakhreddine, with its distinctive octagonal-shaped minaret, the original building dating to 1493. Built in Mamluk style, the mosque consists of a large square room with high arches resting on a central pillar. Quranic verses, along with the date of construction, are carved into the western façade.

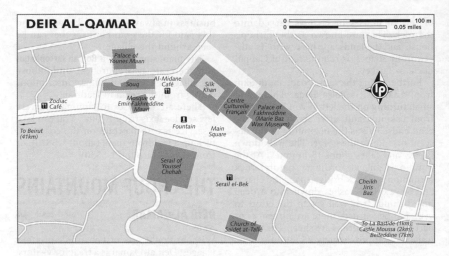

**MT LEBANON &
THE CHOUF MOUNTAINS**

Steps behind the mosque lead up to what was once the town's **souq**, still housing a few shops and a café.

PALACE OF YOUNES MAAN قصر يونس معن
The palace of Younes Maan, governor of Deir al-Qamar while his brother, Fakhreddine, was in exile in Italy, dates to the 18th century, but is now a private house and closed to visitors. However, the elaborate entrance is particularly fine and definitely worth a look.

SILK KHAN
Dominating the main square is the huge silk khan and its warehouse. It dates to 1595 and takes the form of a huge rectangle, incorporating an open courtyard surrounded by arcaded galleries that were once used as stables and servant quarters. Part of the 1st floor, which originally housed the main part of the khan, is now the **Centre Culturelle Français** and can be visited.

PALACE OF FAKHREDDINE قصر فخر الدين
Next to the silk khan and warehouse is Fakhreddine's palace, dating to 1620. It is built on the site of an earlier palace that was destroyed during a battle with Youssef Sifa, Pasha of Tripoli, in 1614. According to local lore, Fakhreddine vowed his revenge and took Youssef's castle at Akkar near Tripoli, tearing it down and lugging the stones all the way back to Deir al-Qamar. He then brought in Italian architects, who rebuilt the palace in an Italian Renaissance style.

Nowadays the palace houses the **Marie Baz Wax Museum** (☎ 511 666; adult/child LL10,000/5000; ☼ 8.30am-6pm winter, until 7pm summer), owned by the once powerful and renowned Baz family. Inside is an eclectic jumble of figures relating to Lebanese history – some more loosely than others – including Lady Hester Stanhope in a strange Medieval princess-type get-up complete with conical hat, a jovial-looking George Bush (senior) and a Jumblatt (see p323) with no head. If you possibly can, try to get hold of the free services of the elderly museum attendant, who'll bark out – from memory – the names and dates of every single obscure figure in the entire place (though largely in French). The oil paintings and relics of the Baz family, an elderly member of whom still lives in one room of the premises, themselves make it poignant enough to warrant a visit. There's also a pleasant cafeteria in the courtyard.

On the corner of the square, the **Cheikh Jiris Baz** was once the Baz family's summer palace, but now stands empty and forlorn. There are plans afoot to turn it into a hotel once tourism picks up – worth checking as you go through – and if you're nice enough to that elderly attendant, he might unlock the palace and let you take a look inside. The owner also has plans to set up a pub/nightclub in an ancient cellar next door to the wax museum, with food and music: check if it's in operation as it's bound to be atmospheric.

SERAIL OF YOUSSEF CHEHAB
سراي يوسف شهاب

On the opposite side of the road from the square itself is the 18th-century Serail of Youssef Chehab, built into the hillside on several levels and hiding a grisly past. Not only did Emir Youssef Chehab assassinate several of his relatives here, but the central courtyard was also the site of a massacre during the anti-Christian violence in 1860. Nowadays the building is noteworthy for its beautiful stonework and houses **municipal offices** (☼ 8am-1pm Mon-Sat), parts of which you can wander through during office hours.

CHURCH OF SAIDET AT-TALLÉ
كنيسة سيدة التلة

The words *deir al-qamar* mean 'monastery of the moon', and the lunar motif can be seen carved in stone on a figure of the Madonna in the Church of Saidet at-Tallé, which sits on the lower slopes of the town. The crescent moon was a symbol of Phoenicia's pagan cult and the Madonna standing on it could be taken as a symbol of Christianity superseding the pagan religion; on the other hand it could simply be incorporating the old religion into the new. The original church was built in the 7th century on a temple dedicated to Astarte, but was destroyed by an earthquake a century later. Fakhreddine reconstructed the building in the 16th century and it was enlarged again in the 17th century.

CASTLE MOUSSA
قلعة موسى

About 2km out of town in the direction of Beiteddine is the extraordinary **Castle Moussa** (☎ 041 144; www.moussacastle.com.lb; admission LL7500; ☼ 8am-8pm summer, 8am-6pm winter), another waxworks place, but this one definitely worth a visit. Popular with Lebanese tour groups, who visit by the bus load. It's filled with strange mechanical tableaux, a life-size recreation of the Last Supper and probably the biggest collection of guns and weaponry you'll ever see in your life. Don't miss this outsider art-type affair, testament to the love of a woman and the stubbornness of its creator (see The Things We'll Do for Love, p320).

FAKHREDDINE

Nationalist hero, brilliant administrator, connoisseur of fine architecture and all-round Ottoman-era gentleman, Fakhreddine (Fakhr ad-Din al Maan II) is credited with being the first to unify Mt Lebanon with the coastal cities, foreshadowing the modern state of Lebanon.

Appointed by the Ottomans in 1590 to pacify the unruly Druze of the Chouf Mountains (many of whose ringleaders were members of his own family, the Maans), he proved more than up to the job. Initially his fiefdom was confined to the district of Sidon and the Chouf, but he was soon granted Beirut and eventually extended his rule to include the Qadisha Valley and Tripoli. While it became clear that their governor was not the subservient puppet they had hoped for, the Ottomans were occupied with revolt in Anatolia and Persia and initially left him more or less to his own devices.

Fakhreddine did more than simply grab territory, and began an ambitious programme of development in Lebanon. He was exiled to Tuscany from 1613 to 1618, for entering into an alliance with one of the Medicis, but returned, inspired by his time abroad, and set about modernising his dominions, developing a silk industry and upgrading olive-oil production with the help of Italian engineers and agricultural experts. Their influence can still be seen in some of his buildings in Deir al-Qamar. Trading links with Europe were also strengthened and European religious missions were allowed to settle in the areas under his control.

Consolidating his power at home, Fakhreddine developed links with the Maronite Christians in the north and encouraged their migration to the south, where they provided labour for silk production. He modernised the ports of Sidon and Beirut, turning them into busy trading centres. In all, the economy flourished under his rule and his power grew to the extent that he controlled areas of what are now Jordan and Israel.

Alarmed at their vassal's growing independence, however, the Ottomans reacted, sending their Syrian and Egyptian governors to attack his territory and bring it back under Istanbul's control. After fleeing to a nearby cave, Fakhreddine was captured in 1633 and taken to Istanbul. Two years later he was executed, like so many historical figures a victim of his own success.

Sleeping & Eating

our pick La Bastide (☎ 505 320, 03-643 010; d/family r US$60/80) About 1km past the town on the left hand side, on the way down to Beiteddine, this is a nice place to stop over for a night if you're exploring by car and heading south or east, via Beiteddine, from Beirut. . It's clean, friendly and comfortable with 20 lovely, airy, flower-patterned pleasant rooms, many with wonderful views across the valley, and the family-sized ones with kitchenette.

Al-Midane Café (☎ 03-763 768; salads & sandwiches from LL6000; ❤ 10am-10pm) A great choice for a drink, snack or nargileh on Deir al-Qamar's main square. Open later in summer if the clientele is in the mood, it serves up decent club sandwiches and salads, and on weekends and summer evenings has live music until the wee hours.

Further back towards the coast, the **Zodiac Café** is a decent place to grab a coffee or doughnut. There is also a series of snack bars and small grocery shops for picnic supplies along the main road.

Getting There & Away

Service taxis en route to Beiteddine go through Deir al-Qamar and can drop you off there. The fare from Beirut's Cola bus station is LL5000. If you're planning to visit both places in the same day, which makes a great full-day excursion, you could continue to Beiteddine and then walk back (6km) to Deir al-Qamar, a pleasant, downhill walk. Keep in mind that service taxis are scarce after dark.

BEITEDDINE   بيت الدين
☎ 05

Some 50km southeast of Beirut, Beiteddine is the name of both a village and the magnificent palace complex that lies within it. The palace, former stronghold of the 18th-century governor Emir Bashir, can be seen from across the valley as you approach, a cross between traditional Arab and Italian baroque (the architects were, in fact, Italian) with its grounds descending over several terraces planted with poplars and flowering shrubs.

There were three other palaces in the vicinity, built for Emir Bashir's sons. Of these only one, Mir Amin Palace, is still standing and is now a luxury hotel just beyond the main part of the village (see p322).

Sights
BEITEDDINE PALACE   قصر بيت الدين
This magnificent early-19th-century **palace complex** (☎ 500 077; admission LL7500; 9am-5.30pm summer, 9am-3.30pm winter) was built over a period of 30 years, starting in 1788, and became the stronghold of Emir Bashir, the Ottoman-appointed governor and leading

THE THINGS WE'LL DO FOR LOVE

The fulfilment of the life-long quest of one enterprising Mr Moussa, who as a child was beaten by his teacher for dreaming of living in a castle, Castle Moussa is also a tribute to his first love, a young lady named Saideh who refused to marry him unless he became wealthy enough to support her in style. After working for several years in archaeological and monument restoration (which included, his website declares, installing 'ancient colons' in front of the National Museum of Beirut), in 1962 he finally began work on his castle to realise his fantasy and to turn 'sand to gold' as his mother once predicted he would. The result was an entire castle from scratch, built largely by Mr Moussa's own two hands, complete with carp-stocked moat, drawbridge, crenellated turrets and all.

Once finished, the industrious Mr Moussa went about filling the castle's many rooms with wax models depicting scenes from traditional Lebanese life, along with excerpts from the Bible (don't miss the plastic toy animals heading on a conveyor belt to a shrinelike ark) and a tableau in which Mr Moussa, as a child, is being perpetually beaten by his teacher – all enhanced with mechanical movement. Sadly Mr Moussa's teacher died before he could witness the kitsch result.

These days, Mr Moussa is still often to be found greeting visitors at the entrance to his castle - ask if he's around and you'll find out whether his castle managed to win the hand of the fickle Saideh after all. But here's a hint: standing on his drawbridge, gazing up at his hard-won stones on a sunny September afternoon, he sighed and patted the hand of a young newlywed heading for the ticket desk. 'Behind every great, or crazy man,' he smiled, 'is a good woman.'

member of the Shihab family. It is the greatest surviving achievement of 19th-century Lebanese architecture and an impressive symbol of Bashir's power and wealth. Most areas except the courtyards and old stables are kept locked, so it's hard to see anything for just the price of your ticket. A guide with an all-important key can be had for about LL10,000 unless you manage to tag along inconspicuously behind another group.

The name Beiteddine itself means 'house of faith' and the original site was a Druze hermitage, which was incorporated into the complex. The palace was built after the Shihab family took over from the Maan dynasty. Partly due to family disagreements, Emir Bashir decided to move from Deir al-Qamar and build his own palace, which would reflect the increasing power and glory of his reign. Architects from Italy, and the most highly skilled artisans from Damascus and Aleppo, were hired and given free rein to try out new ideas. The result was this huge edifice, more than 300m long, built high on a mountain overlooking the valley. The grounds below the palace are terraced into gardens and orchards.

During the French Mandate the palace was used for local administration, but after 1930 it was declared a historic monument and placed under the care of the Department of Antiquities, which set about restoring it. In 1943 Lebanon's first president after independence, Bishara al-Khouri, made it his official summer residence and brought back the remains of Emir Bashir from Istanbul, who had died there in 1850.

The palace suffered tremendous losses following the Israeli invasion, when as much as 90% of its original contents are reckoned to have been lost. But in 1984, the Druze leader Walid Jumblatt ordered its restoration and declared it a 'Palace of the People'. As such, it contains several museums housing various collections, most impressive being a magnificent collection of **mosaics**.

The palace consists of three main courts: **Dar al-Baraniyyeh** (the outer courtyard to which passing visitors were admitted freely), **Dar al-Wousta** (the central courtyard, which housed the palace guards and offices of the ministers) and **Dar al-Harim** (the inner court and private family quarters). Beneath Dar al-Wousta and Dar al-Harim are huge vaulted **stables**, which held 500 horses and their riders, in addition to the 600 infantry that formed the emir's guard. Part of the stables now houses the mosaic collection.

From the ticket office at the entrance to the palace, you pass through a corridor and turn left into the 60m-long courtyard Dar al-Baraniyyeh, where public festivals and gatherings took place. It was from here that the emir would leave for his hunting expeditions or to fight wars. To your right, running along the northern side of this courtyard, are the guest apartments. It was the custom of noble houses to offer hospitality to visitors for three days, before asking their business or their identity.

The restored upper floor of this guest wing is now used to exhibit the **Rachid Karami Ethnographic Collection**. This large collection includes pottery from the Bronze and Iron Ages, Roman glass, Islamic pottery, lead sarcophagi and gold jewellery. There is also a scale model of the palace and, in other rooms, a collection of weapons and costumes. The cloistered ground floor is often used to house temporary photo exhibitions.

At the far end of the outer courtyard, directly ahead of you on entering the courtyard, is a double staircase leading up to the entrance to Dar al-Wousta, the central courtyard. It's known as the 'tumbling staircase' because of the tale of a sheep that escaped the butcher's knife and headbutted an eminent pasha down the stairs. Head this way and through an arched passageway and you'll reach the central courtyard. The entrance is decorated with an inscription of welcome and a decorative **marble portal**. Inside is a beautiful, fragrant and tranquil courtyard with a fountain; the southern side, to your left, overlooks part of the gardens and the valley beyond. The apartments and offices off the courtyard are set along graceful arcades, the palace rooms richly decorated with marble, mosaics and marquetry, and furnishings in traditional Oriental style. The walls and ceilings are of painted, carved cedar wood embellished with Arabic calligraphy. In one room, directly to your left as you enter the courtyard, an inlaid marble **water fountain** is built into the wall, which both cools the room and makes conversation inaudible to eavesdroppers. This is one of the rooms that you'll most likely need a guide with a key to access.

MT LEBANON & THE CHOUF MOUNTAINS

The **entrance to the third court** is a beautiful façade that leads through to the lower court (the kitchens and hammam) and the upper court (the reception rooms). Again, the rooms are lavishly decorated. On the ground floor, immediately beyond the entrance is the waiting room, known as the **room of the column**, named for the single column supporting the vaulted ceiling. Beyond this is a two-level **reception room** *(salaamlik)* with a mosaic floor and inlaid marble walls.

The huge **kitchens** are also well worth a look. In their heyday they catered for 500 people a day. Endless trays of food would have been carried out to set before the divans and sofas of the court and their visitors. To the north of the kitchen is the large **hammam**, a series of domed rooms luxuriously fitted out in marble with carved marble basins and fountains.

Bathers would move between the cold, warm and hot chambers before reclining to rest in the anteroom. In a small shaded garden, usually kept locked, to the north of the hammam is the **Tomb of Sitt Chams**, the emir's first wife. The ashes of Bashir are also reported to be in the tomb.

But the star of the Beiteddine show is housed in the lower part of the palace, which contains one of the most spectacular collections of **Byzantine mosaics** in the eastern Mediterranean, if not the world. These were largely excavated from a former church at Jiyyeh, near Sidon, the ancient city of Porphyrion, which was discovered by workers digging on the coast in early 1982. The area was then under the control of Walid Jumblatt, who had the well-preserved mosaics brought to him, so he could keep them safe from looters throughout the war. The magnificent collection includes some 30 room-sized mosaics and dozens upon dozens of smaller ones.

The designs are often geometric and stylised, reflecting the austere nature of early Christianity in the area. There are also graceful depictions of animals, including leopards, bulls, gazelles and birds, and a pair of fighting deer who almost leap from the mosaic. Set among the stone arches and vaulted ceilings of Beiteddine's former stables and along the walls of the palace's lower gardens, the mosaics are a stunning visual treat.

Festivals & Events

A **festival** is held in Beiteddine every summer in July and August, featuring a wonderfully eclectic mixture of international and Arab musicians, singers, dancers and actors. Check the festival website (www.beiteddine .org) for full details of the year's events.

Sleeping & Eating

There are no budget sleeping options in Beiteddine and if you're looking to stay nearby, the best bet is the lovely La Bastide (see p320) in Deir al-Qamar .

Mir Amin Palace (☎ 501 315-18; www.miramin palace.com; s/d US$123/155; ❄ ☐ ☒) The only hotel in Beiteddine itself is the luxurious Mir Amin, set on the hill overlooking Beiteddine Palace, the restored palace of Emir Bashir's eldest son. There are 24 individually and beautifully decorated rooms and even if you're not staying here, it's still well worth dropping by for a drink on the terrace, where views are spectacular. The hotel also has a couple of good restaurants with Lebanese and Continental cuisine where you can expect to spend at least US$30 to US$40 per person for a meal. Rates are cheaper during the low season.

In the town itself, there's a selection of snack places, though nothing of note. It's better either to bring a picnic to eat on the grass amid the mosaics, or head into Deir al-Qamar down the road for a bite on the square.

Getting There & Away

To get to Beiteddine with your own transport, take the coastal highway south from Beirut as far as Damour, then follow signs east. Service taxis from Beirut's Cola bus station serve the route and the fare to Beiteddine is LL5000.

The service-taxi stand in Beiteddine is close to the palace on the main square; keep in mind that you're unlikely to find service taxis running after dark.

MOUKHTARA   المختارة

About 9km south of Beiteddine is the town of Moukhtara, the seat of the Jumblatt family and de facto capital of the Chouf. The Jumblatts' 19th-century stone palace dominates the town. Consisting of three large buildings, it has its own hammam, a garden with a collection of Roman sarcophagi and

WHO ARE THE JUMBLATTS?

Travelling around Lebanon, you're bound to come across the name and face of Walid Jumblatt, leader of Lebanon's Druze, on numerous occasions. The family from which he hails, however, have been famous for far longer than his lifetime, rising to prominence and settling in the region in the 15th century, to escape persecution from an Ottoman governor.

Walid Jumblatt's grandmother, Nazira, was one of the first major notables of recent Jumblatt generations. In the 1920s, when the family's position was threatened due to the assassination of Walid's great-grandfather Fouad, Nazira came to the aid of the Druze community, both keeping the Jumblatt dynasty alive and assuming the leadership of the community until her son Kamal came of age. The unprecedented spectre of a woman leader was difficult for many to accept (particularly close male relatives), but eventually she won them over and remained in power until Kamal grew up.

Kamal Jumblatt, Walid's father, was a powerful figure in his own right, making his mark on Lebanon in cultural, philosophical and political spheres, and crucially by being the most prominent anti-government leader in Lebanon during the civil war. In 1949 he founded the Progressive Socialist Party, which, officially at least, was nonsectarian and opposed to the essentially sectarian nature of Lebanese politics. With mostly Druze followers, however, it was also a forum for this particular sect itself and during the civil war had one of the strongest private armies of any of the warring factions. In 1977, Kamal Jumblatt was assassinated, allegedly by pro-Syrian factions, and his only son Walid took the political helm.

Walid Jumblatt's political career has been characterised, say many observers, by his tendency towards being a 'political weathervane', changing allegiances, policies and alliances frequently and yet usually managing to come out on top. Though initially a supporter of Syria after the civil war, he has recently become more anti-Syrian in his standpoint, also joining the call for the disarmament of Hezbollah (through whom, he claims, Iran and Syria are attempting to take over Lebanon); he has often claimed that he fears for his life on this account. Walid Jumblatt frequently returns to his sleepy home town of Moukhtara (see opposite) where he holds public audiences to listen to the personal gripes of his loyal Druze followers, probably quite a break from his place in the rather more turbulent national and international political arenas.

a waterfall that tumbles into an ornamental pool. There are public reception rooms that are sometimes open to visitors.

Every weekend when he is in residence, Walid Jumblatt, head of the family and leader of the Druze, spends his mornings listening to the complaints of his mostly Druze followers. If you happen to be there then, you will see the long line of petitioners as they wait to see their leader.

Apart from the overwhelming Jumblatt presence, the town is picturesque and has a number of traditional red-tiled buildings that make for a pleasant wander.

Getting There & Away

Service taxis to Moukhtara leave from Beirut's Cola bus station and cost LL6000 each way, but the town only really warrants a trip if combined with Deir al-Qamar, Beiteddine or the Chouf Cedar Reserve. Keep in mind, especially when planning your return trip, that service taxis can be infrequent.

CHOUF CEDAR RESERVE

محميّة ارز الشوف

The largest of Lebanon's three natural protectorates, the **Chouf Cedar Reserve** (☎ 05 502 230, 03-682 472; www.shoufcedar.org; admission LL5000; ♡ 9am-7pm) represents a quarter of the remaining cedar forests in the country and 5% of Lebanon's entire area. The reserve marks the southernmost limit of Lebanese cedar *(Cedrus libani)* growth, and incorporated within the protectorate are six cedar forests. Of these, the Barouk and Maaser ech-Chouf forests have the largest number of ancient trees – some are thought to date back 2000 years. Hunting and livestock-grazing bans are strictly enforced and a number of species of flora and fauna have returned to the area in recent years. More than 200 species of birds and 26 species of wild mammals (including wolves, gazelles and wild boar) either live in or pass through the area.

Also within or just outside the reserve's boundaries are a number of historical sites.

LEBANON'S CEDARS

There are three or four species of cedar tree *(Cedrus libani)* throughout North Africa and Asia, but the most famous of these is the Cedar of Lebanon, which was mentioned in the Old Testament. In antiquity the cedar forests covered great swathes of the Mt Lebanon Range and provided a source of wealth for the Phoenicians, who exported the fragrant and durable wood to Egypt and Palestine.

The original Temple of Solomon in Jerusalem was built of this wood, as were many sarcophagi discovered in Egypt. Today, however, only a few of the original groves still exist, due to a slow-but-sure process of deforestation that has taken place over the last millennia, and although new trees are now being planted, it will be centuries before they mature.

Of the few remaining ancient trees, most are in the Chouf Cedar Reserve and there are some more in the grove at the Cedars, above Bcharré. Some of these trees are thought to be well over 1000 years old: their trunks have an immense girth and they can reach heights of 30m. Naturally, there are strict rules about taking any timber from these remaining trees and the souvenirs for sale nearby are made from fallen branches.

These include the remains of the rock-cut fortress of **Qab Elias** and **Qala'at Niha**, in addition to the **Shrine of Sit Sha'wane**, a woman saint venerated by the Druze and still a site of pilgrimage for local residents.

Since not all parts of the park are reliably open to visitors (the reserve is desperately in need of extra funds to finance the employment of 60 more rangers when currently there are only 10), the best way to explore Chouf Cedar is to head to the ranger hut at the Barouk entrance, relatively well signposted from the main road. Here you'll find incredibly helpful, friendly rangers just bursting with information on the reserve, its wildlife and hiking trails. There are about eight trails currently open to the public, ranging from 40 minutes to four hours in length. If you take (for an extra donation) a warden along with you on a hike, you'll gain an invaluable insight into some of its most beautiful features, and might get to see trees believed to be more than a millennium old.

Also at the ranger station is a small shop selling local produce, since one of its outreach projects involves aiding local communities and promoting cottage industries. The honey, preserves, olives and olive oil on sale are marvellous additions to a picnic in the mountains.

If you want to stay overnight in the area, contact the **Association for Forests, Development and Conservation** (www.afdc.org.lb), which runs an ecolodge in a forest just 7km from the reserve. It's also worth checking with eco-tour company **Esprit-Nomade** (www.esprit-nomade.com) to see if there's a day trip scheduled to the area, which usually includes lunch, a guide and transport to and from Beirut.

The only entrance open to the public at the time of research (due to understaffing caused by shortage of funds) was at the village of Barouk, which can be accessed without calling ahead. If you don't have your own vehicle, the best way to get here is to negotiate a taxi from Beiteddine, some 10km away.

Tripoli & the North

Northern Lebanon is considered by many people – locals and visitors alike – to be the country's greatest, greenest, cleanest natural asset.

The gorgeous World Heritage–listed Qadisha Valley, hidden deep beneath the mountains east of Tripoli, provides a tranquil escape for hikers from the fast-paced Lebanese development of the cities and the coastal strip. The valley snakes up to the pretty, sleepy town of Bcharré, birthplace of legendary Lebanese poet Khalil Gibran. Further east from Bcharré is the Cedars – where a few of the country's treasured trees remain – home to Lebanon's highest altitude ski resort and a good starting point for hiking in summer. Meanwhile, the small town of Ehden, located on the valley's northern rim, provides quaint respite from the searing coastal heat, with a lovely central square that's the perfect place for sipping arak late into the night. The creation of the Lebanon Mountain Trail and a growing Lebanese interest in adventure sports, such as rafting and paragliding, sees the region becoming more enticing than ever to visitors. Still, it remains sparsely populated, and while you're enjoying the abundance of tracks and trails, you're unlikely to encounter more than a handful of other intrepid trekkers.

A dramatically different face of Lebanon's north lies in tightly-packed Tripoli, with its busy medieval souqs, historic fortress and the workaday port of Al-Mina. Lebanon's second city, Tripoli was once planned as its capital, but today has little in common with cosmopolitan Beirut, exuding a more provincial, and slightly bruised-and-battered feel. Tripoli's economy was hard hit by the 2007 crisis in the outlying Palestinian refugee camp of Nahr al-Bared and is still recovering; nevertheless, the city makes a fascinating place to explore, preferably with one of its famous, sticky pastries in hand.

HIGHLIGHTS

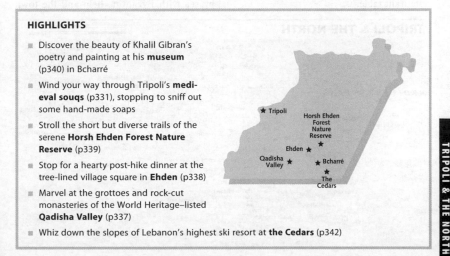

- Discover the beauty of Khalil Gibran's poetry and painting at his **museum** (p340) in Bcharré

- Wind your way through Tripoli's **medieval souqs** (p331), stopping to sniff out some hand-made soaps

- Stroll the short but diverse trails of the serene **Horsh Ehden Forest Nature Reserve** (p339)

- Stop for a hearty post-hike dinner at the tree-lined village square in **Ehden** (p338)

- Marvel at the grottoes and rock-cut monasteries of the World Heritage–listed **Qadisha Valley** (p337)

- Whiz down the slopes of Lebanon's highest ski resort at **the Cedars** (p342)

TRIPOLI (TRABLOUS)

طرابلس

☎ 06 / pop 237,909

Tripoli (Trablous in Arabic), 85km north of Beirut, is Lebanon's second-largest city and the north's main port. Famous for its medieval Mamluk architecture, old city souq, huge fortress and teeth-clenchingly sweet pastries, its charms were sadly overshadowed in 2007 by the deadly and drawn-out confrontation between Palestinian militants and the Lebanese army, centred on the Nahr al-Bared refugee camp around 16km from the city centre. On 20 May 2007, militants and Lebanese police began battling it out in Tripoli itself, before fighting moved to Nahr al-Bared; Lebanese soldiers finally took control of the camp in September 2007. Alleged ties between the militant group and Al-Qaeda lent events a particularly sinister and gloomy edge.

Its image tarnished as a result, Tripoli is currently struggling to entice tourists back to its markets and monuments. Certainly, there's plenty to keep a visitor entertained for a couple of days, and with one good budget hotel and one excellent top-end choice, there are accommodation options for every pocket. Since few tourists currently make it this far north, you'll have no problem finding an available room or restaurant table.

If you're arriving direct from Beirut, though, you may be in for something of a culture shock. Tripoli may be Lebanon's second-largest city, but in many ways it couldn't be more different. Where Beirut is glitzy, Tripoli is demure and down-to-earth. Though there is some nightlife to be had, it's low key and based in the port of Al-Mina rather than in Tripoli proper. It's wise, therefore, to dress down a little, leaving your best figure-hugging combinations for the streets and clubs of the capital.

HISTORY

While there is evidence of a settlement in Tripoli as far back as 1400 BC, its past is likely to go back even further. By the 8th century BC, what had been a small Phoenician seaside trading post had grown with the arrival of traders from Sidon, Tyre and Arwad (Aradus, which became Tartus in Syria). Each community settled within its own walled area, giving rise to the Greek name Tripolis, meaning 'three cities'.

During the rule of the Seleucids, and later the Romans, Tripoli prospered but a massive earthquake in AD 543 altered the geography of the port area completely and razed most of the town. It was quickly rebuilt but by AD 635 a general of Mu'awiyah, the governor of Syria and founder of the Umayyad dynasty (AD 661–750), besieged the city and attempted to starve it into submission. The inhabitants of Tripoli escaped by sea with Byzantine help and the town

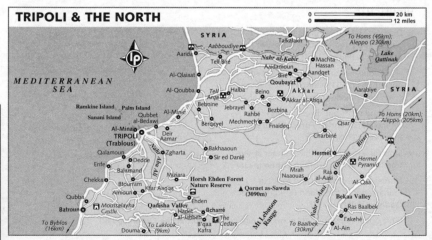

TRIPOLI & THE NORTH

was resettled by a military garrison and a Jewish colony.

Between 685 and 705 the Byzantines captured and resettled the city. It was then recaptured by the Muslims and incorporated into the Umayyad and, later, Abbasid caliphates. By the end of the 10th century, as the Abbasids were losing their grip on the region, the Shiite Fatimids took control of Tripoli. They held onto it until 1069, when one of the city's judges, from a family named Banu Ammar, declared Tripoli's independence. Under Ammar rule, the growing city became a centre of learning renowned for its school, Dar al-Ilm (literally 'Abode of Knowledge'), with a library containing some 100,000 volumes.

When the Crusaders, led by Raymond de Saint-Gilles of Toulouse, first arrived in 1099, the Ammars persuaded them to bypass Tripoli, bribing them with lavish gifts. However, Tripoli's agricultural wealth was too glittering a prize and Raymond returned some three years later. Tripoli's rulers brought in reinforcements from Damascus and Homs, but Raymond defeated the three armies with only 300 men. He then built a fortress, the Citadel of Raymond de Saint-Gilles, on a hill inland from the busy port area and controlled land trade coming into the city.

Tripoli's leaders launched repeated raids on the fortress, eventually mortally wounding Raymond. Just before he died he signed a truce guaranteeing safe passage in and out of the city for its inhabitants and this lasted only until his successor, Guillaume Jourdain, took over and once again imposed the blockade with the assistance of the Genovese fleet, which blocked the city from the sea. After four increasingly desperate years under siege, the city finally fell to the Crusaders in June 1109. The victors sacked the city and set fire to the magnificent library at Dar al-Ilm.

Tripoli became the capital of the County of Tripoli and the Crusaders managed to hang on to the city for 180 years, during which time the economy, based on silk-weaving and glass-making, prospered. Academic traditions were revived too, although this time it was Christian schools, rather than Islamic ones, that led the way.

The Mamluk sultan, Qalaun, took the city of Tripoli in 1289, massacring most of the population and razing the port city.

Qalaun built his new city around the Citadel of Raymond de Saint-Gilles and once again the area flourished: the souqs, mosques, madrassas (schools where Islamic law is taught) and khans that form the bulk of present-day Tripoli's monuments are testament to the city's economic and cultural prosperity in Mamluk times. The Turkish Ottomans, under the rule of sultan Selim I, took over the town in 1516. When the *mutasarrifa* (administrative district) of Mt Lebanon was created in 1860, Tripoli was still ruled by the Ottomans; however, it fell within the boundaries of the French Mandate of Greater Lebanon in 1920.

Since independence in 1946, Tripoli has been the administrative capital of northern Lebanon. Conservative and predominantly Sunni Muslim, it was perhaps natural that the pro-Arab nationalist forces, led by Rachid Karami, based themselves here in the civil war of 1958. The labyrinthine old city was almost impossible for outsiders to penetrate and Karami's men held out for several weeks.

In the 1975–91 round of fighting, Tripoli suffered a lot of damage – especially during the inter-Palestinian battles of 1983 – but it still fared better than the south of the country. Both during and after the war, the city's population grew rapidly, swelled by refugees, including large numbers of Palestinians, most of whom today reside in the UNRWA-administered Beddawi and now-infamous Nahr el-Bared refugee camps on the outskirts of the city.

ORIENTATION

Tripoli comprises two main areas: the city proper, which includes the broad streets of modern Tripoli and the labyrinthine old city; and Al-Mina port, 3km to the west along the sea front. The geographical centre of town is Sahet et-Tall (at-tahl), a large square next to the clock tower where you'll find the service-taxi and bus stands. Most of the city's cheap hotels are clustered close to the square.

The old city sprawls east of Sahet et-Tall, while the modern centre is west of the square, along Rue Fouad Chehab. Between Rue Fouad Chehab and Al-Mina are broad avenues lined with shops, apartment buildings, internet cafés and restaurants. In Al-Mina you'll find a rather run-down waterfront promenade, which becomes at-

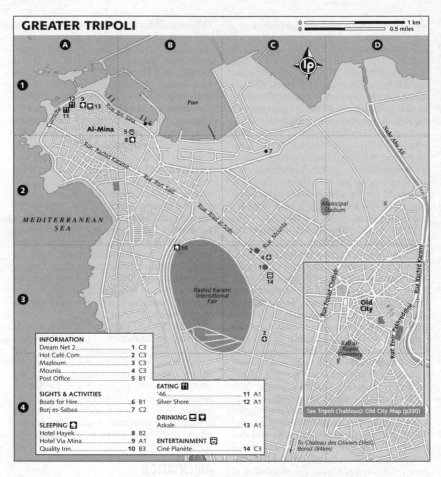

GREATER TRIPOLI

INFORMATION		
Dream Net 2	1	C3
Hot Café.Com	2	C3
Mazloum	3	C3
Mounla	4	C3
Post Office	5	B1

SIGHTS & ACTIVITIES		
Boats for Hire	6	B1
Burj es-Sabaa	7	C2

SLEEPING		
Hotel Hayek	8	B2
Hotel Via Mina	9	A1
Quality Inn	10	B3

EATING		
'46	11	A1
Silver Shore	12	A1

DRINKING		
Askale	13	A1

ENTERTAINMENT		
Ciné Planète	14	C3

See Tripoli (Trablous): Old City Map (p330)

To Chateau des Oliviers (3km);
Beirut (84km)

mospheric towards nightfall when locals stroll beside the big ships of the port, the city's main concentration of bars, the fabulous Hotel Via Mina, and boats taking visitors out to the Palm Islands reserve.

INFORMATION
Emergency
Ambulance (☎ 140)
Fire (☎ 145)
Police (☎ 112)

Internet Access
Most of Tripoli's internet cafés are congregated along the main roads leading towards Al-Mina. The following listings are a couple of the most pleasant:

Hot Café.Com (Map p328; ☎ 622 888; Rue Riad al-Solh; wireless connection per hr with own laptop LL1500, with café laptop LL2500; ⏱ 9am-midnight) A large, airy place owned by a friendly Australian expat, this is a great place to check your mail while munching on breakfast, lunch, dinner or a huge slab of chocolate cake.

Dream Net 2 (☎ 03-858 821; Rue Riad al-Solh; per hr LL1000; ⏱ 8am-midnight) On the opposite side of the road from Hot Café.Com, a little closer to the cinema complex, this doesn't have the atmosphere of the first but is a fine place to get things done.

Medical Services
Mazloum (Map p328; ☎ 628 303) and **Mounla** (Map p328; ☎ 210 848) are good private hospitals. There are plenty of pharmacies dotted along

Rue Riad al-Solh, further along on Rue Port Said and on Rue Tall in the old city.

Money

There are ATMs all over town, many on Rue Riad al-Solh. US-dollar travellers cheques can be exchanged into any denomination at the **Walid M el-Masri Co Exchange** (Map p330; Rue Tall) for US$2 per cheque.

Post

There are two post offices in Tripoli. The **main post office** (Map p330; Rue Fouad Chehab; 🕑 8am-5pm Mon-Fri, 8am-noon Sat) is near the Bank of Lebanon building, just south of Abdel Hamid Karami Sq, and the other **branch** (Map p328; Rue ibn Sina) is in Al-Mina.

Tourist Information

Tourist office (Map p330; Abdel Hamrid Karami Sq; 🕑 8am-5pm Mon-Sat) Friendly, helpful staff who'll try hard to help you with general enquiries and permits to visit the Palm Islands Reserve (p333). Recently, the office's opening hours have become sporadic outside high summer, so persevere if you find it closed.

SIGHTS & ACTIVITIES
Old City

The compact old city dates largely from the 14th and 15th centuries (the Mamluk era) and is a maze of narrow alleyways, colourful souqs, hammams, khans, mosques and madrassas. Though many of the monuments are poorly maintained, some still displaying damage from the civil war, it's an atmospheric and lively place to take in the sights, sounds and frequently the smells, as locals come to pick over stalls laden with fruits and vegetables, butchers take the hatchet to swaying sides of beef, and tailors and jewellers ply their trades as they have done for generations.

Almost all of Tripoli's 40-or-so listed monuments are contained within the old city, each with its own numbered plaque. These plaques are often extremely well hidden and you might have to search around a bit to find them. Some monuments are completely ruined. Others are locked, but a key is usually kept in a nearby shop or house – ask around and a key will usually appear, often attached to a grinning old man.

CITADEL OF RAYMOND DE SAINT-GILLES

The city is dominated by the vast **citadel** (Map p330; Plaque 1; admission LL7500; 🕑 8am-6pm, closes ear-

lier in winter), known as Qala'at Sanjil in Arabic. In AD 1102 Raymond de Saint-Gilles occupied the hill that overlooks the valley, the town and the coast. He decided to transform this position, which he called Mont Pelerin (Mt Pilgrim), into a fortress. The original castle was burnt down in 1289, and again on several subsequent occasions. It was rebuilt (1307–08) by Emir Essendemir Kurgi, and had additions right up until the 19th century. As a result, only the foundation stones remain of the original construction.

The first entrance is a huge Ottoman gateway, over which is an engraving from Süleyman the Magnificent, who ordered the restoration (yet again) of 'this blessed tower, that it may serve as a fortified position until the end of time'. After this there is a bridge across a moat dug by the Crusaders. Inside the castle is a muddle of architectural styles and features, reflecting the different occupants and stormy history of the city. Though it's fun to explore independently, take a guide from near the entrance if you really want to know more about the citadel's history. There's no fixed fee for a guided tour, but expect to pay somewhere in the region of LL20,000.

The best exterior view of the castle can be had from the east bank of the Nahr Abu Ali, perfect if you're able to ignore the cascades of rubbish floating by in winter, and the pungent aroma of muddy river bed during the summer months.

MADRASSAS

From the top of the citadel, walk down the set of steps directly in front of you. When you reach the street, turn left then take the first right and walk along Rue Rachid Rida. Take the first right and soon you'll see the 14th-century **madrassas of Al-Machhad and Al-Shamsiyat** (Map p330), adjacent to the entrance of the Great Mosque. Opposite the entrance are two more 14th-century madrassas, **Al-Khairiah Hassan** and **Al-Nouriyat**. The latter is still in use and has distinctive black-and-white stonework around its doors and windows, and a beautiful inlaid mihrab.

HAMMAM AL-NOURI حمام النوري

Opposite the Al-Khairiah Hassan and Al-Nouriyat madrassas, look right and you should see the entrance to the now derelict Hammam al-Nouri (Map p330), a large public bath built around 1333. If you ask

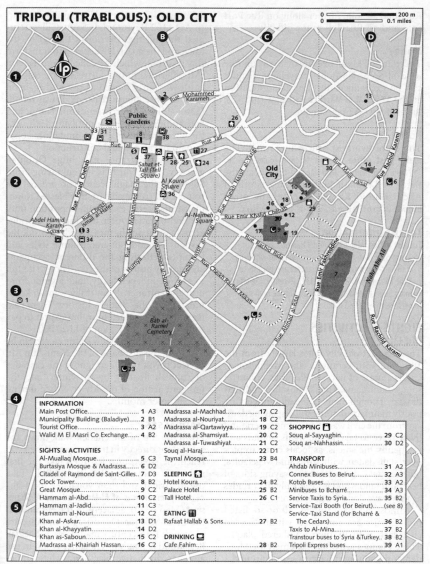

TRIPOLI (TRABLOUS): OLD CITY

INFORMATION		
Main Post Office	1	A3
Municipality Building (Baladiye)	2	B1
Tourist Office	3	A2
Walid M El Masri Co Exchange	4	B2

SIGHTS & ACTIVITIES		
Al-Muallaq Mosque	5	C3
Burtasiya Mosque & Madrassa	6	D2
Citadel of Raymond de Saint-Gilles	7	D3
Clock Tower	8	B2
Great Mosque	9	C2
Hammam al-Abd	10	C2
Hammam al-Jadid	11	C3
Hammam al-Nouri	12	C2
Khan al-Askar	13	D1
Khan al-Khayyatin	14	D2
Khan as-Saboun	15	C2
Madrassa al-Khairiah Hassan	16	C2

Madrassa al-Machhad	17	C2
Madrassa al-Nouriyat	18	C2
Madrassa al-Qartawiyya	19	C2
Madrassa al-Shamsiyat	20	C2
Madrassa al-Tuwashiyat	21	C2
Souq al-Haraj	22	D1
Taynal Mosque	23	B4

SLEEPING 🏠		
Hotel Koura	24	B2
Palace Hotel	25	B2
Tall Hotel	26	C1

EATING 🍴		
Rafaat Hallab & Sons	27	B2

DRINKING 🍸		
Cafe Fahim	28	B2

SHOPPING 🛍		
Souq al-Sayyaghin	29	C2
Souq an-Nahhassin	30	D2

TRANSPORT		
Ahdab Minibuses	31	A2
Connex Buses to Beirut	32	A3
Kotob Buses	33	A2
Minibuses to Bcharré	34	A3
Service Taxis to Syria	35	B2
Service-Taxi Booth (for Beirut)	(see 8)	
Service-Taxi Stand (for Bcharré & The Cedars)	36	B2
Taxis to Al-Mina	37	B2
Transtour buses to Syria &Turkey	38	B2
Tripoli Express buses	39	A1

politely, the owner of the juice stand in front of the entrance should let you past to have a wander around the remains of the hammam beyond.

GREAT MOSQUE الجامع الكبير
Built on the remains of a 12th-century Crusader cathedral dedicated to St Mary of the

Tower, construction of the Great Mosque (Map p330; Plaque 2), known as Jami al-Kabir in Arabic, began in 1294 after the cathedral was destroyed by the Mamluks. It was completed in 1315, and probable traces of the 700-year-old structure can still be seen in the mosque's attractive northern entrance, while the distinctive square minaret may once have been the original cathedral's bell tower. Inside, a large courtyard is surrounded by porticos on three sides, and a domed and vaulted prayer hall on the fourth.

Women are expected to don one of the gowns provided and cover their heads before entering the Great Mosque.

MADRASSA AL-QARTAWIYYA المدرسة القرطاوية

Attached to the east side of the Great Mosque is Madrassa al-Qartawiyya (Map p330; Plaque 3), which was built by a Mamluk governor of the same name in the early 1300s, over the baptistery of the old cathedral. Famed for its fine workmanship, the madrassa has an elegant façade of black-and-white stone facings, topped by a honeycomb-patterned half-dome above the portal. The back wall is also made with black-and-white stone and has some beautiful Arabic inscriptions. Inside, the prayer hall is topped by Tripoli's only oval dome and has a finely decorated south-facing wall and *minbar* (pulpit).

MADRASSA AL-TUWASHIYAT المدرسة الطويشية

Back out on the street, Madrassa al-Tuwashiyat (Map p330; Plaque 9), a law school with an attached mausoleum that dates back to around 1471, is on the main street of the gold souq (Souq al-Sayyaghin). Built of sandstone in alternating black-and-white patterns, it has an unusual, finely decorated portal that towers above the building's ornate façade.

HAMMAM AL-ABD حمام العبد

Close by the Madrassa al-Tuwashiyat is Tripoli's only functioning bathhouse, **Hammam al-Abd** (Map p330; basic bath LL12,000; ⏰ 8am-10pm), built in the late 17th century and situated at the end of a narrow alleyway. Sadly, it's only for men (unless you're travelling with a group of women and can arrange to reserve the entire bathhouse in advance). Expect to negotiate an extra fee if you'd like a massage thrown in.

KHAN AS-SABOUN خان الصابون

Virtually next door to the hammam is Khan as-Saboun (Map p330; Plaque 10), meaning 'Soap Khan', which was built in the 16th century and began life as an army barracks. Abandoned for many years, it was later re-

incarnated as a market where local farmers sold their olives and olive-based products – soap in particular – from the small shops surrounding the courtyard. By the 18th century, when Tripoli's soap industry took off, the khan became famous for its high quality soaps and formed the centre of the soap industry. In recent years, the khan has been brought back to life by the Hassoun family; see A Slippery Business, p332.

KHAN AL-KHAYYATIN خان الخياطين

Beside Hammam Izz ed-Dine is the beautifully restored stretch of tailors' shops known as Khan al-Khayyatin (Tailors' Market; Map p330; Plaque 12). Built in the first half of the 14th century, it is one of the city's oldest khans.

SOUQ AL-HARAJ سوق الحرج

At the northern end of the old town is **Souq al-Haraj** (Map p330; Plaque 21), which is thought to have been built on the site of a Crusader church. Its high, vaulted ceiling is supported by 14 granite columns, two at the centre and 12 ranged around the sides, which are probably a leftover from the earlier structure. Today the souq specialises in mats, pillows and mattresses.

KHAN AL-ASKAR خان العسكر

Just around the corner from Souq al-Haraj is Khan al-Askar (Soldiers' Khan; Map p330; Plaque 33), which consists of two buildings joined by a vaulted passage. It is thought to have been built in the late 13th or early 14th century, and was restored in the 18th century.

Other Sights & Activities

AL-MUALLAQ MOSQUE جامع المعلق

To the south of the Great Mosque is **Al-Muallaq Mosque** (Hanging Mosque; Map p330; Plaque 29). It's a small, 14th-century mosque that gets its name from its unusual position upstairs on the second floor of the building. It has a simple interior and leads down to a courtyard garden.

HAMMAM AL-JADID حمام الجديد

Almost opposite Al-Muallaq Mosque is Hammam al-Jadid (New Baths; Map p330; Plaque 30). While certainly not new – it was built around 1740 – it was in use until the

A SLIPPERY BUSINESS

The city may only have a handful of traditional soap-makers today but historically soap played an important role in Tripoli's economy. Some locals go so far as to claim that soap was actually invented here, and though this is something of a stretch – soap production probably dates back to at least the ancient Egyptians, if not earlier – it's undeniable that, by the 18th century, Tripoli soap was a highly prized product in Europe.

Tripoli's soap was traditionally made with olive oil, honey, glycerine and other natural ingredients, which were melted together in a huge vat, coloured with saffron and other natural dyes, and scented with essential oils. The soap supplied the local hammams as well as households and a collection of soaps of various sizes, symbolising purity, would be given to brides as part of their trousseau.

Towards the middle of the last century, increasingly cheap mass-production of soap almost killed traditional soap-making in Tripoli. In recent years, however, in line with the world's growing interest in natural, 'boutique' cosmetics, its handmade soaps have made a comeback. The Hassoun family is largely responsible for bringing Tripoli's soaps to the attention of the world. If you wander into their shop, **Khan al-Saboun** (☎ 874 483; www.khanalsaboun.com; ꗨ 10am-5pm Sun-Thu), which dominates Tripoli's traditional soap khan, Khan as-Saboun, you're sure to find someone happy to explain the various soap-making processes as well as to take you on a tour of their vast collection of soaps for sale. There are 400 kinds on offer, including soaps in the shape of letters of the alphabet and a soap whose scent remains on your skin for two days. A bar of laurel soap costs US$2 and a bar of clay soap, US$4. Look out, also, for the huge soap carved into the shape of an open volume of the Quran.

Outside Tripoli, be sure to look in on the Musée de Savon (p367) in Sidon, which beautifully illustrates traditional soap making practices.

1970s and is the city's best-preserved and largest hammam (with the exception of the still-functioning Hammam al-Abd). It was donated as a gift to the city by As'ad Pasha al-Azem, governor of Damascus, and no expense was spared in its construction. Draped over the portal is a representation of a 14-link chain carved from a single block of stone.

A huge, glass-pierced dome dominates the main chamber and brings a dim light to the pool and fountain below. The floor and fountain are laid with slabs of marble in contrasting colours. Several smaller chambers, also with glass-pierced domes, lead off the main room.

BURTASIYA MOSQUE & MADRASSA
جامع ومدرسة البرطاسية

By the river, across the street from the eastern entrance to the Khan al-Khayyatin, is Burtasiya Mosque and Madrassa (Map p330; Plaque 19). Built by the Kurdish prince Sharafeddin Issa ben Omar al-Burtasi in 1315, its square, towerlike minaret and black-and-white stonework are particularly fine. Inside, the intricately decorated and inlaid mihrab makes the visit worthwhile. Look for the mosaic in its half-dome.

TAYNAL MOSQUE
جامع تينال

Standing on its own to the southeast of the cemetery, but well worth the few minutes' walk it takes to get there, Taynal Mosque (Map p330; Plaque 31) is one of the most outstanding examples of Islamic religious architecture in Tripoli. Built in 1336 by Sayf ed-Din Taynal on the ruins of an earlier Carmelite church, it still has a partially preserved Carmelite nave in the first prayer hall. Other recycled elements, including two rows of Egyptian granite columns topped with late-Roman capitals, were taken from an earlier monument. The simplicity of the bare stone walls contrasts beautifully with some of the Mamluk decorative elements, in particular the entrance to the second prayer hall, a masterpiece of alternating black-and-white bands of stone with Arabic inscriptions, marble panels with geometric designs and a honeycomb-patterned half-dome.

Al-Mina
المينا

The port district of Al-Mina ranges along the coast to the northwest of modern Tripoli. Until a few decades ago the avenues linking Al-Mina to Tripoli's Old City ran between orange groves; in recent years, as Tripoli expanded, concrete became the order of the day. Although the history of the port stretches back far further than the medieval city, there are barely any traces of an ancient past left standing today. Instead, the area has a run-down seaside air, with families strolling along its Corniche and flocking to its ice cream parlours during summer weekend evenings.

BURJ ES-SABAA   برج السبع

The only monument of any interest in Al-Mina is Burj es-Sabaa (Lion Tower; Map p328), a miniature fortress at the far eastern end of the harbour. Named after the bas-relief decorations of lions that used to line the façade, the building dates from the end of the 15th century and was probably built by the Mamluk sultan, Qaitbey. It is an exceptional example of Mamluk military architecture with a striking black-and-white striped portico, and older Roman columns used to reinforce the walls horizontally. The entire ground floor is one vast chamber that was once decorated with paintings and armorial carvings, traces of which can still be seen.

BOAT RIDES

Along the seafront there are lots of **boats for hire** (Map p328), waiting to take visitors to the small islands just offshore. A return trip takes about two hours (with enough time for a swim) and costs LL7000. If you're part of a group, you can negotiate to hire the entire boat (between 10 and 12 people) for LL70,000. A trip to the Palm Islands Reserve should be negotiated separately.

PALM ISLANDS RESERVE

Six nautical miles northwest of Tripoli lies the Palm Islands Reserve, which consists of three islands and covers a rough area of 5 sq km of land and sea. Declared a protected site by Unesco in 1992 and dedicated as a nature reserve in 1993, the islands are a haven for endangered loggerhead turtles, rabbits, rare monk seals and over 300 species of migratory birds that stop here to rest and nest. Of these, seven are considered threatened worldwide, while 11 are rare in Europe.

The largest of the islands, Nakheel (Palm Island), supports most of the turtles and contains some 2500 palm trees, with paths laid out for visitors. There are beaches from which you can swim between the islands, or

picnic while watching the wildlife – though barbeques are forbidden.

Tragically, the 2006 war between Israel and Hezbollah disturbed the delicate ecosystem maintained on the islands. A large-scale oil spill in Beirut, caused by the Israeli bombing of the Jiyyeh power plant, blackened the coast's beaches. Oil coated the Palm Islands' rocky shorelines, killing bacteria and algae, which are crucial food for marine life and turtles. Oil also spread across the surface of the water, presenting a danger to both turtles and migrating birds. Large quantities of oil, having sunk down to the sea bed, endangered bottom-living aquatic life. For more on the oil spill, see Oil Spill Lebanon (p259).

Clean-up and monitoring programmes undertaken by a World Conservation Union mission to Lebanon have sought to minimise the damage to the Palm Islands, but the long-term impact is still hard to assess and efforts to restore the reserve's shores to their former pristine condition are still ongoing.

Currently the islands are only open to the public between July and September, though they may be closed during this period if environmental work or studies are being undertaken. You can pick up a free permit at the tourist office, and will need to negotiate a fare from one of the boat owners at Al-Mina port. Expect to pay somewhere around LL30,000 per person return.

SLEEPING

In the fallout from the events in Tripoli in 2007, some of the best and longest-established of Tripoli's budget accommodation options have closed down. Moreover, with no decent midrange options and only one really worthwhile top-end choice within easy reach, it's currently not an ideal base for exploring the north beyond the city itself.

Budget

Hotel Koura (Map p330; ☎ 03-371 041, 03-326 803; off Rue Tall; s/d/tr US$15/30/45, dm/d without bathroom US$10/15; ✦) Without doubt the very best of the budget bunch, this small hotel is run by a charming family whose grandmother can often be found reclining on the couch in the living room. The nice, simple rooms with stone walls are available in different configurations, depending on how many guests they have staying. There's a central shared lounge area, breakfast is included in the price and the owners can organise day trips.

Hotel Hayek (Map p328; ☎ 601 311; Rue ibn Sina; dm/s/d/tr US$15/20/30/35) A friendly, family-run business in Al-Mina, offering clean, basic rooms with sea views. The hotel is above a billiard parlour-café on a street running parallel to and behind the Corniche. The entrance is at the back of the building. Rates include breakfast.

Tall Hotel (Map p330; ☎ 628 407; Rue Tall; s/d LL30,000/35,000; ☒) Not particularly welcoming and even downright weird if few guests are in residence, this is a place to be considered if everything else is full. It's difficult to spot the entrance – look for the red, misspelled 'Tell hotel' stencilled high on the building – and, if you do make it this far, minimal lights illuminate spaces inside, making it fairly hard to find your room.

Palace Hotel (Map p330; ☎ 429 993; Rue Tall; s/d/tr US$20/40/50; ☒) Located in what appears to be, from the street, a well-kept and freshly painted old building, the interior hardly lives up to its promise. Still, it does retain some sort of charm, with high ceilings and stained glass windows, and is adequate as long as you're not planning on hanging around longer than to sleep and shower. Though the eerie reception room is straight from the vaults of Hammer Horror and management take a while to warm to you, it's safe and clean and rates can

probably be negotiated down a little – though you may find the US$5 charge for turning on the air-conditioning a bit steep.

Top End

Quality Inn (Map p328; ☎ 211 255; www.qualityinn tripoli.com; Rashid Karami International Fair; s/d/ste US$88/100/150; ☒ ☒ ☒) Unless you're desperate to stay in a large, desolate and fairly pricey hotel, this is really one to avoid in favour of the other two top-end choices. Rooms are standard and rather dated, the two huge pools – one indoor and one outdoor – are often drained if the hotel is quiet, and eating options are limited. Standing near the derelict Rashid Karami International Fair (see All the Fun of the Fair, below), the biggest benefit is a surfeit of parking spaces.

our pick **Hotel Via Mina** (☎ 222 227; www.viamina .com; Al-Mina; d from US$100; ☒ ☒ ☒) The place to splash out in style in Tripoli, this hotel is a hidden gem tucked away in a pretty, quaint backstreet of Al-Mina. With cool, minimalist rooms, a beautiful Arabic-tiled lap pool, courteous staff, an impressive iron spiral staircase, wireless internet throughout, and a bar and library in which to relax downstairs, it's a perfect little boutique hotel to retreat to after the rigours of Tripoli's souqs. To get there, turn off the Corniche at Tasty café and take a left onto the small street running parallel to the rear of the '46 restaurant.

ALL THE FUN OF THE FAIR

If you're heading from the old city towards Al-Mina, it's hard to miss the vast, oval-shaped derelict grounds with the Quality Inn sitting on its edge. This overgrown and unkempt open space comprises the grandly titled Rashid Karami International Fair, commissioned in 1963 and designed by world-famous modernist architect Oscar Niemeyer, who is most famous for his public structures in modernist masterpiece-or-monstrosity Brasilia.

Abandoned midconstruction at the outbreak of the civil war in 1975, the fairground comprises huge, geometric concrete forms, a massive open-air pavilion, and exhibits many similarities in overall design to its Brazilian cousin. Sadly, it has never been used as anything other than a military post and now lies neglected and forlorn.

Recently a call has been mounting for the demolition of the site, one proposition involving building a theme park in its place. In response, the Association for the Safeguarding of the International Fairgrounds of Tripoli has been formed to press for the site's preservation as a modern architectural monument.

Meanwhile in Brazil, Oscar Niemeyer, aged 100 in 2007 and himself a living monument, actively continues his modernist work. In 1996, aged 89, he completed the startling Niterói Contemporary Art Museum in Brazil, which many consider his best ever work, and in 2003 he designed the Serpentine Gallery Summer Pavilion in London. In 2006 he married Vera Lucia Cabreira, his longtime love, and is currently busy updating old projects and instigating new ones.

Chateau des Oliviers (Villa Nadia; ☎ 411 170, 03-634 546; www.chateau-des-oliviers.com; d from US$110; ✕ 🐾) This modern mansion makes an eccentric stay for a night or two. Converted into a hotel by its owner Nadia Dibo, former guests, including Greg Dobbs of ABC News, rave about their wonderful experiences on the chateau's website. Set high on a hill a few kilometres south of the city in the Haykalieh region, it's imbued with the charming host's own unique sense of taste, and a stay here, listening to tales of her former incarnation as a couturière in Paris, is an experience to be remembered forever. Getting to the hotel is the only snag, with few road signs to guide the way: from the Beirut–Tripoli highway, turn into the Haykal road when you reach the Hypermarket a few kilometres before Tripoli. The hotel is up past the Haykal hospital.

EATING

Tripoli's eating options aren't especially illustrious and it's best to wander the areas detailed below, then pick out something that takes your fancy.

Around the clock tower and branching out into the old city are plenty of fast-food vendors, selling boiled sweet corn from pushcarts and felafel from street stalls. If you're planning on taking a picnic out of town, the souqs are the place to pick up fresh fruit, bread, cheese and olives.

Tucked away in tiny alleyways there are also a few small hole-in-the-wall canteens serving up cheap shwarma and other simple dishes.

On Rue Riad Al-Solh, in the area around the cinema, there are plenty of national and international chain restaurants, including Pizza Hut, Pain d'Or and the like, intermingled with local concerns offering up cheap grills and mezze.

Along the Corniche in Al-Mina are a number of ice cream parlours, heaving with locals on weekend evenings, while a straggle of floating coffeehouses dispense hot drinks and snacks on the water itself. In the small streets behind the '46 restaurant are a number of nice bars that offer probably the most fun evening dining in town, all with the same sorts of mezze menus, along with pizzas, pastas and grills.

Rafaat Hallab & Sons (Map p330; Rue Tall) This is the place to sample Tripoli's famous sweets.

You're sure to come across a number of other branches all over town, dispensing, among other delights, gooey, sticky baklava, pistachio-topped *asmaleyye*, crunchy filo *aash el-bulbul* (nightingale's nests), and tea or coffee with which to wash them down. Prices start at around LL1500 per portion.

'46 (Map p328; ☎ 212 223; Corniche, Al-Mina; ⏱ 7am-1am) Named after the year the owner's father opened the restaurant, '46 has a solid Italian/international menu. The friendly waiters, relaxed atmosphere and large windows overlooking the Corniche make it a cut above Tripoli's other dining choices. A rich, spicy pasta Arrabiata goes for LL9000; the 'Rockford filet' – allegedly involving steak and blue cheese – is LL16,000. The entrance is at the back of the building; you won't miss the restaurant when cruising the Corniche.

Silver Shore (Map p328; ☎ 601 384/5; Corniche, Al-Mina; meals around US$35; ⏱ 11am-8pm) Easily the best seafood restaurant in town and right next door to '46, this place specialises in dishes accompanied by its own secret-recipe hot sauce. Strangely, it closes fairly early in the evening, but makes a great choice for a long lunch.

DRINKING

A conservative town by Beirut's standards, Tripoli is certainly not the place for bar hopping. But the cobbled backstreets of Al-Mina, focusing on the small square just beyond the Hotel Via Mina, will have your best choice.

With cafés spilling out along the pavement until late into the evening and crowds of young guys congregating on corners with their scooters, it has a livelier vibe than anywhere else in town.

Café Fahim (Map p330; Rue Tall) This cavernous old café on the square echoes atmospherically with the clack of backgammon pieces from groups of old men perched on plastic chairs and often ensconced in a cloud of nargileh smoke. The outdoor terrace is the best place in town for a nice cup of tea (LL1500) and some serious people-watching.

Askale (Map p328; ⏱ 4pm-1am daily) With a pub and restaurant, this is a great place to enjoy the laid-back atmosphere over a beer, a nargileh and a tasty snack: wonderful Greek salads go for LL7000.

ENTERTAINMENT

If people-watching doesn't appeal, you can always check out the latest-release English-language movies at **Ciné Planète** (Map p328; ☎ 442 471; City Complex, Rue Riad al-Solh; tickets LL10,000)

SHOPPING

Exploring the old souqs is the best way to shop in Tripoli. If you are looking for jewellery, there is a whole souq devoted to gold, Souq as-Sayyaghin (Map p330) or, for a more modest souvenir, the Souq an-Nahhassin (Map p330) has an array of brass goods. Even if you don't want to buy, it is well worth a visit just to see the metalworkers making pieces by hand in the same way that they have done for centuries. For traditional handmade soap, head to Khan as-Saboun (Map p330; see also A Slippery Business, p332). Note that many shops in the souqs close on Friday.

GETTING THERE & AROUND

The timings, availability and costs of bus services may vary depending on the security situation. For services running from Tripoli, it's a good idea to check a day or so in advance of travel. If you have a hire car, Tripoli is an easy two-hour motorway drive north from Beirut.

To/From Beirut

Three companies – Connex, Kotob and Tripoli Express – run coach services between Beirut and Tripoli. Smaller Ahdab minibuses shuttle back and forth regularly throughout the day. All these services leave from Zone C of Charles Helou bus station in Beirut, where there's a dedicated ticket booth for the buses. There's no need to book ahead.

Ahdab Runs minibuses between Tripoli and Beirut (LL1500, around two hours, every 15 minutes from 6am to 8pm). They depart from Rue Fouad Chehab and Rue Tall.

Connex Runs 20 daily express 'luxury coaches' from Beirut to Tripoli, via Jounieh and Byblos (LL2500, 90 minutes, every 30 minutes from 7am to 8.30pm); and from Tripoli to Beirut (every 30 minutes 5.30am to 6pm).

Kotob Runs 10 older buses (it takes longer but is cheapest) from Beirut (LL1500, up to two hours, every 15 minutes 6am to 6.30pm), stopping to let passengers off and on at Jounieh (LL1500, 30 minutes), Byblos (LL1500, one hour) and Batroun (LL1500, 90 minutes); and from Tripoli (every 15 minutes from 5am to 5.30pm) it makes the same stops.

Tripoli Express Runs smaller buses between Beirut and Tripoli (LL2000, 90 minutes, every 10 to 15 minutes from 5am to 6pm).

Service taxis heading to Beirut (LL5000) leave from near the service-taxi booth, just in front of the clock tower.

To Bcharré, the Cedars & Baalbek

Minibuses from Tripoli to Bcharré leave from outside the Marco Polo travel agency, just along from the tourist office (LL2500, 80 minutes, three to four buses daily between 9am and 5pm); and there are services from Bcharré (hourly 6am to 2pm). Those wanting to travel on to the Cedars will need to organise a taxi at Bcharré (LL20,000).

Service taxis heading to Bcharré (LL6000) and the Cedars (LL10,000) leave from Al-Koura Sq.

When there's no snow or ice and the spectacular mountain road is open (usually early April to mid-December) it's possible to take a taxi from Bcharré to Baalbek (around US$50, 90 minutes).

To Syria, Turkey & Jordan

Kotob runs buses for Aleppo in Syria (LL8000, almost five hours, every hour from 9am to 1pm), and to Damascus via Beirut (LL10,000, three hours) on Tuesday, Thursday and Saturday. It also runs a bus to Amman in Jordan (LL37,500, five to seven hours).

Transtour runs buses to Aleppo in Syria (LL8000, almost five hours, hourly 9am to midnight daily); to Homs (LL5000, two hours, every 30 minutes from 8.30am to 11pm); to Damascus (LL8000, four to five hours, twice daily at 5am and 3pm), and to Istanbul in Turkey (US$45, once daily).

Service taxis to Homs (LL7700), Hama (LL9000) and Aleppo (LL15,000) leave when full from Sahet et-Tall. Service taxis from Tripoli don't go to Damascus.

Around Town

Service taxis travel within the old and new parts of Tripoli (LL2000) and to Al-Mina (LL2500).

AROUND TRIPOLI

ENFE انفه
☎ 06 / pop 13,964

A sleepy seaside town on the coast 15km south of Tripoli (look for road signs to 'Anfeh' if you're driving the highway from

Beirut or Tripoli), Enfe's name – which means nose – recalls the shape of its coastline. Unless you're really looking for somewhere quiet and local to wind down, there's not much to detain you for long.

Today a largely Greek Orthodox town, during the Crusades this was the town of Nephim, a fiefdom of the County of Tripoli. The lords of Nephim played an important role here and later moved to Cyprus in the 13th century.

Today there is very little left of the Crusader castle, which stood on the thin peninsula jutting out into the sea, except for a few ruined stone walls. The castle is still remembered, however, for its sadistic history: the lord of Nephim, Count Bohemond VII, walled up his rivals, the Embiaci, in the castle.

Several vaults carved into the rock remain, and the most interesting relics are two **Crusader moats**, one of which is more than 40m long.

Enfe is also home to four **churches**, one of which, Our Lady of the Wind, is Byzantine and has the remains of painted murals. The Church of the Holy Sepulchre dates from the time of Bohemond in the 12th century and is still very much in use.

Since the coast is clean and attractive in this part of Lebanon, it hasn't escaped the concrete coastal sprawl that dominates the coastline. Up beyond the salt pans – shallow pools where seawater is left to evaporate – you'll find the big resort of **Marina del Sol** (☎ 541301; apt per night US$125), with apartments that are rented or leased, usually by the season. Nearby is **Las Salinas** (☎ 540970) with the same resort facilities at similar prices. Both are quite soulless, and set away from the village on the northern end of town. Of the two, Las Salinas is the best equipped, with a cinema, internet café and scuba diving facilities. The best overnight option, however, can be arranged through **L'Hote Libanais** (☎ 03-513766; www.hotelibanais.com) which offers bed and breakfast in a private home for around US$60 per double.

Enfe is on the service-taxi route between Tripoli, Byblos and Beirut, so it is easy to get to; simply ask the driver to drop you at the turn-off.

You will probably be charged the full service-taxi fare to Tripoli (LL5500). A taxi from Tripoli will cost about LL8000.

QADISHA VALLEY
وادي قاديشا

Widely regarded as one of the most beautiful spots in the whole country, the Qadisha Valley is the place to go for long days of solitary hiking amid waterfalls, rock-cut tombs and monasteries, with barely another wanderer in sight.

A long, deep gorge that begins near Batroun in the west, the valley rises dramatically to its head just beyond the lovely, quiet mountain town of Bcharré. Villages with red-tiled roofs perch atop hills, or cling precariously to the mountain sides; the Qadisha River (Nahr Abu Ali), with its source just below the Cedars, runs along the valley bottom, while Lebanon's highest peak, Qornet as-Sawda, towers above.

The word 'qadisha' stems from the Semitic word for 'holy' and the valley's steep, rocky sides have made it a natural fortress for persecuted religious minorities for millennia. From the 5th century onwards, Maronites made this area their refuge and the valley is scattered with beautiful rock-cut monasteries, hermitages and cave churches to explore as you hike through the region. Today, most of the villages perched atop the cliffs surrounding the valley remain almost exclusively Maronite.

Because of its natural beauty and rich heritage the Qadisha Valley was recognised as a World Heritage site by Unesco in 1998, one of six World Heritage areas in Lebanon. Recently, the Lebanon Mountain Trail (see p338) has awakened renewed interest in the area, opening up to visitors exciting possibilities for long-distance trekking through the region.

If you're in the mood for a shorter walk, however, **Esprit Nomade** (www.esprit-nomade.com) offers regular eco-treks, frequently along the most remote and stunning parts of the valley.

Although the valley is nearly 50km long, the main area of interest is the higher 20km section from Tourza to the Qadisha Grotto, which contains four monasteries and numerous natural delights.

To learn more, a good source of information on the valley and its treasures can be found at www.qadishavalley.com.

THE LEBANON MOUNTAIN TRAIL

The Lebanon Mountain Trail, an ambitious project financed by a US$3.3million grant from the United States Agency for International Development (USAID), plans to link the walking trails of the Qadisha Valley to those of both the north and the very south of Lebanon. The country's first long-distance hiking path will stretch some 400km along Lebanon's mountain ranges, from Al-Qbaiyat in the north of Lebanon to Marjayoun in the south.

Currently under the supervision of ECODIT, a US-based consultancy company, the burgeoning trail aims to connect many of Lebanon's best ancient and natural features – its nature reserves, archaeological remains and most picturesque villages – rather like a giant dot-to-dot puzzle, its deputy manager Karim El-Jisr explains, and all at an altitude of 1000m and above.

Recognising the importance of both environmental and cultural sensitivity, ECODIT has teamed up with a whole host of notable Lebanese ecologically minded organisations, to ensure that the trail only enhances Lebanon's mountain landscapes. Along with offering advice on culturally sensitive behaviour, safety and hiking ethics while on the move, it also gives full details of the numerous eco-trekking outfits that run guided hikes along its portions, many of them in the Qadisha Valley area, along with the telephone numbers of independent guides who can truly take you off the beaten track.

Undaunted by the 2006 war, which saw the temporary suspension of the project, ECODIT plans to have the entire route up and running – or walking – by 2009, allowing hikers to see a unique side of Lebanon, with bird's-eye views most of the way.

For more information, visit the trail's website at www.lebanontrail.org.

EHDEN   اهدن
☎ 06 / pop 20,888

On the northern rim of the Qadisha Valley, around 30km from Tripoli, this popular summer resort has a picturesque old centre dominated by a lively tree-lined main square fringed with cafés, bars and restaurants – though beware that outside of the summer season you're likely to find almost everything locked up and packed away. The whole town advertises itself, quite curiously, as a wi-fi zone, so if you're hiking with your laptop for company, it's a good place to stop and reconnect with the world.

Sights & Activities

If you're approaching Ehden from the Tripoli direction, one of the first indications that you're in town is the sight of the tiny Our Lady of the Castle **chapel** on a hill northwest of the village. Thought to have originally been a Roman look-out post, the unmistakable modern addition has an immense Our Lady balanced on a construction that looks like it could be a Raëlian space ship docking on earth. Some might also speculate that Our Lady herself is actually a giant, cleverly disguised antenna, responsible for providing the town with its wireless services.

Back in town, a small street opposite the square leads up to St George's Church,

where there is an equestrian **statue of Youssef Bey Karam**, a 19th-century nationalist hero who led rebellions against Ottoman rule with the support of other religious communities, as well as his fellow Maronites. He was killed by the Turks near Ehden and his mummified body, dressed in a traditional gold-braided costume, lies in a glass-topped sarcophagus against the southern wall of St George's Church. His descendants remain prominent in the area.

Just beyond the main square you'll find the **Church of Sts Peter & Paul**, parts of which date back to the 13th century, and which contains the grave of Lebanese painter Salibael Douaihy. Next door is the **Friends of Horsh Ehden Nature Reserve office**, which, when open during the summer months, can provide maps and information on the Horsh Ehden Forest Nature Reserve (see p339).

Sleeping & Eating

Most people who visit the Qadisha Valley stay in either Bcharré or the Cedars, but there are alternatives in Ehden – keep in mind that it's very quiet outside summer. During summer, some of the cafés on the square have rooms to rent above them; ask inside the cafés for details. They're usually cheap and cheerful, with a great – if a little noisy – location in the thick of the fun.

Belmont (☎ 560 102; d $50-60) This reasonable old-style hotel close to the entrance to town offers a variety of clean, decent rooms, some with views and balconies. It may be closed outside high season.

Grand Hotel Abchi (☎ 561 101; d/ste US$60/85) This large, quite modern hotel offers solid value in a central location and continues Ehden's spaceship theme with its odd 1970s-built, flying-saucer-shaped restaurant.

Ehden is well known for its restaurants overlooking Nebaa Mar Sarkis (Mar Sarkis Spring) where it emerges from the hillside to the northeast of the village. A host of places cluster around the source, all serving traditional Lebanese food with huge mezze spreads and, on balmy evenings, live music and dancing. Most are open in summer only. For Italian dishes, steaks and seafood, browse the numerous cafés lining the square.

Outside summer, the only place in town reliably open is the **Eden Café** (☎ 03-116 780; ◷ 9am-9pm) behind the square – you'll spot the yellow awnings. Hearty bowls of onion soup go for LL5000, and decent salads range from LL5000 to LL8000. The café also has nice rooms to rent above it in the summer.

Getting There & Away

If you're not trekking with an eco-minded trekking operation (see p382 or the Lebanon Mountain Trail website, www.lebanontrail.org for details) by far the quickest and easiest way to explore this part of Lebanon is with your own transport, even just for a day or two.

Otherwise, if you are taking a service taxi from Tripoli to Bcharré, ask the driver to drop you at Ehden or any point you fancy en route along the north side of the valley. If you want to get to the south side of the valley, it's best to go to Bcharré and get a taxi from there. A service taxi from Tripoli to any point from Ehden to Bcharré will cost LL6000. There are also microbuses that ply the rim of the valley; they pass Ehden around five or six times a day and cost LL3000.

HORSH EHDEN FOREST NATURE RESERVE   محمّية حرش اهدن

Just over 3km from Ehden, well signposted with brown road signs, is the nature reserve of Horsh Ehden, a 17-sq-km mountainous ecosystem. You can arrange a guided visit by contacting the **Friends of Horsh Ehden** (☎ 560

950 in summer, 660 249 in winter; www.horshehden.com) or guide yourself around one of the nine short marked hiking trails, the longest of which is just over 2km and should take 45 minutes to complete.

There's a map of trails online, at the entrance to the reserve and also outside the Friends office, next door to the Church of Sts Peter & Paul in Ehden.

Although the reserve covers less than 1% of Lebanon's total area, some 40% of the country's plant species have been found within its borders. There are 1058 species of plants, 12% of which are considered threatened. The reserve has one of Lebanon's largest stands of native cedar, mixed with varieties of juniper, conifer, wild apple and others.

The area is a nesting place for birds and provides a refuge for some of Lebanon's endangered mammals. Wolves and hyenas have also been spotted here, as have wild boars.

Though you can't stay in the park itself, **La Reserve** (☎ 561 092, 03-751 292) at its entrance has chalets and a restaurant, and arranges guided walks, all during summer months only.

KFAR SGHAB   كفر صغاب

The cute village of Kfar Sghab, 4km south of Ehden on the road to Bcharré, might seem unremarkable except for its profusion of well tended flower beds and road-side shrines.

Australians, however, particularly Sydneysiders, passing through here might be surprised to see a sign announcing 'Parramatta Rd' on the main street. More surprising still, if you say hello to almost any of the 750 inhabitants of the village you're likely to hear 'g'day mate' thrown back at you. There's even a Para Cafe just off the main road in the centre of the village. The reason for this surreal connection between the village and a used-car strip in Sydney? A staggering 15,000 Australian Lebanese trace their roots back to this area.

Many returned to Lebanon when the civil war ended and built smart new summer homes here, which you'll see lining the road and the hillside.

BCHARRÉ   بشرّي
☎ 06 / pop 13,756

A pretty, welcoming town in the heart of the Qadisha Valley, Bcharré is a terrific place for stopping off en-route to the Cedars or to base yourself for a few days while

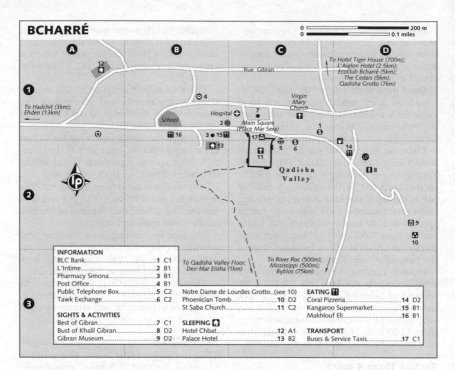

exploring the wild valley below. Famous as the birthplace of Khalil (or Kahlil, as some locals insist) Gibran and the stronghold of the right-wing Maronite Christian Phalange party, the town makes a pleasant stroll and a good place to stock up on picnic provisions to fill your rucksack.

Orientation & Information
Dominated by the St Saba Church on Place Mar Sera, the main square, the town is small and easy to wander around. Both east and west along the main road are small supermarkets and pharmacies. **Pharmacy Simona** (☎ 672 2727; ☼ 8am-8pm) is a well-stocked, English-speaking option. To the east of the square is moneychanger **Tawk Exchange** (☎ 671 305), which also does Western Union transfers; just after it is the BLC bank which has an ATM machine. A block north of the main road is the **post office** (☼ 8am-1pm).

L'Intime (LL2000 per hr; ☼ 11am-11pm daily) is the town's main internet café. For telephone calls, there's a public telephone box on the square and many of the supermarkets sell prepaid cards.

Sights & Activities
GIBRAN MUSEUM
Fans of the famous poet and artist Khalil Gibran (1883–1931) will love this **museum** (☎ 671 137; www.kahlilgibran.com.lb; adult/student LL3000/2000; ☼ 9am-5pm Mar-Nov, 10am-5pm Nov-Mar, closed Mon). In keeping with his wishes, Gibran, who emigrated to the USA in the 19th century and published his most famous work, *The Prophet*, in 1923, was buried in a 19th-century monastery built into the rocky slopes overlooking Bcharré. The museum, which has been set up in this monastery, houses a large collection of Gibran's paintings, drawings and gouaches, and also some of his manuscripts. His coffin is in the monastery's former chapel, which is cut straight into the rock. The views of the valley from the museum's terrace are quite amazing. There's also a good gift shop, selling a number of collections of Gibran's work in translation.

NOTRE DAME DE LOURDES GROTTO
مغارة سيدة لورد
Part way up a small path near the museum is a small cave with a spring. The site is

dedicated to the Virgin Mary. Local legend has it that she took pity on a Carmelite gardener-monk, who had to carry water up to the monastery each day to water his vegetable patch. Small candles and statuettes sit on an altar that has been built around the spring.

PHOENICIAN TOMB
Just up the hill from the grotto is a large stone obelisk thought to date back to 750 BC. At the base of the obelisk is a burial chamber and ledges for four coffins.

QADISHA GROTTO مغارة قاديشا
This small **grotto** (admission LL4000; ☺ 8am-5pm, Jun until first snow) extends about 500m into the mountain and has great limestone formations. Not as extraordinary as Jeita Grotto (p303), but it's still spectacular. The grotto is a 4km walk from Bcharré; follow the signs to the L'Aiglon Hotel and then take the footpath opposite. It's then a very picturesque 1.5km walk to the grotto.

Sleeping & Eating
Hotel Tiger House (☎ 03-378 138; tigerhousepension@hotmail.com; Rue Cedre; dm US$10 incl breakfast) On the high road out of town towards the Cedars, this is a comfortable option with very friendly owners. Outside summer, you're

likely to have a room to yourself for the bargain price of a dorm bed.
Ecoclub Bcharré (☎ 03-832 060; www.ecoclub-becharre.org) Also situated near town is the Ecoclub, which has dorm beds for around US$20 in a hostel near the Cedars ski lifts (see p342) and organises eco-minded activities from Bcharré all year. See also the website for the **Lebanese Youth Hostel Federation** (www.lyhf.org) for more details.
Palace Hotel (☎ 671 460; s/d/tr US$30/40/48; ☒) In the centre of town, this is a clean, decent option, open all year round. Breakfast is an extra US$4.50.
Hotel Chbat (☎ 671 270; s/d/tr US$45/70/85; ☒) Built in 1955 on the side of a hill in the upper part of Bcharré, this homely, welcoming hotel has lovely views across the Qadisha Valley from its rooms, many of which have a sitting room attached. It has two restaurants, both serving hearty Lebanese food, and is a comfy place for a drink beside a roaring fire in winter. Breakfast is included in the room rates. The hotel also has a couple of dormitories, which are popular with school skiing groups.

There aren't many restaurants in town, but there are a couple of options for a decent lunch. **Makhlouf Eli** (☎ 672 585), on the western side, is a small restaurant with a rooftop terrace and fantastic views. It serves

---

KHALIL GIBRAN (1883–1931)

The short-lived Khalil Gibran remains today Lebanon's most famous and celebrated literary figure, though much of his life was spent in the USA, to which he emigrated with his mother and siblings when he was aged 12. Though from a family originally too poor to afford schooling, the young boy blossomed into a philosophical essayist, novelist, mystic poet and painter, whose influences included the Bible, Nietzsche and William Blake. He is mostly remembered in the West today as author of the visionary *The Prophet,* which consists of 26 poem-essays.

During his teenage years in Boston, Gibran was spotted as an artistic talent and introduced to avant-garde artist Fred Holland Day, who championed his work. In 1904, he held his first public exhibition, having published his first literary essays the year before, and met Mary Haskell, his benefactor for the remainder of his life.

In 1908, Gibran began a two-year period of study under Auguste Rodin in Paris, while continuing to write literary essays and short stories. Though his early writings were largely in Arabic and Syriac, works published after 1918 were mostly written in English. His work was rediscovered in the 1960s in the USA: lines from *Sand and Foam* of 1926 – 'Half of what I say is meaningless, but I say it so that the other half may reach you' – are said to have inspired John Lennon's lyrics for the Beatles song 'Julia'.

When Gibran died of TB and cirrhosis of the liver in 1931, his body was returned to Lebanon according to his last wishes and he now lies in a casket at the Gibran Museum (opposite) in Bcharré. Some of his personal possessions are with him in the former monastery building, including an ancient Armenian tapestry that portrays a crucifixion scene in which Christ is smiling.

mezze and sandwiches for about US$5. Coral Pizzeria is an outdoor cafeteria almost directly beneath the waterfall at the eastern edge of town and has pizza and snacks (summer only).

Along the road at the head of the valley, just outside Bcharré, are several restaurants that take advantage of the views along the gorge. River Roc is a restaurant–nightclub with Lebanese food for about US$20. Mississippi, next door, has similar prices and also sells snacks.

The Australian connection (see Kfar Sghab, p339) continues with the well-stocked Kangaroo Supermarket, where the owner, a returnee from Sydney, stocks a few Australian specialities.

Getting There & Away

The bus and service-taxi stop is outside the St Saba Church in the centre of town. For details about getting to Bcharré from Tripoli, and from Bcharré to Baalbek, see Getting There & Around, p336.

THE CEDARS   الأرز

☎ 06

The Cedars is Lebanon's oldest ski resort and to most visitors will feel the most akin to European ski destinations. With its chalet style hotels and string of wooden-hut souvenir shops lining the main road up to the slopes, it has more charm out of the winter season than the country's other ski resorts.

The village takes its name from the small but famous grove of trees that stands at an altitude of more than 2000m on the slopes of Jebel Makmel, about 4km from Bcharré. The grove represents a tiny remnant of a vast cedar forest that once covered the mountains of Lebanon (see Lebanon's Cedars, p324). A few of these slow-growing trees are very old and it's thought that some may reach an age of 1500 years. Known locally as Arz ar-Rab (Cedars of the Lord), they are under the protection of the Patriarch of Lebanon, who built a chapel in the cedar grove in 1848; each year in August there is a festival here presided over by the patriarch.

A fence protects the grove but you can visit all year round, although the cedars look particularly dramatic in winter when they stand against a backdrop of snow. Occasionally access to the grove is restricted, especially when the snow is melting and the ground is soft, so that roots are not damaged by people walking on them.

About 2km further up the road is the ski station, where there is a cluster of

---

SKI FACTS: THE CEDARS

- **Altitude** 1950m to 2700m
- **No of Lifts** Eight (five beginner, one medium, two advanced)
- **Adult Day Pass** US$20 Monday to Friday, US$27 Saturday and Sunday; after noon: US$10 Monday to Friday, US$17 Saturday and Sunday
- ☎ 03-399 133
- **Opening hours** 8.30am to 3.30pm Monday to Friday, until 4pm Saturday and Sunday

People first started coming to ski at the Cedars in the 1920s and the first lift was installed in 1953, making it Lebanon's oldest ski resort. While it is less developed than many of the other resorts, it is the second-most popular, particularly for those who actually ski, rather than spend their time flashing designer outfits in village bars. The season usually starts earlier (mid-December) and finishes later (April) than the other resorts. The runs are more challenging, with numerous off-piste opportunities for more adventurous types. Equipment can be rented from a number of locations including Ski Total and Al-Inshirah Ski Shop, both at the base of the lifts, and a full set should cost US$5 to US$12 per day. There are Red Cross teams on hand at weekends.

A new gondola, planned for the end of 2008, will take skiers up to an altitude of 2870m – the highest accessible summit – with a refuge and viewing platform at the top. At the same time, the building of a new road is underway between Bcharré and the Cedars to reduce driving time up the twisting mountain road; it's due for completion in time for the Lebanon-hosted 2009 Asian Ski Championships.

equipment-hire shops and snack places around the ski lifts.

The road continuing beyond this point leads out into the wilds of the Bekaa Valley and eventually on to Baalbek, and makes for a gorgeous drive during the summer months when you might spot paragliders, along with eagles, surfing the thermals high over the bleak landscape. From roughly December to April, the road is closed due to snow.

Hiking

During the summer months you can hike to Lebanon's highest peak, Qornet as-Sawda (3090m), starting from the ski-fields entrance. To get to the top and back should take around five hours, and you'll need to be relatively fit. The ascent is usually possible between April and October, though in spring you may need to rent snow-shoes for parts of the hike if the snow hasn't completely cleared.

The first part of the trip to the top of the ski lift takes about two hours; from here hike north along the path for another hour to reach the peak. The views are spectacular and the hiking isn't too difficult, although sometimes the path is not as clear as it should be. Also, the signs for each peak have blown off and only the posts remain. Remember to dress warmly – the peaks are windy and there can be snow up here as late as May. For those who think this sounds like far too much effort, take a vehicle along the road out of the Cedars towards Baalbek, then when the road splits off for Baalbek, continue to the left up the mountain. The road leads over Dahr el-Qadib and the view is quite magnificent.

Sleeping & Eating

Most of the hotels situated further away from the slopes offer a free drop-off and pick-up service, so you won't have to trudge the few kilometres up the hill with skis over your shoulder.

Hotel Mon Refuge (☎ 671 397; s/d/apt US$15/30/120; ⊠) This hotel has pleasant rooms, and apartments that sleep 12 (the apartments have a fireplace). Breakfast is US$5 extra. Downstairs is an inviting restaurant-bar (meals US$8 to US$15) that serves a mixture of Lebanese and Western food.

Alpine Hotel (☎ 671 517; d US$30) On the road between Bcharré and the Cedars, this is cosy

and quite simple. If you are staying for a few days, the Alpine offers half board for US$40 per day. In summer, the hotel touts good discounts and you can get a good room for around US$10 per person per night.

St Bernard Hotel (☎ 03-289 600; s/d/ste US$70/90/150; ⊠) An old lodge near the forest grove, it offers warm rooms, a good restaurant and the advantage of only being a couple of minutes from the slopes.

Centre Tony Arida (☎ 678 195, 03-321 998; ⊠) Next door to Mon Refuge, this place has everything from chalets that sleep up to eight people for US$300 per night (half price in spring and autumn) to a nightclub, restaurant and a large selection of ski equipment for hire. Tony is a former ski champion–turned–jovial host, and he presides over his empire with good-natured gusto.

L'Auberge des Cèdres (☎ 678 888; www.smresorts .net; s from US$110, d from US$145, luxury tents sleeping 2 from US$205, chalets sleeping 6 from US$435) At the top end of the village's accommodation options is definitely L'Auberge, which offers year-round respite for weary city dwellers in its collection of rooms and self-contained chalets, log cabins and luxury tents, known respectively as La Grande Ourse, La Petite Ourse and La Belle Etoile. With fabulous food, roaring fires and inviting touches such as fresh croissants delivered to your chalet each morning, it's a place for year-round entertainment. In summer, the resort can arrange balloon flights over the mountains, along with riding, hiking and quad biking. In winter, when you tire of skiing, snowmobiles are available.

Cedrus Hotel (☎ 677 777; www.cedrushotel.com; d/ste US$180/306; ⊠) One of the smartest and most luxurious places to return to after a day out on the piste, this is new and conveniently situated, with a highly regarded French restaurant called Le Pichet, a piano bar, and facilities to arrange snowmobile trips across the mountains.

Getting There & Away

There are service taxis to Bcharré (LL7500) and the Cedars (LL12,000) from the Rue Tall taxi stand in Tripoli. Outside the ski season there are only a few service taxis to Bcharré and you will have to take a regular taxi from there to the Cedars. The fare is about LL18,000 but you may be able to haggle the price down. In Bcharré, the taxis congregate by St Saba Church and charge US$20 for a half-day tour around the Qadisha. There is a minibus at 7am to Beirut's Dawra bus station for LL5000 (double-check that it's running beforehand). When the road is open you can also get a taxi to take you to Baalbek (US$60) across the incredibly scenic mountains.

THE QADISHA VALLEY FLOOR
The best way to hike into the valley is to take one of the steep goat tracks that leads out of Bcharré and down to the valley below. If that's too strenuous, you can drive a car to Deir Mar Elisha and park it there while you walk along the valley floor. A hike from Bcharré to Deir as-Salib takes about six hours, there and back. A steep return hike from Bcharré to Deir Mar Antonios Qozhaya, around 12km in total, will take the whole day, counting stops for photographs, breathers, exploration and a picnic lunch.

Remember to bring plenty of water; the river water is not clean enough to drink. Navigational directions for the following points of interest are given for walking the valley floor from roughly east to west, beginning at Bcharré and heading towards Deir Mar Antonios.

Deir Mar Elisha   دير مار شعيا
Dramatic and beautiful, the monastery of Mar Elisha (St Eliseus) is built into the side of the cliffs below Bcharré. The Lebanese Maronite Order, the first order to be officially recognised by the Roman Catholic Church, was founded here in 1695. The building goes back much further – by the 14th century it was already the seat of a Maronite bishopric. It was restored in 1991 and turned into a museum, where there are displays of books and other artefacts relating to the monastery's history. The museum is on two storeys; to the right of it is a chapel containing the tomb of the Anchorite of Lebanon, François de Chasteuil (1588–1644).

You can get to the monastery from one of the tracks below Bcharré or take the main road heading east from Bcharré and, after 3km, turn off at the small blue sign for the Qadisha Valley. A narrow road winds down to the monastery.

Chapel of Mar Chmouni
كنيسة مار شموني
Built under a rocky ledge in the Middle Ages, this chapel has two constructed naves, one in a natural rock formation. Sadly, the 13th-century paintings that adorn the walls have been covered with a layer of plaster.

The chapel is at the eastern end of the valley at the point where Wadi Houla (Houla Valley) and Wadi Qannoubin meet. You can follow a steep path down from Hadchit or you can get there along a path on the valley floor or, from Bcharré, take a track down to the valley floor and from there follow the path east for around 1km.

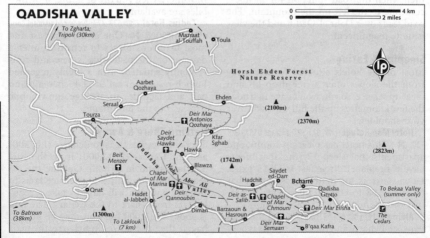

Deir as-Salib   دير الصليب

This rock-cut monastery can be reached by a steep path to the right from the valley floor or from the village of Hadchit. As well as a chapel, there are a number of caves that were used as hermits' cells. Derelict and increasingly ruined, there are nevertheless still traces of Byzantine-era frescoes inside these.

Deir Qannoubin   دير قنّوبين

Continuing along the valley bottom, you will eventually come to a track to the left with a signpost to Deir Qannoubin. The name Qannoubin is derived from the Greek *kenobion*, which means 'monastery'. This is a very ancient site. Some sources say that it was founded by Theodosius the Great in the late 4th century.

Local legend has it that at the end of the 14th century, the Mamluk sultan, Barquq (who was briefly overthrown in 1389), escaped from imprisonment in Karak Castle (now in Jordan) and sought refuge in the Qadisha before returning to Egypt to reclaim his throne. Such was the hospitality shown him that he paid for the restoration of the monastery. From 1440 through to the end of the 18th century, Deir Qannoubin was the Maronite patriarchal seat. Nowadays it is a working convent.

The church is half-built into the rock face and is decorated with frescoes dating from the 18th century. Near the entrance is a vault containing a naturally mummified body, thought to be that of Patriarch Yousef Tyan. Deir Qannoubin can also be reached by a path leading from the village of Blawza, on the valley's northern rim; the walk takes about an hour each way.

Chapel of Mar Marina   كنيسة مار مارينا

Just to the west of the monastery is the chapel-cave of Mar Marina, where the remains of 17 Maronite patriarchs are buried. The chapel is dedicated to St Marina, born in Qalamoun, who lived her life at Deir Qannoubin.

Deir Saydet Hawka   كنيسة سيدة حوقا

Continuing on the main track past the signpost for Deir Qannoubin, and bearing right at the fork, you will eventually see Deir Saydet Hawka (Chapel of Saydet Hawka) on the right. This is a small monastery, thought to date from the 13th century, which consists of a chapel and a few monks' cells within a cave. It is associated with an attack by armed Mamluks against the natural fortress of Aassi Hawka, which is in a cave high above the monastery. The cave is only accessible to experienced rock climbers.

The monastery is deserted for most of the year but is used to celebrate the Feast of the Assumption of the Virgin with a high mass on the evening of 14 August. You can get there via a path from Hawka (about 30 minutes one way) or via the valley-floor path.

Deir Mar Antonios Qozhaya

دير مار انطونيوس قزحيا

Continuing on the main track, you will eventually come to Deir Mar Antonios Qozhaya. This hermitage is the largest in the valley and has been continually in use since it was founded in the 11th century. It is famous for establishing, in the 16th century, the first-known printing press in the Middle East.

The **museum** houses a collection of religious and ethnographic objects as well as an old printing press that was used to publish the Psalms in Syriac, a language still used by the Maronites in their services. A popular place of pilgrimage, the hermitage also has a souvenir shop that sells all manner of kitsch religious knick-knacks. To see the museum you need to knock at the main building and get one of the monks to open it up for you.

Near the entrance to the monastery is the **Grotto of St Anthony**, known locally as the 'Cave of the Mad', where you can see the chains used to constrain the insane or possessed, who were left at the monastery in the hope that the saint would cure them.

If you're not hiking, you can reach the monastery by car from Aarbet Qozhaya on the northern-valley rim. The road is small, unsignposted and tricky to locate, so it's best to stop off at the village and ask a local for precise directions.

B'QAA KAFRA   بقاع كفرا

Back up above the valley, just off the road between Bcharré and Hasroun, is B'qaa Kafra, the highest village in Lebanon (elevation 1750m) and the birthplace of St Charbel. The saint's house has been turned

THE HERMIT OF QADISHA

As you explore the delights of the valley, you might begin to think that hermits and ascetics are the stuff of Qadisha legend. However, at least one modern-day hermit has made his home in the Qadisha Valley, hailing originally from another mountain region thousands of miles away. Father Dario Escobar, who inhabits a hidden cave cell near one rock-cut chapel, is a 72-year-old Colombian monk who is happy nowadays to call the Qadisha his home. Though he'll hospitably open the door to passers-by, he values the tranquillity and opportunity for a simple existence afforded by life on the valley floor – and, unlike others who have high hopes for the tourism generated by the Lebanon Mountain Trail, hopes it won't become too popular.

So if, as dusk draws in over the craggy mountains towering overhead, you see a grey-bearded, black-hooded figure tramping the ancient goat trails of the Qadisha Valley, do not fear. Chances are it's not an apparition of a long-dead medieval monk, but rather Father Escobar, on his way back home to his well-appointed cave for a cosy ascetic supper.

into a **museum**, which commemorates the saint's life in paintings. It is open daily, except Monday, and there is a shop and café at the entrance. The village now has a new convent named after St Charbel and there is a church, Notre Dame, across the way from the museum. St Charbel's Feast is celebrated on the third Sunday of July.

DEIR MAR SEMAAN   دير مار سمعان

Just past the turn-off for B'qaa Kafra, as you head east, is a small path leading to Deir Mar Semaan, a hermitage founded in 1112 by Takla, the daughter of a local priest called Basil. Concrete paths lead down to the spartan four-room hermitage carved into the rocks, where Mar Samaan (St Simon) supposedly lived. Access to the caves involves squeezing through doorways. Inside there are votive candles and offerings. There are also traces of frescoes, and remains of water cisterns. The walk takes about 15 minutes.

DIMAN   ديمان

In Diman, on the south side of the valley, is the summer residence of the Maronite Patriarchy, which moved here from Deir Qannoubin in the 19th century. You can't miss it – it is a large modern building on the valley side of the road. The church is not old but is well worth a look for its pano-

ramic paintings of the Qadisha Valley and religious scenes by the Lebanese painter, Saliba Doueihy. These date from the 1930s or '40s, when the spire of the church was built. The grounds behind the building lead to the edge of the gorge and have views across the valley.

AMIOUN

Back down towards the coast, Amioun stands above the highway to/from Chekka. It is easily noticeable from the road because of the rock-cut tombs that have been hewn out of its southern cliffs. These are either Phoenician or Roman burial vaults. Perched atop these cliffs is the old part of the village, a beautiful mixture of Ottoman stone buildings and narrow winding streets.

High up in the centre of the village is the 15th-century Cathedral of St George, which was built on the ruins of a Roman temple (itself built on Neolithic remains). The site was an important place of worship under the Romans, and pagan rites were reputedly practised well into the Christian era. An earthquake destroyed the temple in the 4th or 5th century AD but elements, including a couple of columns, have been incorporated into the church. A stone iconostasis (screen), with fine painted icons, contrasts with the plain vaulted interior of the church.

The Bekaa Valley
وادي البقاع

The beautiful, fertile Bekaa Valley has not had an easy time of it in recent years, with visitors to the region frequently discouraged by ominous press reports of Hezbollah activity and cannabis farming. Baalbek, infamous as Hezbollah's strategic headquarters, took a battering in the 2006 Israel–Hezbollah War for this reason, with up to 20% of its buildings destroyed. Moreover, the region's most notorious crop – its high quality cannabis or 'Red Leb' – bloomed prolifically before and during the civil war, a draw-card for some and a deterrent for others. Though you'll doubtless see the yellow Hezbollah flag flying in towns and villages across the region, and while cannabis production is currently witnessing a comeback, there's much, much more to the Bekaa Valley than this. With a diverse and friendly population encompassing a high percentage of Christians alongside its Shiite majority, fabulous food and wines, and two stunning world-class ancient sites, don't let its erstwhile unsavoury image discourage you from travelling here.

Despite its name, the Bekaa Valley is actually a high plateau between the Mt Lebanon Range and Jebel Libnan ash-Sharqiyya (Anti-Lebanon Range). For millennia the Bekaa Valley, dubbed 'hollow Syria' by the Greeks and Romans, was a corridor linking the Syrian interior with the coastal cities of Phoenicia. The many invading armies and trading caravans that passed through left traces of their presence, which can be seen in a host of small sites around the valley, but most magnificently at the Umayyad city of Aanjar and the gorgeous temples at Baalbek.

The Bekaa Valley has always been an agricultural region, fed by the Nahr al-Aasi (Orontes River) and the Nahr Litani. In Roman times, this grain-producing area was one of Rome's 'bread-baskets'. Today, deforestation and poor crop planning may have reduced the fertility of the land, but the valley's wines are famous throughout the region and are gaining global renown. Combining temple tours with wine tasting is the way to get the best of the Bekaa Valley.

HIGHLIGHTS

- Marvel over the spectacular temple complex at **Baalbek** (p354)
- Learn to appreciate arak and mix your mezze at Lebanon's favourite **riverside restaurants** (p350) in Zahlé
- Wander the stunning stones of **Aanjar** (p351), the Middle East's only remaining Umayyad town
- Sip something warming in the bar of Baalbek's historic **Palmyra Hotel** (p360)
- Nose the bouquet and taste the wine at the **Ksara Winery** (p351), Lebanon's most famous vineyard

Baalbek ★

Zahlé ★
★ Ksara Winery

Aanjar ★

THE BEKAA VALLEY

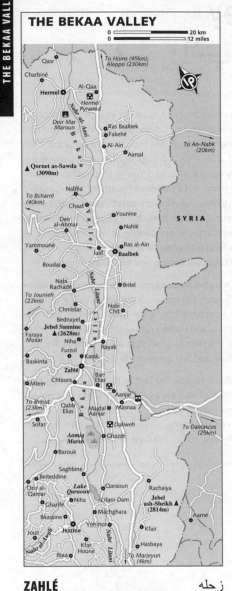

THE BEKAA VALLEY

mon with Beirut than with Baalbek. Known locally as Arousat al-Beqa'a (Bride of the Bekaa), it's set along the steep banks of the Birdawni River (locally known as 'Bardouni'), which tumbles through a gorge, cutting a burbling channel through the centre of town, down from Jebel Sannine to the north.

Zahlé is a predominantly Greek Catholic town, with the highest concentration of this denomination in the entire country, and its beautiful, ornate Ottoman-era houses, lining the riverside Rue Brazil, survived heavy bombardment during the civil war. The town is probably most famous for its open-air restaurants, known as the Cafés du Bardouni, that jostle along the river on the town's edge. During summer weekends and evenings, these are packed with locals and Beirutis enjoying some of the finest Lebanese mezze in the country, washed down with generous quantities of arak (see Arak, p350).

The town's merry modern aspect, however, belies a darker past. In the 19th century, Zahlé was hard hit by communal fighting between Druze and Christians and many of its inhabitants were killed in the 1860 massacre. Some 25 years later, the opening of a railway line between Beirut and Damascus (which is no longer in operation) brought some prosperity to the town. At around the same time, more than half the town migrated to Brazil (after which the main street is named), from where they sent remittances, further increasing the town's prosperity. Zahlé's gracious stone houses date from this time.

In 1981, Zahlé came under fire again, bombarded by Syria after the Phalangist party attempted to build a road linking the town to the ski resort of Faraya. Since, by that point, the Phalangists were closely aligned with Israel, the road represented a serious threat to Syria, whose troops were stationed in large numbers throughout the Bekaa Valley. Like the rest of Lebanon, however, Zahlé proved resilient to the damage, which was quickly repaired, and no traces are evident today.

Keep in mind when planning a visit that from November to April most of the restaurants are closed and the town is relatively quiet, except at weekends and Christmas. In summer, it makes a pleasant lunch stop en route from Beirut to Baalbek, and is an ideal place to stay if you intend to spend a few days exploring the valley.

ZAHLÉ ز حله

☎ 08 / pop 79,803

If you're arriving in Zahlé after some temple-gazing in quiet, conservative Baalbek, you'll probably find it a sharp and extremely pleasant contrast. Lively, bustling and even quite glitzy, this attractive resort town, enjoying a cool altitude of 945m, shares more in com-

Orientation & Information

Most of Zahlé's amenities are scattered along the main road, Rue Brazil, and Rue St Barbara running parallel. This is where the banks, bureaux de change and the **post office** (8am-5pm Mon-Fri, 8am-noon Sat) can be found.

Ambulance (☎ 140)

Centre Culturel Français (Rue Brazil) Has a small library and organises cultural events.

Dataland Internet (Rue Brazil; per hr LL5000; 8am-midnight)

Khoury General Hospital (Rue Brazil) Towards the head of the valley.

Police (☎ 160)

Tourist Office (8.30am-1.30pm Mon-Sat) On the 3rd floor of the Chamber of Commerce building, just off Rue Brazil, this tiny office isn't always open at its designated times, particularly in low season. Worth a try, but don't be surprised to find it looking deserted.

Sleeping

Hotel Akl (☎ 820 701; Rue Brazil; s/d/tr LL35,000/50,000/65,000, s/d without bathroom LL25,000/40,000) Without a doubt this is the best budget choice in town. In a dilapidated but character-filled old house, the hotel benefits from a good, central position and rooms have balconies and lots of natural light. The rooms at the rear overlook the river, and those with attached bathrooms are bigger and brighter, though all are clean and reasonably comfortable. Check, however, that cheaper rooms have some form of heating in the colder months. There's a large communal lounge with TV, piano and fireplace for the winter, and the friendly manager – along with her French-speaking mother – is very helpful and loves catering to international visitors.

Arabi Hotel (☎ 821 214; s/d US$55/66;) Right at the heart of the outdoor eating scene on the Birdawni River, rooms at the front of the Arabi Hotel can get quite noisy in summer; in winter, doubles can be had for around US$40. There's also a restaurant and a small casino – in case you're in the mood for a flutter afterwards.

Hotel Monte Alberto (☎ 810 912-14; www.montealberto.com; d/tr US$60/70;) Located high above town, this hotel commands amazing views. To make the trip between the town and the hotel there is a charmingly kitsch funicular, topped only by the hotel's revolving restaurant. The rooms are clean, cosy and comfortable. Rates include breakfast.

Grand Hotel Kadri (☎ 813 920; www.grandhotelkadri.com; Rue Brazil; s/d/ste US$105/125/160;) The most sophisticated of Zahlé's hotels is located along the Rue Brazil strip in a beautiful, historic building that served as an Ottoman hospital during WWI, and as home to the chief of the French army during the French mandate. Rooms are nowadays

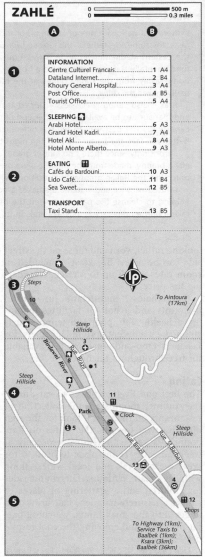

ZAHLÉ

0 — 500 m
0 — 0.3 miles

INFORMATION	
Centre Culturel Francais.................1	A4
Dataland Internet.................2	B4
Khoury General Hospital.................3	A4
Post Office.................4	B5
Tourist Office.................5	A4

SLEEPING	
Arabi Hotel.................6	A3
Grand Hotel Kadri.................7	A4
Hotel Akl.................8	A4
Hotel Monte Alberto.................9	A3

EATING	
Cafés du Bardouni.................10	A3
Lido Café.................11	B4
Sea Sweet.................12	B5

TRANSPORT	
Taxi Stand.................13	B5

To Aintoura (17km)

Steep Hillside

Steep Hillside

Park

Clock

Steep Hillside

Shops

To Highway (1km); Service Taxis to Baalbek (1km); Ksara (3km); Baalbek (36km)

THE BEKAA VALLEY

ARAK

If there is a national drink of Lebanon, or indeed the Middle East, then this is it. An acquired taste for some Westerners, this aniseed-flavoured drink has become a universal favourite in the eastern Mediterranean under several guises – ouzo in Greece, raki in Turkey – but all are fundamentally the same thing. Like a holiday romance, it doesn't feel the same when you get home: away from the sunny climes of the Mediterranean, you might crave the sunshine that really makes the drink.

Arak is also curiously classless – sipped at both the smartest dinner and the humblest café – and manages to be available at either end of the alcohol market (US$4 to US$20 per 1L bottle). Experts say the best way to tell the difference is by how you wake up the next morning: the better you feel, the better the arak the night before.

Surprisingly, since there's no hint of grape, arak is a by-product of the wine industry. It's actually a brandy, made from the bits the wine press leaves behind – the red grape skins and pips – much like the Italian grappa, but additionally flavoured with aniseed.

Diluted with ice and water, arak makes a good partner for Lebanese mezze, with the flavour helping to cleanse the palate between the different dishes – and if you're hooked enough to take a bottle home, try El Massaya arak, in its trademark tall elegant blue bottles.

---

looking rather worn and those on the street side can be noisy. Breakfast – included in room rates – isn't up to scratch, considering the prices.

Nevertheless, significant low-season discounts and a host of facilities including a health club, pool and tennis courts still make it a decent option. Unusually, for Lebanon's top-end hotels, wi-fi is available for free throughout the hotel.

Eating

The best and liveliest places to eat during the summer months are the collection of restaurants on the river – look for the sign directing you towards the 'Cafés du Bardouni'. Packed with visitors, especially at weekends, they're the place to head to for great mezze, arak and local wines, along with ice-cream parlours, fairground rides for children and a scattering of places to smoke a leisurely nargileh. Eat, drink and linger into the small hours, watching bats flit overhead and enjoying the cool respite provided by the river.

Lido Café (☎ 818 656; cnr Rue Brazil & Rue St Barbara; pasta LL7000, mains 14,000; ☉ 7am-late) Back in the centre of town, this is a solid all-day eating option. Not as expensive as the riverside places and open all year round, its pasta dishes and grills make a good change for those suffering mezze overload – though hummus is still on the menu, should you so desire it. There's often live music or a DJ at weekends, attracting Zahlé's younger residents.

Many hotels also have restaurants. The one attached to the **Arabi Hotel** (☎ 821 214; meal per person US$20-40) is one of the most famous in Zahlé: a mezze on its outdoor terrace is a wonderful way to spend a lazy evening, fuelled by decent quantities of arak. **Hotel Monte Alberto** (☎ 810 912-14; meal per person including drinks US$15-25) has summer and winter terrace restaurants, while its Al-Ourzal Café, with the best views in town, serves up mezze feasts.

For snacks, try **Sea Sweet** (Rue Brazil) – this branch of the popular countrywide bakery has delicious Lebanese pastries to take-away.

Scattered along Rue Brazil, in both directions from Sea Sweet, are a number of good juice bars and snack places that serve breakfast for a few dollars.

Getting There & Away

Minibuses from Beirut to Zahlé (LL3000, 90 minutes) leave from the southwest side of the roundabout at Beirut's Cola transport hub. Service taxis (LL6000) leave from the same spot. Both minibuses and service taxis will drop you off at the highway turn-off, which is just over 1km from the centre of Zahlé.

If you want to be dropped at the centre of town, you'll need to get off at nearby Chtaura (LL3000, one hour) and catch a service taxi (LL1500); specify that you want to be dropped in town and not at the highway turn-off.

To get to Baalbek from Zahlé, take a service taxi (LL3000, 30 minutes) from the main taxi stand on a square off Rue Brazil, or walk down to the roundabout at the southern end of town, where the highway begins, and from there take a microbus (LL1500, 45 minutes).

KSARA WINERY   كسارة
☎ 08

Lebanon's oldest and most famous **winery** (☎ 813 495; www.ksara.com.lb; Ksara; 9am-4pm) was originally the site of a medieval fortress (*ksar* in Arabic) and while the fortress may be long gone, the grapevines that were planted here in the early 18th century still flourish. The chalky soil and dry weather is perfect for growing grapes, and production here thrived. In 1857, Jesuit priests took over and expanded the vineyard until it was sold to its present owners in 1972. In recent years, both its red and white wine varieties have won a whole slew of international awards.

One unique aspect of the winery is its extremely spacious underground caves, where the wine matures.

The caves were first discovered in Roman times and were expanded during WWI. There are now nearly 2km of tunnels, where the temperature stays between 11°C and 13°C throughout the year – the ideal temperature for the wine.

The 45-minute vineyard tour takes you to the caves as well as through the various processes involved in wine production. Wine-tasting, along with yummy cheeses and cold cuts, finishes the tour and there's an opportunity to purchase your favourite vintages – along with the winery's own arak and brandy – from the shop. For an overview of Lebanon's wineries, see Lebanese Vineyards, p352.

Getting There & Away
A service taxi from Zahlé heading south will drop you in Ksara village (LL1500), a five-minute walk from the winery. Otherwise a taxi will take you there, wait for you and drive you back for US$15, though you may have to barter to get down to this price. If you're driving, head south from Zahlé towards Chtaura along the main highway; the winery should be signposted to your right.

AANJAR   عنجر
☎ 08 / pop 2400

Also referred to as Haouch Moussa (Farm of Moses), Aanjar is a small, predominantly Armenian town founded by refugees who fled Turkey and the 'Great Calamity' genocide of 1915, which is said to have claimed the lives of well over a million Armenians. First housed in the eastern Karantina district of Beirut, Lebanon's Armenians gradually spread across the country, many coming to rest in the Bekaa Valley, and particularly in Aanjar, in the early years of the 1940s.

During the summer months Aanjar's population swells, as hundreds of members of the Armenian diaspora arrive to visit. Though for many years Aanjar was home to the Syrian army's military base in Lebanon – along with its much-feared intelligence unit – Syrian withdrawal from Lebanon has left the little town tranquil and it's a pleasant, leafy place to spend a day or two relaxing and relishing the quiet. In years when Lebanon's tourism is flourishing, the town also hosts a summer festival, with concerts performed – as at Baalbek – within its ancient site.

Aanjar's most remarkable feature is its impressive, and extensive, complex of Umayyad ruins, probably dating back to the rule of the sixth Umayyad Caliph Walid I in AD 705–715. Its discovery came about almost by accident when, in the late 1940s, archaeologists were digging here in the hope of discovering the ancient city of Chalcis, founded around 1000 BC. Instead, they uncovered a walled town with a Roman layout that dated from the first centuries of Islam. Almost all periods of Arab history have been preserved at other sites in Lebanon, but traces of the Umayyads are strangely absent, so Aanjar has great historical significance. Moreover, since the settlement only seems to have been inhabited for a brief 50 years – after which the Umayyad dynasty was overthrown by the Abbasids – it serves as an atmospheric snapshot of a very specific period in the country's history.

Sights
UMAYYAD CITY   المدينة الاموية
The 1300-year-old **city** (admission LL6000; ☽ 8am-7pm summer, 8am-5.30pm winter) is walled and fortified, cut into four equal quarters and separated by two 20m-wide avenues,

LEBANESE VINEYARDS

Lebanon is one of the oldest sites of wine production in the world, and the Bekaa Valley has always been its prime vine-growing region. Because of its favourable climate (some 240 days of unbroken sunshine each year) and chalky soil, the Bekaa Valley's vines need little treatment and the grapes generally have a high sugar content.

Here are a selection of Lebanon's main wineries (it's best to call in advance to make an appointment, especially out of summer), where you can taste and get tipsy amid rolling Lebanese countryside.

Ksara
Lebanon's oldest winery, Ksara is well worth a visit when you're in the Zahlé neighbourhood. See Ksara Winery p351 for details.

Kefraya
'A soul, A Vine, A Great Wine' is the motto of **Château Kefraya** (☎ 645 333/444; www.chateaukefraya.com; Chateau Kefraya, Zahlé), Lebanon's largest wine producer. Not far from Zahlé, the vineyard welcomes visitors to its award-winning winery, which has won dozens of prizes worldwide and many awards for its Lacrima d'Oro, a fortified white wine. If you're dropping in between 25 August and 1 September, you'll witness the annual grape harvest; if you're there at other times, stop for lunch at its sophisticated Dionysus restaurant, where fine French cuisine complements some of the winery's best labels.

Château Musar
The smallest of the commercial producers, the Musar name is also the one recognised by most wine buffs. It is also the only winery not working out of the Bekaa Valley (the winery is in Ghazir, above Jounieh), though its grapes are grown down in the valley and transported there by truck. Started as a hobby winery in 1930 in the basement of a 17th-century castle, it turned professional when Gaston Hochar, its original proprietor, encountered a British viticulturist, who was stationed in Lebanon during WWII. Gaston's son, Ronald, still runs the winery, which visitors are welcome to **tour** (☎ 01-201 828, 328 111, 328 211; www.chateaumusar.com.lb) by appointment. Call or email for directions.

Massaya & Co
A trendy winery run by two dynamic brothers, **Massaya** (☎ 03-735 795; www.massaya.com) is best known in Lebanon for its excellent arak served in distinctive, tall blue bottles (see also Arak, p350). Massaya's success story begins in 1992, when Sami Ghosn, then a successful LA architect, returned to his family's Bekaa Valley land following the drawn-out civil war and decided to put down roots. Soon joined by his brother Ramzi, a restaurateur in France, it wasn't long before they branched out beyond their popular arak and their wines are highly thought of today. Call to make an appointment, which can also involve a gastro-feast at the winery's Le Relais restaurant, and enjoy the tranquillity of a stroll amid the vines.

Domaine Wardy
Though less a winery to stroll around than the others, **Domaine Wardy** (☎ 930 141/2; www.domaine-wardy.com) is definitely one to look out for on restaurant wine lists; products include a deliciously spicy Christmas wine, a fruity rosé and a couple of good, strong araks. With no insecticides or weedkillers used in production, and a percentage from purchases donated to support the preservation of Lebanon's cedar forests, it's not even a guilty pleasure.

the cardo maximus and the decumanus maximus.

Built in the very early days of Muslim rule, the influence of previous cultures remains strong in the architecture of the city and the layout is typically Hellenistic–Roman. Much of the site's building materials appear to have been recycled from earlier Byzantine, Roman and Hellenistic structures in the same area: note the columns and capitals in the partially reconstructed colonnades lining the streets. The tetrapylon, a four-column structure placed where the two streets intersect, is another Roman element, although the stonework, with its alternating layers of large blocks and narrow bricks, is typically Byzantine.

The Roman effect can also be seen in the public baths, just inside the entrance. As with all Roman baths and many later hammams, these contain three main sections: a place to change; the bathing area (consisting of chambers with cold, warm and hot water); and an area to relax and chat. In the bathing area to the left of the entrance there are two faded but reasonably intact mosaics.

In the southwestern corner of the site is a warren of foundations, thought to be the remains of residential quarters. Across the cardo maximus is Aanjar's most striking building, the great palace, which has had one wall and several arcades rebuilt.

Also interesting is the little palace, where you can find Greek stone carvings of leaves, shells and birds. The remains of a third palace, possibly housing the great palace's harem, can also be made out, as can the traces of an early mosque.

Because it sits on a main east–west trade route, historians have speculated that Aanjar was a commercial centre: around 600 shops have been uncovered here (you can still see some of them lining the southern part of the cardo maximus). Other theories suggest that the presence of two palaces and public baths indicates that it may also have been an imperial residence or strategic outpost.

To get the very best from a trip to the ruins, consider employing the services of a registered guide, who'll usually be found sipping strong coffee at the café just to the left of the entrance, and who can bring the site to life better than any written description.

MAJDAL AANJAR   مجدل عنجر

The village of Majdal Aanjar is several kilometres south of Aanjar. Above the village on a hill are some extremely weathered Roman ruins, including a temple whose cella (inner chamber) is still intact, a scattering of fortifications, and a couple of underground passageways. The temple is thought to date from the 1st century AD and in the 7th and 8th centuries it was converted to a fortress by the Abbasids.

The site is rarely visited, despite some half-hearted restoration efforts. To get

there, pass through the village of Majdal Aanjar (note the 13th-century square minaret as you pass) and follow the road (and signs) to the top of the hill. While the last part is extremely steep and best undertaken on foot, the views are worth the effort.

Sleeping

Challalat Anjar Hotel (☎ 620 753; s/d/ste LL75,000/ 90,000/140,000; ❄) Aanjar's only hotel, situated amid the restaurants at the end of town, is simple, bright and airy, with, the brochure proclaims, 'very considered prices'. It has a decent restaurant and live music outside on the terrace every night during the summer.

Eating

The area around Aanjar is famous for its Armenian food and, thanks to trout farms, its fresh fish. One of the best is the Shams Restaurant (☎ 620 567) on the right hand side of the road into Aanjar, about 500m from the main Damascus highway. In addition to the fresh fish, there's the usual selection of mezze and grills available. A meal without fish costs between US$8 and US$15; with fish it's considerably more.

Alternatively, follow the signs for 'Restaurants Aanjar' down the town's main street. There you'll find a whole series of nice Lebanese restaurants spread around gardens, many with water wheels, streams or children's playgrounds.

Getting There & Away

If you are taking a service taxi heading south or to the Syrian border from Zahlé, you will have to get out at Aanjar town and walk from the highway (about 2km) to the site. If you follow the signs you'll see the Shams Restaurant on your right. After this, take the first left, which takes you to the site entrance. If you don't have your own car, negotiate a return trip from Zahlé with a taxi driver who will wait for you (allow one hour for a visit – two if you are very thorough). The trip, if you opt for a one-hour stay, should cost about US$15.

LAKE QARAOUN & LITANI DAM

بحيرة القرعون وسدّ الليطاني

☎ 08

Way down south in the Bekaa Valley is the Litani Dam (also known as Lake Qaraoun Dam). Built in 1959, the dam created a lake of 11 sq km. The Litani is the longest river in Lebanon – it rises in the north of the Bekaa Valley, near Baalbek, and flows into the sea near Tyre. Although built for the practical reason of producing electricity and providing irrigation, it is an attractive spot to visit. Keep in mind that the waters are not safe for swimming. It's at its best in the spring and early summer, when the water level is highest.

There is a visitor centre at the southern end of the lake (the dam end) on the eastern side. A few kilometres further along the road north is the small town of **Saghbine**. From here the views of the lake are quite extraordinary and the **Macharef Saghbine Hotel** (☎ 671 200; s/d/ste US$35/45/60; ❷ ❷) takes great advantage of it. It's a modern hotel with large rooms, a restaurant, a bar and a swimming pool. Open all year, it makes a great stopover if you're on a self-drive trip.

AAMIQ MARSH   عميّق

Halfway between Chtaura and Lake Qaraoun, at the foot of the eastern slopes of Jebel Barouk, lies Aamiq Marsh. Formed by the Nahr al-Riachi (Riachi River) and its underground source, this is Lebanon's last major wetland, covering some 270 hectares, and consisting of marshes, ponds, willows and mud flats. The area is a haven for migrating and aquatic birds, and more than 135 species have been observed here. The wetland was in an increasingly perilous state until recently, when a Christian nature-conservation organisation, **A Rocha** (http://en.arocha.org/lebanon/), headed by British couple Chris and Susanna Naylor, stepped in and began working with local landowners to improve the area. It now makes a popular destination for Lebanese school and college groups.

In September 2007, long-proposed plans for an eco-tourism facility at Aamiq finally came to fruition and work began on the project. Check A Rocha's website for up-to-date information on the status of the area for visitors.

It is difficult to get a service taxi to the far south of the Bekaa Valley, so you will have to negotiate hard with a taxi driver to take you. Hitching is possible, but the best thing is to rent a car for a day or two from Beirut.

BAALBEK   بعلبك
☎ 08 / pop 31,692

Baalbek, the 'Sun City' of the ancient world, is home to the most impressive ancient site in Lebanon and arguably the most important Roman site in the Middle East. The ancient city has long enjoyed a reputation as one of the wonders of the world and mystics still attribute special powers to the courtyard complex. Its temples were built on an extravagant scale that outshone anything in Rome, and the town became a centre of worship well into the Christian era. Standing beneath the temple's colossal columns, watching the setting sun turn the stone a rich orange, is a highlight of any visit to Lebanon.

Modern Baalbek is the administrative centre of northern Bekaa Valley and is home to one of the most historic, atmospheric hotels in the whole Middle East. There are numerous reminders of Hezbollah's supremacy here (their yellow and green flags are everywhere), but the town's population is mixed Muslim/Christian, and you won't see masked militia men brandishing Kalashnikovs on the streets. According to locals, the armed wing is situated elsewhere; here, it's long-term policies, rather than long-range missiles, that concern its party members.

Since Baalbek is, nevertheless, a conservative region of Lebanon, it makes sense not to wander around in shorts – both men and women – or any other kind of revealing clothing, though you'll undoubtedly see a few Lebanese women from out of town strutting their stuff, and snagging their stilettos on Baalbek's pavestones.

An internationally famous arts event, **Baalbek Festival** (www.baalbeck.org.lb) takes place here every summer (July and August) and features opera, jazz, poetry and theatre. In 2006, it was cancelled due to the Israel–Hezbollah war, but most years it strides on regardless of the political or economic climate.

History
The site was originally Phoenician and settlement here is thought to have dated back as far as the end of the 3rd millennium BC. During the 1st millennium BC a temple was built here and dedicated to the god Baal (later Hadad), from which the city takes its name. The site was chosen for its nearby springs and ideal position between

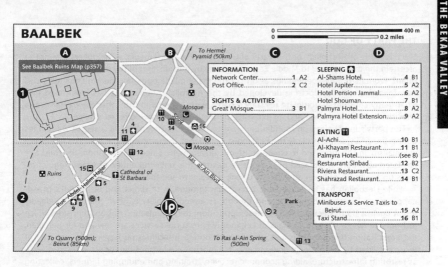

the Litani and Al-Aasi Rivers. It was also located at the crossroads of the main east–west and north–south trade routes.

For all its outward serenity and grace, the site was, in its time, host to sacred prostitution, along with all manner of licentious and bloodthirsty forms of worship. According to ancient tablets from Ugarit, which describe the practices of the Phoenician gods, Anath, the sister and wife of Baal:

> …waded up to the knees, up to the neck in human blood. Human heads lay at her feet, human hands flew over her like locusts. She tied the heads of her victims as ornaments on her back, their hands she tied upon her belt… When she was satisfied she washed her hands in streams of blood before turning again to other things.

Following the conquest of Alexander the Great, Baalbek became known as Heliopolis (City of the Sun), a name that was retained by subsequent Roman conquerors. In 64 BC, Pompey the Great passed through Baalbek, and made it part of the Roman Empire, instigating an era that would see the city rise and flourish. A few years later, in 47 BC, Julius Caesar founded a Roman colony here because of its strategic position between Palmyra, in the Syrian desert, and the coastal cities, naming the new colony after his daughter Julia. The town soon became occupied by Roman soldiers and building works began; it wasn't long before Baalbek was recognised as the premier city in Roman Syria.

The construction of the temples was a massive undertaking. Work is thought to have begun in 60 BC and the great Temple of Jupiter was nearing completion only 120 years later, in AD 60, during the reign of Nero. Later, under Antonius Pius (AD 138–61), a series of elaborate enlargements was undertaken, including work on the Great Court complex and the Temple of Bacchus. His son, the hard-nosed and bloodthirsty Caracalla, completed them, but building work was still ongoing when Rome's rulers adopted Christianity. When you stroll freely around the site, bear in mind that it's estimated that some 100,000 slaves worked on the project over the centuries.

The building of such extravagant temples was a political act as much as one of piety. On one hand, the Romans were attempting to integrate the peoples of the Middle East by appearing to favour their gods; on the other, they set about building jaw-droppingly immense and beautiful structures to impress indelibly upon the worshippers the strength of Roman political rule and civilisation. Even so, the deciding factor in building on such a massive and expansive scale at Baalbek was probably the threat of Christianity, which was beginning to pose a real threat to the old order. So, up went the temples in an attempt to 'fix' the religious orientation of the people in favour of pagan worship. By this time there were no human sacrifices, but temple

THE BEKAA VALLEY

THE PARTY OF GOD

Much is made of Hezbollah, or the 'Party of God', in the Western media, as onlookers attempt to ascertain the threat posed to Middle Eastern security by this offshoot of the Iranian Revolutionary Guard. From its humble beginnings as one of the many militia operating during Lebanon's civil war, following a Shiite doctrine developed by the Ayatollah Khomeini, it has blossomed into what many consider a legitimate resistance party, with 14 seats in the Lebanese parliament, a television and radio station and an extensive network of countrywide social services.

The party's initial aims, on foundation, were to bring to justice those accused of war crimes during the civil war (particularly the Phalangist Christians), to eradicate the influence of 'Western colonialism' in Lebanon, and to create an Islamic government. Since its instigation, the third aim has been abandoned, replaced by a desire to destroy the 'unlawful entity' of Israel. Regular attacks on the north of Israel attest to its ongoing desire to see this carried out.

While Hezbollah has an undeniably bloody background, with direct and brutal links to kidnappings, murders and bombings, and though its armed capacity is often touted as a deadly threat against both Israel and its Lebanese opposition, the organisation has another side, which few outside get to glimpse. In areas of Lebanon where social services are few and far between, the organisation runs hospitals and schools, with outreach facilities far beyond the capacity of those provided by the national government. Its branches are responsible for activities as diverse as restoring infrastructure, aiding economic recovery, training and equipping farmers, collecting rubbish, dispensing drinking water and providing childcare for infants, as well as a 'Martyrs Institute,' which provides for the families of 'martyrs' killed in 'battle'. All this, says Hezbollah, is financed through 'donations by Muslims'; others argue that the money comes direct from high-level Iranian pockets.

Either way, for many impoverished people in the Bekaa Valley, southern Lebanon and south of Beirut, Hezbollah has proved a vital lifeline, offering health, security and education where there is none on offer through other channels.

prostitution remained, while Baalbek had become one of the most important places of worship in the entire Roman Empire.

When Constantine the Great became emperor in 324, pagan worship was finally suppressed by Rome in favour of Christianity, and building work on Baalbek was suspended. However, when Julian the Apostate became emperor in 361, he reverted to paganism and tried to reinstate it throughout the empire. There was a terrible backlash against Christians, which resulted in mass martyrdom. When the Christian emperor, Theodosius, took the throne in 379, Christianity was once again imposed upon Baalbek and its temples were converted to a basilica. Nevertheless, the town remained a centre of pagan worship and was enough of a threat to warrant a major crackdown by Emperor Justinian (527–65), who ordered that all Baalbek's pagans accept baptism. In an attempt to prevent any secret pagan rites, he ordered parts of the temple be destroyed, and had the biggest pillars shipped to Constantinople, where they were used in the Aya Sofya.

When the Muslim Arabs invaded Syria, they converted the Baalbek temples into a citadel and restored its original name. For several centuries it came under the rule of Damascus and went through a period of regular invasions, sackings, lootings and devastation. The city was sacked by the Arabs in 748 and by the Mongol chieftain Tamerlane in 1400.

In addition to the ravages caused by humans, there was also a succession of earthquakes (1158, 1203, 1664 and most spectacularly in 1759), which caused the fall of the ramparts and three of the huge pillars of the Temple of Jupiter, as well as the departure of most of the population. Most of what remains today lies within the area of the Arab fortifications; the Temple of Mercury, further out, is virtually gone. By erecting walls around some of the buildings, the Arabs unwittingly preserved the temples inside the sanctuary.

During the period of Ottoman rule, Baalbek was slowly forgotten and in the 16th and 17th centuries, few visitors stopped to admire what was left of the once magnificent ancient site. In 1751, eight years before Baalbek's biggest earthquake, English architects James Dawkins and Robert Wood rediscovered the ruins, at which point nine of the Temple of Jupiter's columns were still standing. But it wasn't until a century and a half later, when Kaiser Wilhelm II visited Baalbek in 1898 while on a tour of the Middle East, that a study of the ruins was seriously undertaken. The Kaiser immediately contacted the Sultan of Turkey for permission to excavate the site and for the next seven years a team of archaeologists recorded the site in detail. By this time Baalbek was once again frequented by visitors, who, instead of bowing in prayer, helped themselves to sculptures and inscriptions.

After the defeat of Turkey and Germany in WWI, Baalbek's German scholars were replaced by French ones who, in turn, were replaced by Lebanese. Over the next decades, all the later structures cluttering the site were removed and the temples were finally restored as close as possible to their 1st-century splendour. In some parts of the site, work is still ongoing.

Orientation & Information

The town of Baalbek is small and easily explored on foot. From Zahlé or Beirut, you enter the town via the main road, Rue Abdel Halim Hajjar, the street on which you'll find the town's two banks. It intersects with the other main road, Ras al-Ain Blvd.

Scattered down the main road from the Palmyra Hotel are a number of ATMs. Neither of the banks cash travellers cheques and none of the hotels or restaurants seem willing to accept credit cards.

Network Center (Map p355; per hr LL3000; ☉ 9am-1am) It's up a side street between the Palmyra and Jupiter Hotels.

Post Office (Map p355; ☉ 8am-5pm Mon-Fri, 8am-2pm Sat) Heading along Ras al-Ain Blvd, it's up a side street before the Riviera Restaurant.

Sights

BAALBEK RUINS

The **site** (Map p357; adult LL12,000, child under 8 free; ☉ 8.30am-30min before sunset) also houses a free **museum**. A good free map of the site, entitled *Heliopolis Baalbek 1898–1998: Rediscovering the Ruins*, is produced by the German

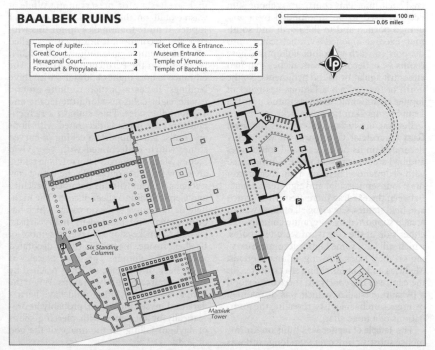

BAALBEK RUINS

Temple of Jupiter...........................1	Ticket Office & Entrance.................5
Great Court...................................2	Museum Entrance.........................6
Hexagonal Court............................3	Temple of Venus...........................7
Forecourt & Propylaea....................4	Temple of Bacchus.......................8

0   100 m
0   0.05 miles

Six Standing Columns

Mamluk Tower

Archaeological Institute and is available all over town. Terrific multilingual guides can be found (or will find you) around the ticket office and charge around US$14 for one hour; see A Guide's Life, p57, for insights from one of Baalbek's accredited guides. The entrance to the main site is currently at the southeastern end of the temple complex. Note that at the time of writing, a new entrance to the museum complex was planned and under construction: the new entrance, when finally completed, will be opposite the Palmyra Hotel, behind an area designated as a new car park.

After passing the ticket office, you enter the ruins via the monumental staircase leading up to the **propylaea** that has a portico flanked by two towers and a colonnade along the façade. This would originally have been covered by a cedar roof and paved with mosaics. The column bases supporting the portico bear the inscription 'For the safety and victories of our lord, Caracalla'.

Through a central door you move into the **hexagonal court**. There is a raised threshold, which separates the propylaea from the sacred enclosure. This courtyard is about 50m deep. It used to be surrounded by a columned portico and to the north and south four exedrae opened symmetrically onto the portico, each with four columns. These rooms were decorated with niches that had either triangular or round pediments. To the north of the court is a famous bas-relief of Jupiter Heliopolitan that was found near the Lejuj Spring, 7km from Baalbek.

Beyond the hexagonal court is the **Great Court** (Sacrificial Courtyard). It was richly decorated on its north, east and south sides and had a double row of niches surmounted with pediments. There are a number of exedrae: four semicircular and eight rectangular. Between the exedrae there are niches, which also held statues. Covering all of these was an arcade supported by 84 granite columns. To either side of the courtyard were two pools, which still have some highly decorative carving on their sides showing Trions, Nereids, Medusas and Cupids riding sea creatures. In the centre of the courtyard there once stood a Byzantine basilica, which was dismantled by French archaeologists, revealing the foundations of a huge altar.

The **Temple of Jupiter** was built on an immense substructure over 90m long, and was approached by another monumental staircase that rose high above the surrounding buildings. It consisted of a cella in which the statue of the god was housed and a surrounding portico of 10 columns along the façade and 19 columns along the side, making for 54 columns in all. These columns are the largest in the world – 22.9m high with a girth of 2.2m. Today only six of these remain standing with the architrave still in position. It was thought in the old days that Baalbek had been constructed by giants and a quick look over the side of the temple to the foundation stones beneath reveals some of the largest building blocks to be found anywhere on earth. One of these megalithic blocks measures 19.5m by 4.3m and is estimated to weigh over 1000 tonnes – how it was moved and positioned so precisely remains a mystery.

From the south side of the temple is a wonderful view of the so-called **Temple of Bacchus**. This was in fact dedicated not to Bacchus but to Venus/Astarte, and is the most beautifully decorated temple in the Roman world. Completed around AD 150, it is also in a great state of preservation. While it wasn't built on the scale of the Temple of Jupiter, it more than makes up for this with style and decoration. Ironically it was called 'the small temple' in antiquity, although it is larger than the Parthenon in Athens. The entrance is up a flight of 30 stairs with three landings. It has a portico running around it with eight columns along the façade and 15 along the sides. They support a rich entablature; the frieze is decorated with lions and bulls. This supports a ceiling of curved stone, which is decorated with very vivid scenes: Mars; a winged Victory; Diana taking an arrow from her quiver; Tyche with a cornucopia; Vulcan with his hammer; Bacchus; and Ceres holding a sheaf of corn. The highlight of the temple is the doorway, which has been drawn and painted by many artists, its half-fallen keystone forever a symbol of Baalbek. Inside, the cella is richly decorated with fluted columns. The 'holy place' was at the back of the cella, which is reached by another staircase with two ramps. When the temple was in use, this would have been a dark and mysterious place, probably lit dramatically by oil lamps with piercing shafts of daylight falling on the image of the god or goddess.

In the southeastern corner of the Great Court is the **museum** (entered from the parking area, near the ticket office), housed in a large vaulted tunnel that may originally have been storerooms or housing for pilgrims. Note that this may also be moved during renovation works to the site: if it's no longer there, just ask a guide or ticket vendor for directions. As well as some beautiful artefacts from Baalbek, the well-lit exhibits give a thorough history of the temple under loosely grouped themes. One fascinating display explains Roman building techniques, showing how the massive stone blocks used in the Temple of Jupiter were manoeuvred into place.

In a side room is a foray into Baalbek's more recent history, with a description of Emperor Wilhelm II's visit. More interesting are photographs by the German photographer Herman Burckhardt, who visited Baalbek at the turn of the 20th century. His pictures are an invaluable record of daily life at the time.

OTHER SIGHTS
Near the main ruins, about 300m from the acropolis, is the tiny exquisite **Temple of Venus** (Map p357) – probably dedicated to Fortuna rather than Venus – a circular building with many fluted columns. Inside, it was decorated with tiers of tabernacles and covered with a cupola. During the early

---

THE LARGEST STONE IN THE WORLD
Stopping off to see the world's largest cut stone at the quarry on Sheikh Abdullah hill, you'll undoubtedly hear the tale of Baalbek native Abdul Nabi Al-Afi, who saved it from life at the bottom of a rubbish dump. Measuring 21.5m by 4m by 4.5m, lying on its side, locals call this stone Hajar al-Hubla (Stone of the Pregnant Woman), and local folklore has it that women can touch the stone to increase their fertility. Al-Afi, a retired army sergeant, single-handedly saved the site from obscurity, and his friendly young son, who runs the tiny gift shop at its edge, will be happy to provide information on his father's remarkable one-man litter-picking story. In case you're on the lookout for a Hezbollah souvenir, the shop itself is definitely also worth a browse.

Christian era it was turned into a basilica and dedicated to St Barbara (who joined the saintly ranks when her pagan father tried to kill her for converting to Christianity – he got his comeuppance when a bolt of lightning reduced him to a smouldering heap). A copy of this gem of a temple was constructed in the 18th century in the grounds of Stourhead in Wiltshire, England.

To the east of the propylaea stands the ruined Umayyad or **Great Mosque** (Map p355), which was built from the stones of the temples using many styles of columns and capitals. Lebanon's only Umayyad ruin other than Aanjar, it was built between the 7th and 8th centuries. There is an ablution fountain surrounded by four columns in the centre of the courtyard. On the right, immediately after the entrance, are rows of arched colonnades with Roman columns and capitals, clearly taken from the temple complex. At the northwestern corner are the ruins of a great octagonal minaret on a square base.

To the southeast of Baalbek's centre is the source of the **Ras al-Ain spring**. The area has pleasant, shady parks along the spring and is the site of occasional festivities with horses and camels and side stalls. At the head of the spring is a ruined early **mosque**, which at some point was thought to be the Temple of Neptune.

About 1km south of the centre of Baalbek, to either side of the road on Sheikh Abdullah Hill, is the **quarry** where the massive stones used to build the temples originated.

Sleeping
Al-Shams Hotel (Map p355; ☎ 373 284; Rue Abdel Halim Hajjar; d US$6) This hotel has only three very basic rooms with washbasins and a shared toilet and bath. Beds are uncomfortable and it's a musty and forgettable place to stay. All the same, with so few tourists currently making it as far as Baalbek, you're likely to get the whole room – if not the whole place – to yourself for that same princely US$6.

Hotel Shouman (Map p355; ☎ 03-796 077; Ras al-Ain Blvd; dm/d LL10,000/25,000) Close to the ruins, this hotel has the added advantage of great views from three of its five rooms. There are hard beds and a simple-but-clean shared toilet and shower. Enter via a stone staircase; the pension is on the 1st floor. Room 1 is a triple with a great view of the ruins.

Hotel Jupiter (Map p355; ☎ 376 715, 370 151; Rue Abdel Halim Hajjar; s/d/tr US$10/20/25) This friendly place is a decent option. Entered via an arcade next to Restaurant Chich Kabab near the Palmyra Hotel, it has large rooms off a central courtyard. These are light and all have fans.

Hotel Pension Jammal (Map p355; ☎ 370 649, 03-716 072; Rue Abdel Halim Hajjar; r per person US$15) Favoured by the German archaeologists working at the archaeological site, this is a good midrange option. Prices are per person whether you take a single, double or triple, and there are rooms available on both sides of the road. Breakfast is included. Those on the southern side, above an immense ballroom, are especially nice and fairly cosy even in winter months, since most have black pot-bellied boilers.

our pick **Palmyra Hotel** (Map p355; ☎ 370 011, 370 230; Rue Abdel Halim Hajjar; s/d/tr US$38/53/63; ⊠) Just opposite the ruins, the Palmyra is one of the most wonderful colonial-era relics dotting the Middle East, its guest book an impressive testament to how glamorous travel in the region once was. Having said that, you'll either love it or find it hair-raising: 'faded grandeur' is putting it mildly, and on winter nights it's cold, draughty and downright spooky.

During WWI, the Palmyra was used by the German army, and in WWII it was the British-army headquarters in the area. Its guest list includes General de Gaulle, who slept in twin room No 30 in case you want to do the same; and Jean Cocteau, whose original drawings – many of which were done at the hotel itself – still adorn the walls.

For those more interested in a good night's sleep, the hotel has a newer, more comfortable extension a few doors down. The five rooms are more expensive (US$100), but are lavishly furnished and the salon has amazing views of the ruins. Guests can enjoy breakfast at the hotel's restaurant (p360) for US$5 per person.

Eating

The restaurant scene is not particularly noteworthy in Baalbek; your best bet is the cheap eateries on Rue Abdel Halim Hajjar.

Al-Khayam Restaurant (Map p355; Rue Abdel Halim Hajjar) This small place is the best of the cheapies. It serves absolutely delicious felafels (LL1000) and shwarma (LL1500), and huge, filling hummus and felafel plates with salad go for LL2000.

Restaurant Sinbad (Map p355; Rue Abdel Halim Hajjar) Directly opposite Al-Khayam, and in direct competition, Sinbad serves up the same sort of simple, tasty meals at similar prices.

Al-Achi (Map p355; ⊠ 6am-8pm) A hole-in-the-wall bakery crammed with good pastries. Especially yummy are the custard-filled chocolate éclairs for LL2000.

Riviera Restaurant (Map p355; ☎ 370 296; Ras al-Ain Blvd; mezze around LL2000) On the way to the

---

HASHISH HARDSHIP

The Bekaa Valley was once the centre of Lebanon's infamous hashish production. Throughout the civil war years, an estimated 10,000 tonnes of hashish were exported from Lebanon each year, a lucrative US$500 million annual trade controlled by a cartel of just 30 Lebanese families. When Syria arrived in Lebanon, it got in on the act too, and used its tanks and artillery to protect the marijuana fields.

In a bid for American respect around the time of the Gulf War, Syria attempted to put an end to the industry, encouraging farmers instead to cultivate tomatoes, tobacco, potatoes and grain. The new produce, however, could not compete with cheaper Syrian goods; farmers' incomes plunged and, unsurprisingly, some returned to their former, more lucrative trade. During the 1990s, Lebanese government clampdowns resulted in bulldozing hashish crops, further injuring the industry and leaving some farmers destitute.

As a result of recent instability and the 2006 war, however, Lebanon's government has turned its attention to other fields, and the Bekaa Valley's are flourishing once more. Currently, 10kg of hash can yield a farmer US$10,000, a sum unthinkable for any other crop. Most production is hidden away in the north of the Bekaa Valley, so you're unlikely to spot it while on the road. Though officially disapproved of by Hezbollah, the organisation turns a blind eye to an industry that supports one of the country's otherwise poorest regions, where farmers truly profit from being green-fingered.

spring, this serves basic but tasty food in its outdoor eating area in the summer months.

Shahrazad Restaurant (Map p355; top fl, Centre Commercial de Yaghi & Simbole; shwarma from LL3500) While the food is your standard Lebanese fare (chicken shwarma sandwich/kebab LL3500/ 6000), the views of the ruins from this sixth floor restaurant are great. It is accessed via a lift at the rear of this small shopping centre in the souq.

Palmyra Hotel (Map p355; Rue Abdel Halim Hajjar; mains from US$8) The hotel's restaurant serves decent Lebanese food all day. The cardboard diorama near the restaurant entrance sports authentic bullet holes, created by a drunken army reveller one snowy New Year's night. The cute 1960s 'snug' bar is a great place for a stiff drink and a yarn or two about the Palmyra's glory days, late into the evening.

Getting There & Away
The only public transport options to get from Beirut to Baalbek are the minibuses (LL4000, two hours) and an array of service taxis (LL6000) from the Cola transport hub. Be warned that the drive over the Mt Lebanon Range can be a white-knuckle experience, particularly in the winter months. Minibuses and service taxis both stop in Baalbek just down from the Palmyra Hotel.

For information about how to get to Baalbek from Zahlé, see p350. For information about how to get to Baalbek from Bcharré or Tripoli, see p336. Keep in mind that the road across the mountains to the Cedars and Bcharré is closed due to snow during winter.

AROUND BAALBEK
If you've got your own car, there are a number of sites to the north of Baalbek well worth exploring. Currently it's perfectly safe to explore the north Bekaa Valley, though unadvisable to drive in the dark due as much to your unpredictable fellow drivers as to the chance of being car-jacked. Still, before heading out it pays to check with a local or two in Baalbek, to ensure the security situation hasn't changed.

Hermel Pyramid   هرم الهرمل
Around 50km north of Baalbek, in the middle of nowhere, is a lonely 27m-high monument sitting on the crest of a small hill, which can be seen for miles around. It is a solid square-base construction with a pyramid on top, large sections of which were restored in 1931.

Its north side depicts two deer standing on what appears to be a hunting trap; its south side is largely worn away, but shows what might have once been a bear. Its east side has reliefs of a speared boar being attacked by hunting dogs, and its west has a bull being attacked by two wolves. Nobody is quite sure what this strange monument is meant to be or why it is standing alone. It closely resembles some of the tower tombs at the Valley of the Tombs at Palmyra (p209) to the east in Syria, and some believe it's a prince's tomb dating from the first or second century BC.

Unfortunately the inscriptions are no longer there, so the pyramid may always remain an enigma.

Nahr al-Aasi   نهر العاصي
☎ 08
Near a bridge that crosses the Nahr al-Aasi (Orontes River), about 10km southeast of Hermel Pyramid, is a scattering of restaurants specialising in trout; you'll spot the restaurants when driving the road from Baalbek to the Hermel Pyramid.

For some great rafting and kayaking in this area, contact **Assi Club Hermel** (☎ 03-445 051, 03-163 014; www.assirafting.com), which can arrange day trips and overnight accommodation. Be sure to ask for driving instructions, as starting points for rafting and kayaking differ depending on the sort of trip you choose.

Deir Mar Maroun   دير مار مارون
Overlooking Nahr al-Aasi, about 200m from Ain ez-Zerqa, sits the ancient rock-cut monastery of Mar Maroun. To reach it you can either take a 3km hike or a 12km-long drive from Hermel. Inside the monastery are several tiers of cave-like cells connected with spiral staircases. The monastery was established in the 5th century by St Maron, the founder of the Maronite church, and was destroyed by Justinian II in the 7th century – hundreds were put to death as heretics. The survivors of this persecution fled up to the mountains and across to the Qadisha Valley (p337).

The South

Less visited than other parts of Lebanon, the South is rich in history – both ancient and modern – making the currently accessible parts well worth exploring. The principal towns of Tyre and Sidon, known respectively in Arabic as Sour and Saida, are full of archaeological treasures, surrounded by lush plantations of bananas, dates and oranges and populated by welcoming locals.

The picture, however, is far from rosy. Hardest hit by the civil war (not to mention a historic lack of interest by Beirut's powerbrokers) the South seems to encounter yet another hurdle every time it attempts to get back onto its feet. Following Israel's withdrawal from Lebanon in May 2000 – before which much of the South was under Israeli or proxy South Lebanon Army (SLA) occupation – the South initially saw a resurgence in tourism as Lebanese and overseas visitors arrived, curious to see this isolated and previously out-of-bounds region. But the 2006 war between Israel and Hezbollah effectively put a stop to its tourist industry once again.

While visitors might initially be wary, those who do make it this far will be in for a treat. Both Sidon and Tyre remain fascinating places to visit, with locals more than willing to stop in the street to help a lost-looking tourist poring over a guidebook. While there are often limited accommodation and restaurant options available, with many businesses closing down or frequently changing hands, the lure of the region's beaches and souqs, along with the ancient treasures of Tyre, will quickly allay any qualms about visiting the area.

HIGHLIGHTS

- Get lost in the atmosphere of **Sidon's souqs** (p367), while snacking on fresh *sanioura* biscuits, the local delicacy

- Relax on the sand at a swanky **beach club** (p369) on the coastal strip between Sidon and Beirut

- Stop off at Tyre's splendid Roman remains and do a lap of its impressive **Roman hippodrome** (p376)

- Walk off a delicious seafood lunch enjoyed at Tyre's **Le Petit Phoenicien** (p377) with a stroll through the tranquil **Tyre Beach Nature Reserve** (p376)

- See how suds are made at the **Musée du Savon** (p367) in Sidon

★ Sidon (Saida)

★ Tyre (Sour)

THE SOUTH

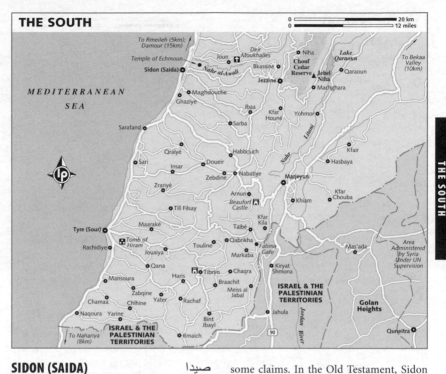

SIDON (SAIDA)   صيدا
☎ 07 / pop 170,516

The port city of Sidon (Saida in Arabic), famous in modern times as the birthplace of assassinated former prime minister Rafiq Hariri, is approached from Beirut, 40km to its north, through thick citrus orchards and banana groves. Although not as well organised or commercial as Byblos – its closest equivalent in terms of harbourside charms – this once grand and wealthy Phoenician city exudes a strong feeling of 'living history' with its mosques, khans and vaulted souqs still very much in everyday use. There are few concessions made here to tourists, which means the selection of hotels and restaurants isn't particularly extensive. But what it lacks in facilities it makes up for in workaday charm and mysterious medieval alleyways ripe for the exploring, along with the most tempting aromas wafting from the souq-based food stalls.

History
The ancient town of Sidon was settled as early as 4000 BC, or 6800 BC according to

some claims. In the Old Testament, Sidon is referred to as 'the first born of Canaan', which may have originated from the town's possible founder, Saidoune ibn Canaan. The word for 'fishing' or 'hunting' is *sayd* in modern Arabic.

As early as the 14th and 15th centuries BC, Sidon had a reputation as a commercial centre with strong trade links with Egypt. The city rose in prominence from the 12th to 10th centuries BC, its wealth generated from trading murex, a mollusc that produced an expensive, highly prized purple dye that over time became known as the colour of royalty and was eventually exploited to the point of extinction. Geography helped, too: like many Phoenician cities, Sidon was built on a promontory with an offshore island, which sheltered the harbour from storms and provided a safe haven during times of war.

In common with the other Phoenician city-states, Sidon suffered from conquest and invasion numerous times. In 1200 BC the Philistines destroyed the city and its fleet of trading ships, allowing Tyre to

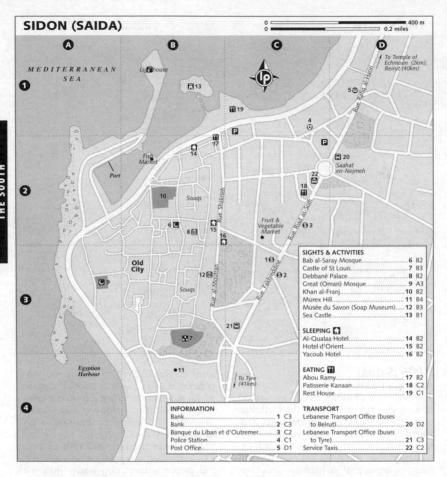

SIDON (SAIDA)

SIGHTS & ACTIVITIES
Bab al-Saray Mosque	6 B2
Castle of St Louis	7 B3
Debbané Palace	8 B2
Great (Omari) Mosque	9 A3
Khan al-Franj	10 B2
Murex Hill	11 B4
Musée du Savon (Soap Museum)	12 B3
Sea Castle	13 B1

SLEEPING
Al-Qualaa Hotel	14 B2
Hotel d'Orient	15 B2
Yacoub Hotel	16 B2

EATING
Abou Ramy	17 B2
Patisserie Kanaan	18 C2
Rest House	19 C1

INFORMATION
Bank	1 C3
Bank	2 C3
Banque du Liban et d'Outremer	3 C2
Police Station	4 C1
Post Office	5 D1

TRANSPORT
Lebanese Transport Office (buses to Beirut)	20 D2
Lebanese Transport Office (buses to Tyre)	21 C3
Service Taxis	22 C2

eclipse Sidon as the most important Phoenician centre. Although often under Tyre's control, or forced to pay tribute to the Assyrians, Sidon recovered its status as a trading centre, only to be destroyed in 675 BC by the Assyrian king Esarhaddon.

The city's golden age came during the Persian Empire (525–332 BC) when the city was the capital of the Fifth Province, covering Syria, Palestine and Cyprus. Apart from murex, Sidon was famed for its glassmaking, which was considered the best in the world. During this period the Temple of Echmoun (p370), about 2km northeast of the city, was built. Inscriptions found there reveal that Phoenician Sidon was built in two sections: the maritime city, Sidon Yam;

and the upper part, Sidon Sadeh, which was built on the lower spurs of the Mt Lebanon Range, upwind from the sickening smell produced by the murex dye works.

Sidon also became known for shipbuilding and provided experienced sailors for the Persian fleet. The king of Sidon was admiral of the fleet and successful in campaigns against the Egyptians in the 6th century BC, and later against the Greeks, giving Sidon a degree of independence from its Persian overlords. This lasted until the middle of the 4th century BC, when Phoenician rebellion, centred in Sidon, incurred the wrath of the Persians. Heading a huge army, King Artaxerxes Ochus arrived to beat the Sidonians into submission. According to

Greek historian Diodorus, residents locked the city gates, employing a 'scorched earth' policy, setting fire to the city rather than surrendering it. More than 40,000 people died in the ensuing inferno, weakening the city to such an extent that when Alexander the Great marched through in 333 BC, its residents were in no position to resist him and surrendered without a struggle.

Under the Greeks, Sidon recovered and enjoyed relative freedom and a sophisticated cultural life. Later the city came successively under the control of the Seleucids and the Ptolemies. Emperor Augustus, however, put an end to Sidon's independence when he brought it under direct Roman rule.

During the Byzantine period, the aftermath of the devastating earthquake of AD 551 saw Sidon fare better than most other Phoenician cities, and it soon became home to Beirut's famous School of Law, which was hastily moved from the wreckage of Beirut. In 667 the Arabs invaded and the city took on the Arabic name Saida, still widely in use today, remaining a wealthy centre, administered from Damascus.

In 1110 Baldwin I, King of Jerusalem, besieged the city and the Sidonians gave up after 47 days of resistance. In 1187 Saladin took the city and razed the ramparts to the ground in an attempt to render it useless as a Crusader base. It failed to deter the Crusaders, however, who hastily recaptured it. Subsequent battles for control saw Sidon passing to-and-fro between the two sides as many as five times, before finally falling to the Mamluks in 1291.

Sidon's fortunes rose in the 15th century when it became a trading port of Damascus. While the city flourished again in the 17th century under the rule of Fakhreddine (Fakhr ad-Din al-Maan II), who encouraged French merchants to the city to set up highly profitable trading enterprises between France and Sidon, prosperity was temporary. In 1791, the Ottoman pasha of Acre, Ahmad al-Jazzar, drove the French from the town and Beirut took over as the centre of commerce. An earthquake in the 1830s, followed by bombardment during the Ottoman–European campaign to remove Bashir Shihab II, helped ensure the city's fall into relative obscurity.

In the early part of the 20th century the area around Sidon was developed for agriculture, particularly fruit, evidence of which you'll see on roads leading to the town. During the civil war Sidon was fought over variously by the Palestinians, Syrians, Israelis, Hezbollah and the Shiite militia Amal, and again suffered greatly, both economically and through human and architectural casualties. In the postwar period, it benefited from being the birthplace of

---

TRAVEL WARNING

Following Israel's 2006 offensive in southern Lebanon, the area remains troubled and its future uncertain. At the time of writing, the main north-to-south highway connecting Beirut with Tyre was still closed in one section, due to an unrepaired motorway bridge, the target of an Israeli air strike. Thousands of UN Interim Forces in Lebanon (Unifil) troops remain stationed in the region, and there are several Lebanese army checkpoints on the roads between Sidon, Tyre and beyond.

At the time of writing it was wise not to venture too far off the main roads between Sidon, Tyre and Jezzine. A roadside bomb attack on Unifil troops on the main road between Marjeyun and Khiam on 24 June 2007 left three Spanish and three Colombian peacekeepers dead, and there are suggestions that there may be other bomb attacks planned. Therefore, some foreign offices also advise staying away from bars and restaurants popular with off-duty Unifil soldiers in Tyre.

In addition to this, the area is still littered with land mines, along with yet more unexploded ordnance and cluster bombs dating from 2006 (see Action Against Mines, p378). If you do decide to venture into the countryside beyond Tyre, do not wander off the roads.

Before attempting any trips to the South, it's best to keep up to date with the situation by checking the internet and print news sources. If you wish to travel outside Sidon or Tyre, it's best to check first with locals, your embassy or the Unifil troops you'll encounter on the road.

For more information on the location and work of Unifil, see the UN's Unifil pages at www .un.org/Depts/dpko/missions/unifil/.

former prime minister Rafiq Hariri, whose eponymous foundation channelled huge amounts of money into the city's reconstruction. Meanwhile other wealthy Sidon financiers such as the Audi and Debbané families (see Building Foundations, below) are sponsoring the ongoing restoration of the souqs.

Orientation
Most of the sites of interest to visitors, including the Sea Castle and souqs, are along or just off the seafront, where you'll also find plenty of good eating options and Sidon's best hotel.

The centre of town, around Saahat en-Nejmeh (a huge roundabout), is most useful for its bus and service-taxi stands, and is also the location of the police station. Rue Riad as-Solh, which runs south off Saahat en-Nejmeh, has plenty of banks with ATMs, moneychangers and travel agencies. The Audi Foundation at the **Musée du Savon** (Rue al-Moutran) provides free maps of the old city listing many of Sidon's heritage buildings.

Information
EMERGENCY
Ambulance (☎ 140)

INTERNET ACCESS
At the time of writing, there were few reliable internet cafés in Sidon. Those that exist tend to change hands regularly. Ask at your hotel for the name and location of the newest option in town.

MONEY
Dozens of moneychangers and banks with ATMs are clustered on Rue Riad as-Solh, close to Saahat en-Nejmeh.

POST
Post office (☎ 722 813; Rue Rafiq al-Hariri; ☺ 8am-5pm Mon-Fri, 8am-noon Sat)

TOURIST OFFICE
Tourist office (☎ 727 344; Khan al-Franj; ☺ 8.30am-2pm Mon-Sat) A small office that can provide you with maps of the historic centre of Sidon.

Sights
With the exception of the Sea Castle, all Sidon's sights are free to visit. Though opening hours are provided, it's worth noting that these may change as a result of the season, day of the week, or whim of those in charge of unlocking the front doors.

SEA CASTLE   قلعة البحر
Built by the Crusaders in 1228, the **Sea Castle** (Qala'at al-Bahr; LL4000; ☺ 9am-6pm, closes earlier in winter), connected to the mainland by a fortified Arab stone causeway, sits around 80m offshore on a small island that was formerly the site of a temple to Melkart, the Phoenician version of Hercules. One of many coastal castles built by the Crusaders, it was largely destroyed by the Mamluks to prevent the Crusaders from returning to the region, but its renovation was ordered by Fakhreddine in the 17th century.

BUILDING FOUNDATIONS
Founded in 1979, Rafiq Hariri's foundation continues to carry out work instigated by its billionaire poor-boy-made-good founder, despite his assassination in Beirut in 2005.

The activities of the foundation, many of which centre around his birth city of Sidon, include education, health care and the conservation of historic structures, as well as a USA-based branch, launched in 1995, dedicated to sending Lebanese students to study at major American universities and colleges. In Sidon itself, the Hariri Foundation has renovated a number of historic buildings damaged during Lebanon's bloody and turbulent years: the Great (Omari) Mosque, shelled by Israeli military planes in 1982; the Khan al-Franj (Khan of the Foreigners); and around 500 old city homes.

Meanwhile the Audis, another wealthy family, continue to do their own bit towards Sidon's reconstruction and restoration. The city's soap museum is part of the Audi foundation's commitment to the regeneration of the old city, while the foundation frequently organises cultural events. Likewise, the Debbané family has gifted the city its historic palace home to become a museum showcasing Sidon's glorious past.

The building consists of two towers joined together by a wall. The rectangular west tower, to the left of the entrance, is the best preserved, measuring 21m by 17m, and has a large vaulted room scattered with old carved capitals and rusting cannonballs. A winding staircase leads up to the roof, where there is a small, domed Ottoman-era mosque. From the roof there is a great view across the old city and fishing harbour. The east tower isn't as well preserved and was built in two phases; the lower part dates to the Crusader period, while the upper level was built by the Mamluks.

On summer days when the shallow water surrounding the castle is calm, you can see many broken columns of rose granite lying on the sea floor; archaeologists believe there's much more to be discovered further off Sidon's coast.

KHAN AL-FRANJ خان الفرنج
The largest, most beautiful and best preserved of the many khans built by 17th century Fakhreddine is **Khan al-Franj** (Khan of the Foreigners; admission free; ☼ 10am-6pm), donated to the French by Fakhreddine to encourage trade relations. The khans all followed the same basic design, with a large rectangular central courtyard, fountain, covered arcades (used for stables and storage) and a galleried second storey providing accommodation for merchants and travellers.

In the 19th century, the Khan al-Franj was Sidon's principal khan and the city's centre of economic activity, also housing the French consul. Today, it has been painstakingly restored courtesy of the Hariri Foundation.

GREAT (OMARI) MOSQUE الجامع الكبير
Facing the northern tip of the harbour is the **Great (Omari) Mosque**, said to be one of the best examples of 13th-century Islamic religious architecture. Originally a fortified Knights Hospitaller structure and converted to a mosque after the Crusaders were driven out of the Holy Land, it was heavily damaged during the civil war and underwent a lengthy restoration. The main prayer hall once housed the Church of St John of the Hospitallers and its original walls can still be seen. There are two entrances to the mosque: one down a maze of covered streets in the souqs to the north of

the mosque; the other on the eastern side of the building (once the site of a palace built by Fakhreddine). Inside is a large courtyard surrounded on three sides by arched porticos and bordered on the fourth side by the prayer hall. There are two mihrabs (niches indicating the direction of Mecca) on the southern wall of the prayer hall, with a modern *minbar* (pulpit) in-between. You can visit the mosque outside prayer times; remember to dress modestly and women should bring a headscarf.

BAB AL-SARAY MOSQUE جامع باب السراي
The oldest mosque in the city is **Bab al-Saray Mosque**, which dates back to 1201. Located just east of the old Bab al-Saray (Saray Gate), it boasts the largest dome in Sidon and an enormous supporting column made from black stone, allegedly imported from Italy. The beautiful stonework has just been restored through a *waqf* (religious endowment). The mosque sits in the corner of a square, which has a pleasant **outdoor corner café** built on the site of the original *saray* (palace). It may not always be open to non-Muslims, so check before entering and, as with the Great (Omari) Mosque, remember to dress appropriately.

SOUQS الاسواق
The old covered **souqs** are the city's highlight, lying between the Sea Castle and the Castle of St Louis. This is where, in labyrinthine alleyways, shopkeepers ply their trades in workshops the same way they have done for centuries. Officially there are some 60 listed historic sites here, many of them in ruins, though renovation work is ongoing.

Scattered throughout the souqs are several coffeehouses and plenty of tiny canteens dishing out cheap, simple and tasty Arabic dishes; there are also a huge number of pastry shops where you can buy hot bread and biscuits. The delicious *sanioura* (a light crumbly biscuit) is a speciality of Sidon and the souqs are also famous for producing orange-blossom water (see The Essence of Summer, p368).

MUSÉE DU SAVON (SOAP MUSEUM) متحف الصابون
Although Tripoli may take credit for being the centre of the traditional soap-making industry, Sidon has Lebanon's first **museum**

THE ESSENCE OF SUMMER

Distilled from the fragrant blossoms of the orange tree, orange-blossom water – along with rose-water – is a speciality of Sidon and it's well worth picking some up to take home while in town. It's said that their correct method of distillation was finally perfected in the 10th century by Avicenna, an Arab physician. Nowadays, both remain popular in the Middle East for enhancing numerous dishes, both sweet and savoury, and orange-blossom water is the defining ingredient in the misleadingly named popular local *digestif*, *café blanco* (orange-blossom water in boiling water).

The trick, in cooking, is to use the distillations sparingly – just a drop or two at a time – orange-blossom water being stronger in flavour than rose-water. Orange-blossom water is particularly yummy when added to fruit salads, salad dressings or Arabic rice dishes, while rose-water can give a delicate flavour to custards, pastries and halva. Both also make lovely cooling summer drinks: add a few drops to a sugar syrup, then stir them into iced water, cocktails or iced tea to conjure a taste of the Middle East wherever you are.

High-quality versions of both are made by Matbakh Saida, and sold in the Musée du Savon's attached café.

(Soap Museum; ☎ 733 353; Rue al-Moutran; entry free; ⊙ 9am-6pm Sat-Thu), courtesy of the Audi Foundation, dedicated to the craft. Located in the old city in the Khan al-Saboun, a 13th-century stone building adapted for use as a soap factory in the 19th century, it once produced soap to meet the needs of the hammams (bathhouses).

The well laid-out galleries and trilingual (Arabic, English, French) explanations take you through the entire soap-making process – referred to in the museum's brochure as 'saponification' – from the massive stone tub where the raw ingredients were mixed together to the shaping and cutting of the still-warm liquid.

The museum has a stylish café, which also sells books and locally produced treats such as figs in syrup, preserved goats cheese and orange-blossom water, and a boutique selling bath products that make great gifts.

DEBBANÉ PALACE

Created by the wealthy Debbané family, this interesting 18th-century **palace** (☎ 720 110; www.museumsaida.org; admission free; ⊙ 9am-6pm Sat-Thu) is tucked away in a narrow souq alleyway on your left as you head from the harbour road to the soap museum. It's well worth a look-in.

CASTLE OF ST LOUIS   قلعة المُعِزّ

The ruins of this once-impressive **castle** stand on a mound to the south of town. The present structure dates back to the Crusaders, who built on the site of an earlier

Fatimid fortress – as reflected in the local name, Qala'at al-Muizz (Fortress of Al-Muizz) after the Fatimid caliph Al-Muizz li-Din Allah, who fortified the site. The English–French name comes from Louis IX, who rebuilt and then occupied the fortress when he retook Sidon from the Ayyubids in 1253. After the Arabs retook the city it was restored, but it later suffered at the hands of the Mamluks. This, coupled with centuries of pilfering, has left the structure in poor condition.

The hill on which the castle is situated is thought to have been the ancient acropolis of Sidon. Archaeologists have uncovered remains of a theatre here, but the site remains largely unexcavated. There is a low wall, with an entrance gate, around the base of the hill. Since this entrance to the site is usually unlocked and unattended, it's generally possible just to wander in for a look around.

MUREX HILL

Just south of the Castle of St Louis is an artificial hill, **Murex Hill**, about 100m high and 50m long, partially covered by a cemetery. This is Sidon's ancient garbage dump, largely formed from the crushed remains of hundreds of thousands of murex shells, the by-product of the city's famed dye. It took 10,000 murex molluscs to make just one gram of purple dye which, in Roman times, was worth three times as much as gold when used on silk. Traces of the shells can be seen on the embankment heading south from the castle.

Sleeping

BUDGET

Hotel d'Orient (☎ 720 364; Rue Shakrieh; dm/s with fan US$5-7, d with fan US$10-12) Grim, grimy and with nothing but the price to recommend it, this is really only one for if you find yourself stuck in Sidon with only a few spare lira rattling in your pocket. It's on the right-hand side as you walk from the harbour to the soap museum: look for a faded 1st-floor sign.

MIDRANGE

Yacoub Hotel (☎ 737 733; Rue al-Moutran; s/d US$40/65; 🖭) Clean, quiet and comfortable, housed in a converted 200-year-old building, this is a great place to spend the night. You'll see it signposted off to the left on your way up from the harbour to the soap museum.

Al-Qualaa Hotel (☎ 734 777; www.alqualaa.com; s/d US$65/70; 🖭) Probably Sidon's best choice, this newly opened hotel in the thick of the seaside action, on the main road in front of the port, is in a beautifully restored building comprising a maze of antique-filled passageways and light, airy rooms, most with sea views.

Eating

Al-Qualaa Hotel (☎ 734 777; 🕒 8am-midnight) A rooftop café at the hotel serves nice mezze lunches and an additional terrace is the perfect location to enjoy a leisurely evening nargileh. It's a great place for soothing souq-aching feet.

Rest House (☎ 722 469/470; mezze LL4000, grills LL10,000; 🕒 11am-11pm) Sidon's upscale option is this government-owned venue, overlooking the Sea Castle. It's a restored Ottoman khan, with vaulted ceilings and inlaid marble and stonework. The shaded garden terrace is on the edge of the sea and has a nice view of Sidon's seafront. Food here is traditional Lebanese, with good mezze, seafood and Lebanese wine.

The best place for cheap eats is the stretch of felafel, seafood and mezze joints surrounding the Al-Qualaa Hotel on the seaside road, opposite the Sea Castle. A very popular local choice here is **Abou Ramy** (☎ 8am-9pm), though all the places offer comparable quality and prices and are packed at weekends. Wandering the souq, you'll also smell tempting, cinnamon-tinged aromas wafting from tiny eating establishments. Follow your nose to a cheap and delicious lunch in its atmospheric hidden alleyways.

If you want to sample *sanioura*, a speciality of Sidon, try **Patisserie Kanaan** (☎ 729 104; Saahat en-Nejmeh; 🕒 6am-11pm) a decent place for a rest and a cup of coffee.

Getting There & Away

Buses and service taxis from Beirut to Sidon leave from the Cola bus station (see p290). To Sidon, OCFTC buses (LL1000, one hour, every 10 minutes from 6am to 8pm daily) leave from the southwest side of the Cola roundabout. **Zantout** (in Beirut ☎ 03-223 414) also runs 14 express buses a day to/from Sidon (LL1500, 30 minutes, every hour from 7am to 8pm daily). Minibuses (without air-con) to/from Sidon cost LL1000 (LL1500 in the evening) and service taxis cost LL2500. Buses depart from the Lebanese Transport Office at Saahat en-Nejmeh, and service taxis from the service-taxi stand just across the roundabout.

A service taxi from Sidon to Tyre costs LL3500 and a minibus (leaving from Saahat en-Nejmeh) costs LL1000. The Zantout bus from Sidon to Tyre (LL750, one hour, around every hour from 6am to 7.30pm daily) leaves from the Lebanese Transport Office at the southern end of town on Rue Fakhreddine, the continuation of Rue Riad as-Solh, near the Castle of St Louis.

AROUND SIDON
Beach Clubs

Along the old coast road running between Beirut and Sidon are a number of wonderful beach clubs that make a welcome change from the capital's scene. All are equipped with pools, beach access – often involving real sand, a rarity in Beirut – and a variety of restaurants and bars. Unlike Beirut's beach clubs, many here don't charge an entry fee and most are open from 10am till late from around May to October. For full listings of all the possibilities for taking to the sands, go straight to the website Lebbeach (www.lebbeach.com), a site that tells you what's most sizzling on the beach scene. Three of the current best are listed below.

O Cap (☎ 07-990 780; www.ocaponline.com; 🕒 9am-late) Stylish and relaxed with a great Italian restaurant and good facilities for kids, this place is about 15km north of Sidon, in Rmeileh.

Oceana (☎ 03-998 080) Further north up the coast near Damour is this bigger beach

---

CHECKPOINT ETIQUETTE

Though you'll find Lebanese army checkpoints dotted throughout the country, there's a higher concentration in the historically trouble-ridden south. Generally, as a tourist, you'll be waved through with a nod and often even a smile, but make sure to always have your passport and car rental papers to hand in case they're requested.

As a general rule, always stop at the checkpoint and wait for the minuscule, almost imperceptible hand signal that serves to wave you through. If you don't, you'll probably be asked to reverse and try again – before being waved through anyway. Two other common-sense measures are to refrain from taking any photos in the area, and to switch on the car's interior light when passing checkpoints at night, especially when there are no street lights.

---

club, able to fit 2500 sunbathers into its pools, beaches and sun lounges. Frequently the scene of all-night parties, it's yet another of the places that Lebanon's young and beautiful come to be seen. Look for the road signs directing you there from the Beirut–Sidon highway.

Bamboo Bay (☎ 07-995 042; entry at weekends LL20,000) in Jiyyeh is another ultra-luxe beach resort with all the necessary ingredients for unwinding beneath the rays, including an extensive spa and good Mediterranean restaurant.

Temple of Echmoun   معبد أشمون

For a more cultural afternoon than hitting the southern sands, this Phoenician **temple** (admission free; ☯ 8am-dusk) is about 2km northeast of Sidon on the Nahr al-Awali. The whole area is filled with citrus orchards and the riverbanks are a favourite summer picnic spot with locals. The region has long been a fruit-growing area and the site of the temple is known as Boustan al-Sheikh (Garden of the Sheikh).

Echmoun was the principal god of the city of Sidon and was associated with healing. This is the only Phoenician site in Lebanon retaining more than its foundation walls and it requires a little imagination to picture it in its prime. Brochures are available at the site.

The temple complex was begun in the 7th century BC and the following centuries saw numerous additions to the basic building. Some of the ruined buildings, such as the Roman colonnade and the Byzantine church and mosaics, are far later than the original Phoenician temple and are an indication of how long the site retained its importance as a place of pilgrimage.

The legendary story of Echmoun closely follows that of Tammuz and Adonis. Echmoun began as a mortal youth from Berytus (Beirut). The goddess Astarte fell in love with him; to escape from her, he mutilated himself and died. Not to be thwarted, she brought him back to life in the form of a god, hence his story was linked to fertility and rebirth. He was still primarily a god of healing and is identified with the Greek Asklepios, the god of medicine, and the Roman Aesculapius. It is from the snake motif of Echmoun that we get the serpentine symbol of the medical profession; the image of a serpent coiled around a staff was found on a gold plaque at Echmoun.

The temple complex has a nearby water source for ritual ablutions. It was customary for people coming to the temple to bring a small statue with the name of the person who needed healing. Many of these votive statues depicted children and wonderful examples can be seen at the National Museum in Beirut (see p270).

Between the 6th and 4th centuries BC Sidon was known for its opulence, culture and industry. During this era, one of the rulers was Echmounazar II. His sarcophagus, discovered in 1858, had inscriptions on it relating that he and his mother, Amashtarte, built temples to the gods at Sidon, including the Temple of Echmoun. The sarcophagus is now in the Louvre in Paris.

Archaeologists rediscovered the temple built by Echmounazar II during the excavation of Boustan al-Sheikh earlier this century. It was destroyed by an earthquake around the middle of the 4th century BC. Although never rebuilt, the site retained its reputation as a place of healing and was used by both pagan and Christian pilgrims. The site remained popular until the 3rd century AD, though it was by that time in ruins.

As you enter the site, there is a **colonnade of shops** on the right that probably did a roaring trade selling souvenirs to pilgrims.

On the left are the remains of a **Byzantine church** just past what was a large courtyard with some very faded 3rd-century-BC **mosaics** showing the seasons. On the right is a **Roman processional stairway**, which leads to the upper levels of the site. The stairway was added in the 1st century AD. Also on the right is a **nymphaeum** with a fountain and niches containing statues of the nymphs.

Further along on the right is one of the most interesting artefacts, the **Throne of Astarte**, which is flanked by two sphinxes. The throne is carved from a solid block of granite and is in the Egyptian style. There is also a very worn **frieze** depicting a hunting scene.

GETTING THERE & AWAY
From Sidon you can take a taxi to the site (LL6000) or get a service taxi (LL1000) or minibus (LL500) to the turn-off on the highway at the funfair and then walk the 1.5km past orchards to the ruins.

Joun   جون
Joun is a large village in the midst of olive plantations above the river, Nahr al-Awali. Its claim to fame is that it was the home for many years of the famous traveller Lady Hester Stanhope (see The Antics of Lady Hester, below).

To reach her home, pass through the village and after about 2km turn left at the sign for the 'Stanhope Tyre Factory'; unsurprisingly, not one of Hester's own business concerns. Follow the road, bearing right at any forks, and eventually you will find yourself at the ruins of her once-substantial house. Fifty metres to the southwest was her tomb, which lay in the shade of an olive grove. Though the simple step-pyramid grave is no longer there, her final resting place remains a picturesque spot and is ideal for picnicking.

GETTING THERE & AWAY
Joun is about 15km northeast of Sidon but is tricky to reach without a car. Your only

---

THE ANTICS OF LADY HESTER
The Middle East has always attracted intrepid women explorers and adventurers, and Lady Hester Stanhope was one of the more extreme examples. She was born into an affluent but eccentric life in London in 1776, the daughter of the domineering Earl of Stanhope and Hester Pitt, sister of William Pitt, the future prime minister of England.

She grew up without a governess and later became close to her uncle, William Pitt. When he was appointed prime minister, she moved straight into 10 Downing Street alongside him to play political hostess. Her first love was Sir John Moore, who took Hester's favourite brother, James, to serve with him in Salamanca. Both were killed in action, and when her uncle also died, Hester was left homeless and broken-hearted.

To assuage her grief, Hester decided to travel abroad and in typical colonial fashion, she and her retinue travelled in luxury throughout the Middle East. Her greatest moment of glory was riding into Palmyra in Syria on an Arab stallion at the head of her travelling procession. For more on Lady Hester and Palmyra, see The Good Things in Life Aren't Free…, p206.

By the time Hester arrived in Joun, her name was known across the Arab world. Having installed herself as a guest in the house of a Christian merchant, she announced that she liked the house so much that she would stay there for the remainder of her days. When it became clear that she meant this literally, the merchant protested to the local emir; Hester wrote directly to the sultan in Constantinople, who wrote back 'Obey the Princess of Europe in everything'.

Once she possessed the Joun house, Lady Hester became increasingly eccentric, reportedly forsaking books, instead communing with the stars. Although greatly respected by local people, among whom she liberally distributed money until she bankrupted herself, she gradually became a recluse, only receiving a few European visitors who would wait at Sidon for word of whether she would see them. The poet Lamartine was one such visitor, as was the son of a childhood friend, Kinglake (author of *Eothen*), who reported that at their meeting, she was wearing a large turban of cashmere shawls and a flowing white robe.

When she died in 1839 she was totally alone and in debt. The British consul had to be sent to take care of her burial and her remains were hurriedly placed alongside those of a young officer in Napoleon's Imperial Guard – reputedly a former lover – in a grave behind her house.

other option is to arrange a taxi from Sidon; a return trip should cost around US$25.

Jezzine   جزّين
☎ 07 / pop 14,030

One of the South's most famous summer resorts and worth a few hours of wandering or waterfall-watching, particularly after the winter rains, Jezzine sits 950m up on the western slopes of Jebel Niha, 22km from Sidon and below one of the eastern Mediterranean's largest pine forests.

Known for its 40m-high waterfalls, cool summer temperatures and production of distinctive, hand-wrought cutlery and swords, the town has a long history, although most architectural remains have gone. One monument worth visiting is the **Farid Serhal Palace** (admission free; ✆ 10am-6pm Sun-Thu), an Ottoman-style building with lavish interiors and displays of antiquities. A new forest on the edge of town, inaugurated in April 2007, is home to 600 new budding cedar trees. If you're keen on investing in some new cutlery, which in traditional Jezzine style is colourful and bone-handled, drop in on **S&S Haddad** (☎ 03-683 369) on the main street.

In the valley below Jezzine is **Fakhreddine's Cave**, where Fakhreddine, like his father before him, hid from the Ottomans. His father eventually died there, but Fakhreddine was found and taken to Istanbul. Entrance to the cave is free and the site unguarded; ask a local for walking directions down from the town centre to the valley and the cave.

A good lunch option is **Rock Fall** (mezze from LL3500, mains from LL8000; ☎ 781 041), open all day, which serves up traditional Lebanese food and tasty mezze right next to the waterfalls.

To get to Jezzine, take a service taxi (LL3500) or taxi (LL9000) from Sidon.

TYRE (SOUR)   صور
☎ 07 / pop 142,755

Tyre, 81km from Beirut, has a long and colourful history. Suffering dreadfully during the civil war and from Israeli incursions, the city remains full of Unifil troops, more than 13,000 of whom are stationed throughout the South. Predominantly Shiite like most of the South, you'll probably notice, on the outlying roads toward the city centre, scores of posters depicting Hassan Nasrallah, the Shiite cleric and Secretary-General of Hezbollah (see Who is Hassan Nasrallah?, p374), and Iranian clerics and leaders including the Ayatollah Khomeini.

Tyre, like much of the South, has traditionally met with indifference at the hands of Beirut's Maronite power brokers. Nevertheless, determined to override its troubles, you'll find the people warm and welcoming and the city definitely warrants a visit – if only a day trip from Beirut – for its souqs and wealth of Unesco World Heritage-listed Roman remains.

History

Tyre's origins date back to around the 3rd millennium BC, when the original founders are thought to have come from Sidon to establish a new port city. Tyre fell under the supremacy of the pharaohs under the 18th Egyptian dynasty, from the 17th to 13th centuries BC benefiting from Egypt's protection and prospering commercially.

Towards the end of the 2nd millennium BC, Tyre became a kingdom ruled by Abibaal. His son, Hiram I, ascended the throne in 969 BC and forged close relations with the Hebrew kings Solomon and David. Hiram sent cedar wood and skilled workers to help construct the famed temple in Jerusalem, as well as large amounts of gold. In return he received a district in Galilee that included 20 towns.

Under Hiram's reign, Tyre flourished. Hiram changed the layout of the city – he joined the offshore island (the older part of the city) with another small island and linked it to the mainland via a narrow causeway, and his ties with King Solomon helped develop trade with Arabia and North and East Africa. Such was Hiram's success that the Mediterranean Sea itself became known as 'the Tyrian Sea', and Tyre its most important city.

After Hiram's 34-year reign ended, however, Tyre fell into bloody revolution, even as it continued to expand its trading links. The city paid tribute to the Assyrians but remained close to the Israelites and was ruled by a succession of kings. The most famous woman of ancient Tyrian legend was Princess Elissa, also known as Dido. Embroiled in a plot to take power, when it became clear that she'd failed Dido seized a fleet of ships and sailed for North Africa. She founded a new port on the ruins of

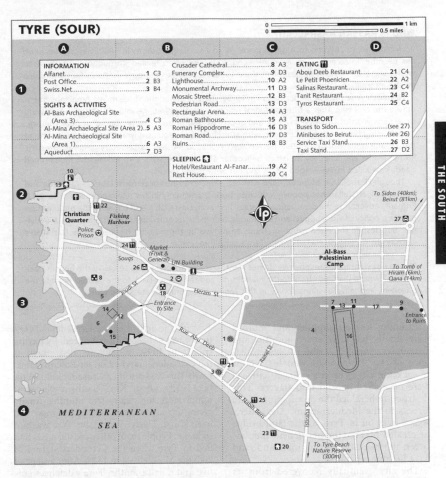

TYRE (SOUR)

0   1 km
0   0.5 miles

INFORMATION
Alfanet..................................**1** C3
Post Office............................**2** B3
Swiss.Net.............................**3** B4

SIGHTS & ACTIVITIES
Al-Bass Archaeological Site
(Area 3)...............................**4** C3
Al-Mina Archaelogical Site (Area 2)..**5** A3
Al-Mina Archaeological Site
(Area 1)...............................**6** A3
Aqueduct..............................**7** D3

Crusader Cathedral.................**8** A3
Funerary Complex..................**9** D3
Lighthouse...........................**10** A2
Monumental Archway.............**11** D3
Mosaic Street........................**12** B3
Pedestrian Road....................**13** D3
Rectangular Arena.................**14** A3
Roman Bathhouse..................**15** A3
Roman Hippodrome...............**16** D3
Roman Road.........................**17** D3
Ruins...................................**18** B3

SLEEPING 🏠
Hotel/Restaurant Al-Fanar........**19** A2
Rest House...........................**20** C4

EATING 🍴
Abou Deeb Restaurant............**21** C4
Le Petit Phoenicien.................**22** A2
Salinas Restaurant.................**23** C4
Tanit Restaurant....................**24** B2
Tyros Restaurant....................**25** C4

TRANSPORT
Buses to Sidon......................(see 27)
Minibuses to Beirut................(see 26)
Service Taxi Stand..................**26** B3
Taxi Stand............................**27** D2

THE SOUTH

Kambeh, which became known in time as Carthage, near modern-day Tunis. This became the seat of the Carthaginian empire.

The rise of Carthage gradually saw a corresponding fall in Tyre's fortunes. Weakened as a power, the Tyrians sued for peace when the Assyrians conquered the Levant and became their vassal state, but when Assyria's power weakened, Tyre rebelled against its overlords. Assyrian attempts to keep Tyre in line led to periods of war throughout the 7th and 6th centuries BC.

With the fall of the Assyrians in 612 BC, Tyre was peacefully controlled by the Neo-Babylonians until 586 BC, when it once again rebelled, leading to a 13-year siege by the Babylonian king, Nebuchadnezzar.

The inhabitants stood firm behind the high walls of the island-city and the siege failed.

More successful, however, was the campaign of Alexander the Great. In 332 BC he marched along coastal Phoenicia exacting tribute from all its city-states. Tyre, in time-honoured tradition, resisted and prepared for a long siege. The city was considered impregnable, but Alexander began building a sea bridge to reach the city, under a constant hail of missiles from the Tyrians. Meanwhile, on the mainland, Alexander's engineers were constructing 20-storey siege towers, the tallest ever used in the history of war. After several months these great war machines lumbered across the land bridge and the battle for Tyre began in earnest.

WHO IS HASSAN NASRALLAH?

Born ninth of 10 children to a greengrocer in an East Beirut suburb in 1960, Hassan Nasrallah has become, in recent years, a figure recognised, and often reviled, throughout the Western world. Secretary-General of Hezbollah since 1992, he provides the organisation's face and voice on the international arena.

Nasrallah's rise to prominence began in 1975, when he joined the Shiite militia Amal movement during the civil war. After a brief period of religious study in Iraq, he joined Hezbollah following Israel's invasion of Lebanon in 1982 and soon became popular for his brand of fiery rhetoric, interspersing his activities in Lebanon with stretches of religious study and periods representing the organisation in Iran. In 1992 he replaced Abbas al-Musawi as secretary-general, after the former leader was killed by an Israeli helicopter attack. Nasrallah's own eldest son, Muhammad Haadi, was killed in 1997, aged 18, in combat with Israeli forces.

Though Hezbollah is often branded with the same extremist or terrorist label as Al-Qaeda and the Taliban, Nasrallah has publicly criticised both, particularly in his televised reaction to 9/11. Primarily advocating the destruction of Israel, however, Nasrallah's lead has seen the organisation pursue a policy of kidnappings and bombings, alongside its nonviolent political and social activities. But despite the often brutal methods employed by those under his leadership, Nasrallah's website (http://english.wa3ad.org/) offers a simple message:

'We do not want to kill anyone. We do not want to throw anyone in the sea. Give the houses back to their owners, the fields back to their landlords, and the homes back to the people. Release the prisoners, and leave us alone to live in this region in security, peace and dignity.'

Running low on supplies and morale, Tyre finally fell after seven months and Alexander, enraged at the dogged resistance of the Tyrians, allowed his troops to sack the city. The city's 30,000 citizens were massacred or sold into slavery. This destruction heralded the domination of the Greeks in the Mediterranean. Alexander's legacy lives on in Tyre, as the land bridge he created became the permanent link between the old city and the mainland, and Tyre became a peninsula.

The city eventually recovered from its devastation and, after a period of Seleucid rule following Alexander's death, became autonomous in 126 BC. In 64 BC, Tyre became a Roman province, then the capital of the Roman province of Syria-Phoenicia.

Later Tyre became one of the first Lebanese towns to adopt Christianity and was the seat of an archbishopric, with 14 bishoprics under its control. In the Byzantine period, flourishing silk, glass and murex industries, producing the prized purple dye, saw the city prosper.

The Arabs took the city in AD 635, and its prosperity continued. The Umayyad caliph, Mu'awiyah, transformed the city into a naval base and it was from here that the first Arab fleet set sail to conquer Cyprus.

With the arrival of the Crusaders, Tyre's future was to become less assured. By paying tribute in 1099, the city avoided attack as the Crusaders marched on Jerusalem. It narrowly survived another Crusader encounter (1111–12), when King Baldwin placed it under siege for nearly five months, finally giving up after some 2000 of his men had been killed. Twelve years later Tyre was not so lucky. People from other coastal cities had fled to Tyre when the Crusaders started to take the Middle East in 1124. After a siege of five and a half months, Tyre's defences collapsed and the Christian army occupied city and the surrounding fertile land.

The Crusaders rebuilt the defensive walls and Tyre remained in Crusader hands for 167 years, until the Mamluk army of Al-Malik al-Ashraf retook the city in 1291. At the start of the 17th century, Fakhreddine attempted to rebuild and revitalise Tyre, but without much success. Following the fall of the Ottoman Empire, Tyre was included in the French Mandate of Greater Lebanon, and then incorporated into the Lebanese republic.

Once the State of Israel was established in 1948, Tyre's precarious position close to the sealed border further marginalised the city, which was already sidelined by Beirut and Sidon. Along with the rest of the South it suffered greatly during the drawn-out civil war, and Israel's long occupation of the adjacent border area left the city depressed long after the 1991 cease-fire. In recent years, the city has slowly begun to recover, but it suffered further setbacks in 2006 when the summer war between Israel and Hezbollah wrought new damage and left Beirutis – who, until then, were beginning to repopulate its hotels, beaches and restaurants – once again afraid to venture so far south. Currently Tyre is in the midst of yet another period of reinvention and renewal, attempting to struggle back to its feet, as it has done – successfully – for centuries.

Orientation
The old part of Tyre lies on the peninsula jutting out into the sea, covering a relatively small area. The modern town is on the left-hand side as you arrive from Beirut. The coastal route goes all the way to Tyre's picturesque old port, around which are a few cafés and restaurants. Behind the port is the Christian quarter, with its tiny alleys and old houses around shaded courtyards.

To the left of the port the road forks southwards and goes around the excavation site of one of the Roman archaeological sites. There are several streets running parallel between the northern and southern coastal roads, and that's where you'll find banks, moneychangers, sandwich stalls, travel agencies and the souq.

Information
INTERNET ACCESS
Alfanet (☎ 347 047; off Rue Abu Deeb; per hr LL1500; ☯ 10.30am-1am) Just north of the main roundabout, a reliable option for checking your email.
Swiss.Net (☎ 03-446 154; Rue Nabih Berri; per hr LL1000; ☯ 9am-midnight)

MONEY
There are banks and ATMs clustered around the service-taxi stand in the town centre.

POST
Post office (☎ 740 565; ☯ 7.30am-5pm Mon-Fri, 8am-1pm Sat) Near the service-taxi stand.

Sights
ARCHAEOLOGICAL SITES
In 1984 Tyre was declared a World Heritage site by Unesco in the hope of halting the

damage being done to archaeological remains by a combination of hasty urban development and years of conflict. There are three sites within the city: Al-Mina (Areas 1 and 2), on the south side of the city, Al-Bass (Area 3), on the original mainland section, and a medieval site in the centre of town. It's well worth taking a guide at the entrance to one of the sites, who'll bring the ruins to life with their specialised knowledge for around LL10,000 to LL15,000 or LL20,000 for larger groups.

Al-Mina Archaeological Site
In an impressive setting leading down to the ancient Egyptian (south) harbour, **Al-Mina excavations** (Areas 1 & 2; adult/child LL6000/3500; ☯ 8.30am-30 min before sunset) incorporate remains of Roman and Byzantine Tyre. Upon entering, a double line of columns to the right is thought to be part of the **agora** (market place). Further down is a long **colonnaded road** leading directly to what was the southern harbour. The marble sections of the pavement date back to the Roman era, while the black-and-white **mosaic street** is Byzantine. To the right of the road, below a modern cemetery, are the remains of an unusual **rectangular arena**, with five rows of terraced seating cut in to limestone. In the centre was a pool that may have been used for some kind of spectator water sport.

Beside the arena, and covering the area heading south towards the harbour, was the settlement's residential quarter. The remains are of small rooms, some of which have mosaic paving.

Across the colonnaded main road is the ruin of an extensive **Roman bathhouse**. Measuring some 40m by 30m, the complex did not fare well during the civil war. However, you can still see the vaulted mud-brick basement and several rows of stone discs, which were used to support a hypocaust (raised floor heated by hot air flowing underneath).

Crusader Cathedral
About a five-minute walk to the north of Al-Mina site, the remains of the **Holy Cross Cathedral** can be seen from the road. Foundations and granite columns are all that remain of the 12th-century building, giving scant indication of its importance in Crusader times. Beneath and around the cathedral is a network of Roman and Byzantine roads and

other buildings, one of which may have been the original temple of Melkart, the ancient god of the city.

Al-Bass Archaeological Site

On the landward side of Tyre, about 20 minutes on foot from the other sites, is the enormous **Al-Bass site** (Area 3; adult/student & child LL6000/3500; ☽ 8.30am-30 min before sunset). A colonnaded east–west road, possibly a continuation of the road at Al-Mina site, takes you through a vast **funerary complex** containing dozens of highly decorated marble and stone sarcophagi. The more elaborate have reliefs depicting scenes from Greek mythology and Homeric epics. Most are from the 2nd and 3rd century AD, but some date back as far as the 2nd century BC, and there are Byzantine coffins from as late as the 6th century.

A huge, triple-bay **monumental archway** stands further along the colonnaded street. Originally the gateway to the Roman town, it dates to the 2nd century AD. Behind it, to the south of the road, are traces of the city's old **aqueduct**, which brought water from Ras al-Ain, 6km south of Tyre. According to travellers' accounts, it was almost intact during the 19th century, but it did not fare so well in the 20th century.

Beyond the arch is the largest and best-preserved **Roman hippodrome** in the world. The partly reconstructed hippodrome is 480m long and once seated some 20,000 spectators. It was used for very popular and dangerous chariot races. *Metae* (turning stones), which you can still see, marked each end of the long, narrow course. The tight, high-speed turns at the *metae* were the most exciting part of the race and often produced dramatic spills and collisions.

FISHING HARBOUR & SOUQS

Small, but bustling with activity, the **fishing harbour** is the most picturesque part of Tyre, with its brightly coloured wooden boats and old-fashioned boat repair shops. There are also a couple of fish restaurants and cafés that overlook the water and make a good vantage point for watching the scene.

Behind them, running from east to west, lie Tyre's Ottoman-era **souqs**, which aren't as extensive as those of Sidon and Tripoli, but are still lively and interesting to explore.

As you walk around the northern side of the harbour, you come to the city's **Christian quarter**, where there are six churches (one ruined) reflecting Lebanon's multitude of Christian denominations. They are surrounded by narrow, winding residential streets, some lined with old houses, and make for a pleasant wander. Heading south, past the **lighthouse**, there are fantastic views of the sea.

TYRE BEACH NATURE RESERVE

Established in 1998, this small reserve – cut in half by the Rachidiye refugee camp – is an important sanctuary for birds, endangered turtles, bats and other wildlife, as well as containing a beautiful stretch of golden sandy beach.

The reserve is made up of two 'zones': the conservation area, which is open to the public 8am to 5pm every day except Sundays, and the recreation area, open all the time. There is no entrance fee, but a donation is highly appreciated and goes towards continuing the reserve's valuable work.

For more information on the reserve, including hiking and route maps, visit www .destinationlebanon.gov.lb and follow the links to Tyre coast.

Activities

SWIMMING

One of the best places to go for a dip is at the Rest House (see opposite), whose sandy beach offers kayaking and surfing for those not content to simply laze on the sands.

Near the Rest House, the northern portion of the **Tyre Beach Nature Reserve** is open to the public for swimming.

Festivals & Events

The annual **Tyre Festival** (☎ 791 252; www .tyrefestival.com) is held (in stable years) in late July/early August at Al-Bass archaeological site and includes a mix of local and international singers, artists and musicians. If you're in Tyre at the beginning of the Islamic year for **Ashura** (see Islamic Religious Holidays, p231) you can witness the Shiites mourning the death of Imam Hussein ibn Ali over a 10-day period that culminates in a procession.

Sleeping

Though Tyre has a couple of midrange hotel options, they're not really up to much, and it's currently best to either go for the budget or the top-end options listed below.

BUDGET

Hotel/Restaurant al-Fanar (☎ 741 111; www.alfanarre sort.com; d US$40, with sea views US$50, incl breakfast) Run by a friendly family, al-Fanar's location right on the edge of the sea near the lighthouse (*al-fanar* is Arabic for lighthouse) is hard to beat. It has a cute little pub and a decent restaurant dishing up homemade food and fish dishes. Good discounts can be negotiated out of the summer season (October to May).

TOP END

Rest House (☎ 742 000/740 667; www.resthouse -tyr.com.lb; d/ste US$75/110, with sea view US$100/130, incl breakfast; ✷ ☒) A light and airy luxury hotel, its chalet-style rooms are popular – in good years – at weekends with city-dwellers down from Beirut. With a nice beach and pool, it makes a relaxing place to return to after tramping the ruins all day.

Eating

There is a fair choice of restaurants in Tyre and, despite its large Shiite population, alcohol is served at all but the budget options.

The cheaper joints are mostly clustered on or near the roundabout on Rue Abu Deeb: follow your nose – and the local crowds – to find the favourite of the moment. The perenially popular Abou Deeb Restaurant dominates the roundabout and serves tasty, filling felafels (LL1200) and shwarmas (LL2000).

Le Petit Phoenicien (☎ 740 564; Old Port; mezze LL3000-5000, fish LL40,000-70,000; ✆ noon-11pm winter, noon-2am summer) Also known locally as 'Hadeed', after the family that owns and runs it, this is considered the best place for seafood in Tyre. With a nice location overlooking the water and friendly staff, it's

a great place to linger over a long, languid lunch while watching the fishing boats. Along the same lines, though without the sea view, the Salinas restaurant, just next to Rest House, comes highly recommended by locals.

Tanit Restaurant (☎ 347 539; mezze LL4000, grills LL15,000; ✆ 10am-late) Just around the corner from the port, both the restaurant and its bar are very popular with locals and off-duty Unifil troops. It serves up an eclectic range of cuisine, from Chinese stir-fry to steak and salads.

Tyros Restaurant (☎ 741 027; Rue Nabih Berri; mezze LL4500, grills LL6000-7500; ✆ 8am-late) This is a huge place that's extremely popular with locals, especially on weekends when it's advisable to drop in during the afternoon to book a good table in advance. It has a great atmosphere, the food is delicious and there's frequently live classical Arabic music on Saturday nights.

Getting There & Away

From Beirut, microbuses (LL2000, after 8pm LL3000) are the fastest direct option between Beirut and Tyre. Depending on traffic, they take between one and two hours and leave every 15 minutes or so from around 7am to 9pm. Large minibuses also ply the Tyre to Beirut route, depending on demand (LL2000 to LL3000, one to two hours, 6am to 8pm).

The first bus from Tyre to Sidon (LL1500, 30 to 45 minutes) leaves at 6am daily from the roundabout north of the entrance to the Al-Bass site. The last leaves at 8pm.

A service taxi from Beirut's Cola transport hub costs around LL7000. From Sidon, a service taxi will cost LL4000.

QANA'S TRAGEDIES

Sadly, Qana is best known not for its Biblical debate but for its frontline position, 12km north of the Israeli border, and for two incidents, a decade apart, in which Israeli Defense Force troops were charged with causing tragic civilian deaths.

The first incident took place on 18 April 1996, during Israel's Operation Grapes of Wrath, when a Unifil compound in the village was shelled by Israeli artillery. Reports indicated that 106 civilians – who had taken refuge there from the heavy fighting outside – were killed and another 116, along with four Unifil soldiers, injured.

The second occurred on 30 July 2006, when Israeli air strikes hit a civilian building. Human Rights Watch stated, following the incident, that 28 people were confirmed killed – of them, 16 were children who were sheltering in a basement from air strikes. Thirteen more were categorised as missing.

ACTION AGAINST LAND MINES

The south is scattered with unexploded ordnance of all kinds, including land mines and cluster bombs dropped by Israel, which have so far killed or seriously injured more than 200 civilians.

Cluster bombs, when dropped or fired, disperse hundreds of small 'bomblets' randomly over a large area which, according to Human Rights Watch, linger unexploded on the ground, with the same deadly threat as land mines, for many years. Lebanon is not the only country to be affected by this outfall of war: the group estimates that dozens of people in Southeast Asia die or are maimed every year by cluster bombs distributed by US troops during the 1960s and 1970s.

No one knows the exact amount of ordnance left behind in the south in the aftermath of 2006, but the UN Mine Action Coordination Centre (UNMACC) states that 800 separate cluster bomb sites have been identified. By November 2006, the Mine Action Coordination Centre, in association with Unifil and the Lebanese Armed Forces, had managed to locate and safely detonate 58,000 bomblets. They estimated that one million unexploded bomblets – out of an estimated total of around four million fired – remained to be cleared. Human Rights Watch said 90% of these were fired during the final 72 hours of the war.

Despite the efforts of various teams working to clear the area, the cluster bomb threat remains. In November 2007, the winter storms saw huge hailstones hitting the ground near the village of Marjeyun, detonating a number of hidden cluster bombs in the area.

Alongside the cluster bomb threat, UNMACC estimates that there are another roughly 15,300 items of unexploded ordnance on the ground in southern Lebanon, including air-delivered rockets and air-dropped bombs of between 220kg and 900kg.

For more information on the current situation in the region, visit the Mine Action website at www.maccsl.org.

AROUND TYRE

Visiting the area around Tyre may not always be possible, depending on the security situation. Ask the Lebanese soldiers at the frequent checkpoints, or check with your hotel, Unifil staff or locals in Tyre for up-to-date advice.

Tomb of Hiram   قبر أحيرام

Around 6km southeast of Tyre, on the road to Qana, is a huge limestone tomb with a large pyramid-shaped top, rising to an overall height of almost 6m. Although some scholars contend that it dates back to midway through the 1st millennium BC, most likely to the Persian period (525–332 BC), it is locally known as Qabr Hiram, and has traditionally been associated with Hiram, the famous king of Tyre, who ruled some 500 years earlier.

Below the sarcophagus are large stone steps (now blocked) and a rock-cut cave, which were first discovered by the French theologist and historian Ernest Renan. When he started excavations at the foot of the tomb in the mid-19th century, he found an even earlier staircase connected to the mausoleum's foundations. There are other signs of tombs in the area as well as a sanctuary.

Qana   قانا

This small **Shiite village**, 14km southeast of Tyre, was tragically catapulted into international consciousness in 1996 for the Israeli massacre of civilians and UN soldiers sheltering at a base here (see Qana's Tragedies, p377).

The village is at the centre of a scholarly debate as to whether it's in fact the biblical Cana, where Jesus performed his first miracle of turning water into wine. Until recently it was assumed that the Israeli village of Kefr Kenna was the site of biblical Cana, but the 4th-century historian Eusebius seems to support that Cana was near Sidon, as do the 3rd-century writings of St Jerome. Further proof for the claim is centred on early Christian **rock carvings** and a grotto 1km outside the village. The worn carvings depict 13 figures, said by proponents of the Qana-as-Cana position to be Jesus and his disciples. The cave, just below the carvings, could possibly be where he and his followers hid from persecution. Elsewhere in the village, large basins have been excavated and are said to have contained the water that was transformed into wine. Without more definitive proof no doubt the debate will continue, but the site is worth a visit.

To reach the carvings, go down the steep path next to the school, about 1km before the village (if you're coming from the Tomb of Hiram). The spot is marked by a modern, white-marble stone with black Arabic script. The track leads into a deep valley and it is a five-minute walk down to the grotto and carvings. The site is not supervised, so you can visit any time. The stone basins are between two back gardens of village houses, and you will need to ask the villagers (who are usually only too happy to help) for directions, or get your taxi driver to show you.

GETTING THERE & AWAY
You can take a service taxi from Tyre to Qana (LL2500) but they aren't frequent. A taxi from Tyre is about LL8000; LL10,000 for a return trip. The memorial to the bombing victims is at the UN base, 2km beyond the town.

THE SOUTH

Lebanon Directory

CONTENTS

This directory contains information specific to Lebanon; for more general information refer to the Syria Directory (p226).

ACCOMMODATION

All the accommodation options listed for Lebanon have been divided into budget, midrange and top-end categories; budget accommodation comes in at under US$40 per double room, midrange between US$40 and US$90, and top end at $90 and above. Prices are quoted for a room in high season, from around June to September, except for ski resort regions, where the prices represent rooms in ski season, between December and March. Prices are listed in US dollars or in Lebanese lira (LL), depending on which is used by the establishment itself.

During festival and holiday periods such as Christmas, Easter and Eid al-Fitr, and throughout school summer holidays, room prices can rise by 50% or more, as Lebanon is swamped with returning expats and partying Gulf Arabs. It's worthwhile booking well in advance during these times, especially for Beirut's budget options, as they tend to fill up fast. See Holidays section for Syria (p231) and Lebanon (p385) for more details. During the low season – roughly October to May – prices can fall by 40%, and similarly in high season if the security situation is shaky. Even in high season, it's always worth asking about discounts on stays of more than two nights – competition between hotels in Beirut, particularly in the midrange and top-end categories, is fierce, meaning that you're often in a strong position to bargain.

It's important to remember that outside summer, many of Lebanon's summer hotspots shut up shop. On one hand, this can mean that only limited accommodation is available; on the other, that you'll likely get terrific service and good prices, since hotels won't be rushed off their feet. If in doubt, call in advance to check whether the place you're heading for is open.

Camping

The concept of camping in Lebanon is very slowly starting to grow in popularity. Still, there are very few camping options outside summer camps for children, or camping trips laid on for organised groups. For independent camping, there are just two choices: Camping Amchit Les Colombes (p311), a few miles north of Byblos, with pretty basic facilities but a good position overlooking the sea; and La Reserve (p316), a resort with its own relatively luxurious tents in a gorgeous location high up above the Adonis Valley, close to the Afqa Grotto.

Hostels

A great alternative to budget hotels, worth exploring especially if you're heading off the beaten track, is Lebanon's network of hos-

tels. The **Lebanese Youth Hostel Federation** (www
.lyhf.org) lists nine hostels serving the country
from north to south, though there is no hostel in Beirut itself. Most are situated in small
rural villages, which you might otherwise
miss out on your travels, and have beds for
US$10 to US$15 per person, per night.

Hotels

BUDGET

In general, Lebanon isn't big on budget
hotel accommodation; even in Beirut,
there are few budget places and most have
only a handful of rooms. Budget lodgings
have also suffered the brunt of Lebanon's
recent upheavals – which kept large numbers of tourists and travellers away – and
several old, established places have sadly
closed down.

This means that budget stays require a
little extra planning and it might be necessary to take day trips to destinations where
budget accommodation is scarce. Luckily,
given Lebanon's diminutive size, this is easily done: few places are more than two or
three hours drive from Beirut, traffic and
mode of transport permitting.

When choosing a budget hotel, keep in
mind the season in which you're travelling.
If it's summer, check the room has a fan
or air-conditioning, especially on the coast
where humidity can be extremely high and
temperatures unrelenting. Likewise, check
that your room has some form of heating
if you're travelling in winter, when even
the lower regions are chilly in the mornings
and evenings.

MIDRANGE

Beirut, in particular, has lots of midrange
hotels, most situated in the Hamra area,
which offer good value, a central location,
and sometimes even a small swimming
pool on the roof. Outside Beirut, midrange
hotels can vary quite wildly in terms of facilities, so check exactly what you're being
offered – in terms of air-con, satellite TV,
heating or bathroom facilities – before accepting a room.

The very best midrange option in Lebanon can be arranged through L'Hote Libanais (p281), a Beirut-based organisation
supplying quality B&B accommodation in
real Lebanese family homes and tiny, characterful inns.

TOP END

Generic top-end hotel chains swamp Beirut, with all the bells and whistles you'd
expect from international luxury brands. In
other parts of the country, what you'd wish
for from a top-end hotel might not be exactly what you get and you may find yourself disappointed with what's on offer. Most
notably, swimming pools – even indoor
ones – may be closed in low season or if
there aren't many guests in residence, and
hotel breakfasts might not be up to much.
Two fabulous exceptions are Hotel Albergo
(p283) in Beirut and Hotel Via Mina (p334)
in Tripoli, two world-class boutique hotels
guaranteed to wow you with dozens of winning touches.

Rental Accommodation

Long-term rental apartments are available
in Beirut. You may see ads posted around
the American University of Beirut (AUB)
area (p271), often in English. Otherwise,
grab a copy of the Ministry of Tourism's *Hotels in Lebanon* guide, which has
furnished-apartment listings, or check the
classified section of the *Daily Star* newspaper. Many more reasonably priced places
fill up quickly at the beginning of university
semesters (February and October) and are
usually rented for their duration. Apartments are also available in coastal towns
north of Beirut, but are usually booked out
well in advance of every summer; similarly,
long-term ski resort rentals are usually
booked out for the winter season, particularly in places such as The Cedars (p342)
and Faraya Mzaar (p299).

ACTIVITIES

If you decide to go it alone on any land-
based activity, remember that there is a
very real danger of land mines in parts
of Lebanon, particularly in the south (for
more information see Staying Safe, p244).
Always seek local advice on the safety of
your intended route.

Caving

Lebanon has a number of spectacular caving
opportunities. The Jeita Grotto (p303) and
Afqa Grotto (p314) may be Lebanon's most
famous caverns but there are more than 400
other explored cavities throughout the country, including some holes with depths of up

to 602m – among the deepest in the Middle East. From small chambers in the rock to huge caverns, Lebanon's rugged mountains have enough crags and holes to keep most spelunkers happy for a very long time.

There are a few spelunking clubs in Lebanon, which organise trips throughout the country:

Association Libanaise d'Etudes Speleologique (ALES; www.alesliban.org, ales@alesliban.org; ☎ 03-666 469) Offers group trips into Lebanon's subterranean world, from beginners to advanced.

Groupe d'Etudes et de Recherches Souterraines au Liban (GERSL Caving Club in Lebanon; ☎ 03-275 353, 03-240 013) The group organises weekend expeditions from May to October.

Cycling

Though risking life and limb on two wheels in Beirut traffic might not be such a tempting thought, there are a few places in the country where cycling can be a pleasure, rather than an extreme activity. The Horsh Ehden Forest Nature Reserve (p339), Chouf Cedar Reserve (p323) and the Cedars (p342) are just some of the areas that are ideal for mountain biking.

Beirut by Bike (☎ 03-435 534) arranges bike tours around Beirut and elsewhere, as well as renting out bikes by the hour, day or week (p280). It's a good starting point for finding out more about cycling in Lebanon.

Ladies on Bikes (☎ 03-825 823) arranges night-time tours of the city, usually on Tuesday and Thursday evenings.

Blue Carrot Adventure Club (☎ 03-552 007; www .blue-carrot.com) organises mountain biking expeditions, along with hiking, snowshoeing, and a host of other adventurous activities.

If you decide to hit the road alone, remember that even outside the big cities Lebanese drivers aren't expecting cyclists around those hairpin mountain bends. Be highly vigilant, and don't cycle at night.

Paragliding

With its dramatic mountain scenery, Lebanon is prime paragliding territory and the sport is gradually being established here. The season is usually from May to October, depending on the weather, and the prime areas are The Cedars (p342) and Faraya Mzaar (p299).

Club Thermique (☎ 03-288 193/237; www.club thermique.com.lb), based in Ajaltoun, offers paragliding courses ranging from one to seven

days, as well as equipment rental, ballooning, snowboarding and 'eco' activities.

Skiing

Most of Lebanon's resorts are accessible on a day trip from Beirut and the ever fun-loving Lebanese ensure the après-ski scene is worth sampling. The season lasts from early December to April, depending on the snow. The mountains are relatively close to the sea, so the air around the slopes is humid. In the morning, when the air is coldest, this can mean icy conditions; by the afternoon, with the rise in temperature, the snow becomes wetter. If you're looking for good powder skiing, head straight for the Cedars (p342); otherwise, Faraya Mzaar (p299) is your best bet.

Cross-country skiing and snow-shoeing are growing in popularity and equipment can be rented at resorts. Most of Lebanon's trekking clubs also organise snow-shoeing day trips in winter. See Trekking (below) for more information.

Ski Lebanon (www.skileb.com) operates an absolutely fantastic website for all things ski-related in the country. You can book hotels, check out ski schools and get important tips, as well as information on snow conditions and snow-cams. For more details on ski resorts in Lebanon, see the individual boxed texts for Ski Facts: Qanat Bakiche & Zaarour (p298); Faraya Mzaar (p299); Laklouk (p316); and the Cedars (p342).

Trekking

Lebanon has fabulous trekking opportunities scattered through its mountains and gorges. There are well-maintained trails in Horsh Ehden Forest Nature Reserve (p339), the Chouf Cedar Reserve (p323), and along the Qadisha Valley floor (p344). The website for the **Lebanon Mountain Trail** (www.lebanon trail.org) has a great page of links to trekking organisations offering responsible trekking across the country; the three following listings are all excellent groups, operating with an 'eco' slant.

Esprit-Nomade (☎ 70-813 001; www.esprit-nomade .com) Arranges weekly hikes, treks and snow-shoeing, and promotes responsible ecotourism.

Lebanese Adventure (☎ 03-360 027, 03-213 300; www.lebanese-adventure.com) Runs outdoor activities throughout the country each weekend. Its moonlight hikes, with overnight camping, are especially memorable.

Liban Trek (☎ 01-329 975; www.libantrek.com) A well-established trekking club that arranges day and weekend treks throughout Lebanon. It also organises other mountain sports.

Water Sports

Much of Lebanon's swimming is from rocks or artificial platforms built out on jetties, since its sandy public beaches aren't currently well-maintained enough to recommend them.

The rocks, nevertheless, make for good snorkelling and there are often water-sports facilities at the private beach resorts. Water-skiing, jet-skiing and sailing are popular during summer and equipment can be rented from most resorts.

The Riviera Beach Club in Beirut offer swater-skiing in summer for the hefty sum of US$120 per hour.

There are good swimming pools at almost all the larger top-end hotels and resorts, and fantastic beach clubs dotted along the coastline. Expect to pay between US$10 and US$25 per person per day (unless you're staying at the resort), depending on the level of luxury. The best are in-and-around Beirut (p279), Byblos (p311) and Sidon (p369).

For surfers, Batroun (p313) is where you'll find the closest thing to a community of like-minded individuals. Surfers should check out www.wannasurf.com/spot /Middle_East/Lebanon/ for more information on surfing spots around the country, and windsurfers can log on to www.batroun windsurfers.cjb.net for details.

BUSINESS HOURS

Shops and private businesses in Lebanon are generally open from 9am to 6pm Monday to Friday, and 9am to mid-afternoon on Saturdays. Banks are open 8.30am to 2pm Monday to Friday, and 8.30am to noon on Saturdays. Post offices and government offices are open 8am to 5pm Monday to Friday, and 8am to 1.30pm on Saturdays.

Restaurants have no standard opening hours; in Beirut, many stay open all night. We've indicated opening hours, where possible, throughout the book.

CHILDREN

For general tips on travelling with children, see Children (p228) in the Syria Directory.

Sights & Activities

There are plenty of activities for children of all ages in Beirut and the surrounding area; see Beirut for Children (p280) for details. If you're planning on travelling country-wide with children, it's worth investing in *Family Fun in Lebanon* by Charlott Hamaoui, Sylvia Palamoudian and Dunia Gardner, which is available at most Beirut bookshops.

Ancient sites such as Baalbek (p357) and Aanjar (p351) are, to their detriment and children's delight, fairly bereft of railings, guards and 'keep off' signs, so children should have fun scrambling over ancient remains. Older kids, meanwhile, will probably enjoy wandering the souqs of Tripoli (p329) and Sidon (p367) just as much as their parents. Most of the country's nature reserves have easy marked trails, which little legs can manage.

For seasonal activities, many summer coastal beach clubs are well set up for children, with kids' pools, playgrounds and sometimes even dedicated kids' clubs available for visitors.

In winter, Ski Lebanon (see Skiing, opposite) offers ski day-trips from Beirut to Faraya Mzaar, including lunch and a full day of ski school, for seven- to 16-year olds.

CLIMATE

Given the diverse topography, it's not surprising that the weather here varies quite considerably from region to region. Broadly speaking, Lebanon has three different climate zones – the coastal strip, the mountains and the Bekaa Valley.

The coastal strip has cool, rainy winters (mid-December to February) and hot Mediterranean summers (June to September). The Mt Lebanon Range, stretching roughly the length of the country and including the climbable Jebel Sannine and Lebanon's highest peak, Qornet as-Sawda in the north, can concentrate the summer heat and humidity on the coast to a stifling degree. During the spring (March to May) and autumn (October until mid-December), the weather on the coast is warm and dry with occasional showers. October and April can see very heavy rainfall.

The mountains have a typical alpine climate; fresh breezes keep the summer heat at bay, which is why many people head to the mountains to escape the oppressive heat

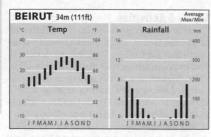

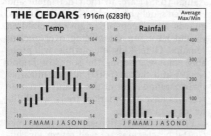

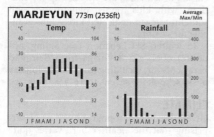

CUSTOMS

There is no problem bringing most items into Lebanon, such as cameras, videos or computers, and no censorship of books and magazines – though it's a sensible precaution not to bring with you any maps or material relating to Israel and the Palestinian Territories. Duty-free allowances are 400 cigarettes and one bottle of spirits or 200 cigarettes and two bottles of spirits.

DANGERS & ANNOYANCES

See Staying Safe (p244) for detailed information on safety concerns in Lebanon.

DISCOUNT CARDS

There are no discount cards for seniors in Lebanon. Student cards are of little use at archaeological sites and museums, unless you're Lebanese or under 12. If you do want to pursue a student discount at an archaeological site, it may be possible by applying direct to the Ministry of Tourism, who will grant you a special permit for entrance at a reduced price. Unless you're planning several successive visits to the same site, however, it's not worth the leg- and paper-work.

EMBASSIES & CONSULATES

See Embassies & Consulates (p230) in the Syria Directory for general information on what your embassy or consulate can – and can't – do for you.

EMBASSIES & CONSULATES IN LEBANON

Nationals of New Zealand should contact the UK embassy. Embassies and consulates in Lebanon include the following:

Australia (Map p275; ☎ 01-974 030; fax 974 029; Embassy Complex, Serail Hill, City Centre)

Canada (☎ 04-710 591, 713 900; Coolrite Bldg, Jal al-Dib)

Egypt (Map p265; ☎ 867 917; Rue Thomas Edison, Ramlet al-Bayda, Beirut)

France (Map p265; ☎ 01-420 000; Rue de Damas, Achrafiyeh, Beirut)

Germany (☎ 04-914 444; near Jesus & Mary School, Mataileb, Rabieh)

Italy (Map p275; ☎ 01-985 200/300; Place d'Etoile, Beirut)

Jordan (☎ 05-922 501/2; Rue Elias Helou, Baabda)

Netherlands (Map p277; ☎ 01-204 663; Netherlands Tower, Achrafiye, Beirut)

Spain (☎ 05-464 120/5; fax 05-464 030; Palace Chehab, Hadath)

Turkey (☎ 04-520 929, 412 080; Tobi Bldg, Rue 3, Zone II, Rabieh)

during the summer months. There is heavy winter snow, which lasts from December to May on the higher peaks. At certain times of year you can stand on the warm coast and look inland at snow-covered peaks.

The brochure clichés are true: it is indeed possible to go skiing in the morning and swimming in the afternoon, although few people actually do it. The Bekaa Valley has hot, dry summers and cold, dry winters with snow and frost. The valley is set between two parallel mountain ranges and the wind can blow fiercely, especially in winter.

COURSES

Except for language courses in Beirut (p279) and ski lessons in the ski resorts (see Skiing, p382), there are few courses designed for those not resident in Lebanon long-term.

UK (Map p275; ☎ 01-990 400; fax 990 420; Serail Hill, Downtown, Beirut)
USA (☎ 04-543 600, 542 600; fax 544 604; Rue Amin Gemayel, Awkar)

FESTIVALS & EVENTS
These days it seems that no large town in Lebanon is worth its salt without some sort of festival in one of its floodlit ancient sites. Many towns and villages also have their own small festivals, which can be anything from local fairs to folkloric performances, and are usually held during the summer months. See p246 for information on Lebanon's major festivals.

GAY & LESBIAN TRAVELLERS
There's a thriving, if clandestine, gay and lesbian scene in Lebanon, concentrated in Beirut. For more information see Gay & Lesbian Beirut, p288. Remember, however, that homosexuality is illegal under Lebanese law so discretion is advised, both in public and when checking into a double hotel room.

HOLIDAYS
Public Holidays
See p231 for details and dates of Islamic religious holidays. Following is a list of other holidays celebrated in Lebanon.
New Year's Day (1 January)
Feast of Saint Maroun (9 February)
Easter (March/April) The most important event on the Christian calendar, with Western and Orthodox Christians celebrating on different dates, which vary from year to year.
Labour Day (1 May)
Martyrs' Day (6 May)
Assumption (15 August)
All Saints' Day (1 November)
Independence Day (22 November)
Christmas Day (25 December)

INSURANCE
See the Syria Directory (p232) for tips on insurance matters.

INTERNET ACCESS
There are internet cafés in all Lebanese cities and in most smaller towns. Most charge between LL2000 and LL4000 per hour. Many regular cafés, restaurants and hotels now have wi-fi access, which is rarely free and mostly accessed through prepaid cards. See Internet Access (p268) in the Beirut chapter for more details.

If you're staying long-term, the country now has more than a dozen ISPs; here are three reputable ones:
Cyberia (☎ 01-744 101; www.cyberia.net.lb)
Inconet Data Management (IDM) (☎ 01-512 513; www.idm.net.lb)
Terranet (☎ 01-577 511; www.terra.net.lb)

LEGAL MATTERS
Drug smuggling, long a problem in Lebanon, has been heavily clamped down on and carrying any kind of narcotics (including marijuana/hash) is a foolish undertaking with a heavy jail sentence attached. Remember that if you do fall foul of the law, your embassy can do little to help other than contacting your relatives and recommending local lawyers.

MAPS
For details of city maps, see the Information sections in individual destination chapters.

There are few good road maps of Lebanon, a problem compounded by the fact that Lebanon's roads – both major and minor – aren't numbered, and there are few road signs, even on motorways. One of the better countrywide maps is the *Lebanon Tourist Map* published by Paravision. It has a scale of 1:200,000, costs around LL12,000 and is available from most Beirut bookshops.

To minimise guesswork along the way, employ the services of friendly locals at regular intervals, and take comfort in the fact that Lebanon's a small country – so you can never really go too far wrong.

MONEY
The currency in Lebanon is the Lebanese lira (LL), which has remained relatively stable over the last few years, with an exchange rate hovering at US$1 = LL1500.

Banknotes are of the following denominations: 1000, 5000, 10,000, 20,000, 50,000 and 100,000 and there are also LL250 and LL500 coins.

US dollars are widely accepted throughout the country, and higher-end establishments rarely quote prices in anything else.

For details of exchange rates see the inside front cover of this guide.

ATMs
There are ATMs throughout the country and all dispense cash in either US dollars

or Lebanese lira. As always, though, keep some extra cash with you as insurance.

Cash

If you're travelling with US dollars you only need to exchange a small amount into lira for tipping, service taxis etc. Try to stick to US$50 and US$20 notes, which are more readily accepted than larger denominations. A stock of US$1 bills is useful to have for tipping and small items. Note that change will usually be given in lira.

Most banks will exchange cash if it is in British pounds or US dollars. There are many banks in the capital and all but the smallest village has at least one bank.

There is no black market in Lebanon.

Credit Cards

Credit cards are accepted by almost all hotels of midrange and above, midrange restaurants, petrol stations and many shops. They may not be accepted by budget hotels and restaurants. Cash advances are easily available in most banks, although transactions are far quicker at ATMs. If you are planning on hiring a car remember that almost all reputable companies will insist on a credit card deposit.

International Transfers

There are Western Union offices that can arrange international transfers in almost all major towns in Lebanon. For more information, contact them at their headquarters in Beirut (☎ 01-391 000).

Moneychangers

There are many private exchanges on and around Rue Hamra in Beirut, and all the smaller towns have at least one exchange shop. You may find it a problem changing money in some of the smallest villages.

Before using moneychangers try to find out what the current exchange rates are. Either ask at a bank or check the previous day's closing exchange rates in the local newspapers. The rate you'll be offered will never be the same as the published rate, as it includes the moneychanger's commission, but you can always try to bargain with them to bring the rate closer to the published rate. If you're not happy with the rate offered by one moneychanger, try another. The commission varies from 3% to 5% for changing currency.

Tipping

It's usual practice to tip waiters, hotel porters, guides and Beirut's numerous parking valets: something around LL2000 or over, depending on the service, will always be appreciated. Waiters in restaurants generally receive an optional 10% tip – again, depending on the quality and quantity of their attention – but won't chase after you with rebukes if you leave less. Remember to check your restaurant bill before tipping, though, since some places add a 15% service charge automatically to the bill.

Travellers Cheques

Travellers cheques may be a smart way to change money, but they can be time-consuming, depending on the bank or currency exchange shop you find yourself in. Fees are usually around US$1 per US$50 of cheques.

PHOTOGRAPHY & VIDEO

For general photography tips, see the Photography & Video section (p233) in the Syria Directory.

Camera Equipment

There are plenty of shops selling memory cards and batteries for digital cameras all around Beirut, particularly along Rue Hamra. Outside Beirut and the larger cities you may have problems finding memory cards, though batteries (rarely rechargeable) are widely on sale everywhere. 1GB memory cards go for around US$25, while a pack of four AA batteries will cost roughly US$5.

Restrictions

You shouldn't have any problems taking photographs in Lebanon, with the exception of military areas. As always, when people are going to be featured in your photo, it's polite to ask first; when it comes to women and residents of conservative Muslim areas this is particularly important. If you happen to be near an army checkpoint, go up to the soldiers first and explain to them what it is you want to photograph – they usually won't object. Do not, however, try to take photos of the soldiers themselves, or military installations unless you've been given permission. If you offend they will not hesitate to ensure you wipe the images from your digital camera.

POST

Lebanon's postal service, **LibanPost** (www
.libanpost.com), is nowadays quite dependable.
Letters less than 20g in weight cost LL500
within Lebanon, LL1250 to the Middle East
and Cyprus, and LL1750 to everywhere else.
Delivery time to Europe or North America
is usually within seven to 10 days. You can
post them from the yellow tin boxes you'll
see on the street, often attached to buildings, but it's more reliable to send them
direct from the post office.

Packages weighing up to 30kg can be sent
from LibanPost offices: you'll just need to
sign a declaration form that gives the General Security forces the authority to open
and check the parcel. Many post offices also
offer a variety of other services, including
Western Union money transfers, sale of
prepaid cards for mobile and public tel-
ephones, faxing and photocopying.

Most Lebanese use courier services for
sending parcels: **DHL** (☎ 01/03-629 700; www.dhl
.com) has several offices in Beirut. A second
option is **Federal Express** (Map p275; ☎ 01-987
000; www.fedex.com/lb; Chaker Oueni Bldg, Riad al-Solh
Sq, Downtown, Beirut).

Receiving mail from around the world
generally takes several weeks, but Beirut's
LibanPost (Map p272; ☎ 01-344 706; 2nd fl, Matta Bldg,
Rue Makdissi, Hamra, Beirut) branch in Hamra has
a poste restante facility. If you know the
hotel in which you'll be staying and let the
desk staff know, most will keep hold of your
incoming mail for you.

SHOPPING

See Shopping (p289) in Beirut for information on the city's best shopping districts.
Outside Beirut, the best places for souvenirs
are the souqs of Tripoli (p329) and Sidon
(p367), and the shops in the old centre of
Byblos (p310).

SMOKING

Smoking is a lifestyle in Lebanon, and nonsmoking areas in restaurants, if they're
designated at all, still tend to experience
wafting smoke from the much larger smoking areas. Added to this, nargileh smoking
is incredibly popular – especially among
teenagers. If you find the often thick smoke
hanging over cafés and restaurants hard to
handle, it's best to eat before 9pm, when
most places will still be quiet and smoke-

free, and avoid the lunchtime rush between
around noon and 2pm.

SOLO TRAVELLERS

See the Syria Directory section on solo travellers (p235) for details.

TELEPHONE & FAX

The countrywide telephone codes are as
follows:

Beirut ☎ 01
Jounieh, Byblos and **Kesrouan** ☎ 09
Mount Lebanon (north) ☎ 04
Mount Lebanon (south) ☎ 05
North Lebanon ☎ 06
South Lebanon ☎ 07
Bekaa Valley ☎ 08
Mobile phones ☎ 03 or 70

If you're taking your mobile phone from
home along, many nowadays work on a
local Lebanese network, though you'll of
course pay heavily for the privilege of making and receiving calls, and sending text
messages.

Otherwise, it's a good idea to invest in
a prepaid calling card for both local and
international calls.

Cards come in two types: the Telecard
costs LL10,000 or LL30,000 and can be
used in the many card-operated telephone
booths on the city's streets. The alternative
is a prepaid Kalam card that costs LL15,000
or LL45,000 and allows you to make calls
from any phone, public or private, by using
a code. Cards can be bought from newsa-
gents, post offices, newspaper kiosks, or

CHANGING TELEPHONE NUMBERS

At the time of research, some telephone
numbers in various areas of Lebanon were
in the process of being changed. There appears to be no discernable pattern to the
changes: some numbers in some areas had
already changed, while their neighbours'
numbers remained the same.

We have included the newest phone numbers available where possible and have ex-
cluded the numbers of some establishments
whose numbers were likely to change in the
near future. If you find that you are unable
to get through, dial 120 from within Lebanon
to speak to a local operator.

anywhere an 'OGERO' sign is displayed. Local calls cost LL100 to a land line and LL300 to a mobile phone.

Unless you're planning on staying in Lebanon for a while, it's probably not worthwhile investing in a local pay-as-you-go mobile phone. There's quite a bit of bureaucracy involved and they can end up being pretty pricey, often between US$250 and US$300. If you're hiring a car, however, you can frequently rent mobile phones through the larger car-rental agencies. Phones usually cost about US$6 per day, plus a deposit and call charges.

Many LibanPost offices – as well as stationers and some internet cafés – offer fax services, as do all but the most budget hotels.

TIME

See the Time section (p236) in the Syrian Directory for details.

TOILETS

See the Toilets section (p236) in the Syria Directory for what to expect.

TOURIST INFORMATION

Beirut's main tourist office is a great starting point for countrywide information; see p269 for details.

Outside Beirut, the larger towns all have decent local tourist offices and can advise on festivals, events and security issues in the vicinity.

The Ministry of Tourism has an excellent website with a travel planner (www.destinationlebanon.gov.lb), while Getting Started in Lebanon (p247) lists other useful websites.

TRAVELLERS WITH DISABILITIES

Considering the number of people who were disabled during the civil war, it is curious that Lebanon is not more disabled-friendly.

People with disabilities are rarely seen on the street, which is not surprising given the difficulties of navigating the potholes, rubble and anarchic traffic. Buildings and archaeological sites do not have wheelchair ramps and bathrooms are generally not modified for access. The exception is the newly constructed inner city, which has Braille in lifts (elevators) and wide-access doors.

VISAS

All nationalities need a visa to enter Lebanon, though visa costs and requirements are frequently changing. For the most up-to-date information, go to the website of **Lebanon's General Security Office** (www.general-security.gov.lb). In an effort to encourage tourists back to Lebanon, tourist visas are currently free of charge.

Citizens of Jordan and Gulf Cooperation Council Countries (Kuwait, Saudi Arabia, United Arab Emirates, Qatar, Bahrain and Oman) are entitled to a free three-month visa at the airport.

Citizens of the countries below are entitled to a free one-month tourist visa, extendable to three months, issued at Beirut airport: Andorra, Antigua and Barbuda, Argentina, Armenia, Australia, Austria, Azerbaijan, The Bahamas, Barbados, Belarus, Belgium, Belize, Bhutan, Brazil, Bulgaria, Canada, Chile, China, Costa Rica, Croatia, Cyprus, Denmark, Estonia, Finland, France, Great Britain, Georgia, Germany, Greece, Hong Kong, Hungary, Iceland, Ireland, Italy, Japan, Kazakhstan, Kyrgyzstan, Latvia, Lithuania, Liechtenstein, Luxembourg, Macedonia, Macau, Malaysia, Malta, Mexico, Moldova, Monaco, The Netherlands, New Zealand, Norway, Palau, Panama, Peru, Poland, Portugal, Russia, Saint Kitts and Nevis, Samoa, San Marino, Singapore, Slovakia, Slovenia, South Korea, Spain, Sweden, Switzerland, Tajikistan, Trinidad and Tobago, Turkmenistan, Venezuela and Yugoslavia.

The same visa policy applies in principle at all Syrian-Lebanese border crossings, though visas may not always be issued free of charge (previous fees of LL50,000 may sometimes apply).

For other nationalities, visas can be obtained in advance at any Lebanese embassy or consulate; you'll need two passport-sized photographs and probably a letter of recommendation from your employer to say that you are returning to your job. Visas are usually issued the next day but can take longer.

If you're planning onward travel into Syria, it's crucial to note that you cannot get a visa to enter Syria from Lebanon. Only passport-holders from countries that have no Syrian consulate may obtain visas at the Syrian border, so if you want to travel overland, make sure you have a valid Syrian visa before you go to Lebanon.

If you have an Israeli stamp in your passport, or have stamps from Egyptian or Jordanian crossing points into Israel, you will be refused entry into Lebanon. For more information on entering Lebanon, see p390.

Visa Extensions

To extend your one-month visa to a three-month visa, you must go to the **General Security office** (Map p265; ☎ 1717, 01-429 060/061; Rue de Damas, Beirut; ☿ 8am-1pm Mon-Thu, 8-10am Fri, 8am-noon Sat, closed Sun) in Beirut at least a few days before your first month ends. Take with you a passport-sized photo, your passport, and photocopies of your passport ID page and the page where your entry visa was stamped.

WOMEN TRAVELLERS

Women travelling in Lebanon will notice a huge difference in attitudes towards them compared with most other parts of the Middle East, with the exception of Israel and the Palestinian Territories. In Beirut, less is definitely more in clothing terms, and it's common to see women in the most startlingly low-cut, figure-hugging combinations, even when loading up on supermarket groceries in the middle of the day. In make-up terms, though, more is usually not enough: Lebanese women enjoy being primped, preened and powdered to the hilt.

However, if you are travelling alone, you may want to be a little more restrained than your Lebanese sisters, even though you'll mostly find Lebanese men courteous and welcoming.

Generally, along the coast between Byblos and Sidon you can wear almost anything you like, and bikinis are standard issue at the beach. Outside the coastal strip – and especially in the more conservative or Muslim areas around Tripoli, Baalbek and Tyre – it's sensible to adopt a more conservative style of dress. If you are planning to visit a mosque, you'll need to make sure that your arms and legs are covered and that you take a headscarf with you. Some mosques provide women visitors with a black cloak at the door.

In the midrange and top-end hotels, security is usually very good and women need not be concerned about being hassled. In budget hotels it might be more of a problem, and it pays to remain vigilant – though there's no reason to be worried. As a rule, keep the door locked when you're alone inside your hotel or hostel room and take local advice on where, and where not, to walk alone in the evening.

In order to feel more secure, you can also consider only taking shared taxis in which another, local, woman passenger is already present.

For additional advice, see Tips for Women Travellers (p239.

WORK

Though Lebanon is a great place to live, with the economy in poor shape this is not the best time to look for work. Lebanese are highly educated and most speak at least two or three languages fluently, so competition is stiff: unless you're fluent in both French and Arabic, you're at a distinct disadvantage. English-language publications do sometimes need writers and copy editors: you should enquire with them directly (see p269 for details).

One option for those men and women of Letters is the **American University of Beirut** (AUB; Map p272; ☎ 01-340 460; fax 351 706; www.aub .edu; Rue Bliss, Beirut), as the language of instruction is English. For most faculty positions you need a PhD.

If you do have a job, work permits are not difficult to get, although your employer must prove that there is no Lebanese person capable of doing the job.

You need a health insurance policy that guarantees repatriation of your corpse should you die in Lebanon (presumably a war-time hangover), a letter from your employer (either in Lebanon or abroad) and roughly US$667 per year for both the work and residency permit.

Other options include coming in on a tourist visa and renewing it every three months, up to a maximum of four times. However, there are periodic crackdowns during which renewals are no longer issued, and customs and passport control check the number of stamps in your passport carefully upon arrival in the country.

Transport

GETTING THERE & AWAY

Heading to Syria and Lebanon is fairly straightforward, especially if you are coming from Europe or the Middle East where there are a range of airlines and a number of direct flights to both Damascus and Beirut. From other regions, flights again are fairly straightforward, just expect a couple of stops on the way. There is also the option, for those with a bit of time, of travelling overland.

ENTERING SYRIA & LEBANON
Entering both countries is very easy from a bureaucratic standpoint: all you need is a non-Israeli stamped valid passport and a valid visa. Syria and Lebanon refuse to admit anyone who has ever visited their neighbour, Israel and the Palestinian Territories. The evidence immigration officials will be looking for is any kind of incriminating stamp in your passport. This can include arrival/departure

stamps from Ben-Gurion Airport, or similar stamps from border crossing points, such as Rafah and Taba on the Egyptian border or any of the crossings with Jordan.

There's also a question on some visa application forms that asks, 'Have you ever visited Occupied Palestine?' to which a yes response will see your application turned down flat. If you are doing a trip right through the Middle East, you can save yourself some potential trouble and leave Israel & the Palestinian Territories as the last stop on your itinerary. And should you plan on going there after Syria, keep it to yourself.

Immigration at the airports in both countries is quite efficient, but the customs staff at Beirut often check travellers' luggage.

The level of attention you receive entering either country by road is purely at the whim and boredom or stress level of the staff working at the border point. Regardless of their attitude, be unfailingly polite – despite the journey you've endured to get there.

See Departure Tax (left) for information regarding taxes.

Passport
Make sure that your passport is valid well beyond the period of your intended stay. If your passport is just about to expire, immigration may not let you into the country. Also, make sure it has sufficient space for any new visa stamps that you're liable to pick up.

You should get into the habit of carrying your passport at all times while in Syria and Lebanon as you often need to present it to change money, cash travellers cheques, buy long-distance bus tickets and, in some destinations, even to make telephone calls. In Lebanon there are still many Lebanese army checkpoints, although the officials rarely ask to see your ID these days. However, if you are stopped and you don't have any ID, it will create delays and hassles.

AIR
Airports & Airlines
SYRIA
Syria has two international airports, one in Damascus and the other in Aleppo, plus a third, in Lattakia, which is international

THINGS CHANGE...
The information in this chapter is particularly vulnerable to change. Check directly with the airline or a travel agent to make sure you understand how a fare (and ticket you may buy) works and be aware of the security requirements for international travel. Shop carefully. The details given in this chapter should be regarded as pointers and are not a substitute for your own careful, up-to-date research.

in name only. Damascus has regular connections to Europe, Africa, Asia and other cities in the Middle East, while Aleppo has more limited services. Most air travellers arrive in Damascus but there are some direct flights from Europe and other Middle Eastern destinations to Aleppo.

The **Damascus International Airport** (DAM; ☎ 011-543 0201/9) is 32km southwest of the city centre. There's a branch of the Commercial Bank of Syria (CBS) linked to Cirrus, Maestro, Visa and MasterCard and a sometimes 24-hour tourist office with free city maps, plus desks for the major car-hire companies. Note, the bank will *not* change Syrian pounds back into dollars or any other hard currency.

On the plus side, there is a duty-free store that takes Syrian pounds and US dollars, and is seriously cheap.

For information on how to get to and from the airport, see p118. Syria's national carrier **SyrianAir** (Syrian Arab Airlines; www.syriaair.com) flies to Europe, Delhi, Mumbai and Karachi in Asia, many Middle Eastern destinations and North Africa, and it's not a bad airline for short-haul travel.

The following major airlines offer services to and from Damascus:
Air France (AF; in Damascus ☎ 011-221 8990; www.airfrance.com)
British Airways (BA; in Damascus ☎ 011-331 0000; www.britishairways.com)
Cyprus Airways (CY; in Damascus ☎ 011-222 5630; www.cyprusairways.com)
EgyptAir (MS; in Damascus ☎ 011-223 2158; www.egyptair.com.eg; airline code MS)
Emirates (EK; in Damascus ☎ 011-9934; www.emirates.com)
Etihad (EY; in Damascus ☎ 011-334 4235; www.etihadairways.com)

Gulf Air (GF; in Damascus ☎ 011-222 1209; www.gulfairco.com)
Lufthansa (LH; in Damascus ☎ 011-221 1165; www.lufthansa.com)
Royal Jordanian Airline (RJ; in Damascus ☎ 011-231 5577; www.rja.com.jo)
SyrianAir (RB; Airport office ☎ 222 9001; www.syriaair.com)
Turkish Airlines (TK; in Damascus ☎ 011-221 2263; www.turkishairlines.com)

LEBANON
There is only one airport in Lebanon, **Beirut Rafic Hariri International Airport** (BEY; ☎ 01-628 000; www.beirutairport.gov.lb). There are no direct flights to the USA; though connections to Europe, Africa and Asia are frequent. The arrivals hall is well organised, and immigration procedures are reasonably straightforward, although customs can be slow if luggage is being checked. Facilities inside the airport are still somewhat thin on the ground, but some car-rental agencies and exchange places are open. For details on getting to and from the airport, see p291.

The national carrier, **Middle East Airlines** (MEA; in Beirut ☎ 01-737 000; www.mea.com.lb) has an extensive network, including flights to and from Europe and the Arab world. The airline has a pretty good safety record, is serviceable enough and good for regional connections.

The following airlines fly to and from Lebanon:
Air France (AF; in Beirut ☎ 01-977 977; www.airfrance.com)
Cyprus Airways (CY; in Beirut ☎ 01-362 237; www.cyprusairways.com)
EgyptAir (MS; in Beirut ☎ 01-973 330; www.egyptair.com.eg)
Emirates (EK; in Beirut ☎ 01-734 535; www.emirates.com)
Gulf Air (GF; in Beirut ☎ 01-323 332; www.gulfairco.com)
Lufthansa (LH; in Beirut ☎ 01-347 007; www.lufthansa.com)
Malaysia Airlines (MH; in Beirut ☎ 01-741 344; www.mas.com.my)
Middle East Airlines (ME; in Beirut ☎ 01-737 000; www.mea.com.lb)
Royal Jordanian Airline (RJ; in Beirut ☎ 01-379 990; www.rja.com.jo)
Syrian Arab Airlines (RB; in Beirut ☎ 01-375 632; www.syriaair.com)
Turkish Airlines (TK; in Beirut ☎ 01-999 849; www.turkishairlines.com)

TRANSPORT

Tickets

As Syria is one of the more popular Middle East destinations you will probably find discounted fares, particularly from Europe. Prices vary from one agency to the other, so take the time to call around. If you're planning to tour either Jordan or Turkey as well as Syria, you should consider flying to Amman or Istanbul, as a greater range of airlines serve those cities with a wider spread of fares.

For Beirut, it really depends where you're coming from. Online agencies will give a reasonable discount, but to save money you'll be taking a connecting flight or sometimes two.

BUYING TICKETS

Unless you have a travel agent who really knows their stuff and can get you good discounts, online booking is the way to go, whether it be through the airline themselves or through an agency such as Expedia. Surfing the internet is a quick and easy way to compare prices. The most important thing is to make sure you buy a ticket that works for your kind of travel – if you have a date by which you have to be back in your country of origin, a nonrefundable, nontransferable ticket (which is generally cheaper), if your trip is 'open-ended', a more expensive unrestricted or flexible fare is a better option. Always think carefully before you buy a ticket that cannot easily be refunded.

Most airlines offer frequent-flier deals that can earn you a free air ticket or upgrades. To qualify, you have to accumulate sufficient mileage with the same airline or airline alliance. Many airlines have 'blackout periods', or times when you cannot fly for free on your frequent-flier points. If you're in a frequent-flier programme, always try to use an airline that is a partner in that alliance should your normal airline not fly where you want to go.

STUDENT & YOUTH FARES

Full-time students and people under 26 have access to better deals than other travellers. The better deals may not always be cheaper fares but can include more flexibility to change flights and/or routes. You have to show a document proving your date of birth or a valid International Student Identity Card (ISIC) when buying your ticket and boarding the plane.

From Asia

For both Damascus and Beirut, flights generally land in Dubai first. Saudi Arabian, Emirates, Gulf Air and Qatar Airways all offer connecting flights to Damascus that add about US$100 to a return flight to Dubai. For Beirut it's similar, with Gulf Air, Malaysia and Emirates offering the best deals. Return flights from Kuala Lumpur to both Damascus and Beirut start at around US$1000 from online agencies, if you book well in advance.

From Australia & New Zealand

From Australia, low-season fares to Damascus and Beirut start at A$2300 return with Emirates, with a stop in Dubai. Other airlines may have two stops. From New Zealand, return low-season fares with Emirates or Cathay Pacific start at NZ$3000; expect a couple of stops. Depending on the airline, the stop in Asia is usually Singapore or Kuala Lumpur and then Dubai in the Middle East. Round-the-world tickets start at A$2420 from Australia or NZ$2880 from New Zealand.

From Canada

From Canada, flights are via one of the European capitals and sometimes via the USA as well. Return flights to either Damascus or Beirut with Air Canada and British Airways start from around C$1500 from Vancouver or C$1400 from Toronto.

From Continental Europe

Airlines including Air France, Austrian Airlines, Alitalia, KLM, Royal Jordanian Airline, Gulf Air, Middle East Airlines and SyrianAir offer regular flights to Damascus and/or Beirut from most European cities. KLM and Air France have direct flights to Beirut from Amsterdam and Air France and Austrian Airlines offer direct services to Damascus from Amsterdam. From Paris, Air France offers direct flights to Beirut and Damascus. Alitalia also has direct flights to both these cities from Milan as does Lufthansa from Frankfurt.

Depending on the airline and number of stops (direct flights are generally more expensive) return flights from these cities to either Damascus or Beirut go from around €200 to €500.

From the Middle East & North Africa

Middle East Airlines has regular flights to Beirut from the Middle East capitals of

CLIMATE CHANGE & TRAVEL

Climate change is a serious threat to the ecosystems that humans rely upon, and air travel is the fastest-growing contributor to the problem. Lonely Planet regards travel, overall, as a global benefit, but believes we all have a responsibility to limit our personal impact on global warming.

Flying & Climate Change

Pretty much every form of motor travel generates CO_2 (the main cause of human-induced climate change) but planes are far and away the worst offenders, not just because of the sheer distances they allow us to travel, but because they release greenhouse gases high into the atmosphere. The statistics are frightening: two people taking a return flight between Europe and the US will contribute as much to climate change as an average household's gas and electricity consumption over a whole year.

Carbon Offset Schemes

Climatecare.org and other websites use 'carbon calculators' that allow jetsetters to offset the greenhouse gases they are responsible for with contributions to energy-saving projects and other climate-friendly initiatives in the developing world – including projects in India, Honduras, Kazakhstan and Uganda.

Lonely Planet, together with Rough Guides and other concerned partners in the travel industry, supports the carbon offset scheme run by climatecare.org. Lonely Planet offsets all of its staff and author travel.

For more information check out our website: lonelyplanet.com.

Amman, Abu Dhabi, Kuwait and Dubai. It also offers flights to Beirut from the African cities of Cairo, Abidjan (Ivory Coast), Accra (Ghana) and Kano (Nigeria).

SyrianAir has regular connections to Beirut from many Middle East and North African cities including Amman, Abu Dhabi, Algiers, Bahrain, Cairo, Dhahran, Doha, Dubai, Jeddah, Khartoum, Kuwait, Muscat, San'a, Sharjah, Riyadh, Tehran and Tunis.

Both Turkish Airlines and Middle East Airlines have direct flights from Istanbul to Beirut. Turkish Airlines offers direct services from Istanbul to Damascus. Check the airlines' websites for fares between cities.

From the UK

From the UK there are a number of airlines offering flights to both Syria and Lebanon. Emirates, Etihad, British Airways (Damascus only) tend to offer the best routes. Other flight options from London to Damascus include KLM via Amsterdam, Alitalia via Milan or Air France via Paris. At the time of writing return flights from London to Damascus or Beirut started from around £415.

From the USA

Although there are no direct flights from the USA, there are quite a few options for getting to either Syria or Lebanon. Flights to Damascus and Beirut are via one, sometimes two, European capitals (usually London or Paris) or another Middle East city (usually Dubai). Return fares from New York with airlines including British Airways, Emirates, Etihad, Royal Jordanian and Air France start from around US$900 for a restricted fare, while return fares from Los Angeles start from US$1300 for a restricted fare. Another option from the USA is to buy a return to London and from there buy a cheap fare to either Damascus or Beirut. If you are travelling to Syria or Lebanon as part of a bigger trip, expect to pay around US$2500 for a round-the-world ticket that takes in Beirut or Damascus.

Discount travel agents in the USA are known as consolidators (although you won't see a sign on the door saying 'Consolidator'). San Francisco is the ticket consolidator capital of America, although some good deals can be found in Los Angeles, New York and other big cities.

A good place to scope fares is **Kayak** (www .kayak.com), while the following agencies are recommended for online bookings:
www.expedia.com
www.sta.com (for travellers under the age of 26)
www.travelocity.com

TRANSPORT

LAND
Border Crossings
The only land borders open to Lebanon at the moment are those with Syria. Despite the Israeli withdrawal, the southern border is closed with no immediate sign of opening – especially considering that it's been dusted with a light sprinkling of unexploded bomblets from cluster bombs.

Whether leaving Syria by land (or air), have your yellow entry card, or the equivalent you received upon getting a visa extension, ready to hand in. There may be a small fine to pay if you don't have it – which could be awkward if you have made sure to spend your last Syrian pounds before crossing the frontier.

If you've overstayed your visa limit in Syria without getting the required visa extension, reports indicate you can get away with being a day or two over, but for anything more you must get an exit visa from an immigration office. If you don't, you risk being turned back.

BRINGING YOUR OWN VEHICLE
It's no problem to bring your own vehicle to Syria. A *carnet de passage en douane* is apparently no longer needed. Instead, drivers arriving with vehicles have to buy what amounts to a temporary customs waiver at the border. This costs about US$50, plus possible bribes to grumpy customs officials. Third-party insurance must also be bought at the border, costing US$36 a month. This supposedly also covers you for Lebanon, but double-check. The real value of these compulsory insurance deals is questionable, so make sure your own insurance company will cover you for Syria. There is also a US$100 diesel tax payable if your vehicle uses diesel fuel.

If you are bringing a foreign-registered vehicle into Lebanon, there is a hefty charge levied at the border (refundable when you leave). This is calculated on a sliding scale depending on the value of the vehicle. Unless you have large amounts of cash to leave as a deposit, this ruling effectively makes it unfeasible to bring your own car into Lebanon. A better plan would be to arrive by bus or service taxi and then rent a car locally.

See also Car & Motorcycle for Syria (p400) and Lebanon (p403) for more specific details.

Iran
There is a service connecting Damascus (and Aleppo) to Tehran by rail. The route is Damascus, Aleppo, then into Turkey – Malatya, Lake Van (where there's a ferry) – and on into Iran – Tabriz, Tehran. The departure from Tehran is 8.15pm Saturday, arriving in Damascus at 7.20am Tuesday; the reverse journey departs Damascus at 7.21am on Saturday, arriving in Tehran at 6.45pm Monday. The first-class fare is €39.90. For departures from Aleppo, see p193.

Jordan
There are two border crossings between Syria and Jordan that are only 3km apart: at Nasib/Jabir and Deraa/Ramtha. Nasib/Jabir is the main post and if you're catching a service taxi or bus you'll use this one. If you're travelling by train or by local transport, you'll use Deraa/Ramtha. For details see Crossing Into Jordan, p131.

BUS
There is one JETT bus daily in each direction between Amman and Damascus. You need to book in advance as demand for seats is high. For details of departure times and prices from Damascus, see p117.

SERVICE TAXI
Service taxis are faster than the buses and depart much more frequently. Between Damascus and Amman costs JD5.500 (S£385) either way. Service taxis run between Damascus and Irbid for JD4 (S£300).

TRAIN
At the time of research there was talk of upgrading and revitalising the Hejaz Railway, a narrow-gauge line that was meant to link Damascus to Medina for the annual pilgrimage (see The Hejaz Railway, opposite). Services will be suspended while work takes place in 2008, and no date has been provided as to when services will resume. If it's anything like the interminably delayed Hejaz Station development in Damascus, it could be years. Train-watchers and nostalgics should be warned that the locomotive was a Romanian diesel-run machine, not a romantic, sooty steam job, although some travellers have had the luck to get the sooty version on the Syria leg. It remains to be seen what trains will be used when the line is rejuvenated.

THE HEJAZ RAILWAY

Begun in 1907, the Hejaz Railway was the last grand vision of the dying Ottoman Empire. It was an ambitious scheme to connect Damascus to Medina in Saudi Arabia by rail. Ostensibly, this was to facilitate the annual pilgrimage to Mecca but, perhaps more importantly, it was a way of consolidating Constantinople's hold on the region – the trains were as useful for troops as pilgrims.

This underlying military significance very quickly proved the undoing of the line. When war broke out in 1914 the Hejaz became a strategic target and it was this railway that was repeatedly blown up by Lawrence of Arabia.

The line never, in fact, reached Medina and with the dissolution of the Ottoman Empire that followed the Allied victory, there was never any need for it to be completed. In recent times desultory talks on the possibility of resurrecting the Hejaz Railway in its full glory have concluded that such a project would only be viable if the line were reconnected to the European rail network – a long-term goal of more visionary thinkers in the Middle East, but still some way from becoming reality.

Saudi Arabia & Kuwait

It is possible to go direct from Syria to Saudi Arabia by bus, via Jordan. There are also irregular services all the way to Kuwait. For details inquire at the Baramke terminal in Damascus.

Turkey

BUS

You can buy tickets in Istanbul for buses to Aleppo (approximately 24 hours) or Damascus (30 hours), costing US$24 to US$30, depending on which company you travel with and regardless of whether you are going to Aleppo or Damascus. Buses leave daily, usually with five or six departures between about 11am and early evening. The journey usually involves a change of bus at Antakya, the last major Turkish city before the border.

The buses cross at Bab al-Hawa, the most convenient and busiest border post between the two neighbours. The volume of traffic means delays are frequent, with waits of up to a couple of hours. One way to side step this is to buy a bus ticket in Istanbul to travel only as far as Antakya, and from there make your own way to Syria. Take a local bus from Antakya to Reyhanli from where you can catch a *dolmuş* (shared taxi; can be a minibus or sedan) to the border; after crossing on foot (a long and sweaty 2km in summer) you can try to pick up a lift on the Syrian side.

Alternatively, from Antakya you also have the option of catching a *dolmuş* south to Yayladaği (these go from beside the Etibank, opposite the entrance to the bus station),

from where you pick up a taxi or hitch the few kilometres further to the border. Once across (crossing takes just 15 minutes), you're only 2km from the Syrian mountain village of Kassab, from where regular microbuses make the 45-minute run to Lattakia on the Mediterranean coast. To get to Kassab from the border, walk about 10 minutes to the main road at the point where it curves sharply to your right, and then flag down any northbound microbus. Southbound microbuses will be heading from Kassab to Lattakia, but they'll probably be already full and won't pick you up here.

You can also cross from Gaziantep: take a *dolmuş* to Kilis, then another to the border, walk across then take a taxi for around US$2 to Azaz in Syria from where a bus to Aleppo is just S£20.

From northeast Syria it's also possible to cross into Turkey at Qamishle (see p224). From Damascus and Aleppo, there are direct buses to Istanbul and several other Turkish destinations, including Ankara. From Aleppo to Istanbul with Etihad buses, for instance, takes 17 hours and costs S£2000.

TRAIN

Syria used to be the terminus for the *Tarsus Express*, the eastward extension of the famed *Orient Express*. The *Tarsus* set off from Istanbul's Haydarpaşa station and terminated at Aleppo, where travellers could then change trains and catch a service that went via Lattakia down through Beirut and to Haifa in Israel and the Palestinian Territories. Aleppo

TRANSPORT

was also the starting point for services to Baghdad and through to Tehran. Sadly, that sort of rail travel came to an end in the Middle East soon after WWII, when poor relations between the newly emerging states of the region meant minimal cooperation and locked-down borders.

However, a limited form of rail travel between Turkey and Syria has persisted, and there is one weekly service that continues to run between Istanbul and Aleppo/Damascus. It departs Haydarpaşa station at 8.55am Sunday morning, arriving 2.34pm in Aleppo (€25.20) the following day, terminating at Damascus at 8.06pm (€33.20). The sleeper supplement is €23/23 (Aleppo/Damascus) for a single or €15.40/15.40 per person in a double. For further details check the website for **Turkish Railways** (www.tcdd.gov.tr).

For details of train services from Aleppo on the Syrian side, see p193.

Also see the website www.seat61.com for other useful travel information, instructive photos and often amusing travel stories.

OVERLAND TOURS

For people with time to indulge, Syria can be visited as part of an overland trip taking in a combination of three, four or more countries – typically Turkey, Syria, Jordan and Egypt. You travel in a specially adapted 'overland truck' with anywhere between 16 and 24 other passengers and your group leader. Accommodation is usually a mix of camping and budget hotels and everyone is expected to pitch in.

Travelling in such a self-contained bubble, the success of the trip very much depends on the group chemistry. It could be one long party on wheels or six endless weeks of grin and bear it and judicious use of your iPod. And no, you don't get to vote anyone off.

Following is a list of well-regarded tour operators:

Dragoman (www.dragoman.com) Istanbul to Cairo (or vice versa) through Turkey, Syria, Jordan and Egypt in four to 6½ weeks. Longer trips available as well.

Exodus (www.exodus.co.uk) Trips include a 'Middle East Encompassed', which comprises 16 days through Lebanon, Syria and Jordan.

Kumuka (www.kumuka.co.uk) Masses of routes offered, including dedicated explorations of Egypt, Jordan or Syria.

Oasis Overland (www.oasisoverland.co.uk) Syria, Jordan and Egypt in 21 days or Turkey, Syria, Jordan and Egypt in 37 days.

GETTING AROUND

TRAVEL BETWEEN SYRIA & LEBANON

You cannot get a Syrian visa in Lebanon, but you can get a Lebanese visa at the border when entering from Syria. For more details, see Visas, p388.

There are four different crossing points from Lebanon into Syria: Masnaa, on the Beirut–Damascus Hwy; Al-Qaa, at the northern end of the Bekaa Valley; Aarida on the coastal road from Tripoli to Lattakia; and Aabboudiye on the Tripoli to Homs route. Always check that the borders are open before setting off.

Air

At present there are no flights between Damascus and Beirut.

Bus

Buses to Syria from Beirut leave from the only 'real' bus station, Charles Helou, just east of Downtown.

You must go in person to buy your ticket and, if possible, it's best to book a seat the day before you travel.

The first bus to Damascus leaves at 5.30am, and they run every half-hour until 7am, after which they leave hourly. Buses to Aleppo (ask for Halab) start at 7.30am and leave at half-hourly intervals until midday. There are also three buses a day (10.30am, 2pm and 5.30pm) to Lattakia, six to Homs (7.30am, 9.30am, 1.30pm, 5pm, 7pm and 9.30pm) and four to Hama (9.30am, 5pm, 7pm and 9.30pm).

Tripoli also has extensive bus services to Syria. A number of bus companies are clustered around Jamal Abdel Nasser Square in the city centre, many offering air-con and on-board videos. There are frequent departures to Homs, Hama and Aleppo in the morning, from around 9am until midday; there are not as many buses in the afternoon. Buses travelling to Lattakia and Damascus are fewer in number and tend to depart in the afternoon. For average prices and travel times, see Fares Between Syria & Lebanon, opposite.

From Damascus, private buses travel to Lebanon. Buses leave from the Baramke terminal, which is about a 15-minute walk to the west of Martyrs Square.

FARES BETWEEN SYRIA & LEBANON

Note that these prices and times are approximate, as at the time of research all of the services were suspended as all borders except the Damascus–Beirut border between Lebanon and Syria were closed due to the political troubles in Lebanon. It was thought the other borders would not be opened until the Lebanon parliament voted in a new President, which it had still not done as of early April 2008. Note also that travel times do not include the border crossings, which depend on the traffic; at times of political tension they can get very busy. How long it takes also depends on who is manning the border and what kind of mood they're in.

Bus

Route	Cost	Duration
Beirut–Aleppo	LL10,500/S£250	6hr
Beirut–Damascus	LL7000/S£175	3hr
Beirut–Hama	LL9000/S£250	6hr
Beirut–Homs	LL8500/S£250	4hr
Beirut–Lattakia	LL9000	4hr
Tripoli–Aleppo	LL8000/S£175	4hr
Tripoli–Hama	LL6500	2hr
Tripoli–Homs	LL6000/S£150	1½ hr
Tripoli–Lattakia	LL6000	2hr

Service Taxi

Route	Cost	Duration
Baalbek–Damascus	LL9000/S£300	1½ hr
Baalbek–Homs	LL9000	1½ -2½ hr
Beirut–Aleppo	LL21,000/S£300	5hr
Beirut–Damascus	LL15,000/US$10	3hr
Beirut–Hama	LL15,000	4hr
Beirut–Homs	LL15,000	3hr
Beirut–Lattakia	LL15,000	3hr
Beirut–Tartus	LL12,000	2hr
Tripoli–Hama	LL9000	2hr
Tripoli–Homs	LL7000	1½ hr
Tripoli–Lattakia	LL9000	2hr

From Aleppo, the buses leave from the bus station tucked away just behind Baron St, not two minutes from the Baron Hotel. Again, the services to Beirut are mainly privately operated buses.

Service Taxi & Taxi

If you do prefer to take a taxi, either service or private, in Beirut they depart from the Cola bus station and taxi stand or from Charles Helou bus station.

In Tripoli these services depart from Jamal Abdel Nasser Square. The service taxis leave when they are full but there is seldom a wait of more than 20 minutes or so. Service and private taxis travel to and from Damascus, where you can change to continue on to Jordan.

A private taxi from Beirut to Damascus costs about US$70, although during tense periods politically when Beirutis head to Damascus to escape potential danger, taxi drivers will increase the prices.

Tours

See the Tours sections under Damascus (p103) and Beirut (p280) for details of tours around each individual city.

LOCAL TOUR OPERATORS

Local tour operators offer a variety of tours – most (with a couple of exceptions) offer one-day excursions starting and ending in Beirut.

There are some longer tours available which include Syria and/or Jordan.

TRANSPORT

Adonis Travel (www.adonistravel.com) Offers tours either within Lebanon or across Syria, Lebanon and Jordan.

Campus Travel (Map p272; ☎ 01-744 588; www .campus-travel.net; Maktabi Bldg, Rue Makhoul, Hamra, Beirut) Travel agency focusing on student travel. Arranges skiing trips, tours in Lebanon and to neighbouring countries, such as Syria and Jordan.

Esprit-Nomade (☎ 70-813 001; www.esprit-nomade .com) Offers hiking, rural tourism and responsible ecotourism with innovative programming in Lebanon.

Jasmin Tours (www.jasmintours.com) Based in Damascus, this company offers a variety of Syrian tours, including hiking, culture and nature tours. It also offers tours of Lebanon and Jordan.

Lebanese Adventure (☎ /fax 01-398 982, 03-360 027; www.lebanese-adventure.com; Sioufi, Achrafiye, Beirut) Different outdoor activities throughout Lebanon are arranged each weekend. It can also tailor-make excursions for a minimum of five people.

Liban Trek (☎ 01-329 975; www.libantrek.com; 7th fl, Yazbek B, Rue Adib Ishac, Achrafiye, Beirut) A well-established trekking club that arranges weekend treks throughout Lebanon. It also organises trips to Syria, Jordan, Egypt and Turkey, as well as other mountain sports.

Nakhal & Co (☎ 01-389 389; www.nakhal.com; Ghorayeb Bldg, Rue Sami al-Solh, Badaro, Beirut) Lebanon tours cover Aanjar, Baalbek, Beiteddine, Byblos, The Cedars, Sidon, Tripoli and Tyre. It also organises tours from Lebanon to Syria.

Saad Tours (☎ 01-429 429, 01-427 427; www.saad tours.com; 8th fl, George Haddad Bldg, Rue Amin Gemayel, Sioufi, Achrafiye, Beirut) A consortium of tour operators that offers sightseeing trips in Lebanon and tours to Syria and Jordan.

Tania Travel (Map p272; ☎ 01-739 682; www .taniatravel.com; 1st fl, Shames Bldg, Rue Sidani, Hamra, opposite Jeanne d'Arc theatre, Beirut) It has tours to Aanjar, Baalbek, Bcharré, Beiteddine, Byblos, The Cedars, Deir al-Qamar, Sidon, Tyre and day trips to Damascus.

SYRIA
Air
The national carrier, SyrianAir (www .syriaair.com), operates a very reasonable (if monopolistic) internal air service and flights are cheap by international standards. Unless you're on a cash-rich, time-poor itinerary it may make more sense to catch the bus; the Damascus–Qamishle flight is perhaps the only exception to this.

Sample one-way fares (return fares are double) from Damascus:

Aleppo (ALP) S£1200 (1 hr)
Lattakia (LTK) S£811 (1 hr)
Qamishle (KAC) S£1306 (1¼ hrs)

Bicycle
A growing number of independent travellers are choosing to cycle Syria, both as a destination in itself or as part of a wider bike tour around the Mediterranean, Middle East, or indeed overland from Europe to Asia. Cycling Syria can be hard work for several reasons: Syrians are not used to long-distance cyclists, which means you need to pay extra attention on the roads; the extreme temperatures, especially in summer, need to be taken into account; plus, you need to carry a fairly hefty amount of gear, including complete tools and spares, because you cannot rely on finding what you need on the way.

On the plus side, cyclists manage to meet more people and therefore are the recipients of wonderful Syrian hospitality – receiving fantastic welcomes everywhere they go, showered with invitations to stop and eat or drink and frequently offered accommodation for the night.

PRACTICALITIES
Carry a couple of extra chain links, a chain breaker, spokes, a spoke key, two inner tubes, tyre levers, a repair kit, a flat-head and Phillips screwdriver, and Allen keys and spanners to fit all the bolts on your bike. Check the bolts daily and carry spares. Fit as many water bottles to your bike as you can or wear a hydration pack – the desert heat is unforgiving.

Make sure the bike's gearing will get you over the hills, and confine your panniers to 15kg maximum. May to mid-June and September to October are the best times for cycling; in between, bring lots of extra water. In your panniers include: a two-person tent (weighing about 1.8kg) that can also accommodate the bike where security is a concern; a sleeping bag rated to 0°C and a Therm-a-Rest; small camping stove with gas canisters; MSR cooking pot; utensils; Katadyn water filter (2 microns) and Maglite. Wear cycling shorts with chamois bum and cleated cycling shoes. Don't fill the panniers with food as it is plentiful and fresh along most routes.

It's also a good idea to carry a Dog Dazer or something similar. Wild, biting mutts are a big problem, particularly on the Desert Hwy out to Palmyra and Deir ez-Zur. If nothing else, carry a big stick or a pouch of stones.

Bus

Syria has a well-developed road network and, partly because the rate of private car ownership is at a low level, public transport is frequent and very cheap. Distances are short, so journeys are rarely more than a few hours. About the longest single bus ride you can take is the nine-hour trip from Damascus to Qamishle in the northeast.

A couple of different classes of bus ply the same routes, the best being the 'luxury' buses, followed in distant second by the Pullmans.

LUXURY BUSES

At one time the state-owned bus company, Karnak, had a monopoly on the road, but today a crop of private companies, running what are commonly referred to as 'luxury' buses or 'luxury Pullmans' rules the roads. Routes are few and the many operators are all in fierce competition. Consequently, fares vary little and the buses are all pretty much the same: large, newish, air-con – comfortable. Travelling with **Kadmous** (www.alkadmous .com) is highly recommended.

CHEAP PULLMANS

The orange-and-white buses of the state-run Karnak company were once the deluxe carriers on the Syrian highways – however competition has forced them off the roads. So now the cheap category of buses left is the Pullmans (not 'luxury Pullmans'). These are old, battered stock – in the more extreme cases genuine rust buckets – for which a punt on a ticket is akin to a gamble on whether the vehicle's going to make it or not. This is the cheapest way of covering long distances between towns. These vehicles have their own 'garages', quarantined well away from those of the luxury buses. At the same 'old bus' stations you'll usually find boxy minibuses, which run the same long-distance routes offering a bare minimum of comfort at an even cheaper price. You pay your money and take your chances.

MINIBUS & MICROBUS

While buses – of whatever vintage – connect the major towns and cities, short hops and out-of-the-way places are serviced by fleets of minibuses and microbuses. Minibuses on many of the shorter routes, for example, Hama–Homs, Tartus–Lattakia and Homs–Lattakia.

The term microbus (pronounced '*mee-crobaas*' or just '*mee-cro*') is a little blurred, it typically refers to those modern (mostly Japanese), little vans that are white with a sliding side door, and squeeze in about 12. These have set routes but no schedules, leaving when full. Passengers are picked up/set down anywhere along the route; just yell out

BUS STATIONS & TICKETING

Most Syrian towns and cities have a central or main bus station, which is home base for the various 'luxury' companies. There's often a second or third station too, devoted to second and third ranks of buses. These stations, known locally as *karaj* (garage) are basic affairs, no more than an asphalt lot with a row of prefab huts serving as booking offices for the various companies. Annoyingly, there's no central source of information giving departure times or prices, so it's simply a case of walking around and finding out which company has the next bus to your desired destination.

With so many companies, departures are frequent, and it's rarely necessary to book in advance. Just show up at the station and something will be heading off your way sometime, usually about right now.

Beware the touts – particularly persistent at Aleppo, Damascus and Homs – who will attempt to steer you to the bus company paying the greatest commission, irrespective of the time of the next bus. Start by heading straight for the Kadmous or Al-Ahliah office, and if they don't have a bus departing any time soon, then walk around and start asking the times of the other companies' buses.

Buying tickets is straightforward, but you need your passport so the ticketing person can enter your details in the log. It's wise to carry your passport at all times anyway, in case of random ID checks. Seats are assigned.

for the driver to stop or flag him down from the roadside. Destinations may be written in Arabic on the front of the bus. At the microbus station just listen out for somebody shouting the name of your destination.

SERVICE TAXI
Share taxis, which are also called service taxis (ser-*vees*), are often old American Desotos and Dodges from the '50s and '60s, although there are fewer of these on the roads than there were in the past, unfortunately. There's a chronic shortage of spare parts but ingenuity and improvisation keep them running. Although more modern vehicles have begun to appear, most drivers persist with their old favourites – largely for their robustness and size (good for squeezing people in).

Share taxis only operate on some major routes and in some cases seem to have succumbed to competition from microbuses. Share taxis can cost a lot more than the buses: unless you're in a hurry, or you find yourself stuck on a highway and it's getting late, there's really no need to use them.

Car & Motorcycle
DRIVING LICENCE
Theoretically, to drive a car or motorcylce in Syria you do require an International Driving Permit (IDP), but on the ground your own national licence should generally be sufficient. If you do decide to drive into Lebanon, you will need an IDP, the vehicle's registration papers and liability insurance. It is possible to service most common makes of vehicle in Lebanon. Petrol, available in the usual range of octanes and lead-free, is sold at most petrol stations.

FUEL & SPARE PARTS
Standard unleaded costs around S£28 a litre. It is advisable that you bring a good set of spare parts and some mechanical knowledge, as within Syria you will not always be able to get the help that you may need. While there are plenty of motorcycles in Syria, most are not the common Japanese brands, but Chinese copies, so you'll need to bring plenty of spare parts with you.

SYRIA: ROAD DISTANCES (KM)

Damascus to Beirut = 127km

	Aleppo	Ath-Thaura	Bosra	Damascus	Deir ez-Zur	Hama	Homs	Lattakia	Maalula	Palmyra	Qala'at al-Hosn	Safita	Seidnayya	Suweida	Tartus
Aleppo	---														
Ath-Thaura	150	---													
Bosra	501	651	---												
Damascus	355	505	146	---											
Deir ez-Zur	321	201	567	421	---										
Hama	146	296	355	209	401	---									
Homs	193	343	308	162	354	47	---								
Lattakia	187	337	494	348	508	147	186	---							
Maalula	311	466	204	58	420	167	120	306	---						
Palmyra	353	194	366	220	201	207	160	346	230	---					
Qala'at al-Hosn	252	402	367	221	414	106	156	179	179	219	---				
Safita	261	421	386	240	432	125	78	120	120	238	32	---			
Seidnayya	339	489	176	30	420	196	149	335	335	250	208	227	---		
Suweida	462	614	39	107	528	316	269	455	167	327	328	347	137	---	
Tartus	287	437	404	258	450	143	96	90	90	256	73	31	245	365	---

TRANSPORT

HIRE & INSURANCE

Europcar and Hertz are the only international car-hire firms in Syria and both are recommended over the local companies for safety and insurance reasons.

Hertz's cheapest standard rate is US$49/309 per day/week for a Renault Clio, including all insurance and unlimited mileage. Europcar is more expensive, starting at US$62/412 per day/week for a Peugeot 106 (plus insurance). The local companies can be cheaper.

There's also a minimum rental of two/three days for limited kilometres/unlimited kilometres, which is standard with rental companies in Syria. Europcar also charges an additional fee of 75% of the daily rate if the car is returned to a town other than where it was rented.

A plethora of local companies has appeared since the early 1990s but many don't offer full insurance. Another problem with local agencies is maintenance. Vehicles are prone to breakdowns and poor back-up service translates to you hanging around for a day or two waiting for your hire car to be fixed or replaced.

You need to be at least 21 years old to rent a car in Syria, although some places require that you be 23. Most companies will require a deposit in cash of up to US$1000, or you can leave your credit card details.

Budget (Map pp82-3; ☎ 499 9999; opposite Four Seasons Hotel, Damascus)

Europcar Saahat Umawiyeen, Damascus (Map p80; ☎ 222 9300; Sheraton Damascus Hotel & Towers); Sharia Shoukri al-Quwatli, Damascus (Map p80; ☎ 222 9200; Le Meridien Damas); Damascus International Airport (☎ 011-543 1536).

Hertz Damascus (Map pp82–3; ☎ 011-223 2300; www .hertz.com; Cham Palace); Damascus International Airport (☎ 011-23 2300).

Cars & Drivers

An alternative option is to hire a car and driver for a day. You can usually manage to get a big old Mercedes taxi or a modern smaller car to ferry you around for a full day – no insurance necessary and no deposit. You should be able to arrange something similar through your hotel, but make it clear how many hours you want to be out and where you wish to go, and get a firm agreement on this and the price beforehand. The standard rate for a full day is US$100 for the car and driver (regardless of how many passengers

there are), but try to negotiate, especially if you want one for several day trips. We've had drivers recommended by hotels who've fallen asleep at the wheel, didn't know where they were going and had to stop at every village or had a recurring habit of steering us towards souvenir shops. If you want one for a few days, we suggest giving them a one-day test drive and see how it goes.

ROAD RULES

Traffic runs on the right-hand side of the road, while the speed limit is generally 60km/h in built-up areas, 70km/h on the open road and 110km/h on major highways.

The roads are generally quite reasonable in Syria, but if you're travelling extensively, you will come across places that are signposted in Arabic only. The best advice is to find someone and ask – point at your destination in the book if necessary. Always take care when driving into villages and other built-up areas, as cars, people and animals all jostle for the same space.

Long-distance night driving is not really recommended, as not all drivers believe in using headlights, and general lighting is poor. Truckers testing their manhood by overtaking in a suicidal fashion are a major concern, as are wayward children; sheep and goats accompanied by an inattentive shepherd; camels; and farmers and their tractors.

Hitching

Although, generally speaking, Lonely Planet does not advocate hitching because of the small but potentially serious risk it involves, unless you have your own transport hitching can be considered as an option to access some of Syria's more remote sites. In fact, as so many locals don't own cars, it is an accepted means of getting around. Money is never expected and any attempt to pay is unequivocally refused.

Despite the hospitality of many Syrians, people who choose to hitch will be safer if they travel in pairs and let someone know where they are planning to go. Women should never hitch alone.

Local Transport
BUS

All the major cities have a local bus and/or microbus system but, as the city centres are compact, you can usually get around on foot. This is just as well because neither the buses nor the microbuses have signs in English (and often no signs in Arabic), though they can be useful (and cheap) for getting out to distant microbus or train stations, especially in Damascus.

SERVICE TAXI & TAXI

Taxis in most cities are plentiful and cheap. In Damascus they have meters, although many drivers are deliberately unaware of their existence. Despite this, if you get into a taxi and ask how much it is to the bus station (or wherever) you will often be told the correct fare and bargaining will get you nowhere. If you are catching taxis, always ask at your hotel how much the fare should be before you leave. To avoid the hassle, in Damascus there is a new taxi company, **Star Taxi** (x9207), with good drivers, vehicles, meters that work and services to the airport, Jordan and Lebanon.

Although they are not in evidence in Damascus, some other cities, notably Aleppo, are served by local service taxis that run a set route, picking up and dropping off passengers along the way for a set price. For the outsider, there is no obvious way to distinguish them from the normal taxis. If you can read Arabic, it's easy. Regular taxis have a sign on the doors reading 'Ujra medinat Halab, raqm…' (City of Aleppo Taxi, Number…), while service taxis have a similar-looking sign reading 'Khidma Medinat Halab' (City of Aleppo Service) followed by the route name.

Should you end up sharing with other people and the taxi doesn't take you exactly where you want to go, you're probably in a service taxi.

Train

Syria has potentially an excellent railway network, with more than 2000km of track connecting most main centres. The main line snakes its way from Damascus north to Aleppo via Homs and Hama before swinging southeast via Raqqa to Deir ez-Zur. At that point it turns northeast to Hassake and finally to Qamishle. Trains also operate on a couple of secondary lines, one of which runs from Aleppo to Lattakia, down the coast to Tartus and then on to Homs to connect with the Damascus line.

However, the reality is that train travel is rarely an attractive option. The first draw-

back is that there are never more than three or four services a day between any given destinations (often fewer) and some arrive and depart in the dead hours of morning. Not only does this disrupt your sleep, it also means that most journeys are made in complete darkness so you don't see any scenery. Rolling stock is 1970s Russian with all the levels of comfort that implies. To compound matters, the stations are often awkwardly located a few kilometres from the centre of town and are poorly catered to, with little or no public transport (Aleppo and Lattakia, to name two, are exceptions).

Nevertheless, there are some good options. The line between Aleppo and Lattakia passes through, under and over some beautiful scenery as it snakes its way across the barrier of the Jebel an-Ansariyya and down to the coast. There are four services a day, all travelling during daylight hours. Readers have also commended the overnight service from Aleppo down to Damascus on sleek new trains, which seems a sensible way to cover ground if you're short on time (it saves wasting a day on a bus), plus it saves on at least one night's hotel bill.

Steam train buffs might appreciate the summer service up the Barada Gorge – see p125. It goes nowhere in particular but there's fun in getting there.

LEBANON

Lebanon is a tiny country; although there are no internal air services, you don't really need them. You can drive from one end of the country to the other in half a day, depending on traffic congestion. Most visitors use the ever-useful service taxis (servees) to get around. A huge number run on set routes around the country, although you may have to use more than one to get to where you want to go. If you're going to less-travelled areas, taxis can add up and it could be worth your while to rent a car.

Buses and minibuses also link the larger Lebanese towns, and there are two bus companies with extensive routes throughout Beirut and the outlying areas.

Bicycle

The terrain in Lebanon is extremely steep once you leave the coastal strip and it really suits a mountain bike. The state of some of the urban roads also demand a rugged all-terrain type bike. Keep in mind that the traffic problems described under Road Rules (p404) will also present a hazard to the cyclist and extreme care should be taken when riding anywhere in Lebanon. Having said that, the scenery is beautiful and the air in the mountains clear, although it would be best to avoid the summer months, when heat exhaustion can be a real hazard.

Bus
Buses travel between Beirut and Lebanon's major towns; see Bus & Microbus (p290) in the Beirut chapter for details.

Car & Motorcycle
DRIVING LICENCE
Most foreign (or national) licences are acceptable in Lebanon, However, an International Driving Permit (IDP) is theoretically required, and therefore recommended.

FUEL & SPARE PARTS
Petrol, including unleaded, is readily available and reasonably priced (about LL1100 per litre for unleaded).

HIRE & INSURANCE
If your budget can cover renting a car, it is the best way to see the most beautiful areas of Lebanon. Cars can easily be rented in Lebanon and, if you shop around, for surprisingly reasonable prices. If there are three or four of you, it becomes a very feasible way to travel, even if you're on a tight budget. Most of the big rental agencies are in Beirut (see p291 for a selection of car-rental companies), although a few can be found in other cities. If you shop around, you can find a small two- or three-door car for as little as US$40 per day with unlimited kilometres. A more luxurious model (Mercedes, for example) will be more like US$250 per day. If you want a local driver, it will set you back an additional US$30 to US$60 per day.

All companies require a refundable deposit if you are not a credit-card holders, and offer free delivery and collection during working hours. The minimum age for drivers is 21 years, but some rental agencies will charge extra if you are under 25. You cannot take hire cars over the border into Syria.

LEBANON: ROAD DISTANCES (KM)

Beirut to Damascus = 127km

	Amioun	Baalbek	Batroun	Bcharré	Beirut	Beiteddine	Byblos	Hermel	Jezzine	Jounieh	Marjeyun	Sidon	Tripoli	Tyre	Zahlé
Amioun	---														
Baalbek	97	---													
Batroun	24	113	---												
Bcharré	37	60	53	---											
Beirut	82	83	58	111	---										
Beiteddine	125	88	97	154	43	---									
Byblos	47	119	223	75	36	78	---								
Hermel	117	62	133	80	146	150	155	---							
Jezzine	153	109	129	182	71	29	107	179	---						
Jounieh	61	101	37	90	21	64	14	167	92	---					
Marjeyun	185	115	160	175	102	85	138	185	56	124	---				
Sidon	123	124	99	152	41	42	77	187	30	62	61	---			
Tripoli	222	109	33	49	91	134	55	102	162	70	193	132	---		
Tyre	161	163	137	190	79	80	115	225	48	101	79	38	170	---	
Zahlé	133	36	105	96	47	52	79	99	73	65	78	88	138	126	---

TRANSPORT

ROAD RULES

The first rule of driving in Lebanon is: forget the rules. Driving is on the right side of the road, unless the vehicles in front are not fast enough, in which case one drives on the left. The horn is used liberally because nobody uses their mirrors. In other words, anarchy rules: if you like aggressive driving, you'll do just fine. If you're a nervous driver, you might be too intimidated to nose your way out of the car-rental garage. If you do take the plunge (and it's surprisingly easy to unlearn the rules of the road), stay extremely alert, particularly on mountain roads, where cars hurtle around hairpin bends without a thought to oncoming traffic. The only other thing to remember is that you must stop at ALL military checkpoints. See the boxed text Checkpoint Etiquette (p370) for tips on getting through them with your dignity intact and your underwear unsoiled.

Hitching

Hitching is not very common in Lebanon – the tourists who venture off the service-taxi routes tend to either rent cars or private taxis. This may be to your advantage if you decide to try hitching a lift. The novelty of foreigners increases your chances of a lift – it helps if you look foreign. The usual precautions apply, though: never hitch alone if you are a woman. With many private cars instantly turning into taxis when they see a foreigner, there is a chance that the driver will expect payment. There does not seem to be a very polite way out of this situation, except to ask first if the driver is going to charge you for the ride. Travellers who decide to hitch should understand that they are taking a small but potentially serious risk. People who do choose to hitch will be safer if they travel in pairs and let someone know where they are planning to go.

Local Transport
BUS

Beirut and its environs now have two bus services, one operated by the privately owned Lebanese Commuting Company (LCC), the other by the state-owned OCFTC. They both operate a hail and ride system and have a fare of LL750 for all except the most distant destinations (such as Byblos and far-off suburbs). For route details, see Public Transport in the Beirut chapter (p291).

SERVICE TAXI & TAXI

Most routes around towns and cities are covered by service taxi and you can hail one at any point on the route. The only way to find out if the driver is going where you want is to hail him and ask. If the driver is not going where you want he'll (and it's nearly always a 'he') respond by driving off. If he's going in your direction the acknowledgment to get in may be as imperceptible as a head gesture. You can get out at any point along their route by saying 'anzil huun' (I get out here), to the driver. Occasionally when the drivers have an empty car they will try and charge you a private taxi fare. To let him know that you want to take the taxi as a service taxi, be sure to ask him 'servees?'.

Taxis are usually an elderly Mercedes with red licence plates, generally with a taxi sign on the roof and smoke belching from both the interior and the exhaust. The fare for all routes around towns is LL1000, unless the driver feels that you should pay LL1500 for the pleasure of his company. The fare to outlying parts of towns is LL2000. Try and pay at the earliest opportunity during your trip. It's a good idea to keep a few LL1000 notes handy for these trips.

If you do wish to take a service taxi as a private taxi, make sure the driver understands exactly where you are going and negotiate a price before you get in. Prices vary according to destination, and the typical fares are listed in the Getting There and Away section of each destination. If you have a lot of sightseeing to do in out-of-the-way places, you can hire a taxi and driver by the day. Haggling skills come to the fore here, but expect to pay at least US$50 per day plus tip.

You can order taxis by phone from a number of private companies; they'll take you anywhere in Lebanon and some also have services to Syria and Jordan. See p292 for contact numbers.

Health <small>Dr Caroline Evans</small>

CONTENTS

Prevention is the key to staying healthy while travelling in the Middle East. Infectious diseases can and do occur in the region, but these are usually associated with poor living conditions and poverty and can be avoided with a few precautions. The most common reason for travellers needing medical help is as a result of accidents – cars are not always well maintained and poorly lit roads are littered with potholes. Medical facilities can be excellent in large cities, but in remoter areas they may be more basic.

BEFORE YOU GO

A little planning before departure, particularly for pre-existing illnesses, will save you a lot of trouble later. See your dentist before a long trip; carry a spare pair of contact lenses and glasses (and take your optical prescription with you); and carry a first-aid kit.

It's tempting to leave it all to the last minute – don't! Many vaccines don't ensure immunity for two weeks, so visit a doctor four to eight weeks before departure. Ask your doctor for an International Certificate of Vaccination (otherwise known as the yellow booklet), which will list all the vaccinations you've received. This is mandatory for countries that require proof of yellow fever vaccination upon entry, but it's a good idea to carry it wherever you travel.

Travellers can register with the **International Association for Medical Advice to Travellers** (IMAT; www.iamat.org). Its website can help travellers to find a doctor with recognised training. Those heading off to very remote areas may like to do a first-aid course (Red Cross and St John Ambulance can help) or attend a remote medicine first-aid course such as the one offered by the **Royal Geographical Society** (www.rg s.org).

Bring medications in their original, clearly labelled, containers. A signed and dated letter from your physician describing your medical conditions and medications, including generic names, is also a good idea. If carrying syringes or needles, be sure to have a physician's letter documenting their medical necessity.

INSURANCE

Find out in advance if your insurance plan will make payments directly to providers or reimburse you later for overseas health expenditures (in many countries doctors expect payment in cash); it's also worth checking that your travel insurance will cover repatriation home or to better medical facilities elsewhere. Your insurance company may be able to locate the nearest source of medical help, or you can ask at your hotel.

In an emergency contact your embassy or consulate. Your travel insurance will not usually cover you for anything other than emergency dental treatment.

Not all insurance covers emergency air evacuation home or to a hospital in a major city, which may be the only way to get medical attention for a serious emergency.

RECOMMENDED VACCINATIONS

The World Health Organization recommends that all travellers, regardless of the region they are travelling in, should be covered for diphtheria, tetanus, measles, mumps, rubella and polio, as well as hepatitis B. While making preparations to travel, take the opportunity to ensure that all of your routine vaccination cover is complete. The consequences of these diseases can be severe and outbreaks do occur in the Middle East.

MEDICAL CHECKLIST

Following is a list of items that you should consider packing in your medical kit.

- Antibiotics (if travelling off the beaten track)
- Antidiarrhoeal drugs (eg loperamide)
- Acetaminophen/paracetamol (Tylenol) or aspirin
- Anti-inflammatory drugs (eg ibuprofen)
- Antihistamines (for hay fever and allergic reactions)
- Antibacterial ointment (eg Bactroban) for cuts and abrasions
- Steroid cream or cortisone (for allergic rashes)
- Bandages, gauze and gauze rolls
- Adhesive or paper tape
- Scissors, safety pins and tweezers
- Thermometer
- Pocket knife
- DEET-containing insect repellent for the skin
- Permethrin-containing insect spray for clothing, tents and bed nets
- Sun block
- Oral rehydration salts
- Iodine tablets (for water purification)
- Syringes and sterile needles (if travelling to remote areas)

INTERNET RESOURCES

There is a wealth of travel health advice on the Internet. For further information, the website for **Lonely Planet** (www.lonelyplanet.com) is a good place to start. The **World Health Organization** (www.who.int/ith) publishes a superb book, *International Travel and Health*, which is revised annually and is available online at no cost. Another website of general interest is **MD Travel Health** (www.mdtravelhealth.com), which provides complete travel health recommendations for every country, updated daily, also at no cost.

The website for **Centers for Disease Control and Prevention** (www.cdc.gov) is undoubtedly a very useful source of traveller's health information.

FURTHER READING

Lonely Planet's *Travel With Children* is packed with useful information including pretrip planning, emergency first aid,

immunisation and disease information, and what to do if you get sick on the road. Other recommended references include *Traveller's Health* by Dr Richard Dawood (Oxford University Press), *International Travel Health Guide* by Stuart R Rose MD (Travel Medicine Inc) and *The Travellers' Good Health Guide* by Ted Lankester (Sheldon Press), an especially useful health guide for volunteers and long-term expatriates working in the Middle East.

IN TRANSIT

DEEP VEIN THROMBOSIS (DVT)

Deep vein thrombosis occurs when blood clots form in the legs during plane flights, chiefly because of prolonged immobility. The longer the flight, the greater the risk. Though most blood clots are reabsorbed uneventfully, some may break off and travel through the blood vessels to the lungs, where they may cause life-threatening complications.

The chief symptom of deep vein thrombosis is swelling or pain in the foot, ankle or calf, usually but not always on just one side. When a blood clot travels to the lungs, the clot may cause chest pain and difficulty breathing. Travellers with any of these symptoms should immediately seek medical attention.

To prevent the development of deep vein thrombosis on long flights you should walk about the cabin, perform isometric compressions of the leg muscles (ie contract the leg muscles while sitting), drink plenty of fluids, and avoid alcohol and tobacco.

JET LAG & MOTION SICKNESS

Jet lag is common when crossing more than five time zones; it results in insomnia, fatigue, malaise or nausea. To avoid jet lag try drinking plenty of fluids (nonalcoholic) and eating light meals. Upon arrival, seek exposure to natural sunlight and readjust your schedule (for meals, sleep etc) as soon as possible.

Antihistamines such as dimenhydrinate (Dramamine) and meclizine (Antivert, Bonine) are usually the first choice for treating motion sickness. Their main side-effect is drowsiness. A herbal alternative is ginger, which works like a charm for some people.

IN SYRIA & LEBANON

AVAILABILITY & COST OF HEALTH CARE

The health-care systems in the Middle East are varied. Reciprocal arrangements with countries rarely exist and you should be prepared to pay for all medical and dental treatment.

Medical care is not always readily available outside major cities. Medicine, and even sterile dressings or intravenous fluids, may need to be bought from a local pharmacy. Nursing care may be limited or rudimentary as this is something families and friends are expected to provide. The travel assistance provided by your insurance may be able to locate the nearest source of medical help, otherwise ask at your hotel. In an emergency contact your embassy or consulate.

Standards of dental care are variable and there is an increased risk of hepatitis B and HIV transmission via poorly sterilised equipment. Keep in mind that your travel insurance will not usually cover you for anything other than emergency dental treatment.

For minor illnesses such as diarrhoea, pharmacists can often provide valuable advice and sell over-the-counter medication. They can also offer advice on when more specialised help is needed.

Medical Facilities
DAMASCUS
Shami Hospital (Map p80; ☎ 373 5090-04; Sharia Jawaher an-Nehru) This private hospital has an excellent reputation among expats; many doctors speak English.

ALEPPO
Al Razi (City Hospital) (☎ 2676-000-02; Abou Firas Al Hamadani) Well-respected hospital close to the centre.

BEIRUT
American University of Beirut Hospital (Map p272; ☎ 01-350 000, 354 911; Rue Sourati) Considered one of the best hospitals in the Middle East, with English and French spoken.

INFECTIOUS DISEASES
Diphtheria
Diphtheria is spread through close respiratory contact. It causes a high temperature and severe sore throat. Sometimes a membrane forms across the throat requiring a tracheostomy to prevent suffocation. Vaccination is recommended for those likely to be in close contact with the local population in infected areas.

The vaccine is given as an injection alone, or with tetanus, and lasts 10 years.

Hepatitis A
Hepatitis A is spread through contaminated food (particularly shellfish) and water. It causes jaundice, and although it is rarely fatal, can cause prolonged lethargy and delayed recovery. Symptoms include dark urine, a yellow colour to the whites of the eyes, fever and abdominal pain. Hepatitis A vaccine (Avaxim, VAQTA, Havrix) is given as an injection: a single dose will give protection for up to a year while a booster 12 months later will provide a subsequent 10 years of protection.

Hepatitis A and typhoid vaccines can also be given as a single dose vaccine, hepatyrix or viatim.

Hepatitis B
Infected blood, contaminated needles and sexual intercourse can all transmit hepatitis B. It can cause jaundice, and affects the liver, occasionally causing liver failure. All travellers should make this a routine vaccination. (Many countries now give hepatitis B vaccination as part of routine childhood vaccination.) The vaccine is given singly, or at the same time as the hepatitis A vaccine (hepatyrix).

A course will give protection for at least five years. It can be given over four weeks, or six months.

HIV
HIV is spread via infected blood and blood products, sexual intercourse with an infected partner and from an infected mother to her newborn child. It can be spread through 'blood to blood' contacts such as contaminated instruments during medical, dental, acupuncture and other body piercing procedures and sharing used intravenous needles.

Countries in the region that require a negative HIV test as a visa requirement for some categories of visas include the United Arab Emirates, Egypt, Iran, Iraq, Jordan, Kuwait, Lebanon, Libya, Qatar and Saudi Arabia.

HEALTH

Leishmaniasis

Spread through the bite of an infected sand fly, leishmaniasis, in its cutaneous form, can cause a slowly growing skin lump or ulcer. In its visceral form it may develop into a serious life-threatening fever usually accompanied by anaemia and weight loss. Infected dogs are also carriers of the infection. Sand-fly bites should be avoided whenever possible by using DEET-based repellents.

Malaria

The prevalence of malaria varies throughout the Middle East. Many areas are considered to be malaria-free, while others have seasonal risks. The risk of malaria is minimal in most cities, however check with your doctor if you are considering travelling to any rural areas. It is important to take antimalarial tablets if the risk is significant. For up-to-date information about the risk of contracting malaria in a specific country, contact your local travel-health clinic.

Anyone who has travelled in a country where malaria is present should be aware of the symptoms of malaria. It is possible to contract malaria from a single bite from an infected mosquito. Malaria almost always starts with marked shivering, fever and sweating. Muscle pains, headache and vomiting are common. Symptoms may occur anywhere from a few days to three weeks after the infected mosquito bite. The illness can start while you are taking preventative tablets if they are not fully effective, and may also occur after you have finished taking your tablets.

Poliomyelitis

Polio is generally spread through contaminated food and water. It is one of the vaccines given in childhood and should be boosted every 10 years, either orally (a drop on the tongue) or as an injection. Polio may be carried without symptoms, although it can cause a transient fever and, in rare cases, potentially permanent muscle weakness or paralysis.

Rabies

Spread through bites or licks on broken skin from an infected animal, rabies is fatal. Animal handlers should be vaccinated, as should those travelling to remote areas where a reliable source of post-bite vaccine is not available within 24 hours. Three injections are needed over a month. If you are infected and you have not been vaccinated, you will need a course of five injections starting within 24 hours or as soon as possible after the injury. Vaccination does not provide you with immunity, it merely buys you more time to seek appropriate medical help.

Rift Valley Fever

This haemorrhagic fever is spread through blood or blood products, including those from infected animals. It causes a 'flu-like' illness with fever, joint pains and occasionally more serious complications. Complete recovery is possible.

Schistosomiasis

Otherwise known as bilharzia, this is spread through the fresh water snail. It causes infection of the bowel and bladder, often with bleeding. It is caused by a fluke and is contracted through the skin from water contaminated with human urine or faeces. Paddling or swimming in suspect fresh water lakes or slow-running rivers should be avoided. There may be no symptoms. Possible symptoms include a transient fever and rash, and advanced cases of bilharzia may cause blood in the stool or in the urine. A blood test can detect antibodies if you have been exposed and treatment is then possible in specialist travel or infectious disease clinics.

Tuberculosis

Tuberculosis (TB) is spread through close respiratory contact and occasionally through infected milk or milk products. BCG vaccine is recommended for those likely to be mixing closely with the local population. It is more important for those visiting family or planning on a long stay, and those employed as teachers and health-care workers. TB can be asymptomatic, although symptoms can include a cough, weight loss or fever months or even years after exposure. An X-ray is the best way to confirm if you have TB. BCG gives a moderate degree of protection against TB. It causes a small permanent scar at the site of injection, and is usually only given in specialised chest clinics. As it's a live vaccine it should not be given to pregnant women or immunocompromised individuals. The BCG vaccine is not available in all countries.

Typhoid
This is spread through food or water that has been contaminated by infected human faeces. The first symptom is usually fever or a pink rash on the abdomen. Septicaemia (blood poisoning) may also occur. Typhoid vaccine (typhim Vi, typherix) will give protection for three years. In some countries, the oral vaccine Vivotif is also available.

Yellow Fever
A yellow fever vaccination is not required for any areas of the Middle East. However, the mosquito that spreads yellow fever has been known to be present in some parts of the Middle East. It is important to consult your local travel-health clinic as part of your predeparture plans for the latest details. Any travellers from a yellow fever endemic area *will* need to show proof of vaccination against yellow fever before entry into Syria and Lebanon. This normally applies to travellers arriving directly from an infected country, or travellers who have been in an infected country during the last 10 days. However it's a good idea to carry a certificate if you have been in an infected country any time in the last month, to avoid any possible difficulties with immigration. There is always the possibility that without an up-to-date certificate you will be vaccinated and detained in isolation at your port of arrival for up to 10 days, or even repatriated. The yellow fever vaccination must be given at a designated clinic, and is valid for 10 years. It is a live vaccine and must not be given to immunocompromised or pregnant travellers.

TRAVELLER'S DIARRHOEA
To prevent diarrhoea, avoid tap water unless it has been boiled, filtered or chemically disinfected (iodine tablets). Eat only fresh fruits or vegetables if cooked, or if you have peeled them yourself, and avoid dairy products that might contain unpasteurised milk. Buffet meals are risky – food should be piping hot; meals freshly cooked in front of you in a busy restaurant are more likely to be safe.

If you develop diarrhoea, be sure to drink plenty of fluids, preferably an oral rehydration solution containing lots of salt and sugar. A few loose stools don't require treatment but, if you start having more than four or five loose stools a day, you

should start taking an antibiotic (usually a quinolone drug) and an antidiarrhoeal agent (such as loperamide). If diarrhoea is bloody, persists for more than 72 hours, or is accompanied by fever, shaking chills or severe abdominal pain, you should seek medical attention.

ENVIRONMENTAL HAZARDS
Heat Illness
Heat exhaustion occurs following heavy sweating and excessive fluid loss with inadequate replacement of fluids and salt. This is particularly common in hot climates when taking unaccustomed exercise before full acclimatisation. Symptoms include headache, dizziness and tiredness. Dehydration is already happening by the time you feel thirsty.

A good indicator is the colour of your urine – aim to drink enough water to keep it pale and diluted. The treatment for heat exhaustion is fluid replacement with water or fruit juice or both, and cooling by cold water and fans. Treat salt loss with salty fluids such as soup or broth, and add a little more table salt to foods than usual.

Heatstroke is much more serious than heat exhaustion. This occurs when the body's heat-regulating mechanism breaks down. An excessive rise in body temperature leads to sweating ceasing, irrational and hyperactive behaviour and eventually loss of consciousness and death. Rapid cooling by spraying the body with water and fanning is an ideal treatment. Emergency fluid and electrolyte replacement by intravenous drip is usually also required.

Insect Bites & Stings
Mosquitoes may not carry malaria, but can still cause irritation and infected bites. Using DEET-based insect repellents will prevent bites. Mosquitoes also spread dengue fever.

Bees and wasps only cause real problems to those with a severe allergy (anaphylaxis). If you have a severe allergy to bee or wasp stings you should carry an adrenaline injection or something similar.

Sand flies are located around Mediterranean beaches. They usually only cause a nasty itchy bite but can carry a rare skin disorder called cutaneous leishmaniasis (see p408). Bites may be prevented by using DEET-based repellents.

Scorpions are frequently found in arid or dry climates. They can cause a painful bite which is rarely life threatening.

Bed bugs are often found in hostels and cheap hotels. They lead to very itchy, lumpy bites. Spraying the mattress with an appropriate insect killer will do a good job of getting rid of them.

Scabies are also frequently found in cheap accommodation. These tiny mites live in the skin, particularly between the fingers. They cause an intensely itchy rash. Scabies is easily treated with lotion available from pharmacies; people you come into contact with also need treating to avoid spreading scabies.

Snake Bites

Do not walk barefoot or stick your hand into holes or cracks. Half of those bitten by venomous snakes are not actually injected with poison (envenomed).

If bitten by a snake, do not panic. Immobilise the bitten limb with a splint (eg a stick) and apply a bandage over the site, firm pressure, similar to a bandage over a sprain. Do not apply a tourniquet, or cut or suck the bite.

Get the victim to medical help as soon as possible so that antivenin can be given if necessary.

Water

Tap water is not safe to drink in the Middle East. Stick to bottled water or boil water for 10 minutes, or use water purification tablets or a filter. Do not drink water from rivers or lakes, this may contain bacteria or viruses that can cause diarrhoea or vomiting.

TRAVELLING WITH CHILDREN

All travellers with children should know how to treat minor ailments and when to seek medical treatment. Make sure the children are up to date with routine vaccinations, and discuss possible travel vaccines well before departure as some vaccines are not suitable for children aged under one year old.

In hot, moist climates any wound or break in the skin may lead to infection. The area should be cleaned and then kept dry and clean. Remember to avoid contaminated food and water. If your child is vomiting or experiencing diarrhoea, lost fluid and salts must be replaced. It may be helpful to take rehydration powders for reconstituting with boiled water. Ask your doctor about this.

Encourage children to avoid dogs or other mammals because of the risk of rabies and other diseases. Any bite, scratch or lick from a warm-blooded, furry animal should immediately be thoroughly cleaned. If there is any possibility that the animal is infected with rabies, seek immediate medical assistance.

WOMEN'S HEALTH

Emotional stress, exhaustion and travelling through different time zones can all contribute to an upset in the menstrual pattern. If using oral contraceptives, remember some antibiotics, diarrhoea and vomiting can stop the pill from working and lead to the risk of pregnancy – remember to take condoms with you just in case. Condoms should be kept in a cool dry place or they may crack.

Emergency contraception is most effective if taken within 24 hours of unprotected sex. The **International Planned Parent Federation** (www.ippf.org) can advise you on the availability of contraception in different countries.

Tampons and sanitary towels are not always available outside major cities in the Middle East.

Travelling during pregnancy is usually possible but there are important things to consider. Have a medical check-up before embarking on your trip. The most risky times for travel are during the first 12 weeks of pregnancy, when miscarriage is most likely, and after 30 weeks, when complications such as high blood pressure and premature delivery can occur. Most airlines will not accept a traveller after 28 to 32 weeks of pregnancy, and long-haul flights in the later stages can be very uncomfortable. Antenatal facilities vary greatly between countries in the Middle East and you should think carefully before travelling to a country with poor medical facilities or where there are major cultural and language differences from home. Take written records of the pregnancy including details of your blood group in case you need medical attention while away. Ensure your insurance policy covers pregnancy, delivery and postnatal care, but remember insurance policies are only as good as the facilities available.

Language

CONTENTS

Arabic is the official language of both Syria and Lebanon. Though French is also widely spoken, and English is rapidly gaining ground, any effort to communicate in Arabic will be well rewarded. No matter how bad your pronunciation or grammar might be, you'll often get the response (usually with a big smile): 'Ah, you speak Arabic very well!'. Greeting officials, who are often less than helpful, with *salaam alaykum* (peace be upon you), often works wonders.

Learning a few basics for day-to-day travelling doesn't take long at all, but to master the complexities of Arabic would take years of consistent study. The whole issue is complicated by the differences between Classical Arabic (*fus-ha*), its modern descendant MSA (Modern Standard Arabic) and regional dialects. The classical tongue is the language of the Quran and Arabic poetry of centuries past. For long it remained static, but in order to survive it had to adapt to change, and the result is more or less MSA, the common language of the press, radio and educated discourse. It is as close to a *lingua franca* (common language) as the Arab world comes, and is generally understood – if not always well spoken – across the Arab world.

For most foreigners trying to learn Arabic, the most frustrating aspect is the spoken language (wherever you are), as there's virtually no written material to refer to for back up. Acquisition of MSA is a long-term investment, and an esoteric argument flows back and forth about the relative merits of learning MSA first (and so perhaps having to wait some time before being able to communicate adequately with people in the street) or learning a dialect. All this will give you an inkling of why so few non-Arabs, or non-Muslims, develop the urge to embark on a study of the language.

ARABIC OF THE LEVANT

The Arabic dialects of Syria and Lebanon belong to a group known as Levantine Arabic. As it happens, these spoken varieties are not too distant from MSA, but in any case, the words and phrases we offer in this language guide reflect local speech, with any significant differences between the two dialects marked either (Leb) or (Syr). For a more comprehensive guide to Levantine Arabic and the other principal languages and Arabic dialects of the Middle East, get a copy of Loenly Planet's compact but comprehensive *Middle East Phrasebook*.

PRONUNCIATION

Pronunciation of Arabic in any of its guises can be tongue-tying for someone unfamiliar with the intonation and combination of sounds. Pronounce the transliterated words slowly and clearly.

This language guide should help, but bear in mind that the myriad rules governing pronunciation and vowel use are too extensive to be covered here.

Vowels

Technically, there are three long and three short vowels in Arabic. The reality is a little different, with local dialect and varying consonant combinations affecting their pronunciation. This is the case throughout the Arabic-speaking world. More like five short and five long vowels can be identified; in this guide we use all but the long 'o' (as in 'or').

THE STANDARD ARABIC ALPHABET

Final	Medial	Initial	Alone	Transliteration	Pronunciation
ـا			ا	aa	as in 'father'
ـب	ـبـ	بـ	ب	b	as in 'bet'
ـت	ـتـ	تـ	ت	t	as in 'ten'
ـث	ـثـ	ثـ	ث	th	as in 'thin'
ـج	ـجـ	جـ	ج	j	as in 'jet'
ـح	ـحـ	حـ	ح	H	a strongly whispered 'h', like a sigh of relief
ـخ	ـخـ	خـ	خ	kh	as the 'ch' in Scottish *loch*
ـد			د	d	as in 'dim'
ـذ			ذ	dh	as the 'th' in 'this'; also as **d** or **z**
ـر			ر	r	a rolled 'r', as in the Spanish word *caro*
ـز			ز	z	as in 'zip'
ـس	ـسـ	سـ	س	s	as in 'so', never as in 'wisdom'
ـش	ـشـ	شـ	ش	sh	as in 'ship'
ـص	ـصـ	صـ	ص	ş	emphatic 's'
ـض	ـضـ	ضـ	ض	ḍ	emphatic 'd'
ـط	ـطـ	طـ	ط	ţ	emphatic 't'
ـظ	ـظـ	ظـ	ظ	ẓ	emphatic 'z'
ـع	ـعـ	عـ	ع	'	the Arabic letter *'ayn*; pronounce as a glottal stop – like the closing of the throat before saying 'Oh-oh!' (see Tricky Sounds, opposite)
ـغ	ـغـ	غـ	غ	gh	a guttural sound like Parisian 'r'
ـف	ـفـ	فـ	ف	f	as in 'far'
ـق	ـقـ	قـ	ق	q	a strongly guttural 'k' sound; also often pronounced as a glottal stop
ـك	ـكـ	كـ	ك	k	as in 'king'
ـل	ـلـ	لـ	ل	l	as in 'lamb'
ـم	ـمـ	مـ	م	m	as in 'me'
ـن	ـنـ	نـ	ن	n	as in 'name'
ـه	ـهـ	هـ	ه	h	as in 'ham'
ـو			و	w	as in 'wet'; or
				oo	long, as in 'food'; or
				ow	as in 'how'
ـي	ـيـ	يـ	ي	y	as in 'yes'; or
				ee	as in 'beer', only softer; or
				ai/ay	as in 'aisle'/as the 'ay' in 'day'

Vowels Not all Arabic vowel sounds are represented in the alphabet. For more information on the vowel sounds used in this language guide, see Pronunciation on p411.

Emphatic Consonants To simplify the transliteration system used in this book, the emphatic consonants have not been included.

LANGUAGE

a	as in 'had'
aa	as the 'a' in 'father'
e	short, as in 'bet'; long, as in 'there'
i	as in 'hit'
ee	as in 'beer', only softer
o	as in 'hot'
u	as in 'put'
oo	as in 'food'

Consonants

Pronunciation for all Arabic consonants is covered in the alphabet table opposite. Note that when double consonants occur in transliterations, both are pronounced. For example, al-hammam (toilet), is pronounced 'al-ham-mam'.

TRICKY SOUNDS

Arabic has two sounds that are very tricky for non-Arabs to produce: the 'ayn and the glottal stop. The letter 'ayn represents a sound with no English equivalent that comes even close. It is similar to the glottal stop (which is not actually represented in the alphabet), but the muscles at the back of the throat are gagged more forcefully and air is released – it has been described as the sound of someone being strangled. In many transliteration systems 'ayn is represented by an opening quotation mark, and the glottal stop by a closing quotation mark. To make the transliterations in this language guide (and throughout the rest of the book) easier to use, we have not distinguished between the glottal stop and the 'ayn, using the closing quotation mark to represent both sounds. You should find that Arabic speakers will still understand you.

TRANSLITERATION

It's worth noting here that transliteration from the Arabic script into English – or any other language for that matter – is at best an approximate science.

The presence of sounds unknown in European languages and the fact that the script is 'incomplete' (most vowels are not written) combine to make it nearly impossible to settle on one universally accepted method of transliteration. A wide variety of spellings is therefore possible for words when they appear in Latin script – and that goes for places and people's names as well.

The whole thing is further complicated by the wide variety of dialects and influences, and the problems Arabs themselves

often have in deciding on an appropriate spelling. In Jordan, for example (where English is likely to play a part), the transliteration of the same Arabic words may be very different from what would be rendered in Lebanon and Syria, where French is a key factor. Not even the most venerable of western Arabists have been able to come up with a satisfactory solution.

While striving to reflect the language as closely as possible and aiming at consistency, this book generally anglicises place, street and hotel names and the like the way the locals have done. Don't be surprised if you come across several versions of the same thing.

ACCOMMODATION

I'd like to book a ...	biddee ehjuz ...
Do you have a ...?	fi ...?
(cheap) room	ghurfa (rkheesa)
single room	ghurfa mufrada
double room	ghurfa bi sareerayn

for one night	li layli waHde
for two nights	layltayn
May I see it?	mumkin shoofa?
It's very noisy/dirty.	kteer dajeh/wuskha
How much is it per person?	'addaysh li kul waHid?
How much is it per night?	'addaysh bel layli?
Where is the bathroom?	wayn al-Hammam?
We're leaving today.	niHna musafireen al-youm

address	al-'anwaan
air-conditioning	kondishon/mookayif
blanket	al-bataaniyya/al-Hrem
camp site	mukhayam
electricity	kahraba
hotel	funduq/otel
hot water	mai sukhni (Leb)
	mai saakhina (Syr)
key	al-miftaH
manager	al-mudeer
shower	doosh
soap	saboon
toilet	twalet (also bet al-mai in Syria)

CONVERSATION & ESSENTIALS

Arabs place great importance on civility and it's rare to see any interaction between people that doesn't begin with profuse greetings, enquiries into the other's health and other niceties.

Arabic greetings are more formal than in English and there is a reciprocal response to each. These sometimes vary slightly, depending on whether you're addressing a man or a woman. A simple encounter can become a drawn-out affair, with neither side wanting to be the one to put a halt to the stream of greetings and well-wishing. As an *ajnabi* (foreigner), you're not expected to know all the ins and outs, but if you come up with the right expression at the appropriate moment they'll love it.

The most common greeting is *salaam alaykum* (peace be upon you), to which the correct reply is *wa alaykum as-salaam* (and upon you be peace). If you get invited to a birthday celebration or are around for any of the big holidays, the common greeting is *kul sana wa intum bikher* (I wish you well for the coming year).

After having a bath or shower, you will often hear people say to you *na'iman*, which roughly means 'heavenly' and boils down to an observation along the lines of 'nice and clean now, eh'.

Arrival in one piece is always something to be grateful for. Passengers will often be greeted with *il-Hamdu lillah al as-salaama* – 'thank God for your safe arrival'.

Hi.	marHaba
Hi. (response)	marHabtain
Hello.	ahlan wa sahlan or just ahlan (Welcome)
Hello. (response)	ahlan beek/i (m/f)

It's an important custom in Lebanon and Syria to ask after a person's or their family's health when greeting, eg *kayf es-saHa?* (How is your health?), *kayf il'ayli?* (How is the family?). The response is *bikher il-Hamdu lillah*, (Fine, thank you).

Goodbye.	ma'a salaama/Allah ma'ak
Good morning.	sabaH al-khayr
Good morning. (response)	sabaH 'an-noor
Good evening.	masa' al-khayr
Good evening. (response)	masa 'an-noor
Good night.	tisbaH 'ala khayr
Good night. (response)	wa inta min ahlu
Yes.	aiwa/na'am
Yeah.	ay

No.	la
Please. (request)	min fadlak/fadleek (m/f) or iza bitreed/bitreedi (m/f) (Leb)
Please. (polite)	law samaHt/samaHti (m/f)
Please. (come in)	tafaddal/tafaddali (m/f)/ tafaddaloo (pl)
Thank you.	shukran
Thank you very much.	shukran kteer/shukran jazeelan
You're welcome.	'afwan or tikram/tikrami (m/f)
One moment, please.	lahza min fadlak/i (m/f)
Pardon/Excuse me.	'afwan
Sorry!	aasif/aasifa! (m/f)
No problem.	mafi mushkili/moo mushkila
Never mind.	ma'alesh
Just a moment.	laHza
Congratulations!	mabrouk!

Questions like 'Is the bus coming?' or 'Will the bank be open later?' generally elicit the response: *in sha' Allah* – 'God willing' – an expression you'll hear over and over again. Another common one is *ma sha' Allah* – 'God's will be done' – sometimes a useful answer to probing questions about why you're not married yet.

How are you?	kayf Haalak/Haalik? (m/f)
How're you doing?	kayfak/kayfik? (m/f)
Fine thank you.	bikher il-Hamdu lillah
What's your name?	shu-ismak/shu-ismik? (m/f)
My name is ...	ismi ...
Pleased to meet you. (when departing)	tsharrafna/fursa sa'ida (Leb/Syr)
Nice to meet you. (lit: you honour us)	tasharrafna
Where are you from?	min wayn inta/inti? (m/f)
I'm from ...	ana min ...
Do you like ...?	inta/inti bitHeb ...? (m/f)
I like ...	ana bHeb ...
I don't like ...	ana ma bHeb ...

I	ana
you	inta/inti (m/f)
he	huwa
she	hiyya
we	niHna
you	into
they	homm

DIRECTIONS

| How do I get to ...? | keef boosal ala ...? |
| Can you show me (on the map)? | mumkin tfarjeeni ('ala al-khareeta)? |

SIGNS

Entrance	مدخل
Exit	خروج
Open	مفتوح
Closed	مغلق
Prohibited	ممنوع
Information	معلومات
Hospital	مستشفي
Police	شرطة
Men's Toilet	حمام للرجال
Women's Toilet	حمام للنساء

How many kilometres?	kam kilometre?
What street is this?	shoo Hash-shari hayda? (Leb)
	shoo Hal shanki had? (Syr)
on the left	'ala yasaar/shimaal
on the right	'ala yameen
opposite	muqaabil
straight ahead	dughri
at the next corner	tanee mafraq
this way	min hon
here/there	hon/honeek
in front of	amaam/iddaam
near	qareeb
far	ba'eed
north	shimaal
south	janub
east	sharq
west	gharb

HEALTH

I'm ill.	ana maareed/a (m/f)
My friend is ill.	sadeeqi maareed (m)
	sadeeqati maareeda (f)
It hurts here.	beeyujani hon

I'm ...	andee ...
asthmatic	azmitrabo
diabetic	sukkari
epileptic	saraa/alsaa'a

I'm allergic ...	andee Hasasiyya ...
to antibiotics	min al-mudad alHayawi
to aspirin	min al-aspireen
to penicillin	min al-binisileen
to bees	min al-naHl
to nuts	min al-mukassarat

antiseptic	mutahhi
aspirin	aspireen/aspro (brand name)
Band-Aids	plaster

EMERGENCIES

Help me!	saa'idoonee!
I'm sick.	ana mareed/mareeda (m/f)
Call the police!	ittusil bil polees! (Leb)
	ittusil bil shurta! (Syr)
doctor	duktoor/tabeeb
hospital	al-mustash-fa
police	al-polees/ash-shurta (Leb/Syr)
Go away!	imshee!/rouh min hoon!
Shame (on you)! (said by woman)	aayb!

condoms	kaboot
contraceptive	waseela lee mana' al-Ham
diarrhoea	is-haal
fever	Harara
headache	wajaa-ras
hospital	mustashfa
medicine	dawa
pregnant	Hamel
prescription	wasfa/rashetta
sanitary napkins	fuwat saHiyya
stomachache	wajaa fil battu
sunblock cream	krem waki min ashilt al-shams
tampons	kotex (brand name)

LANGUAGE DIFFICULTIES

Do you speak English?	bitiHki ingleezi?
I understand.	ana afham
I don't understand.	ana ma bifham

I speak ...	ana baHki ...
English	ingleezi
French	faransi
German	almaani

I speak a little Arabic.	ana baHki arabi shway
I don't speak Arabic.	ana ma beHki arabi
I want an interpreter.	biddee mutarjem
Could you write it down, please?	mumkin tiktabhu, min fadlak?
How do you say ... in Arabic?	kayf t'ul ... bil'arabi?

NUMBERS

0	sifr	٠
1	waHid	١
2	itnayn/tintayn	٢
3	talaata	٣
4	arba'a	٤
5	khamsa	٥
6	sitta	٦
7	saba'a	٧

8	tamanya	٨
9	tis'a	٩
10	'ashara	١٠
11	yeedaa'sh	١١
12	yeetnaa'sh	١٢
13	talaatash	١٣
14	arbatash	١٤
15	khamastash	١٥
16	sittash	١٦
17	sabatash	١٧
18	tamantash	١٨
19	tasatash	١٩
20	'ashreen	٢٠
21	wāHid wa 'ashreen	٢١
22	itnayn wa 'ashreen	٢٢
30	talaateen	٣٠
40	arba'een	٤٠
50	khamseen	٥٠
60	sitteen	٦٠
70	saba'een	٧٠
80	tamaneen	٨٠
90	tis'een	٩٠
100	miyya (meet before a noun)	١٠٠
200	miyyatayn	٢٠٠
1000	'alf	١٠٠٠
2000	'alfayn	٢٠٠٠
3000	talaat-alaf	٣٠٠٠

PAPERWORK

date of birth	tareekh al-meelad/-wilaada
name	al-ism
nationality	al-jenseeya
passport	jawaz al-safar (or simply paspor)
permit	tasriH
place of birth	makan al-meelad/-wilaada
visa	visa/ta'shira

SHOPPING & SERVICES

I'm looking for ...	ana abHath ... aa'n
Where is the ...?	wayn/fayn ...?
bank	al-bank
beach	ash-shaati'/al-plaaj/al-baHr
chemist/pharmacy	as-sayidiliyya (Syr)
	al-farmashiya (Leb)
city/town	al-medeena
city centre	markaz al-medeena
customs	al-jumruk
entrance	al-dukhool/al-madkhal
exchange office	al-masref/al-saraf
exit	al-khurooj
hotel	al-funduq/al-otel
information desk	isti'laamaat
laundry	al ghaseel
market	al-sooq

mosque	al-jaami'/al-masjid
museum	al-matHaf
newsagents	al-maktaba
old city	al-medeena al-qadeema/
	al-medeena l'ateeqa
passport & immigration office	maktab al-jawazaat wa al-hijra
police	ash-shurta
post office	maktab al-bareed
restaurant	al-mata'am
telephone office	maktab at-telefon/
	maktab al-haalef
temple	al-ma'abad
tourist office	maktab al-siyaHa

I want to change ...	baddee sarref ...
money	masaari
travellers cheques	sheeket siyaHiyya
What time does it open?	emta byeftaH?
What time does it close?	emta bi sakkir?
I'd like to make a telephone call.	fini talfen 'omol maaroof (Leb)
	mumkin talfen min fadlak(Syr)
Where can I buy ...?	wayn/fayn feeni eshtiree ...?
What is this?	shu hayda/hada? (Leb/Syr)
How much?	addaysh? (also bikam in Syr)
How many?	kim waHid?
How much is it?	bi addaysh?
That's too expensive.	hayda kteer ghaalee (Leb)
	hada ghalee kheteer (Syr)
Is there ...?	fee ...?
There isn't (any).	ma fee
May I look at it?	feeni etallah 'alaya? (Leb)
	mumkin shoof? (Syr)
big/bigger	kbeer/akbar
cheap	rkhees
cheaper	arkhas
closed	msakkar
expensive	ghaali
money	al-fuloos/al-masaari
open	maftuH
small/smaller	sagheer/asghar

TIME & DATE

What's the time?	addaysh essa'aa?
When?	emta?
now	halla'
after	b'adayn
on time	al waket
early	bakkeer
late	ma'qar
daily	kil youm

today	al-youm	3rd	Rabi' al-Awal
tomorrow	bukra	4th	Rabay ath-Thaani
day after tomorrow	ba'ad bukra	5th	Jumaada al-Awal
yesterday	imbaarih	6th	Jumaada al-Akhira
minute	daqeeqa	7th	Rajab
hour	saa'a	8th	Shaban
day	youm	9th	Ramadan
week	usboo'	10th	Shawwal
month	shahr	11th	Zuul-Qeda
year	sana	12th	Zuul-Hijja
morning	soubeH		
afternoon	ba'ad deher		
evening	massa		
night	layl		

TRANSPORT
Public Transport

Where is ...?	wayn/fayn ...?
airport	al-mataar
bus station	maHattat al-baas/
	maHattat al-karaj
ticket office	maktab at-tazaakar
train station	maHattat al-qitaar

Monday	al-tenayn
Tuesday	at-talaata
Wednesday	al-arba'a
Thursday	al-khamees
Friday	al-jum'a
Saturday	as-sabt
Sunday	al-aHad

What time does ...	ay saa'a biyitla'/biyusal ...?
leave/arrive?	
boat/ferry	al-markib/as-safeena
(small) boat	ash-shakhtura
bus	al-baas
plane	al-teeyara
train	al-qitaar

The Western Calendar Months

The Islamic year has 12 lunar months and is 11 days shorter than the Western (Gregorian) calendar, so important Muslim dates will occur 11 days earlier each (Western) year.

There are two Gregorian calendars in use in the Arab world. In Egypt and westwards, the months have virtually the same names as in English (January is *yanaayir*, October is *octobir* and so on), but in Lebanon and eastwards, the names are quite different. Talking about, say, June as 'month six' is the easiest solution, but for the sake of completeness, the months from January are:

Which bus goes to ...?	aya baas biyruH 'ala ...?
I want to go to ...	ana badeh ruH ala ...
Does this bus go	hal-baas biyruH 'ala ...?
to ...?	
How many buses	kam baas biyruH ben nahar ...?
per day go to ...?	
How long does the	kam sa'a ar-riHla?
trip take?	
Please tell me when	'umal ma'aroof illee lamma
we get to ...	noosal la ...
Stop here, please.	wa'if hoon 'umal ma'aroof
Please wait for me.	'umal ma'aroof unturnee (Leb)
	'umal ma'aroof istanna (Syr)
May I sit here?	mumkin a'ood hoon?
May we sit here?	mumkin ni'ood hoon?

January	kanoon ath-thani
February	shubaat
March	azaar
April	nisaan
May	ayyaar
June	Huzayraan
July	tammooz
August	'aab
September	aylool
October	tishreen al-awal
November	tishreen ath-thani
December	kaanoon al-awal

1st class	daraja oola
2nd class	daraja taaniya
ticket	at-tazaakar
to/from	ila/min

Private Transport

I'd like to hire a ...	biddee esta'jer ...
Where can I hire a ...?	wayn/fayn feeni esta'jer ...?
bicycle	bisklet
camel	jamal
car	sayyaara

The Hejira Calendar Months

1st	MoHarram
2nd	Safar

donkey	Hmaar
4WD	jeep
horse	Hsaan
motorcycle	motosikl
tour guide	al-dalee as-siyaaHi/
	al-murshid as-siyaaHi

Is this the road to ...?
Hal Haza al-tareeq eela ...?
Where's a service station?
wayn/fayn maHaltet al-benzeen?
Please fill it up.
min fadlak (emla/abee) Ha
I'd like (30) litres.
biddee talaateen leeter

diesel	deezel
leaded petrol	benzeen bee rasa
unleaded petrol	benzeen beedoon rasas

(How long) Can I park here?
(kam sa'a) mumkin aas-f hon?
Where do I pay?
fayn/wayn mumkin an addf'aa?
I need a mechanic.
bidee mekaneesyan

The car/motorbike has broken down (at ...)
al-sayyaara/-mutusikl it'atlit ('an ...)
The car/motorbike won't start.
al-sayyaara/-mutusikl ma bit door
I have a flat tyre.
nzel al-doolab
I've run out of petrol.
mafi benzeen or al-benzeen khalas
I've had an accident.
aamalt hads

TRAVEL WITH CHILDREN

Is there a/an ...?	*fee ...?*
I need a/an	*biddee ...*
car baby seat	*kursee sayyaara leel bebe'*
disposable nappies	*pamperz* (brand name)
nappies/diapers	*Ha fa daat*
formula (baby's milk)	*Haleeb bebe'*
highchair	*kursee atfaal*
potty	*muneeyai*
stroller	*arabeyet atfaal*

Do you mind if I breastfeed here?
mumkin aradda hon?
Are children allowed?
Hal yousmah leel atfaal?

Also available from Lonely Planet:
Middle East Phrasebook

Glossary

Abbasids – Baghdad-based successor dynasty to the *Umayyads*. It ruled from AD 750 until the sacking of Baghdad by the Mongols in 1258.
abd – servant of
abeyya – woman's cloak
ablaq – alternating courses of coloured stone
abu – father, saint
acropolis – citadel of an ancient city (usually Greek)
ain – well, spring
al-muderiyya – town hall
Amal – Shiite militia turned political party
Amorites – Western Semitic people who emerged from the Syrian deserts around 2000 BC and influenced life in the cities of Mesopotamia and Phoenicia until 1600 BC
apse – semicircular recess for the altar in a church
Arab League – league of 22 independent Arab states, formed in 1945, to further cultural, economic, military, political and social cooperation between the states
architrave – the lowest division of the *entablature*, extending from column to column. Also the moulded frame around a door or window.
Arz ar-Rab – 'Cedars of the Lord'. The local name for a small remaining group of cedar trees near Bcharré.
AUB – American University of Beirut
Ayyubids – an Egyptian-based dynasty founded by *Saladin*

bab (s), abwab (pl) – gate, door
bahr – river
baksheesh – tip
baladi – local, rural
beit – house
bey – term of respect
Bilad ish-Sham – the area of modern Syria, Lebanon and Palestine
bir – spring, well
birket – lake
burj – tower

caliph – Islamic ruler. The spiritual and temporal leader of the Sunni Muslim community, or 'umma' (note the institution of the caliphate was abolished in 1924). Also spelt 'khalif'.
capital – the top, decorated part of a column
caravanserai – see *khan*
cardo maximus – the main north–south street of a Roman-era town
cella – inner part of temple that houses the statue of a god or goddess
centrale – government phone office

chador – one-piece head-to-toe black garment worn by Muslim women
chai – tea
Chalcolithic – period between the Neolithic and Bronze Ages, in which there was an increase in urbanisation and trade and the occasional use of copper
cornice – the upper portion of the *entablature* in classical or Renaissance architecture
cuneiform – wedge-shaped characters of several different languages, including Babylonian

dabke – an energetic folk dance that is the national Lebanese dance
decumanus maximus – the main east–west street of a Roman-era town
deir – monastery, convent
donjon – castle keep or great tower
Druze – a religious sect based on Islamic teachings. Its followers are found mainly in Lebanon, with some in Syria and Israel.

eid – Islamic feast
Eid al-Adha – Feast of Sacrifice, which marks the end of the pilgrimage to Mecca
Eid al-Fitr – Festival of Breaking the Fast, which is celebrated at the end of *Ramadan*
emir – Islamic ruler, military commander or governor
entablature – upper part of the classical temple, comprising the architrave, frieze and cornice, supported by the colonnade
exedra – a room or outdoor area with seats for discussions
ezan – call to prayer

Fakhreddine – a Lebanese nationalist hero. Appointed by the Ottomans in 1590 to pacify the Druze, he unified the Mt Lebanon area. Also spelt Fakhr ad-Din.
Fatimids – a Shiite dynasty from North Africa that claimed to be descended from Fatima, daughter of the Prophet Mohammed, and her husband Ali ibn Abi Taleb
frieze – central part of the *entablature*
funduq – hotel
furn – oven

Green Line – line that divided Beirut's eastern (Christian) half from its western (Muslim) half

hajj – pilgrimage to Mecca
hakawati – storyteller
halawat al-jibn – a soft cheese-based, doughy delicacy drenched in honey or syrup and often topped with ice cream

hamam – pigeon
hammam – bathhouse
hara – small lane, alley
haram – the sacred area inside a mosque
haramlik – family or women's quarters
hejab – woman's headscarf
Hejira – migration. Usually refers to Mohammed's flight from Mecca in AD 622. Also the name of the Islamic calendar.
Hezbollah – Party of God, radical Shiite political party based in Lebanon. Its guerilla arm, Islamic Jihad, was largely responsible for expelling Israel from the south of Lebanon.
Hyksos – Semitic invaders from Western Asia, probably from Asia Minor (ie Anatolia) famed for their horseman-ship. They introduced the horse to Pharaonic Egypt and ruled there from 1720 to 1550 BC.
hypocaust – raised floor in Roman bathhouses, heated by circulating hot air beneath it
hypogeum – underground burial chamber

iconostasis – screen with doors and icons set in tiers, used in eastern Christian churches
iftar – breaking of the day's fast during *Ramadan*
imam – a man schooled in Islam and who often doubles as the *muezzin*
Islamic Jihad – armed wing of *Hezbollah*
iwan – vaulted hall, opening into a central court, in the *madrassa* of a mosque

jalabiyya – full-length robe worn by men and women alike
jebel – mountain or mountain range
jezira – island
jihad – literally 'striving in the way of the faith'; holy war

Kaaba – the rectangular structure at the centre of the grand mosque in Mecca (containing the black stone) around which pilgrims walk
kalybe – open-fronted shrine
kanjar – dagger
karaj/karajat – garage/garage of
Karnak – Syrian government-run buses
khan – a travellers' inn
kineesa – church
kiyaas hammam – goat-hair bags used as loofahs
kubri – bridge
kufeyya – distinctive black-and-white or red-and-white headdress worn by traditional Muslim and Bedu Arabs
kursi – a wooden stand for holding the Quran
kuttab – Quranic school
Levant – literally 'where the sun rises'. Region of the Eastern Mediterranean from Egypt to Greece.
loggia – colonnaded arcade providing a sheltered exten-sion of a hall

madrassa – school where Islamic law is taught
mahatta – station
maktab amn al-aam – general security office
Mamluks – military class of ex-Turkish slaves, established about AD 1250, that ruled much of Syria and Lebanon from Egypt and remained in power in the latter until 1805
manakeesh – a type of flat bread
mar – saint
maristan – hospital
Maronite – Lebanese Christians who embrace the Monothelite Doctrine that Christ had two natures but only a single divine will
mashrabiyya – ornately carved wooden panel or screen
matar – airport
medina – old walled centre of any Islamic city
meghazils – spindles
mezze – starters, appetisers
mihrab – niche in the wall of a mosque that indicates the direction of Mecca
minaret – tower of a mosque from which *ezan* is made
minbar – pulpit in a mosque
muezzin – mosque official who calls the faithful to prayer five times a day from the *minaret*
muqarnas – stalactite-type stone carving used to decorate doorways and window recesses
murex – a kind of mollusc from which the famous purple dye of Tyre comes
mutasarrifa – an Ottoman administrative unit, eg Mt Lebanon

nahr – river
nargileh – water pipe
nave – central part of a church
nebaa – spring
Neolithic – literally 'new stone' age. Period, based on the development of stone tools, that witnessed the beginnings of domestication and urbanisation.
nymphaeum – monumental fountain

oud – literally 'wood'. Used for both a kind of lute and wood burned on an incense burner.

pasha – lord. Also a term used more generally to denote a person of standing.
Phalangist – member of the Lebanese Christian paramilitary organisation, founded in 1936
PLO – Palestinian Liberation Organisation
propylaeum – monumental temple gateway

qa'a – reception room
qahwa – coffee or coffeehouse
qala'at – fortress
qasr – palace

rais – waiter
rakats – cycles of prayer during which the Quran is read and bows and prostrations are performed
Ramadan – ninth month of the lunar Islamic calendar, during which Muslims fast from sunrise to sunset
ras – headland

saahat – square
sabil – public drinking fountain
Saladin – founder of the Ayyubid dynasty, warlord who retook Jerusalem from the Crusaders. Also spelt Salah ad-Din.
saray – palace
Seleucids – royal dynasty (312–64 BC) whose rule extended from Thrace to India at its peak. Founded by Seleucus, a Macedonian general in Alexander the Great's army.
serail – Ottoman palace. Also spelt 'seraglio'.
servees – service taxi
sharia – road, way
Sharia'a – Islamic law, the body of doctrine that regulates the lives of Muslims
sheesha – water pipe
Shiism – a branch of Islam that regards the prophet Mohammed's cousin Ali and his successors as the true leaders
shwarma – meat sliced off a spit and stuffed in a pocket of pita-type bread with chopped tomatoes and garnish. Equivalent to the Turkish döner kebab.
SLA – South Lebanon Army
souq – bazaar, market

speos – rock-cut tomb or chapel
stele (s), stelae (pl) – stone or wooden commemorative slab or column decorated with inscriptions or figures
Sufi – follower of the Islamic mystical orders, which emphasise dancing, chanting and trances in order to attain unity with God
sultan – the absolute ruler of a Muslim state
sumac – reddish, lemony dried herb, delicious in salad
Sunni – main branch of Islam. Based on the words and acts of the Prophet Mohammed, with the *caliph* seen as the true successor.

tabla – small hand-held drum
tell – artificial mound
tetrapylon – four-columned structure

ulema – group of Muslim scholars or religious leaders, a member of this group
Umayyads – first great dynasty (661–750) of Arab Muslim rulers, based in Damascus
umm – mother of
Unifil – United Nations Interim Force In Lebanon

wadi – desert watercourse, dry except in the rainy season
waha – oasis
waqf – religious endowment

zaatar – thyme-like herb
zawiya – hospice and religious school
zikr – long sessions of dancing, chanting and swaying carried out by Sufis to achieve oneness with God

THE AUTHORS

The Authors

TERRY CARTER   Coordinating Author

Terry has lived in the Middle East since 1998, moving to the United Arab Emirates (UAE) after many years toiling in Sydney's publishing industry. Having erroneously concluded that travel writing and photography was a far more glamorous occupation than designing books or websites, he's been writing and shooting photos for magazines, books and websites for several years. He's always angling for an excuse to scout out second-hand *ouds* (Arabic lutes) in Syria or to hit some off-piste snowboarding in Lebanon. Based in Dubai with wife Lara, Terry has a Master's degree in media studies. Terry and Lara jointly researched and wrote all of the Syria chapters, as well as Itineraries, Destination Syria & Lebanon and Transport, and cooauthored the History and The Word on the Street chapters.

LARA DUNSTON   Coordinating Author

Australian-born Lara Dunston may have travelled to over 60 countries, but Syria and Lebanon have remained firm favourites since she and husband Terry first visited 10 years ago. Based in nearby Dubai, the couple makes a habit of heading to the Levant every chance they get for the cuisine, culture, shopping and social life. Holding degrees in film, writing and international studies, Lara has worked in filmmaking, PR/media relations and academia. With husband Terry she has authored over 25 guidebooks and her travel writing has appeared in magazines and newspapers around the globe. They also blog about their travels.

AMELIA THOMAS

Amelia Thomas is a writer and journalist working throughout the Middle East and beyond. She has worked on numerous Lonely Planet titles and particularly loves traipsing around the Middle East's atmospheric old Victorian hotel relics. Amelia has three toddlers – with a fourth baby on the way as this book was researched – who enjoy tagging along on far-flung jaunts. Her book *The Zoo on the Road to Nablus* tells the true story of the last Palestinian zoo. Amelia researched and wrote all of the Lebanon chapters and coauthored the History and The Word on the Street chapters.

LONELY PLANET AUTHORS

Why is our travel information the best in the world? It's simple: our authors are independent, dedicated travellers. They don't research using just the internet or phone, and they don't take freebies in exchange for positive coverage. They travel widely, to all the popular spots and off the beaten track. They personally visit thousands of hotels, restaurants, cafés, bars, galleries, palaces, museums and more – and they take pride in getting all the details right, and telling it how it is. Think you can do it? Find out how at lonelyplanet.com.

Behind the Scenes

THIS BOOK

This 3rd edition of *Syria & Lebanon* was coordinated by Terry Carter and Lara Dunston, who jointly researched and wrote all of the Syria chapters, as well as Itineraries, Destination Syria & Lebanon, and Transport. Amelia Thomas researched and wrote all of the Lebanon chapters. Terry, Lara and Amelia coauthored the History chapter and The Word on the Street chapter. Greg Malouf and Geoff Malouf wrote the Food & Drink chapter for both editions, and Dr Caroline Evans the Health chapter.

For the previous (2nd) edition of this book, Andrew Humphreys conducted preliminary research in Syria. Terry and Lara researched and wrote the Lebanon chapters, conducted further research in Syria, and compiled and wrote the introductory and closing chapters.

This guidebook was commissioned in Lonely Planet's Melbourne office, and produced by the following:

Commissioning Editor Kerryn Burgess
Coordinating Editor David Carroll
Coordinating Cartographer Julie Sheridan
Coordinating Layout Designer Pablo Gastar
Managing Editors Brigitte Ellemor, Geoff Howard
Managing Cartographer Shahara Ahmed
Managing Layout Designer Adam McCrow

Assisting Editors Susie Ashworth, Gennifer Ciavarra, Laura Crawford, Shawn Low, Anna Metcalfe, Stephanie Pearson, Martine Power
Assisting Cartographer Diana Duggan
Cover Designer Wendy Wright
Project Managers Eoin Dunlevy, Sarah Sloane
Language Content Coordinator Quentin Frayne

Thanks to Sin Choo, Jennifer Garrett, Lisa Knights, Adriana Mammarella, Raphael Richards, Averil Robertson, Wibowo Rusli, Jacqui Saunders, Cara Smith, Celia Wood

THANKS
TERRY CARTER & LARA DUNSTON

Since our first trip to Syria 10 years ago, the country has ranked among our favourites in the world. Numerous visits since have confirmed that Syria is home to some of the friendliest and most hospitable people on the planet, so this is a huge *shukran* to those of you who were so generous with your time and knowledge: Nagham Omran, Ayman Kreiker, Greg Fisher, Naim Turki, Heike Weber, Bannoura Awad, Abu Shady, Gabi and the Talisman staff, Ghaith Machnok, Sawsan Khalifeh, Boushra Abdoh, Samia H Saheb, Samar Dahdouh, Missak Baghboudarian, Father Zakai at St Ephrem's Clerical Seminary, the kind people at Mar Musa monastery, Muna of Lattakia, Muhamad

THE LONELY PLANET STORY

Fresh from an epic journey across Europe, Asia and Australia in 1972, Tony and Maureen Wheeler sat at their kitchen table stapling together notes. The first Lonely Planet guidebook, *Across Asia on the Cheap*, was born.

Travellers snapped up the guides. Inspired by their success, the Wheelers began publishing books to Southeast Asia, India and beyond. Demand was prodigious, and the Wheelers expanded the business rapidly to keep up. Over the years, Lonely Planet extended its coverage to every country and into the virtual world via lonelyplanet.com and the Thorn Tree message board.

As Lonely Planet became a globally loved brand, Tony and Maureen received several offers for the company. But it wasn't until 2007 that they found a partner whom they trusted to remain true to the company's principles of travelling widely, treading lightly and giving sustainably. In October of that year, BBC Worldwide acquired a 75% share in the company, pledging to uphold Lonely Planet's commitment to independent travel, trustworthy advice and editorial independence.

Today, Lonely Planet has offices in Melbourne, London and Oakland, with over 500 staff members and 300 authors. Tony and Maureen are still actively involved with Lonely Planet. They're travelling more often than ever, and they're devoting their spare time to charitable projects. And the company is still driven by the philosophy of *Across Asia on the Cheap*: 'All you've got to do is decide to go and the hardest part is over. So go!'

Akkam, Mohamad Saleh, Mamdouh Akbik, Radwan Al Taleel, Ibrahim Tawil, Saeed Zozoul, Hassan Al Kazaz, Mahmoud Shahin, Elham Bakir, Mouna Atassi, Mohamed Fayyad, Mohammad Hussein, Chiara Chierici, Farida Chadri, Maj Greitz and Maria Fernandez Coll. A *shukran kebira* to our beloved Dr George back 'home' for providing food, lodging and counselling during write-up.

AMELIA THOMAS
Thanks to Kerryn Burgess, Terry Carter, Lara Dunston and the rest of the team at Lonely Planet for their help, advice and flexibility on what proved to be a very challenging project. Many thanks go to Nich Hastings, my valiant travelling companion who took to Beirut traffic like a pro to a stock-car rally, and to Zeina Boufakhreddine, Mr Moussa, Mr Baz, Charbel Saliba, the people at Ya Libnan and SkiLeb, Anis at Bar Louie and fossil hunter extraordinaire Pierre Abi-Saad, along with all the other wonderful, hospitable people who make Lebanon a joy to travel in.

OUR READERS
Many thanks to the travellers who used the last edition and wrote to us with helpful hints, useful advice and interesting anecdotes:

Zafar Ahmad, Ahmed Albanna, Evi Allemann, Elie Amatoury, Deboncourt Amélie, Bent Schiermer Andersen, Maja Arnold, Mahdis Azarmandi, Malek B, Mohammed Barri, Dimitris Basias, Alain Bertallo, David Bertolotti, Yasmine Beydoun, Colin Biggs, Mike Bissett, Patricia Blessing, Cheryl Boescloeteu, Kim Boreham, Florian Von Bothmer, Eden Brandwein, Catherine Brew, John Bushby, Alistair Campbell, Ryan Cardno, Yee Cheng, Elizabeth Chipp, Hana Cmakalova, Simon Corder, Andy Cox, M D, Siska D'Hoore, Tim Dean, Esteban Derlings, Richard Desomme, Kapil Dhawan, David Dibden, Belika Douma, Mark Duncan, Klaus Dunder, Logan Elliot, Hendrina Ellis, David Evans, Dan Eyles, Tim Eyre, Erik Feenstra, Regula Forster, James Gallagher, Kaj-Martin Georgsen, Christina Gerhardt, Bahi Ghubril, Hannah Goldstein, Caroline Green, Chris Hall, Mike Hall, Susan Harris, Zeid Hashim, Hussein Hirji, Harald Hofmann, Mark Hunting, Russell Huntington, Trygve & Karen Inda, Taha Jassim, Maeve Jennings, Sara Junker, Hasan Kadoni, Najat Keaik, Alexis Keech, Thomas H F Kidman, Pablo Kimos, Catherine Koch, John Koeing, Claudia

Kuehn, Tamas Kutassy, Olivier Lourme, Francisco Chong Luna, Yoshifumi Manabe, Mika Minetti, Jesper Nissen, Elvira Pacheco, Brigette Palmer, David Patel, Doris Paulus, Matt Pepe, Laure Perrier, Lucy Pettman, Anne Poepjes, Liam Pounder, Matthew Pusey, Gerwin Ramaker, Spela Repic, Felix Rollin, Elisabeth Rona-Laser, Christophe Sap, Deepak Sapra, Beth Sargent, Bert Saveyn, Tim Schindel, Berit Schrickel, Ulrich Schröter, Gianluca Serra, Gabriella Serrado, Jennifer Skilbeck, Sonja Steiner, Per Steinoe, Gary Mark Stocker, Jochen Stührmann, Franc Sumandl, Graeme Thorley, Christian Tobutt-Somers, Donald Toney Jr, Henk Der van Laak, Brian Vickery, Claus Virmer, Nikky Wilson, Michelle Witton, Keiji Yoshimura

ACKNOWLEDGMENTS
Many thanks to the following for the use of their content:
Globe on title page ©Mountain High Maps 1993 Digital Wisdom, Inc.

SEND US YOUR FEEDBACK
We love to hear from travellers – your comments keep us on our toes and help make our books better. Our well-travelled team reads every word on what you loved or loathed about this book. Although we cannot reply individually to postal submissions, we always guarantee that your feedback goes straight to the appropriate authors, in time for the next edition. Each person who sends us information is thanked in the next edition – and the most useful submissions are rewarded with a free book.

To send us your updates – and find out about Lonely Planet events, newsletters and travel news – visit our award-winning website: **www.lonelyplanet.com/contact.**

Note: we may edit, reproduce and incorporate your comments in Lonely Planet products such as guidebooks, websites and digital products, so let us know if you don't want your comments reproduced or your name acknowledged. For a copy of our privacy policy visit www.lonelyplanet.com/privacy.

BEHIND THE SCENES

बोमे français

मनशफे

MANchafé

Index

INDEX

000 Map pages
000 Photograph pages

INDEX

INDEX

INDEX

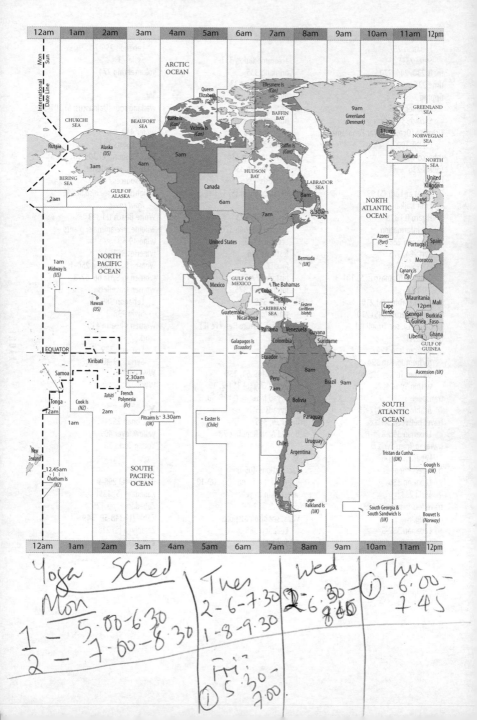

Yoga Sched
Mon
1 — 5.00-6.30
2 — 7.00-8.30

Tues
2 - 6-7.30
1 - 8-9.30

Wed
2 - 6.30-
8.00

Thu
① - 6.00-
7.45

Fri:
① 5.30-
7.00

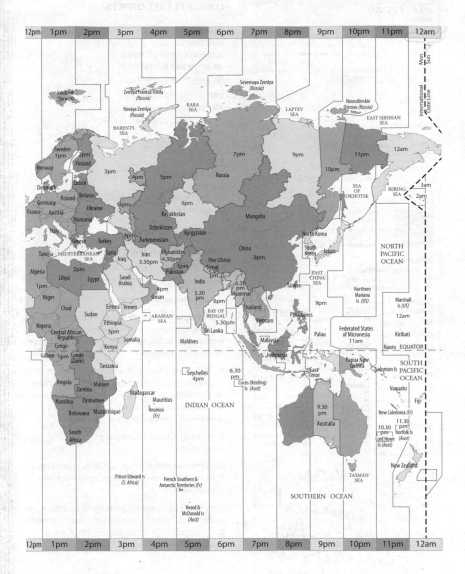

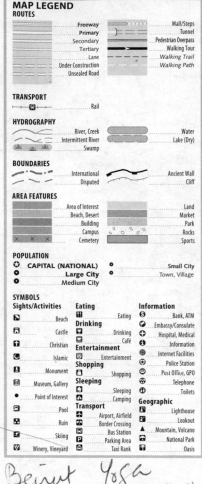

MAP LEGEND
ROUTES

Freeway	Mall/Steps
Primary	Tunnel
Secondary	Pedestrian Overpass
Tertiary	Walking Tour
Lane	Walking Trail
Under Construction	Walking Path
Unsealed Road	

TRANSPORT
Rail

HYDROGRAPHY
River, Creek
Intermittent River — Water
Swamp — Lake (Dry)

BOUNDARIES
International — Ancient Wall
Disputed — Cliff

AREA FEATURES
Area of Interest — Land
Beach, Desert — Market
Building — Park
Campus — Rocks
Cemetery — Sports

POPULATION
○ CAPITAL (NATIONAL)
● Large City — ● Small City
● Medium City — ○ Town, Village

SYMBOLS

Sights/Activities
- Beach
- Castle
- Christian
- Islamic
- Monument
- Museum, Gallery
- Point of Interest
- Pool
- Ruin
- Skiing
- Winery, Vineyard

Eating
- Eating

Drinking
- Drinking
- Café

Entertainment
- Entertainment

Shopping
- Shopping

Sleeping
- Sleeping
- Camping

Transport
- Airport, Airfield
- Border Crossing
- Bus Station
- Parking Area
- Taxi Rank

Information
- Bank, ATM
- Embassy/Consulate
- Hospital, Medical
- Information
- Internet Facilities
- Police Station
- Post Office, GPO
- Telephone
- Toilets

Geographic
- Lighthouse
- Lookout
- Mountain, Volcano
- National Park
- Oasis

LONELY PLANET OFFICES

Australia
Head Office
Locked Bag 1, Footscray, Victoria 3011
☎ 03 8379 8000, fax 03 8379 8111
talk2us@lonelyplanet.com.au

USA
150 Linden St, Oakland, CA 94607
☎ 510 250 6400, toll free 800 275 8555
fax 510 893 8572
info@lonelyplanet.com

UK
2nd fl, 186 City Rd,
London EC1V 2NT
☎ 020 7106 2100, fax 020 7106 2101
go@lonelyplanet.co.uk

Published by Lonely Planet Publications Pty Ltd
ABN 36 005 607 983

© Lonely Planet Publications Pty Ltd 2008

© photographers as indicated 2008

Cover photograph: Camel beside the monumental arch of the ruins at Palmyra, Mark Daffey/Lonely Planet Images. Many of the images in this guide are available for licensing from Lonely Planet Images: www.lonelyplanetimages.com.

Printed through Colorcraft Ltd, Hong Kong.
Printed in China.